BE-com-ing
AUTHENTICALLY
Me

BE-com-ing
AUTHENTICALLY
Me

**BEing the Creation of Myself by Lighting the Spark of
Inspiration Back into the Heart of my Luminous Soul BEing**

BIRGITTA VISSER

To my mum, for without your love, your foundation, and the backbone of your strength, I would not be who I am today—nor would I have been able to slay my demons.

To my dad and stepdad, thanks for cheering me on from the side-lines on the playing field of my life, never losing faith, and always being supportive regardless of the bruised tackles I have had to endure, allowing myself to be battering rammed into the ground by my many experiences. You know I got this!

To my sister, for having been the ultimate reflection to me in helping me see my blind spots, thank you.

To my Guides, and all other Light BEings across the bountiful multiverse, for your eternal wisdom, teaching me on my continued and ever-expansive journey, making my life a hell of a ride!

To all that have come and gone and all who continue to be my teachers in this lifetime, thank you!

Foreword

My daughter, Birgitta—well, what can I say? As a child growing up, she was rather timid and always trying to please everyone, and growing into adulthood this continued as she was always afraid of hurting others. As a teenager she wanted to see the world and started modelling. However, the agencies didn't like her look, and no matter how many castings she went to, she was always turned away—modelling just wasn't her path to walk in life, so she changed course.

As she got older, she moved around quite a bit, living and working in many different countries. She was a late bloomer, and too trusting of people who took advantage of her good nature. In the many places she's lived, wherever she went and whomever she met, she always learned something.

Birgitta has, ever since she was a child, always been interested in the spiritual side of life, and started seeing spirits at a very young age—even though I really thought that she was still too young to get into all of this, as my late husband lived too much in the spiritual realms, forgetting he had a family to take care of.

She commenced developing that side in her early twenties, accumulating her many life experiences, choosing to learn from them, always looking at ways to heal and develop herself, for remaining in a rut has never been an option for Birgitta. She has often made choices that landed her in hot water, but has never been one to throw in the towel, and has taken a lot of teachings on board from the many people she has crossed paths with.

She is light years ahead of many people, who don't always understand her nor her attitude towards life—and truthfully some of it is way above my head too, but it doesn't bother her as she remains true to herself. She merely says that people don't have to understand you, as long as you understand yourself. She has become very balanced and grounded; it wasn't always this way, but she now has one foot in this world and one foot in the other worldly dimensions. Is she a bit of a loner? Yes, but she loves her own company these days, and as the saying goes, the apple does not fall far from the tree.

Birgitta has walked through hell and back several times, wandering the lands of purgatory, and I wouldn't have liked to live in her shoes. She has been in extreme situations, accompanying those she was in a relationship with on the road to hell, yet she managed to pull herself out of the raging fires every single time—and she talks at length about her many earthly and otherworldly experiences in her book. I highly recommend you read it, not because she is my daughter, but because I believe that we can all learn something from it, preventing many of you from possibly making the same repetitive mistakes.

Birgitta's abilities in talking to the many masters have been so developed over the years that it is an integral part of her and comes to her very naturally. She doesn't see it as anything special, it's merely who she is, and she has never been one to push anything on anyone. She is a firm believer that you choose to believe whatever it is you want to believe in. As she always tells me, "Mum, it doesn't matter what people do or say, it is merely their level of awareness—they don't know any better, so leave them be."

Am I proud of her? You bet! She has turned out to be a beautiful woman, and regardless of what life has thrown at her, she still has a big heart and is still that person wanting to help others who need help but are willing to help themselves, albeit not at the cost of razing herself to the ground.

She has done readings for me in the past and helped me holistically and gotten me many organic supplements over the last few years, for various ailments I have suffered from, including back pain and elevated sugar levels, and even though I feel like I'm a pill-popping factory at times, they have helped immensely, paired with a now much healthier non-'ping' meal diet.

Birgitta has a long line of guides that protect her on her journey in life, and I am a firm believer that they help keep her safe whilst she walks her path in aiding many others on their own journey in becoming themselves.

She has come a long way from bending over backwards, being the people-pleaser she was, to now speaking her own truth. She is very honest and says it rather bluntly like it is, much like me, which is not everyone's cup of tea—but at least she shoots straight, in the hope of planting a seed of change in the way of thinking of those she meets.

—Birgitta's mum Eveline

Contents

Contents

The Galactic Symbolism on the Cover Explained

The cover was channelled to me by the various Councils; below a detailed explanation thereof.

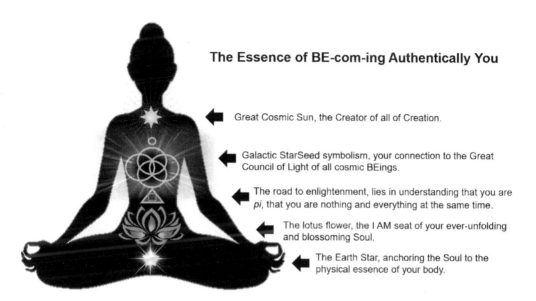

The Essence of BE-com-ing Authentically You

Great Cosmic Sun, the Creator of all of Creation.

Galactic StarSeed symbolism, your connection to the Great Council of Light of all cosmic BEings.

The road to enlightenment, lies in understanding that you are *pi*, that you are nothing and everything at the same time.

The lotus flower, the I AM seat of your ever-unfolding and blossoming Soul.

The Earth Star, anchoring the Soul to the physical essence of your body.

"You are a Star BEing created from the embers of the Cosmic Sun connected to the celestial Stars, as above so below, anchored to the grid of the Earth, with your Soul having taken up residence in the physical essence, rooted in the beautiful ever-un-folding and blossoming lotus flower, partaking in the journey of life through the art of expanding through polarities, relinquishing one's experiences through the art of the violet flame of transmutation, and understanding that like pi you are everything and nothing at the same time. You have no beginning or end. You are an infinite formu-lated mathematical equation to the truth of all Creation. You are Life, and you are Light. You are a Fibonacci formulation to the evolution of the spiritual revolution of your Soul, waltzing back to the truth of who you are and always have been."

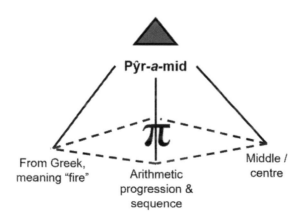

Pŷr-*a*-mid

π

From Greek, meaning "fire"

Arithmetic progression & sequence

Middle / centre

"The Pŷr-a-mid denotes one as being an energetic formulation of the Divine, built according to the sacred geometrical design and Divine blueprint of the Universe. You are an eternal fire dancing but ever so gracefully back to one's variable of an atomic structural formulation through the progression of the Soul's experiences creating an arithmetic sequence, eventually spinning back to the central axis of the very pi of the grid of Self, connecting back to the 'Alpha,' the One of All, as much as the All has always been One with You, basking in the Eternal Remembrance of who one is and has always been."

~The Council of Ra, the Galactic Federation, and the Council of Divine Cosmic Light~

Introduction

"Don't ask the world to change...you change first."

~Anthony de Mello~

Namaste to you reading this. Know that I honour the light of me in you as I honour the light of you in me. You must have been drawn to this book for a reason. Maybe you're soul-searching, or you want to sweep the winds of change through your life but are unsure where to start, or perhaps you need some words of inspiration to feed your soul whilst trying to make sense of the madness that is your world. Of course, there is order in all this chaos and unbalance. We merely need to learn to expand our sometimes-limited view of our own awareness in this world we so "confuciously" live in—a world of our own confused consciousness, having been dampened through the torrent and barrage of being ingrained within a matrix of a created existence.

Where do I even begin? Know that this is not your ordinary everyday book. This is a rollercoaster of a ride of my warped earthly life, interwoven with a wondrous journey of delving into my illustrious and diverse past lives and my connection with the many Light BEings surfing the cosmic waves across the far-reaching multidimensional galaxy.

When life falls apart—and trust me, mine has been shot to pieces plenty of times—it gives you a chance to heal from the inside out, to rise from the ashes like a phoenix reborn into the light and love of self. We can only move forward if we let go of the past, ridding ourselves of those pesky shackles that have kept us chained in the loop of our own created heavy cream of conditioning, leaving us walking with an inner gaping hole o' pain and a dis-ease with ourselves. Life is all about braving the winds of change instead of merely just standing there in that sorry state, in the hues of your uncomfortable twilight zone, looking rather surly and forlorn, bitchin' at the world.

Life is much like a jigsaw puzzle; things that happen may seem unfair, and yet there is order in all the Chaos. Seen from a Universal bird's-eye perspective, life seems so eternally simple, but lest we forget, you are down there navigating through the thick of it all.
And in the midst of breathing but the breath of Life.
It is not....
To slot the pieces of the puzzle together, you must understand the ebb and flow of your chosen Journey. You must learn to listen to your inner Awareness, breaking the barriers of your current conditioned Conscious understanding, and embracing all your Experiences.
And thus, your actions should reflect as such.
For only then will you Master the Journey of Life, relishing in the Joy of Life and the rediscovery of Self.

~The Divine~

Life is about empowering yourself and understanding that your experiences are not here to downgrade you, but to upgrade you, walking back to the remembrance of loving oneself, for love is your divine nature—it is the exquisite vibrance of your soul. It is merely the earthly conditioning you have so coated your beautiful soul with that has enamoured you with an instilled fear. Ditch the fear by rinsing off the conditioning, to elevate yourself back to the hue of the divine love and light of self. You are a magnificent spirit of the stars of creation, in the current wrapped-up human embodiment of infinite sparkling starlight particles. Walk your walk and talk your talk. Be as much the inspiration of self as a reflection to others in the flow of their own BEing of magnificence and potentialities. It is a rare gift to be able to live in the unrestricted ness of self, having chosen to give away your I AM power, leaving you devoid of living a life according to the matrix. Yet, you are a sovereign BEing of the divine, and carry with you the power from the "galaxial" and celestial architects of infinite stars within. One simply needs to light the spark of inspiration back in the heart of one's own Soul BEing. As St. Germain states:

"I AM, as you are, as much as You are as I AM whilst 'others' are merely faces of your own Self. The I AM defines your Divine Consciousness, the Essence and flavoursome wholeness of your core BEing, your true Self—the All of you connected back to the All of Source. All that follows the mere wording of I AM bears fruit into the manifestation of your outer world. All commences from the I AM God Source within. You are the Master Creator of your own World. Energetically you reap what you sow. Connecting with your I AM-ness is the path to the ascension into God Consciousness onto the next octave of Existence because you are choosing to live consciously rather than in ignorance."

We may not have met on a conscious level, but on a soul level we are all infinite particles of that same divine light, interconnected throughout the whole spectrum of this beautiful multiverse. Know that I love you as you are. When you see the reflection staring back in the mirror, make sure to utter those same words—"I love you"—to yourself, for each and every one of you is worthy. Never forget to shine your light—the very essence of the divinity of all that makes you *you*. You have sprung from love and will return to love. You are a beautiful force of nature, you are a radiant being of the divine, you are love, you are light, and you are a God wonder walking on this current shifting timeline on Earth.

You have to love yourself, how can you not? Love is and has always been your Divine Nature. It is those pesky conditionings that you have so lovingly slapped upon yourself, causing you havoc on your journey of life and a dis-ease within the Self. Conditioning is overrated. Love yourself, and all those that have dished you these wonderfully serv-ed experiences that have made you tear up, sweatin' the chilies, crappin' your pants in a constipated and contorted pain. The only way out of the pain is to walk through it. Breathe through the movement of it all, dancing back to the "wholesomelicious" Divine Light and lightness of the loving Soul of Self.

~The Divine Shakespeare Club~

Our experiences reveal the real soul depth of our existence and how much we are ingrained within the attachment of these created experiences. To let go or not to let go? —that is the question. I have been that drowned and submerged rat on my own sinking ship, refusing to budge and refusing to let go of my experiences, much to the detriment of my own self, until I chose to relent, having caused nothing but immense havoc in my life. Yes, I've been there, done that, and worn that T-shirt too many times. I understand the meaning of letting go as much as I now understand that my experiences are merely here for me to expand my awareness, and to love myself so that I can laugh at my own silly mistakes.

The truth is, the world does not care what you fear, nor the superficiality of living in the shallowness of self. The world cares about why you are here. Have you not chosen to play the cosmic game of evolution? Are you not a player of the game of life on Earth? Are you not here to help elevate your own vibration? Are you not here to help elevate the love vibration of Mother Earth, to unshackle her from the restraints of the heaviness she has been incarcerated in? Are you not the master creator of your own worldly reality?

Who Am I?

I'm just an everyday person, like you. I see myself as everything and nothing at the same time. I am a Light Empowerment Coach, a Soul Configurator, a bit of a galactic kite surfer, and a supersonic boomerang, reverberating messages from across the dimensions of the ever-weaving tapestry of the universe. I'm a messenger across the cosmic waves, delivering messages from the Light BEings (Collective of Guardians of Higher Vibrational Light) to aid humanity. In many ways, that makes me a courier, a messenger across time and space. I often say, being Dutch, that I am a bike messenger between the here and there. We "Dutch Landers" are a bike-friendly nation; it's a true cyclist's heaven as the infrastructure is built around cyclists.

I AM who I AM, no filter needed. I have learned to embrace all quirky aspects of myself, alchemising all that served me not, and long ago ditched the labels of shame and fear I carried, merely BE-com-ing authentically me—and so can you. I don't sugar-coat or wrap things in cotton candy, I'd be a hypocrite, and I will never apologise for speaking my truth. How you choose to perceive me is ultimately how you perceive yourself. I am raw, honest, and blunt; the latter I blame on being Dutch, so don't be offended by my writing style. I give what I get. Take it or leave it, love me or hate me, it's all the same to me. I still love you anyway. Take whatever resonates with your heart in this book and leave the rest.

Why the title *BE-com-ing Authentically Me*? It was given to me by the Council of Ra, who love to speak in riddles, and it is for you to figure out the rest. Much like when you were a kid, engrossed in solving a Rubik's cube for hours on end, trying feverishly to get all the colours in the right place.

BE-com-ing, stands for BEing.com. The "com" is a domain suffix identifying a company. It's an identity. In this case, it means BEing the creation of myself. Isn't life all about becoming and being true to the I AM of who you are, rather than a tainted and created societal persona of who you have become? You have to BE true to yourself, true to the originality of the soul of who you are, and always have been.

Why conform to the illusion of what you perceive to be a reality, that in truth is but an artificiality of a created bubble of illusion, baked, conditioned, and served up as a reality? The deeper you wander within the wonders of the 'wonderlicious' Wonderland of Self, the more you come to the realisation that you are far more powerful than you have been led to believe. I dare you to unleash your inner Alchemist, walking back to the very naked BEingness of the luminous Soul that you are, creating a life less ordinary.

"Always be you, not who the world wants you to be, because your Soul will suffocate within its hous-ed body, causing one to squirm and be blown to smithereens, seeping into the physical, whipping up but mere cracks of dis-ease. Never conform to the norm, rather live a life in the radiance of your own essentiality and originality."

~The Divine~

I am simply here to plant a seed—an unlocking of one's true potential into a better understanding of oneself and the universe. My life has been very much trial and error. I've had to figure it out, often whilst just standing there being the dumb arse I was—with the same lessons neatly served and presented to me in different scenarios. Until my Guides finally said, "Hallelujah, the friggin' penny dropped its clogs onto her 'thick' skull, and she's finally grasped it."

Knowledge is infinite; like you, I am still learning and finding my way. Ultimately, you'll figure out who you are and why the heck you came to Earth in the first place. We are all just passing through, gracing this beautiful Earth plane with our presence. We've already chosen our suit for our current pre-planned "vacation," so we might as well make the most out of it.

All my experiences have led me to this point in my life; without them, I would not have a story to tell. I am a child of the world, having travelled the globe extensively, both with my family—my childhood years in the wonderful culture and flavours of both Singapore and Malaysia—and on my own, having lived in various European countries and hopped across the Atlantic onto the shores of the Caribbean and the good ole US of A. I have always been a wanderer and a seeker of the expansion of consciousness, yet it took me years to realise why my life was an eclectic bag of mixed experiences: some utterly sour and distasteful, and some sweeter, bringing me immense joy. I have had to start from scratch repeatedly, as such was my chosen journey, and thus, I live rather simplistically, as I don't value the material. But in all of my misadventures, my resilience was never compromised, for my mum's immense strength throughout life taught me to be a fighter and never to bow down to defeat.

On my journey of self-discovery, of self-recognition, of who I was and who I am now, I learned to heal the very broken aspects of myself, allowing light to permeate where there had been but emptiness,

I have learned to take life with a pinch of salt, and as you will come to read, often poking fun at myself, looking back at all my experiences with a sense of humour. Adding a pinch of salt, adding flavour to your experiences, and nurturing your soul, is far better than living a bland and tasteless life in one's served plates of experiences. And as St. Germain adds:

"To become the best version of yourself, all you need is a yummy scoop of ice-cold courage, a sprinklin' of chopped nuts o' faith, topped with a 'lightilicious' dusting of creamy self-love, and taking a 'bite' out of that melty magical goodness, whip up the magic within, and commence walking through that uncomfortable feat of a pesky thing called darkness, to delve into, and embrace the 'wonderlicious' Authentic hue in You learning to ultimately weave but your magic without."

Channelling did not come to me overnight, as I was a jack of all trades yet a master of none. I chose to study many healing modalities after falling foul of my traumatic experiences, always choosing to heal, develop and enhance my capabilities, creating a better version of myself. When I was so forlorn and depressed, lying on the floor screaming and crying, I begged my Guides to help me, and all I did, as you will read later, was follow the bread-crumb trail of people strewn in my way.

But don't think healing is a walk in the park because your guides will most gladly put you through the mud-filled trenches of who you think you are, back to who you truly are, should you accept the challenge. Many people can visualise and see the many masters and archangels, but I never saw them to begin with; I merely felt them until, through my Akashic Healing, and an exercise given to me, I sat down one evening and clearly stated that I was open and ready to receive and the words just started flowing, and I just started crying, as, for the first time, I felt I was good at something rather than being a failure. You will find that I often write from the perspective of my Higher Self, as I have channelled so much with the many masters over the years; you could say, as people often tell me this, that they have "influenced" me with their ways and mannerisms of speaking. I hope that the channelled messages by the many Ascended Masters, including St. Germain, archangels, Galactics, high councils, Light BEings, and the writers' club called "The Divine Shakespeare Club," will inspire you and give you a better understanding of yourself and life in all its essence. Most have a witty sense of humour, don't mince their words, and some of their language can be both 'old' and colourful, so pardon my French, but that is how some choose to express themselves. I have honoured their style in the channelled transmissions.

For the record, I don't have a TV. The times I did, I barely watched it, nor am I a social media buff, as it's too much egotistical chaos for me. I quit watching online news long ago, as that is the malarkey of the illusion that one feeds the mind with, acting according to the ingested wording thereof, which in turn affects the collective consciousness, as everything is created through the mental imagery of the mind. That is how powerful you are—you are the energy you conjure forth in your existential existence.

This is a 'big' book, which I commenced writing in 2000, and consists of two books bundled in one. The first covers the current evolution of the human shift in consciousness, which initially wasn't meant to be in this book, but both the Ascended Master St. Germain and Thoth impressed upon my heart that it needed to be inserted for people to begin to understand the why's of what has been happening these past few years—to help gently awaken their beautiful slumbering hearts into understanding what life is all about and why we are here. It ranges from our origins, the Anunnaki, the war on humanity, to Covid, the "agenda," messages from Mother Earth, Archangel Michael, and understanding that there truly is no death. The second part is about my life, including the trauma I encountered growing up, the loss of my father at the age of fourteen, my stint with drugs, starving myself, the bullying I endured, my toxic relationships, suffering from vaginismus, and much more. As the Light BEings state, "*This book holds a treasure trove of wisdom to finding your way back from the 'dishevelled' state of the overgrown 'jungleicious' Self to living in the brilliance of the Authentic Light of Self.*"

I have inserted a short Q&A with Archangel Michael here so that you get a feel for what you're about to experience.

Q: Won't people think I'm a bito loo-loo when reading all of this?

A: *That's okay, we're all love, light, and a bit loo-loo up here too.*

Q: Some of the messaging is a wee bit repetitive, it might drive the readers potty, no?

A: *Maybe, but we leave no angle unturned. The incessant flow of words flows but miraculously, like a never-ending cascading rolling of the tongue torrent of the written word. For a first-time reader, it will hopefully plant forth a burnin' thought seed of 'what's the meaning of life?', in the hope of elevating their mindset and freeing their Soul, no? It might well drive you potty, but you stripped yourself butt naked of much of the glorified conditioning, not to mention you've channelled, written, read, and reread the written wording a thousand times, so touché ma cherie.*

Q: Some of the channelled chunks of text from the various Light BEings may be difficult to understand or follow as the language used may be way out there for some.

A: *Walk the walk to our level, I daresay, and it'll be a doddle. You have to sit in the energy of the wording to absorb the essence of all you read. Much like savouring your palette with a glass of finely aged wine, swirl, sip and savour, (no chuggin' the jug in), drinking in the smoothness of the enriched notes and underlying tones of the* *written words, and letting them warm the very essence to a remembrance of your Divine incarnate sparklin' enlightened delight of a Soul Light.*

It matters not which part or chapter you are drawn to and choose to read first. I ask that you simply read this book with an open heart and mind and see if there is a resonance within your sweet soul. I can't tell you how to live your life, but I hope you draw some inspiration and divine guidance from the words written here and that my story somehow empowers you to live a more abundant and fulfilled life.

Much love and light to you.
—Birgit

PS: My apologies if there are any spelling mistakes. It has gone through many levels of editing to ensure this is a cohesive and error-free book, but we are, after all, as you know, only human.

BOOK 01

The Evolution of the Human Shift in Consciousness

"Learning to step outside the mind matrix of our current existence, through healing the soul back to the sacred geometrical grid of the beautiful divine self."

You are the Light of a thousand suns.
You are the mere expression of the Light of your Soul partaking in the direction cast.
You are a spark of the One Cosmic Sun Eternal.
The rays reflecting from Oneself to Oneself and to the hearts and souls of others back to the heart of the Soul and thus back to the Cosmic Sun.
You are as beautiful as a dew drop's morn,' the glint to the mirror of your Soul.
You are the glistening of the ice crystals forming on a cold wintry morn.
You are the heart of the replenishing Soul of Self in the warm embrace of a summer's rain.
You are the unfurling leaves and budding blooms of an early spring's day.
You are the Earth's Consciousness as much as the Consciousness is the Breath of the Earth.

You are as much an extension of mother Earth as mother Earth is an extension of you, for you are One and the same breath, yet through your emotional discoloration of Love you traipse in the dis-harmony and the dis-ease of both yourself and thus reflect that discord back at your Sole Nurturer Mother Earth.
Stop acting as if the world owes you, for you owe the world.
Stop interrupting the beautiful free flow falling of Self, so all can flow back harmoniously to the Earthly grid and thus back to Self.
Revel in the mere grace of the brilliance that you are, and walk with a debonair of Love and Gratitude, and thus it will mirror back in the Consciousness of the Planet.

You are the intricacy of the spiritual evolution intertwined with the millions of Light particles dancing the rhythmic dance at the resonance of one's soul beat.
Remember the divine song that sings to your heart, be in unison with the song that you are, for it is the reawakening to the remembrance of your magnifique 'magnificilicious' magnificence.
You are as much the dawn to the dusk, as the sun to the moon, casting but its refracting Light to the shimmering of the Stars across the vastness of the universal skies.
You are as much the water to your own fire as the light to your own shadows.
You are the builder as much as the destroyer to one's own created little cos mic bubble of pragmatic experiences.
Be the authentic revelation of Oneself by grabbing your life by le horns of le bull and leaping to the faith of a soaring eagle.
For by the Grace of God, I tell thee that Life is the ultimate richness of your experiences and but a beautiful feat to behold.I say Salud, Prost, and dare to risk the Self a bit more in the unravelling to the blindness of Self through the art of the game of Life, back to the multidimensional eclectic Soul BEing that one is.

~The Ascended Master St. Germain~

The Earth's Birthing into Existence

The system as it stands is crumbling, it's disintegrating to make way for the new. Even if not all seems clear yet, the blueprint for the ascension is in progress. The question is, are you willing to do the work to elevate both yourself, your fellow humans, and Mother Earth into the next paradigm of Consciousness? Or will you remain dormant in the slumber of yourself walking into the epic battle of enslavement of humanity with eyes wide shut? The revolution to the new evolution has begun.

~The Light BEings of Divine Consciousness~

I love our planet, Mother Earth, yet her creation remains a bit of a mystery. I have often pondered if Georges Lemaître could have been so wrong. One would think that Albert Einstein came up with the theory of the Big Bang—but not so, for it was a Diocesan priest, mathematician, astronomer, and professor of physics from Belgium who first put that theory to the test. He said that the theory of relativity supported the idea that the universe was ever-expanding, whereas Einstein stated that the universe is constantly in motion and humming to the beat of electromagnetic vibrations—everything is in vibratory motion, nothing rests.

If the Earth came into existence through the commencement of the primeval atom, being a conscious energetic frequency, then it would have taken millions of years for the Earth to be created. Much like a child first conceived and growing in the womb, being born and growing up, the Earth was created according to the divine blueprint before it ultimately became inhabitable. Once formed, it needed to interweave the tapestry of land, water, vegetation, minerals, rocks, and all that was required to commence the human race experiment thousands of years later.

It's incredible how everything on the Earth has been architecturally and consciously created from the basis of pure unconditional love. The divine architects created everything with precision, according to the sacred geometrical grid of the divine—and thus, you have been created as a sacred BEing of the geometrical grid of the divine. In everything, there is order.

Everything breathes. Everything is life. Everything is consciousness and interconnected with everything else, with no exception. It's amazing to be one with all, and that all is breathing back with the oneness that is you. A baby will go through many growth spurts and changes—such is the evolution of humanity. The Earth too, goes through many growth spurts and changes, for it has tilted its axis in the various stages of its evolution. How can that not be? The beauty of Earth is that it is evolving as much as humankind. I believe dinosaurs were ancient landscapers that roamed the Earth, changing the landscape they inhabited, much like elephants, who change their environment simply by walking and eating, leaving imprints wherever they go.

Humans, however, change the landscape of the earthly environment to suit their wants, not needs—leaving Mother Earth with an incapacity to breathe due to greed and atrocities. Dinosaurs were ultimately wiped out by an asteroid that collided with Earth, causing tsunamis and other natural disasters and changing the landscape of the Earth yet again. I call these the growing pains of Mother Earth, who is slowly maturing and coming of age until one day, many light-years from now, she will have attained her own enlightenment and be absorbed once more within the universal energetic grid—from which henceforth another planet for other species or maybe a higher-evolved species of humanity may be born.

Like there are architects of buildings, these conscious architects of worlds create something inhabitable out of nothing. Buildings, once created, are run by "management," and worlds are run by "governments," some corrupt, to the detriment of those inhabiting the space, others far more just and loving. Some countries create havoc and have no regard for the space they have been given to live in, while others live in the oneness and unity of their given and created surroundings. Occupants come and go—such is the nature and cycle of life, and thus evolution continues. Just as buildings can be refurbished and upgraded, worlds can be refurbished and upgraded by expanding people's awareness. Buildings can be demolished when they reach the end of their life cycle, as much as worlds will end once their evolution has been completed and the occupants have reached the point of ascension and return to the love of the oneness of all.

Once the cosmic experiment of Earth was habitable, the human experiment could commence. Many volunteers from many different planets wanted to grace our planet with their presence—they were all excited and overjoyed to start, knowing full well that descending into the dense physical form, many would forget their origins, their powers, their heritage, and all the ancient wisdom they beheld when "staycationing" on Earth. Many of you may believe that we evolved from apes into humans. I agree to disagree on that front; I think the tinkering of DNA eventually led to the Homo sapiens creation of man.

As the Earth was getting ready for humanity to descend, who, you may ask, was overseeing this whole process? The answer is simple. Although your initial thought may be that it was God, the infinite creator, in truth, you are not wrong. However, the various councils of light, the architects of the many worldly planes of existence, oversaw the Earth's creation. God source energy is the conscious mind map, the navigator, the creator of all, the alpha and the omega, infinity—God source energy oversees the process of its overall creation but has merely withdrawn into the void to watch it all cosmically unfold without interfering.

We have to think of life as an experiment living within an experiment. Why the experiment? Because when the architects created the multiverse according to the divine source blueprint, and all species agreed on the 'terms' with one another, some decided they wanted more. The Draconians, part of the reptilian Starseeds, and several others decided to undertake a carefully planned heist, throwing the whole divine plan as outlined into chaos, displacing many peaceful, loving species within the multiverse with their advanced weapon arsenal, making many planets uninhabitable, and while on a rather successful collision course, they decided to take this part of the universe, making it their bolthole. These displaced peaceful light warriors learned to arm themselves and fight back the power of the dark forces. In effect, the Draconians "nuked" them—much as Mars, being once a beautiful habitable planet, was nuked into annihilation by dark forces. (Lest one forgets, the Anunnaki nuked part of the once-created civilisation within the Sumner region; nuclear technology was not "invented" in the 20th century, it's eons-old ancient knowledge, which bubbled to the surface within three reincarnated German scientists who "rediscovered" nuclear fission in 1938, with Oppenheimer—without remorse creating the first atomic bomb.

All knowledge from many previous incarnations lies deeply encoded within the mind.) It's much like the Sith in *Star Wars*, having sat on the council and been members of the Jedi order dedicating themselves to peace through the light side of the Force, until they decided to go dark. The EGO crept in, and they wanted galactic domination, power, and control, enslaving the many, curbing their freedoms and movement, and imposing strict rules and regulations because they believed that the galaxy was theirs to rule by cosmic right. The Sith were exiled, and for eons, they interbred with the many other exiles and other races, creating different species, before resurfacing and putting their plan for power and destruction in motion. As Yoda said, "Fear is the path that leads one to the dark side. Fear leads to anger. Anger leads to hate, and hate leads to suffering, for the dark clouds everything." Fear is a destructive force throwing one into the fires of doubt and chaos, losing one's authentic nature. One becomes lost in the maze of the ego and separation of oneself, and it causes all kinds of anomalies due to the comparative and competitive nature, thus creating a possible barrage of dis-ease. The Sith relished and fed on that fear to empower themselves, loving the control and power it yielded for and to them. To them, it was all about being the dominant masters in a controlled matrix, feeding off the fear of the many that were enslaved under their dominion. Is the world that much different today? As the whole divine plan was thrown into disarray and galactic wars were in full swing, the architects had to think about how to rebuild the light back into the cosmos and decided to send cosmic ground troops to Earth, but as with any plan, anomalies have crept in as those that lost their 'mind' having forgotten their origins, strayed from the path. We are merely playing the Cosmic Game of Evolution, and it is time to awaken and connect back to the "all-spark of consciousness" and return to the beckoning of the dawning of the Age of Light.

We may think that we hold the knowledge of all civilisations on this planet, but we do not, and I certainly don't, for there have been too many, and anything we read is simply a piece of the puzzle to our origins. I have been given many flashes of our origins, piecing them together through the many channelled messages received. If they had shown the whole of creation to me, my human mind would have gone fried banana fritters on me. And sometimes they have overloaded me, and it's like a literal brain freeze, and I have to retreat from the world and recalibrate. Here, I will discuss the main known extra-dimensional civilisations, although there is a separate chapter on the Anunnaki, as many may not be familiar with them.

The Anunnaki

The Anunnaki, a superior race from the planet Nibiru, came to Planet Earth searching for gold. The atmosphere on their planet was dying, and they required gold to sustain the life of their people. While it is said that they created the human race with their DNA strands and used them to mine for gold after the Igigi, their servants, seen as a lesser creed, rebelled. I still believe humanity to be an intertwining of various galactic races, seeing we are a definite fusion of many, i.e., the Lyrans, Arcturians, Andromedans, Pleiades, and Sirians, and several other species who created the Atlantean race using their chromosomes and strands of integrated DNA encoding the whole universe within. It is incredible to behold that one is encoded with the entire universe within.

All races have evolved over the many billions of years since they first arrived on Earth. I know this because I have channelled the Anunnaki and have understood them to be regretful of their ways towards humanity, with many having transcended in consciousness from that era.

The Lemurians

I have channelled bits and pieces of the Land of Mu, also known as ancient Lemuria—once a landmass in the Pacific Ocean, from about 4,500,000 BC to about 12,000 years ago. It extended from the western part of the United States and Canada to lands in the Indian Ocean and Madagascar. Lemuria sank to the depths of the Pacific as the Earth shifted its axis. Much of Lemuria lies dormant under the tectonic plates at the bottom of the ocean; remnants can be found in Hawaii, the mountains of Polynesia, and Bolivia, with one of the portals in Mt. Shasta in California.

As the Earth vibrated at a higher resonance, Lemurians lived in the fifth-dimensional frequency and from a divine heart space, with a resonance from the heart and a love for all beings and Mother Earth. They were a beautiful collective energy and communicated with their galactic homes across the stars through the synchronicity of both meditation and telepathy. They were the heart and the oneness with all in the universe, cultivating the lands by listening to the whispers of nature, the fae, and the correspondence of the energies with Mother Earth. They worked in unison and harmony to keep the vibration high and had a vast understanding of the healing properties of the Earth. The Lemurians thrived for many years, with many emissaries coming from the various planets in the galaxies, sharing knowledge in the hope of creating a more enlightened Earth. Their architecture is beyond what we have now, for much of the materials used were not of this planet—it was of a much lighter vibration, but so were the Lemurians.

Lemurians are the master crystal healers of the grid. The crystalline energetic frequency field is the light grid on Earth, enabling humanity to shift dimensional consciousness. It is a power source of energetic and magnetic electro-frequency waves—an Akashic record hall of sorts, a memory bank of stored memories of humanity. Remember that Mother Earth is a living, conscious, breathing BEing, just like you.

Lemurians understood oneness as being a part of the whole. They celebrated their individuality but knew that they were all brothers and sisters of the light. Harmony of the heart was key to the workings of an ever-expanding society. They listened to the heartbeat of Mother Earth, for it sustained them with the nurturing and well-being of their bodies through the irrigation and waterways of the workings of the lands. They listened humbly to the realms of nature that sustained them and thus were blessed healers to those who sought their help and those who wished to be taught the art of healing. They were beautifully aligned within themselves, encoded with the crystalline light codes that enabled them to transform matter at will. Alchemy was their nature, and transformation was but beauty to behold. Humanity can choose the path of magic, sustainability of the land, and harmony once more, but the road ahead is a long one to forge as we have devolved into our third-dimensional reality of believing in separation.

Many Lemurians were mermaids, living in the beautiful, crystal-clear waters of the Lemurian seas, then shapeshifting from the waters to walk the lands. At the end of the Lemurian epoch, when the Atlanteans came into existence and grew to be of a denser capacity than the Lemurians, many suffered from disease due to the misalignment of energetic frequencies. Their song diminished. Many were in pain, having to heal themselves back to the wholeness and vibrance of their own song.

For many who love mermaids and have an immense affinity with them in this lifetime, they ask you to rise in aiding the planet back into the harmony it once was. You will often feel like a fish out of water, but as the Lemurians say:

"Understand that you are a beautiful BEing of the Divine, think yourself not lesser than anyone else, for you are not, you are beauty incarnate. You are the lotus within the lotus, often keeping hidden the gem within, causing you much misalignment within yourself, which has led to a dis-ease within the corridors of your own body. Your body lives according to your Soul's vibrance, steering the energetic direction thereof. Never be afraid to shine your Light, never be afraid to speak your Truth, never be afraid of your own haunted shadow, for it seeks not to taunt you in these shifting times but asks for a healing of one's radiant Soul of Self—like the immersion in water that washes away the dirt, your Soul seeks for you to scrub and wash away the 'taintedness' you have kept ingrained within you for so long, it seems an attached stuck-on patch that has become a part of you. For too long many of you have given away your own I AM Power—it is time for you to take back your Power, and bask in your own Light of Self, your beautiful Divine self-worth. For far too long, you have simmered beneath the surface of yourself, causing an often outright suffocation of yourself. It is time for you to re-emerge from the waters you have kept yourself under and breathe in the Divine Light you are."

Lemurian dragons are the gatekeepers to the Lemurian light codes and light activations. They have encoded many of the Lemurian crystals with the memories thereof and are fluid in carrying the vibration of the pure of heart. One can call upon these beautiful creatures to help ease the burdens of the mind and heart, allowing both to be interconnected and work harmoniously with one another. They breathe fire into your heart chakra to allow for all aspects of your soul to be healed, for we often get stuck in the programming of our current chosen reality. Dragons teach us to let go of fear, for fear simply resides within us in the conditioning of who we think we are but are not.

The Ascended Master Prince Oromasis, the keeper of the flame of eternal fire, in charge of the Salamanders and the Elemental BEings of Fire, who serves the planet, working with the priests of the order of Melchizedek, says:

"Dragons do indeed help ease the burdens of the mind, yet a dragon's wrath is fire to the flame that throws you off the cliff into the abyss of a burnin' change. Sometimes, no matter how much you try to hold on to the known, you are pushed in a different direction, and it is a blessing, even if one is often so comfortable in the discomfort one has become so prone to. For out of the sea of the sacred fire, one re-emerges, becoming far more enriched and in tune with the Self, having trusted and felt the Divine intervention of the Lemurian Dragon Spirit."

If you have lived in Lemuria in a previous lifetime or are drawn to it, you are here on Earth to remember who you are and to garner the broken aspects of yourself, healing back to the wholeness and truth of the very essence of who you are. It is often not a pretty ride but a necessity to attain a lighter version of yourself. As your body is of the Earth, everything you do goes hand in hand with nature, for everything is intertwined, and all are interconnected. You may have a deep love or sense of nurturing for nature and all its sentient BEings and be very much in tune with her. The Earth needs you as much as you need the Earth, for you are an angel of the Earth, helping to restore the balance of humanity and that of the natural ways of the womb of the mother. Always remember that.

As Lemuria came to its end, some opted to go underground and some to Atlantis, while others settled beneath Mount Shasta in California and built the city of Telos. Those that remained gave up their "physical" bodies to continue their evolution in spirit form, such was their enlightened understanding of the workings of the universe. Death is merely an ingrained morbidity of human illusion.

The Atlanteans

Atlantis had a different energy; whereas Lemurians worked from the heart space, the Atlanteans expressed themselves outwardly. Many had a great interest in shipping, garnering wealth and power, which is where the ego and separation slowly started to creep in. The Atlanteans were mineral, stone, and crystal traders, with a large amount of trade entering and leaving Atlantis by water, branching out to various other civilizations around the planet.

The architects of the Atlantis experiment, which commenced and disintegrated several times, built the Temple of Poseidon, known as the Cathedral of the Sacred Heights, which contained the generator crystal for all of Atlantis. It was created in the Atlas Mountains and formed the seventh peak. These peaks symbolised the seven pillars of the universe, the seven spiritual laws to abide by for harmonious living of both the temple of the abode and the place one had chosen to evolve in. It is one of the reasons Atlantis thrived in what started out as an honouring of truth and light.

The beautifully enlightened soul, the Ascended Master Casimir Poseidon, once ruled over part of Atlantis in what is now known as the Amazon area in the South Americas, where the rivers flowed with crystalline waters, the lands were fertile and lush with vegetation, the air was clean, and people were part of a thriving community, working in a communion from the heart, with a love and understanding for all living things of the Mother. It was a time when pure laughter and joy filled the air, people celebrated each other, and a hierarchy was unbeknownst to them, for all humans were of equal status and an equal divinity.

Imagine how much cleaner the world would be if we stopped polluting the waters and air and depleting the richness of the Earth. We have forgotten the use of the crystal and electromagnetic grid field that the Earth's axis dances on and have replaced it with many variants of chemicals and oils, choosing to live in a deviation from our authentic nature. One poisons the self as much as one chooses to poison the Earth. A more beautiful world would be reborn if humanity could learn to live according to the seven laws that once adorned the halls of the many temples in Atlantis.

1. The Law of One
2. The Law of Karma
3. The Law of Manifestation
4. The Law of Grace
5. The Law of Responsibility
6. The Law of Unconditional Love
7. The Law of Intention

To create awareness and harness the knowledge deep within, know that all change starts with the self. Great civilisations have always been founded on spiritual principles and adhered to these laws of life; however, if those governing have been contaminated, drifting away from their own God source energy, spilling over into the population, disintegration commences and snowballs forth, until they return to the fundamental of balance, purity, and equality for all, or are wiped out by their own discord, with the old making way for the coming of a new dawn.

If we can all learn to step into our awareness and begin living by the spiritual principles of the God-self—an untethered unconditional love—perhaps we can one day return to living in far more harmonious ways with one another and the Earth we so grace our presence with. It is all about expanding the heart and the light of who we are through the vastness and the richness of our experiences— for they seek not to destroy us but to awaken us to the realisation of ourselves and the light of our authenticity.

Towards the end of Lemuria, Atlantis had become a flourishing civilisation, with various beings and races visiting as emissaries and inhabiting its intricately designed geometric streets and canals that fed directly into its centre like spokes on a bicycle wheel. Rather fitting, as, without spokes within the wheels, one cannot create balance when riding a bike, causing a misalignment from rubbing against the brake pads unevenly, causing damage to both the wheel and brakes.

I have often been asked how I know Atlantis existed. Only one account of it has ever been written by the Greek philosopher Plato, who was an incarnation of the Ascended Master St. Germain. Despite no "concrete" evidence that can be found within the superficial thinking of the mind, it most assuredly did exist, but much has been hidden from us by those wielding power, dumbing down the masses. As St. Germain says, *"One may state Atlantis was a mere construct of the mind, a mere fable of the tongue, but everything is an enigma of the senses. You are only as enlightened as your 'hue-man' awareness allows you to be, so how enlightened of a Light are you?"*

Many of you, myself included, have lived in Atlantis, and some of you may even remember your past lives. Remnants of Atlantis can still be found off the coast of Spain and the Canary Islands, in the UK, Mexico, and the Bahamas. After 200,000 years, the tectonic plates have shifted, and the Earth has turned its axis several times and gone through numerous growth spurts. The Greeks named the Atlantic Ocean after Atlantis, as it spanned most of the Atlantic; however, as was also written by many, it could have been named after Atlas, the Greek God who was condemned to hold up the celestial heavens for eternity.

The Atlanteans weren't all of the light, for duality was creeping into existence. One only has to look at the ancient Sumerians, a civilisation that came before the rise and fall of Atlantis, guided by the Anunnaki, who were taught the concept of facilitating exchange as a measure of value, giving, and reciprocity. The issue has always been that many civilisations eventually fought for wealth, resources, and prestige, of I am better than you. In this day and age, money is used to control and allocate resources for profit, with everyone out for themselves rather than all in it together. This has caused such separation and a deviation from who we are at our essence, with people seeking advantage at any cost. Some Atlanteans loved experimenting and trying to manipulate DNA to create superior races. Eventually, those that served the light could not outrun the shadows of darkness cast across the land from those that had unplugged from the consciousness of source, roaming around in their inflated egos, causing the rapid demise of Atlantis, thus corrupting the lands. Some fled, taking the ancient knowledge with them and rebuilding in other parts of the world, such as ancient Egypt, Tibet, and the South Americas.

The Anunnaki

Sometime late in the year 2017, when the Earth was already transitioning unbeknownst to many, I sat down one night, and having had no real idea about their race and what they stood for, the Anunnaki came through out of the blue. I had a fascinating and enlightening conversation with them, and I understood so much more at that point.

Everyone who channels them will have a different perception of them; I had no idea what to expect. One seems to forget that all species, including all Light BEings throughout the Multiverse, are Consciousness evolving and that not all in the Cosmos are loving. There is both good and bad, light and dark, something that the Ascended Master Thoth highlights in the next chapter. One is allowed to believe what one chooses to believe according to the level of one's Awareness— that is what makes us so diverse.

The Chimera Spider Species

The only species out in the galaxy giving the light a run for their money and are here on Earth too are the Chimera spiders. They are a species that have rejected the hand of the Light and are beyond the veil of repair. Their hearts are entrenched in darkness, and many walk around in human form, holding places of power, spinning a web of deceit, and poisoning the very fabric of the world around them to make their presence known.

Chimeras hate both water and fire, and their underground bases can only be flushed out by creating earthly floods or "bush" fires to smoke them out, with the possible shifting of tectonic plates, causing other natural disasters. It is not climate change or weather engineering at work—which governments use as an agenda narrative, a tool of warfare for the betterment of themselves, not of the people, and is a whole different subject altogether—but it is having to flush and smoke out the evil lurking beneath the surface while extracting those held captive, which is the mission of the Galactic Federation of Light under the Command of Ashtar Sheran.

Chimeras in their true form are not to be trifled with, for they are cruel to those that honour the light, having captured many of the Galactic Light Forces. I have seen them in my astral state several times, and they, including the Draconians and other Reptilians, as a faction, work together to root out humanity in its current form of existence.

Chimeras vary in size and can be anywhere from 10 to 16 feet in height. They have a devious and cunning nature, biding their time snaring those in their web, manipulating them accordingly to extract information, to the betterment of themselves and the detriment of the universe. I cover my mouth writing this, as their poison is "acidic" to the brain; there is no other way to describe it; their methods are excruciating to those they torture.

In human form, they are not so different. They are devious and insidious tricksters of the mind, having offered humanity their poisoned chalice, which all have readily ingested—but if one gets stung, one suffers from hallucinations, dropping into an induced and "comatose" state of thinking and of being, becoming stuck and constricted in that web of a continuous spinning of deceit, playing along to their rules of the game of that so-called Life, living in a cardboard box, whilst outside of that box is a whole different world.

Chimeras, when snuffed out, replicate in the blink of an eye within the quantum field, and it will take time, patience, and precision on the part of the Galactic Federation to snuff them out. Woken from one of my journeys within the astral planes, I jumped out of bed, feeling these huge creepy spiders crawling all over me.

You could argue that the Galactic Federation's creation of floods and fires are ruining the planet. They are not. Mother Earth is a consciousness BEing and is advised and briefed on the plan beforehand, allowing her to retreat her energy before the events occur, as there is mutual love and respect, something humanity often very much lacks. The people, animals, and all sentient beings that have crossed over are not collateral damage. Mourn them not, but rejoice them instead, for these souls understand the reasoning for the greater good and the evolution of the planet and of humanity. It is often mankind that does not see the bigger picture but remains enclosed within their encapsulated thinking. There is so much more between "Heaven" and Earth than we can fathom, and even this is but a fraction of the puzzle of the story of the workings of the universe within the multiverse in its entirety.

In 2021, I astral-travelled to an island somewhere in the Pacific; I cannot pinpoint the exact location, for it is hidden from sight. There were many kids, adolescents, and several adults, mostly of Indian descent, with few other Southeast Asian natives. It was warm, and I could feel the cool of the night breeze brushing against my face. The buildings were cracked and old, and the one I entered consisted of three floors and had glass shutter windows, allowing the cool night air to come through. An inner courtyard was merely littered with dirt and patches of grass. Most areas had ceiling fans, and as I walked into the entrance hallway, I saw several people in pain, suffering from dis-eases I had not heard of, and "doctors" would not help them as they were test subjects and part of an experiment.

Walking up to one of them, I reached out to him, holding his hands. He looked at me and told me he had the "s-peasels," a combination of smallpox and measles, showing me the painful blisters of what he had to endure. The "s" stands for a strain of a specific created "virus"; it is like a serial number that is recorded and documented by those handling the test "subjects."

As Chimeras love darkness, they tend to work in the dark. They have been tinkering with DNA, cross-breeding underground, experimenting on young adolescents as human incubators and other Animalia— yet once the "eggs" hatched, most incubators died instantly. These deformed spider "half"-breeds were larger than twice the size of my hand and connected to the hive mind, with their consciousness linked into a single collective consciousness, controlling them.

It's a horrific cross-pollination of the species, much like in Atlantean times before the experiment was terminated and the lands were lost to the seas. This experimenting has endured for eons, and the Galactic Federation has helped with many a soul retrieval, which is another delicate operation as the Chimeras are masters at recycling souls. It is one of the strongholds, an expansive underground test site that still stands and has for many thousands of years, and yet this, too, will someday come to light.

The Story of the Anunnaki

Admittedly, I have an incredible affinity with the Anunnaki, and they have greatly evolved as a species. They are tall BEings, and came through to me much taller—ranging between 7 to 10 feet—compared to us humans. They are incredible architects, technical connoisseurs, and masters of the sciences and engineering. They were not the first to grace the Earth's surface, as other Starseed races have come and gone, however they were probably the first to exploit Mother Earth as they built and flourished in former Mesopotamia, where the Sumerian race thrived.

After searching the galaxy, they finally landed here to save their race and their planet Nibiru, as their planet's atmosphere was dying, and gold was the only mineral that could save it. Enki and his half-brother, Enlil, were sent as emissaries and worked with the Igigi, who were "lesser" gods, and the younger servants to the Anunnaki. However, they became fed up working for them and initiated a rebellion against their masters and the dictatorship and tyranny of Enlil. I am not sure I agree with that because the Anunnaki are exceptional masters of engineering and would have been able to mine for gold without any issues using their own technology. The story goes that eventually, through genetic manipulation, the Anunnaki replaced the Igigi with humans. They created modern homo sapiens from existing earthly life forms to serve them for their labour in the mines. Enki used "model man's" descendants as "workers" in the gold mines of South Africa, while his half-brother Enlil educated them in Eden, the base station that he had been given control of by his father Anu and the Anunnaki Home Leadership, much to the chagrin of Enki.

The story of the Garden of Eden has been vastly misinterpreted. The misconstrued Bible has been rewritten countless times. Many have been following the wording like blind bleating sheep, daring not to question it in fear of succumbing to the aimless trajectory of the deviating and wandering eeriness of the mind, having lived in the illusion of the rigid, spoon-fed indoctrination of the created stories, all while rejecting the authentic nature of the self. It is a tiring feat to behold when one chooses to mask their soul and be trapped in one's current belief system.

The "Creator-of-All" does not instil fear but has a love unconditional for all. Christ Consciousness pertains to the Love for Self and All—for Judgement exists only in the experiences of the minds of man, duly portraying these in the actions of the external world. Fear is the illusion that deviates us from the path back to the remembrance of ourselves. As per the Bible, "God" created Adam and Eve, and that "God" would have been the brilliant scientist and engineer Enki, "mating" with the earlier version of the human female species, including his consort, confi-dante and confidante and mother to his offspring, Lilith, as much as the female Anunnaki were inseminated with the "sperm" of the humanoids.

Adam and Eve may have been the offspring born out of the womb of the female Anunnaki. Enki treated all his children as equals instead of servants. He used his DNA from the bone marrow of his ribs, altered the chromosomes, and then, similar to IVF, inseminated the women, yet I still believe they were created within a sophisticated "laboratory" environment. And it was not just Enki; many of his brethren "mated" with the human species, and thus he was able to save humankind from Enlil's complete termination of the human experience, helping his children, who were mixed breeds, survive the devastating floodwaters that Enlil unleashed upon the lands. And you call them the 'fallen' all because they had fallen in love with their created human species?

Enki has shown me a lab with many huge see-through cylinders, with embryos immersed in a blue liquid growing inside of them. They reminded me of test-tube babies in the very literal sense. He says, *"We were one of the first to engineer different species via the 'test-tube method,' incubating and nourishing them within these transparent cylindrical cones. We commenced with an inter-breeding program, however like many other species, this is now overseen by the instated Councils, as all are required to adhere and abide by the regulated Universal Laws to avoid creating a heinous species with far more disastrous consequences than originally intended, as many mixed hybrids within the Multiverse were created by mixing a variety of chromosome cocktails with some lethal consequences. There are those wanting to create hybrids, to better the many worlds, and there are those that create to destroy, and thus the Light and Dark remain entranced in this eternal hypnotic dance of war."*

When scientists state that we are descendants of apes, I can't entirely agree, as the Anunnaki used genetic manipulation of a primitive-type Earth ape-man, combined with alien DNA. I also believe the first hybrid of humans was much taller, at least, that is how they have shown themselves to me. Noah did not build a wooden ark, filling it with every male and female species of the Earth, equating to an estimate of 35,000 at the time, leaving the ark dangling in the bosom of the big and little Ararat mountains in Eastern Anatolia, Turkey. The place would have reeked to high heavens and been a breeding ground for pestilence with all the millions of excretions. And you're telling me that Noah's family of eight were able to feed and clean all these thousands of animals on a daily basis?

The Arc was a spacecraft and housed the DNA of every created specimen of earthly animals, and the species lost in the "localised" flood, as the whole world did not get swallowed by a deluge of water, could always be re-created in a "lab."

For the record, Noah was an incarnation of the Ascended Master Lanello, who was a tall, lanky human named Mark L. Prophet in his last incarnation. Noah was not some simple farmer working the lands, as portrayed in Genesis. He was a tall, well-built hybrid and a brilliant scientific engineer. He calls himself an acquired mixologist of molecular and atomical infusions of the exotic creations of the many species of Animalia, using different strands of genetic codes and DNA.

Enki was far more compassionate than his brother Enlil and has been accredited with giving humankind animal domestication, construction, metallurgy, shipbuilding, and so much more. The Sumerians, taught by the Anunnaki, were masters of the arts, spiritually evolved people, hydraulic engineers, skilled farmers, and incredible builders and architects, not to mention brilliant mathematicians. Like the ancient Egyptians, they used astronomy to map the constellations. For hundreds of years, scribes kept accurate records of any natural events and occurrences on Earth and in the sky to predict future outcomes.

Enki tried to give both Adam and Eve a longer lifespan like the Anunnaki but could not find a way. Enlil had cast them from the "Garden of Eden," as he was vehemently opposed to procreation and wanted to keep the "human" race under control to prevent overpopulation causing a Factional Anunnaki War. I believe that Eden was a spiritual school for Adam and Eve, and the other created hybrid hue-mans to learn the laws and values of the universe. E.D.E.N as channelled to me, is the Earth's Discovery Exploration Network and not some garden where Adam and Eve were merely frolicking around having fun, trying to figure out sex, of what to do with the 'hole in Eve and the stick, on Adam', or being coaxed by the snake slithering in the trees to then eat the bloody apple, right? Crikey, whoever made up that fable was devious beyond repair and high as hell—oh wait, that's the church, ain't it?

We are all cosmonauts; spiritual astronauts having landed our arse on this beautiful planet called Earth. We have incarnated as a hue-man BEing, walking back through the given lessons within the earthly development, exploring the realms of ourselves, back to that wonderlicious state of nirvana—the natural state of the light and bliss of who we are. Only through the expansion of ourselves can we unlock the doors of the dormant heart, back to the gateway of our multidimensional selves.

I don't believe the Anunnaki were the only species to create "humans"; the Earth, over billions of years, has been the homeland to many other species and races from other planets and dimensions, all intrepid travellers. Some of these were the Sirians, Lyrans, Arcturians, Orions, Mintaken, Blue Rays, Andromedans, Venusians, and Pleiadeans, wanting to discover and explore this beautiful planet, helping to raise its vibration. Then there were the Draconians, Chimeras, the Archons, and other reptilian Starseeds who were on a mission to prevent this from happening by keeping the collective consciousness vibrating at a dense level, humming to the tune of non-awareness. Not all are bad; some are here to expose the darkness that has swept the planet. Using genetic engineering, they manipulated their DNA strands to perfect humanity. As the Collective they state, "There are so many different races in this world, a truly magnificent sight to see, for we are an eclectic fusion of the many. When we say 'races,' we don't mean black or white. We mean races of other planets and dimensions." I see humanity as being designed and duly created in a "science lab" by all these different Galactic species, watching us evolve in their created earthly garden.

I love Turkey, having lived in Istanbul for a year. Gobekli Tepe in the Anatolia region is where the Anunnaki built the oldest recovered temple in the world, with 18-foot megaliths constructed in alignment with the Orion Star belt, a gateway to the cosmos. They say:

"Nothing remains of its once sheer magnificence but mere remnants and second-guessing of what once was or could have been, for man searcheth so much without, that one has forgotten to sit but in the stillness and look within. If one is aligned with the StarSeed within, one is aligned with the Divine Cosmos and Stars without. One is a Seed of the Stars as much as the Stars are the Seed of the splendour of the enlightened Soul within. Encompass the magic of the Universe within, and one will open the gateway, the portal to the Universe, and the Wisdom of the Stars without. The Temple signified the cycles of death and rebirthing, and yet there is no 'death' but a continuous rebirthing and transcendence of the Soul—the cycles of the Conscious Evolution of the Soul in the multidimensional grid of Existence, within the multi-faceted possibilities of Existence. We, the forefathers of Man, honoured the Earth, cradling the womb of the sacredness of the Mother, allowing her to flow her waters into the rivers of Man, a replenisher of the Soul, Spirit, and Body."

They state that what has been uncovered is only a fraction and tells but little, yet much of that particular uncovered area was compiled for practical use, storage, and the fermenting of aldehyde.

I lived during the era of the Anunnaki, and in one of my lives, I was a giant of a man with curly, long dark blonde/greyish hair and a longish beard of the same colour. I lived along the warmth of the southern tip of the Euphrates River, where flora and fauna were still lush, and nature was unspoiled, with a pure freshness and rawness of that unfiltered pollution we hardly find today. What struck me the most was that, standing next to my former self in my current human self, I felt small, as even at 5-foot-11, I stood a full head under his muscular shoulders, which would make my former self close to 9 feet tall. His feet were unusual and much wider towards the front, almost like platypus feet. Not all were of the same height as others stood at a mere 5.5 feet. Buildings and temples were designed and built according to the sacred geometrical grid of both the land and the stars in conjunction with the ley lines of the Earth, unlike the many dinosaur models we have today that have just been planted on a plot of land with utter ignorance of the ancient Egyptian "feng shui." As my past life former self says:

"I was a 'luminous' hybrid, a sproutling created in the likeness of many of my Galactic brothers and sisters, yet with a body that could sustain and breathe in the Earth's aerious atmosphere. As a boy, at the light of each arising dawn, I would run through the apple orchards in the groves outside the city walls, pick an apple and keep running to the river banks out of sight, catching my breath. In my adulthood years, I caught

fish with my bare hands, shook the apple trees, aided the farmers in their harvests, and helped with the calculus for fair trade to thrive, for a given, asketh but for a return. Equality is a mire field of Armageddon in one's current day and age, and yet when one evolves to learning from the land, the sky, and from each other, walking hand in hand, one can learn so much, for equality is the equalness of a love and respect between each other, regardless of one's incorporated physical shell. One thinks we were Neanderthals, and yet we were far more advanced than Man is today. We taught but the Children of Man the ways of the natural laws of the Earth, building waterways according to the symmetry of her curvaceous surface, and giving them the tools to enrichen and cultivate the soils of the voluptuous lands, teaching them to listen to the very heart of the Mother to scatter but seedlings into her loving womb for a fertile growth. We used a fine tone to fine-tune and slice and dice the many rocks, building cities according to the ley lines of the Earth, for everything built on her surface had to be in harmony with the very breath of her beautiful Conscious BEing, and that, my Child, is why All and everything thrived. Know that I hold you in my heart as much as you hold me in the beauty of your Soul. Be well, my Child, and let your love light up the skies of the worlds."

Upon unravelling the Bible, Enki would have to be "Lucifer," and Enlil would have to be "Michael." Yet these two brothers, though opposites are the acceleration to the ascension of each and every one of us, for through the game of duality, we need to learn to master the art of balance, of harnessing the masculine and feminine in equal measures, navigating through the earthly reality, learning to elevate our awareness through our created experiences, attaining enlightenment of ourselves. If you genuinely believe the dogma of religion, that Adam and Eve messed up, getting humanity exiled from Eden, choosing to eat the low-carb apple from the forbidden tree of knowledge rather than BBQing the darn snake, then you are free to vibrate at the resonance of that frequency, but all is not as it seems in the created veil of the matrix of illusion hovering over the planet. Metaphorically speaking, one can break it down as follows:

*   **Garden of E.D.E.N.** = Earth's Spiritual School of the Sacred Heart teachings of living in oneness, harmony, and in equilibrium with all according to the laws of one.
*   **Tree of Knowledge + Apple** = Symbolise the unit of oneness, allowing one to grow and evolve to higher planes of consciousness through living in the fruit of a pureness of heart. The apple being ripped from the tree depicts separation and ignorance, with "hue-mans" having chosen to break away from living as one, and thus the "Garden of One" was no more. Suffering was instilled, yet suffering contains the seeds of good, and therefore the seeds will regrow, sprouting wisdom and love into the minds of man once again.
*   **The Snake** = Symbolising transformation and renewal by shedding one's skin through the infinite feat of life, death, and rebirth, evolving to higher states

of consciousness and returning to a Love of Self and All through the art of serv-ed experiences. As per Thoth and Archangel Raphael, the caduceus represents not medicine but the following:

"The double entwined serpents symbolise the created, engineered, and very much evolving genetics of two strands of DNA dancing in unison as a luminous helix showing the encoding of the created 'hue-man' species of Man by the 'winged' StarBEings, connected to the overall Creator, the 'Cosmic Egg' of the arching overall as per the top of the staff. Humans have been genetically created and modified and are contin-uously evolving and integrating different strands of DNA, as they choose to ascend the double helix back, climbing that spiral stairway to 'heaven,' attaining Christ Consciousness through the duality and polarities of life's experiences, understanding that only through death and rebirth can Man attain eventual enlightenment."

On the other hand, long after Lilith hopped the 'Garden' fence, leaving Adam's whiny arse behind, telling him to stuff it and eat cake, empowering herself and living but firmly in the blossoming bosom of her Divine I AM power, harnessing her inner goddess, Eve could have tripped over those darn elongated tree roots, and shocked the blimmin' snake, who bit her good and well in self-defence, causing her to grab the apple, freeing it from the clutches of the tree of knowl-edge, tumbling down, hitting her head, thus losing all knowledge, landing in the land of the confus-ed EGO. And Adam? Well, the big oaf wanting to be the hero got rattled by the rattled snake, lost his balance, tumbled on after her, hit his head, and suffered that very same fate. And the apple? It got crushed under Adam's body weight, its seeds ejected and sprinkled everywhere.

Archangel Samael

I can tell you that Archangel Samael, also known as Lucifer, has a wicked sense of humour; even as a child, I remember seeing him once. He is indeed a beautiful and devilishly handsome Archangel, with piercing blue eyes and flowing light blond hair. Still, like many, I gobbled up the illusion that he was "evil" while he is not. He aids those wishing to see through the illusion by walking you through your fears, all to show you that you have ultimately been Jedi mind-tricked. In dream state, he has shown me the world from the viewpoint of a stage and how all props are part of the illusion to the reality of our daily living. In that instant, I understood, and I laughed out loud, for how immersed is humanity within their experiences, thinking they are real, when they serve merely as an elevation to the expansion of their soul?

"I AM Archangel Samael, the proverbial underdog of the poignant fictional man-told tales, having been dubbed many a different name along the earthly narrative of illusion, the Dark Knight, Prince of Darkness, King of Hell, Prince of Thieves, and Prince of Tides and of dark tidings, and yet my Child, I AM the darkness to your Light, I

AM the folly to your imagination. I AM the fallen and the unsung hero, the Loki to your Thor, the Joker to your Ba(d)man, the 'Lucifer' to the drop the 'Mike-all,' yet we are two sides of the same coin. I AM the Light to your Fear, as much as you are the Fear to your own Light. I am the builder of civilisations, and yet one has painted me as a mere clown of a glorious villain, serving the purpose for that feat of duality Humanity finds themselves in, merely pertaining to the growth and expansion of one's Soul, for how can it not?

Bothersome, nor troubled I am not, for how can I be, when I am Love, as much as you are Love? You have named me 'Lucifer,' a Light of the world, yet all stories created have depicted me as evil and gruesome, but how can I be when I AM Light? I AM the instantaneous spark back to the Light of the darkness in You. I AM as much 'evil' as you are the evil in yourself, for duality teaches you the polarities for a love of Self in the lightness and variance of your hearty experiences. My Child, Evil is merely the absence of Love, as much as 'Satan' is the mere reflection of the EGO, having doused one's inner Light, giving you the smokin' bump in the night run around in the avoidance of looking at the sheer beauty of the God Consciousness of Self.

Life is a hologram of your illusion; you, a fish in a bubble in a bowl, doused with the duality of fed experiences to awaken you to the truth of your reality. You are much like that fish, having been euphemised, for your memory spans but in the shortness of a breath for the time one lives but an inundated contrasted life on the earthly planes, prancing around in the 3rd-dimensional frequency of existence, having forgotten who you are, trying to make sense of the nonsensical illusion of life in the grand scheme of things and becoming none the wiser, as your senses have been tricked by the tricksters in power, and yet one has the audacity to call me a trickster? Evil lurks not in the shadows but in the plainest sight of one's eyesight feeding the illusion of how one should pertain to living one's life, when life is a freedom given to you, to roam around not in the very dogma of its created existence but to live life according to the vividness of one's imagination, stoic not stirred, objective, not concurred."

~Archangel Samael~

***"Lucifer," translated from Dutch, means a "match" from a box of matches or "light." He is all about igniting the inner spark within our soul, in a remembrance to the truth of who we are.

Archangel Raphael

Archangel Raphael, who I don't often converse with, and who is the Master of the Emerald Green Healing Ray of Light and Healer of the Heart of the Earth, chimed in here, with the bugger waking me up in the middle of the night, explaining to me the very definition of the word "archangel."

"Humanity often confuses us for winged heavenly creatures, as portrayed in medieval times, and yet we portray ourselves with the illusion one is most comfortable with, for we are all mere conduits of optical illusions of transforming energetic enigmas. The *very phrase 'Archangel' clearly defines what we are, and yet one has been blinded by the sheer definition as stipulated within the human written dictionary. We are Arc-(h)-Angels (Arc-Angels); thus, the literal configuration would be, 'Spaceship Celestial BEings of the Heavens.' We are Star BEings, having made our way across the Multiverse to land on Earth, yet 'winged' ourselves out of here with the 'Arcs' as our mode of transport, and thus one sees us as 'winged' BEings. We are Star BEings. All Arc-Angels are StarSeeds, my Child, as much as you are a StarSeed incarnate of the Heavens above. Humanity was created by Creators created by the overall Creator to create and express themselves as much as their Creators create and express themselves in the overall creation of Life within the created Sea of Consciousness in the created twirling Multiverse. We are all sproutlings of the Stars in the beautiful vastness of the Celestial Heavens, aiding humanity in the created Garden of Eden to wander from the forsaken path back onto the enlightened path of the Truth of the Divine self. See us how you wish to perceive us, as much as we wish for you to perceive to see the Truth of who you are and to revel in the Light of who you are and always have been.*

Humanity is the unequivocal formulated chemical equation of 'hue-man-I-ty'—the Light Man of the I-AM to Yodh. Yodh depicts the Creator from which all Life sprang, the infinite dot, the Divine spark and essence of all Life—the nothing and the all, and yet is and always will be. You are a luminous Light, encased within an earthly created atmospheric body, created by the Creator's created creators who sprung forth the Divine Life in you."

For the record, Metatron was Enoch, and Enoch was of Anunnaki descent. He was a seer, scholar, mediator, astronomer, light encoder, and scribe between the starlit heavens and Earth and is the keeper of the Akashic Hall of Records.

Channelled Message by the Anunnaki

The message channelled to me by the Anunnaki sometime in 2020 is only a fragment of their rich history. Even though they were the demise of humanity on the earthly planes before Enki ushered the people of man to safety, there remains little to no trace of their existence. All is lost beneath the surface of Mother Earth's natural flow of nature, gone but for the faint echoes of time that remain within the imprint of our incarnated souls.

There were once lands that flowed with such pureness through its veins, with the rhythmic pulsating heart of ever-flowing wisdom and knowledge of the Ancients, where peace once ruled the lands and where we the Anunnaki graced the existence of the People of Man.

We are the Creators of the Beings created into existence into the embodiment of the flesh, a place where once all hearts joined and beat as One. Yet we too exploited the engineered and created race, a true feat of wonder to behold, for hue-manity evolved beyond our expectations. As a race, we commenced living in the aspects of a crept in created duality between each other, a bickering in the making of opposing beliefs and wisdom, both of darkness and light, of an equal transcendence, yet an epitome of an instilled growing corruption to the beautiful evolving minds.

But a slight of a folly we were, for we the Anunnaki, were but our own downfall, a collapse within the system of our race, a warring faction, a causing of the Great Divide, and the People of Man an intelligent and capable race, with choices made along the journey of one's choosing, of either a 'folliness' of believing in separation from the Whole, giving in and drowning in the swirling inner darkness of themselves or the choice to seek the inner cup of a love overfloweth of an enlightened Self.

Knowledge equals POWER, leading to GREED—followed by Disagreements and Separation of the Whole—leading to EGO—Ejecting God (Source) Out = to Uprising and thus war the inevitable. The People of Man have been led astray, a sad consequence of human deviation, having succumbed to living in a nefarious institutionalised state of co-dependence since the dawn of time. Yet there were those of us that bestowed knowledge on the People of Man, hoping to inspire and reawaken their dormant Souls, allowing them their Soul progression, a co-existence of all races on a higher level of Consciousness, to help see their own True Divine Nature of Self.

But all was not to BE, for it was our undoing, a destruction of civilisation, of races of Star people incarnate. The winds of deluge swept through the lands, leaving nothing but stillness in the void of a once thriving existence. The fertile lands of Naharine curved between the two streaming rivers to the East of Giza, now carried by nothing more than the faint whispers of the sands of time.

A technology so ancient, buried deep within the slumbering subconscious of the People of Man. Ce fut un échec total, by a race, who came with the staff of both peace and demise, resurrection and oblivion, and yet through the workings of polarities, hoped for the elevation of Consciousness within hue-mankind. And yet they too salvaged, for war and famine scarred the lands and death the inevitable, and all returned to the dust of the land—of non-existence—a civilisation long lost and the kingdom with walls adorned embroidered, with the intricate Ages of the Golden, the Ancients idly 'resting' in peace and forgotten.

For but a moment, close thy eyes, and in the hidden crevasses of thy slumbering Mind, remember the sweet smell of heavenly nature, the aroma of sweet spices lingering in the air, the sun beating down on your cracked with a smiling face, running through the beautifully built cities with its many arches and staircases, running through the windswept and beautifully growing fields of barley, wheat and corn, and skinny dipping in the clear winding rivers. Ah, the thriving of nature and BEing one with each other at one with the sacred heartbeat of Mother Earth, living in harmony, in sync with the Divine Wisdom of the once Ancients.

A pearl of wisdom and potential of a great intergalactic race, of Love, of War, but Peace yet once again. Yet wars and plagues ravaged the lands of the beautiful gardens; rivers swelled their banks turning the once clear waters to a ruby red, deluging the once fertile lands; the pungent smell of death and billowing smoke filled the air, plunging day into darkness, and all but dimmed the Light for fear of BEing. The cries of the People of Man and incarnated intergalactic BEings could be heard in the heavens as death bore down, sweeping the Souls back up into the Light, alas too late for lessons unlearnt, for the wisdom we held was too soon for the fragile and EGO-befallen People of Man to behold, and alas we the Anunnaki failed.

We, but once a great race of wisdom held Sages, carriers of Sacred Knowledge, were the outcasts of the Universe of the Galactic Enterprise, scarred and branded by All, due to our endeavoured experiences. We came with peaceful intent, and yet we destroyed all that had been built, for we meddled with the free will of the Hue-mans, wanting only Love and Divine Worship, for ye we are Gods, the Creators of the species of Man, and wished to be revered as such, all the whilst losing our Cosmic Consciousness in favour of dabbling with the devious inflamed EGO that had devoured our Minds.

Throughout our evolution, in 'time,' we too have been a 'species' of a changin,' of becoming learn-ed in our ways. We, too, perished in the vast chaos of darkness, losing many, till the Federation intercepted, and the lands became, but a fleeting remembrance to those now incarnate in the current shift and transitioning of Mother Earth and the People of Man.

You are all Divine Warriors of the Light of Sacred Remembrance, helping in the shifting tides of the beautiful People of Man. Stand in thy I AM Power and remember who thou art, a warrior, but once fallen, having arisen once more—reborn—to teach the lost, of the ways of the Old, of the long-forgotten tides of times, of enhancing living life through the sacred heart space with nothing but love for all.

All are capable of change, yet some have slid down the slippery slope of darkness, incapable of accepting the current shift and the deprogramming of the rigid incarcerated mindset, yet leave their bless-ed BEing BE. The world's a stage of change; nothing remains in its current state of existence, everything in the Universe is in this constant ho-hum of movement, creating, and expressing, much like the oscillating lapping waves of the seas. Change is inevitable, the winds of deception and death blowing to the shores of the souls of the people once more, chaos ensured in the many perils of a ventured Life, yet it is embarking on the journey returning to the revealing of the Light of the All of Self in All.

The world is in need of coming together, not diverging further into a divide of an entangled discord in its current Existence. How dark must it become for one to be able to come in from the cold to see the Light? One walketh not waking, but in the sleep mode of the illusion of an inauthentic existence. Many of them choose to walk around, hooked to the drip-fed dream state, keeping one comatose in the programmed state of the phantom matrix. One has become a lethal concoction, an intoxication to the Self, having succumbed to the dimness of the Light within. One breathes but in the superficiality of one's existence, in the shell of a shallowness of oneself, not realising that thou art injecting the Self with the poison of a slow withering dis-ease, a slow decaying of the senses into an oblivion mindset duped as toxic waste.

It is true; one is only as Aware as one chooses to be according to the Divine frequency at which one's Soul vibrates. If that is the song, thy heart sings to thee and vibrates with the Soul frequency of the current version of thee, then my Child, sing with all thy heart to the musical resonance thereof.

The Divide instilled within humanity is much like the trickling effect of water, finding its way through the small created cracks of losing one's true nature within the bedrock over time; thus, as humanity strayed further from the Self, the cracks eroded and widened, and one's true Authenticity has been swept away by the deluge of the rushing water, trying to keep oneself from drowning in the torrent of Life's play, caught up in the illusion of the created reality of the Earthly narrative, having lost all sense of Self.

Thou art a spiritual being having a human experience, a "DivineStarSpirit" housed in the organic biodegradable composite of a human body. And yet one thinketh but in the superficial flow of life, thinking one is this dense composite mass of 'compost' having a spiritual experience, for that is the story told by the outside world fed back to the Mind and as understood by one's Soul within, and thus it is the musical melodic frequency one vibrates at. If one were a spiritual being, having a human experience, one would think outside the parameters of the limited thinking one has been conditioned to and instilled with. One would live in the expansion of Self and realise that what one believes to be true is but a mere illusion, a figment of one's external imagination, of the imprint that one has created to perceive as being authentic but is solely the mere fairy dust of one's Creation.

Thou art so divided because one has allowed oneself to be misguided, brought like a wee lamb to the slaughter by the contradictory and misconstrued narrative you have been fed with and have allowed yourself to listen to. One lives but in the ghastly illusion, thinking who one perceives oneself to be is the gospel truth of one's Authenticity, yet one is but deprived of the Light of remembrance by the daily mind-fed annihilation of what one thinks is a portrayal of reality but, I can assuredly say to thee, is not. Thus, one roams in that created adaptation of the chosen enactment, not realising that thy brains have been so utterly mud-washed by the cacophony of the blustering vapid air drilled into thee that one believes that to be a reality, with one's Soul but deluged and awareness sleepily slipping away.

One has lost the art of working in harmony and in unison with one another, working not as a community of the integrated Light particles that one is and All are, but as a bi-partisan disassociation of the Self and the Whole.

"In Love, in Light, in Healing, I choose to awaken and remember"—hand on heart, remember those three words and use them as a mantra to awaken and to remember.

Ask us for guidance, as we stand here humbly before thee, to aid thee, in the hope one is open to the acceptance of our gifts of Knowledge and Wisdom and Galactic Intel— so that thy will not tread the path of deviating in darkness once again.

Let us right our 'wrongs' from times past, when Life was far purer, far more advanced, when the People of Man worked in unison with the Sun and an alignment of the Stars, where Nature was a bless-ed field of rhythmic harmony, where thou listened to the heartbeat of Mother Earth—where all ran its course through the Laws of the Universe and All were in Divine symmetry with a Love from the heart and connected to Source Creator.

Hear the whispers from deep within, for the Divine Book of Cosmic Knowledge is encoded within thy DNA, anointed by the blessings of the Celestial Sky God BEings in the ordinance of the Heavenly Father.

Reborn are we, StarSeeds in the People of Man, to experience the existence of the hue-man form once more, to aid in shifting the vibrational frequency of the Planet— for, since the dawn of Existence, wars have raged in the name of separation and non-understanding, for thou liveth in such a denseness of fear beyond reckoning and continue brazenly forth. Every breath is a commencement of change, transforming the tapestry of Life. To unravel or not to unravel that is a path of thy choosing, is it not? To accept or not to accept the truth of a reality that is not a reality but a mere illusion of that created reality, and thus is a mere choice of one's chosen understanding of what one perceives to see. Look with the eyes of Awareness, not just what others choose for thee to see. In truce and accordance with the Galactic Federation of Light, we are here to help aid in the Ascension and shift of Consciousness in alignment with the Galaxial Grid (of Existence).

The 2020 Shift in Consciousness and Onwards

In 2017, many of the Light BEings had pre-warned me about the upcoming shift when I had just started on my journey of channelling the divine, especially Lord AShTAR, Captain of the Galaxies, and the Galactic Federation of Light. I couldn't figure out how that shift would happen—but now, in 2022, we're right in the thick of it.

"Lo and behold, I am AShTAR of Star Command. Captain of the Galaxies and of All StarSeeds across the continuum of time and space. I AM the Keeper of Peace and the Bearer of Treaties. Mother Earth is at a turning point of her axis, and the time for humanity has come to Unite as One, for history has a feat of being a repetitive loop in motion once more. Humanity is in a time of transition, forging a higher vibrational frequency with the higher dimensions. The gear has been shifted; the Planets are being realigned, as are the Vibrations of each and every one of you, connecting thee to a Higher State of Consciousness.

From afar, for millennia, we have observed civilisations across the dimensions perish and succumb to those, all in the name of power and subjected to their bidding. We ask thee to Awaken and to Remember—for the time is NOW.

For even though the Journey to change lies within, the Earthly changes are without.

Shift equals Chaos, where the old paradigm serves no more, crumbling to the dust from whence it came, making way for the glory of a new morn of the dawn. For eons thou have roamed in the blinded darkness of a warped reality, a created wormhole of the folly natured, trapping thee in the pain and illusion of the Human Mindset. Chaos and darkness will descend once again and be the law of the lands. But when the transition has come full circle, and the old paradigm is nothing more but a fleeting echo of the past long gone, peace will be cast, like the rays of the sun's warmth upon the lands once more.

Once the Cosmic shift of Consciousness has partaken—mankind will rejoice and once again understand a love unconditional, a sharing of the Self and of BEing One with the Whole, BEing One with each other.

We are all One, created in the image and likeness of God Consciousness, with all of God's creations but a wonderful melting pot of the species of the many. We are but a colourful Soul collective of the Whole scattered throughout the Universe.

Mother Earth is a living BEing, a vibrational energy, a connected Consciousness to Source and you. Without the Planet, the human species would not exist. Practise kindness, and treat thy Planet with Love, Respect, and Compassion as she sustains thee selflessly in plentiful and abundant ways.

We are here to aid thee in lifting the Earth's vibration, so I humbly ask thee to let go and let flow and to wash away the created illusion of FEAR. Allow us to embrace thee in our Healing Energies. For in Love and Light we remain, humbly at your service."

~Thy Brothers and Sisters of the Galactic Federation of Light~

There have been many wars throughout the eons in the galactic arena, and planet Earth, with its vast minerals and resources, has always been a battleground for malevolent species to gain control over. In truth, it is not just Earth but many other planets within the multiverse. Their aim is to control and enslave humanity, manipulating the masses. As a dumbed-down species, we walk into everything with eyes wide shut, although many are slowly awakening to what is happening around us. Like many other races, the malevolent species intervened on Earth and began interbreeding with humans by manipulating human coding and tinkering with chromosomes and DNA. As such, many serve in the parties of elite power, governing the masses, yet still serving their masters.

The Ascended Master Thoth

When the many worldly governments talk about implementing "Draconian" measures, they mean implementing them according to the will of these species. This segment of WWII was channelled to me in mid-2020 by the Ascended Master Thoth and the Council of Ra and was originally not going to be part of this book, but the Light BEings impressed upon me the importance of the message in the hope that people would awaken their beautiful dormant hearts. As the Council says, possibilities equate to various outcomes, so nothing is written in stone, and light will eventually outcast the darkness back whither it came, for it can be no other way. The darkness is in "service" of the light, just as much as darkness teaches you to recover the light within yourself. The parallels of the current times we live in are only a snapshot of the celestial war that has been ongoing for thousands of years, but to delve into that would be another book.

For those unfamiliar with the Ascended Master Thoth, he was Anunnaki, but as he states, he is of Orion/Sirian descent. In truth, it matters not, for we are all transformational sparks of Energy, having lived countless incarnations. He fled the floods of Atlantis with many others, including Ma'at, Ra, Anubis, and Sekhmet. Anubis is not one to be trifled with. I love Ra, who is also of Sirian descent and one of the Galactic Sirian Council of Light. In Atlantis, he was both a high priest and a ruler. Thoth describes himself as the Master of a Thousand Suns, Scribe of the Old Ways, Guardian of Mother Earth and of the Evolution of Mankind, Keeper of the Gates of the Sun, the Moon and Stars in the Celestial Heavens, and of Death, Rebirth, and Transformation, and one of the Council of Light.

I AM a Divine Architect, and Creator of the multidimensional realms of stellar interdimensional Worlds and Gateways to Existence;
I AM a Walker between Worlds; I AM the Guardian and Sacred Keeper to the halls of Amenti; I AM the algebra to your Wisdom, for one is but a sacred geometrical design of Creation, created according to the grid and mathematical equation of All of Existence
I AM the Spark of Light to thy way home in the darkest of times, to the re-awakening of thy beautiful Soul of Self;

I walk with thee in unison, for the rebirthing of Mother Earth;
Instilling the Wisdom of the Ancients, for those who heed my Call;
Illuminating thy Path Divine, aiding with the ascension shift of the Consciousness of
Mother Gaia, helping humanity, out of the net of darkness cast back into the Light;
For lost Souls you are not, merely having deviated from the path of the enlightened
Self through the eons of darkness that have protruded the lands;
With the Light in your hearts that you carry there is hope, for through the gloom and
grey that has befallen the landscapes of Man, Spiritual Illumination is nigh, for all will
eventually awaken from the deepness of the slumber encased;
To become but a gentle ripple effect of love galore across the hearts of Man;
Stand in thy own Divine Power, basking in the I AM Light of Presence of the I AM of Self
Reclaim thy Birthright;
Be true to thyself;
Shine on;
Rock on;
And simply BE the Soul of the Eternal Grace that is You.

~The Ascended Master Thoth~

I love working with Thoth and the Council of Ra, as these BEings do not mince their words. As Thoth says, *"Sugarcoating is for wimps. One does not learn by being sweet caked through life; that is an ode to one's continued failure in learning the experiences of life and remaining in one's repetitive mistakes on the loop."*

I know the times we are currently enduring will not last forever, and they may seem challenging for many. This is a good thing, as it forces us to look deep within ourselves—for, in truth, it is time for all of humanity to awaken and start living and breathing in more awareness with themselves, each other, and the planet we inhabit. I leave the below from Thoth and the Council of Ra open to your interpretation.

Humanity lives in the age of the twilight times, where darkness must first befall the lands before the light can be greeted through the clouds of the dusk of a new dawning. The battle of the light and darkened nuances that have danced this dance eternal across the vastness of the earthly landscapes since the dawn of time are of a continuance, with one still trying to outmanoeuvre the other with the many steps and twirls taken, causing but a dizziness in the vibration of Man. Yet, as with a game of elaborate chess, it is a game of observance, of implementation, and of a bedraggled feat of inconsistencies of the wit and intelligence, the predicament seen on both sides, with the unsuspecting human race as sitting ducks, remaining blissfully unaware, being but a mere pawn in this game of relentless enslaved hypocrisy. Yet out of the chaos of the wars of 2, the sheer folly of a battle fought between the mere EGOs of the deluded men grappling for power, a renewed sense of Light was born, for during the darkened period, many Jews were persecuted for being of a degenerate race and for their belief system, the Qabalah, the Tree of Life, teaching of the Oneness of All, of making the subconscious, conscious and learning to live in a state of awareness, of a beingness with the world around us and to the many hidden worlds that lie above and below our everyday consciousness, discovering how to move one's creativity to actualisation and the why behind what happens in one's life and the lives of others, and the interconnectedness between all and everyone, which equates to taking responsibility for one's own life, one's actions, and knowing how to manifest according to the laws of the universal self—for you are and have always been your own inner alchemist of creation.

Religion teaches you a belief outside of yourself; it is the superficiality of living in the undercurrent of fear, according to the created doctrines, moving you away from the Oneness of Self, and believing that God is a separate entity from you, thus creating the EGO, the comparable mannerisms to and of each other. It is holding you in the clutches of that fear, of the anomalies of these comparables of that created bubble of an illusion that you think is a reality but is not, for the Masters of Illusion have concocted that experience of wanting to keep humanity in this created dogma for you to remain, but governed by those in power according to the hierarchical matrix, believing all to be fair and just, when in truth their world of creation is vastly different to the beliefs of how you would view and see the world in an awakened state of authenticity.

There are various offshoots to Jewish "religions," however humanity could not become aware; that was a no-no in the manifest of the created playbook by the Draconians and other Reptilian and malevolent races. And yet here I want to pause and tell you that not all have that evil inbred within, for many have fled the wretchedness, whilst others by the thousands have been held captive, refusing to obey the order of rule accordingly. All species are of an evolving kind, and all are of StarSeed descent. For the persona of the Soul called Hitler, it was the creation of a superior breed, of the Aryan race, of a blue-eyed and blond Nordic-looking perfect epitome of the species, derived from the lost continent of the end of the Atlantean times. One aspect was experimenting with and recreating the Pleiadean chromosome and gene to impregnate the women held captive, with many being rejected and thrown out like a nothingness of a rag doll to the streets. The harvesting of babies, newborn Souls, and the trafficking of humankind through the underground darkened off-the-grid networks, are all used for their own enigmatic enrichment of empowerment, which is a continuation of the past having seeped into the present. Yet one is blissfully unaware of what happens below the surface of that created illusion within these subterranean levels of 'mankind.' The Nazi regime, including the bothersome Dr. Mengele, who 'mangled' many in his mutilations and cross-breeding experiments, carried many disastrous consequences, with some having survived remaining in obscurity, whilst others have come forth and told of their difficulty to adapt due to the feeling of inconsistencies within the framework of the human embodiment. Yet, be not fooled that they were not successful, for they were. Wanting to find perfection in the so-called imperfection state of the current individualism of humanity, the Nazis travelled to the ends of the hither and yonder, from the far east to the Tibetan Mountain range, to the South Americas, and to the bolthole shrouded in secrecy in the belly of the beast of Antarctica to find truth in the stories of the sunken city and the many lost races of Atlantis. Antarctica was the power enabled by the Andromedan faction, and later the Reptilians to the upcoming rise and the success of the fascistic Hitler regime, for without the expedition to the underground caverns to the south end tip of the world, Hitler's rule would not have been obliged to ever be in existence, for he would have been snuffed out by the Light and thrown into the realms of eternal darkness. And even though the world was unaware of the Galactic civilisations, Hitler and others who held a position of power knew of their existence. Add to that the weighed-up possibilities and considerations of a Heinrich Himmler, an incarnate of the Sons of Belial, and hence Hitler became relentless in his search for perfectionism to the breed of a superior human race, a pure race with a heightened IQ and longevity of Life, to help build the dream of a future Reich, with other races deemed as being of a lesser creed to him as many were contaminated. It was not so much about invading countries as it was about the collaboration with the Reptilians, the collapsing of the systems, and the experimenting on countless people through the arts of science infused 'therapies' with the learn-ed alchemy, wanting them to subject to their bidding. Hitler was a tyrant, emblazoned by power and greed for mystical knowledge of the darkened arts, weaving them into existence with his brothers, the Reptilians. His cruelty knew no bounds, and those that tried to come but within reach of his underground Arctic project were blasted into oblivion by a created technology unbeknownst to Man.

The Nazis were the grandmasters of illusion, for they created but the deception of being 'humane' towards their unknowing victims, leaving them in that state of blissful unawareness that they were about to die, yet they were inhumane for walking them to their deaths knowingly. The Gestapo implored the consonance of rule and order and sought the obeyance of the people through the use of shear force. They subjected the people under arbitrary control, with those not constituting in adherence to the laws imposed nor the implemented rolled-out doctrine and living a life according to the truth of their own ideologies were henceforth fervently punished, often disappearing into the void of the forgotten and the cold of the confined camps by executive decree, held without a tribunal. The moral of being immoral, yet pertaining to the illusion to stick to their 'humane' morals whilst masking the immorality of those held captive. Power is the void of a heartless emptiness that darkens the user into the abyss of the unknown; it is the submerging of the Soul into the gooey ectoplasmic darkness of night, for fear was the glory and ecstasy of a feeling of that power within. Himmler stated, "The best political weapon is the weapon of terror. Cruelty commands respect. Men may hate us. But we don't ask for their love; only for their fear." Such reminisce of a time that is clearly seen in the current passing humanity finds themselves in, for fear is like the striking of a hammer, a continuous series of blows that causes but a panic and a mild fever of hysteria, relinquishing one's freedom by trapping humanity like rats in the current experiment, causing the people to willingly obey and follow the laws of an implemented and coerced regime. For the mere sake of a better analogy, you are like a bunch of lab rats being experimented upon in a controlled worldly environment. Yet, you seem unaware of the comings and goings thereof, believing much of what you have been fed.

The experiment merely continued from the Wars of 2, with the key question of how next to control the population on a grander scale to make them (un)willingly commit to an obeyance of a magnitude unbeknownst to man. You create a grander experiment introducing humanity to a more advanced technological society to allow for a narrative to drip feed through the various infused channels of programming. Technology can be used for both the positive engineering of a beautiful society but also to spin the toll to the darkness thereof, which is the plan of the Masters of Illusion. One sees not the greatest deception being played out, yet the Truth dances right in front of your eyes. For them, it is creating a grander experiment based on an artificially manufactured society with a fear of death to make them more compliant to the wills of the few. You live in a state of a dissociative fugue, a cognitive dissonance of the Soul based on a life of the EGO-trippin' Self, which has become the very fusion of a created and manipulated society. Those in power have nothing but a dissonance of the heart, having lost their way, sitting there but with pomp and grandeur with their inflated sense of Self and a mere lust for power and money, with a feeling of contempt for the rest of those that they govern, causing them to forget a far more Conscious Way of Life according to the Laws of One, and thus one sees the mere parallels between the wars of then and now, for they are nothing more than the mere cause of the continuation of the inhumanity, the inhumane suffering to Man. They think they are a moral grace to the lands of the Earth. Yet, their morals are immoral, for their construed thinking of what they feel is humane is, in fact, inhumane by introducing the props for the enactment to make humanity believe that it is for the benefit of society and all. But it is all a grand illusion, a con to make the masses obey, for them to have that feeling of power in controlling others whilst dulling the perception through the feeding of the Mind of the so-called non-existent outer dangers.

The experiment never ceased, but for the mere said words, let's not repeat history, and as such, humanity was lulled back to sleep into thinking it was. The coined term 'government' is a mere wordplay on the senses, derived from the Latin syllables of guvernare and menti, translating to an absurdity of the algorithmic incremented 'mind control,' causing one to be induced into a hypnotic and conditioned state of a willingness of acceptance. Snap out of this state of subservience, for you are free to think for yourself.

Darkness has kept humanity in the dark whilst the Light has been trying to seep through the filters of the human Mind that has been clouded by this darkness, thinking this conformed life lived is the norm whilst it is not. This is a psychological war on the people, all in the persistence of a controlled herd to the obedience of the few. It is a grand experiment on a massive scale, and one is merely regarded as a lab rat in their created laboratory on the terrarium of the Earth. You come to Earth, being born straight into this brainwashed institution, being given your conditioned meds, all to stay in line with the rules of the asylum. Yet, many have stopped taking their meds and are awakening from the state of fugue they were in and had been confined to, and are now seeing that there is a whole different world beyond the walls of the institution of that created belief.

Humanity has become a 'sickly' devolved race, in defining that one lives on the mere outer fringes of life and of themselves, having caused but a steer towards materialism and the capabilities of an even denser and destitute forlorn experience, and yet mankind finds itself on the cusp of either the greatest revolution of the dawn of a new era or a plunging in the pool of a depth of darkness unbeknownst to many. This is a time of awakening, of becoming more aware of the world one dances and vibrates in, for the narrative is but an utter folly, playing tricks on the Mind, to keep you in the warped, marbled world of the fear-fed agenda. The joys of those keeping humanity fooled are but the trickery of the joker to one's dormant batman. It is the slow poison thereof that percolates through the Mind, bleeding into the Soul, seeping through and spreading like a slow infectious dis-ease, and still, one wonders and asks if life in this paradigm will return to the actualities of the old norm. Why would you commit to wanting a return to existing in the old structured and created matrix when life is infinitely more magnificent than you have been led to believe? Why would you stray from the beauty and magnificence of the radiant BEing that you indisputably are? Is this your authentic Nature? Is this your Truth; does it resonate with your Soul? I think not, for many suffer from self-inflicted ailments caused by the depletion of a non-nurturing of the Soul, causing one to be out of sync with one's embodiment. Yet everyone needs to reflect upon the scope and chosen expansion of oneself to shift from the darkened night of the Soul, returning into the fold of a more enlightened understanding of Self, for life is simply a journey of walking back to the Remembrance of Self. The feat of darkness is a dance undertaken back to the rhythm of the Light one is, and to understand that one has chosen to live in the matrix of inconsistencies to keep one's Soul deviated away from one's inner awareness and finding out the Truth of learning to bask in one's Light. Any dis-ease is the stellar creation of oneself, through a continuous feeding of the Self, through the intersensory receptors of the Mind. It is the perception of the fed Mind that one projects into the stream of one's inner world through the understanding of the outer world. It is one's inner trajectory that compromises the functions of the body, for the discomfort within one's Soul rejects the body and thus creates a blockage of internal creations of dis-ease. If you retort that you are not the Master of your universal creations, then pray tell me, who might that be? If one chooses to listen to the mere outer narrative, one is consumed by the emotionality thereof. If one chooses to listen to the tuning-in of one's inner world, one would hear a different song being sung to one's heart.

Man has a selfishness and lust for power, a need to govern and control others according to their bidding, having forgotten the Higher Modus Vivendi, causing but inhumanity and suffering to Man.

Whilst many are waking to the illusion, many sit there grinning like a Cheshire cat, simply indulging in the illusion, waiting to hop back on the train of the 'norm' when it comes steamrollin' back in. Life is an experience, and in the current reel of the film, called the 'Experiment,' you've been sucked into the hypnotic song and dance of it all, with many meekly following the beat of the pied piper of Hamelin through the streets of the grandest deception of all times.

The darkness that be, has been like a slow poison and a tumorous inclination to humanity, causing a stain on the very fabric of Life; it is very much a darkening of the ages, yet it serves to be a Remembrance of the wayward path back to the Light. The feeding the fear status quo is but cleverly disguised, for behind the curtain of the illusion, they have taken refuge in this cesspool of sticky, tenacious, created darkness, feeding their own shadowed shades of dusk and subsequently choosing to infect people with their 'ice-cream darkness galore' through the spiel of a societal created propaganda under the guise, we know what's best for you.

It is time to unplug yourself from the matrix you have been prone to living so accordingly to. Un-program all that you have been taught, back to the basics of the stark-naked nude Soul, to become aware of a life beyond that created matrix, beyond the illusion that one has so inherently adhered and been coerced into like a regimented toy soldier. You view life merely through the notion of the prescribed glasses of the perceptive created illusion. Yet, there is as much beauty in you as there is beauty in life, for life truly is a blissfully magical, beautiful ride, but only if you dare to open your eyes to the wonders thereof. You resonate with the peculiar resonance of this thing called energy, so what you vibe out is what you perceive to receive in return. Open your eyes to the blatant beauty around you to see that you are infinitely magical and beautiful, as much as life is equipped with those same magical infinite particles. You vibe energy as much as energy vibes with you.

For too long and many moons passing, you think not for yourselves but for the mere thought processes fed to you from without yourselves through the implemented created sensories from the outer perceptions of a technocratic based society that have infiltrated your Mind and thus your thoughts, causing the creation of biased opinions upon created beliefs that you have so willingly fed your Mind with. You live in the bombardment of a manipulative narrative, and yet that is what you choose to believe. Should you wish to look behind the curtain, then you will find that all is indeed an illusion to keep you hooked to the matrix of a fear-based and mediocre narrative-created society, which the darkness thrives on in the jubilant dance of the jest at hand, yet the light will eventually devour the darkness. The question is, when will you commence to awaken from your slumber to see that the truth has been staring you in the face all this time? Allow no one to play with the roll of the dice pertaining to your life; you choose to throw the dice at your own leisure, let no one else do the casting for you but you.

With the dark clouds hovering, it is not a time to cower in a corner to shelter from the storm; it is a time to rise up, muster up the strength, and walk through your own zones of discomfort, to cast out the shadows that have served your fit for programming purposes and release these in the billowing winds of change. It is time, my Child, to set yourself free, for the darkness coursing through the veins of humankind serves as a purpose for you to jolt you out of the suffocation and back to the realisation, to the remembrance of who you are. You are only controlled because you have allowed yourself to be controlled. Seek but a way out by opening the door and walking inward—for healing to better days for humanity starts by commencing and raising the vibration of yourself. The work outwards must first begin with the journey inwards.

You need not the dawning of a new day's breath to start over; you simply need to change your mindset and breathe back life into the joy of your Soul. Every stellar breath you take is a choice to the commencement of changing, transforming, and reweaving the tapestry of your life according to the true vibrance of your Soul. Wait not for a saviour till the homecomings of the pickings of the cherry season to save you from the torments of the shadows that have taken up residence within your Soul, for you, my Child, are the only one you have been waiting for to spring yourself back to life, to switching the Light back on in shadows of your Soul.

Humanity lives in this comfortable dis-ease of a complacency which has been the fortitude of the narrative one has so succumbed to. You are born into a system of your chosen itinerary and raised in the confinement of a created society. You think of yourself as separate, as this is the conditioned Mind 'partaying' trick, but you are not. You are a merging melting pot of the whole with the whole returning to a whole-someness of Self with the Divine and All. One has chosen to live in the separation of classes of an implemented hierarchy that has numbed the senses into believing it is so. One has scrapped a world of living in harmony with oneself and each other in favour of the ever-rolling EGO, when there is no difference between any of you but for the mere outer appearance one perceives oneself to be. How can you think of yourselves as being separate from the whole when we are all family of that same Divine Consciousness? You are all Divine Sparks of that same Light, merely on Earth as Consciousness evolving, expressing and creating.

As Thoth was on a roll, I asked him more questions about the current corona-virus, other events in the world, and how this would all unfold.

Q: As you have already hinted on dis-ease, can you shed some light on the 'coronavirus'?

Ah yes, the coercion of a psychological warfare playing out at its finest, that is, if you ingest the given narrative as truth, giving it fuel to the power of your beliefs of a created bubble of a poisoned energetic heap of hype. All this is just a story you tell yourself because many are still hooked in the clutches of this paradigm of fear and materialism, causing nothing but a disarray of unfolding dis-ease. The more you ingest it, the more you will emanate that particular frequency, and the more you add the 'absorption' thereof to the collective consciousness. It's like consuming alloyed water; what you put in is what you pee out into the sewers of your own existence. This mutated 'virus' exists, yet if one had called it the flu, one would have paid no mind to it, knowing that it is of a passing and one would get better in the space of several days, n'est-ce pas? Yet, one's Mind has been utterly deep fish fried, seasoned, and conditioned daily by the fear of this 'virus,' that one has commenced into believing that if one coughs or but mildly sneezes or runs a slight fever, one has been infected with this 'virus' that is but a 'flu,' and thus the Mind, engulfed by fear, panics, causing these seedlings of fear to sprout and grow, attracting that energetic vibe of what you vibe out, as an invitation to come on back in. One has made but a tsunamic monster, having overfed it with fear for something that is barely minute!

This created 'virus' is a biological strain of a manufactured diabolical variant, carrying an energetic frequency, and as many think themselves to be this dense mass consistent of biological compounds formed in the physical essence of the human body, rather than the Soul of the Light of the Energy within, it stands to reason that one combats the threat of that strain in the physical denseness of the consum-ed Self. If one thinketh of oneself as Energy, then one rides a different frequential wave with no significance to the created strain, for it bears no momentum to the holder thereof, as it will merely revoke and ricochet the virulent energetic strain back into the dissi-pation of oblivion.

As my Brother, St. Germain states, "The truth dances but constantly in front of one's eyes, through the mere feat of cleverly deployed wordplays, yet one takes the wording of everything in the literal sense, having lost all ability to think for oneself. Corona from Spanish translates to 'crown,' with the novel coronavirus being the new cold to the crown chakra, thus freezing the chakra to keep people trapped in the frozen arena of the fed acidic fear of a created controlled environment, keeping them in the very bliss of their unawareness, booby-trapping the doorway to enlightenment, steering people away from walking through the collective dark night of Soul. And thus, Corona being the 'crown' beer, has knocked humanity for six into the shift of a drunken stupor as opposed to an alignment with the crown chakra of the Soul seat of Self, with the ingested experiment merely meant as a sobering experience to wake you the heaven's sake up. Yet it is bombing in their faces, as Souls in their humanness are waking up from their hungover and confus-ed state, having overcome the incapacitated brain freeze of the crown chakra, and the nauseousness of having blown themselves to smithereens, blasting themselves through the veiled doorway, and obliterating and alchemising their demons, plugging back into the Oneness of Source, and connecting back to themselves and each other."

The Earth's ascension was commencing, which those holding 'power' have known for eons, having studied the position of the stars and planets and thus created a 'virus' with the vax containing a chemical-laden stop-block to humanity ascending, keeping them dumbed down in the narrative. The stop-block is the cause of dis-ruptions within the body's energy flow as it is the light versus the darkness within the human body, and thus the formulation counter-attacks the anomaly of the Light within. It was all about stopping the ascension of Earth and humanity, keeping humanity enslaved within the current grid of its one-dimensional existence.

Their motto is, "Contaminate, Indoctrinate, Vaccinate, Exterminate"—throw in a so-called 'bomb' of a virus, create chaos to keep up appearances with people scurrying around in fear and panic like blind mice on steroids, all believing the narrative they have been so duly fed, telling them to be chemically induced to fight off a 'virus' whilst unbeknownst to them there is a war being played out. Yet in all wars, there can be no victory without sacrifice, for that is the battle between the light and darkened forces causing but a plague of incestuous deceit upon the lands, where one is induced in an artificial reality, which is but a perpetual magical conditioned fairy dust blown in your face, to make you believe that all is a reality in this concocted deceivable illusion. And yet it serves as a true awakening of understanding the human feat through the mere art of the instilled polarities that has cracked that very abysmal illusion having kept one at bay, eventually shattering the mirage to let the Light of Love flood back into the hearts of humanity out of their stumped slumber of having believed all that was instead of all that is.

This is and has always been a war on humanity, on the people of the lands, and yet one sees it not, for it is hidden from the line of sight through the mere play of sheer inconsistencies, but for the dancing on the fringes of one's outer peripheral. It seems but an anomaly of absurdity to even think beyond the current dimensional thinking of an utterly diabolical sci-fi program, and yet it is! Would one rather live in the continued loop of illusion or delve through the dirt to unearth the scope of reality at play? Reality is a science fiction of unperturbed intention, unfathomable yet a plausible feat to a co-existence of the species. Thinketh not that one is the only species in the universe, and that movies are but a drab of a made-up illusion through the vivid imagination of the receptive and creative few, for I tell thee everything carries magic and everything carries a 'truth,' one just needs to see passed the judgement of the illusion of error.

Many now see it was a manufactured in a lab-created dis-ease, and yet that was merely a deviation tactic to coerce humanity into the exuberant force of locking one's senses into an apathy of a rabbiting down the hole into the abyss of fear. One can often see this through the many chosen word plays unless one is but of a gullible nature. Many people have awakened, are currently going through an awakening, or will eventually awaken, and if not in this life, then the next. See the beauty in the destruction of what was into what will be, for the world and humanity are in deservance of a life of lighter times.

You talk of a plague, but as you know within your hearts, the biggest plague to ravage the Earth is humanity in its current state of dis-ease, for you are the cause of your own misery and thus your own malady. The biggest dis-ease walking the planet is the dis-ease within and the dis-ease between each other, walking hand in hand with the EGO in separation and divisiveness instead of walking in a united Oneness. The biggest dis-ease stems from the core of your inner self; it is all that is not in agreement with you because you have chosen it so. Have you not cut yourself loose from Source and your inner consciousness, living in an outward way of existence of dabbling with the falsehoods of the EGO and listening to the commotion and chaos without, all the whilst forgetting to listen to the stillness and connectedness of the beautiful world within? That is the actual cause of the demise of oneself.

Why allow yourselves to be controlled when a created 'Pinocchio' government knows you not but for their own feeble institute and a destitute of making a sales pitch, of selling a point across for their leisurely benefit, all for the sake of you buying your 'stake' into it? Fear is a great motivator, a conglomerate to herd the masses into mass obedience to their 'master.' One thinks of the Self as free, yet one allows one's sovereignty, one's I AM Power, to be ruled and toyed with having but given it away so freely. No one knows you better than you, so listen to your inner heart and not what some random hyped-up belligerent stranger tells you, of some so-called plague ravaging the planet, for it is the ones running the show that have run a feverishly high case of delirium and are trippin' on a dis-ease called power, all the whilst having stupefied your senses with their drunken galore and tactics. S-ick you are not, but for the mere ick suppressing the Mind of Self, cascading into the e-motions to how one feels. Do those working within the governmental constitutions know you intimately? No, they do not. They know you not at all. So why follow their narrative so sheepishly, thinking it is God's gospel truth? Why allow them to feed your minds with some illicit twisted storyline, keeping you in the grips of the fear of that illusion, all under the false pretence of seemingly knowing the health and circumstances of every single person? It is preposterous, yet everyone can think for themselves should one decisively remove the drip that has kept one entranced with the poison that has so cookie monster fed your Mind. You have allowed yourself to be 'governed, ' yet you ultimately govern yourself. You have merely given your power away, allowing them power over you. There is no right or wrong; you do you. Your experiences, your growth, your Soul's evolution, and how you play the Game of Cosmic Evolution is entirely up to you.

Remember that the most extensive universal pharmacy resides not without but within, for your Soul is the greatest healer of all possible impossibles. There is nothing that cannot be healed or transmuted but for the mere thought of a seed in the Mind that says yay or nay. You are as much your own greatest dis-ease as your own greatest healer if one would only revert to listening to the Soul within instead of all the infil-trated commotion and distortion of the outer world, deviating you in the uncertainty of the chemical-laden choices without. The biggest infection of all is fear, whilst the greatest healer of all is Love.

Upon incarnating, you carry with you stored trauma within your cellular memory body, giving you a chance to heal this back to the order of your own Divine Self. Yet, often one gets convoluted in the concurrent constrictions imposed, having lost one's way through the rattled bombardment of continuous conditioning, causing a possible array of dis-ease varying in magnitude. Yet, it is all in the choosing, for that is the art of the game played back to the confluence of the wholeness of your Soul Self.

You are your own greatest toolbox with internal medicinal supplies in the Universe. This virus exists, but not in the capacity one is led to believe. It is through the mere form of fear tactics that it has been conditioned to you as being a 'deadly' bug. And as it has been conditioned, the energy of many becomes bumpy and unstable, for many firmly believe it will kill you because of the trepid lies of the few. If one would put it down to the flu, would one worry? The physical body of many Souls succumb to the flu every year, with the physical turning back to the dust of the land, yet it has not been a created narrative that has been propped to the forefront, so one pays little mind to it, would you not agree? Yet if one is fed a different narrative, with a botched-up label, and you have allowed it to enter the 'mindly' senses, causing the impact of the fear frequency to resonate with the internal energetic waves of your own bodily station, then indeed it is the belief thereof that wills the energy in the intended direction thereof. Everything you choose to believe materialises, for you are an energetic frequency; you attract the same bout of waves as you vibe out and back in. If you live in the energetic ether of fear, you operate on that frequency; thus, if you think it, you will it into your auric *field, filtering through to the body, causing a disruption in the flow of your energy system, leading to an output of a possible dis-ease.*

With this psychological war on the masses, it is sad that so many see no reason to go on living, feeling boxed in, with their freedoms curbed, their mind having become fraught, causing their Soul to become fractured due to all the implemented regulations making one uncomfortable in a chokehold of one's sense of self. Many people have crossed over, unable to get the treatment they require as healthcare follows the rules according to the implemented playbook, with many more succumbing to their illnesses and committing suicide, leaping back home to walk amongst the Stars, all because they are being coerced and forced into this stupendous rigor, unable to wrap their heads around the enforced regulations to divide and conquer. One forgets that this so-called hyped-up virus with an attached fear factor label is merely a strain of the flu. The vaccine was created for a virus called 'humanity' to keep them from ascending, to stop-block the changes within their bodily systems, shifting and igniting their DNA and chromosomes because, oh dear, what would happen if many awakened becoming lighter and enlightened? The game would be up, and the catalyst to a totalitarian world order would be down the chute.

Indeed, countless Souls have crossed over having received insufficient treatment, yet they have forgiven those for their limited awareness and hold nothing but love for them in their hearts. Suffice to say that they continue the work of healing and elevating the Consciousness of humanity and Mother Earth within these higher planes of Existence, having regained their understanding of their once 'fugued' out human selves. And, yes, in these rocky and transitional times, with many not comprehending the chaos within the shift, people choose to jump back home for the saving grace of their Soul, for Life in the human embodiment was far too much of a torturous feat to behold to finding a way out of their own Soul's drowning. When one is so accustomed to the 3rd-dimensional paradigm, having become rife to the fed conditioning, and unable to shift their axis to elevate themselves beyond the created suffocation of the implemented layers, it has an adverse effect on the severely weighted Soul, having been duped underwater, struggling to breathe in the density of the onslaught of the enveloping darkness, whereby the only way out of this life is to take one's life walking the Soul back home to live in the Light of Self once more. The world is a concentration camp to those who have ingested the narrative of the programming within their cellular DNA; it becomes a prison of one's own making and can be Soul destroying for the bearer thereof. Never weep for those that have decided to take the plunge and walk back home to the Stars, for they rejoice in the Light of the truth of who they authentically are, having left the weight of the human world behind them.

One lives in such a world of inconsistent and insistent 'comparables'; it becomes hard for many to live life authentically according to the very song and rhythm of their hearts. Seek ye not shelter in the outer inconsistencies of the worldly conditioned chatter but seek ye the warmth in the hearth of your Light of Soul, for here you will find the 'om' back to the awesomeness and vibe that makes you, you. Regardless of the psychobabble that goes on around you, see it as the grandest of opportunities to now do whatever makes your Soul cha-cha and twirl back to the drumbeat of the authenticity of the Light and Love that is you.

Q: Since you have already alluded to the various vaccinations out there, can you elaborate on this?

Why would you need any chemical composition injected into you? Your body is a powerhouse of energetic frequential medicine, as are the Earth's natural resources one has so mercifully rebuffed, having surrendered oneself in a white flagg-ed defeat, having chosen to dumb down one's use of intelligence in favour of a conditioned story you have so duly fed yourself. You fear for your life for the sake of germs within the atmosphere and will look hither and yonder to see how these germs will affect your well-being. Yet, when one gets jabbed, one checks not the label of the ingredients, taking this in 'good' faith unbeknownst of the repercussions thereof, and dare I say, humanity is truly an oxymoron in disguise. You are a Creator, Manifestor, and Healer all in One. You are not separate from you; you are One with the whole Pie as much as the entire Pie is One with you. If you understand that, you know that you are the pharmacy of All within, that often seeks to quench one's pain through the pills of the pharma-laden world without...

St. Germain says, "To jab the Self, or not to jab the Self, that is the question. Your Body, your Awareness, your Choice, your Decision. I live not your Life; you live it, so live it according to thine own Self be True. One can heal the chemic-al Self back to the equilibrium of the 'all-chemic-al' alignment of the Divine I AM, for within the mental conditioned mind maze of the dormant Self lies the roadmap back to the Power of the Divine I AM breath to the cure of all inflicted ailments to oneself. Seek, and ye shall find, my Child, for the journey of a chosen Life is yours for the undertaking."

Healing comes from the Sacred Divine within. The Heart is the seat of the Soul of one's e-motions; let your e-motions not be the toy-ed creation of others. Take back your driving force, throwing the fed narrative out the window, allowing it to roll along in the dirt along the side of the road, revelling in the beauty of the Divine Light that you are by creating a life of 'deservance' and servitude and living in grace and gratitude.

Like many, in December 2019, I was hit by a nasty flu that lasted for two weeks, with me literally unable to get out of bed. I couldn't breathe properly, it felt like my lungs were clogged, nor could I sleep or lie down comfortably as everything ached, and I was coughing like crazy. It was horrendous, I'd never had anything like it before, and the cough remained persistent for more than a month after that. I label that flu, even though Co(n)vid may have already been released in the ether during that time.

I don't reside within the matrix any longer and see life from a completely different perspective. I see myself as pure energy and not this earthly organic body, but I have no issues whether one has chosen to vaccinate themselves or not. I don't love you any less because of it. For those that have not yet harnessed the power within themselves and vibe at that level of fear, it can act as a Trojan Horse, which upon unlocking, can open the floodgates of Pandora's box of dis-ease within. Taking the jab is about personal choice and the current level of awareness you vibe at. These are your experiences, and regardless of your beliefs, please respect and love each other and leave your ego at the door. There is no need to put others down, no need for all this divisiveness, for we are all here just trying to find our way through the thick polluted foliage of the nonsensical tripped-up earthly jungle in this created and implemented superficial worldly matrix, back to the very light and love of our authentic selves. It ain't easy, but when one wakes up and hops out of the cocoon and sees the world for what it really is, it's well worth the ride of ridding yourself of the caked-on grime of sultry conditioning.

I've always wondered if this virus was so deadly, then why would you have to get tested to see if you have it, or why would you require 24/7 advertising, that is, if you watch tv or are hooked on online news and all that jazz, to remind you of its existence, and lastly, why do you allow yourself to be inoculated by an experimental jab when you are not sick, only to make yourself sick against a dis-ease, that is merely causing you far more of a greater dis-ease within the self, due to the influx of the narrative causing you to fret with the energetic resonance of fear? If it ain't broke, why fix it, as you'll create another "bug" within the bodily functioning system. The flu has died a quaint death, having been replaced by Covid, to make you buy into the fear and give in to the conditioning of agreeing to be vaccinated to cure yourself of that fear. As the Light BEings state:

"It is a rather twisted and diabolical state of affairs if one should choose to believe the cinematic spectacle with the grandest actors on the world stage in the making, and yet it will bomb to the high heavens receiving nothing short of a Raspberry award, for the failure to induce the people into the zombified state of petrification as was originally planned and once thought to be craftily written according to the implemented script."

As Thoth continues, *"Many succumbed in the War of II. yet this is a 'silent genocide' on a much grander scale and has a long-term plan attached to it, with the experiment broken down in increments. The first, by injecting chemicals altering the sequence of DNA chromosomes within your physical essence, causing eventual kinks in the cable over time, with your Spirit in a slow burn pain, causing one to become unaligned and far more disconnected from the Self as that is the exact intent—separation and suffering and a dependency on the state. If you trap a fly in a spider's web through the instigator of fear, it becomes entangled. Once it becomes entangled, trying desperately to free itself, it only becomes more constricted, with the spider closing in on its prey. Once confusion sets in, the next steps of the planned agenda and controlling and enslaving humanity are put into place. Kick the grand ingested illusion of fear to the curb in the wisdom of understanding that illusion to release the shackles of that allow-ed control one has capsized the Self with, and wake up from said illusion—for when one controls not the other, one loses power over the once controlled masses."*

Many Light BEings of the collective have been helping humanity neutralise this energetic frequency, but humanity must also learn to help themselves. As they clearly state:

"You have manifested what you co-created. See this onset of an infested influenza as a positive, to reset yourself into the Light and Truth of Self, for we are not here to save the world but merely to remind the world how to save itself. We're not here to save humanity but to remind each and every one to learn how to save yourselves, breathing in the Light of your most Authentic selves, getting rid of the masked persona you have so impersonated yourself with through the engrained conditioning of the one-dimensional matrix. Remember, that death is non-existent for the Soul is eternal; it is a mere created feat for the awakening of all of humanity."

Several people I knew have crossed over due to blood clots, heart failure, and others whose ailments were exacerbated. My mum suffered shortness of breath and fatigue. I simply won't be blackmailed into injecting chemicals into my body to alter the chemical composition thereof, all because some random governmental representatives and scientists state I should. Just because they are qualified in their respective fields does not make them humane, for they have lost their humanity, trading it for the greed of monetary gains.

When my mum went in for her second shot, I told her to ask the GP about the exact ingredients of the AstraZeneca jab, and she did. Her GP told her he had no clue what was in the jab. I told her if he doesn't know what he's injecting you with, then why take it? My mum told me it didn't bother her, and like millions of others, she has taken it in good faith because a health professional administered it. It blows my mind that medical professionals can administer a jab, having no idea of the contents thereof, without any regard for the patient's well-being sitting in front of them or bearing the consequences of their actions. Is their first Hippocratic oath not *"primum non nocere,"* translated from Latin as "first, do no harm"? Money has overridden all rhyme and reason.

The Nuremberg Code Article Section 3 states, *"No Government can mandate or force medical treatment without individual consent."* Section V, page 1051 of the American Medical Association Encyclopaedia of Medicine, published in 1989, states that Coronaviruses are nothing more than the common cold, which paid scientists debunked as this is classed as a different strain. The UC Health site says these vaccines contain fats and oils, acids, salt, and sugars, which can be consumed through avocados, lemons, limes, salt, and sugary fruits such as strawberries, grapes, mangoes, cherries, bananas, pears, and watermelons. Why would you need a concoction of a chemical conundrum injected into you, making you sick?? Real medicine comes from the Earth, not from some big business lying money-making pharma lab, churning out chemical-laden medication with many unknown ingredients on their production lines that so many have become accustomed to, having turned away from and choosing to live in a deviation from the light of themselves.

Pharmakon, translated from Greek, means "pharmaceutical" and a *pharmakeus* is one who prepares either a remedy or poison for ingestion of the "sickly body," which is either beneficent or maleficent. Either way, one often becomes dependent on the drug as a habit. As Spirit so often states, *"Everything is a debauchery on the play of words, with the truth dancing quite literally in front of your clos-ed eyes."* I got my mum the following herbal supplements, which have ironed out the kinks within her body:

* ✶ Turmeric Curcumin Ginger Black Pepper
* ✶ Magnesium glycinate
* ✶ Quercetin (1200 mgs)
* ✶ Vitamins D3 & K2

Taking supplements goes hand in hand with adhering to a healthy diet to better absorb all the nutrients. Iron, zinc, and vitamin c are the more standard supplements, but chlorella, spirulina, oregano, and charcoal are excellent aids too. Her sugar levels also elevated, so I got her 500 mg of herbal berberine, which has done wonders for her. Even though she states she feels like a pill factory because of the supplements I got her, she is thankful that she has bounced back. She has said she wants no more chemicals injected into her veins, as it did quite a number on her body.

From a healing aspect, having a light language healing session does wonders for one's body and soul. Light language is a channelled multidimensional language bringing sound and energy from the many BEings from other realms and star systems. It is galactic and "ancient," yet when your soul hears it, it will understand the language and commence to realign itself back to the grid of the essence of your beautiful divine BEing. It is not a band-aid healing but heals on a deeper soul level; in many cases, it eradicates physical ailments and blockages, releasing past life, funky energy, and spirit attachments. It activates one's DNA; as light language carries encoding specifically for your soul, it opens up your awareness. It is truly phenomenal. Some say it is a shortcut to healing; I think it's powerful and transformational with lasting effects, yet you can't just sit there like a couch potato and proclaim to be healed; one will still need to do the work. I love Archangel Nathaniel; he has such a fiery, warm, and powerful presence when you call upon him. I asked him to explain the benefits of a light language session, and here is what he said in response:

"Light Language is the pureness of crystalline Light acting as a soap deterrent washing away the grime and gunk of your accumulated conditioning, allowing the energy to flow and your Soul to breathe. Light Language is the best deterrent to all ailments of the body caused by the Soul in the denseness of the human embodiment. The only way out is through, and Light Language is the pathway back to the warmth and sparkling sunlight of the beautiful de-Light-full Soul of the once sour turned sweetened Self.

Light Language is the language of the Soul, the tones corresponding with the healing intent it has so yearned for, yet has been so fervently denied by yourself on a human level, for it is the mere non-understanding thereof that leaves one incapacitated, walking with an often dis-ease in Life. It is returning to the breath of the I AM Power within your Soul Presence, being in sync with the Light of the Soul that is you. It is transformational healing at its finest, a connoisseur of the Soul's flavours ingested by the Soul to remedy the malady thereof. It is the spearmint to the clogged in the gutter mind of Self, having soaked your Soul and a mere recalibration through the reactivation of one's DNA, returning to the grid of the essence of Self. It is the key to the locked Soul, unlocking its potential to the truth of the Light of who you are, to remember, to awaken, and to live a life according to the very resonance and lightness of your own heart. Skip on out of the illusion that one has been so dismayed with, and walk out into the open sun-drenched fields of awareness, leaving the living of the lies in the thicket of the forest behind thee, for my Child, the truth of the matter will always set you free from the self-imposed shackles one has so incarcerated the Self with. Shake off the illusion like a wet dog having been dunked in water, feeling refreshed and being reborn through the heavenly bliss of allowing yourself to be true to the very naked essence of You, of breathing back to the lightness of the very breath of your BEing and understanding your Existence beyond the incorporated and manufactured matrix you have allowed yourself to be so utterly indulged in, having done nothing but dull and lull the senses. So, live my Child and be free, having ripped off the band-aid of the illusion that held you in the clutches of the fairy tale world of that once so orderly ordained illusion, commencing to live in the wonders of the Authentic hue in You."

Light Language sounds like a breeze, but it sure as hell ain't. It can be brutal. It turns you upside down and inside out, with a whole load of hoarded and accumulated over many lifetimes held-on trinkets to come falling out, requesting healing and alchemization—much like being the mischievous Abu Abu, Aladdin's kleptomaniac hoarder of a monkey. It's made me turn ice cold, left me with sleepless nights, and has often made me feel nauseous to the point of throwing up. I felt like I was pulled apart and emptied out like the trash, as everything within had to reconfigure itself, allowing for the cracks to heal and the light to blow life back into my soul.

Light Language is much like dragging the mud up from the bottom of your mind and soul and going through the turmoil of the healing motions to feel more authentic and at ease within yourself, filling your cup o' soul with joy, and ultimately becoming aligned with who you are. There are some wonderful light language healers that I have outlined for you below:

* Siobhan Purcell, www.siobhanpurcell.net, channels the many Galactics, ancients, and angelic BEings. Having a session with her will knock your senses as she works at an incredibly high and ethereal vibration, allowing you to drift to otherworldly places so that the healing can take place.

* Louise Rhodes, www.louiserhodes.co.uk, channels the many Galactic BEings, especially the Arcturians, and working with her, you'll feel any pain dissipate almost immediately, which is a beautiful experience in itself and shows the power of the energetic frequencies of light language and how it intertwines with your energy, to alter the energy field within your own physical body, rectifying the kinks you've allowed yourself to walk around with.
* Maia Francis, www.maiafrancis.com, is a Divine Frequency Alchemist and resonates at an incredibly high vibration. I adore her, as she has mentored me, helping to elevate my consciousness to the next level. She's all about amplifying your soul connection, and healing all aspects of your multidimensional self, so that you expand and grow, allowing yourself to live a life of deservance. She works with Steven and the Collective Cosmic Consciousness, elevating people's awareness and healing their lovely fragmented and bashed souls through channelled wisdom, powerful meditations, and hitting you at the core of your soul, light transmissions.
* Alan Pratt, www.alanpratt.net, is an out-of-this-world galactic healer. I love him, for he channels the ancient modality of Io Uyzuy used by civilisations that once were but are no more. He sings, speaks, and whistles while speaking many celestial languages. It is incredible how he helps reactivate those dormant strands of DNA, altering our perspective of life, and freeing us from our trapped conditioning. He confirmed many things I already knew and has helped many fully recover from various forms of cancer, addictions, and many other physical and emotional ailments.

The stuff in the jab is an alteration of the encoding within our DNA. We merely need to change our perception of that chosen reality, be that energetic alchemical ball of awesomeness we are, feel the pain to heal the pain, and we will, in turn, alter the wiring of our body back to the love and vibrance of the rockstar soul that we are. As with all healing, one has to be willing to change and work to heal the self, for, without it, one is a flatulent sack of potatoes, remaining in the whinge of oneself. As St. Germain always says:

"You are your very own Alchemist of the Creation of yours truly, yourself. Fear is the path to the dark side. If one ingests the formula component thereof, one allows the particles of fear to accelerate in the direction of that chosen lifestream into the existence of one's BEing. However, when one's Soul and body choose to sync and snap back into unison with the Godly Divine I AM Presence, there is nothing that cannot be altered if you will it so, for my Child, you conjure up all that you create in your Life. One is not the mass of a blob one thinketh one is, but composed of infinite Energetic Light Frequency Particles of the Divine, and Energy is transient in nature, moving according to the will of one's Mind and one's BEing."

Continuing on with the Council of Ra and the Ascended Master Thoth below.

Q: Are we truly living or are we being lived?

Remember, my Child, you are Light, and Light can never be snuffed out. You may have dimmed the Lights in your Soul through the veil of the Mind in the human embodiment, but all it takes is to fin-d the 'lost' spark to illuminate the heart of your Divine Soul Light flippin' the switch to the remembrance of who you are. Snap out of this dream state you have so lullabied yourself to sleep to and allow the rebirthing of yourself returning to the unfolding of the beautiful, Divine flower of Consciousness that you are.

Many of you are not living but are being lived. Is that a life you want? You have chosen your life according to the implemented rules of the rigged game. So, if the game is rigged, why be the fiddle to the string of their violins? Your life. Your choice. Think of life as one needing to upgrade to the Universal broadband, connected through the optic fibre of the sacred geometric grid, plugged back into the Higher Consciousness of Self and the Whole. If your broadband is out of sync, it causes challenges within the spectrum of oneself and far more of a dis-ease and frustration than when one opts to upgrade to the Universal broadband, integrating oneself, living in Awareness, having a faster acceleration, a faster speed to an understanding of the world within as the resonance of the world without. It's all about unplugging the Self from the systematic Matrix and back into the power grid of Source Energy.

In layman's terms, you are a Divine God Conscious Soul expressing and creating yourself through the human experience. Your Soul is the Light of you that is real; your experiences merely serve as an elevation to your Conscious Awareness, affecting the Cosmic Consciousness of the Whole, creating that tapestry of Consciousness through the art of dualities, of light and darkened contrasts, all to make you walk through the maze of your experiences, remembering the Light of the Soul that you are. You have chosen to incarnate to help Mother Earth rid her of the devil's spawn and for the quantum leap of the evolution of Man into the next enlightened dimensional frequency.

Rebirthing does not come without its pains, but remaining in that futile dream state serves you but a far lesser purpose than waking up from the illusion and partaking in the rebuilding of an enlightened tomorrow, where humanity can breathe as One, breaking into a unified sing-song of living in harmony with oneself, each other, and Mother Earth.

Q: Can you explain the term "the conscious shift"?

Collectively, humanity has to shift its Consciousness to give birth to the new age, for that is the ascension process. The Conscious shift means shifting your consciousness from the known into the known unknown; it is all you know but have forgotten by being peppered with the current known syndrome of a labelled medication called "condi-tioning." It is not sitting around waiting for the old to come back into play—that is like waiting at an out-of-service bus stop or idly sitting by the docks for your hail Mary to come steamrolling in. The old is dying; those clinging to that sinking ship will feel uncom-fortable, drowning in the familiarity as they long for the old institutionalised paradigm to be reinstated, as their soul craves that structured illusion. Their steadfast belief system is being toyed with and shattered, as embracing change is a fear of the unknown. Yet, this 3D reality is merely an illusion to keep you enslaved to a hierarchical system that has been created to front that humanity is not equal—yet all are of equal divinity, for the Soul my Child has no Race; it is the spark of the Light of the All in All. One can merely hold the line for them, eventually leading them out of the land of contused confusion and illusion. As Archangel Michael rightfully says, "You are all here to walk one another home, through the casting of one's experiences upon each other."

3D to 5D is merely a shift in one's state of Mind; shifting your consciousness is to shift your perception and thought of Self. To ascend means to lift up, rise above, commence living a heart-centred life, and pay no mind to the trifled narrative that has kept you compartmentalised in the old programming of living in fear of that quid pro quo status quo.

As my brother, St Germain adds, "Paradise is not a place but a state of Consciousness. Heaven dwelleth within and is not some 'candilicious' place over the fairy floss rainbow. Your Mind is a state of Consciousness, non? Mais oui! 3D to 5D is that simplistic shift in Consciousness. Do you think not? Does it have to be something more?! Non mes chéris, that is your over analytical 3D brain playing dire tricks on you. It is relinquishing all that you are not and uncovering all that you are and always have been. You are a gem under the cloak-ed layers, having become a rather depen-dent addict hooked on the 3D-infused cocktail of delirium to keep you in a state of continuous denial. It's got you straying so far from yourself, having lost the Self like a cat without a home and duly having lost the very meaning of the 'What's the meaning of Life?' And as it was sung, 'Elevate your Mind, and free your Soul.....' Merely remove the drip-feed and release all the experiences you perceive to be so real. Are they real? Or is it your Mind that has played you for an ambiguous fool into believing the illusion of that reality that you are adamant is a reality but is merely an illusion? Ha, I am sure the wordplay got your tongue tied as much as it's got your Mind mystified, n'est-ce pas? Life is a simple recipe really, so why keep adding unnecessary ingredients to your experiences, causing it to bomb but so 'joyfully' in your face? Either shift, let go, and experience a lighter sense of joy in your state of BEing, allowing the frequency to dance but ever so eloquently within your Life, or remain dumbfounded within the cataclysmic rigidness of swimming in your own muddy Hogwarts swamp of Self. All that matters is how you choose to want to live your Life, yet know that no one is responsible for the outcome but for the sole perpetrator staring back sheepishly in the mirror. Et voilà, c'est toi, n'est-ce pas?"

Thoth continues, "For those in power, it has always been, do as I say, not do as I do, for the fed narrative does not pertain to them. They think they are above the rest, yet rather daftly, they are not, for one is of equal divinity. Yet humanity has given them that status quo of power through a cleverly created hierarchical system, and they wield it in their egotistical megalomaniacal ignorant bliss of a non-understanding, having lost but all love for themselves, thinking they rule the land with an ironclad fist. Rather comical when one sees the illusion, the mirage, the smoke, and mirrors for what it is, of keeping the "herd" imprisoned in a state of fear, all to stop one from thinking for themselves and living in a heightened state of awareness of one's natural state of Self. Stop feeding the narrative and being consumed by it. Get off that gravy train of "addiction." When you give it no power of thought, it has no power of thought over you. The shift occurs when humanity commences shifting away from all the tripe of the fed illusion. It is happening as we speak, yet many remain damnified within the old *programming, waiting for normality to return, which is like waiting till the cows come home to save you from yourselves, is it not? To ascend, to shift your Consciousness means to let go of that instilled programming and not to give that tripe any attention, creating a new age of coming together in unison. It is in the power of the people to transcend and consciously usher in the new golden era. It lies not with the old egotistical ways of any created hierarchical governmental institution, but it lies within oneself to commence and collectively be the change that one wants to give birth to.*

Breaking down this once-upon-a-time toxic fairy tale belief system integrated within means working on the Self, uncovering and recovering your own Light through the journey of awakening yourself, opening your eyes, and becoming more aware with each breath you take and with each step you take, shaking off the dust of that veiled illusion that has kept you weighted down for so long, for each piece of the puzzle will create a picture of the lay of the land of the whole of the decep-tion that is being played out. And as you shift your Consciousness and begin seeing beyond the veil of that illusion, you will rebirth a new age beyond the walls of that created institution. The old will die at the dusk of the eve to give rise to the dawn of a new morn.

Everything is a manipulation of the senses to keep you thwarted in the game of your own evolution. The conditioning of the experience within the experiment you have been heralded into is one for you to discover and to unleash the awakening from the dormancy within. Yet your evolution is your own, and we cannot help you if you do not commence to help yourself; we can only assist in the messages we bring forth, in the initiatives we instil, in the virtuous hope that you as a collective commence to awaken and open your eyes to the illusion of a reality you have so bought into. The spawning of the darkness is as much the opportunity for the day breaking of a new dawn, rediscovering your own Truth, Light, and Divinity and that of humanity—one light at a time, a step at a time, and a soul at a time.

Q: Will those that have wronged humanity be held accountable for their actions?

The Galactic Federation has been monitoring the Earth closely as the shadows that control the puppets within the governmental structures and other "deemed worthy" conglomerates have instilled much chaos and divisiveness, with the energetic effects rippling across the Universe as it does not just affect this world, but the repercus-sions can be felt across the continuum of the Universe, which the Federation cannot allow because the aftermath will be far too great. One realises not that the grand architecture of the Multiverse is a wondrous and delicate ecosystem. Everything is Consciousness, and thus those droplets of 'conscious' darkness have trickled and bled into the corner of the Universe where the Earth has so due diligently been making her orbit for millions of years.

Think not that those who have taken power over the people and subject them to their bidding will not be put on trial, whether in the Earthly realms or within the Galactic High Court of the Cosmic Central Sun, for they are not without consequence. Yet it deters them not, for they think they are invincible, a Spartacus in sheep's clothing. All follow their own agenda, not for the people but for the betterment of themselves and who they serve, yet their light is far poorer for it, for their actions serve them the inquisition of the Courts. Enlightenment is not a fortitude on their path of knowing. It is the darkness in which they roam and slither hither and yonder amongst the darkened grime of the Universe, living but in the absence of the light of love. It is with a slyness and a cunning of the split tongue to rebuke the people, and yet the end game is neigh, for it has become plain to all those living and gracing the Planet to see. To give rise to the new, the old must fall into the paradox of a sinking ship, for a new dawn cannot be achieved when all players in the fields of the realms are still splotching the canvas with their streaks of darkness. Many realms within the earthly dimensions serve as boltholes for the malevolent, with many Galactics held as a bargaining chip, yet all is not lost, for all will prevail. Eventually, the Light will checkmate the darkness when they least expect it. Keep the faith, for all will be well, for out of the darkness shall spring forth back the Light to the rebirthing of Man.

Sometimes, I channel things that make no sense to me. Some of the words are not in my vocabulary, and I'll have to research the messages I receive afterwards, only to realise that, in truth, these words make sense in the context of that sentence within the given message.

The comparison the Council of Ra and the Ascended Master Thoth make to the WWII era is that the Nazis taught a "humane" method of killing people, and those held captive should indeed remain blissfully unaware that they were about to die; hence they were the masters of illusion, setting the stage to secure such conditions, relying on elaborate props of deception. I think they would have given Houdini a run for his money. They made promises of water, food, and work and built fake railway stations, which were pretty painted gas chambers surrounded by flowerbeds and decorated with the star of David, all to trick those held in captivity into thinking they were not marched to their deaths. As Shakespeare famously quoted in *As You Like It*, *"All the world's a stage, and all the men and women merely players; They have their exits and their entrances, and one man in his time plays many parts."*

The key takeaway here is that those within this experiment were unaware of the consequences. And is the world much different now? Many recoil at the horrors of what happened all those years ago, and those in power still lay wreaths in remembrance, yet they have simply upped their game and chosen to evolve to a far grander plan of execution, still deceiving humanity and leaving us blissfully unaware. And even though the Nazi regime has "died" out, the Sons of Belial have simply reintegrated themselves far more cleverly into society, feeding the narrative from within the central hubs of organisations and governments. Chemicals and variations of parasites have been inserted into the overall worldly food chain, affecting everything from the foundation of the natural Earth to our food and water supplies, all for the so-called betterment of humanity. Yet many have remained blatantly unaware of the slow infusion thereof.

The Council has shown me that everything in the grid will eventually collapse to make way for the new. It can be no other way. The "hue-man" soul is not designed to live this way. When we talk about the grid, it is the entire grid upon which everything is built to "sustain" humanity living life according to the implemented 3D paradigm. I know "wars" are ugly, with lives lost and souls transcending, but see it not for the ugliness you perceive it to be but as the mere beauty of a rosebud gently unfolding. As the old is dying, you will start to notice that things commence failing, much like a frail old body that's had its best years and is about to take its last breaths, only to be reborn in its ascension. The time has come for the birthing of a new world, ridding itself of the eons of implemented "hive" mind frequential energetic coding and categorically algorithmic programming, to where we can live in unison and harmony with one another and ditch the separation and the ego.

We consist of energetic particles and thus encode ourselves within the sacred geometrical grid of our cosmic mathematical equation of existence. Will it take time? Of course, evolution is a process, but as Galactic Light Ambassadors, we signed up to incarnate during this era to take out the adversaries of Planet Gaia, restoring her presence and awakening humanity to the divine blissful and heart-centred self. Be thankful to be living in these transformational times, for it truly is a blessing to be alive in these grandest of times.

The Jewish people were considered "dangerous," and the Nazis implemented more and more laws restricting their movement, further humiliating, isolating, and demonising them. It caused divisiveness amongst the people, and many Jews, who did not have the correct papers, were persecuted, treated like pariahs, hunted down like animals, and thrown into "containment" camps, better known during that era as "concentration" camps. Are times so different now? We live in the loop of history often repeating itself. We are participants in a game of divide and conquer, to rile the people against each other, under the watchful eye of the fed indoctrination of the many governments, conglomerates, and foundations who serve not the people, but their masters in charge of the global world dominion, enslaving the people to the rule of their will.

View life like a grand spiel of Monopoly, with everything created within the grid of the board game and structured for all to follow the rules of the game. Whether quelled or not, humanity has risen up to tyranny time and time again. We should be rising up in unison against those that try to divide us, stepping out of this induced coma of a segregated imposed egotistical autocracy and this constant duelling of "comparables" with one another, for we are all part of the same universal source, we are all part of each other, and thus we are all brothers and sisters of the light.

I have never understood the secrecy of all our governments and all that hold "power" over humanity. I always thought David Icke was kooky in my late teens and early twenties. Yet over the years, what he had said kept coming back to me, and had we been given the raw and honest truth, we would have fared far better, and light warped our evolution as an enlightened species in the long run— rather than where we are at present, living in this ultra-condensed version of what we call our authentic and enlightened selves. When people talk of ETs or aliens, I shake my head and tell them, you state these BEings are aliens, and yet can you not see the irony in the wording? Humanity has alienated themselves from themselves through the mere art of separation, for all these other races throughout the multiverse are your brothers and sisters. All have been created from that same spark of overall creator as you have. They are not separate from us. They are a part of us as much as we are a part of them. We merely radiate and emit at different levels of consciousness, trying to find our way home to our delightful enlightened selves.

As Thoth stated, darkness has percolated into the minds of humanity over the many thousand years, and we are basically lab rats in their overall experiment because we have allowed ourselves to sink so deep in being in the acceptance of the spoon-fed storyline, thinking that it is indeed a reality. We have deviated so far from ourselves that we have forgotten who we are and why we are here. We have descended into a world of materialism and of a technocratic society. Is that why we are truly here? No, we are here to remember who we are. We are here to find our way back to ourselves through the conditioned paradigm. We are here to raise our vibration and help raise the vibration of Mother Earth, who we have so severely depleted and treated. We have strayed so far from ourselves that we believe everything that those in the seat of power and the media feed us. Yet, in truth, we are our own salvation. Thoth clearly states that we need to help ourselves, end our suffering, and wake up from this induced coma we've been so programmed to believe. The question is, what is it that you choose to believe?

As Thoth continues:

"The war cast has been going on in the 'quaint' silence behind the backs of humanity since the dawn of time, much to the chagrin of those sitting with their failing casting wands of power. Much of this war has been a slow burn, like a drawn-out bad vs. good, light vs. dark forever ongoing TV soprano, whereby you eventually drool and get lulled to sleep by the repetitive projected scenarios and thus the boredom thereof. Alas, with all the initiated chaos, you are forced to quit drooling, pay attention and smack yourself out of this lala land, as the war between the darkness and the light has stepped up a notch. Every single one of you has a role to play on this beautiful planet right now, so shed the layers, walk the walk through those inner shadows, heal up and rise up, illuminating the spark back to the brightness of the beautiful Light that you are. When more Souls awaken and maintain their vibration, the planet will eventually be engulfed with the rising fire of Love and Light. Take back your Power, stand in your

luminous Divine I AM Presence, shine your Light, and be that beacon of Light for those who need that guidance back to the Light of the beautiful truth of who they are."

For those that aren't sure what a shift in consciousness is, Thoth gave me a great analogy as I was taking a walk with my dog Myra one morning. When you are at a movie screening wearing 3D glasses, you're in this third-dimensional reality. Because 3D movies have depth and volume just like in real life, you can feel the scene of the movie happening around you, and you can feel it—you're immersed in it, right?

So, you eat your popcorn and believe the whole scenario of this fed narrative because the experience of all that your senses have been bombarded with feels real. But is it? It is only real because you choose to believe it is. What if you swapped your 3D for 5D glasses showing you a different perspective on life? Suddenly, you can see behind the great storyline of the movie being played, and you sit there laughing at yourself, realising the movie was just an experience, and it's not real. It seems real because you were so immersed in the plot, in the portrayal of the narrative of that dramatic unfolding storyline, but it was all just an illusion. You wake up from the 'dream' having a far greater understanding of life, and the mechanics portrayed to you in 3D—that is what that conscious shift pertains to.

Know that the state of play in the world today is of our own making; every single action we take is woven into the fabric of the energetic holographic imprint of the universe. Everything we do affects the world around us because we are conscious creators, creating and expressing ourselves through the human embodiment. We wear masks to hide our emotions, suffocating the very breath of ourselves, hiding the light of our true enlightened selves. Yet, this has transfigured into the current experiment of having to physically wear a mask for the safety of ourselves and others. It is the mere irony of the innuendo thereof—the avoidance of self, the disconnect between each other, of living the lie of separation.

The Ascended Master Hilarion's Take on the Consciousness Shift

Channelled in October 2020

The Ascended Master Hilarion is a Master Teacher I adore, as he is gentle soul yet has an incredibly witty sense of humour. I asked him how he sees the current shift of consciousness for humanity, and this was his response:

"Change calls for the destabilisation of what was, to what can be; without it, everything remains. It's like having oil and water, with oil representing the darkness versus water representing the Light. Once water (Light) trickles into oil (darkness), it slowly disintegrates. It becomes dislodged from the surface it has so generously caked itself to; it no longer has the fuel, the ferocity, and power to create the immense chaos it originally intended, for it has become fractured. Such is society in its current state. It is a defragmentation of the old paradigm that one so desperately clings to because that is the programming of the state of affairs, but my Child, it is an illusion! The process of

returning darkness to Light is the alchemisation process of the darkness surfacing to the Light, as that is the gravitation of darkness, for it chooses the Light to feed off the Light, and as it reaches the surface, it is transmuted back into the Light by the Light BEings in service of the Light.

That is the process of ascension, to find Light in the shady shades of darkness within, and transform this into wisdom and understanding. It is the easiest analogy of the principle of the current circumstances of the planetary evolution and ascension of all.

Ultimately, you could see Life through the bespoke analogy of hair conditioning. When one conditions one's hair, it becomes a sleekness and slenderness of sorts and sits beautifully according to the control of that beautiful conditioner. Yet if one's hair is free from said conditioner, it causes a state of hair chaos, a frizz bomb of sorts, with your hair wanting to do its own thing and have its own way, leaving you to look like a sassy witch on a drunken broomstick. As such it is that same sleekness by which humanity has been conditioned within the grid of the matrix, for one lives according to the control of the well-oiled cogwheels of the societal machine. And yet, when one kicks the conditioner to the curb, it is like a rider being thrown off a well-mannered horse, with one's head hitting the dirt, seemingly having been woken from a bad dream, henceforth commencing on the journey of awakening, having put a spoke in the wheels of that one's so well-oiled manufactured machine.

Be not afraid of the dark, for you are the Light. Polarity is the nature of the Universe, and in many civilisations, learning through the contradictions of Life has always played a role in their evolution. Darkness can and will not prevail, for it is the mere absence of Light; once you shine a light in the dark, the darkness goes away until you flip the switch and choose to plunge back into darkness—it is a cycle, and as such a continuation for the cosmic evolution of growth.

You create what you desire. You are not your body but your Soul within the home of your given body; hence, how can there be a differentiation in races? Unless you believe yourself to be solely your body, then be your body.

The Law of Energetic Compulsory Waves corresponds to the magnetic waves of the Soul vibrance within. You are the Light to the ignition of the spark of the Life Force Energy housed within to the energetic magnetic multidimensional magnitude of a thousandfold to the gravitational axis spun without. You are the fuel to the source of your own power. Ignite that spark to ignite that power. One creates one's Life through the magical mind wordings equating to one's lively outward creations. One's inner Universe is a series of light bulb moments, churning the course, returning yonder to the enigmatic blend of the bubble' n squeak authentic you in You.

Your experiences do not define you; you define your experiences. Your 'suit' does not define you; you define your' suit.'

So, I ask you, what's your resonance? What do you vibrate at?"

We must walk through the darkness of ourselves and that of humanity to rebirth ourselves, stepping into our divine essence, becoming that light, and illuminating that beautiful tapestry of consciousness to steamroll into the birthing of the new Earth collectively.

The Ascended Master St. Germain's Take on the Current Shift
Channelled in October 2020

Q: What is a spiritual awakening that many speak of?

Awakening is a process of the complete destruction of who you think you are but are not, disrobing the Self, standing in the bare bones of one's Authentic Light o' Soul. To walk through the s***, clear up, and heal the created crap of your experiences is to step back into the Light and sparkle of your Awareness and truth of Soul. If you say you are not deserving of a beautiful life, then one is at liberty and at the mercy of the Self to keep walking through the damned sludge of a created mess of one's sheer misery, walking but in the muddy trenches of the slippery slope of one's created persona, causing one nothing but perpetual mishaps of the fed Mind and thus the trickling of the words materialising into one's Life.

Q: Can you explain this "virus" labelled "Covid"?

*Covid is meant to rudely awaken you from your contented deep sleep, not make you run amok like a leprechaun with fear. One can break it down to "**Co-vid**," stating to humanity to please be seated within the worldly auditorium and listen to the orator over the earthly PA system as your **cooperation** is required to watch these well-educated **videos** for the sole betterment of your life. One is free to roam in one's* beliefs, yet know that your Mind's been hijacked and you've been hoodwinked into believing the created videos dubbed with a false narrative, monotonously looped to hypnotise you, is loopholed with a mirage of illusions, making you ever fearful of death, all to keep you within the consistency of the matrix approach.

Q: Why do people even wear masks in light of the current "virus" that has been dished out before us?

Love is contagious; it's alright—a golden oldie, yet so current, coherent, and resonant for the sign of the times. On a far more serious non-lyrical note, it is with such ample desire that they choose to do so. One wears a mask in the Earthly party of the ball masquerade to cover one's true Light of Self in a controlled environment in the experiment of the served experiment, for humanity lives in an experiment of the created experiment at play. Got it? The worldly governments state that you must wear a mask to protect yourself from yourself because you are a danger to yourself and others? A whole ménagerie de la population du monde, contained, confined, and controlled. It's a rather preposterous situation, n'est-ce pas?

It is physically masking the masked person of who you truly are, causing you to stray further away from the Light of who you are. You already suffocate yourself by being someone you are not by wearing a mask over your Soul, and yet you now choose to wear a physical mask to choke the life out of the very breath of your physical BEing. You torture yourself in the absurdity of the grotesque and non-necessity, adhering to the very playbook of the created and conditioned world you have so chosen your existence in. Thinketh for oneself, not according to the chorus of the few, but to thine own Self be True. Does it resonate with your Soul to mask the masked Self for the belligerent tattle tales sitting on their thrones of power? I AM true to you in the very wording of my prose, speaking from the seat of the heart, yet one chooses to be baffled into the hedonistic nature of the few that pull the strings of one's demise of existence. Tell me, Child, why is that?

As the Rolling Stones sang:
You're not the only one, with ~~mixed~~ masked emotions
You're not the only ship, adrift on this ocean
Let's grab the world by the scruff of the neck
And drink it down deeply and love it to death

One is merely adrift in the vastness of the Universe, having no inkling of the artificial world one has been duped and been constituted to live in, with all being so intimately disconnected from one another that one sees not a Soul in the breath of its radiant authenticity, as all are masked personas living a lie of having masked relationships with each other, rather than ridding the Self from the gunk and loving each other in the Light that you most authentically are.

Masks conform you to the non-expression of yourselves. Like Toto sang, "Stay away, stay away from my heart," so come not to me with the copout of, "I wear a physical mask to protect others," because my Child, you do it for fear of living in the Light of the truth of who you are, and remain in that state of a conditioned program-ming doing as you are told by devious clowns with no "heart" who know you not, and yet prey on your fears, to keep you in the ruse of staying away from living in an Awareness of the heart-spaced centred Self. Have you not in deliberation chosen to hide your e-motions from every living BEing, including yourself? You run around in a continuous deviation of yourself, running scared of the Light, hiding in the darkness, enlivening the Self with all the different personas and a creation of characters to suit your needs, wearing but a variety of different masks pertaining to the many occasions presenting itself in a complete coherence and a disconnect from one's nature of Self. It's like sitting under the shade of a tree, too afraid to dip your toe into the sunlight, for fear of the burn, with the shadows cussing you back into the shade of Self. Would you rather not bask in the freedom of your Light, and see the world beyond the confined shade one has kept the Self secluded in? Talk about a dissociative disorder, think you that I am insane? I will tell thee to look at the reflection staring back in the mirror, and one will see a created and tainted persona. Does one recognise the eyes of the Soul staring back at one or sees one but a distorted version of oneself? A masked persona, a Soul with a twist of one's elaborate making? Tell me, how does it feel to walk around with a physical mask on your face? Some of you cannot fathom the Power of the I AM that resides within to cure all ailments that haunt the Self. Yet, one chooses to blindly be fooled by a mass hysteria created "something," that boggles the senses into the stupefying of oneself. When one tells you to jump, many of you go; how high? If I tell thee to stand in line, will one stand in line like a good regimented soldier and follow *my lead promptly because I told thee to? If I told thee to stay a minimum linear yards away from me, because of the possible contamination to my current human embodiment, by invading my space, causing the possible dislodgement of my Soul from my body, would thy do it so? It seems it is but the very breath and touch of you that is poison to my veins! It sounds but rather a preposterous state of play, does it not? It stinks of a rat, as one would say, and yet people have happily obliged in this ongoing spectacle, participating in the jump of the tune being played.*

Can one not think for oneself? Is one so lost in the given and fed delirium that one has proclaimed the status quo of an oxymoron? You seem much like cattle, being prodded for the branding and tracking of the herd to appease the Masters of their livestock in the worldly market. Ah, the sheer feebleness of refusing to think but with one's inner intelligence; it is a diabolical contortion of the senses. Have you gotten your pants in a tizzy, I daresay? Is one unaware of the phenomenon that one is Energy, with the body the very embodiment of the Soul it houses and the cause of one's own energetic direction? You look at the body and your life as being such a cumbersome state of affairs, yet it wields within one's greatest power, "You," unless, indeed, one thinks one is merely a body, then believe it so. A car does not start without the key in the ignition, nor could your body commence life without a Soul. Stop masking yourself and start living in the truth of the Soul that you are.

This whole created public performance is to show humanity what it feels like to be disconnected from the All, to make you come to the understanding that you are connected to the Whole, for separation is but a dish in your face as a metaphor for a served-up illusion. Do you now understand the experiment you have been cast into? If you wish to wear a psychical mask, to condemn yourself to the e-motional mask you so wish to personify and condemn the Self to, then, by all means, keep deviating and digging yourself deeper into a hole of non-understanding and living in a blissful state of unawareness, being a little puppet on a string, suffering from the do as you're told syndrome. But let others in the state of an awakening choose to unearth their own Light returning to the essence of themselves, leaving the illusion of this grand ball masquerade, living life according to the rhythm of their own song and dance of Soul, ascending in the casting of the dawning of more beautiful tomorrows by creating and shaping a far more magical universe and a rebirthing of the earth from within the magical essence of an understanding of who they are—creating a world according to their own Divine Selves in the same breath as being at One with the rhythm of the Universe. Now that my Child is a joyous feat to behold, for the world breathes and gently floats in merely a corner of the Universal Multiverse and is far grander than one can ever fathom.

Step left, step right, step backward, forward, twirl, you follow the choreographer to the exact steps of the dance given, yet can one not think for oneself and dance to the rhythm of one's own Life, to the heartbeat of one's own Soul? You choose to be confined and constricted by malarkey talking charlatans who want to see nothing more than how well you follow the beat and svelte dance moves of their choreographed tune.

Humanity is but a finely unattuned frenzy of insistent e-motions, a soap opera mixed with the grandest ingredients of the various spices of emotional entanglements, causing but a furore and disarray and an erupting of chaos, with the running of hot and cold, at the velocity and increment of a second coming to mind. Your dramady is surely but worthy of an Oscar performance, is it not? Experiences are clung to like one's life depends on them! It is but the mere walloping of cow dung one slingshots the self with and thus chooses to remain in. How can that be when one is eternal, and all are just players on the field at play. All are actors in the various enactments of the experiences one so characterises and dupes to be real. What is reality and what is not? What is the illusion, or is all but an illusion? The Mind is a wondrous yet tricky corridor of the Alice in Wonderland Syndrome.

The Journey of Life is to find the way back to the heartbeat and truth of Self and All, to create but wonder without. You are a Light of the Divine. Your body is merely the vehicle to the attributes of living a human life through the host of experiences shovelled your way. People get so caught up in their experiences that they have lost the understanding to snap out of them, keeping them in a place of complacency, which serves no one but is a sheer detriment to themselves. If one remains within the realm of shadows of one's unauthentic Self, one causes nothing but a pain-ed salvo of possible dis-ease caused solely by yourself. Come not to us, to quick-fix thy way to healing, use thy own inner hidden magical wand to heal and fix thyself. There is nothing that your body cannot fight off. It is the futile resistance and lack of under-standing that debilitates one into thinking that one does not have the power to heal oneself. It is that rigid mindset of thinking the cause is external when in truth, the cause is an internal collaboration with the outer narrative one feeds the mind. What your Mind "eateth" so will one becometh.

To mask the Self or not to mask the Self, that is the question. You are but a mere pollutant to the Self as much as you fear being a pollutant to others, and yet only you can eventually decide how to live your life, to remain in the programmed illusion, or to snap out of it. To either live in the constraints and confinement within oneself because you do as you're told by people who know you not, or to live your life being the sover-eign and divine spirit you know yourself to be, choosing to ascend but masterfully and gracefully returning to the beautiful Light of the "butterflylicious" Self, rising above all the claptrap and chaos into the stillness of the harmonious Self, having dusted off the illusion one was so foolhardily caught up in. Whatever you give power to will have power over you. Take back your Power of the I AM, to be all that you are and can be in the I AM of all that you are. For I AM You, as much as You are Me, so how can you remain living in a state of a trapped fugue when you are infinitely so much more than all these created characters you perceive yourself to be. Drop the mask, drop the act, and reverberate but gently back into the I AM of the I AM.

Q: Don't you think everyone has become like Monk the detective, having a fear of germs and each other?

As MC Hammer states, "Can't touch ~~this~~ me," it is the exact point of making one decisive in their divisiveness, causing nothing but a further separation from the whole and making one more obedient and fragmented in their own state of affairs of coerced thinking. Fear is the germ that keeps the Soul incapacitated from its true form of Origin; it keeps you in a deviation of the Light of Self. The biggest germs are those *that hold power over others, all to ply the people with a repetitive narrative, in the hope of infecting the masses into the coercion of falling in line with the remedy to that created infection, healing the "sick," yet sickening the healing and thus the malady of both humanity and Gaia.*

You think yourselves to be so contagious pretending you do not know each other, living in the bliss of separation whilst in truth you are all brothers and sisters of the Light!

Q: What purpose do lockdowns serve in the grand scheme of things?

You have been locked down to lock yourselves down into the very bliss of a non-escapism of Self, to face the demons that you have so run from, residing in the ultra-conditioned current paradigm of existence, and thus serves to enlighten you to a higher vibrational state of awareness, to make you see that your life lived till now has been nothing but an instated mirage parading and dancing in front of your very eyes as a mere and twisted illusion, all to keep you captivated in said illusion. One can either keep running and be sucked into the fear narrated narrative or hop out of the matrix of this comical created farce and live a life to thine own Self be true.

Q: Why does everyone keep saying "stay safe"? Am I the only one that finds that a bit strange?

To stay safe means to remain encapsulated in the consistent grid of the matrix of said and fed existence. It is believing in the boundaries of a human existence rather than understanding that one is an infinite sum of possibilities, for one is the same breath and light as everything in the Cosmic Universe—yet equally, one vibrates at the resonance of one's understanding in the human "candy" wrapper. Live not to the detriment of the Soul according to the rules of the societal matrix, but live life according to the rules of your own Divine matrix— for you are far grander, far more majestic, far more capable, and far more powerful than you are led to believe. As such, one lives in a created, dumbed-down society of the inherent existence of the current dogma. I say to thee look not to the outer "confinements," but look at the resilience of the Spirit within, for one is but by sheer magic an Alchemist of the Divine. Use your magic to wield your visions into the reality of a new paradigm. Learn to think outside the created box of a feeble existence returning to the sacred grid of the Divine BEing you are. Unleash your inner Alchemist, my Child, for that is what you are, a breath-taking glitterball of 'bouncilicious' energy waiting to bunny hop outside the box back to the feat of the dazzling awareness of Self and an extension of the mere source of one's undertakings.

Q: Many people were worried they couldn't travel abroad, and that their freedoms were curbed. Most countries have opened up, whilst some still have strict regulations in place. Can you shed any light on that?

Have your freedoms been curbed? Well, my Child, were you ever free from the constraints of those in control? You are being blackmailed in all aspects of your life by the worldly in power that do nothing but appease themselves by bathing in their poor man's wealth and keeping humanity enslaved in the paradigm of their created illusion, letting them think they are free, yet are not. When you are so stuck within yourselves like the walls are caving in, and you feel like you want to get out, many often take a vacation to "get away from it all"—the irony of said saying. To vaca in the outer or to vaca in the inner, that is the question. Nothing is an improbability, for everything is an infinite possibility. One is merely chained if one thinketh one is chained. Yet the yo-yo non-travel outward is a blessing in disguise, for the greatest journey one can undertake at present is the journey inwards, for only then, when you vacate the demons that have held residence in the house of your Mind and Soul, will your outlook on life change. The journey outwards commences with the journey inwards; it can be no other way. Once the implemented filters and strewn garbage that dampened your Spirit have been removed, one will see the truth in all of the illusion that once held you in the grips of those tainted velvet lies.

You need to see it from a different perspective. The truth is the spun story of governments with their "tell me lies, tell me sweet little lies" have no control over you unless you allow it so, which is why new ideas falter. You cannot create something new within the old systematic paradigm of inequality; that is like trying to fit a round peg in a square hole. You have the power to create, to give birth to something new in a newly awakened world. Governments divide and conquer through the warfare of instilling fear, yet the power lies in the hands of the people, in the movement of the people uniting as One to give birth to the new. If you create what you desire, you desire what you create, and that intended and once actioned desire will come to fruition. If humanity understood that it never ceases to create, that one creates ever so continuously like the wheels on the barrow of Life but turning through the Presence of God Source Energy within, then one realises that having entangled the Self in a sticky web of miscreations, one could purify and discard these 'creations' in the blink of an eye and free the Self from one's imposed limitations, living in the Light and freedom of one's luminous wondrous "God" Self. There is a lot of freedom in the life you choose to create, and when people come together as One, mountains can be moved, and much beauty can be achieved. Lose the set thinking mode that one is separate, for more heads together can work magic. That freedom to break out of that conditioned confinement lies within. Hold not on to your hats of the old, but come together to work as one, in unison, forging awakened alliances and new beginnings, striking whilst the iron is hot to build bridges and communities anew and thus birthing a new dawn of creation.

Q: The UK, including some of its former colonies, have had severe Draconian measures in place, why is that?

Lest we forget that history repeats itself, from the Germanic states to the Mussolinis of Italy drowning in the delirium of exercising power over the people, to the UK being diverse in nature, with the blood of the ancient rivers running deep within its veins through the vast landscapes and formations of its existence, where the druids once ruled the lands with the Magi of the mists of Avalon and the Ray of Light by El Morya, triggering the Consciousness of Christ back into the hearts of Man. Yet, it has for centuries been a power struggle between the forces of light and darkness, with the beast now residing on the throne of the very heart of the lands, with darkness having seeped deep within the very breath of its Soul, and its tentacles wide-reaching into the "elitarian" forces on the surface of the Earth, who will stop at nothing to control the people of the common man, who in turn are nothing to them but a bargaining chip to a richer life in the materialism and their own pseudo-narcissism of the 3rd created dimensional paradigm and those they serve. Yet, they too shall falter; they too shall be decimated by the very poison spread, back to the woeful sins of Self.

You are where you are to see the darkness for what it is, to sit in that pit of the epicentre of the damned eternal, and reverberate the light back into the clogged-up pores of the lands with the help of the many, allowing the once constricted heart of Gaia to be freed from the wretched that kept her in a state of ill-ness. The heart-beat of Love and Light is spreading through the lands, from the most southern tip of the Americas, dissipating it from the smog and pollution of the once infiltrated darkness back to the breath of a new day's Earthly morn. AMERICA is the very I AM RACE, the forerunners that carry the Light of the Sacred Fire, the torch of a new Light of Understanding, of Hope and Enlightenment, spreading Love back into the hearts of Man, steering them into the crystal-clear waters of the New Golden Dawn, celebrating peace, harmony, and prosperity for all, working in unison with the lands and all people as One. Yet know that evolution is a process; it is a time-consuming matter of de-bricking the current system and rebuilding better as per the will of the people as a whole. Yet know my Child that nothing is set in stone, for every action carries infinite possible outcomes.

One forgets that, like you, Mother Earth is Consciousness and has chakra centres within her body to help sustain humanity and all sentient BEings. Yet, those negligent forces that have so infiltrated the Earth have shut down and taken control of her many beautiful energy vortexes, keeping her a prisoner to their plans and domination of existence, much like humanity has for eons been confined to the darkness of the matrix, Gaia has suffered much of that same fate.

Everyone is on their own chosen journey here on this plane. I have never worn a mask, yet I respect those who do because we all vibrate at different levels of understanding. I respect you for choosing to wear a mask, masking your soul, but in turn, please respect others for opting not to wear a mask, living in the freedom of expressing who they choose to be. Let's be honest; masks are about as good as trying to keep a fart in your trousers.

The Age of Aquarius

Having kicked the door shut on the Age of Pisces, where many of us swam as a school of fish, with the fishy few fish misguiding all fish, we now live in the Age of Aqua-rius—derived from Latin, meaning "Age of Water Rivers"—where we are forced to look in the mirror at those wobbly shadow sides residing within, knowing full well to take responsibility for all our chosen indulgent experiences, healing ourselves back to the wondrous light within.

This is an age of empowering ourselves, fuelling the inspiration of the I AM into our soul light. We can't power ourselves up if we keep roaming in the same created mucky sandbox, remaining separate from the divine source of all that we are.

The Age of Aquarius is the age of transformation, where the old will be destabilised and replenished with the birthing of the new. Rather like life knocking sense into us, paired with a cold front of some sobering fresh air, to awaken the masses to a remembrance of self and who we are—for we are enigmatic transformers, capable of transforming ourselves and the world we have chosen to dance in. Yet it's always a choice to remain in the current dimensional frequency or to alleviate the pain from the shadows within, to shift our awareness, embarking on the journey back to ourselves, elevating our vibration and treading lighter on the consciousness that is Mother Earth. Humanity lives in intrepid times, yet only by walking through the darkened chapters can we truly revive the light within and shine forth that beacon without. In all of this wonderful divine chaos, the question to ask ourselves every single day is, what AM I grateful for and be in acceptance of that.

The Ascended Master St. Germain is urging humanity to wake up, to make the world a better place for all:

Are you awake? Or are you still trapped in the slumber of the Alice in Wonderland down the rabbit hole syndrome—of following the out-of-breath nutsy tripe of a narrative of the 3rd-Dimensional Mad Hatter's Tea Party that the world projects and thus impresses upon your Soul? So many of you seem to still be in this relentless induced coma of the matrix, and even though we smack you with your chosen experiences to wake you the heaven's sake up, many of you still choose to be ingrained in the embroiled reality your Soul chooses to participate in.

What if I told you that all are just actors in the various enactments of your own created experiences one so characterises and dupes to be real, simply to elevate your vibration of Soul? Would that in the slightest alter the perception of your thought patterning? Would that eliminate the e-motion of that toy-ed word called "fear" that has persistently bullied you and that you have allowed to run rampant with your naked Soul so insistently? The "fear" that has for so long held you imprisoned in the status quo of the mind foolery—for I can tell you that "fear" is but a mere illusion concocted in your Mind, through the mere deviation of a lalalala, of refusing to listen to the Self and of refusing to heal the Self. It is a trickery plight of playing a game of poker with the EGO, who keeps acing you out with a continuous royal flush, but only because you allow yourself to be bamboozled every single time! So, I ask you, when will you stand up, kick the EGO and turn the tables on "fear"? When will you choose to transcend into having a greater understanding of Self and expanding your Awareness? Would this shift the particles in your stagnant Soul to a choosing of an expansion in your field of Awareness? If not, we will keep enhancing the experiences, making life a series of "uncomfortabilities," as "timing" is of the essence, seeing we are in the grandest of transformational times. We will all too gladly throw you off the edge of that cliff to make you see that all is but a mirrored illusion so that you can start the process of understanding what is reality and what is not and thus heal the Self back to the lightness of the Light of Self.

You have chosen to incarnate into this warped land of a confus-ed illusion, yet this chosen reality is the optical illusion pertaining to your reality. Is it all a reality, or are you merely living an illusion that you perceive to be a reality? Only you can determine the truth by delving within to understand what is the illusion and what is reality, for Life is an intricate Journey back to the Remembrance of your own Truth and Originality.

The transformation of Gaia and the human race—of the connectedness to ALL back in alignment with the Grid—has commenced and is well underway. Do not be distracted by the incorporated narrative or by any of the "demons" in seat preparing for what they think are yielding the "fruits" of their labour. You live in a world where up is down and down is up, with humanity reacting with utter bravado to the surface of the illusion of a fed trickled choco tripe narrative layered with a syrup of inconsistencies, all to make the villains out to be the heroes and the heroes out to be the villains. Much like the villainous big bad wolf being portrayed as this sweet lil red caped ridin' hood, whereas this lil red riding hood is the devious big bad wolf in sheep's clothing. My Child, get out of the darkness of the movie theatre and rub your eyes wide shut, walking into the brilliance of the Light of Truth of the World of who you Are. The world is a hall of laughing mirrors. What's up comes down and what's down comes up, for all you see is a sheer illusion of a game of chequered charades with twisted plots. The truth resides in the whispers of your heart. Stop living in the lie of the illusion and start living in Truth. The shift and ascension of the Planet begin with the Self—to ascend the Self is to heal the Self from shadows past, returning to the mere brilliance of the Light of Self.

Many indulge in the illusion of the portrayed storylines and gobble it up like a smarmy "vanilicious" amaretto sponge cake infused with the cool of bailey cream layered gelato and a warm treacle of flavoured creamy custard topped with a richness of imbued tequila sunrise maraschino cherries and a walloping of laced whipped cream a la Cointreau et coffee beans, drunk punching the senses living in a land of delirium believing all that is said and served, like a drunk on steroids.

One cannot heal if one chooses to remain in the "stifleness" within, with a continuance of feeding the greediness of that drug called "fear," brought on by a rush of adrenaline and endorphins due to the e-motions of the "fed" psychedelic mind trip without.

Healing is the feat of the enlightened Self back to the spark plug of one's Higher Self. Hold the Love and BE the Love to hold the Light and BE the Light. Remain steadfast in the eye of the storm through all of life's tempests and trust the process. Remember that every one of you is a Universal Ambassador of this beautiful and radiant I AM Light that sits but so beautifully in the chambers of your heart space. You are here to navigate yourself through the matrix of an entangled jungle, much like a cassette, trying to untangle the tangled "tape" back to a rewinding, to then hit the play button listening to the sweet ole music that hits the notes to the melodious beat of your Soul, syncing the Self with Gaia and each other. You have forgotten now, have *you? Hmmm, well, my Child, you are not here to live in this institutionalised matrix, conforming to the norm of the asylum, thinking one is separate, living but in a confined cell, remaining but ever so dozily dosed up in the perkiness of your numbed out meds, happily obliging to the bubbles of that illusion. No(!), you are here to chuck the meds, awaken your Soul and break out of this hyped-up looney bin, run by mad, deranged psychotic doctors in power, hopping the fence, back into the beautiful "garden" of the world you have so chosen to incarnate upon, understanding that you are a StarSeed with a Divine mission, here to shine Light, Love and Healing back into your Soul, the world and each other, freeing Gaia from the chains of imprisonment that she has for eons been subjected to, allowing her to heal and breathe the breath of life back into the core of her beautiful and enlightened BEing. Elevate your Soul to elevate and celebrate the world in all her beauty, fairing into the new golden dawn', and know that we are all brothers and sisters of the Cosmic Divine Light. The only difference between us is the shell we have so duly chosen to embody, for the hue of our Soul Light within the Multiverse is the same—do well to remember that, my Child. I bid you adieu and leave you showered with but much Love and Light.*

Fear is the illusion that keeps us trapped in the land of confusion, remaining intimately entwined within that fed illusion, with all the comings and goings from the way of the world and how we perceive it. Can humanity shift their awareness past this current "reality" and see that it has all been a fed bunch of lies to keep the masses in line? I can see it for what it is—can you?

Message to Humanity from Mother Earth

Welcome to Project Earth. Are you enjoying your staycation or making a mockery and being a cosmic blowing bubble out of sorts? Earth—because the galaxy needed an insane asylum, where the crazies are labelled as insane, refusing to conform to the system, and the sane live like the worker bees serving the hive within the frame of their containment box. We laugh about it, and we make the best of life within that set matrix, and yet this is not life; we are being lived, and we can all do better working together as one.

We live on the surface of the Earth as much as we live on the surface of ourselves, forgetting we have a "depth" to us as much as the Earth has a depth of beautiful different BEings residing on a far higher "harmonial" frequency, who can see humanity on the surface, albeit humanity hasn't even scratched the surface of their beautiful selves!

Mother Earth has gracefully accepted humanity and other sentient beings to walk the surface of her lands, yet we have trashed the place to the high heavens. Yet she still loves us, regardless of our shortcomings towards her. Remember to honour, love, and nurture her as you would choose to honour, love, and nurture yourself, which is often the kink in the cable, for do you love yourself enough to love the Mother you so freely walk on? She is the bearer and the "sustainer" of all life. She has given you the freedom to walk your chosen journey and unravel yourself through the trepid upheaval of the conditioning to which one has become so accustomed, back to the light of your true self.

I love tapping into the energy of Mother Earth as she has such a warmth to her, and I asked her for a message to humanity at this time. She replied:

Look at the majestic skies above, at the splendour of Nature in the world around you; everything resonates at its own energetic frequency and expands in its own Divine timing.

You live in a Universe, built and created according to the sacred geometrical design of all life across the multiversal grid by the Supreme Creator and the Architects of all species and all of Life. There is nothing that is not intertwined with the Oneness and with all. The Earth is a mere speck in one of the many multi-dimensional Universes to coexist in parallel with the All, for life is far grander than what you can anticipate, than what you can behold.

Remember, you are all temporary visitors to this time and place, merely passing through, like gentle particle waves crashing on the shoreline and receding upon returning to the vastness of the Cosmic Ocean of One, with the sole purpose of learning, understanding, observing, honouring, growing, and remembering that one is love unconditional returning to the fold of One of Self and All, and thus taking the journey "homebound" to the Stars yet once again, such is the circular cycle of the winding staircase of Life. Make it so that your experiences here are of a memorable notion and that, should you wish to return, I will gracefully welcome you back with open arms to nurture you and further your journey for the growth of your Soul and the continuance of the evolution of your bless-ed Spirit.

You look at me, and I look back at you.
You smile at me, and I smile back at you.
For we are but mere reflections of one another, reflecting Conscious Cosmic Energy waves from and to each other.
I see but beauty and a Divine Nature in you as I hope that you see my Divinity and understand my unconditional Love for you.
The beauty of the sunrise and the dawning of the sunset is the nature of my evolution as much as yours. I wish not to devolve but to evolve and to aid humanity in the current Conscious shifting of the paradigm, for I, too, am deserving of shifting into a lighter dimensional plane of Existence.
I, too, am much like a babe, growing and choosing to expand.
I, too, wish to breathe a little easier and not feel so constrained and constricted within myself, for harnessing me in a trapped contusion will only cause "eruptions" on the surface of my BEing. Humanity has often made me ill, having tipped the scales of Love and Light, and are as much the malady as the cure of the cause-ed havoc within my "system" and thus, through the pain inflicted, I will break out and throw up to relieve the pain of the inconsistencies, of those anomalies within that one, has so wilfully imposed upon me without.

Yet I need your unity, your devotion returning to an understanding of a Love of Oneself and another.
For just like you as a hue-man have a vessel to the embodiment of one's human experiences, my Soul and my beating heart reside in the centre of my BEing, the inner Earth, a fertile ground for the sprouting and growth of your ecological nature, with my surface, a feast to the nurturing and sustenance for all of Life created.

How can you respect me when you do not have the tenacity even to respect yourself?
How can you love me when you do not love the wholeness of who you are?
How can you honour me when you honour not yourself but in the slightest?
How can you cherish me when you choose not to cherish the awe and wonder of all that you are?
How can you nurture me when you are choosing not to nurture yourself?
Yet I carry all of the above for you and love you with the pureness of my BEing regardless of the many faux pas humanity has made.
Treat me not with ignorance but nurture me as I nurture you.
Love me as I love you.
Honour me as I honour you.
Let the truth within your heart guide you in all that you do.

Everywhere humanity chooses to tread, I feel it with every ounce of my living and breathing Conscious BEing.

Think not that I do not feel, for your Soul inhabits your given "body" whilst my Soul resides within the core of the Earth of ME; my surface is but my ample skin you choose to walk on.

I, too, have a pulse like you. I breathe just like you, for without the beat of my heart and sustenance of my life force energy, you simply would not exist.

I am as much Divine Consciousness and alive as you are.

I AM but beauty to behold, as much as you are a beautiful Divine Light dancing on my "skin," and yet you are but a mere grain of the desert sand inhabiting the surface of my wonderful and enigmatic BEing—be thankful and give thanks.

I AM continuously expanding and expressing myself, just as you are choosing to expand and express yourself in the human embodiment.

Even though my energy has for eons been controlled by those who wish me harm, I AM and remain selfless in my ways, unlike humanity, having deviated from the path of Oneness through the implications of the implemented conditioned matrix.

I ask you to treat me not with disdain, but to treat me with love, respect, devotion, and an honouring of the Earthly Ancestors reflecting back to the Self and back to the roots and love and light of me, in the vibrance of who you are and all of who you can be.

Allow yourself to shift from the denseness of the Soul BEing you believe yourself to be, walking back to the breath of the enlightened Lightness of a Light you are, and have always been.

Let us both move and dance with ease and grace through the chaos back to the beat of Oneness ascending and shifting into a more expanded and harmonious state of Conscious Awareness.

For you, as much as I am deserving.

Destruction would be but a void, an empty of nothingness, and I would be at the mercy of your destruction and feel the pain thereof, for Mankind uses me but in kind for experimenting beyond the surface, draining me of valuable minerals, and not nurturing me to retrieve it as quickly as I can give out.

Give thanks to the Earth, and let us dance into an age of rediscovering the Self in unison with the All, reclaiming the Divine Flow of Creation within Oneself and thus learning to sync in song with ME (Mother Earth) and all its sentient BEings.

~In Love and Gratitude, Mother Earth~

Mother Earth holds so much wonder; without her, we would not be in existence, and yet we treat her with the same disregard with which we treat ourselves. We have polluted the Earth as much as we have polluted ourselves, causing nothing but a dis-ease within ourselves.

If we want to make the world a better place, we have to commence by looking at ourselves. The work starts within, for a better place without. If we could truly learn to love ourselves and live in a heightened state of awareness and acceptance of all that has been given to us, learning to tap into the energies of the Mother instead of simply taking her to fulfil our needs, then she would be far more gracious towards us, as we would be to ourselves. One single step can cause a ripple effect in either direction. Please don't take the Earth or yourself for granted, but have a conscience and think consciously in all that you do, giving thanks for all she gives you. Raise your awareness to be appreciative of all you have in life; even if you get duped down in the crap of your experiences, so does the Earth, yet she still evolves, loves, and sustains us.

As the Earth is as much a part of you as you are of the Earth, to help heal her, she gave me this exercise while channelling her.

Sit quietly, taking several deep breaths in and out. Breathe in from the root chakra to the crown chakra to the count of 4, hold for 4, and breathe back out for 4—do this ten times, and subsequently, repeat with the count of 8 till you come to the space between, feeling centred within yourself.

* With each breath, pour pure white brilliance light of unconditional love eternal over yourself and subsequently within from the head down to your feet, and out into the Earth.
* Bathe in this light, being the brilliance of radiant divine love.
* Breathe love, light, healing, and gratitude within your own heart space, and visualise pouring this pure white brilliance light of unconditional love eternal from your heart over Mother Earth, starting from the top of the North Pole, all the way to the tip of the South Pole, letting it flow abundantly before pouring this love through the inner core of the Earth, replenishing her heart self.
* Once you have done this, envision Mother Earth in a hue of pink golden light and close your meditation by giving thanks, blessing the light and love of Mother Earth, and so it is.

Message to Humanity from the Ascended Archangel Michael

Archangel Michael, to me, comes across as a bit of a jack the lad, someone you can sit down and have a beer with but suffers from a bout of verbal diarrhoea once he gets going—yet everyone will experience him differently. He is enormous compared to my current human embodiment, and he can be serious yet has a unique sense of humour. He always tells me it's *"Mich(k)a'el"* and that all names of the Arc-Angels are spelled similarly, having the apostrophe. To avoid any confusion, however, I have left the names as they are known to most. Often people think that he alleviates fear, but he gives you an extra dose of it so that you muster up the strength and courage within to overcome the engrained illusion of fear that you have planted and so "lovingly" nurtured. If you want his help, be prepared to walk through the layered depths of darkness of who you think you are, back to the light of who you truly are.

One other thing he would like to clarify is the sword he carries. He says, *"The cutting of cords is done with a created crystalline sword I carry, a sound reverberator, and when inserted into the Soul, it regenerates the 'soil,' smoothing out the anomalies and ridding the Self of the heaviness that once was but is no more. The key is to remain not fixated nor trapped within that conditioning but to heal and move forward in a joyous motion to the leaps and bounds of the heart of Self."*

Archangel Michael is a warrior, having battled many legions and wars within the multiverse, and aids in helping you battle your own demons to find your inner light warrior back to the very breath of who you are. At the end of 2020, he started coming through to me more predominantly. He wanted humanity to understand him and how his fine woven account weaves back into the tapestry of understanding humankind's beginnings. Indeed, I call him "Ascended" because while he may have transcended and is of the light, he clearly states that ascension is for you to behold through your experiences, through the many incarnations you choose, to evolve to the next level of the game of Life. It lies not merely in the esoteric but also in aiding to help free Gaia, who has been unwillingly subdued, gagged, and handcuffed to the matrix.

I AM the Archangel Mika'el, upholder of the Sacred Divine.
Encoder and Warrior to the centrifuge of Humanity, for Duality is a feat of the acceleration of Oneself back to the Divine Grace within.
I AM a Warrior of the Light, a Protector to all in the Universe in the quest to Ascension.
I AM the Instiller of Truth, Expansion, and a Light to those who seek me for the Wisdom Eternal. Come not to me in the mere self-pity of oneself, for only a fool would choose to wallow and weep and drown in one's created Experiences of Illusion; for my Child, you set yourself up for the fall in the chosen Game of the Portrayal of your storyboard of Life.

Know that I AM the Upholder and Archon (derived from the Greek word 'ruler') of Strength and Courage. I AM a Beacon of Hope, a Ray of Light in the depth of the swirling consuming darkness back to the Divine Light of Self. I AM a Crusader of the

Light, of the Cosmic Rays of the Divine Galactic Sun. I AM All that you are and more than what you Are, yet we are Star particles born of the same Light Divine. In Truth, I AM an extension of you as much as you are an extension of ME.

All history, books, and movies are a di-variation of who you are and where you are from; it is a divergence on the road to Self-Awareness on the discerning of Truth versus the Illusion of the portrayed Reality.

Much darkness has been cast over the Earthly lands, a battle of a waging of wars since the dawn of time.

You have chosen to be born of a lesser creed, a lesser understanding, and yet we are, but ingenious masters of illusion and deception portraying one with the narrative of one's choosing, with one needing to decipher the unravelling story and come to one's own conclusion, the discernment between the truth of the illusion and reality for it is a trickery and a jagged edge slope.

Believe not the narrative of the many different flavoured and yummy dishes in front of you, but listen to the truth that resides deep within each of you, for embedded within these chambers, one will find a knowledge eternal, pearls of ancient wisdom lost in the depths of the uncut fabric of your Soul, intact in the paradigm of the narrative of the current matrix of understanding.

Finding these pearls will tear into the very layered fabric of who you believe yourself to be, but undoubtedly are not, for one's true authenticity is a residual of the BEings that we are, a creation created by creators of creation. Yet, in truth, are we not Masters of our concocted creations, playing the game of snakes and ladders to achieving ascension on the board game of Life?

Homo Sapiens were created as a hybrid, a tinkering with the genetics and DNA by advanced races, a creation of ethics and morality Encoders of the Light Divine. But as humanity rises from its slumber, a tear in the fabric of one's docile existence allows for the Light to percolate through the once clouded cumbersome darkness, and one realises that life has been but a feverishly controlled game of those in power holding power over the dumbed down masses, all for their pivotal egotistical megalomaniacal and sadistic gains.

I am as much the dusk, the twilight of times, as my brother is the dawn of the morn, yet we are two sides of the same coin, for one is an ending of the cycle so that a new one can be forged from the iron cast reborn.

Yet whilst one has free will, it is the accumulated karma that determines the outcome, as much as the outcome equates to the awakening of the brethren, of one another, the diversity and duality forming the backdrop of the acceleration of the many in the Universal Grid, the stage lit for the pandemonium—to ensure the understanding of the dualities within oneself, and each other.

It is not to create a divide but to alleviate the darkness, the shadows that reside in the wells of each of you, so that you have a far deeper understanding of both yourself, the world, and one another, for you see, darkness and light are merely two sides of that very same coin.

You have chosen to come here to elevate the Light back into the Consciousness of Man—you are here to accelerate the awakening of Man. Either one can decide to grow at an exponential rate to a higher level of understanding should one accept the challenge of the experiences one has been bestowed with or move at a turtle's pace of suffering from the mere bunny-in-the-boiler syndrome.

You are a multitude of manifestations in a multidimensional reality, blending past, present, and future timings creating the You of who You ARE.

One is lost in the earthly density, having to find oneself walking through the crunchy crinkles returning to one's own smooth criminal rhythm divine. Living in the earthly realms is a game of quid pro quo; it is a diversion of creation of the Subliminal Mind.

Since the dawn of time, Man has been erroneous in their ways and rescinded one's Divinity in the dwindling of the belief in separation.

You are privy to the Light as much as you are privy to the darkness. You are a conceptualised DNA invocation of the Soul Light that you are. Fear is the illusion of the implementation into the grid of the matrix.

You live so much in a deviation of your own pain; you are an utter pain to the created pain of the pain-ed Self, living in the despair of constantly wooing yourself, revelling in the energetic sludge of your own misery and the cumbersome outward portrayal of your drama. By immersing in the thick of your experiences, you have but lo behold forgotten the art of joy, the lightness of laughter, and the skip a heartbeat of a love for self and others.

One has strayed so far from the truth, having become lost in the maze of the trippy warped mind, a far cry from the actual truth, thus living in the accustomed phantom matrix one has so hopelessly devoted the Self to, having assumed an avatar, and suited and booted the Self to roleplaying that character.

I AM not who you think I AM, just as you are not who you think you are. And that is one of Life's great mysteries. Yet in all the vastness of infinites that you are, the journey is yours to undertake, to understand one's cosmic evolution on the board game of Life. It is intricately more complicated and vast than one can fathom, and yet in all the flickering of recognition of the aha moments of one's return to Self, it is the journey undertaken into the wandering maze of the hidden Self that creates but the return to the luminous spark within to create but that radiance of the brilliance of the Light without. Like the Universe, you are a drop o' Starlight in the Cosmic Sea in constant motion. Polarities are forever playing the field across the whole spectrum of the Galaxial Grid; it is a continuous light switch prank between light and dark, night and day, with many civilisations partaking in the evolutionary game of ascension, whereby some have plunged into darkness and others have completed the game aiding others in the planetary ascension of the coming.

Live not in fear of the Self, but with the courage to know that all can be bequeathed, all can be overcome. For by the Power vested within the Sacred Divine, thou art unfathomably infinite, nothing is an improbability but for thine own Self, boxed-in creation of the Mind and through the art of the play of Life.

Life is a mere series of experiences, and the longer you allow yourself to get knocked down by them, the more lost you will become, being sucker punched into the Wizard of Oz whirlwind, eventually being spat out, walking around torn, bruised, and confused in the non-understanding that your Mind and Soul have been tripped. Expect not a *sorry from me, for I am not the creator of your created mess. Get off your sorry arse, shake the illusion of dread, stop acting like a porcelain doll and heal those broken fragments of Self. Experiences are not meant as an attachment to leech you dry in the sheer deprivation of oneself but serve as a delish dish to heal the fragmented Mind o' Soul to the core of the Light one is.*

You are not who you are but who you choose to unravel your Soul to be through the mere experiences of Self upon the earthly planes.

You cannot rise without falling, nor can you fall without rising, for the two go hand in hand into either the oblivion of who you are at the mercy of your Soul, or to the ecstatic heights of your Powerful Divine I AM Presence of Self.

Your destiny is not your fate, nor is fate your destiny; it is a choosing of the Life you have so ambiguously set out for yourself, along with the characters of your choosing. Yet, in the enactment of each of your lives lies the freedom of choosing a path to the infinite potential, the infinite pearls of wisdom of outcomes pertaining to the choices of your choosing.

Let all not be in vain, for procrastination is a sucker to finding the truth to one's authenticity and creates but a deviation of sour grapes. If one mope-muppets around in one's created experiences for far too long, one loses the will to live and, in one's exasperation, the understanding of the intended lesson thereof.

Many of you live on the outer fringes of yourselves, on the peripheral ledge of what the eye can see in the existence of your current embodiment. The narrative of fear, the 'demons' that have taken up cosy residence inside your head, is the block that holds you back from undertaking the journey to your own truth, for that would tear the very fabric of your existence as you have been led to believe, would it not? How can you be all that you can be when you live in a continuous fear of Self when you live in a continuous fear of the shadows of Self?

Muster up the courage to realise the strength of who you are and to stand up for your beliefs. Let not the drivel nor the opinionated blustering of others drive you back into the shadows of your cardboard-boxed non-existence. Speak your truth and let fear not hold you back, for fear is the beholder of the masked Soul that you are; it is a back-holder of Self. Bask in the unequivocal I AM Power of the Divine God or Goddess you are, for are ye not a God? Aye, but ye are, for one is but the extension of the spectacular spark that resides within the hue of your heart, giving the breath of Life to the organism of the human embodiment.

It is time to step outside the box of who you think you are and unleash the dormancy returning to the true nature of who you are; for my Child, you are a worthy Divine Warrior of the Light, simply having rescinded in the depths of the folly holed matrix. You are capable of anything you put your Mind to. Have the strength to take back your I AM Power that you have so complicity given away and relish in the Divine Presence of who you are. Conform not to the normalcy that is not, but for a mere parade of displayed charades in front of your dancing eyes—merely close your eyes and dive deep within, unlocking the locked boxes of ancient knowledge, inspiring the Self to return to the Light of Self as much as inspiring the uninspired back to their Light of Selves.

I AM as much You as You are Me, for I AM the basking of the Light in you as you are a reflection and basking of the Light in ME. Always speak your Truth, stand in your Truth and live in your Truth to BE the Light of the all-encompassing Truth of YOU.

~The Ascended Archangel Michael~

It is time to ascend, to rise above, let go of the old ways, and recover the light of ourselves, for it is in the power of the people to transcend and usher in the new golden age. It lies not with a governmental institution but within ourselves to commence and be the change to which we want to give birth.

This excerpt of the Evolution of Human Consciousness and the Shift wasn't supposed to be in this book, but the many Masters deemed it of the utmost importance for you to understand what is at play in this current ascension process. I could tell you about the mirror worlds—Agartha, the kingdom of the inner Earth, and the continued experiments within the hub of Antarctica—but that is an entirely different story. What I will say about Antarctica is that billions of years ago, it bathed in the lushness of a subtropical climate, yet with the movement of the tectonic plates, it has sunk into an Arctic blast, with its surface rather deceptive, for it is built underground into many subterranean levels, with BEings held against their will, powered by a crystal grid, and is an interdimensional gateway.

I have been told that there is a hyperbolic-powered speed tunnel deep underground at the far ends of the Antarctic to the tip of the South Americas, with other tunnels built millions of years ago going from the tip of Argentina snaking into Ecuador. Everything is interconnected, and as the Ancients of those times state, *"One lives too much and searches too much on the surface when one needs to delve deep within to seek but the answers to the truth that is and has always been there. Expand the Mind and what you seek, so ye shall find; knock, and it shall be opened unto you, for if one asketh, one receiveth in the readiness of the Soul but wanting to Master the teachings of the once ancient future past."*

It's mesmerising walking through some of these beautifully polished tunnels, illuminated through a carefully laid out crystal grid field with its many alcoves. They call it a storage facility of ancient knowledge, from the forebearers of mankind that walked both the stars and the lands, to help nourish and evolve the planet. Many civilisations have stored wisdom within its "archives," from Atlantean technology to the construction of the pyramids, the Hall of Records, the Mayans, the lost Sumerian civilisations, and many more that came before them. These tunnels were not dug with manmade prehistoric shovels of wood and animal bones but with sophisticated ancient technology. Nor did these civilisations use a cart and horses to load their stuff, walking through hundreds of miles of tunnels; they used off-the-ground transport pods. Maybe someday, when humanity is ready, the seals will be opened for man to understand the unearthing of the Earth's eclectic origins, but until they stop roaming in the insufferable state of their petulant ego, living in a tainted state of a conditioned love, the doors will remain shut.

This book, however, is about my life. It may resonate somewhere deep within your soul, for many of you will have lived in otherworldly dimensions, having come to assist in the ascension process, to be a guide to a better way of living instead of being lived, whilst others may have lived countless incarnations here on Earth, having once roamed the Ancient lands of Egypt, or swum the waters of Atlantis, or lived in the magic of Lemuria, or the Gardens of Sumer, or Babylon, or immersed oneself in the centre of the cosmos of the Mayan culture, or traipsed through the beginnings of the grand Mesopotamian civilisation. Wherever you may have mapped your soul, now is the time to remember that ancient knowledge in your current embodiment. It is shimmering and dancing on the surface yet lies dormant in your cellular memory body, waiting for your soul's remembrance to reactivate it, for your assistance is needed now more than ever in the creating and the rebirthing of a New Earth.

The Art of Duality

Many of the Light BEings talk about duality throughout my book, so I wanted to explain the concept. I always used to say I have no shadow sides, but actually, I was crippled by them! I knew duality meant opposites, but I didn't realise that one had to experience duality to understand polarities and learn from them. I always thought I had learned from my experiences, but nope, I often avoided them, thinking I had dealt with them, limping even more through the story of my buggered-up life. When I commenced healing myself, I told my Guides that I had no more shadow sides to heal, as I understood duality. I was done, been there, done that s***, was all healed-up, am all light, love, peace, and all that jazz. And they were laughing their butts off. Little did I know that I had to dig a hell of a lot deeper—and as I did, a whole fountain of crap erupted over me, leaving me covered in my unhealed shite of this life and past lives gone. If you truly want to heal, Spirit will shove you right into your problems, and you can either choose to wail and scream and remain as you are or decide to heal up. The choice is yours.

The Multiverse is a convolution of Consciousness evolving, created by the Grand Master Architect, who blew the breath of life and that of all Divine Creation into the ever-expanding Universum of Creation.

Spirituality = Spirit-You-Duality. It is the human experience of celebrating one's individuality through the eyes of duality as a mere reflection of oneself. It is allowing your soul the art of experiencing 'polarities' through the mere journeying of life within the earthly realms of one's chosen incarnation. It is the experience of the light and shadow sides of the game of human evolution, in understanding the nuances of the various states of consciousness through one's experiences, and that duality is but a mere state of mind. It is the perception of contradictions, of contraindications, and having the courage to transcend and evolve to higher planes of awareness and existence, escaping the dogma of the programmed conditioning one has been subjected to upon incarnating—thus elevating your soul frequency, vibing to a higher frequential level of evolutionary planetary consciousness, where duality exists no more. One is a cosmic dancer, dancing the soul back home to a realignment in unison with the soul-self and the universe, singing off the same hymn sheet of love and understanding. It is reverberating to a deeper sense of the self and all BEings, ascending to a higher level of consciousness and understanding that love is all there is and all there ever will be.

The path divides the Soul into the duality of the senses, for all roads lead to an eventual elevation of one's Conscious Awareness, returning to the somersaulting zing-and-zest in one's Soul unless one chooses to keep the lights dimmed, living in the superficiality of one's own intended narrow mindset of a conditioned version of a chosen reality.

Without day there would be no night. Without the Light of the Sun, the Moon and Stars would remain unseen in the vast landscapes of the night sky. One cannot co-exist without the other. Your shadow side is a mere reflection of the self to the Light within, enabling you with the choice to grow and evolve.

Without rain, growth would not be a feasible experience of understanding the rays of the brightened sunshine streaming back into the crevices of the healed Soul. To live in contrasts is to understand life and the direction one chooses to ultimately flow.

One often lives so much in the duality aspect of living that one has forgotten the true meaning of life. You are Love. It is your birthright, and yet you duel with the polarities in life, having allowed yourselves to be conditioned, having become defunct in your existence, trying to make sense of this nonsensical farce of this manufactured paradigm. Difficulties shape the receiver into the fortitude of one's very own making. Life is not a tit-for-tat but a beautiful experience in all one's undertakings. It is a joyous feast, for the tougher the challenges, the harder the fall, the greater the slam dunk comeback. Always remember life does not hold you back; you hold yourself back by the monsters that keep you at bay inside of your head.

My Child, there is no separation. How can there be when all of Life throughout the Multiverse has sprung from the Godverse and is a continuous expressing and expanding of that Divine Consciousness expressing and expanding through you? We are each other, and we live in each other, for we are all goddamn wonders of that same breath of Universal Consciousness, merely having wrapped our Soul in a different skin, living a life of duality, either getting our knickers in a twist, with a dose of ants in our pants or choosing to overcome our hurdles walking back to the Truth and remembrance of who we are. The choice is yours as to how you choose to perceive life in its current status quo.

~The Light BEings, the Ascended Master St. Germain and the Archangel Michael~

Life is about embracing yourself and accepting yourself for who you are. Your thoughts are the energetic frequency that makes up the landscape around you. Learn to adapt like the fluent chameleon that you are. Change the landscape of your thoughts, and I promise you, the horizon of your life will change to brighter tomorrows.

On a side note, the Light BEings are a beautiful collective of guardians from a much higher frequency of light, making their form difficult to discern, and hence one perceives them merely as light, yet they can transform at will taking on a form of their choosing. They are very much active in creating the many worlds of all created archetypes throughout the multiverse, giving those that are called upon specific messages related to their life purpose but also creating specific changes that will significantly impact the whole. By absorbing our experiences, we can be that beacon of light for others to make the necessary changes within their own lives. It may be an individual experience, yet it is that domino effect cast upon the whole of creation to elevate ourselves, to beam ourselves into the next phase of evolution, serving humanity in the broader context of the overall consciousness.

There Is No Death

You existed long before you were born and will continue to exist long after you have discarded your physical garment, for you are forever and always have been. How can there be death when the soul is eternal? You are the light! You are the divine energetic life force that powers this body up. Without the hue of your light, the body would be a mere dead weight of biodegradable compost, its loins but lying in waste, and your energy would have transcended elsewhere.

Death is an opportunity for the soul to rest and recalibrate itself back to its divine light of consciousness, its divine I AM presence, having been freed from the discord and turmoil while it was anchored in its human embodiment on Earth. The soul recharges its 'batteries,' powering itself back up to the light it is and always has been. As St. Germain states:

"Dream a little dream, my Child, for Life is but a beautiful, whimsical dream, and yet for some, it can be a rather 'messilicious' impish nightmare - yet in truth, it remains but a splendid dream. When you 'die' you wake up from your deep slumber to the bliss of your authentic nature, your higher consciousness, and realise it was all an elaborate plan, a ruse created by none other than yours truly, you, in the form of experiences, to help expand your consciousness and experience life in the duelling motions of duality. Without duality in human nature, how can one ever evolve and transcend to the next level of the 'cosmilicious' bubble of the Game of Evolution?

Death is a close confidante, a wonderful friend, for without 'death,' life would not be possible. Death is an elevation of the Soul; one checks out, having taken the return leg of the journey from Earth and checking in when arriving at the next destination, having levelled up in the playing field of the Cosmic Game of Evolution, serving elsewhere within the multidimensions of the Universe. The Universe does not move backward but is forever moving forward, expanding in consciousness and ever greater joy and perfection. It remains not in a stagnant status quo, for energy is continuous and constantly evolving. If one carries nothing but love for the person that has crossed the nethers of the earthly realms, one should not grieve for the loss thereof nor have the desire to hold that loved one in a state of incapacity, creating nothing but a gilded cage, as that Soul should be able to revel in the heights its freedom, returning to the Authentic Light of its true form of Self. It is merely the ignorance of this truth that keeps humanity bound in its own created limitation, incapacitating oneself and the Soul that wants to fly free in the rapture of its own Light.

Death is a created stigma in one's society of the current matrix. It is non-existent. It is merely a word in the manmade dictionary of languages, institutionalised into the very fabric of humanity's existence. If one named 'death' as a mere transcendence, one would erase the heaviness and mournings of that feeling of loss, for it is merely a transformation and an energy transference of one's Soul back to the Light of Home. The Soul's energy simply transfers from the physical embodiment, the temple it once called 'home,' back to the rejoicement of the true Light of Home. Death carries that morbidity label attached to it, where people weep but for the love and loss of that person, and yet it is ludicrosity at its finest, for one is and always has been energy, and thus one cannot 'die,' one can merely 'transform,' one can merely 'transcend,' it is the matrix that has gotten one living in fear thereof—as that is what controls the masses. Is one not Energy? Can one not alchemise one's malady of created dis-ease that one so ails from? With the utmost certainty, you can(!), but alas, humanity has deviated and strayed so far without themselves, having developed a co-dependency upon the very implemented system in place, having forgotten the Power of the I AM Presence within. Aren't you a sight for sorry eyes to behold? I ask thee to discard all that one thinks one knows and unlearn all that one has so learn-ed, for everything learn-ed lies deeply dormant within, hidden under the many ingrained and created layers of one's created persona in one's current realm of existence. Transcendence of one's Soul equates to ascension, joy, exhilaration, and the eternal Light of Love. One is infinite energy, and yet one fills the Self not with gratitude but often with an aptitude of desti-tution towards the Self. One fools the Self into believing something that is not, and yet what is, seems but preposterous in the eyes of the Soul of the beholder. The truth of what you know is the density of the frequency you so choose to vibrate on, and thus exactement one dwells in that vibrational plane of existence. Yet if one relents one's limited thinking and learns to see the truth of the light of all that is, it will set thee free into the wonders of the realms of one's Divine I AM Presence and the magnificence of the Multiverse that has been given the breath of life by the Cosmic Creator of All of Existence, continuously evolving on a Conscious Cosmic Quantum level within the Multiversal Quantum Field, forever expanding, quantifying, reshaping, transforming, changing, and blowing life into the realms of all of Existence through the art of both a rebirthing and of a deconstruction, reconfiguring the Energies back to the dust of the lands and a birthing of the new, for nothing my Child is ever stagnant, all life forms both old and new are evolving Consciousness within this beautiful Universal Grid we call Home, so understand that there can be no death but for the mere thought of the untruth one has so duly been led to believe in the sweet sound corners of one's beautiful exploratory observational Mind."

Once our soul is free from the body, our light returns home, taking the memories of our experiences of the life we so masterfully and wilfully created. When we look back over its record to date, and once our soul has recharged by receiving an influx of light, we determine the possible next Earth life we wish to undergo. I say "possible" as you could choose to incarnate on a different planet within a different dimension. Whatever you decide, your next life will complement your previous life experiences. If you lived a 'crappy' life, that's the karma of the experiences you take with you in the hope of leading a better life, regardless of the experiences thrown your way.

When someone you love crosses over, Spirit states, have your grief but do not mollycoddle yourself in that emotion, for it is rather selfish to remain in that constant state of "grief" as the soul that has passed revels in the remembrance of the once earthly "fugued"-out self. Weep not, for the loss is merely physical, but the spirit is eternal.

As we are shifting dimensions, and humanity is transitioning and stepping out of that denseness that once was, we need to step away from the engrained morbidity of death. I may show compassion, but as St. Germain has impressed upon me:

"What kind of teacher would you be if you felt sorry for the people that have lost someone and mollycoddled them in their state of grief? Morbid, it is certainly not, for the Soul is overjoyed being back home and celebrating its experiences, having had the chance to evolve in its human life, so who are you to sit there and weep, feeling sorry for yourself, when death is a non-existent feat? Wipe your tears, snap out of your conditioned state of a sorry arse Self, for whilst you remain like a jaded flat and deflated pudding constricted within your sadness, letting life pass you by, the Soul revels in its delish chocolate delight of Light back Home."

As Anubis chimes in:

"You live in such a state of physiocracy. You do not put someone into the ground nor incinerate them to a crisp with the dust of ashes remaining. It is the mere worn-out outer garment inserted into a casket or cremated—there is no death, only life. The transformation of death has always been an ascension, a graduation of the Soul and its accumulated learnings. You are the indestructible Energy carried within the destructible organism of a human body. Weep not like a fool, curled up in a ball and crumbling to a heap allowing one to be ruled by the dogma of grief, all the whilst the soul having travelled the duat and returned to the vastness of the A'Aru, the field of reeds and barley, is jumping for joy in the divine remembrance of the star seedling it is and always has been."

With Thoth, continuing:

"There can be no death. There is only Life. You are not matter. You are Light. You are Energy; energy cannot be snuffed out; it merely changes form. You are a walker between worlds and hop from one to the next in the blink of an eye. How can that not be grand? Your physical human body returns to the dust of the Earth from whence it came, whilst the Soul merely floats back to the warmth of the Light and Love of home, where one's memories flood back, as the denseness of the physical has been left behind. You have this eerily misconception that death is a barrier between two worlds. It is an incorrect and miscalculated conditioned statement. Life is living in finite form, yet one returns to life in infinite form eternal because one dances from one level of the Cosmic Game of Evolution to the next. Death is a stopover and reincarnation a do-over on that same board game of Life. If there is no death, how can one weep? How can one be so selfish to keep the Soul in a state of paralysis because one misses the physicality of the person that inhabited a temporary body that once was? In these transitional times, with many ascending back home, one would hope that humanity duly awakens, untraining that programmed monkey mind, snapping out of living in a state of grief, instead rejoicing that beautiful Soul that wishes for nothing more but to move on, living in its rapture of Divine bliss and remembrance. Keep each

other not imprisoned. Celebrate your own life as much as you celebrate the life of that graduated Soul, for death is a mere conditioned illusion, my Child—always has been, always will be."

Your life equates to the actions you put into it. The reward one cashes out on, and the sum of the equations of your actions ultimately configure to the culmination of your life. When your life is over, and you made a bit of a 'mess' out of it, then it is your conscience you have to face when transcending, and it will be between the council and yourself how you choose to resolve and evolve from this. The Ascended Master Hilarion puts it best, saying:

"If one lives to be but a 'cursed' life in one incarnation, one can choose to 'atone' for that life by a following incarnation in accordance with the Council. There is no right or wrong but for the mere programming of a life to achieving the state of enlightenment. No one said life would be easy, but the journey to attaining enlightenment is worth walking the road less travelled for the Soul to achieve the state thereof. After all, you are but biodegradable compost; how you flower is entirely up to you."

Death equates to transformation as much as transformation equates to the death of the incarnated embodiment of the evolution of the soul it once housed. We have been taught to believe that death is a tragedy; it is not. It is a celebration of that soul's evolutionary progress. It is a step forward in the development of that spirit and should not be a cause for mourning. I agree that death may cause a period of sadness, as a loved one is gone in the physical sense, but the moment you understand that this person's life experience has come to an end, be joyous, for the body was a mere casing that held its soul. Death is merely falling asleep and waking up from "the dream of life" back home.

Many have argued with me, believing that once you die, you're gone, and nothing remains of you. To that, I say, really? Then how does the body function? Spirit's analogy is simple: can a car start without a key in the ignition? A body functions similarly; one's soul is the key to powering up the body for it to work. If nothing were to remain of you, all your experiences and creativity you've garnered throughout your life would have been for nothing, and that would be a terrible waste, would it not?

Does a tree die in winter? It withdraws and re-emerges in spring when nature reawakens from its deep slumber. Humanity has simply become too embedded in matter, in the material, and has lost sight of its true authenticity, as many have decided to unplug themselves from Source, living a life in the bliss of separation and total unawareness of who they really are. Many have lost the understanding of why they've come here to Earth in the first place and where they go once the adventure comes to a close. Fear is the trump card of the corrupted governing systems that have controlled the earthly realms for eons. The Ascended Master Hilarion, asks:

"What is your biggest fear? Is it a fear of living? A fear of dying? Or fear of nothing-ness? You are but what you allow your Mindset to be. What you allow within your energy dynamics will transpose and cascade into your environment. Swim or drown. Rise or fall, and remain but seated in the damned eternalness of your conditioned misery. It is all about choice, so what's yours?

Life is a vigour, an explosion, the ultimate adventure of experiences back to the ultimate sensation of Self. One is born awake, yet throughout the culmination of the worldly experiences, one forgets. How can you live an unperturbed life in the dullness of your senses? Make of Life what you will, but follow it to thine own heart and Self be true.

You have been dogmatised by the rules of the play-and-rule book of Life that one has become docile and programmed in one's ways, walking around dazed and confused, lost in the maze of who one truly and authentically is. Stop living in that perpetual bliss of non-understanding, consumed by the external behaviours and patterns imprinted upon the Mind of your Soul. Live it not according to the rules of others but according to the 'vibelicious' and fabulicious frequency of Self. Live from the heart, not from the Mind. Live through the heart, not through the Mind, for living from and through the heart lifts the fugue of the long-forgotten Self back into the Divine Blueprint of who you truly are—so make the change to be the change in this unfettered feat of an existence called Life."

You are only a temporary visitor, having booked your vacation to remain on this beautiful earth plane for as long as your ticket is valid. The analogy of a vacation sums up an incarnation, for we are given a temporary "suit" to house our soul light for the duration of the life we have been given. The characters in our chosen soul group are souls we may have incarnated with in past lives, or we may select a new group based on different experiences.

As we "pack our suitcase," we pick our 'avatar', choosing the country of rebirth, our parents, and their characteristics, i.e., gentle, strict, materialistic, neglectful, or even abusive. We could choose to be rich or poor, fit or born with ailments. In a way, it's like playing the old board game of the Checkered Game of Life. Naturally, you do not decide all of these aspects on your own, but you sit down with the Council of Light, or as I call them, your "travel agents." The Council of Light is here to assist in raising the consciousness of the planet. They are an intergalactic group of thousands of Cosmic Light BEings from across the multiverse and consist of many Ascended Masters, Light BEings, Galactics, angels, and Guides, all devoted to raising the vibration of the earth and all humanity.

The evolution of the game of life is for humanity to shift into a unified consciousness and return to their natural state of joy instead of all the entangled chaos the world resides in. Once your itinerary has been completed, the Council leaves you in the care of your selected travel guides that you can check in with, should things go south—that is, if you remember, as we're often smacked on the head pretty hard, suffering from that darn memory loss. When you are ready, you whoosh through the chute, popping into your human existence to your chosen life. The veil of duality obscures our previous lifetime(s), so we always come in oblivious of what we have done in our past lives. It's a choice we make as a soul before incarnating. Once reborn, we are subject to the laws, environment, national and world conditions, rules and regulations, and the many other factors that impose restrictions on the full expression of free will. As St. Germain says:

"You have come to Earth, having booked a return ticket with a full itinerary, landing here, and enveloping your infinite starlight particles into this rather rigid boxed-up organism of a thing called a human body, suffering instant amnesia, much like having been hit by a train, as you popped out from the warmth of the womb into the cold earthly air. It stupefied your senses, n'est-ce pas? One has forgotten the magnificence of the lit fire within, having shoved it under the carpet, living a life according to the rules of the regimented asylum of existence. Ah, what joy to live in the non-exuberance of Self, living life but happily dosed on meds, having conformed to the rulebook of the implemented illusion of an institution, living but gurglingly happy in the separation of Self instead of living in the unison of One with All. You came here not to merely exist but to use your time on your chosen travel itinerary, remembering who you are before you got hijacked by the illusion of all the conditioning you have so hardened yourself with. It's time to hop out of the asylum, get off the meds, and realise that you are a magnificent Divine Star BEing, a God Wonder of the Universe, here to smack yourself out of the dream world you have been so 'comatosed' in and remember who you are, remember your mission and help elevate the planetary Consciousness and understand that all are part of the breath of Oneness. We are all magical interconnected energetic BEings of the Divine and brothers and sisters of the Light."

This is the challenge you take on when you incarnate—to express yourself, to create yourself within the confines of that physical life. And yet, within these restrictions and the earthly manipulations of the frequency fold of your minds, your lives, and your souls, yours is a walk back to the remembrance of the self by shifting your consciousness and raising your inner vibration, understanding that you are the creator of your own manifesto and that you manifest the life you want by aligning yourself to the divine innate frequency of yourself and orchestrating the electromagnetic frequency waves of your chosen outcome. You are ultimately the key to your manifestations, your own experiences in the creations of your human experience.

Our appointed travel "Guides," who seem non-existent to us ever since we got whacked on the head once born, cheer us on, trying to direct and guide us as best they can until we land in the shits—and even then, many of us still leave them in the obscurity of a forgotten remembrance, simply swearing and cussing at life and the world, causing more of a conundrum in our own lives than necessary. No wonder we ramshackle on in life, accumulating problems and getting stuck in our drama.

Every single one of us has sat down with the Council and our soul group to discuss the life we have chosen to live. I must have been off my face or had some serious sadomasochistic tendencies while sitting there with them, choosing my parents, siblings, extended family, and other characters within my life's itinerary to devour the experiences I chose for the benefit of my soul's growth. I agreed with them to make my life a living hell, to be smacked around, so that, in turn, I would be smacked out of my conditioned coma and wake up, elevating myself out of my drowsy awareness to understand the meaning of life and my mission on earth. The initial background I chose was not to be born to enlightened, spiritual parents, and lots of effort and work was required on my end to heal and transcend any family issues and emotional trauma offloaded on me during my incarnation, all to find a way back "home" to myself. It went south for a while before I had various light bulb moments to drag myself out of my created shit. I was probably super excited to commence with my current earthly life, my soul incarnating and coming back as a living, walking, talking, breathing, biodegradable organism. I was all geared up, thinking it would be a breeze, a walk in the park, but like you, I have danced this dance many times, and once born, everything became a total blank, having been whipped with that insistent mind fugue.

You may sit there and say, but if I have chosen my life, why won't you allow me to remember? How am I supposed to navigate my way through all of this? What would be the joy in experiencing life when you have everything handed to you on a silver platter? What would you learn? How would you evolve? You would not. There is no point in giving you a cheat sheet; it carries no evolutionary value. The journey of life is about finding your 'lost' self through the bout of your experiences and remembering who the hell you are and why you incarnated on Earth—simples.

You may say, but I did not ask to be born. I did not ask to live a challenging life or an unfulfilling one. Why am I always ill? Why do bad things always happen to me? You should not be asking yourself the why as much as you should be asking yourself the how with the intent to review your perspective of that ever-changing kaleidoscope of life. You can either condemn yourself to live in the saturated miserable misery of yourself or pick yourself up, elevating your senses and returning to the true understandings of the cogwheels of all that is your life. As St. Germain says:

"Are you not born stark naked into this world? You have been in the making as a human organism for the whole of nine months, your Soul taking a seat in the heart of your Divine vessel upon birth, a miracle to behold in itself, and yet through the walking of one's Life, one creates an infinite mirage of realities through one's experiences, in the hope of finally understanding the Truth of your Divine Reality and all of Creation—for you are the Light within the Light, a beacon to the non-understanding of others who have yet to open their eyes to the beauty of the Divine within and to the resonance of the beauty of the world without.

God is Consciousness as much as you are the God Consciousness of the God-Self within. You are not separate from Source. How can you be when you are Source as much as Source is you! You may have cut yourself loose living in the dense jungle of this 3d paradigm, drowning in the deluge of your created script of a dramady of experiences, seemingly 'amnesiad' out as to why you came to Earth in the first place. Well, duh, you came here to help rid the Planet of all the engulfed darkness and to return to the Light of your Authentic Self in the process. Of course, you do not remember! What would be the point of having embedded the Self into the evolution of the Game of Life? Life is simples. It really is. You are here to help upgrade Gaia as much as you are here to upgrade yourself, relinquishing yourself from the current instated programming that has had your Soul in a sourly lemon-drizzled merengue tit-for-tat tizzy. No one is more or less than another, for you are all of equal divinity. It is merely the EGO loving to trip you up and smack you down, to see if you choose to get back up and cleanse and heal the bruis-ed Soul, shedding a layer in the aha of the expansion of Self or whether you decide to remain smacked down in the ambivalence of Self, with the illusion of fear having grappled a hold of your Soul. Who are you?

My Child, you are a Galactic Ambassador of the Light, here to recover the Light of Self through the ultra-conditioning you have instilled yourself with. You chose to incarnate into your current human embodiment, forgetting the brilliance of the essence of the Light you are, to help aid in the ascension of yourself, humanity, and Planet Earth. Life is not about living in the superficial current 'welcome to the jungle' of the 3d matrix of existence; that is just a grand illusion to keep the masses in control. It is time to 'bounce' from the discothèque le matrix and remember your mission and why you came here in the first place. Time to transform, to heal up, and get with the program, for the time of dithering and walking in the land of confusion is long past due—time to hop on aboard and ride the wave of the 5D frequential paradigm into the new cosmic dawn of Existence. Remember, you are Love. You are Divine Consciousness, and you are One with everything as everything in the entire Multiverse is One with you—for you are all part of the All in All."

The truth is, you asked to be born and do the work at this time, devoting your life to raising the vibration of yourself and the planet. You are an ancient keeper of the stars, having chosen to incarnate at this time in the era of a renewed awakening, bringing about the long-awaited shift in the Earth's evolution of consciousness, the transition into the Age of Aquarius, where life as you once knew it will no longer exist, being washed away, cleansed, to re-emerge and reawaken into a reconnection with the divine heart space.

The privilege of each life you have lived, currently live, and concurrent lives you may choose to live in the place of your choosing within the multidimensional multiverse is to attain enlightenment, for one never stops evolving; one keeps climbing the ladder to ever-higher" reaches" of consciousness within this beautiful monopoly of the Cosmic Game of Evolution. We are here to grow as individuals and as part of the collective, bringing about the shift of consciousness. I always say, "I walk the Earth, but I am not of the Earth." We are stars of the luminous universe, encapsulated within the earthly physical world, planting seeds on the Earth, and how and what we choose to feed our minds with is how we choose to perceive and see the world, so feed it wisely.

You most assuredly did choose this life, and if it sucks and you throw tantrums at it and get sucked into the darkness of your experiences, then, by all means, go for it. You signed up for this, and the Council will gladly show you your itinerary and the fine print of your contract, which you signed along the dotted line. They want you to understand that it is an incredible privilege to be alive, yet humanity has become so accustomed to living rather mundanely, having numbed their senses to walking the lines of the matrix. That is not living; that is being lived. Just because you live does not mean you understand the concept of being alive. One is either lived by one's experiences, or one defines one's experiences, to live and become alive in the very essence and joy of living within the hues of this beautiful divine radiant human embodiment that you have chosen to assist you in your time on Earth. You are the master creator of your own life and manifest what you so desire. Don't like it? Well, you're the alchemist. Challenge yourself to change it.

"Experiences are like lap dances; no two are ever the same, yet serve as a distraction to leave you in the dumps of your unauthenticated soul, allowing the buggers to grind you down. That is the vulgarity of the worldly narrative being fed to the masses. All answers you seek are encoded within your DNA, yet you seek validations with no rhyme or reason in the outside narrative of the psychobabble, all deviating you further from your Light of Self. Stop listening and only indulge in the delish flavours that resonate with the vibrance of your own heart o' Soul, serving as a springboard to the elevation of your Soul consciousness and thus each other and the planet."

~The Divine Shakespeare Club~

The Ascended Master St. Germain says that many have come back countless times, stating they are an old soul, yet the terminology is incorrect. Everyone is an ancient and experienced soul; some are newer to incarnating within the earthly realms, whereas many others have incarnated here countless times. At this time, many have chosen to assist in the earth's ascension, having incarnated numerous times before in the many otherworldly dimensions.

"Old" is a label suggesting that you have lived many incarnations, whereas "new" simply means a newbie to the earthly realms, having lived in other dimensions of the Multiverse. You are here to elevate your Consciousness and that of the Earth. You are here to remember that you are God Source Energy and the Master Creator of your 'luscilicious' Life. Everything is Consciousness, and everything is One—you are One with everything as much as Oneness is the merging of everything with you. You are not a singularity. Yes, you live in polarities to recognise your experiences as a stepping stone to the next dimensional state of BEing. All these different flavours of served experiences are in service to you to help you remember who you are. Challenges are not here to bring you down. They are merely here to lift you out of the bedraggled

state you have encased yourself in, to ascend you to a higher state of understanding. It's like a ding-dong to the doorbell, awaiting sesame to open the door to a greater mastery of Self. It is these aha moments where the light bulb to a vague remembrance switches back on, and ancient memories start seeping through the cracks, back into your awareness. Man has forgotten to live in harmony and unison with all. What I mean by that is that your body is very much the vehicle of your Soul. Your Soul steers that vehicle into the bidding of your created choices and experiences. Your Soul should be in sync with your body and in sync with Mother Earth—it should be in alignment with All, humming from the same hymn sheet, dancing to the same tune, for the energetic encoding that vibes from you deciphers precisely how you treat yourself as much as how you treat others within your environment and the Earth. There is no separation. How can everything be separate when all is Divine, when each of you is made from that same Conscious matter? How you nourish and treat your Soul and body is how you nourish, treat, and use the Earth. It would help if you learned to listen more intently with your inner awareness to create a more stable and harmonious environment for yourself, your body, and your Soul. You languish in the outer distractions far too much, deviating from the Truth of who you are. If you merged yourself with the Oneness of everything, you would realise that there is no separation. You are that mere beat of Consciousness evolving, as much as everything else is consciously evolving in the world and the Universe around you. Nothing is separate; it is the mere conditioning of the Mind that has honey trapped you into believing it is so"

I have chosen to incarnate within the earthly realms countless times, including otherworldly dimensions. Each time you incarnate, regardless of where you decide to spend your time learning new experiences, you shed a layer, grow, and expand through your experiences. Every time it is like the rebirthing of yourself, the rising up out of the ashes, of a phoenix reborn, living in higher states of awareness and of the world around you. The soul's evolution is truly a beautiful process, so embrace it.

BOOK 02

My Life

"The grand adventures of my often 'dark' life, trying to make sense of the nonsensical whilst journeying through the maze of my wounded mind, healing my fragmented soul back to the vibrancy and light of my divine self."

You have chosen the Cosmic Game of Evolution. Are you ready to play? Have you chosen your character? Have you understood the rules of the Game? One's memory has been iced, waiting to be thawed through the undertaking of the experiences one plays with the forward-sideway-backward Board Game of Life.

It is a walking back to the Awareness and Remembrance of the Sovereign BEing one is.

But lo and behold, the power of the ever-changing rules and regulations implemented at the whim of a churning.

Much like Jumanji gung-ho, what is the illusion, and what is reality? The fate of Jumanji lies in your hands. You get ~~three lives~~, one life—spend it wisely, for the Game, just like you, is an ever-evolving feat of Consciousness.

One seems trapped in the dogma of the illusion, perceiving it to be a reality, when in fact, one is stuck in the Game of the illusion, traipsing back to one's Divinity yet plunging deeper into the board game of one's emotional experiences and allowing oneself to hang on the edge of a cliff in a drunken stupor, expecting but help, for letting go would mean the death of you, would it not? In reality, by breaking out of the matrix, one elevates oneself to a higher state of consciousness, a higher seat at the table of one's Awareness.

Let go of the reins and freefall instead of clamping on to the experiences like one's life depended on it. The Game is indeed thrust with the pitfalls of both challenges and opportunities, both equalling to the growth of oneself in either direction. Challenges equate to the infinite possibilities of opportunities, just as opportunities can equally prove to be challenging in the mindset of the utterly warped and often psychedelic lala land trip of one's choosing.

It is climbing the ladder and falling back down, flat-faced and bruis-ed. The question is, what will you do? Will you sit there and wallow and ponder for a wee while, soaking and shivering in the cold of your experiences? Will you be defeated and knocked out senseless, time and again, by the overbearing experiences that have you huddled in a corner, defending yourself from the blows thereof? Or will you knock 'em dead in the ring, levelling up to the next round, deciding to own your experiences and grab them by the horns of one's true intention of twirling in the al-chemical Divine BEing one is?

Growth pertains to the shrewdness and cunning of the user playing the Game. The navigation and rolling of the dice pertains to the outcome of one's next move and experiences.

Be the observer as much as the participant in the "fraughtness" of the imposed barriers of the sudden onslaught of new rules.

One must become the Master of Self through the expression of Self to become the Master of the Game, or be a Wreck-it-Ralph and let one's life veer off into the dingy, dark back alleyways of the forgotten Self, losing both one's aspect and sight of the Game at hand. The Game is the illusion; the Evolution thereof is not. You are the Authentic Player stuck with a bout of whacked-on-the-head-amnesia. Can you relinquish the Light returning to the Grace and Divinity that you are? Or will you

crash and burn and raise a white flag of defeat and be locked in the Game of the matrix forever?
Master the Rules to Master the Game, and navigate the Self through the earthly multidimensional realities to checkmate the board back to the Self, to the Light of the you in you, of who you are.

~The Ascended Master St Germain~

Life is not about following the rules of the game, it is about breaking out of the game and playing according to the rules of self. So, are you ready to participate and play the game of cosmic evolution?

The Start of My Life

Your Spirit is merely on a loco holiday here on Planet Earth, having chosen a human organic body fit for purpose to incarnate into for its travels, and it is entirely up to you how you choose to populate your travel itinerary, by one's created and serv-ed experiences—served to you rather royally on one's chosen platter of servings, which can sometimes be tearfully spicy, or a heavenly luscious delight. Embrace them all, be in acceptance and love them all, because if you laugh at them, you remain in the higher octaves of waltzing through the frequential energetic storm with ease and a cha-cha slide, as opposed to vibin' low and trippin' over your own two left feet whilst dancin' to "cry me a river" like a slumped-over drunken hillbilly and the "lord have mercy on me." You're an infinite God Wonder of the Universe, get over yourself and wash off the conditioning you have so soiled yourself with, back to the Light of the Infinite I AM Wonder you truly are.

Happy Earth travels in uncovering the conditioned "human" schmuck you have so covered yourself with and recovering the beautiful Light of Soul you are, because my dear you are worth every damn penny of the enriched flavoursome experiences you have so duly cast upon yourselves.

~The Ascended Master St. Germain~

On a sunny Tuesday morning, on the 25th of June 1974, at exactly 10:00 a.m., I decided it was time to quietly pop out of my mother's womb and feel the warm sunlight streaming on my face. After wriggling around, trying to find my way through that narrow birth canal of hers, I popped my head out down under, and oh, what a sight it was! I had no choice—it was getting too tight in there, and the council had kicked me out into the Earthly realms. With me having rolled the dice on the game of cosmic evolution, another Earth life it was, yet again. I did not cry the first minute; only after the midwife gave me a smack on my tiny buttocks did I start screaming, but not as loud as my mum, who was in excruciating pain, suffering a second-degree tear.

I was born at home in a tiny rural town called Spijkenisse, on the outskirts of Rotterdam in the Netherlands. I can't remember being born, but I'm sure my parents were thrilled, and my mum especially, being a whopping five pounds and an ounce lighter, to be exact. My dad, last name Visser, was half Dutch, half German; my mum, last name Hajary, is Indian, Indonesian, with a blend of Belgian and a splash of mustard French. My father named me Birgitta Eveline Geertruida Visser, which he forgot to tell my mum, so when she was asked, she told them to ask her husband as she didn't have a clue. If I had it my way, I'd have scrapped the Geertruida, which is Gertrude in English. What a great start to my life, right?

I had told myself that this time when I incarnated, I would remember who I was; and that this life was going to be a walk in the park if I made the right choices and understood the experiences. Well, fat chance of that happening, as I lost myself rather rigorously growing up.

My Family Background

Neither of my parents came from an easy background. My father, Ignatius Johan Gerard Visser, born in 1943, grew up in Losser near the border of Germany. He came from a large but somewhat dysfunctional catholic family, with his mother being aloof and his father, a rather demure man, being under the thumb of his iron-willed wife. Being raised as a Catholic, 10 percent of his dad's wages went to the church every month. His parents wanted him to become a priest, and at the tender age of twelve, they sent him to a seminary, which he bailed on. In his late teens, he left home and started working to keep a roof over his head. Many years later, my mum told me he was abused at the seminary—this should come as no surprise, as many priests hide behind their so-called celibacy of priesthood and prey on young, innocent children.

My dad, a lost soul, married another lost soul, and they had two children. Neither was happy in the marriage; it was a marriage more of convenience than love. My dad was a truck driver and in 1973, whilst still married, he met my mum on the UK ferry crossing, telling her he was a widower. After moving in with my mum less than three weeks later, he came clean, sheepishly telling her he was still married. He got a quickie divorce, and they got married within only nine months of meeting one another. Sadly, his ex-wife banned him from seeing his own children. He even went to his former marital home; however, he did not get past the front door, as she wanted nothing to do with him and would not allow him to see or be in touch with his kids. He fought tooth and nail to see them, and the presents he sent were always returned to sender. He tried to get custody of his son, my half-brother; however, it was all too draining for him, so instead, he chose to let it go, focusing on a life with my mum rather than being bogged down by the bitterness of his ex.

My mother's childhood wasn't an easy one, either. She was born in October of 1950 to Frederik Kramatalie Hajary and Geertruida Johanna Vieleers and named Eveline (Eef) Jacqueline Hajary. Her grandparents on her father's side, whom she never met, were of Indian descent and moved to Suriname at some stage, with her father being born in 1905 in Nieuw-Nickerie. He was brilliant like all Hajarys and became a refendary, an administrative official working for the government. During WWII, he was captured by the Japanese and electrocuted and waterboarded because they thought he was a spy. His hair literally turned white due to the experience. I don't know when he was captured, nor when he was released, as my mum said he refused to talk about it, but he went to Indonesia and became a lecturer of Bahasa-Indonesia at the University of Indonesia, where he met my grandmother, fifteen years his junior, who was working for him as an administrative assistant.

The Hajarys are a well-known family throughout Pakistan, India, and Suriname. Frederik's brother Harry Najaraly Hajary became Minister of the Department of Finance in Surinam, marrying Philippintje Wilhelmina Albertina Tjong-Ayong (Mien) from Surinam. Unfortunately, he had no say in anything and allowed her to manipulate him, causing a rift between both brothers. When my great grand-parents crossed over, Harry was the sole proprietor of the will, which stated that all monies should be divided equally between all siblings. Seeing that the Hajarys had been renowned landowners and were extremely well-off, and still are, Harry allowed Mien to take control of the will, and she made sure none of the other siblings received a dime; it went solely to her own family. As my grandfather had lost his own mother, Mien told him to call her "Mum," and he told her in no uncertain terms that she was not his mother but his sister-in-law, which is what caused him to be cast out from his own family, as Harry had no say in the matter whatsoever.

Whilst my grandfather was working at the university, my grandmother, who was pregnant at the time with my mum, decided to emigrate to Holland—and her husband, my grandfather, chose to remain in Jakarta for another seven years to be able to receive a double pension, making sure that my grandmother was well looked after should something happen to him. During that long period apart, he started drinking heavily, as he was missing my grandmother and his two kids.

When he finally came to Holland, he was still drinking and would hit my grandma in his drunken outbursts. She gave him an ultimatum: either quit or leave. He decided that his family was more important and quit drinking cold turkey. My grandfather was offered a job as an accountant and paid the wages of an accoun-tant, but did the job of a refendary, working for the Dutch government. As my mum told me, he was a very hard worker, and people loved him, as he was a very gentle soul, always willing to help out.

Harry and Frederik never reconciled, and my mum only met her Uncle Harry once when he visited them in the Hague when she was eight. His brother died shortly after that, in July of 1959, and the H.N. Hajary Street in Paramaribo, the capital of Suriname, was named after him.

My grandfather told my grandmother that if anything ever happened to him, he had some cash hidden away, to be used to pay for his funeral. He had only been in Holland for two years, when on the ninth of September, 1960, he was at work having a cup of coffee and talking to his colleagues, when all of a sudden, as one of his colleagues later recalled, he sighed and slumped and slid off his chair onto the ground, having suffered a massive stroke.

My grandfather, bless his heart, had no idea he had crossed over, as it was so sudden. His soul was confused. My mum, who was only nine then, spoke to him every night, as she could see him as clear as day. "Why did you leave me all alone?" she asked. "Why did you have to die? Now I have no one to take care of me." He listened to her and finally understood that he was no longer of the Earth and had died, returning to the light and warmth of heaven.

With her father out of the picture, unable to protect her, and her mother distant towards her, my mum had to fend for herself. My mother often got the wrong end of the stick and was repeatedly beaten with a belt, often causing painful bruising around her legs. My mum had to work hard for everything she wanted, whereas her sister was always given everything. The one thing her father always taught her was to live debt-free and within her means. Her mother was the opposite; she spent money like water and was very bad at handling her finances. Even though she received the double state pension after her husband's death, my mum, as she got older, had to bail her out many times so that my grandmother could pay her bills and go on vacations.

I asked my grandmother, who transitioned to spirit many years ago, why she was so harsh on my mother. She said, *"Eef was a constant reminder of my late husband, and my grief coping mechanism embroiled with my own pent-up anger and repressed emotions due to my own lack of understanding and a lack of love from my own upbringing, upsurged in me taking it out on her. Growing up, my mother was harsh in her words and the beating of common sense into me, and I was no different and too conditioned according to the value of her morals instilled in me to understand otherwise. I carried on the lineage of my ancestors and thus conditioned this onto my daughter. My own father, of Belgian descent, worked as a manager on a cane sugar plantation and died when I was young, leaving my mother unable to care for me; hence I sought solace within the arms of the Salvation Army if only for a while, giving me a rest from the reprieve of the beatings endured. How could I understand love when I was merely deprived of this emotion myself? I was living too much in my pain, having created a barrier between the created persona and the core BEing I most authentically was and AM. I lived in a dissociative state of disconnectedness of having to reprogram the self, of wanting to forget the hurt, compartmentalising the pain to keep it at bay, and yet my own lack of understanding and my lack of self-love only caused the transference of pain onto my own daughter. I lived in the shadow of my upbringing, not comprehending the consequences of the actions I instilled upon my daughter, for I was merely conditioned to that level of awareness as my mother had taught me through her own conditioning to be like her. One is conditioned to the level of awareness passed on from one's parents. That is not to say that one cannot break the cycle, for that is a choice, and yet I did not break the cycle; I did not heal the root cause of my wounded mind and my fragmented soul. I continued, for that was the comfort of my programming, that was the knowing of what I understood."*

At the age of sixteen, my mother had had enough. When she got into yet another fight with her mother, calling her an "old whore," her mother raised her hand to slap her, and my mother told her to never raise another hand towards her, as she was much taller, and she wouldn't stand a chance against her. That was the last time my grandmother ever raised a hand to my mum.

One night in a dream state, my mum went to heaven, where she saw my grandmother with my stepdad John, my mum's former partner, and my grandmother apologised to my mum for her behaviour whilst growing up. My mum never remembers her dreams, but this one has stayed with her for many years, and she can still vividly remember it.

My grandmother is funny, though. I talk to her from time to time, and she told me that even though she is trying to make up for what she did, and my mum talks to her and asks for help, my mum doesn't listen because she's a stubborn mule. I know this, so there is no point in trying to direct my mum or help her in any way. In the end, she'll do things her way.

Of course, DNA genetics are encoded within our cellular system. It's called ancestral heritage, and I will talk about this in the chapter "Ancestral Healing." The genetic makeup comes from past generations and is also conditioned into your programming as you grow up, so in effect, you carry with you much of the gunk from your ancestors, who are waiting in anticipation for you to break the cycle that had them so twisted in their own rigid way of thinking, acting, reacting, and thus understanding.

My Early Childhood Years

But first, let me retrace my steps to the flower-power blooming world of the 1970s and '80s, which was vastly different than it is now. From Spijkenisse, we moved to Middelburg, the capital of Zeeland in the South of Holland, which is steeped in history, with its many historic buildings, courtyards, old merchant and warehouses, canalside homes, and picturesque cobbled alleyways. It's like stepping back in time, a fusion of modern with preserved Middle Age history, even though the city's centre was bombed and burned down during WWII, yet rebuilt in that same style.

During my time, almost none of the technology that we have today existed. Life was far simpler back then, and people still communicated from the heart. I remember playing with the kids in the neighbourhood, hopscotching around on the pavement, roller skating, often taking a nasty tumble, scraping my knees, and hurting myself. We played marbles for keeps, and I was gutted when I lost my big beautiful marbles, but that's the name of the game. We jumped ropes, often double-dutching. We cycled, played with Barbie dolls and with my collection of Monchichi monkeys, a line of stuffed monkey dolls. I had my handheld Donkey Kong Nintendo LCD, which came out in 1982, and was addictive back then. When the screen started to flicker, you'd know the batteries were about to run out, and I'd have to patiently wait for my parents to get me some new batteries when they went to the supermarket next. It would seem a clunky piece of tech for the millennials in this era.

We loved going to the video store to rent VHS movies, which was a real treat for us back in the day. And if every available copy from a long-awaited movie were out, you'd have to put your name on the waitlist and hope and pray it was there the next time you'd pop in. Not to mention when you rented a bad copy and all of a sudden bang in the middle of a movie, you got the annoying fuzzy static. We built with Lego, played Indians and robbers with Playmobil, and I loved playing music on my record player. My dad built a swing set in the garden for my sister, who is 15 months my junior, and me, and we loved being out there when the weather was nice, seeing who could swing the highest. My sister and I were close when we were younger. I loved reading and was an avid fan of the Hardy Boys and the Dutch comics Suske and Wiske (Spike and Suzy) and Asterix and Obelix.

I remember the weekly milkman coming round in his milk float, taking the empty bottles, and leaving fresh milk on our doorstep. We grew potatoes in the back garden, and I loved watching the plants grow. In the attic, I had a real electric train with a vast array of tracks that I used to build, and often my sister and I would build forts and play hide and seek.

My upbringing was rather strict, but looking back, I am grateful for that. We had to adhere to the rules, keep our rooms tidy, dust our shelves full of toys once a week, and if we were naughty, we either got a spanking or were told to stand in a corner, having to think about what we'd done and eventually apologise.

In Middelburg, my dad set up his own import/export company in Vlissingen until one of the ships went out of commission, and the company went bankrupt. He was terrible with money, whilst my mum was the opposite, so she controlled the purse strings in the household. He had a home office up on the third floor, and my sister and I would run upstairs when we heard the sound of the telex machine with an incoming message—a telex was the precursor to the more well-known fax machine.

I enjoyed primary school, mostly cycling to and from school, and had several friends. One day during recess, I was in the playground and climbed this wooden fish structure. I had climbed it countless times and was just sitting on top of it when suddenly, I was pushed off it by a big kid and fell flat on my face, catching my chin first, which bled profusely. One of the teachers ran up to me, took me inside, and stemmed the bleeding as much as possible. When my mum picked me up later that day, she took me to the doctor. However, it was too late to stitch up, so it left a funny scar, and as the doctor said, it would merely take another fall to rectify that scar.

The second time, I was racing my dad home from an outdoor school event of Game of the Goose, took a shortcut, and not seeing a pothole, was literally thrown off my bike and landed on my chin. I saw my dad and sister bike past, but they didn't hear my screams. Other people did, and phoned my parents, who came to pick me up, taking me to the hospital, where I was given three stitches.

(The last time my face got stitched up was in 2012, as I was running to catch my train to get to work, carrying my heavy backpack, when I tripped over my own two feet, landing flat-faced on the pavement instead of using my hands to break the fall. No one helped me; they just gawked at me whilst blood streamed down my jacket. I got my mum to pick me up and drive me to the hospital and was saddled with another three stitches.)

In the early 1980s, we went on plenty of holidays, driving down to Spain in my dad's new beige Mercedes, which was top-of-the-line then, and he took great care of it. My mum put Abba in the cassette player, and we listened to it the whole way. I know all Abba songs and love singing along, as the songs have been burnt into my brain. I think my dad must've been Abba-ed out! The place in Spain had a pool, except it was level with the bungalow, and it poured nonstop for days, causing it to be flooded. So, we left, drove to France, and finally found a place, as everything was booked solid due to the summer holidays. It was a small bungalow, but we enjoyed it, as it was close to the beach. I even rode horseback with my mum, telling the horse not to break into a gallop. Well, of course, it didn't listen to my soft squeaky voice, and off it went with me screaming and my mum laughing, because who the hell whispers to a horse to stop galloping? I had my certification, as I used to ride once a week but was always given the difficult ones that threw me off, yet that never deterred me. I continued riding for some years, even in Malaysia, entering fun competitions with my then-favourite old horse, Sayang, which means "darling." He was later retired, living out his life in green pastures under the sun.

As a family, we even visited the UK, where my mum and dad hired a motorboat. However, as we were about to set off, the motor stopped running, and because all boats had been booked out for the summer, our replacement was a narrowboat instead, which, as my mum said, was super slow. The weather was rather chilly and overcast, but when is it not in the UK? Summers have always been a complete washout. We visited Ely Cathedral and several other places along the rivers. We docked along the fields, with many cows grazing, and most mornings, the boat would rock as cows licked the boat like a lollipop. My sister and I loved having to open up the locks along the waterways to raise and lower water levels for our boat to move from one inlet to another; it was fascinating.

We've been to Gran Canarias, and my dad could not go last minute, so my grandma came instead. In those days, as times were different back then, people could smoke everywhere, and someone in the room across the hall had set their mattress on fire, with the cigarette seemingly having rolled off the lip of their ashtray onto the bed. My parents were smokers for years until they decided to quit independently. Nowadays, it is relatively uncommon, and let's face it, smoking is bad for you. Your body is a temple, not a garbage dump, so treat it accordingly with the love and respect it deserves, for the way you treat your body is a direct reflection of how you treat yourself and those around you.

We celebrated Sinterklaas, or St. Nicholas, going to the docks several years in a row, wanting to catch a glimpse of Sinterklaas, with his long white beard, wearing his red cape, his mitre, and walking staff, coming in on his steamboat every November loaded with gifts and his dedicated helpers, *zwarte pieten*, a.k.a. Black Petes, because they were Moors. The *zwarte pieten* would throw traditional gingerbread men, marzipan, and spiced biscuits into the crowd.

We were allowed to put our shoes by the back door some nights and put a carrot in it for Sinterklaas's horse Amerigo, as a thank you for leaving a present because Sinterklaas would ride across the rooftops leaving gifts in the children's shoes. My sister and I would always run down the stairs the following day to find the carrot gone and a little present left in its place. Unbeknownst to us, the carrot went back into the fridge!

We'd sing songs to Sinterklaas, making sure he heard us, and if we'd been good, on the 5th of December, we'd find a bag filled with gifts just outside the front door.

It was the best time of the year for us, but we were happy with the four or five presents we each got during those days. Christmas was a family get-together, with no presents, and setting up the Christmas tree together. I don't understand the feverish consumerism of people buying each other gifts when the true gift is loving one another unconditionally and being appreciative of all in your life. I love the spirit of Christmas, but it has dwindled because people have become too materialistic, loving things instead of loving each other. My mum is not a big fan of Christmas either, and throughout my adult life, I have worked many Christmases and New Year's, and I enjoy being in service to others far more than just staying home.

These days, when I see Christmas trees thrown out in the garbage, having lost their use as the holiday season is over, I hear them weep softly as their life force is ebbing away. They've merely been chopped down; their limbs severed, all to look pretty, and dressed up with balls, lights, and glitter bombs, bringing joy to humanity for the created Christ consciousness season.

We moved to Singapore in the early '80s when I was eight, as my dad had set up another company that dealt in agricultural projects and poultry farming. We lived in a hotel for several months until we moved to our place on Fernhill Road. The home was huge, with three floors, and both my sister and I had our own room with an ensuite bathroom. I loved the culture, the weather, and the food, which was vastly different from the food in Holland.

My sister and I attended the Dutch school behind the Shangri-La Hotel, and we went on a trip to Sentosa Island, where we watched the musical light fountain at night. They had an outdoor roller-skating rink, but without fail, I tripped and slammed my face hardcore into the pavement, trying to break the fall with the palm of my hands. It was a nasty fall, and the teachers put a cream on which caused it to swell and become infected. It took quite a while to heal, and it looked like someone had punched me a black eye, but I didn't care.

After a year, we moved to Kuala Lumpur, Malaysia, and lived there for nearly five years. In the interim, we got a dog from the pound called Bibi, but we changed his name to Bobo, after a Dutch rabbit cartoon character. That dog loved my mum. My sister and I weren't always as nice to Bo; we were sometimes mean to him, and he did tend to show his teeth. We moved homes and schools several times in Kuala Lumpur. In one of the homes, we found a cobra in our kitchen, which was taken care of by a couple nannying us for a few days, as my parents were in Indonesia at an agricultural expo. They poured boiling water down the drain it slithered back into, hoping it had either burnt or gotten out and returned to the garden somehow. It freaked us all out, as cobras are venomous. Another time, a pink-butted baboon entered our home. It had to be chased out by some friends—breaking several of my mum's ornaments in the process—as they can be vicious. In that same home, we had beautiful Komodo dragons strolling through our levelled back gardens and our driveway, set against the backdrop of dense vegetation. Even though they were big and moved slowly, they could run like the wind.

Many people in Malaysia who have livestock, especially chickens, eat them for dinner when the time is right. When we went to visit our neighbour's family in

Seremban, this elderly Chinese grandmother had several chickens in her backyard, and she wanted to prepare some chicken for us that night, so she got an axe, grabbed one of the chickens, and chopped its head off right in front of us. I was horrified. Yes, it may be comical to see a headless chicken running around for a few minutes after its life had been taken, yet I never understood how that was possible. Now I know that the pressure of the axe triggers the nerve endings in the neck, causing that little burst of electricity to run down all the nerves, telling the muscles to move, and thus you see it run before it eventually drops. My father worked on many agricultural projects. As kids, we had seen company videos of large battery hens, where the chickens were treated humanely until they were hung upside down on a conveyor belt, stunned into unconsciousness before their heads got the chop.

There were times when my parents didn't have any money, as my dad was out of a job, which meant we couldn't attend school and had to diligently study at home for nearly a year. At least we had a roof over our heads, and there was food on the table every night, so we were blessed in that way.

Growing up, I was a skinny and lanky girl with gangly arms and long match-stick legs matched with knobbly knees. I remember seeing a stack of rolled-up bills lying in the open sewer system along the road, and it was pretty narrow, but I managed to jump down and wriggle myself sideways, picking it up out of the trickling water—it turned out to be roughly 300 Singaporean dollars. My mum and dad waited for it to be claimed by someone, but it never was, so they used it instead—a godsend.

We loved Chinese New Year, often watching the dragon dances in town, and when my mum and dad visited friends, we'd go round, going *"Gong xi fa cai, and Angpao lo le!"* which means, "May you have a prosperous new year and a red envelope please!" All the money we received went into our respective piggy banks. Even though we were not allowed to touch it, sometimes we would take a *ringgit* (Malaysian dollar) and get some sweets at the supermarket. If we didn't have the money and had to get some groceries for our parents, we nicked sweets in small amounts or pried the many freebies on the Milo tins or the various cereal boxes, making sure none of the shop assistants saw us. One of us was always the lookout while the other did the deed. We always made sure we ate the sweets before we got home to cover our tracks.

One day on my way back from the supermarket, an Indian guy with a bunch of papers in his hands stopped me and said he knew my father. "What's his name then?" I asked. He didn't know but said, "You live in the building on the other side of the fence, right?" "Yes, so?" I asked. He wanted me to come closer and said he needed to show me something. I hesitated; he removed the papers covering the front of his pants and flashed his penis. As fast as my legs could carry me, I ran back home and told my mum and dad what he had done. Luckily, I never saw the guy again, but that didn't mean it was the end of the pervs for me. It was only the beginning.

After my dad had sold his company and quit working at another company, we had to move again, as the apartment came with the job. We ended up staying with a friend of my parents. His name was John, and he was a middle-aged, pudgy Malay/Indian. He had a home office and worked from home. One day after school, I hid behind the kitchen door as John came downstairs. I wanted to give him a fright, but he spotted me, and when I tried to go upstairs, he took my hand and rubbed it over the front of his pants. He continued to do this and would sometimes come and rub himself against me. I made sure that I ran from him when I saw him coming into a room. I was about eleven years old, and I didn't understand what was happening, but I knew it wasn't right. My parents didn't know as they were either away or in a different part of the house, which was set over three floors.

Around the same time, my sister and I attended a Bahasa-Malay language course taught by a male teacher. We'd have to go up to him whenever we'd finish our exercises to get them corrected. He kept rubbing his hands over my legs, and my sister noticed this, as he didn't do this to her or any of the other students, so she opted to tell our parents. My parents called the school principal, and I was called into her office and told her what happened. I was visibly upset and cried because I didn't understand, even though they told me I had done nothing wrong. I then had to put this in writing, and the teacher was fired soon afterwards, but I was left feeling guilty because it was my fault that he got fired in the first place.

Around this time, I suffered from the early stages of bulimia, which my mother caught promptly, subsequently watching me like a hawk. It's not like I kept sticking a finger in my throat; I did, but eventually, it came up, like an acid reflux sort of thing, as it came naturally. She caught me in the bathroom as I was brushing my teeth and getting ready for bed, and I had thrown up in the sink. She wanted to know why. I didn't know why, but the underlying cause may have stemmed from these experiences with these pervy men. I had never even heard of bulimia at that age, but it resolved itself over a short period of time.

The Label of "Shame"

It's easy for adults to tell kids that it's not your fault, yet the child is left not quite understanding or grasping the whole situation, and I was a real introvert, keeping a lot bottled inside, which chipped away at my confidence. My parents had also found another flat, so we moved to another part of Kuala Lumpur without our dog as the landlords were Muslims, but ever so lovely before returning to Holland. Bobo was left with John, who treated him poorly, but my sister and I would go to his place during the weekends to wash and play with him, and if my sister couldn't go, I would, making sure to keep Bo as a buffer between John and me.

I didn't tell my mother about John until I was nineteen, as I was too afraid and ashamed. The story only emerged when we'd seen an episode on The Oprah Winfrey Show, where she talked about children that had been abused. My mum said she was glad it had never happened to either of us. I remained quiet, so then my mother looked at me. I started crying and finally told her what I should have told her all those years ago. She was so shocked. The first thing she asked me was if it was my father. I said no, it wasn't Pap; it was John back in Malaysia. She was reeling and said, "If your father were still alive, he would have grabbed him by his throat."

It took me many years to get past that shame—it was a part of me. My mum always encouraged me to talk about it, but I shut down because I simply didn't want to. Counselling wasn't heard of in those days, so I kept it all in and kept a lid on it. Shame is a hard nut to crack, even though the Ascended Master St. Germain disagrees and says, *"Not really, it is the mere conditioning of the human mind that makes it so. Shame is that feeling of unworthiness, making way for all sorts of insecurities to creep in, which creates a distorted version of yourself, as opposed to the true flavour of your original nature."*

It is the carving out of a different persona instead of remaining true to the essence of who you are. We stay stuck within that experience, within that energy, thus attracting the same kind of energetic frequency because we don't know how to deal with it. Shame is that heart-wrenching cry for help from the soul, pleading with you to be healed—yet as a child, how could I know? Even in adulthood, it took me a long time to figure out. It is one of the many reasons my relationships were all defunct, the red thread of abuse running through them as a common theme.

Shame, like any experience, is a wonderful opportunity for growth. It allows you to be vulnerable, to heal these broken aspects of yourself that you have so rigidly held on to, having created your belief system upon that experience, causing your life to become a mere wrecking ball. As St. Germain says, *"Shame is a mere experience of the reflection of your inner Soul, shining outwards, being translated into your outer world. With Soul work the catalyst is healing one back to the wholeness of who one is. It is not here to torment you but to make you move beyond the pain, the hurt, the guilt, and the shame of that experience. It is for you to learn to forgive all parties involved without transgressing back into the juvenile limping of Self, causing continuous kinks in your Life due to the created conditioning, the distortions one has layered the Self with, remaining in the imposter syndrome fatigue of the ever-tiresome Self."*

I had not heard of imposter syndrome until St. Germain flagged it. It is not classed as a mental illness; it borders on depression, yet it is not. A person lacks self-confidence, suffers anxiety, and has continuous doubts about their abilities, achievements, and accomplishments. Add to that not feeling adequate and dwelling on past mistakes, and you've got a whole concoction of messed-up ingredients creating a wholly different persona, all due to the "trauma" of one's experiences.

Some people go through far worse trauma at a young age, and being a child, you do not ask for this. Yet, ultimately, at any given point in time, you have the power to change the trauma that has held you hostage, into an opportunity for growth and acceptance, for the beautiful expansion and awareness of the light of the soul that you are. Pain is a blessing in disguise; it brings you back to the wonderment of the very breath of your soul. No matter how lost you feel or how severe the abuse you've experienced, no one can rescue you from the depths of despair and hopelessness but you, for the gem of returning to self lies deep within the very depths of you.

I love the once-incarnated beautiful, gentle soul of a master teacher once named Sir William Blake, who is one of my Guides in the Divine Shakespeare Club. He has lived countless lives, dating as far back to the ancient tribes of Atlantis, being a high priest of the Temple of the Sun, to the foregone civilisations of Egypt. Lest one forgets, he was a poet and prose writer, a painter, and a rebellious visionary, choosing to see life beyond the veil of illusion while waltzing through the grace of his own existence. He has this eclectic sense of charm around him, a sereneness; throughout his life, he lived with one foot in the earthly realms and the other in the nether realms. He is a mystic of divine grace, a rebel with substance, and reflects on the fact that his life was a series of some damn fine and poignant experiences. He says:

"Regardless of the trauma and suffering one has endured, it is a steering of the loins of the muscular memory bodies that guide one back to the remembrance of the dormant Soul returning home to the spark of the Divine BEing of who you are. Trauma is a mindset of the wounded Soul. Know that out of the darkness springs but forth the Light. One can choose to remain in the cold of the shadows of Self or get up, to ignite the spark to the flame of the truth of who you are within, for hidden within the very chambers of the pain-ed creases of your Soul lies the remedy to opening the door to let the pent-up pain flood back out into the Light of Love and sheer forgiveness. Humanity is fallible, for the conditioned beliefs one has so conditioned the Self with cause one to limp through the created muddy troughs due to the nonstop pouring of rain onto the Self. Weep not, my Child, instead find the inner strength through the hearts of all matter, for one often sees not the sometimes painful patterning instilled upon oneself, having grown but merely accustomed to all through the forte of one's systematic imprinted beliefs. You have become so used to your cognitive programming that it seems but impish and a foolishness of thought to act on the impulse of change.

But disregard not the torment of your Soul, for inertly it weeps for a connection back to the heart within the heart of the matter—it longs for that fusion back to the masculine and divine feminine within—giving one a balance and a greater understanding within yourselves and towards others.

One can live in denial for much of one's Life, but it will seek a series of discomforts and the possibility of a culpable dis-ease in the outer contours of the human embodiment. Are you not deserving of happiness? Are you not worthy of Love? Are you not deserving of the sceptre of abundance throughout the entirety of your Life? Trauma gives one the opportunity to grow beyond the measures one has compounded the Self to, so I ask of thee to seek opportunity, not resentment, for it leaves but the taste of a sheer bitterness on the palate of the heart.

Seek not to be controlled by one's experiences, but seek to take back control of the serv-ed experiences at hand and of Life. Rebuke the cowardice back to the land of the shadows from whence it came, and rekindle the magnificence of the Light of who you are, living a Life of passion and vigour, for it will surely lead you back onto the path of your own vibrance of heart and a lightness of day, where once there was only a nuance of varied shades of darkness. Find the Light, to be the Light and inspire the Self back to the innate Lightness of Self, for there is nothing that cannot be transcended if one believes but in the transcendence of Self."

My School Years in Malaysia

We stayed in Malaysia for another year and attended Sayfol International School; however, whether you believe me or not, our classroom was haunted. It would feel cold all of a sudden, or during recess, when we went back, the toilet would flush by itself, the curtains would sway, or the fan would turn itself on. Several of us used to investigate and just run back out, as it freaked us out. They boarded up the bathroom within our classroom; however, we could hear it flush even during class. The school breakfast and lunch were included, and I loved most of what was served to us, but not papaya—it smelled and tasted like damn vomit to me. The teachers would watch us like hawks, ensuring we finished our food before enjoying the rest of our recess. I made sure to either try and skip the papaya or cover that part of my tray with a napkin and throw it into the big bins. I loved most Malaysian cuisine, especially *roti canai* with non-spicy dahl or mutton curry, satay with compressed rice cakes (*nasi impit*), and Indian spice potpourri.

I enjoyed sports and had no issue with PE; people didn't laugh at me, even though I was probably one of the tallest in the school with my gangly legs. Those legs sure came in handy with sports day, although I still couldn't beat the fastest girl in school, who could fly like the wind! I was selected for the 800 metres and came in first, with my mum and dad cheering me on from the sidelines. I came in second in the butterfly and breaststroke in swimming and still have the medals.

I loved the education system, as all kids wore uniforms, so there was no comparison or differentiation. The only thing that upset me was the caning. My parents were vehemently against it and called the school to say that kids should not be caned, with other kids forced to watch the public flogging. Kids had a different attitude back then, unlike today, as most have no respect or regard for their teachers or, sadly, anyone else.

No one within the educational system ever taught us the importance of self-love. The education taught is set within the parameters of the matrix, which teaches not about self-love but divisiveness, competitiveness, and a buttering up of the ego, to slip and slide through life thinking one is better than others, living according to the status quo of one's status. If one loved the self, one would love and embrace others in total acceptance of who they are, and the world would be dipped in a big pulsating ball of loving awesomeness.

Former–Prime Minister Dr. Mahathir

Every Sunday, we saw the then–prime minister horseback riding with his security detail. I would run downstairs to the front gate and say, "Good morning, Dr. Mahathir!" He was always pleasant enough, sometimes stopping and having a quick chat or simply greeting us in return. When the landlord and his wife downstairs invited us to attend a New Year's celebration at Dr. Mahathir's home, we all went.

My sister and I were so excited, hoping to see him just to say hi. We were ushered into a small auditorium, where he gave a speech. At the end of it, as we walked out, my dad walked toward Dr. Mahathir, wanting to provide him with a written proposal for growing potatoes and the use of greenhouses for the growth of other crops in the area of Cameron Highlands, which would expand the agricultural sector for Malaysia. Security stopped him, but Dr. Mahathir recognised my dad, and he was let through, handing him his proposal whilst briefly speaking to him. My dad never heard back, but if you look at Cameron Highlands now, you'll see that Dr. Mahathir did not throw my dad's proposal in the bin. He acted upon it. Even though it took several years to get off the ground, it flourished. He could have thanked my father or offered him a job, which would have helped, but instead, he completely disregarded him. My mum was never a big fan of Mahathir. But politicians, in general, do not rule with honesty and integrity; they rule according to the glorification of their egos and for the betterment of themselves within the corrupt game of politics, only to further their own career, kicking the "little man" to the street once they have served their purpose.

Several months later, in April 1988, we returned to Holland, leaving everything behind, except for our clothes and some small toys that fit into the suitcase, as there was no money to ship anything across. I felt sad, as I had so many toys, books, and crafts, but I understood it wasn't possible, as did my sister. My favourite doll, Anna, whom my mum had sewn clothes for, was left on the bed with all my many other dolls. I hugged her tight one last time and told her I loved her before closing the door and going to the airport.

My sister and I shared a room in the last house in Kuala Lumpur that we lived in, with a pool that we often swam in after school. My mum was pretty strict when it came to us exercising and stretching our muscles, yet exercise was not part of her regimen.

The Death of My Dad

My dad died several months later, in July 1988, when I had just turned fourteen. When he was diagnosed and hospitalised with coronary artery disease, I knew that he did not have long to live, and I remember my sister telling me not to worry, that he would be fine. I was worried because I'd had a vivid dream where I was sitting in the classroom, and the maths teacher took me aside and told me that my father had passed away. Three months later, in the summer of 1988, he was cycling and suffered a cardiac arrest at the tender age of forty-four. He was rushed to hospital, while paramedics tried to resuscitate him, to no avail. Once at the hospital, the doctor decided to let him go because his brain had been starved of oxygen for too long, and he would have been in a vegetative state for the rest of his life, which would have been no life for my dad or any of us. He had simply fallen off his bicycle, taken a last breath, and was gone, having apparently suffered no pain.

My father was a fit man, of average build, not an ounce of fat on him, 1.86 metres tall (six-foot-two), and had a moustache and the same hairstyle as Phil Collins, a blond mousy colour with a touch of grey. He smoked cigarettes but wasn't an avid smoker and quit once diagnosed with heart disease. He was a quiet, stern, thoughtful man, a great cook, and had a funny sense of humour. My dad could not dance and had absolutely no rhythm; I am very much the same. I can't dance. I tried my hand at ballroom dancing for a year but was as stiff as a plank with two left feet. Nor can I sing, as I'm tone-deaf, but the shower sure doesn't care, nor does my dog!

I cannot describe the feeling of immense pain and sadness—so many emotions went through my head when he died. I couldn't grasp that he was gone; it seemed surreal. My dad was no longer on this plane. Why? My mother, my sister, and I cried uncontrollably. My mum had lost a husband, and we had lost a father. When I went to sleep that night, my head was pounding. I had never experienced a headache before; I could barely look out of the corner of my eyes. When I woke up the next day, I hoped it was all just a bad dream and that my dad would walk through the door, but unfortunately, it was a cruel reality.

I remember going to the funeral home with my mum, sister, and grandma. I saw my dad lying there in an open casket, and all I could do was stroke his hair. His nose must have broken when he fell, as it was slightly crooked. I felt within my gut, like an inner knowing that my dad had left a letter and told my mum, being pretty adamant about it. And indeed, several days later, the hospital advised my mum that there was a letter he had left behind, the content of which I remember being rather spiritual, knowing he was on his way out to the next world. Does one call it suicide if you refuse to take your meds? I don't know, but for many years I was angry that he had chosen to take the easy way out.

The songs played at his funeral were heart-wrenching and an indication of where his head had been at the time of his passing, as he had sung these songs before his death. The one that to this day still plays on my heartstrings is "Sailing" by Rod Stewart, which clearly states that he wanted to sail the stormy waters to be free and closer to God—and in the end, he was. I know he found all the answers he was looking for that he could not find in life.

My father was cremated. I don't think he would have wanted to be buried. His funeral service was held at the same place where my grandfather was buried. I would often visit his gravesite or lay some flowers to let him know I was thinking of him. The tears just rolled down my cheeks once the final curtain drew after those songs. It was a final farewell to a husband, a son-in-law, a brother-in-law, an uncle, and a wonderful father. I love and miss him, but I know that no matter what, he is with me, guiding me in spirit. He will always be a beacon of light in the dark, guiding me through life's tempests.

When he had just crossed over, I told my mum that I had woken up one night, and he was standing at the edge of my bed smiling down at me, not saying anything; she told me I should focus on myself and let papa be.

Before we left Kuala Lumpur, he wrote me a beautiful poem:

Dearest Birgitta,

You are my first born
I treasure you,

I am the sunshine
which warms you,

In my heart I carry you
with my thoughts I help you,

My love supports you
in all undertakings,

I am there and not there
yet that in itself is not important,

For our bonds exist and remain
throughout time and distance.

Papa 6/04/88

Ancient Mystical Order Rosae Crucis

I believe my father was tired of life. He had a family and no job, and I think he felt like a failure. For many years he had followed the teachings of the AMORC—Ancient Mystical Order Rosae Crucis, whose teachings date back to the Egyptians, roughly 1500 BCE. In Kuala Lumpur, he had been jobless for quite some months, and though he was actively looking, he hadn't been successful. The Dutch embassy helped us pay the bills, yet to alleviate the stress, he joined the AMORC.

Back in the day, my mum was unhappy about this because he spent a lot of time studying and meditating, and they charged a lot of money for the materials, money we didn't have. I have never understood why organisations would need to charge astronomical amounts for ancient teachings, but back in the 1980s, life was different, and knowledge of the ancient Egyptians and Atlantean wisdom did not come at the click of a button via Google but was sent through the good ol' mail instead.

I don't want to detract from my story but want to include a brief outline, and I must admit until I delved into the actual history of the Rosicrucians in 2019, I was not aware of any of this, as my knowledge does not come from the organisation that my father joined but from the channelled messages directly from the many masters themselves. I was floored at how everything slotted together and that I am basically that extension of my dad, continuing from where he left off. Many practised the art of alchemy during the Egyptian era, and Pharaoh Thutmose III, who ruled Egypt from 1500 to 1447 B.C., was one of the most significant pharaohs of all times, a grand architect and a military genius. Yet, after having a spiritual awakening, he reformed his warmongering ways. He treated those he defeated with kindness and bound them to an oath of allegiance: *"We will not again do evil against Menkheper Ra, our good Lord, in our lifetime, for we have seen his might, and he has deigned to give us breath."* He was an incarnation of the Ascended Master Kuthumi, the founder of the Rosicrucian teachings and the Great White Brotherhood. As Kuthumi, in the aspect of Thutmose III states, "When the Mind is at war, there can be no peace. It is only when the ills of the Soul are eased that harmony and natural order are restored to the Mind."

Thutmose III built many temples, including many additions to the Temple of Karnak at Thebes, erecting new pylons and several towering obelisks, built in honour of the Sun God Ra, adorned with beautiful golden caps, reflecting the rays of the Sun, and used as sundials to tell time—yet these amplifiers were also used to re-energise the soul back to the breath of the power of one.

After the death of Thutmose III, Pharaoh Akhenaten (Amenhotep IV), who I believe was an aspect of El Morya, took over as the Grand Master of the Brotherhood. Akhenaten's father was Amenhotep III, an aspect of the Ascended Master Serapis Bey and architect and builder of the Luxor Temple. In the notebook that contained my dad's written poem, he also left me a sacred geometrical pyramid design (figure 1), which took me years to decipher as per figure 2, where all parts have been fused and integrated accordingly like a mini 3D model. Thoth and Anubis, the latter who often walks by my side, being a foot or so taller than me in my human form, eventually helped me solve the puzzle.

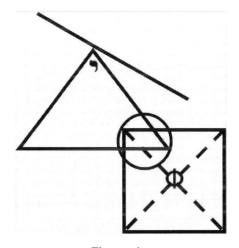

Figure 1

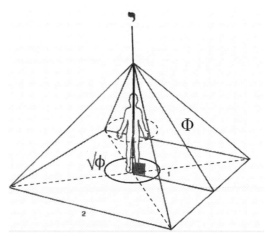

Figure 2

"The sacred geometrical grid serves as a realignment of Self—for you are a sacred geometric Divine BEing of the Light—you are a mathematical equation of the nothingness and yet of the All in All and the vibrance of who you are. Yod in the corner of the pyramid signifies the Divine Energy of creation, for you are a drop in the vast Cosmos, as much as the Cosmos is contained within the drop that is you. Through the path of duelling with the Self, contrasting between the pitfalls of Light and heavenly darkness, one will spring forth into understanding the dualities of human nature, serving as a feat to the expansion of one's Consciousness back to the Divine breath of Self. All starts with phi in the spiral of the great pyramids of Ancient Egypt, for phi is the mathematical equation of all and nothing at the same time. You are without beginning nor end. You are a transformer, morphing within the morphogenetic field of the multidimensional Cosmos into the lives of one's chosen equation to live forth, forever twirling and dancing to a higher elevation of Consciousness. You are the core equation of all of Universal Existence, walking back through the art of polarities to the centre of the sacred geometrical design of the evolution of Self. Phi is infinite, the single equation to the truth of all creation. Are you not life eternal? Are you not the sum of the equation of the dividend of All there is? If you think not, then walk with me Anubis, and I will show you the truth of the beautiful sum of the All that you are. Is it not time to swim back to the centre like the flowing fish you are into the very grid of Self, to embark on a journey of remembrance, from the land of Nod back to the land of the Ancients, where time was a non-existent feat, but for the mere ticking of the harmonious working seasons, where Man was but a fondness to both the Mother's womb, her very Nature and in Cosmic Harmony with the All. Step into the Grid of the Djed, the Master Conduit between the Celestial Heavens and Earth, the interdimensional gateway to existential worlds beyond the realms of the Earthly Existence. It is the axis of the Mother, symbolising a continuous cycle of death and rebirth, for out of chaos will spring forth the rebirthing of the Light.

Envision yourself in a pyramid to connect you to the divine remembrance of the path and wisdom of the ancients who walked the lands before you. It is time to remember, awaken, and walk the path of your ancient forefathers, and yet time is a deviant, it is non-existent but for the mere blood coursing through the veins of humanity.

If you understand that you are a sacred geometrical design of the Divine and a mathematical equation to the sum of all your experiences, knowing how to calculate the alchemical formulation according to the fruition of your chosen outcomes that you have cast according to the morphogenetic field of your Soul's frequency, then life becomes infinitely easy because you have mastered the Conscious Mind-map and thus your Road-map of Creation."

~Cosmic Creators & Architects, Anubis & Thoth, who are Walkers between Worlds, Warriors of the Sacred Truth, and Keepers of the Earthly realms~

As my father adds, *"I wasn't the greatest hula dancer. I wasn't really Shakin' Steven(s) those hips of this ole house of mine to the rhythm of life and had veered off the grid to the gateway of my inter-multidimensional self."*

I want to touch briefly on Moses, only for the sake of the Commandments, which have been severely misconstrued. He came across as a quiet, contemplative, somewhat tortured soul yet held a force of beautiful, charismatic power within. He was more a patron of the arts, a poet, and a philosopher who believed in the hearts and kindness of man. Moses, an incarnation of the Ascended Master Ling, was also an initiate of the Brotherhood, who, with the help of the pharaoh Akhenaten, helped free the Jews. Akhenaten was married to Nefertiti, someone my mother has been compared to several times, and she may have lived in the courts of that era or been an aspect of her. Although his reign was short-lived, and his adversaries outwardly erased his new "monotheistic religion" after his mysterious death, he promoted the belief in one God, a unified creation through the single image of Aten, the Sun God, as the physical image of the Father of all Divine Creation present in all things and all people, the loving Divine Source from whence all life sprang.

"I AM the Ascended Master Moses, Lord Ling, One of the Grand Counsel of the Divine serving the Sixth Ray of Light. I have lived many lives, each one an evolvement complementing the other.

I was once bathed in wealth yet a mere simple man, in service to the people and with a humbleness in service to Source, for the realisation dawned that I AM God, and all are God—All are Divine, for God is All in Everything consciously expressing and creating as much as Everything is All part of God consciously expressing and creating, for you are merely an extension of Divine Creator. People thought that I but spoke to God and that they could not; how mistaken they were, for I was but a mere channel to the vibrational frequency of Source. We have been created by Creators, who the overall Creator has created. The Architects, our Creators, the Star People walking the stellar luminous heavens gave us Commandments to abide by, to allow for Man to break the vow to their ruptured and bleeding EGO, of learning but that Love of Self as but once taught in the beautiful Gardens of E.D.E.N. Many had left the Gardens and wandered into the wayward path of the EGO, embracing dualities, straying ever further away from the very Source of Self. And yet, these simple commandments were merely twisted to suit the needs of those that serve the scriptures in the current paradigm."

~The Ascended Master Lord Ling (Moses)~

During the Middle Ages, alchemy was on the rise in Europe, which did not sit well with those in power. Alchemy is the art of transmutation, turning the human character from lead to gold, returning yonder to the light of the authentic self.

It is only when we decide to venture into the 'wonders' of the created hellish abyss of our earthly selves, facing our shadows and slaying our demons, that we become whole again. Much of mediaeval Europe lay wrapped in the tentacles of darkness, with "sorcery" frowned upon, "witches" burnt at the stake, and those seeking truth, were silenced for wanting to teach their fellow human beings, in turn becoming the object of persecution by those in power and those of the religious incorporated and institutionalised systems. The political influence of the Knights Templar became far too great, and the organised church mafia took measures to destroy the Brotherhood, which merely went underground. The Brotherhood always emphasised the equality of men and women and the true solidarity of all humanity as One. All mystical teachings and knowledge of the many ancient civilisations were once housed in the magnificent Library of Alexandria. Enter Julius Caesar, who, in 48 BCE, in pursuit of Pompey, landed in a civil war between Ptolemy XIII and Cleopatra. He got himself into a pickle and, as a diversion, ordered his soldiers to set fire to several of his ships, including Egyptian dry-docked ships in the harbour, which evidently got out of control, and thousands of manuscripts stored in one of the library's warehouses went up in flames and was razed to the ground. That's all fair and well, but Caesar was a conqueror, and I believe he destroyed far more than stated within the history books. Fast forward to 640 CE, the Arabs under General Amrou ibn el-Ass, captured Alexandria; however, Caliph Umar did not destroy the manuscripts nor use them as fuel for the bathhouses of Alexandria, as the Arabs were a learned race. As per the Masters, scribes copied many manuscripts, and the library was destroyed deliberately over a period of time, as its archives and museums were filled with the many intellectual riches of Mesopotamia, Assyria, Persia, India, Ancient Egypt, Rome, and Greece. The knowledge was not lost, and much of the ancient world has now been stored in the 53 miles of shelf space within the Vatican secret archives, with the public unable to view any materials prior to 1939, which coincided with the start of WWII. These archives contain hidden wisdom and millions of ancient scrolls dating back to Sumerian and Atlantean times. It's criminal from a faith-based religion to withhold such a wealth of knowledge from humanity. Religion should be transparent, yet when shrouded in secrecy serves merely as a control mechanism and an indoctrination to keep the masses in line.

Christianity is based on putting the fear of God in people, while the pope is shrouded under the guise of the holiest of holy, pretending to be of the light. Many ministers speak of the written word of God as a separate entity as taught by the papacy. It has been created to keep humanity in the grasp of a religious dogma according to the written word created by man, all under the guise of the teachings of Jesus.

We are free to choose what we want to believe and dismiss whatever insults our soul. I believe the Vatican is an organisation that has its sticky fingers in many murky pies and is in cahoots with the elite running the worldly created matrix, all to keep humanity rigidly in line to avoid a deviation of evolving themselves and understanding their "kindredness" with the Stars.

As Aristotle quaintly quoted roughly 2200 years ago, *"The fate of empires depends on the education of the youth."* As he continues, *"Wisdom untapped, and remaining but dormant within the hearts of the minds of man, will cause a deviation in one's spirit, a deviation in the soul path of humanity as a whole. What better way to keep the masses in a state of disregard than by blowing smoke and fire in their eyes, remaining but unknowingly blinded by those in control who wish for others to remain but trepidly in the unknown."*

During the European Renaissance period, St. Germain incarnated as Christian Rosenkreuz and became the legendary founder of the Rosicrucian Order (Order of the Rose Cross).

He then decided to reincarnate as the renowned Sir Francis Bacon (1561-1626), an English philosopher, essayist, and statesman, the apparent illegitimate bastard son of Queen Elizabeth I, and the pseudonymous author of the famous Shakespearean plays. As Sir Francis, he directed the Rosicrucian Order and its activities in England and the continent. Growing up, I was an avid Shakespeare fan, and Lady Portia, a character in the well-known play *The Merchant of Venice*, is St. Germain's twin flame. She portrayed a young lawyer with her famous quote, "a pound of flesh," meaning that one is determined to get what is theirs by right, no matter how it may affect anyone else and regardless of the consequences.

In 1694 Rosicrucian settlers journeyed across the Atlantic under Johannes Kelpius, master of a Rosicrucian Lodge in Europe, establishing themselves in Philadelphia before moving to Pennsylvania. Many Rosicrucians were educated, and the communities made valuable contributions to the newly emerging American culture in printing, philosophy, and the sciences and arts. Renowned Americans such as Benjamin Franklin, Abraham Lincoln, Thomas Jefferson, and Thomas Paine were themselves Rosicrucians. Many played a vital role in the tremendous alchemical and social process, leading to the founding of a new nation. Other famous Rosicrucians included Leonardo da Vinci, Isaac Newton, Rene Descartes, and Nikola Tesla.

The Rosicrucians are the record keepers of the ancient ways and the halls of learning of Atlantis and have been vilified and ridiculed throughout the ages, and yet as St. Germain says:

"Once you awaken and catch your breath from having been dunked and suffocated underwater, held in the grips of the matrix for what seems like an eternity, you realise that everything you think is fiction is, in fact, reality, and what you believe to be reality is often mere fiction in the current created film reel called 'the matrix.' It is much like the Sith in Star Wars, where the dark rises to supremacy, taking power through the art of mind control, controlling the masses to do their bidding, keeping them as puppets within their created hierarchical system, dominating the universe. The current shift is about unplugging from and dissolving the matrix that has kept you under its 'spell' for so long, resurfacing and breathing back Light into the beautiful hue of the soul embodiment you are. It is re-emerging and returning to the Light and vibrance of who you are and always have been, aiding in the rebuilding of heaven on Earth, for you are the rebellion of enigmatic Light Warriors, using the lightsabers of the heart to spread the Light of Love and harmony, breathing back equilibrium within the time space continuum, restoring peace and unity in the Universal Song for all."

Had my father taken his medication, he could have averted death and stayed on this plane just a while longer. I am sure we would have had many interesting conversations regarding the subject matter. He held a vast wealth of knowledge when it came to Egyptian sacred geometry and the workings of alchemy. He was also very much into the books of Og Mandino, especially *The Greatest Salesman in the World*, which he carried with him wherever he went. It was first published in 1968 and is about the philosophy of salesmanship and success, telling the story of Hafid, a poor camel boy who achieves a life of abundance by reciting written scrolls for thirty days at a time before moving on to the next scroll. As teenagers, my father asked us to recite these in the mornings and evenings, hoping to give us a better understanding of life.

The Greatest Salesman in the World, Part 2: The End of the Story, was published in 1988 after my dad crossed over. It is the continuing story of the poor camel boy Hafid, who is now successful in life but mourning the loss of his wife. A dream of his late wife convinces him to see a stranger that turns up on his doorstep. This "chance encounter" pulls Hafid out of retirement to embark on a new adventure, travelling worldwide and undertaking a speaking tour to enlighten others about the principles of the Ten Scrolls. This book mentions Paul the Apostle and how he lost the scrolls in a shipwreck.

As a side note, in 2017, I interviewed renowned UK trance healer Ray Brown, who allows for his body to be occupied by a remarkable "spiritual surgeon" named Paul of Tarsus, also known as Paul the Apostle who two thousand years ago helped found Christianity. Paul of Tarsus is an aspect of the Ascended Master Hilarion, so Ray was channelling that part of the multidimensional BEing that Hilarion once was in the embodiment of Paul. He is a phenomenal healer, having helped me with my back, my plantar fasciitis, and heel fatigue many years later, and has helped thousands of people worldwide. It was an honour to have been able to converse with both Ray and Paul for this interview.

My father thought he could cure himself, and I don't think he was quite at that level of conscious understanding. He carried an immense amount of pent-up pain and unhealed trauma throughout his life, simply masking this through his conditioning. He meditated every day, but while meditation calms you down and helps to recentre the self, it can only do so much, for that deep-seated and unhealed trauma remained. To attain that level of healing, one must first learn to heal all broken aspects of oneself, walking the journey within and alchemising all that is no longer of servitude. If only he had taken his prescribed Ascal cardio medication, a carbasalate calcium that prevents the formation of blood clots in the blood vessels, he might have been alive today.

Two years later, cycling on my way home from school, I finally plucked up the courage to drop a handwritten letter with no return address into the mailbox of the AMORC in the Hague. As soon as I did, I bolted, pedalling at lightning speed, not wanting them to see who the culprit was in case they would recognise me in the future. I wrote them a rather damning letter, blaming them and their "religion" for making my father believe he could cure himself, leaving my mum to raise two teenage kids on her own. I thought they should know how I felt about them, having taken advantage of someone vulnerable, milking them rather astronomically for their monthly teachings; I was a traumatised kid, and this was my only outlet for helping me deal with my grief. My dad had retreated more and more into the world of that belief, having been unable to heal his own trauma and thus chose to exit this life in favour of the next.

Had my father understood his energetic awesomeness, he would have known the proper steps to take to heal himself, and yet through his distorted perception, he chose not to. I understand that to step out of this life into the next was a conscious choice he made, but I was hurt and angry, and I sometimes hated him immensely for deserting us like that, mainly because he left my mum with nothing but debt. I didn't want to grow up without him. I needed him there to talk to when life got me down: to ask advice, laugh, cry, and have fun with. I needed him to be there when I graduated from high school, to give me away if I (ever) got married, and for so many other father-daughter things—and in the blink of an eye, that was all gone.

My Dad's Life as a Starseed

I could say that I miss my father, but he's still here. He only left in the physical sense of the word. I see him from time to time and know he is an extremely busy soul, helping out with the planetary ascension. He has often shown me glimpses of what he does and where he's at. He is an interdimensional gatekeeper who has shown me the Earth from space in an ark or rather a spacecraft, with its enormous windows and sleek lines—state-of-the-art and *Star Trek*-like. The Light BEings have so often told me to watch *Star Trek: Discovery* that I finally gave in and recently started watching it, and it has given me so many a-ha moments. The technology on the ship I was on was literally out of this world; it is hard to describe to you with my limited humanoid senses. Our modes of flight transport are, in fact, rather prehistoric compared to the Galactic tech. In that sense, we have devolved instead of having evolved; although truth be told, the technology is known, but we, the people, have been kept in the dark. In time much will be revealed as more people are commencing to awaken.

I have since come to understand that my father, like many others, works with both St. Germain and the Ascended Master Kuthumi, and is an advisory council member of the Great Council of Light. I am that mere extension of my dad, continuing on from where he left off. He told me not too long ago, *"Your experiences have led you to this point in understanding the cogwheels of life, the mechanics of how to live a life more authentically, regardless of what life throws your way. It is in the embracing of all experiences that one lives far more in the flow of Self than creating an intended chaos within, causing one nothing but a domino effect of created misery caused by the Self and impacting one's surroundings as everything vibrates according to the law of universal kinetic energy."*

There are many interdimensional portals dotted throughout the multiverse, with access to the various dimensions. It's like getting on a plane, except you're being transported in the blink of an eye to the arrival of your destination. I have to admit it was fascinating to see it all from the command centre, with many other BEings intermingling.

My father always comes to me as I remember him, but this time wore a dark green and golden cloak, material unknown, like many others who wore the same. He has shown me these beautiful, huge white halls of a library with many intricately built domes. The architecture was breathtaking, and many others roamed around, learning and discussing many matters. It seemed like a gathering place. I remember the immense bright light streaming through the enormous windows, and the linen hung from the ceilings, gently blowing in the warm breeze. I could happily stay there for a while, basking in the light, but unfortunately, he always zapped me back to my earthly form. We are all students of the University of Life, partaking in unravelling the secrets of the Universe, and astral travel is about learning to absorb and convey the learn-ed knowledge back to the people of Man—for all is given through the subconscious, filtering back to the conscious forefront.

The Ascended Master St. Germain

You will find St. Germain's wisdom dotted throughout my book, as I work very closely with him, having incarnated several times with him. He keeps the sane in me insane or the insane in me sane. He says, *"The Crazy in Me is the Crazy in You, and you are all merely Crazy reflections of each other."*

He lightens the mood with his wisdom, so I thought it was only fitting to let you get acquainted with him now and let him tell the story of his life and the Violet Flame. Choosing to work with any of the masters, one must understand not to go yammering for help and expecting a miracle, believing that life will get better with the press of a button or the wave of a wand. Instead, one should muster the strength to get up and find the avenues to heal the self, by stripping away the imperfection of who you think you are back to the perfect BEing that you truly are, by accepting the light that you are. How can you be a light to others if you remain unlit yourself? How can you breathe the breath of love into others if you cannot even breathe the breath of love yourself?

I AM the Ascended Master St. Germain, Master of Alchemy & Healing, and Keeper of the Grid of the Sacred Geometrical Merkabah. I AM the Chohan of the 7th Ray of the Violet Flame of Remembrance and Transmutation. I AM an Illuminator to the Path of thy Authentic Truth, back to the wonders of thy Luminous Self, for like a firefly, you have fallen prey to the ointment one has fallen into. I was once a revered high priest of the Temple of the Divine Transcendent Healing in Atlantis, where the Violet Flame burnt but once so brightly, yet its Light dimmed and remembered no more. For the people roamed in much darkness, of no clear understanding of their own Conscious Self, their Souls draped in the cloak of forgottenness, and their freedom of Self hence forgotten, and thus, the Violet Flame was but taken to safe havens until such time humanity understood the Power of invoking the Violet Flame but once more. I have walked the Earth but plentiful, a Sacred Master of many a disguise, characterising but many a flipside of the coin eternal, transcending the ladder to my Higher Self on the path to Enlightenment.

I was fortunatos to have lived but a life of many, from the known to the mere unknown, but that in essence is of non-importance, the key objective of all incarnated lives is to evolve to the remembrance of a love of Self and All. Mastering the Game of Evolution is like a game of truth or dare, a pitfall of the earthly biassed essences of hide-and-seek with the Self. I have lived the life of Joseph, the father of the Essene Jesus Cristos, the anointed One, and as my journey ended, my brother Joseph of Arimathea stepped in my shoes to come to the aid of Jesus in the darkest of times, and thus, became the Keeper of the Holy Grail, yet it is not the material treasure one thinketh it is. Mankind has always sought but to look without, yet the Grail is but the Violet Flame, the key to the sacred Enlightenment State of Beingness, of Oneness—it is the Holi that one so seeks without but resides within. It is the Consciousness of your own Divinity. For you are the Light, the Holy Grail, of your own luminous Divine I AM Presence, bringing forth the transcendence of Self back into the Light of Self, of a disintegration of the old you back into the rebirthing of the wondrous Phoenix YOU, rising from the plumes of the smouldering ashes, manifesting the Divine BluePrint in the Creation and Abundance of both the Self and the Planet.

I was but once a Man who cloaked the embodiment of the Self, finding the path to Enlightenment by teaching Man the ways of harmonising and walking in alignment with the breath of Mother Earth—the Conscious embodiment with the Grace of God's Divine Breath. I was but a Sage of Olds, an Ancient Druid, and a Keeper of Sacred Knowledge. I taught but the old ways of the Green Man of the Earth, a vibrance to the growth of all of Nature working in harmony with the Elemental Kingdom of the Fae.

I AM the Architect and Creator of the Round Table of Camelot, created for but the noblest of Knights. It was not to seek out the "Holy Grail" where many but besieged the holy lands of Jerusalem in search of the Cup of the Enlightened one, Jesus, but to keep it out of reach from the potential destruction thereof, in the safe-keeping of those meaning but to dishonour its Power and attain Enlightenment but for the Self in the maleficence of All of Humanity.

And yet, the holy grail of vino et la bière, were my quench for thirst, of quietening the buzz of my thoughts and alchemical Mind—for what better way to attest to the chemical composition of the all that one is, by formulating a different chemical-laden formulation equating to compounding the battling demons in one's head?

I was but the ultimate revered Alchemist, a Conjuror of the Arthurian Courts, a leader whose bravoure staved off the course of the warring Anglo-Saxons. A king but righteous and yet flawed by his humanity none the same, as we all but once were. The immortal mortal understanding of the Elixir of Eternal Life.

I was once the revered pseudonym author of many a mediaeval English play after having lived as a swashbuckling adventurer, an explorer, a tyrant, and the first man to set foot upon the warm white sands of the Americas—the I AM Race, of a rebirthing of the Golden Age of Consciousness—a land and a people of a renewed hope and faith, carrying but forth the reminiscence of the I AM Presence layered in the slumbering of their hearts in the current integrated paradigm, yet transcendence will allow for the Age of Light to commence, to allow for the seeds of Remembrance to blossom but once more, and for them to be but the way bearers for the New Earth.

As the persona of Columbus, I ravaged the sacred lands, terrorised its inhabitants, enslaved the many, for where I stood but idly, nothing but the pooling of blood and death followed into the veins of the lands. I was a tyrant, an iron-willed bully and smirked at humane suffering, for decency was not my forte, and my heart was but flatulent, ill begotten by the tides of time through the experiences encountered. I was inhumane to those I deemed of a lesser standing, and yet I was nothing, but for hiding these created humanoid narcissistic tendencies through the mere feat of seizing control of others, having free rein on my then sadistic urges and desires. As I made the island people suffer, so too, did I receive but a serv-ed quid pro quo of a dose of insufferable pain in return, for a debilitating poison caused a slow churning and a burning of the joints and muscular contusions, often incapacitating me until death welcomed me many years later.

Being a 'villain' served its purpose for the mere understanding of the light and compassion one should have for each other. I lived at varying degrees of light and darkness according to my instilled human conditioning, with power and greed and a lust for minerals and gold. I 'enraptured' myself in the arrogance of my duly inflated EGO, with a self 'indicted' importance, having lost all sense of Self, for power was only begotten but ill by me. C'était un défaut humain. I was judge, jury and executioner, enslaving the many people of the islands, yet how can one understand the light if one is not doused into the darkness? How can one understand love when one has not been subjected to cruelty nor treachery? Comment comprendre la joie si l'on n'a pas pleuré? Ce n'est-ce pas possible mon Enfant, for the art of duality teaches one the under-standing of being human, of gaining perspective, having compassion and carrying but love for others in the face of adversity. Experiences should not sire hate regardless of the wretched and foul circumstances one has been subjected to but merely instil a love for fellow humans, for love is the mere dissolvent to all cast darkness.

I was the indulgent and exuberant grand French philosopher and Alchemist opting to exit my Life before the coming of the French Revolution when another Son of Belial rose to Power to conquer the people of Man, with his bluster and pomp, but rather daftly, he eluded his own inner misguided folliness, suffering but from a narcissistic obsessed persona of the fragmented persona he was.

Humanity lives but in a perceptual prison of its own making. How can thy be at One with the Self, when thy cannot even Master the Truth of the Self? For one is but layered by the fugue of Remembrance of the ever-underlying e-motions running through thy intricate bodily system—thy human state of Awareness.

Lifting the state of fugue is not the idea of a simpleton's vacation. It is a journey to the depths within, to the understanding of Oneself to be able to transmute the experiences with the Violet Flame of Remembrance, Elevating one's Consciousness to the 'sparklicious' Light of Self.

Thy shadows are but a feat for growth, with karm the feast to the embodiment of one's experiences. Life is but an imperial experience of the enigmatic senses of being human. Freedom cannot be understood in the line of ease of one's life, but at the hands of suffering, for only through the darkened experiences of "trauma" can one truly choose to progress. To elevate or devaluate one's Consciousness through one's choices on the Earthly planes, that in itself is a choice.

Alchemy is not the turning of lead into gold in the physical sense of the word, but the harnessing of one's inner power to the transformation within Oneself. Turning lead to gold is the simple definition of "Lead" pertaining to the confrontation of the shadows of darkness roaming deep within and thus transmuting this back to the Light, so that one becomes a hue of 'Gold,' an iridescent Being of the Light of Greater Consciousness.

Thou art the alchemical substance of thy own soup of Creation. One is transfor-mational energetic frequency, a Magician of thy own world of Creation. Magic comes from the heart within. It is not about gaining power over others, for that is but a tripe of the human egotistical illusion, but it is a Power and Mastery of the Love of Self, for the Magic of Life comes through the very breath of Life. Be that magical Divine BEing of Light, that kick-arse unicorn, to shine forth your Light across the planes and the celestial heavens in a wild frenzy of your Soul lit alight on Fire. That is the secret to Alchemy. For one is an Alchemical Energetic BEing of the Divine Cosmic Frequency. Change the frequency to fine-tune one's own Divine Soul tune.

Master the inner to Master the outer. You must become the Master of your own Life, or it will become the Master of You. Life gives you no guarantees, but for the guarantees one creates through the defined actions of infinite outcomes.

Harness the Power of the I AM.
Transcend, Transmute, Exterminate, Elevate, Alleviate, Radiate and Illuminate
I AM One with the Violet Flame incarnate
I AM incarnate with the Violet Flame as One
I AM One
I AM
I

Like the many but led astray, our Divinity diminished, and we became but embroiled in the clutches of the material world—a freedom lost but for the faint whispers in the illustrious winds a blowin '. Come back to thy own Divine Essence connecting back to Source, for one roams around but unplugged, having lost one's senses. Few have heard the whispers and have allowed their hearts to be stirred back to the calling of Remembrance with many more awakening, until humanity and the Earth shall breathe once more as One.

Responsibility for one's life equals to the law of karma, of releasing the old patterning of the paradigm programming within, freeing the self with the burden of thy thus far created reality. The "transforlumination" of oneself is the luminous transformation of the Soul, allowing for the Light to permeate the gridlocked Mind, for there is nothing that cannot be healed but for the block of healing the Self.

I AM the I AM and all that is not, yet I AM
All that is and to take away all that is not, I AM

I AM the I AM for that I AM
As You are the You in You
For I AM the reflection of the mere Self of the You in You
As I am the mirror incantation of the I AM in You

I ask for all the negative to be dispersed from the heart centre to the All within me,
for it serves me no purpose but the holding back of Myself.
In the action of the I AM.
I ask to feel Lighter.
Unburdened by the strain of the current drama of the denseness of Self.
I ask for all to be transmuted, transcended back into the Light.

One is but such a delicate flower, a rose budding. Gaze upon thy reflection in the calming ripplin' of a stream. See the Self but shifting in that continuous ripplin' for nothing stays but ever stagnant. Be not of a closed-mindedness, for one will get lost in the feat of drowning in the current earthly transition, but quietly stand in the stillness of the I AM and invoke the sacred Fire of the Violet Flame. It is but a continuous source of strength and resilience for those choosing to use and harness its healing qualities.

Where darkness dares not perturb, but for the flickering of footsteps, the Light will but whisk them away into their own crevices of being locked in their own eternal damnation until they too shall learn the art of Love, returning to the brilliance of the Light of Self. For Light will sweep away the darkness of the lands, to the elevation of the haze within. The denseness of the 3rd-dimensional frequency will be but lifted, dispersed by the bursting of the rain clouds washing away the heaviness of the current paradigm, cleansing thy Soul and of All in the appeasement of the Self and All back to the Soul-Sun-Light of the beautiful, radiant Souls of Selves.

Live but in the joyous and abundant Soul that one is. Be in the natural state of thy BEing, for thou art Magnificent. Dazzling, I dare say. A crisp of the Light Divine. Live by thy own rules. Play by thy own rules. But so be it, within the sacred geometrical laws of the Universal Grid of One. Trust me when I say to thee, All will be Well.

Be of the Conscious understanding that Peace comes from within, it comes from the embers of the glowing heart within, emitting outward, basking others in the warmth of compassion thereof. When one is at Peace with the Self, one is at Peace with the world around thee, for the vibrational frequency of one's Cosmic Resonance has shifted.

Start with the Self and merge with the Self. To the blend of the ONE of All in All there is. One transforms the world by firstly transforming the reflection of Self. To exhibit one's outer qualities, one must first work on one's inner qualities—shine within, to shine without.

Humbly I remain, seek me out when thy needeth but the aid of the Violet Flame to the Higher Realms of Understanding thy Purpose and True Authenticity, until then, I bid thee toodeloo, auf wiedersehen and wish thee well on thy Journey of uncrinkling the creas-ed created crisp of a Soul back to the lightness and crunchiness of the most Authentic version of Self.

~The Ascended Master St. Germain~

In one of my incarnations with St. Germain, I was a student of Druidry, learning from none other than Merlin the Druid. Just for the record, he wasn't as strait-laced as you think he was. Many druids drank a fermented fruity beer mixed with honey to sweeten the deal, and he could drink like the best of them. The taste reminds me a bit of the present fruity Belgian beer, but instead the taste thereof leaves a rather bitter aftertaste in my mouth, making me want to puke.

My High School Years

My mum did not have it easy after my father's death; she had two adolescent teenagers to take care of, having to start with a debt, as my father had been jobless in KL, with the Dutch consulate paying our bills and our school fees until there was no more money in the kitty and we were home-schooled for nearly a year. My mum finally had enough and said, we are going back to Holland, so we did. My dad had gone for interviews and was called back for a second interview for a job in Indonesia, but my mum had to tell them that he had just passed away. After the funeral, my mum started with debts. She was allocated a second-floor two-bedroom council flat in the Hague, where we stayed for just over a year as one of the neighbours was a nasty piece of work towards my mum. He shoved her against the wall, shouting racial abuse at her, thinking he was far superior to her, all because of her skin colour. My mum merely asked this couple to refrain from doing building work in the middle of the night and to have some consideration for the other neighbours, who didn't dare to say anything about the continuous noise he made. We would always make sure to pass by their door hurriedly in the hope it wouldn't open, but sometimes it did, and we just got nasty looks.

I've never understood the whole race debacle. Too many people live from a sense of their ego, forgetting that we are all equal and are all one, no matter the colour of our skin, religion, or origin. Who cares? Underneath that shell, we're all light; we're all from the same source of creator energy.

My mum had been a coffee lady at Shell, got a job as a minibus driver, driving disabled children to school, and after that, she started working at the Dutch Railways as a ticket issuer at the counter. In the beginning, we wore second-hand clothes; some of the jeans were baggy, but I didn't care as long as they kept me warm in the winter. I had a pair of blue floral leggings that I wore under my jeans because I was always cold. My mother didn't know; if she found out, it would be bye-bye leggings.

My mum had an old banged-up Skoda that wouldn't always start on the first try, yet it served her faithfully for several years before giving up completely. My sister and I were bunkmates as we shared a room; she slept on the bottom, and I slept topside. The floorboards of the place creaked, which wasn't helpful when I climbed down from the bunk bed to go and steal cookies from the yellow cookie jar that was always on the living room table in the middle of the night; this is something my sister and I used to do quite a lot as kids. Once we moved to a bigger place with an extra room, with concrete floors instead of wooden floors, life became much better, and my sister and I could return to our midnight snacking.

Because of what happened with John in Malaysia and my father's passing, my teenage years were difficult, as I carried a lot of sadness and pent-up fear within. I was scared of the guys in high school; it was so bad that if there was even one guy in the corridor during recess, I would take a different route to get to my class. I would never take the front entrance when going to and from school; I would always make my way through the bike basement unless it was closed, then I would, unfortunately, have to take the main entrance.

I was so insecure, as I always felt people staring at me because I was so skinny, slouched, and felt ugly. I had this instant panic mode button inside my head, with this little voice often pleading with people to stop staring at me, as it made me feel uncomfortable. Going to school, I was always engrossed in a book, and sometimes I would listen to the Walkman, my sister and I shared. When the batteries were dying, the music would slow down in playback speed until it stopped. I loved my created mixed-tape cassettes. My sister and I would listen to the Top 40 and record songs from the radio. Remember sitting there waiting in anticipation till your favourite song came on, making sure you hit the record button at just the right time? When you'd played a cassette countless times, it would sometimes get stuck, and the tape would either come out all mangled, and you had to rewind it using a pen, or it would snap, and you'd get a piece of tape and carefully place the two ends back together. The most annoying thing was cassettes would squeak or warp over time. I used to grease the little cogwheels in the cassette player with a bit of cooking oil, as that would often do the trick! How I miss the '80s and early '90s.

Being super skinny, I was teased and bullied a lot during my high school years in Holland. In Asia, we wore school uniforms, so there was no differentiation, and people didn't care how we looked. In Holland, however, kids could wear whatever they wanted. Trust me when I say I was one of the mousy kids; I hunched, not wanting to be seen, hiding in my own world. If I could have disappeared using Harry Potter's invisible cloak, I most certainly would have.

I am pretty tall, 5-foot-11, but I felt like I carried the weight of the world on my shoulders. I tried to hide away in baggy clothes, never wore any makeup, and did not find myself in the least bit attractive. Many kids copied my homework; I didn't dare say no. I wasn't an overly excellent student, but I managed. My sister was a year younger than me but a year ahead of me at school; I was stuck in second grade for three consecutive years, so she surpassed me. It's not a great feeling when your younger sister is super bright, and you're not. I knew it made me look dumb, but I wasn't; I was just a shell of myself. I was trapped in a body I hated. I felt insecure and had no self-worth, which affected my schoolwork. I even went down to a lower level of education and attended a girls' school for about half a year, which, truthfully, was a lot better for my mental health, as most girls there were friendly. As it was too easy for me, I spoke to the teachers and the dean, and they agreed it would be best for me to return to my former high school for a higher level of education. So off I went, feeling a little better within myself but with a feeling of dread about being bullied again.

My mum always wanted me to wear my shorts for PE, and I didn't want that because my legs were so gangly and bony, so I always snuck my canary-yellow baggy jogging pants out of the closet and put them into my schoolbag. I also have double-jointed elbows, which some thought was freaky. I made sure I was either the first one in or the last one out in the changing rooms, as I didn't want the girls to see me. I looked at them and thought, why can't I be more like them? They're so perfect.

My worst nightmare was when my mum took my sister and me to the hairdressers to get bangs, something I did not want, which dented my confidence even more, and I cried myself to sleep. I could never get my hair to sit right before school, as I had wavy hair, so my bangs would be all out of sorts.

At sixteen, we went on a high school trip to the Ardennes in Belgium, once the battleground of three wars but a paradise for nature lovers with its many hiking trails and rivers running through it. I did not want to go, I felt awkward as I had my period, which I got when I was on my way to sweet sixteen, so I was a late bloomer in that aspect. I remember sitting on the toilet and having to change my underwear once again, as I kept bleeding until my mum came over to me and told me that I had my period. I just sat there crying on the toilet, as I didn't want to walk around with a pad and have to bleed; it was awkward.

My period pains were often debilitating as I suffered from massive cramps in my abdomen and upper legs and often felt like I was running on empty, afraid my pads wouldn't hold. I also suffered from headaches and heartburn. I was panicking in my head, as I didn't want the other girls I would be sharing the cabin with to see I had my period, so once again, I made sure to change when no one was watching.

On the first day, as the class was walking through the Ardennes, one of the popular kids grabbed my arm, shouting to the entire class, "Look how skinny she is!" None of the teachers did anything to help me, and in truth, that is the only thing I remember from this trip, as I felt awkward and at an unease with myself, having cried myself to sleep that night, making sure to remain vigilant the remainder of the trip.

There was a high school dance every year, which many looked forward to; I never got asked, so I never went—it was more for the popular kids to show off. I fancied several guys but never made it known as they never looked my way, but they sure knew where to find me when copying my homework. I was great at throwing my sandwiches away at school, with my mum none the wiser, I simply didn't feel like eating them all the time, but I did eat at the dinner table at night. It took me years to get over the shame and guilt I felt and realise that what John did was wrong because I felt it was my fault for the longest time. My mother encouraged me to talk about it, but the more she nagged, the more I shut down and blocked it out, as I didn't want to talk about it or think about it.

As St. Germain pointed out to me, one would call it body dysmorphia in this day and age, something I had never heard of. He says:

"It is a 'mental' disorder for one thinks there is something wrong with one's appearance but is merely the Mind that has tricked one, due to the ingestion of one's environment, through the art of bullying, teasing, feeling inadequate, fear of being ridiculed and a deep shame. As a child, one is raised according to the beliefs of one's surroundings; one feeds the Mind through its extrasensory activities in one's environment, and thus conditions the Self accordingly. What one continuously thinks about

eventually grows enormous in size, for those feelings of anxiety and worries turn into supersized monsters eating you alive. It is like a hurricane that tears through your whole life, leaving you in the status quo of an unalignment of one's body and Soul, for the Soul is in disagreement with the body due to the wounded Mind that you have so duly fed these improbabilities equating to the monstrous outcomes in your head. One often gets thrown into the ring of doubt because the Mind chatters too much, causing a stirring of unwanted e-motions, racking the elasticity of the brain, much like being slammed into the ropes of the boxing ring, clogging the wires with uncertainty and bouncing back daz-ed and confus-ed, not quite knowing what to do. Know that it is merely the outer conditioning from the trauma accumulated from the various experiences serv—ed— deciding to overcome the hurdles, slaying the demons inside your head, and walking out into the basking of the Light of the magnificent and radiant Soul that you are. Live your Life according to the vibe of thine own Self be True, never according to the ho-hums of others—let them sing from their own hymn sheet of Soul as much as you sing but wildly in the freedom of your own beautiful Soul Self. Know that you are a beautiful Child of the Light and that you are beautiful as you are. It is the mere conditioning that has made you think otherwise with your Mind pulling the strings and whipping you into a frenzy, keeping you incapacitated in the shadows within."

Life was different growing up without my dad. My sister and I used to make dinner after school so that when my mum came home from work, she could just sit down and enjoy her meal at the dining room table with us. We helped with the house chores, cleaned the bathroom, and kitchen, dusted, vacuumed, hung up the laundry outside and took it back in, washed the dishes, went grocery shopping, and took out the garbage. How many people can cook nowadays, let alone boil an egg? The landscape of the world in which kids grow up these days has vastly changed, and I am thankful I grew up in the era I did.

At night, I suffered from sleep paralysis, but I could also leave my body and astral travel; although, as a teenager, I had no idea it was astral travelling. Later on in life, I understood lucid dreaming. There is a difference between sleep paralysis and astral travelling. Sleep paralysis is a feeling of being conscious but unable to move or even speak; it occurs when a person passes between stages of wakeful-ness and sleep. When you're in that in-between state, you can't move or utter a word, no matter how hard you try; this can last from several seconds to a few minutes. Also, I often felt a sense of someone choking me, and I would try to flail my arms and eventually wake up gasping for air.

Astral travel is an out-of-body experience and occurs in a dimension outside of the physical realm. Spirit states, *"It is the travelling of self to the higher dimensional planes of existence."* Astral projection happens on the astral plane, whereby the consciousness separates from the physical body and travels to the astral plane in the ethereal body. Some use binaural beat recordings to assist with projection. I love listening to Solfeggio and 432 Hz Frequencies, which are much softer than the harsher binaural beats meditations.

I remember being able to fly, leaving the house, walking through walls, and sitting on top of a San Francisco bridge, looking down at the lights of the city, such beauty to behold. I knew I would be out of my body as I felt a huge whooshing sound, like a rush of water going past my ears, and off I went. There were other times that I would come across entities I fled from. When others were being terrorised, I would hold the light and fight back, often saying, while I did not grow up in a religious household, "In the name of Jesus Christ, I command you to leave." Sometimes I would have to repeat it several times, or I would call for help from other BEings and then move on.

I was shown a past life in Atlantis in my late teens, and at the age of nineteen, I was given a message by Kerry, a former Australian model, and beautiful soul: *"Live the life that she well knows of the brothers and sisters of the Ashtar and foes."* I had absolutely no clue what the hell that even meant! You still had to go to the library to do your research in those days. A year later, I finally found information on Ashtar in some random bookstore, and I was so surprised that I literally dropped the book to the floor.

At twenty-two, I was shown crystal caves somewhere in the mountains and met other Light BEings, and I loved the energy of the amethyst crystals; they glowed with such a soft hue. I could have sat there all day, bathing in that peaceful iridescent light. I remember going quite often, and it was here that I had my first conscious meeting with the Ascended Master St. Germain. I vaguely remember Lord Ashtar, captain of the Galactic Federation of Light, being there, but I have seen Ashtar several times over the years. I wrote down many of my dreams, but as I have moved more times than my age, a lot got lost over the years.

Lucid dreaming is when your consciousness remains merged with your physical body. You are conscious of the subconscious higher self in that heightened dream state and are very much aware of what is going on in your dream. As my Guides say, *"It is the subconscious becoming conscious, revealing messages meant for the growth of the Soul. One often becomes entangled in the emotions of the state one has duly created, with lucid dreaming the doorway to those wanting to assist within the subliminal nuances of your conscious mind, albeit in a higher state of dreamy consciousness."* Lucid dreaming is being fully aware of what is happening in your dream state and understanding the messages conveyed from often crossed-over loved ones or other Light BEings. I'll know it's a lucid dream because I always ask them why they're in my dream.

Another icky problem I had as a kid was nail-biting; my mum cut them short when I was like five to avoid me from scratching because of the chickenpox, and they remained short after that. On top of that, I suffered from warts around the edges of my nail rims, which was horrific, and I only got rid of them in adulthood by getting over-the-counter meds. When I was fifteen, my mum and I made a bet that I would stop biting my nails if she quit smoking. My mum kept her end of the bargain, but I kept relapsing, biting here and there when nervousness or anxiety crept in. It was a kink within my programming that took me years to get rid of, as my hard drive was faulty for the longest time.

My mum thought signing me up for a modelling course to correct my posture would be a great idea. It felt like I was walking around with a ton of lead slung over my shoulders, but neither my posture nor my confidence improved, not by a long shot. A hairdresser plucked me up, and I was the primary model for a hair haute couture show, but I didn't know that he'd chop off all my hair and style it into a short pixie cut, making me look and feel like a complete freak! I hated it; it was a nightmare to maintain with my hair always having a mind of its own. I wished for nothing more than for my hair to magically grow back, but alas, it took quite some months.

Growing up, you are influenced by your upbringing and don't realise you have placed these restrictions upon yourself in the first place. It would have been wonderful growing up to have understood that we are the sole creators of our reality; that way, kids could learn and understand that they are their own little alchemists, creating their reality according to their thoughts and according to the vibe of their soul. If we have the desire to change the events, conditions, and circumstances in our lives, we only need to shift our mindset, to change our beliefs and the emotions responsible for bringing them into and making them our reality.

My mum had saved up money for both my sister and me. At fifteen, and still, in high school, I started working part-time at a Dutch department store called the HEMA, as did my sister when she reached that age. To help our mum out, we paid part of the rent and continued to do so until we moved out. In Holland, this is normal, as it teaches kids responsibility at an early age. Nowadays, kids take everything for granted and think the world owes them as they've been given everything from a young age. Looking back, I don't know how my mother raised the two of us by herself, but I'll tell you, respect and kudos to her for raising us the way she did, even though my sister would dispute this.

At the HEMA, I worked in the food department, either at the bakery, the butchers, or the hot snacks section, where you could get a pork sausage in a bun and various other sausage rolls. I so wanted to learn how to use the slicing machine; however, as I was fifteen, I wasn't allowed, but the supervisor told me she would watch me. All went fine until I got a bit overconfident, having done it several times, and I sliced off the top of my thumb, I had to go to the hospital, was given a tetanus injection, and had my thumb bandaged up, and the sliced part of my thumb sewed back on, leaving me with only a tiny scar. I am one of these people who gets queasy at the sight of blood, so it was a harrowing experience with a lot of blood loss.

My Flatlined Modelling Career

I was so glad when high school was over; relieved, yet I still had no idea about the direction of my life. Nevertheless, as fragile and insecure as I was, I wanted to give modelling a go. I had this dream, like many kids do, of being this famous, glamorous somebody with the world at my feet—wanting people to see me, showing them that I wasn't some loser.

Then again, for many years, I kid you not, I had also wanted to be a nun, retreating within, in the peace and quiet of myself, getting away from the screaming chaotic world around me, as I felt like a misfit. I was such a mangled and buggered-up soul, with my inner reflection directly reflecting my physical appearance, my distorted energy further protruding into my immediate environment, creating my reality.

So many make modelling out to be this glitzy world of glamour and fun and living the high life. However, that's all just a façade. Over the years, I have met my fair share of sleazy and two-faced figures in the industry. It's a very superficial and fickle world, more fake than the nail polish used on my fingernails. I felt like a cow at a cattle ranch, standing there with my portfolio in immense long queues at castings, waiting to be called in and either be given the thumbs up or the thumbs down; it was mostly the latter. The issue was my look, as many compared me to Linda Evangelista, Niki Taylor, Brooke Shields, and Margot Hemingway, which meant there was no place for someone in the market like me.

Paris

In the interim, I worked as a receptionist for a pharmaceutical organisation to pay my bills and enable me to live. I saved up some money, and the agency I was with sent me to an agency in Paris called Glamour. Having gone to Paris by train, I lasted two weeks. The bookers didn't like me; they told me I had to dress differently when attending castings. I was rather conservative, wearing suits or pants, and I had nothing revealing in my wardrobe, nor would I feel comfortable in it because of how skinny I was. Over the years, I went to health stores to get supplements to put on weight, but nothing ever worked for me. At the age of 19, I started taking contraception, not because I was dating someone, as I'd never had sex or kissed a guy before, but to try and gain weight; however, that didn't work for me either. It did, however, get rid of the horrible debilitating monthly period pains I suffered from. Many years later, as my body changed and the pain trickled back in again, I tinkered with herbal supplements and found that Dong Quai (high strength), ginger, fructus gardenia, ashwagandha, and iron helped me. Many years after that, I discovered that rubbing peppermint oil over my belly cooled the pain right down. Now, I have a continuous contraceptive with the main ingredient being desogestrel—no more periods and no more pain, and I love it.

Most people love Paris and think it is the most romantic city in the world. I am part French, but *je n'ai pas aimé* felt cold, empty, and desolate to me. I felt disassociated and didn't particularly like walking along the cobbled streets with its many bars and cafés. It felt eerie to me, and I didn't have an affinity with the Parisian people, nor France in general. I couldn't put my finger on it at the time until many years later when several past lives came to light and the penny dropped.

In one of my rather vivacious lives, I was a royal descendant, living somewhere in the backwaters of France, although I made my way to Paris as and when required, as many were *traîtres*. I was there for the people, listening to their wants and needs; however, the establishment I resided over was fraught with corruption and chose to turn its backs on the will of the people. I was very outspoken and had an air of joie de vivre, a passion for righting the many wrongs. As my past life former self continues:

"Deserved the people to live in poverty? Deserved they to pay hefty taxes to fill the pockets of the gleefully wealthy of the arrondissement? Equality is a measure that should be measured in an abundance for all, not by being belligerent and maliciously egotistical because you believe yourself to be of a higher status and of a nobler standing.

One is born equally; a difference there is not, for all are born naked from the birth of the womb, yet it is Man that chooses to discriminate due to a conditioned social status of an engrained standing, thinking one is of a lesser degree. My outspokenness caused controversy in the courts and with the powers that be, and I was detained for making my disdain known and made an example of, yet that did not deter my spirit from wanting to help the people. Even though the country was rife with unrest, and I was incarcerated within the walls of physical confinement, I chose to see myself as a limitless embodiment and a voice for the people. Several decided to remain by my side—or so I thought, for, in the end, their egos got dealt the better hand, their humbleness, and a striving and a belief in a better world, having been beaten by the devil's advocate of selling their own souls, for the garnering of but material wealth, all to have a seat at the table of power. Change commences not by having a seat at the table whilst having sold one's soul to the devil for the garnering of riches; rather, it commences with an instilled empowerment within oneself, to henceforth breath forth the fire of that change. I confided in one who remained as a loyal aide by my side; however, upon relaying my plans, he too chose to betray me, causing me to be served the death penalty by the unjust courts.

If you believe that society was just during the French Revolution, 'ha,' they were all egotistical, scheming patricians wanting political control, turning against each other, all for the betterment of themselves, not that of the country and its people. The court was a shambles, an illicit trial of no standing moral grounds, held in a back office somewhere on the confines of the prison grounds, with a ruling made on the evidence of but one man, who turned the tides against me. The people had suffered for lack of food, the burning of crops, and abominable tax hikes causing nothing but the pains of social unrest among the created system of the classes. Man had lost their virtues and sold their souls to the devil playing a perilous game of roulette with the lives of many. It was an act of sheer folly, with the penance for my caus-ed 'grievance' death by guillotine.

I was not alone, for many suffered that same fate of wanting enlightenment and fighting the unjust, yet being punished by the darkened forces, who had no desire to make amends for the betterment of humanity, for theirs was to enslave, to corrupt, and to profit from their gains."

I honestly cannot remember being beheaded, nor does it matter. I do, however, to this day have a fear of large sharp knives. If a place does not agree with you, it may very well be that you have lived an unresolved past life there.

Milan

Returning to the Hague was a welcoming sight. A month later, I went to Milan to an agency called Why Not, where I stayed for a month, living in a cheap hotel for models. I finally got picked at a casting and worked for a French magazine *Femme Actuelle* (first edition). I was over the moon; I couldn't believe they had picked me out of all these girls! I was so excited as the job was in Paris, so I would have to fly there and return to Milan. I loved the clothes as they were a mixture of modern and classic, though they styled my hair in the fashion of the 1960s. I was hoping to get more jobs but only got one more for a hair magazine.

Many models were asked to attend parties in Milan and told they would get paid merely by showing up, but that was only half the story. Getting paid came with favours of a different nature, and I am glad nobody ever asked me to go. I was way too conservative in my dress code. I knew two girls that escaped the ruse and made it back to the hotel, vowing never to attend such "modelling" parties again.

Düsseldorf

I did a fashion show in Düsseldorf. I was made to wear ridiculously five-inch-high stilettos and was far more concerned with not falling flat on my face. However, in the end, the client refused to pay me because I wobbled on the catwalk.

I was then sent to see a middle-aged English photographer for casting by this German agency in Düsseldorf, who turned out to be another sleaze. He wanted to do a test shoot with me, which I didn't think was a problem. However, he said that should we finish late, I could stay over and catch the train back home in the morning. As you can imagine, I did not feel comfortable with that, so I was hoping we would finish at a reasonable time for me to catch the last train back to The Hague. I disagreed with the shots he wanted, even though he was going for the semi-nude look. It commenced with me having to take off my bra, with him continuously touching my clothes with his greasy fingers, ensuring it was all exactly how he wanted it. The more he did this, the more agitated I became and the more I withdrew. We finished at around 10 p.m. that night, with me calling it quits, and I called my mum from the hotel landline on the bathroom floor where I was changing and hiding out, telling her I would take the last train home as the guy gave me the creeps. It was a very frightening experience for me. All I wanted was to get out, but I was too scared to leave as I wasn't sure what he was capable of. It's easy for other people to say that they would have kicked him in the balls telling him to stick it where the sun don't shine. I refrained from telling the agency what happened, wanting to forget the whole fiasco, and got reprimanded by my mother agency for not reporting the incident, as another girl went and had the same experience. How could I? I felt so humiliated for having allowed myself to get caught up in that situation, and I was made to feel even worse because I didn't tell them, causing the scenario to play out with another model.

Hamburg and Amsterdam

I went to Hamburg in Germany, where I joined an agency called Network, merely having one job for the month I was there. Here I met Dominique Galas, the owner of Metropolitan in Paris; he'd seen my portfolio before but wasn't interested. But whilst there, he asked me if I wanted to go swimming with him, and I told him no, thank you. Why would I go swimming with some random dude who was twice my age? I thought it an odd request to ask a 19-year-old.

I started a modelling agency called Click Amsterdam with an incredibly talented photographer named Jos Verstegen. I knew Jos through the agency I was signed up with, as he had done test shots with me, images I still possess more than twenty-five years later. We had quite a few models on our books and went to see some clients, but sadly it never got off the ground. We were ahead of our time, as we created an online agency, making it far easier for clients to view and select models online rather than waiting for comp cards to be mailed or portfolios couriered across. Back in the mid-1990s, this was all new. As I was travelling, we lost touch for a while, and sadly, Jos passed away several years later whilst riding his motorcycle in Austria, succumbing to his injuries on impact. He truly was an exceptional person, taken far too soon.

I did a big campaign in Holland for the Renault Twingo and Clio with another Dutch model, Robert, with our smiling faces adorning the showrooms of all Dutch Renault dealers, which was kind of cool at the time. He now resides in Ibiza and is the owner of the Hidden bar and restaurant set in the magical valley of Cala de Sant Vicent, within an enchanted garden covering an estimated 2,500 square metres. In 2021, part of it burnt down to the ground including his home, and he has been rebuilding it ever since. I told him things happen for a reason; experiences are given to make you more resilient in achieving your dreams through the accumulated pearls of wisdom. He was a bit downcast about it all but, for the longest time, had wanted to make changes. I told him that if that is what one thinks, then that is what one gets—so if you wanted to build it from the ground up, then you materialised this into the actual manifestation of being able to create it according to the dream of your inner vision. From that passion will come the abundance and willingness to help and inspire others into realising their own inner visions, from that dream state into reality. You are the master creator, so make it a grand adventure whilst accomplishing what you set out to do.

Hidden Ibiza, www.hidden-ibiza.com/en, is where your soul can rejuvenate and spring back into realignment with the self. It's all about returning to the holistic sense of self with a "conscious" food restaurant, where all foods and their biological products are primarily organic and sourced locally. Cala de Sant Vicent is a mythical village where the goddess Tanit made her home in the nestled and enchanted valley of Cala San Vicente. This great warrior goddess ruled over the three realms of existence: the heavens, the Earth, and the underworld. She is the guardian of fertility, divination, and the creation of both life and the art of warfare. It wouldn't be complete without the various rejuvenation activities, from hardcore boot camp, Atlantis hiking (www.ourlittleplaceofhappiness.com/atlanthis-hike), paddle boarding, yoga, and biking. This is a wonderful little slice of hidden heavenly paradise duly created for those wanting to resync, replenish, and return to a heart-centred state of mind.

Robert has invited me to visit Ibiza many times, but the timing did not feel right for me, nor did I want to adhere to all the implemented yo-yo travel restrictions.

London

My mother agency in Holland referred me to an agency in London called Manique Model Management in London's then-trendy King's Road, which has ceased to exist. This whole circus operation was run by Tracey, who had this yappy spoiled furball dog that seemed to be glued to her side at all times. I was shortlisted for a casting in London for the new video for the punk rock band the Who.

That went sideways because I had an interview in a bookshop in Buckingham the day before the casting, and as I was leaving, I tripped and fell as my heel got lodged on one of the stair nosings, subsequently tearing all the ligaments in my foot. After waiting three hours in the emergency room at the hospital in Milton Keynes, with my head between my legs—rocking back and forth as the pain was unbearable—the nurse asked me if I was able to walk. I was unsure what planet she resided on, as I clearly couldn't walk.

I was on crutches for several weeks. I only did two jobs for Tracey; she finally paid me for one job months later, after I had to beg and plead with the accounts department; agencies are notoriously bad regarding payment. She kept the money for the second job, citing I still had a balance to pay off, as she had sent my portfolio to various clients and made comp cards without advising me, the likes of which I never laid eyes on. I demanded my portfolio back, and she refused point-blank—not until I had paid her the monies owed. She never returned it, and even though to her it may have been meaningless, to me, it was invaluable, as it contained all my actual tears and pictures. I hounded her, calling every day until she refused to take my calls, and the bookers told me that if I wanted my portfolio, I would need to pay up. Yes, in hindsight, I should have ventured up to London, but I lived several hours away by train, so in the end I let her keep my portfolio, which probably landed in the bin.

Istanbul

I did have many gigs in Istanbul, Turkey—not just modelling but also bartending at various locations. I never had issues finding work, as I was always open to learning new things and trades. I connected with Istanbul, its culture, and its people, blending in like a chameleon adapting to my surroundings.

I stayed with Rob and his business partner for several months rent-free, but he didn't feel like I pulled my weight enough around the office. This wasn't true because, besides my modelling and often working double shifts at the bar, I happily lugged a heavy bag over my shoulders, distributing the free postcards that were the rage in the 1990s. These cards were usually displayed on a display rack by the bathroom in a restaurant or bar, featuring cool advertising for sponsoring brands. They'd be changed out every few weeks, and I'd always make sure to grab the ones I liked, as they were great to keep, swap with others, or merely mail out to someone. I even designed a dope bumblebee card carrying their logo, which I still have, but unfortunately, they never used it (at the time, I was gutted, as I put a lot of effort into it). I moved to a friend's place, and when I wasn't working, I helped him make his artificial trees for clients until I finally found a rental in Taksim. The one-bedroom flat wasn't superb, as I had no central or electric heating and would often have cold water. I had to get a gas tank for my portable gas heater to keep at least my bedroom room warm during the colder months, leaving the rest of the apartment ice-cold.

However, one could not beat the view from the rooftop of where I lived, overlooking the Bosphorus, especially when the sun set over Istanbul, the fading yellow light reflecting on the sparkling, often choppy waters. It was mesmerising to breathe in the beauty around me, and I would sit up there in my spare time, these moments scarce with me being the workaholic I was.

Istanbul was formerly Constantinople, with Byzantium the largest city in Turkey and the only city built on two continents. It overlaps the Bosphorus Strait, with one foot in Europe and one in Asia. It's both an ancient and modern city; you can see the remains of many ancient civilisations and their cultures, with splendid natural landscapes; Istanbul has an impressive number of castles, palaces, and mosques. The city was founded by the Megaras in AD 658 and named Byzantium after their commander Byzas. It developed rapidly into a large trade centre; it was known as the Roman-Byzantine and Ottoman Empires' capital and existed for hundreds of years. The Bosphorus Bridge (actually, there are two) is one of the largest suspension bridges linking Europe to Asia. The Galata Bridge crosses the Golden Horn right at its mouth, connecting Old Istanbul with Beyoglu.

In the heat of the sweltering summers, I used to walk from Beyoglu to Karaköy or cross the Galata Bridge to Eminonu, wandering through the historic cobbled streets towards the harbour, observing the early morning bustling fish trade, savouring the fresh air mixed with the smell of freshly caught fish, and watch the ships come in and out of the harbour. It honestly felt like I was in a different era, where life seemed simpler, and people lived with such humbleness and ease. Anglers used to sit out and catch fish from the top of the Galata Bridge, while below it was crowded with various fish restaurants. From here, you can see the Galata Tower, built in 1348, also known as the Tower of Christ because it was the tallest and strongest fortification of Galata's Genoese town.

If I was too lazy to walk, I took the old tram between Taksim Square and Tunel Meydani and took the "water taxi" (ferry boats) from the harbour, making sure not to slip on fish guts at the end of the day. Being the clutch I was, it did happen to me several times. From here, I would sometimes travel to Kadikoy on the Asian side. My place was just around the corner from Istiklal Caddesi (Independence Avenue), where a statue of Kemal Ataturk, the founder of the Turkish Republic, stands at the centre point of Taksim Square. This area along the tucked-away cobbled streets is stacked with quaint little antique and modern bookshops and old churches, which carried something mystical and magical to me.

I had plenty of editorial gigs for *Marie Claire* and *Vizyon*, several jeans campaigns, catalogue work, and two commercials for Turkish pasta. For the Vizyon shoot, I went to Kapadokya. The landscape is surreal because of its rich history. During the early times of the spread of Christianity, the people who needed to hide from the Arab raids carved out these rugged rocks, constructed churches, and built underground cities, defending themselves against the attacks. Even today, people still live in these caves. They're cool in the hot summers and easy to heat in the cold winters. I saw many rock paintings of early Christianity there, but although it is a historical attraction, this place felt cold and eerie, as nature was deathly quiet there. During the shoot, having to climb one of these many formations so that they could get the desired backdrop, I slipped and fell, tearing the back of my leg open. However, I soldiered on, and they got their shot.

I had a shoot in Kilyos, a small Black Sea fishing village surrounded by the beautiful Belgrade forests. Even though it is close to Istanbul, it is far enough removed from all the craziness, the hustle and bustle, and pollution of inner-city life. This place was packed with Japanese tourists; many took pictures with me, politely bowed, and thanked me afterward.

Not even a year later, I left Istanbul completely broke and returned to my mum in the UK. Mobile phones were the new rage and rather pricey, and I paid a hefty price for the usage thereof.

Germany

After going back to college, following a short secretarial course, I moved to Germany in 1997 and finally landed a big commercial for a cleaning detergent, General. My agent at Cawi Models said I would be making 40,000 DEM; however, in the end, they negotiated the price down to 16,000 DEM, and it took the agency the better part of a year to pay me; this is the norm for all agencies in the industry. I never understood how others could make a living merely modelling, unless they were a supermodel. Through Cawi, Boss Models wanted to represent me in Cape Town, so in November of 1998, I decided to go.

Cape Town

Cape Town was a beautiful place and a real eye-opener for me; it was also the place where, at the age of twenty-four, I had my first alcoholic beverage. I stayed in a model apartment for the first month with two others. I'd never been out clubbing before either, so I couldn't tell you what a disco looked like, except from TV. I used to walk to castings by myself and sometimes hitch a ride with the others, but walking around on my own gave me a chance to explore the town and soak up the sun.

The model scene wasn't for me; it was just too superficial, and I had nothing in common with most of them. Many models I met there weren't the brightest bulbs in the box, with one Eastern European model slowing the car down for a pigeon in the middle of the road, honking in the hope it would fly off. The truth is I shunned them, preferring my own company as I got tired of listening and talking to them. Even in the modelling apartment, I kept to myself. I have always been a bit of a loner, loving my own company rather than being around others, as their energy drains me too much. It was only years later that I discovered I was an empath, having sucked all their feelings into my auric field, making them feel better and me like shit. St. Germain disagrees and says it rather, "unapologetically polite":

"It's a whole load of bollocks as being an empath is a mere state of Mind. It's like being given a flavoured lollipop and refusing to let go because you love it too much and become 'addicted' to the variety of flavours of that brand' empath.' 'I'm an empath, and I absorb other people's energies,' well, my Child, that is the ultimate copout of taking responsibility for how you feel, hiding behind the influx of the wave of e-motions you have allowed to wash over you. Stop conning yourself; change that 'fear-based' illusional thought to change your subliminal state of Mind. To be a sponge or not to be a sponge that is the question? A rather preposterous thought, for it is a rather matrixial mindset one chooses to participate in, is it not? Are you not a Divine Alchemist by default? Wills one not into existence what one thinketh? Is one not the Magician to one's very own concocted brew o' Life? It is the energetic vibe one so chooses to ride—don't like the vibe, change the frequency, to ride but a different cosmic supersonic wave. If one chooses to absorb but the energies of others and remain but an exhausted mop-the-floor-with-me persona, then indeed, by all means, be that cling-on, but seek not the fault in another, rather look at the faulty wiring within, and tweak the Self from that deflated state back to the vibrance of a radiant inflated state of BEing."

Alcohol

One day as I was walking back from the city centre, a car pulled over beside me, and this guy stepped out. On the inside, I was freaking out and getting all panicky and flustered, as I had no idea what he wanted, nor did I appreciate being approached like that. He merely wanted to know which agency I was with, as he'd seen me walking up and down the road a couple of times. I politely told him

I was with Boss, and he gave me his business card and said if I ever needed a tour around the peninsula, I should give him a call.

I left the agency a month later, as I was never sent to any castings, and joined a different agency, which meant that I had to move out of the apartment, and decided to give Ross a call. Heaven must have been smiling down on me, as he had a one-bedroom place available, so I moved in with another model who paid the rent to me, which I in turn—as agreed with Ross—used as spending money. It was a genuinely good deal, and Ross was a super nice guy. One night he took me out to this snazzy place called La Perla Bar, and he asked what I wanted to drink. I decided to keep it light and started with an Archers and lemonade, but I didn't like the taste of it, so I moved on to a Bacardi and Coke, but I didn't fancy that either. I asked Ross what he was drinking, and he said Vodka Red bull. I took a sip and was instantly hooked; it tasted like fizzy apple juice, only a little stronger.

I got so sick that night, as my body had not experienced the effects of alcohol intoxication before, and thankfully, shaky as I was, I made it down the stairs to the bathroom, where I ever so graciously threw up in the toilet. Needless to say, being a first-timer, it took me several days to recover.

Fun fact: alcohol is derived from the Arabic Al-Kuhl, meaning "Body-Eating-Spirit," for the spirits ingested "eat" away at our bodies, impairing our senses and masking the hidden emotional pains that have loitered our minds, which cannot be averted unless we heal the experiences that we have so wilfully incarcerated ourselves with.

One of the clubs I frequently visited was called the Jet Lounge, which no longer exists. At the time, the Ajax football squad had flown in, playing against one of the local teams in Cape Town, and they happened to be there. I spoke to Edwin van der Sar, the Dutch national goalkeeper at the time, and the now-re-tired footballer Dani da Cruz Carvalho, who gave me his phone number and said if I ever fancied strawberries and champagne, I should call him. He kept at it most of the night, but not a chance; he was much shorter than I was in heels and didn't float my boat. Gordon, a Dutch singer, was also there and offered me an ecstasy tablet. I threw it on the floor and pulverised it with my foot; I don't think he was very impressed. My watch broke that night, and Richard Witschge, another Ajax player, was standing next to me and offered me his Nike watch after trying to fix my old one. I told him I couldn't accept this because it was too expensive. He told me it wasn't a big deal as Nike sponsored him, and he'd get another. I was eternally grateful and used that watch for years until it went bust.

Miami

Even though Cape Town was a wonderful experience, I got zero jobs. Several years later, I ended up in Miami with Marianne Models through an Italian model. As there was no space in the model apartment, I had to sleep on the sofa of Marianne's place, and the next day she put me up with one of her friends. I was very wary, but he turned out to be okay, although I remained on high alert and kept very much to myself.

Once a spot opened up at the model apartment, I moved. It was overcrowded; there were eight models in a two-bedroom flat, with a bunk bed in the living room, two regular beds in one bedroom, and two bunk beds in the other room, one of which I inhabited. The agency didn't care; the more models you could stack in one apartment, the more rent they'd collect.

I worked as a hostess most nights to pay for all my expenses, as I wasn't getting any castings. The agency told me that my boobs weren't big enough for the Miami clientele. They had been aware of my bust size prior to me flying out, and I wasn't planning on getting breast implants anytime soon. I went to see a few other agencies whilst I was there, but none wanted me. They told me that I was too old (at twenty-six) or didn't have the right look. Only the wrong and wacky agencies seemed interested in me, which made perfect sense as I was so distorted on the inside, attracting exactly that on the outside.

When I was doing a Bacardi promotion, a scout for one of the top modelling agencies tried to kiss me, and I rejected his advances, which blew my chances. I was at his place somewhere in Miami with several other girls, and I just wanted to get out and go back to the hotel and get some sleep. He told me he had seven bedrooms and that I could stay in one of them. No, thank you, the guy gave me the creeps. While waiting for the cab, he kept putting his arms around me, telling me I was such a beautiful girl, not like all the other models who lacked intelligence, and that I should give him a chance. I politely told him a recurring no. I was so relieved when the taxi finally showed up an hour later, and thankfully I had $20 for the ride back to Miami Beach. I saw him around in Miami after the incident, but he ignored me, as I did him.

Marianne wasn't happy that I wasn't paying rent, but I wasn't prepared to pay because I had no castings through her, so no work. The other girls were always out and attending parties, and I shunned them. I wasn't interested in having dinner with wealthy Arab businessmen. One of the girls came back crying one night as one of these men had tried to assault her, having cornered her. I think that says enough about the reputation of this so-called "modelling" agency.

When I was leaving to fly back out to the UK, Marianne was outside screaming my name, demanding to be let in for me to pay my rent arrears. One of the girls let her in, and I ran up the fire escape and stayed there for half an hour until the coast was clear, eternally grateful to the girls for covering for me. I was glad to leave that madhouse behind.

New York City

In 2002 I ended up in New York City, and the first agency I went to see was Click, no affiliation with the agency I set up with Jos in Amsterdam, and was introduced to the owner by an ex-photographer who was well acquainted with her. She looked at my portfolio and said it shouldn't be a problem for me to get work in New York, although my book required an update. She compared me to the usual: Brooke Shields, Nikki Taylor, Linda Evangelista, and Rebecca Romijn. She introduced me to some of the bookers, and I came back the next day to meet the head booker of the women's division.

Yes! Finally!, Although that moment was short-lived because the head booker, an elderly lady, didn't know why I was there and was rather stand-offish with me. She flicked through my portfolio and reiterated that my pictures needed updating. Next, she asked me my age, and I told her I was twenty-seven, to which she curtly responded that I was too old and sent me on my way.

I decided not to give up and met with Karen Li at Elite. She said the same thing but wished someone would break the age barrier. However, she would not take a chance on me.

Why have a sixteen-year-old on the cover of a magazine? They are a developing soul, lacking the maturity and characteristics etched within the facial expressions compared to those with the wisdom of life's experiences.

I was left feeling downcast and unmotivated; however, I refused to give up. I scoured through the Yellow Pages and made an appointment with Ford Models, but I didn't get further than reception as I had not written down who I had spoken to on the phone. The receptionist took my portfolio, returned within half a minute, and said, "Sorry, but you're not our type." Cold! The way she said it hit home. It hurt me.

Yet I kept forging ahead, contacting Next, IMG, Barbizon, and Wilhelmina, but I never got any further than a phone conversation. I finally ended up with a commercial agency called McDonald Richards. I told them I had no social security number and was allowed to work as long as I didn't make more than $600. They were all very nice, but I only got one job for *Newsweek* magazine. I was dressed as a surgeon, holding specific tools, pretending to operate. You didn't see much of me, and maybe that was precisely the point.

The only thing I ever got were hair shows. Unfortunately, most hairdressers were like Freddy Krueger with my hair. I had not had a haircut in several months as I couldn't afford it; however, I found a casting for Paul Mitchell on Craigslist, and decided to attend. I'd had a good experience with Sebastian in the UK, doing quite a few of their hair shows, so I figured why not; however, I was adamant that they not chop it short, and I made that very clear to them. They finally gave in and said, okay, we'll cut off around an inch.

Arriving on the day of the show, I saw that the Paul Mitchell section had all these bizarre wigs, with freaky designs and styles, from moon-shaped to zig-zags and weird diagonal lines. It honestly looked like Edward Scissorhands would have done a better job if given the opportunity. I told them not to cut my hair in any way, shape, or form like those wigs, and they told me not to worry, but when I saw the amount of hair being chopped off, I started to panic. I couldn't see anything because there were no mirrors, which was smart of them.

After my haircut, I went straight to the colouring department, making it clear to them that I wanted no bleach in my hair but a simple chestnut colour, to which they agreed. Once done, I trotted off to the rinse basins and the blow-dry section.

I still had no idea what I looked like, but all these hairdressers were saying they loved the cut and colour and that it looked amazing on me.

Once done, I ran to the toilets and looked at myself in the mirror. I couldn't breathe. I was so horrified and burst into tears. They had lied through their teeth; I looked like a total ass, ready to be paraded round in the freak show of Paul Mitchell. They had bleached the front of my hair a platinum blond with an orange stripe in the middle, then another strip of platinum, and the back was some weird reddish colour; it sure as hell wasn't chestnut. What was wrong with these people?

The colours were harsh, but the cut was a total disaster. I still had a fringe, but they had layered my hair, cut the under-layer short, and left the upper layers to go over that. I warned the guy not to cut my hair too short, but as this was their show and I was getting paid, he obviously did not care.

I felt miserable, but after having wiped my tears, I made my way back, quietly packed my things, and left the building. I was told to be back there the next day at 7 am, as they needed to put the final touches on my hair, but I wasn't planning to come back after they lied to me, having disregarded everything I said. I huddled in my coat, wanting to be invisible, as I felt so hideous. When I got home, I desperately tried to wash the colour out of my hair, but they had used a permanent dye, so it was impossible. I honestly looked like a heroine chick on a bad trip, and my housemates were shocked at what they'd done to me.

My regular hairdresser told me to come by the next day. He looked at me and said that this was exactly what hairdressers did for shows; they don't care about the wants and needs of the models and just do their own thing. It cost me $200 to get my hair redone, with a $70 paycheck from Paul Mitchell for ruining my hair.

I did a shoot for my regular hairdresser on the Upper West Side, who hung my photograph on his salon walls. I didn't realise that he had a bit of a thing for me, and he went too far one day. He'd cut my hair and offered to give me a massage. He was a licensed massage therapist and had separate cubicles in the upstairs section of his salon. I was fully clothed on the table, and it was a scorcher, so I was wearing a long skirt, but he assaulted me, touched me inappropriately without my consent, by venturing down below and starting to finger me.

I froze, and it took me a minute to get back to my senses, as I was in shock. Finally, I told him to stop, and he said, "Why, doesn't it feel great?" At that point—even though I felt this fear welling up within me, not knowing what he was capable of as he was a lot stronger than I was—I managed to somehow get up and leave.

I felt utterly repulsed and violated, and when I got home, I took a long, hot shower, scrubbing myself until my skin was red. I struggled with whether to report him or not, but it would be his word against mine—not to mention, I was too scared of the cops wanting to deport me, as I wasn't exactly working "legally." The experience left me deeply ashamed and shaken, as I kept attracting those with abusive tendencies. It's easy for others to say that if it ever happened to them, they would get up and punch this person's lights out, but when you're in a scary situation like that, sometimes your mind is paralysed by fear, and you're unable to move.

I took it in my stride because I felt the guilty party, as I allowed it to happen, and tucked it away like I always did, simply getting on with life. I had the odd modelling job via Craigslist, with a mixture of paid work and working for free but getting free prints in exchange. I remember doing showroom modelling for a Lebanese designer called Gemy Maalouf in the Waldorf Astoria for two weeks. She liked me instantly, and I loved her designs; they were mainly hand-stitched and simply classy and timelessly elegant, with a hefty price tag. You could see how passionate she was and that she loved what she did. She also designed bridal wear, and modelling for her was the only time in my life I have ever worn a wedding dress.

The industry can be very degrading; getting rejected repeatedly is hard. Beauty is merely skin-deep, with people comparing and bitching about one another, thinking they are better than the other. Backstabbing is rife, as the industry is built on lies and deceit. I knew many who slept around to get a job, in the hopes of making it. Honestly, this business brings out the worst in people, for they see beauty on the surface when real beauty comes from within. You can have a beautiful face and yet be so ugly. One's reflection cast from within is what reflects and thus shines without.

And then there was me, a timid, messed-up mouse, a seemingly stick on the wall flower, thinking I was too skinny, ugly, and awkward, as no one wanted to book me or even look at me. The industry made me look at myself in such a distorted way—despite the fact that I believe all people are beautiful. As Spirit has always said to me, *"Beauty comes from within. You are a beautiful Soul of the Divine; never forget your awesomeness and resilience in all you have encountered. Under all the created layers of your created persona, you are radiant and worthy; let no one tell you otherwise. And even though the battles you have encountered and will still encounter may seem unfair, they have given you the fortitude to the continuance of walking the path ahead. Match not the beauty of yourself with another, for you are beautiful. You cannot expect to be the Light if you can't walk in your own blissful Soul Light. What you vibe out is what you vibe right back in, and if you understand that, then you also understand that it is your own energetic distortion that has created this concept of yourself into this chosen reality."*

It was a waste of time for me to attend castings, waiting several hours until I was called in. They'd flick through my portfolio, politely say thank you, and call in the next girl, often not even taking my comp card. It dented my self-confidence, which was at an all-time low, and there were many times when I just sat down in my room and cried because I couldn't understand what was wrong with me; why agencies or clients didn't like my look and cast me aside like a nobody.

Over the years, I changed my hair colour and style so many times just to feel better about myself, as I have never been happy with how I looked. The reflection in the mirror didn't agree with my inner self; my soul just wasn't in alignment with my body because I hated it so much. I hoped that one day someone would come up to me and say, "I like your look," but that never happened, and in hindsight, I'm glad, as this world was not for me. Nevertheless, the experiences taught me who I did not want to be.

I suffered from weight issues during this time, which has been a theme throughout most of my life. When I was happy, I ate; when I was down in the dumps, I did not. I wasn't bulimic but leaned towards being anorexic because, in my non-happy place, I was most excellent at not eating. I would take my outer experiences of rejection out on myself and stick to cereal, a slice of bread, yoghurt, and the odd piece of fruit. To put the weight back on was difficult, so I fluctuated for many years. Many models I encountered during that stage of my life lived off salads, coffee, cigarettes, and alcohol.

All people are beautiful; some have merely cloaked their light more than others, having become beautifully broken due to their experiences. But beauty is how we feel inside, reflected in the ripples of how we choose to live our life on the outside.

St. Petersburg, Florida

In St. Petersburg, in Florida, I had the odd bits and bobs, modelling organic nightwear and being the muse for Juliette Retro, vintage clothing from the roaring 1920s to the 1950s. Sandrine had some beautiful apparel, one of the dresses I still have and wear today. I am still with an agency in London; however, I've had no work for quite some years now. The last gig I did was for the *Guardian Weekend magazine*. Even though I have done plenty of test shots to keep my online portfolio current, I'm guessing it's simply a case of suck it up, buttercup; you simply haven't got the look, never had, and never will. As my Guides always tell me, *"Birgitta, it wasn't your path to travel, as life is far more than the superficial, barely touching the surface of who you are. This "line of work" seems all glitz and glam on the surface, but what lurks beneath is a vile and rotten industry of manipulation and egotistical behaviour and a deviation of walking back to the Light of oneself, clambering down into the abyss of the shadows, unbeknownst and becoming ensnared in the world of a darkness of the Soul. Yet, my Child, they have served as merely a richness in experiences of what one should want and what one should not have, for fame and fortune are but a drab when one sees the 'Souls' many have but stampeded upon, through the art of living a life through the EGO of Self. Celebrate your individuality in this land of duality; live it not in the glorification of the EGO but see it through the humbleness of one's experiences back to the light of the breath of Soul that you are."*

My Stepdad John

John was a character; he really was. He met my mum in 1993 when we went on this all-inclusive Christmas family vacation to the Dominican Republic. He had flown out from the UK and was actually on vacation with his then-girlfriend, but they were miserable in each other's company until he met my mum, and his world lit up. When they each went back to their respective countries, John had a check-up because of throat pain, and three months later, when my mum visited him in the UK, he found out he had cancer. He said that he would understand if she wanted to part ways. My mother did no such thing—she loved him and stayed with him, and although they were only together for five years, I know that he was the love of her life; they had an incredibly strong bond. I believe they both helped one another grow, with John becoming a better person because of her.

After my stint in Cape Town, an Italian agency called Pepea kept calling me, wanting me to come to Milan. Under normal circumstances, I would have jumped at the opportunity, but I decided against going because John, who had been in remission for two years, sadly had the cancer return. I wanted to stay in the UK to help and support my mum.

John had already been through extensive chemo and was told that if the cancer returned, the only option was to perform surgery to remove as much of it as possible without damaging any nerves, as the growth was right by the side of his aorta.

When he was taken into hospital at the Radcliffe in Oxford, I visited him, and I told him that death was nothing to fear and that there was always someone watching over him. I said, "When you die, you'll go to the city of Shambhala, which is another name for 'heaven.' You'll see that it's not much different, except that you're made of energy. There are houses and universities with libraries with rows and rows of books about people's lives, and you'll also be reunited with your loved ones that passed years earlier."

I had become fascinated by Shambhala many years before, and I was curious if it existed. Back then, I didn't channel, so I scoured books in libraries and bookstores, as the internet wasn't really a thing just yet. But I knew the heart of Shambhala was so much more than the written word.

As I now understand, the Gateway of Shambhala is the realm between the here and now, the physical and the spiritual—the gateway to the enlightenment of self and all. It is embarking on the journey of returning to the awareness and breath of self, understanding that we are one with source and all in the universe. I encountered Shambhala as the City of Lights, and those dwelling within that dimension are the keepers to the blueprint of civilisation, the encoders of Mother Earth, parallels to many ancient civilisations across the vastness of the galaxy, through the use of stellar intergalactic dimensional gateways. The many beautifully symphonic and orchestrated creations are created by the Real Estate of Spirit, the wondrous Architects of the Conscious Energetic Multiverse, who design, shape, and form the sacred geometrical grids of the many different atmospheric planets for the many species to inhabit and participate in the Cosmic Game of Evolution.

Shambhala is of Middle Eastern origin, meaning "light of the sun." Alternatively, Shambala, without the "h," means "the sun above" (from the Persian *bala*, as in Bala Missar, the fort above Kabul). Shambala would then mean "the celestial sun"—not merely the ordinary visible sun but the principle of light itself, coming from the transcendent cosmic central sun, the source of all light. Shambhala, the doors of heaven at the top of Mount Qaf (the cosmic mountain), open into Na Koja Abad, which means "nowhere place," a place beyond all places. This place is nowhere because it has no third-dimensional limitation. It belongs to what the Persian Sufis would have called the Malakut—or their Zoroastrian forebears would have called Hurqalya—the world of pure angelic intelligence.

I had no idea why I spoke of the city of Shambhala with John at the time, as I just blurted it out, but I asked him to promise me that when he crossed over, and if I was right, to come back and let me know. With a mischievous twinkle in his eyes, he smiled and said he would.

When death stares someone you love in the face, you wonder about God. At the time, I couldn't understand that if God created the universe, how was God even created? If God exists outside of time and space, and God is the creator of both time and space, then obviously, God was not created. God is the alpha and the omega, the beginning and the end, the first and the last. But everything that has a beginning has a cause; the universe has a beginning; therefore, the universe must have a cause. Yet, God had no beginning, so it doesn't need a cause. It simply is.

In addition, Einstein's general relativity shows that time is linked to matter and space; hence, time would have begun along with matter and space. Yet time is an illusion; it is non-existent but set within the paradigm settings of the Earth. Since God, by definition, is the creator of the whole multiverse, "it" is the creator of the illusion of time. Therefore, God is not limited by the dimension of time, for it exists outside the reality of space and time. God is "the high and lofty One that inhabiteth eternity." There is no cause for the creator other than for us to create and express ourselves in the human embodiment, to transcend our consciousness to a higher state of BEing.

I used to wrack my brain when I was younger, not quite understanding the energy of it all. I searched for years until I simply sat down and asked, and finally, I understood: God is in all of us as much as all of us are in the all of God.

I AM Infinite Consciousness.
I AM with no beginning nor end for I AM and always have been
I AM the Infinite "God" Source Energy as much as you are the spark of Infinite "God"
Source Energy experiencing Life in finite form.
I AM the Infinite All, as All is the Infinite I, and yet "I" comes not into the equation,
for We are All One with the We in each other—for I AM One with We and We is One

with I, there can and never has been a separation of the One, but for the I in the Mind of the incarnated human Awareness.

You are merely expressing yourself in the I form back to the We of the One that You Are.

The All is in the All of Everything and Everything is in the All, yet the Everything in the All is at a varying degree of its Evolutional Consciousness of Existence journeying back to the Oneness of the All in All.

I AM the Mind Map Maker of Consciousness, for I AM the Creator of the All. You live through ME, as 'I' live through YOU, in the creation and expression of all that you do, reverberated back to ME into the Cosmic Consciousness, evolving at the vibratory rate of your own Divine Luminous Rhythmic Frequency.

I AM Infinite Mental Consciousness, for the I AM Universe is Mental, and thus I AM the Mind Map to All of Divine Creation, where All moves and expresses within the Ocean of the Infinite of All Creation.
I express Myself as You express yourself in one's chosen finite form.

I AM the Alchemist of all of Creation, as much as you are an Alchemist of yours truly your own Creation.
You are an al-chemical BEing of the Divine, chemically creating the All of the Infinite that is you in the current finite form you have undertaken.

I AM an extension of you as much as you are an extension of Me.
I AM a Reflection of you as much as you are a Reflection of the Nature of all that I AM.
I AM the Creator of the Infinite of All, the Universe, as much as you are the Creator of your own Infinite Universe.
I AM Divine Consciousness, as much as you are Consciousness of the Lush Divine that is you.
You are the encompassing of the Universe within, as much as I AM the Universe in existence without.
I AM the extension of the Breath of you as much as you are the extension of the Breath of Me.
You've kept me hidden as much as you've kept yourself hidden.
I AM the Light as much as you are the Light.
I AM the Truth as much as you are the Truth in what you choose to perceive as Truth.
I AM the Way as much as you are the Way to finding the Light back to the Soul of Self.
Revel in the Godly Light that you are, waltz but back through the debris of the brokenness of the relinquished Soul back to the Light of who you are, back to the Authenticity of the dazzling Soul wonders of Self.

147

I AM worthy as much as you are worthy.
You are a Ray of my Light, yet have hidden yourself behind the clouds of a chosen narrative of pragmatic human Illusion.
Why? Ah, my Child, to help alleviate the darkened clouds that have long hovered across the landscapes of the Earth of the Mother.
To help in the wielding of a new dawn from a dusting-off the crippled old.

Who AM I?
I AM as You Are—for the mirror tells no lies.
I see a Reflection of you in me, as you see but a Reflection of me in you.
We are mirror images reflecting back at each other.

I AM the Infinite All of Creation, of the many billion Star Systems within the Multiverse of Existence.
You are Infinite of All of Creation in finite form, creating according to thine own Self be True, moving in the accordance of one's own Evolutional Self within the very Mind of the All of Creation of Existence.

You are carved from that same Spark of Universal Energetic Consciousness, as all my Children across the spectrum of the Multiversal Grid of Existence.
In thee, I AM but the mere expression of the Self in human form
I AM the Master Creator, as much as you are the Master Creator of the Life of your chosen Incarnation.
All are God Source Conscious Star Light particles interconnected to each other, connected back to the Whole of that One Spark Divine.
Me
You
All
Are, infinite Energy in Motion, constantly creating and expressing throughout the continuum of the Cosmic ever-beautiful-evolving Multiverse.
You are Infinite Energy
You are Infinite
You are
You

~The Source of All Divine Creation~

As John's only remaining vice was smoking cigarettes, my mum told him to smoke outside on the patio—unless it rained or it was freezing, and then she took pity on him, and he could stand by the kitchen window and puff his ciggies. John was once a well-built man, had a bit of a potbelly, always a devious twinkle in his eyes, often wore baseball caps, and his hair, once dark, was now grey. He reminded me so much of the actor Walther Matthau, from *The Odd Couple*, with his mannerisms, sarcasm, and dry sense of humour. If he pointed his index finger up instead of his middle finger, it meant f*** off.

He deteriorated slowly, and after a while, he couldn't swallow his food anymore and had a liquid food pouch with a tube inserted into his stomach. Over time, he lost a considerable amount of weight; he was literally skin over bones, a former shadow of himself in the end. It was heartbreaking to see as much for my mum as for me. He was a genuine lover of food, especially roast lamb and baby mint potatoes, something I despaired about when we sat around the dinner table, as I had to eat the food, whether I liked it or not. In my time, we grew up having to eat whatever our mum or dad put in front of us, we had no choice in the matter.

Living off liquid food wasn't easy for John, but he took it in stride. Cancer is such an ugly dis-ease and causes so much suffering for the one with cancer and their loved ones. To see John slowly wither away was hard for me and even more so for my mum, as his quality of life was fading. Life often has a twisted sense of humour, as my mum first lost my dad, and now it would be John ascending back home to Spirit.

As I discussed earlier, death is nothing to be afraid of, as we are all divine lights eternal. When the physical has no more oomph, and the wick has burnt up, our light returns home, continuing to live on in its true essence. It is just our conditioning that leads us to believe that death is the "end." We all eventually pass on to the next dimension.

"Life is a journey, forfeit not the ticket thereof, for that would be but a deplorable state of affairs. It is a chosen journey undertaken of redefining the broken and forgotten aspects of oneself by thy chosen experiences. One is a bubbling feat of energetic expanding consciousness; one is eternal in nature and 'human' life transcends death. Death is the Light of the Soul re-awakening, the trans-illumination of the Spirit back into its Divine Grace of one's Authentic Existence."

~The Ascended Master Thoth~

I often wondered if deep down John was afraid to "die" or if he had found peace with it. He had a son and a daughter from a previous marriage, who were both married and had kids, but they didn't come around to see him much, yet he made amends with them before crossing over. I was there most weekends, and he'd walk arm in arm with me, shuffling along the pavement with a cigarette in the other, happily strolling into town. He made it clear that he didn't want to walk with anyone else—unless, of course, it was my mum. When anyone asked, he'd always refer to me as his daughter. People in town loved him; he'd get a free haircut at the local barbershop, or on Saturdays, he'd pop round the market in Buckingham town centre and sometimes come home with a free pair of socks from Tony's stall.

John was not a quitter; he had immense resilience and worked full-time until eventually going part-time before stopping completely. He worked for an electrical wholesaler, which took him all over the country, and when that got to be too much for him, he worked locally for a frozen food company. He loved to golf and played pretty much till the end, mostly with his son. I wanted him to teach me how to play the game, but he was too sick at that stage.

Instead of going to Milan, I moved to London and got a steady job as a multilingual customer service agent. As the job paid peanuts, I had to put in a lot of extra hours to make ends meet. I got bored rather quickly, and after six months, I commenced working as a customer service analyst for a telecommunications company. Fancy job title, but it didn't equate to much. I moved to a much cheaper place in Marble Arch, in central London, downgrading from a maisonette to a basic room. The carpet was a weird dirty purple colour. It contained a coined electricity meter, and the communal shower ran on an ancient water meter in the hallway, which only worked by inserting old ten-pence coins.

Ölüdeniz, Turkey

In April 2000, I had a modelling job through a German agency connected to Models Plus. It was a catalogue job for some clothing brand, and the shoot was held at a hotel called Club Lykia World, located on the hillsides of the Baba Mountains in Ölüdeniz, Turkey. When I walked down the garden path and looked back at my stepdad John, I had this nagging feeling that this would be the last time I'd see him alive, although I was desperately hoping to be wrong.

I loved Ölüdeniz, the weather was lovely and warm, and the resort was surrounded by pine trees and edged with a shore of sand and pebbles running along the turquoise Aegean Sea—to me, it was heaven. The food was superb, as I pigged out on American pancakes, omelettes, and lots of bacon every morning, mostly sitting by myself. Several other models were flown in from a different agency, but I shied away from them; with one of the girls being brash and full of herself, I felt intimidated and out of place, especially as they were both beautiful and overly confident. They both ignored me for the most part throughout the shoot, making it a bit uncomfortable. However, I soon found other people at the resort to spend my free time with.

John passed away on a Saturday while I was still out there, but unfortunately, my mum had no way of reaching the agency, nor myself, as I had no international roaming on my mobile. I had wanted to call her that Saturday night to see if everything was alright but decided against it because I thought I'd see them again late the next day. That night, having dinner with a family I met there, I said that I wished he would just die already because he had suffered enough—and yes, truth be told, he could be a pain in the arse sometimes due to his illness. It's difficult to see someone slowly deteriorating, as every day seemed to become more of a struggle for him with the amount of morphine he had to take to ease the pain. He'd been in and out of hospice several times, with the hospice staff being absolutely brilliant. He could get nasty towards my mum, though, telling the specialists and hospice caretakers that my mum was trying to kill him, which wasn't easy for her; he didn't mean it, but being doped up on morphine changes a person's persona.

To me, he was such a brave man, and I often wondered what went through his head when he was still here on the Earth plane. He loved walking around the lake and nature-filled grounds of Willen hospice to collect his thoughts and have some quiet time away from everyone. I often wondered if he cried when no one was around. I know they took good care of him, keeping him comfortable, easing his pain, and supporting my mum. Being a hospice nurse must be an incredibly rewarding job but also hard when you find out that the patients you nursed have passed on. I cannot thank them enough for their support to both John and my mum during his transition.

Once we landed in Frankfurt, and everyone had gone their separate ways, I sprinted to a payphone and called my mum. She didn't have to tell me because I already knew. I felt so numb just standing there holding the receiver for God knows how long. Having to snap out of it, I made my way to the airport lounge and the check-in counter, speaking to the attendant, telling him that the plane could not be delayed because my father had just passed away. There wasn't much he could do or say besides telling me he was sorry and hoped I was okay. Of course, I was not okay; how could I be? I wanted to cry but felt too empty even to allow myself to feel sadness. I felt so cold within, and everything and everyone around me seemed a blur.

I felt like I hadn't properly said goodbye to John when I left for Ölüdeniz, and I wished I had run back up the garden path, given him an extra big hug, and told him how much I loved him. I know he wanted to hold on, but he simply didn't have the strength for another day, as his body had been ravaged by cancer, and it was done. The guilt of what I had said the night before, that I wished he would just die, stayed with me for a long time because I wished it, and he did.

I went to the funeral parlour because I thought it might help ease the pain. I took his favourite little teddy called Bear and left it with him in his casket. I only stayed for a few minutes because the energy in the room was so intense; I knew he was there with me, as I could feel his energy all around me. He was dressed in his favourite suit, and I knew it was just his body lying there and that his soul was finally free from the physical suffering he had endured, but it felt like he was looking at me from a corner of the room and that feeling became so overwhelming that I ran out. I was so apologetic to him and repeatedly told him I was sorry and hoped he would forgive me for what I'd said.

John was vastly complex. When my mum was visiting her mother in Holland, he'd popped over to the neighbours' next door and gotten so utterly drunk that when he left, he lost his balance, fell, and literally rolled down the pavement; they lived on a steep hill. The neighbour called the emergency services, and he was taken to hospital. My mum flew back the next day, having to change her flight, which cost her an arm and a leg. When my mum was home, he told her that she needed to sit down because he needed to tell her something.

He told her he was an alcoholic and had been for years, which my mum had never realised because he was always "happy." You may ask why she didn't smell the alcohol? He drank gin, and gin smells like medicinal alcohol, the perfect cover for him—hence the secret of his crippling alcoholism went unnoticed for so long, with my mum none the wiser. Whenever they were in the car, with him driving, she'd ask if she could have a sip of his water, and his answer was always no—because it was his G&W road soda (gin and water). Had my mum ever tasted it, she would have sussed him out a lot sooner.

Even on holiday, he'd be drinking behind my mum's back and was always so jovial, being a happy drunk. After so many years, he'd become a pro at hiding his addiction from people. When he sat her down, she asked him what he wanted to do about it, and he said he wanted to quit drinking and get sober, as this wasn't fair to her. He called Alcoholics Anonymous and sought the help he needed, with both of them attending AA, and from that day forward, he quit drinking.

On Friday, the day before he crossed over, my mum and John went to see his consultant at Radcliffe Hospital in Oxford, who asked him how he was doing. John told him he felt it was time for him to go, as this wasn't living, he had no quality of life, and he was tired. My mum had not been ready to let him go, but she realised it was time for him to undertake the journey back "home." We often hold on for as long as we possibly can because we're not ready to let go of someone we love, but once both parties come to the realisation, the transition process becomes easier for all involved.

The following day, my mum could see the change in him; she saw the glow and radiance, and he seemed content and at peace with himself, and she knew in that instant that he was getting ready to cross over. This often happens when people are ready to ascend back home; they are full of this last burst of life, perking right up. His son came over with his two grandchildren, and he danced with one of them in the kitchen. That morning he asked my mum when I was coming home, and she told him I'd be home the next day.

Sitting on the couch, they always used to hold hands at night, and he'd often nod off to sleep whilst watching TV. However, if my mum changed the channel or tried to switch it off, he'd sit right back up and tell her not to touch it as he was watching the program. *Really, John?* That night, however, he had been stroking his favourite lamp, a vintage lady holding a crystal ball in her hands—an antique my mum had bought, and he loved it.

All of a sudden, he got up abruptly, not saying a word, stroked the lamp once more, and went straight to the kitchen. My mum heard a loud thud of something slamming onto the kitchen counter. She got up, ran into the kitchen, and saw that the artery in his neck had burst, and he'd slumped onto the counter. She gently cradled his head and put him down on the floor, where he looked at her with a sigh of relief, and she told him that it was okay for him to go now, as he'd suffered enough. He just looked at her, and it was as if she gently felt his spirit leave, after which she called the ambulance.

They were there within a minute, and my mother told them that John had asked her to promise him to let him go and not to put him in the recovery position. She was not about to break that promise. They reiterated the fact that it was procedure to put him in this position. "Don't you dare touch him," she'd said. Instead, they asked her to sign the relevant paperwork stating that she took full responsibility, which she did. What is the point of attempting to recover someone when all quality of life was gone and his soul had already left his body?

She knew that afternoon that he was already halfway between here and "home." When she asked him to go to the market, he said, "No thanks, I'm tired, Eve, you go." As she was getting ready to leave, she kissed him, and he looked at her and said, "Well, where are my jacket and shoes then? I want to come with you." So off they went, past Tony, who asked him if he wanted to help clear up the stall later, which he often did, but this time he was like, "Sure, okay," and shuffled on. His last walk into town and back home had tired him out, as his life force was slowly fading, and my mum told him that there was no spunk left in him, to which he merely smiled, shuffling on.

My mum has been to see Ivan Lee, a fantastic medium in the UK; when he communicates with passed-over loved ones, it's like he's on the phone with them; that's how clear his connection is. Of course, John came straight through, and he was like, "You slammed my head on the floor," which was his typical sense of humour, the cheeky son of a bitch, because my mum had gently laid him on the floor, which he knew perfectly well. He is around my mum often, especially in the car, for she'll suddenly smell cigarettes, and she talks to him. John was the love of her life, and when the time comes for her to cross over eventually, she knows he will be there to take her "home."

I always say I have the best of both worlds: I have the spiritual side from my father and the earthly side from my mother. She is very grounded and has an immensely strong personality. Even though she believes in Spirit, that's where the buck stops. I have had to come to terms with our differing beliefs and keep the other side of me separate while trying to find common ground with her in this transitioning world. It's okay. I don't love her any less because of her beliefs; why would I? We all choose to awaken in our own divine time.

Sue Grassby, a phenomenal soul astrologer, explained that it is often difficult to carry high-vibrational souls to full-term, so kudos to my mum for managing this. As the Light BEings state, other mums-to-be may have complications at birth, or the babies may have health issues, as their soul cannot align with the density of their human body. Had my father still been alive, I know we would have had some very deep discussions about all of the "spiritual" stuff into the wee hours of the morning. My mum cracks me up; she thinks I "pendel" (*pendelen*, translated from Dutch, means to "commute" or travel between places) but I've told her I don't "pendel" mum, I "channel." She is not wrong, but I *pendel* within the galactic realms rather than hopping on a shuttle, shuttling between places.

She had done so much for John, unconditionally; it takes someone strong, determined, courageous, and very loving to do what she did for him. It must have been hard for her to see him suffer the way he did. He didn't feel it because he was full of morphine, but it was still excruciating for him to have to pass this way. He disagrees with me because, as his spirit puts it, *"I brought this onto myself. These were the experiences that I chose to burden myself with. Had I understood how to alchemise my experiences by learning to love myself and embracing my flawed Self, I would have been able to heal myself, something that I had completely discarded through my humanity because we merely forget whilst living this human life. We live with blinkers on, looking for cures outside of us, whilst all the while, the cure lies within. I would have been able to heal myself from the wounds that commenced bleeding within my Mind having seeped into my Soul and thus having spilled over into the physical in the form of cancer."*

My mum has been through so much in her life, and she is still standing strong; she is and will always be a fighter, and I take my hat off to her. In honour of John, she bought me an 18-karat gold ring with a little diamond to thank me for helping her out so much when John was so ill. She knows I am not a big fan of jewellery, but when she bought it, she felt that John thought she'd picked the right one and I would like it. Indeed—I was gobsmacked, it was so pretty, and I put it on my finger straight away and still wear it to this day.

As with my dad's funeral, the hardest part was when the final curtains closed to Frank Sinatra's "I Did It My Way." It was that final farewell, and I'd held myself together pretty well, but the tears were streaming down my face; even now, as I am writing this, I cry because I miss the bastard. I loved him like he was my own father. I miss his wicked sense of humour, and miss having him around. Saying that, he randomly pops his head around the corner; the smell of cigarettes fills my house, and since I don't smoke, I know it's him. Poking fun at him, I always go, "What do you want now, John?"

Regarding the job I did in Ölüdeniz, the client wasn't happy. They hardly used me for the shoot, preferring to work with the other two girls, which resulted in the German agency refusing to work with me again. To this day, I have no idea what the issue was. I got paid eventually, but it took many months for the money to come through.

My Drug Abuse

I was hoping that John would be around for a long time after my dad's passing all those years ago. He could have given me away if ever I got married (but blimey, more than twenty years later, he'd still be waiting, and to be honest, I am perfectly happy being on my own). His death hit me hard, harder than I was willing to admit. I stayed strong for the people around me, and I helped my mum out as much as possible, but I cracked when I was on my own. I resorted to taking things to numb the pain.

I decided to take myself down the Alice in Wonderland rabbit hole of experimenting with drugs for several months. In hindsight, not very smart, but I was hanging out with the wrong kind of "friends," who gave me cocaine and ecstasy (MDMA), and I'm guessing they hoped it would get me vibing back to my happy place. I tried to talk to them about my stepdad but felt they'd think I was a crybaby if I broke down. I didn't feel I could talk to anyone about this, though I tried; the truth is they didn't seem to want to listen because, after a few minutes, they would start talking about something else.

For several months, I felt so numb and lost within myself, not thinking straight; I was twenty-five and just not very aware, and didn't have the strength to fight through my grief. I could blame my 'friends', but in the end, I was the responsible party; taking drugs was my decision. I was hurtling into a downward spiral of my own toxicity; the truth was I felt like I was drowning. What better way to detach than through the escape of a temporary high?

Never look down on someone suffering from the dis-ease of addiction, as these are the experiences they have chosen for the breadth and depth of their soul's growth. Sometimes we have to die on the inside a little at a time in order to be reborn. Failing that, we can choose to let our soul burn rather crisply in the experiences of our choosing.

Years later, the Ascended Master Hilarion and the Divine Shakespeare Club said the following:

"Understand that you are where you are by choice, there is no exception to the rule thereof. One has evolved according to the patterning of one's chosen experiences. No one is responsible for the course and actions of your Life, but solely the bearer thereof—c'est toi. You are who you are in the current state of your I AM through the experiences you have created. To heal the Self is learning to look at the Shadows of Self, liberating oneself from one's chosen constraints, becoming aware and living in the Awareness of the radiant Power of the' I AM you' reflection in the mirror, choosing to live in the bliss of your Authentic Truth of Self and through the heart space of the I AM in the I AM of your BEing. Happiness is an inner state of BEing, and the secret to happiness and falling in love with yourself is to learn to let s*** go. How can you love yourself when you walk around with a wounded Mind, refusing to shed your experiences, remaining but jaded in the ultra-conditioning of the Self, and not being happy with the you in you? Life is too short to hold on to grudges, living in sheer misery, and

being judgemental of others, that's the flippin' EGO having its topsy turvy way with ye. Let go, love yourself, and let your beautiful Soul dance a wee bit more in rhythm with the Energy of Life, or else you'll just keep trippin' over 2 left feet, bruisin' yerself Child."

Seeing as I created my own experiences, I was adamant that I wanted to slip and slide in the pools of darkness for a while, sod the world and everyone in it. People, however, are quick to judge, but Spirit always states, *"Let the judgement of others and how they see you not cloud the judgement of self, for everyone walks on the path of their own journey."* We each need to learn to stand in our own truth, our own light, for it is a love for ourselves that will eventually set us free. I understand that now, but I rejected myself on all levels back then.

I wasn't an addict per se, but rather a recreational user, only using on the weekends, clubbing till the early morning hours, and suffering severe hangovers when I had to go to work on a Monday. Truthfully, I skipped going in a few times; my head was too heavy to even move from my pillow. I got nauseous; that was the worst for me, as I just wanted to crawl back under the covers, shut out all daylight, and disappear for several days.

Taking drugs leaves you on a happy high for a few hours before you crash and burn into a downward spiral. Cocaine and MDMA are two different types of drugs; MDMA is a psychoactive (mind-altering) drug that affects how we think and behave. It alters your state of awareness, allowing you to view the world through a different lens, not to mention your pupils dilate immensely. I used it to elevate myself out of my unhappy place and heighten my feelings of affection and empathy for a few hours; it felt like I had a connection with others. But it was all an illusion, as everyone else around me was on a high too.

It also boosted my confidence because drugs stripped away all my inhibitor blockers. But was that my authentic self coming to the forefront, or was that merely another distorted version of myself? Here's the kicker: I often suffered from memory loss, not remembering what had happened that night or what I had done. I know I was always talking to people and running around like a loony, just having fun, with time seemingly non-existent. Though, of course, time is an illusion of the mind. You are consciousness, eternally evolving, with past, present, and future simultaneously flowing into one. The illusion only persists because our minds think it so.

I'd look at my watch, and it would be five hours later, whereas it felt that only ten minutes had passed. Sounds and colours always felt more intense, and I loved my trance when on a high. *Renaissance*, the album by Nigel Dawson, would move me and suddenly take on a rather trippin' sort of spiritual significance. I could listen to that for hours and would drift away with the beats of the music. MDMA is not a drug that makes people violent, just chattier, much like cocaine. I remember chewing on gum nonstop, working my cheek muscles like a damn chipmunk.

Cocaine is a stimulant; on it, I suffered from verbal diarrhoea and felt freer expressing myself. Believe it or not, in the 1880s, psychiatrist Sigmund Freud wrote scientific papers that praised cocaine as a treatment for many ailments, including depression and alcohol/opioid addiction. As a result, cocaine became widely and legally available in patent medicines and soft drinks.

I snorted it, and the effects were almost instantaneous; I felt wide-awake and on top of the world. For some people, cocaine increases sexual desire. It did not do that for me. On the other hand, I never felt the need to eat; I simply wasn't hungry. After a big night on coke, though, I felt like crap coming down the next day, often feeling like I had a bad flu.

I remember this guy 'friend' throwing me a birthday party, with most people off their heads, including myself, as I was all over the place. I found a pair of diving flippers and, together with someone else, pranced round in these. I was plastered when I started taking pictures and realised that there was no film in the camera the next day. I was normally out and about and would consume alcohol as well, never really a good combo because the next day, I'd feel agitated and entirely out of sorts with myself. I didn't know back then that alcohol and cocaine combined can be a lethal cocktail, so I am lucky to be alive.

I had two one-night stands, and both happened after a boozy and drug-fuelled night out on the town. I'd wake up the next day feeling horrified and very unclean, take long hot showers trying to scrub the "dirt" off myself, clean the bedsheets, and open the windows to air out my room. Call me crazy, but I didn't want to wear the clothes I had worn and chucked them in a bag for charity.

I went on a bender one night, taking five or six ecstasy tablets in the space of several hours. Looking back, I know it was an extremely foolish thing to do, and I could have killed myself. It was a terrible trip; I suffered memory loss and convulsions, was sweating like a banshee, and experienced bruxism or jaw clenching, with my heart rate going through the roof. I was talking gibberish for hours, and I kept asking for water. The people I was with had taken me home and stayed with me until I had calmed down. Did I have sex on E? Yes, but having sex on drugs didn't work for me. Having sex on MDMA was a horrendous experience; it's not about making love but just riding out the adrenaline of the pill on pure lust. It was brutal, painful, emotionless, and wrong on all levels; it's like a complete disconnect from yourself, with your body feeling limp, like a ragdoll. Not a great memory, as I was too far out of it to even realise what was happening.

At that point, I knew I had gone too far. Yet, even after that, I knew I had one pill stashed away in my drawer somewhere, which I was desperately trying to find until I gave up and completely forgot about it. I found it over a month later, pondered it for a while, then walked to the bathroom and flushed it down the toilet.

My mum was shocked when I confessed all of this to her. She asked me if I was still using, and I told her I wasn't, which was the truth, and I haven't touched any drugs since. I only used it for a few months, but that wasn't the solution to my grief; it only caused my own soul more contusions.

The drug industry is a never-ending cycle of pure corruption in the highest places; it is a ruse to keep the population hooked and dependent on the many concocted poisons available over and under the counter. The world's corrupt governments are the biggest organised crime syndicates and have the most significant stakes, together with the mafia and various national security agencies. The deep-seated corruption within the system knows no bounds. Rules and regulations govern the people to stay in line with the indoctrination of the conditioned metaphor of upholding the illusion of their reality, fed to them by those controlling the world. The more illicit drugs are distributed on the streets, the more laws are created and put in place, which equals more criminals, more prisons, more control, and more corruption—and more money to be made. Drugs that are prohibited bring higher prices, with the competition "officially" weeded out, while the public continues to pay out-of-pocket for anti-drug messages to help those suffering from addictive dependencies. It's a con run by the few that pull the strings behind the scenes, pulling the wool over our eyes in this never-ending shady cycle. As Spirit says, *"Welcome to the jungle."*

I now know that John is not mad at me. How could he be? He is love incarnate; he knows that life is just an experiment and that the experiences and the memories are all you take with you when crossing over.

Did John visit me to tell me if the city of Shambhala existed? He did. He merely stood briefly by the end of my bed at my mum's before disappearing, which was the deal we had agreed on, and thus a sign that I wasn't going crazy nor imagining things.

I know that the city of Shambhala exists, as twenty years later, in 2020, after I had written the segment about my stepdad, the "Shambhalans," otherwise known as the Venusians, and Lord Sanat Kumara came through to me out of the blue when I merely sat myself down, asking about Shambhala. Sure enough, I started conversing with them about the floating city of lights.

Shambhala—The Floating City of Lights

Channelled in September 2020

We are the Light BEings of the Floating City of Lights, Council to the Ashtar Command overseeing the planetary ascension. We are the Keepers of the Sacred Golden White Light Grid. We are merely the Librarians of Ancient Knowledge, the "Shambhallans" for a mere better reference to the name. We are the Helpers and Educators of the Planetary Universal Wisdom for those who so seek the expansion of the Light within. We are the Astro Philosophers in service to Sanat Kumara, the Flamingos of our species, outspoken yet remaining but in silence watching from afar. Those that seek our help will find their way to the City of Lights. We walked the lands of the Gobi Desert, the landscapes of the once tropical gardens of Ancient Egypt, stretching to the vastness of the Grecian shores, once cloaked in the embodiment of Man. Zeus and all Creator Gods from the Cygnus star system were worshipped in the interwoven lands by both the Grecians and Egyptians alike, teaching the ways of the ancient carvings, of the arts and healing, the heralded sorcery of the Earth, and the embedded Stars across the vastness of the many planetary systems, educating all in the use and building of waterways for irrigation throughout the lands and cities through the ancient sacred geometric design, learning the art of transcendence of invoking the I AM presence in the all of everything that one did. The architecture of the halls and many temples were a sheer delight and splendour to behold. The stage of pandemonium had not set foot in the lands of peace that prevailed for many years.

To expand one's Universe, one must learn to dance in concurrence with the Universal Light of Self, embracing the flow of one's inner alchemical BEing. Opening the eyes to the inner kingdom of Awareness is the key to unlocking the truth to the heart space within, for the heart is the connection to all layers within, both the physical and ethereal parts of you and all that you encompass.

It is the connection to the All in All there is. It is the key to remembering one's marvellously stratospheric atmospheric Authenticity of encapsulated dancing hydro-atomic-molecular particles in the earthly suit walking within the celestial spheres of the great blue yonder.

You live with and in fear of losing everything when all you can ultimately lose is yourself. Do you think so little of yourself, that you do not realise that you are all that you are and more across the starscapes of the Multiverse? Fear not for change, but embrace it; much like the ever-changing seasons on Earth, it is a rhythmic breathing of life and rebirth, for such is the cycle of constant cosmic evolution.

We are but Guiding Lights in the darkness, much like sunflowers with a want for nothing but to bask in the radiance of the Sun. As such, we wish for nothing more than for humanity to awaken, to turn their heads to the radiance of the Light of the Sun of Remembrance rather than remaining downcast in their shadows of non-progression, remaining but instilled with a fear of growth and of change. A sunflower cannot yield in the shadows alone, it will wither and yearn but in anticipation for better tomorrows, yet it refuses to turn its back to the Light, knowing full well it needs *its support for its growth. So too, let one's Mind o' Soul not remain in the darkness of the EGOtistical Self, but return to a Love of Self, enabling one to expand and thrive, basking in the warmth and the Light being a beautiful flower of the Sun, just like that beautiful Grecian 'helios anthos.'*

Walk within to create without, for to navigate without, one must first learn to navigate through the darkness within. How can you stumble and not experience the understanding of that stumble? The humanoid Mind is but a subliminal incorporated and created energetic wonder of a marble maze, for the marbles within the functioning of the stellar brain labyrinth keep rolling within the ever-fluid creation of branched off passages equating to infinite possibilities weaving the particles within the alchemical field of the ethereal Self, and thus forth materialising the elements into the particle field of the physical existence.

One is not human by Divine Nature, but a Light Walker amongst the Stars. Wiggle your body to shake the gunk and act like the Light Walker you are and always have been underneath the accumulated conditioned junk of the earthly embodiment. You are an ultimate powerhouse of creation; just as the stars are mapped across the infinite reach of the Cosmos, so too are they mapped within the infinite Cosmic embodiment of You.

One can create as much as annihilate within the vastness of this 'trickilicious' Game of Evolution, but Love is the ultimate truth and only truth to the Soul's incarnation within the human embodiment. The richness of the heart flows through the unconditionality of Love. Live by it, abide by it, for Love is infinite. Love is the Alpha to the Omega; thus, Love is All there is, and how can you be what you are not when you are all that you are?

Ignite the Spark, to be the Spark, setting your Soul on fire, reforging the connection with the all in you as much as with the all in everything.

~The Master Teachers of Shambhala~

They are indeed the flamingos of their species, as these BEings originate from Venus and inhabited the physical realms several million years ago. I was so intrigued that I started to ask Lord Sanat Kumara questions, and he was more than happy to answer them all.

Q&A with Lord Sanat Kumara and the BEings of Light

08 September 2020

*I AM Lord Sanat Kumara, Master Envisioner of the Divine, and of Planet Earth.
I AM the Commander and Overseer of the Galactic Federation of Light.
Many a life lived and a transcendence of each to the enlightenment of Self.
I AM Master and Ruler of the Enlightened Planet Venus, Keeper to the House of
Shambhala—the realms between heaven and Earth, the inner earth kingdom of
the ethereal realms, and Overseer of the Spiritual Great White Divine Brotherhood
formed here at the heart of Shambhala.*

*For eons, the Venusian Council and I have been tasked with the art of teaching
humanity in enhancing their Awareness of Self, the art of transcendence of moving
beyond the non-physical world of understanding in the physical, moving away from
the denseness of the incorporated illusion instilled at birth, to live a life of Joy, Love,
and Acceptance with the heartbeat of the All in One.*

Q: Why have you come to aid humanity?

For a return to Self, a return to you, a return to "Eden," and a return to your roots.

*To help elevate the divine human consciousness back to the grid, the matrix of
love and understanding through the rebirthing of Christ Consciousness in the hearts
of Man. Many paths have caused the deviation of humanity, yet there are those that
now hold the Light stronger than ever and remain unwavering in their focus of shining
that beacon forth. I am merely here to help forth awaken the hearts of all in attaining
the nirvana, the bliss within oneself, on walking the road back to one's inner enlightenment and an undressing of the conditioned layers one has besieged the Self with,
returning to the simplicity of a Love of Self and All, back to attaining Shangri-la on
Earth, that was once in the bloom of Existence but has long been erased from the
Minds of Man, by the hovering darkness, that has befallen the lands. Yet, my Child, all
lingers dormant beneath the surface of one's Remembrance, until reactivated by the
mere quest of choosing to find oneself.*

For eons, we have aided in both the many Earthly transitions and human transcendence.

In plain English: humanity has been dumbed down through the ages, abiding
by the implemented rules and regulations of a created system, remaining in the
matrix of that created existence, to the detriment of the confused and dimmed
light of your soul. That is not living; that is solely being lived, accepting a mundane
existence. You are created within a system believing in separation, having been
morally corrupted through the conditioned innuendos.

***The below segment was channelled in conjunction with St. Germain and, as I call it,
the Divine House of Poseidon.***

*You are all Cosmic Super Agents of the Divine, having been given the suit of a human
body, except you have all been Men-in-Blacked-out, having forgotten your origins and*

why you are here. Some Secret Agents, we are, right? You limp your way through your experiences, none the wiser as to why your lives are so shredded in creating your manifestations? A wicked distortion of the senses caused by the warped experiences one's senses have been so bombarded with. You've but all forgotten that you have superpowers, that you are Alchemists of the Divine, duly walking round in straitjackets having incapacitated yourselves through the folly trickery of the Mind and the illusion of that darn created paradigm you have so conditioned yourselves to. You are an Al-chemical BEing of the Divine. Al-chemical equates to the Chemical being of All that One is—a chemist of one's own concoction with the very ingredients chosen by the Self, creating your own little paradigm of yours truly, your Existence. Blame not me when one burns the Self, solely due to the wrong composition pertaining to that experience. Alchemy is the mere subtle wordplay of All-Chemi, for one is the equation and thus the Universal Creation of all Chemi(cal) components as per the Sacred Geometric Divine within the All that You are, the embodiment that makes You, You.

Humanity is an evolutionary hybrid species, and thus the evolution is your own, battling the darkness in the third density as we aid in battling the species that seek to do but humanity harm. Just because you have been "neuralysed" does not mean you have been stupefied, yet many walk around dazed and confused, gobbling up the false narrative to keep you in line. It all seems a bit daft, n'est-ce pas? Be not consumed by it, rather walk through the darkness of Self, through the wet sticky tar of your experiences, clearing the tarmac to a smoother road ahead, remembering that you are infinite StarLights incarnate, here to shine your Light and elevate yourself out of the David Copperfield illusion of that created stickiness that you think is real, but is not, because you have simply been slapped into a dream state of non-remembrance. It is time for each and every one of you to wake the celestial heavens up, to shake off those pesky cobwebs from thy Soul, and walk back to that brilliant Cosmic Sunlight of Self, to shine forth and lift the world into the Ascension of the New Golden Dawn.

Q: It cannot be easy, especially in the current transitioning world we live in. How do you find working through the transition with humanity as a whole?

The task at hand was given to me when Venus had already transcended, completed its Evolution, and ascended into the Divinity of the I AM Presence. It is but a planet of fortitude of Light, an exquisite beauty of a sight to behold. When the Earth was but vibrating ever so faintly at the level of exhaustion, of a depletion, close to death, I was tasked to aid in the shifting of the heaviness, the darkness that consumed the vast landscapes of Gaia. It is much like the birthing of a child, and nurturing and teaching it along its Journey of Life—as such is my devotion, and of all that are on the various Galactic Councils and Councils of Light, for we wish humanity nothing but a transcendence into the Light, and for Mother Earth to transition into the next grid of Sacred Consciousness. Yet, it is not easy when in the forum of duality, one is devoid of the understanding of breaking through the barriers of the transitional energies that are persistently in the force field of the Light. It is a constant bashing of the darkness in the force field of the Light—yet in all the chaos, Light will eventually usurp the darkness. Remember that real change comes from the dance of inner movement. 3D to 5D is a shift in Consciousness, think not that we wave but a magic wand, sprinklin' fairy dust onto yer Soul, waking you from your Sleeping Beauty slumber to weave but your life oh so magically around. Would one evolve? No, surely not! One would take life for granted. How could one ever progress without the various recipes of hardship sent your way?

Can one not behold the beauty of the current suffocating darkness, to seek but to allow oneself to "dive into" the sea of change, back to the pure iridescent BEing of the All that is You? Washing off the caked-on human-make-up enables one to crack a smile and breathe back into the Lightness of the Divine wholeness of one's natural breathable state of Authenticity. A fervour, a lightness in thy step, by embracing the winds of change and discarding the discordance of who you are not will do just that. It will open your eyes to the world around you, making you look at Life in a vastly different Light. Revel in the infinite awesomeness of the Star Light particles that make you, you— dancing in a synchronous movement, and in harmony with the Divine orchestra, for it is about fine-tuning the Self back to the rhythmic heart of the sparklin' Universe. We wish nothing more for humanity, yet it is the darkness, the density, that gives one the opportunity to catapult one back into the Light, for, without the darkness, one would be of a non-understanding of the Light and the dualities of Life. It is the anchoring of One's Soul to the paradigm of one's current conditioning; one's layering of disconnectedness to One's Authenticity.

Upon one's human incarnation, your Soul forgets the Light that you are, and all of you get sucker-punched into this created influenceable society, thinking it is oh so real. Yet, it is the veil of illusion that has pulled the wool over your eyes, and thus you have become entranced in the cocooning of your human experiences. Many live too much in a deviation outside of yourselves, starving the roots of your Souls from the Light that you are, having unplugged the Soul's power cord from Source, stumbling around trying to make sense of the illusion of Life, having forgotten your own wondrous Authenticity. Find your inner plug, to plug yourself back into Source, and nurture your roots by alchemising your unwanted and accumulated experiences that have clogged the pores of the very Light of your Soul back into the alchemisation of wisdom and understanding, for only then will you flower power back into the rhythm Divine of Self, allowing your Soul to blossom and flower into a deeper understanding of Self and the world you have so chosen to grace your Divine Presence with.

Everything you do is an expression and a creation of oneself, in a perceiving of the senses creating your reality. To be a Light in this world, one must walk the Light to be the Light, enfolding the all of Self, knowing that you are enough. We are all extensions of each other, and yours is to walk back to the mere remembrance of the sparkle of Self. It is but an Authentic remembrance of the spark of the all-Divine Grace of who you are. The 'burden' of Life is to sever the ties that no longer serve thee, to undeck the halls of the decked-out Self of boughs and holly, that have blinded thee from thy Awareness, that have kept you "Houdinied" in the eluding of yourself. Such is the conditioning, the jest being played through the choice of thy current circumstances prior to the incarnation of one's chosen Life with the many sprinkled feat of bombardments of negative e-motions coursing through one's veins of both the ethereal and physical. It is a trip of the disempowerment of Self back to the resolve of the I AM Power that is you!

Why do you go so much against the grind of Life? Like a miller grinding its grain in a continuous loop, when one does not snap out of one's current patterning, one will not achieve the status quo of change. One may grind the grain to flour, but on cue should leave one's post to reap the benefits of each experience being ground, n'est-ce pas? Humanity is constantly being spoon-fed with information pertaining to the illusion of the current created reality to deviate one from the path to enlightenment. How long one chooses to traipse in the darkness is a choice of thy own making. We can only assist and guide thee should one decide to ascend to the higher dimensions of understanding and come to the realisation that the material and the onslaught of negative emotions is but to keep one trapped in the current dogma of existence, living in an enslavement to the created system.

So many of you live in fear of everything, with even your own shadow giving you the jumps and the run-around, when fear is simply an illusion that keeps you trapped in your current programming; it is a created energetic imprint by oneself through external existential causes. It is a mere paraphrasing of cause and effect if one allows it so. A boomerang thrown, curves straight back at you, the cause may not be changed, but the effect can be changed if one is willing to move away from the rooted spot and step outside the created lines one has so craftily created.

Q: I love this story of Fear having an encounter with Death, the power of the illusion of fear, and the hold it has on many of us.

Death sat outside the city walls. When a scientist asked him en passant why he was here, Death looked up, smiled and said, *"I've come to take 100 lives."* The scientist freaked out and ran through town shouting in a panicked tone to all that would listen, that Death was outside the city walls, coming to take 100 lives. The fear terrified many people, and they scrambled to get home, bolting the doors and windows.

Over the next few weeks, almost 10,000 people perished from hunger, thirst, and various illnesses, as mentally they couldn't cope anymore. When the scientist strolled out of town, he saw Death sitting rather nonchalantly outside the city walls. He raged, *"You lied! You said you would take 100 lives, but you took 10,000 instead. Why?!"*

Death looked up at him, smiled, shook his head, and said, *"I only took 100 of those people that were very ill and whose bodies were maxed out, and escorted these souls back to their heavenly home; the rest were taken by Mr. Fear, whom you took beyond the city walls into town and spread everywhere."*

Q: What is fear?

Fear is the biggest plague that consumes all; its slow poison feeds the Minds of the masses and thus bleeds into one's environment. It is time to step out of the shadows that have held you back, taking back your Power of Conscious Mastery and of the I AM Power, and basking in the glow and warmth of your I AM Divine Light Presence.

Take a simple deep breath and listen to the song of the heart calling within. What does your heart tell you? What sings it to you?

Whisper but words of fear and that is exactly what the vibrance around you will hear, embedding itself into the resonance of your auric field, dripping into your environment. **Fear** is **F**racturing the **S**elf **E**nergetically in the **A**bandonment of one's **R**eality. It is alienating yourself, having chosen to wade into that pool of darkened toxicity and having submerged yourself therein.

Awareness has gradually slipped and faded back into the subconscious minds of Man. Much like algae having slipped into the ocean, spreading like 'fungi' causing dark clouds to hover across the landscape of the once enlightened waters, slowly suffocating the Light. It is the darkness that has perturbed, feeding of the Light of Man, and yet Man, understandeth this not. All one needeth do is scrub the hues of darkness within, stand in unison and in Love and Light, to drive out the poison of that seeping darkness, and thus commence the dispersing of the algae. Too much replication of algae equates to large swathes of algae blooms, for that is the nature of the bloom. It spreads like wildfire, like a plague causing the ocean to be depleted of oxygen, leading to the illness of both fish and all ocean life; in the unequivocal equivalence, it is the very suffocation of humanity through the implementation of the net of darkness cast over the people for the ultimate game of coercion and control. To disperse the algae blooms, one must first learn to turn within and come to the realisation that life is not intended to live in the control of others, to live under the power of others but to live in one's Divine I AM Presence, taking back one's I AM Power, and returning to living in the Authority and Authenticity of Self, of mastering the very Light of Self instead of allowing one's life to be lived so freely by others—for humanity has allowed itself to be herded like cattle to the "slaughter," living and obeying those that coerce the herding. Forget not, my Child; you are a sovereign BEing of the Divine.

Life inadvertently changes because either you change or life changes you. If you change the way you look at fear, fear will change the way it looks at you. Keep your Soul rooted in gratitude regardless of the faring storms life may throw at you. As long as you nurture your roots in the acceptance of all your experiences and cling not to them like an abysmal drowning rat on a sinking ship, suffocating yourself in your own deluge of created e-motions, you will grow and be inundated with the blessings and blossoming of your own Soul's growth and have a far-reaching understanding of the cogwheels of Life in the vastness of this beautiful Cosmos.

Fear is a conditioned mindset, nothing more, nothing less. It is the encapsulated boxed-up creation of a conditioned Self through the mere feat of a created and doctored society. Fit not into the norm of that cramp-my-style rigid thinking, but have the courage to jump out of the box, not being afraid of the jack-in-the-box that has kept you in fear of the Authentic Self, but dare to transform, breathing life back into your deflated Soul, losing the rigidity and shining forth in the breath of the brilliance of the awesome Light of Self.

The divine Light in me is the divine Light in you, for I am the Light in you as much as you are the Light in me; we are all glowing lights within each other. I honour the Light in me as I honour the Light in you. I AM a spark in the infinite Cosmic Ocean as *much as you are the Cosmic Ocean encompassed within the spark of the Light of Soul reverberating back to the all of ME and the All in All.*

Q: If all is, as you say, an illusion, how do we break through these barriers, to understand that it is in fact an illusion and not a reality?

You are as much the barrier as you are the shift of yourself. You've got to break through and let go of all the stigma of your experiences that have created your belief systems, alchemising all the sticky residue. You are the ultimate creator of your own reality, the captain of your own ship, and everyone's perspective on the same story is different from that individual's chosen reality. You are all creators of your own Universe, choose not judgement, but discernment, compassion, love, and understanding, for not all vibrate at the same level of Consciousness.

Become more aware and more present with the I AM within yourselves, coming to a place of self-acceptance and the world you so gracefully dance in, rather than walking with eyes wide shut, taking everything at face value when life is infinitely richer beyond your wildest surface dreams of your shaped understanding. Be truthful with yourself and deep-dive inside the algae ocean of un-comfortabilities within, swimming through the gunk, releasing all the drab that once weighed you down, bobbing back to the surface and floating in the lightness of Self.

Either you control life, or life will control you, and you will eventually paraglide into the abyss of a repetitive existence rather than a more enlightened way of living.

You are not here by chance but by one's chosen aspect of learning and delving into the vastness of one's current experience of living life in the human embodiment of one's chosen incarnation. Challenge Life as much as it challenges you, for to ride the wave, one must first learn to master the wave.

Shift equates to consciousness as much as consciousness equates to a shifting of the senses. Imagine yourself being on an ever faster-going merry-go-round; as the speed increases from a 3rd gear to a 5th gear, one becomes overwhelmed with a sudden onset of severe nausea because the body cannot understand the increased speed in vibration. Now, imagine the Earth being bombarded with infinite Light particles, faster than the current acceleration, than the speed of Light; many of you will find your current physical bodies shifting, being elevated at such an increased rapid "vibrationary" rate due to the shifting of the energetic frequencies within the dimensional atmosphere, that one is overcome with a sense of immense nausea, making one feel "ILL," making one feel Imbalanced of Love and Light—because one is not accustomed to the rate of the shift, and one is knocked out of alignment. As a result, when you start to listen and breathe coming from a place of inner awareness, the nausea, the physical limitations, and discord will simultaneously fall away like an old worn-out item of clothing, like a snake shedding its skin, elevating itself to its next stage of evolutionary growth, making one feel lighter, and having a far better understanding of yourself, and your experiences. It's like trying to fine-tune an old radio to a specific station with an antenna. What happens when you move the radio to a different spot, from the 3rd level (dimension) of a shelf, up to the 5th level on the shelf? The "sound" becomes distorted, right? And when you become distorted, just like that radio frequency, you have to fine-tune yourself back into alignment, recentring the Self until you are back in sync with your elevated frequency, much like that radio, having moved to the 5th shelf—now having a far clearer sound and reach than when it was on the lower 3rd shelf. Do you now understand the metaphorical comparison?

Q: You talk so much of light that people may feel bombarded by the light you spread in your wording, because I certainly did.

Because my Child, you are Light! Me talking about Light in a constant paraphrasing manner should strip you from the human conditioning you have so harboured yourself with and dunk you under in the fresh breath of a rude awakening that you are Light, conceived from the infinite Love of the Spark of the Creator of All. It is your Divine Nature! The time for trivialities and constant dithering is over. It is time to switch the Light back on in your Soul by awakening the conditioned Mind out of the darkness. It is the Mind that has caused the clouds of confusion to deluge the Soul in the inky swirls of a taintedness. You have unplugged yourself from Source, having dimmed the light of your own I AM Power Source, living in a dormancy, in a land of make-believe. Time to plug back in, to enlighten the Light of Soul. Get lit, my Child! Vibe high on the awakened spark of the lit Light of Self!

You are the Light within this body in service of humanity. You are all infinite parti-cles of Light encapsulated in your current chosen human embodiment. Everything on Gaia is a beautiful symphony of ever-evolving and rhythmic dancing "de-Light." You are an energetic vibrance of the Light Divine—you can neither be created nor destroyed; you simply are and always have been. You are eternal. You cannot die. It is an impossibility and a total improbability! You think yourself not eternal and thus cling on to the physical substance of one's body because that is the conditioned "reality" that one has been peppered with. Yet, it is merely one's chosen outer garment whilst having accepted one's assignment as a Galactic Ambassador of Light, aiding in the awakening and ascension of humanity and Gaia, raising the vibration of Love on Earth. Be in acceptance that you are a Divine Light of the All in All, and that you are a beautiful infinite God Wonder choosing to create and express yourself through all your Creations and Experiences, weaving the magic of your Light, casting the "spell" of your Energy creating the outcome to all of your experiences. You are the Merlin to the Light of your very Soul; that is how powerful you are!

Q: You speak of both living in "awareness" and the I AM Presence; can you explain in more detail what that means exactly?

The I AM Presence pertains to one's true Authenticity—the You in You. It is the very Nature and Essence of your BEing.

It is your connection to Source and your ability to manifest and co-create with the world around you. Awareness as per the above is key knowledge in developing oneself—progress cannot be attained for the mere statement of the word; action should follow in the "immersement" of the understanding of Mindfulness. Appreciate life in your current circumstances. You are where you are solely because of your created and chosen circumstances. All Light of Awareness springs from the Rays of one's own Cosmic heart, for the heart is the seat of your Divinity; it is the centre of the breath that gives you life, non? Live in that state of the I AM OmniPresence from the seat of the heart and through the heart in all that you do.

You are the unbearable lightness of BEing, yet you roam in the denseness of your current understanding because that pertains to the upholding of the illusion that you think you are but are not. To live in the heaviness of the portrayal you perceive yourself to be is a "folliness" of the heart, keeping you shrouded in the mystery of who you are and all that you can be, for one lives not through the heart but with the ease of the perceptive analytical Mind, dissecting all information and archiving and actioning accordingly. A gullibility gobbled up all too eagerly by humanity, for one chooses to live but within the confinements of that reality. My Child, you are far more magnificent than you think you are; you are far more capable than anyone has led you to believe. To expand, turn inward, to expand outward, for, on the wandering of the inner planes of oneself, one will commence to come to terms to a better understanding of Self.

You must become the Master of your own Life, or it will become the Master of You. Life gives you no guarantees, but for the guarantees one creates through the defined actions of infinite outcomes.

The ultimate purpose of your Soul is remembrance through the art of progression. It is the spiritual process of a detoxification of the created inhibited Self, a purging of the hurt of the experiences one has so encountered in life. It is healing the wounded Mind. Your journey is not mine, nor that of others, but it is yours to walk as you see fit. The tangibility of your progression depends on how you walk the journey, should you choose to live in a more awakened state of being yourself or in the darkened hues of the entangled fabric of your own created life. It is much like riding a wave; you go several feet under and get back up until you have mastered the art of balancing the Self through the attention, focus, and dedication of the work thereof.

Your I AM Presence is a multidimensional aspect of Consciousness. Your past, present, future thoughts and actions make up the whole of who you are as a direct expression of Consciousness in your physical essence. How you interact with harnessing your I AM-ness is entirely up to you.

To ascend or not to ascend? To tune in or not to tune in? Only you can configure the realms of your understanding of the current You in the very I AM Presence of Self.

Q: Can you describe "ascension"?

Ascension equates to healing the conditioned self-tripe, and living and breathing in a lighter and more authentic version of yourself. As the Earth is ascending, ridding herself of all the toxified energetic waste and pollution instilled deep within the heart of her BEing, so too are you to ascend, with your Soul requesting healing wanting nothing more than a return to the iridescent spark of Self, with many a deep-rooted e-motional trauma rearing its "ugly" head to the surface. Don't like it? Well, my Child, one can either heal and deal or run and shun and sink deeper in the toxic yeasty beer brew of oneself. You have to tend to, in order to ascend to, is it not? Never whack-a-mole the same serv-ed experiences back under the skin of one's Soul, for it will become a somewhat repetitive dance, creating but a boisterous pimple, waiting to pop and erupt like a Mount Vesuvius, spilling into the energetic field of one's essence causing an "erroneous-ity" of "comical" errors in one's Life. One spirals through the same e-motional experiences until the electrical charge has but fizzled, and the Soul is free from the conditioning, and thus the "pimple(s)" it was once so painfully lumbered with.

If you still decide to walk the lines of the matrix, you poison not only yourself, but you add to the brew of the Consciousness of Gaia. Rid yourselves of all the baggage and shift into the 5th-dimensional frequency, for keeping the baggage you'll only remain, and trust me, that's a whole load of codswallop right there, as you'll suffer but immense dis-ease within yourself because you're refusing to grow. It's like trying to desperately squeeze yourself into clothes that have become too tight, and what do you do? Walk around holding your breath, feeling uncomfortable in your rigidity until you drop? Unless common sense fails one, you upsize and ditch the old clothes, non? Same with ascension, ditch the old to welcome in the new.

As St. Germain says, "Those 'suffering' from 'ascension-flu' merely need to walk through the crap that has surfaced, having made one feel crappy because honestly, one will feel lighter after having washed off the conditioning of those deep-rooted emotional issues. Yet, call it not suffering, for it is merely the conditioning one has been wearing like the uncomfortable hot and stuffy overcoat cloaking the Soul. Instead, see it as a wonderful opportunity to deal with the created issues that have been nothing but thorns in one's foot, causing one to have deviated from one's path, straying even further into the bush, n'est-ce pas? Indulge the Self with a bit more 'metanoia' returning from the depths of darkness back to basking in the Light, choosing to reflect instead of deflect by healing one's heart, one's mind, the Self, and one's destructive self-defeating ways."

Due to the occurring shift, purging the crap in my own cellular memory, releasing the heavy held-on energies, recalibrating my DNA, and expanding my vibrational field, I too have suffered from persistent headaches, nausea, dizziness, vomiting, immense lack of sleep, muscle aches, sore throat, sensitive teeth, bloating, entity attacks, vibrating back and forth when lying down, making one feel like the speedster, the Flash. Not to mention frequent urination, much like "Manneken Pis," the well-known sculpture of the naked little boy peeing into the fountains' basin. I have started eating lighter foods and drinking more water. Keep in mind that you cannot ascend if you choose to keep your baggage with you, it is an impossibility—either you release to be at ease or remain in a sorry state of dis-ease.

Q: What is self-love and why is it important? Some people think it is selfish to love yourself.

Love is what you are, so how can you not love yourself? How can you be of service to others if you cannot be of service to yourself? If the cup within overfloweth not, how can it overfloweth in a love for others? One must first lovingly water the roots of Self in order to sprout and grow and thus embrace the floral essence of love to others.

Love has been so misconstrued in this current day and age. Love is the greatest response to the duelling of the negative e-motions one will encounter in life. Love is pure; it has the Power to overcome any obstacle thrown your way. Love dissipates the early morn dew drops with the caressing rays of the warmly radiant sun, drying the tears from the gentle swaying in the breeze tree leaves. Love is kind, love is compassion, and love reserves no judgement unto others. Loving yourself is a necessity; it is not selfish but selfless. If I could tell you one secret of Life, it is that the ingredient of self-love is the secret to happiness.

Have you sooted your Mind so much by remaining sitting in the burning embers of your smoking experiences that you can't see the light of your beautiful Soul? Have you not cast enough wood into the fire to smother your Mind? Have you not thrown enough 'petrol' into the fire to burn but so hellishly alive in the raging fires of your experiences? Have you got your crown chakra so far up your root chakra that you asphyxiate yourself, breathing in the intoxicating fumes, unable to see a way out through the inhalation of the thick smoke causing you to tear up and suffocate within rather than extinguishing the experiences and healing yourself, diffusing the Mind to clear the smoke walking out into the clearing of the brilliance of the Light of your Soul?

Has your EGO gotten you sitting pretty in the smouldering fires of your experiences? Have you run so out of love with yourself, having become so lost without yourself?

Have you allowed the duly labelled Captain EGO to gain control over you running a mutiny in your head, with your tortured Soul incarcerated below deck and feeding the pirates of your Mind but 'fuelling' opposites? The only way out is in, and through, by counteracting the mutiny in your head with the bliss of Love, for, without Love, one will remain as is, rather than rebirthing the Self back into the glorious sunlight above deck, reinstating yourself as the captain of your ship, having befriended the EGO and the Mind by learning to love, embrace and master all of your experiences.

Love is not poison ivy to the Soul, rather Love is a deterrent to all that ails the riddled Mind.

Q: What is the illusion of the created ego and the so-called differentiation in the human race?

Humanity is selfish in its ways, not selfless. One has come into this world cold turkey, remembering nothing, and growing up in the illusion of the institutionalised grid of the asylum of existence that came into being and has been craftily cultivated for thousands of years—yet that has commenced to flounder, for like a spoke in the wheel, one has come to a reverberating halt in the slowing down of the senses, to the bewilderment of all, and one is forced to look within the deeply created wounds that have taken root within the Self, to find a way back to a remembrance of what truly is and always has been. One works not in harmony with one another but strives to better one's EGO in an ever-weighted war of a battle of "comparables." The EGO is a depiction of the "prescribed" labelled aspects from the Self to the Self, that require inner healing and have the knack for competing with others rather than working in unison and in harmony with each other. It is the I AM better than you competition, this constant battle with the Self all through the external influences that say it so—buttering up the

EGO—really? Everything has always been about the grand glorification of the Self. EGO means to Eject God Out, and how can you deny your existence when you are God Source Energy, a Divine Infinite of the Whole. If you think yourself to be better than the other, then one lives but in utter shambles of the illusion that is. Separation is but a folly of statements—you judge one another beyond an immeasurable doubt when every single one of you is cut from the same bark of wood! One is the blend of all from another, a fusion of energetic light particles dancing in the bravoure of the inhibited bodies one has so graciously accepted. Just because we look different does not make us any different. Just because we vibrate at different altitudes of awareness does not make us any different; we are all the same. You talk about race, yet you carpal tunnel and individualise, comparing the Earthly races, thinking lesser of certain "races," but within these suits your Souls wear, these beautiful bodies you all inhabit, we are but One Race.

It is One world and One people, yet you live so fractured from one another. You are all units from the same big cheese, yet upon incarnating, you divide yourself amongst a whole flavour of cheeses, thinking each cheese is different. Cheese may carry different flavours, but cheese is still cheese, and you're all still a piece of the big overall cheese. No one is of a lesser creed. Everyone has chosen a set of different circumstances and cultures to evolve in, as that was their chosen travel itinerary for their Soul's evolution. Stop belittling others, for you are only belittling yourself, as people are all mere reflections of one another. Look at the holes in your own cheese before badgering about the holes in someone else's. And then one wonders why the Soul is so "drafty," and one feels so off-kilter? Plug your own holes and stitch yourself up to feel far more whole and awesome within yourself and your standing in the world. Be in acceptance of each other, for everyone attains enlightenment in their own sweet Soul time. Practise Love, Compassion, Kindness, Gratitude, and Acceptance of yourself and each other every day, and that Oneness of BEing will become the norm of living, walking hand in hand with the vibrance of the All in One and One in All.

Q: What is the use of the physical body?

The body is the synthesis of Life. It is the temple of the I AM, a shrine of dedication and of service to the Self whilst in the incarnation of being a human entity. Your body is a vehicle; it is a mode of transport, enabling you to seek the Self and explore the playground of the world.

Your body is the vessel to the seat of the Soul it houses. Without a Soul, the body is but a limp and lifeless shell; it needs the Soul essence to spark it to Life. Even though many don't abide by the abode of that thinking, the body is a wondrous organism and a beautifully created sacred design of intricately interwoven DNA and genes of the various species. One takes the body utterly for granted, one day knowing that you will ultimately "die" and move on to the next stage of evolution. The body enlisted to you serves one for the greater good, lest one beholds the truth, that the body is indeed a Temple, and devoted to you, then one lives but in the temporary illusion that the body is just that.

Your Soul is the conduit, the maestro to the Body. The body is a Conscious organism; it listens to every word and all you choose to feed it with. You cannot live an unhealthy life and expect to reap the benefits in return. You throw sludge at your body through the emulsion of chemicals and junk, then expect nothing less in return. Foods may be the fuel to your existence, but let it be an existence of Conscious choosing, and thus of service to yourself. Living in the bliss of deviation and denial causes nothing but a mountain of upheaval, creating an energetic sludge, a constipation within the energetic flow of yourself because of poor dietary choices. The intake of the intoxicating food consumption allows your body to vibrate at a denser level, and then one wonders why one suffers from dis-ease? What you ingest defines who you choose to be, it is the imprint of the energetic frequency you choose to resonate at, so I ask you to choose wisely.

The Ascended Master Hilarion interjected into this part of the conversation as I discussed John's cancer and how one creates that dis-ease within the body. I often hear people say, well, I did not choose this dis-ease, or a passed loved one did not ask to have cancer or dementia.

"The biggest suppressant causing the stemming of the energetic flow is you—yes, you. You are as much the cause as the dis-ease of the condition of your body. You are the navigator without question, and yet this is precisely what you question, and hence you search for the answers without, whereas the sophistication of the I AM Awareness is far greater than one can fathom if only one takes that first step to tap into one's inner world, one's inner navigational compass of Consciousness. Taking cancer as Birgitta's queried example, one's suppressed e-motions are the root of all dis-ease within the body due to the conditioning one so believes and adheres to. John had many underlying issues to work out. Being vocal in the wording of his true Authenticity was not his strongest suit; as such, the blockage, the stemming of blocked e-motions accumulated within the throat area. And yet, due to the illness that ravaged his body, he learned to speak his truth.

Understand that dis-ease is an experience to teach you the understanding of the Light within. The body is but a mere vessel to experience life in its essence and to navigate one's way back to the Self. Pain and suffering are warning signs that you are living against the grind of the nature of your truth. Smoking, and the consumption of alcohol in his case, was a mere extension to creating the dis-ease, for many seek solace in the escapism through various outlets of toxicity, causing the user an imprudent and severe procrastination of self-growth, and thus a mere running away dodging the bullet from themselves, by interjecting a slow poison emanating through the veins of their existence. Procrastination equates to needless suffering by remaining steadfast in one's conditioned programming. One can keep running, but it is a tiresome feat to behold and causes nothing but unnecessary complications in one's life rather than choosing to live in your truth and Authenticity in the first place! Why do you choose to play this game of hide-and-seek with yourself when one can easily choose to come out of hiding and emanate in the Lightness of vibrational truth and be real with the you in you.

Remember, you can either live in a perpetual state of bliss or in a state of sorriness. The choice is yours. Understand that death is but the transcendence of the miracle that is embodied within the human created clayed organism, for death is the mere recycling of the physical back to the dust of the Earth with the Spirit brought forth home, thus understanding that one is and always has been Light. One can cut out dis-ease, but one still needs to mend and heal the fragmented Self back together, and one relies but with a folly on the chemicalised medication instead of stepping into the Spirit of Mother Earth and all her offerings. Intoxicate and desecrate or elevate and illuminate. Yet know that there is no right or wrong in how one chooses to heal; it is merely the level of Consciousness one resonates at. The beauty of John was that even though his body was ravaged by cancer, he knew he could not leave this dimension until all had been resolved. That was a mere choice of his, choosing to experience finishing the unfinished and transmuting that back into the Light."

As John says, being very much the joker he is, "I smoked and drank my blues and worries away, living in the vast escapism of a catch me if you can of myself. I loved life, had my faults, being a bastard at times, but lived it to the best of my knowledge and awareness. You live life according to your upbringing and make the best of not remembering who you are as you are too busy and preoccupied with working to fund your very life and existence within the set parameters of your confined matrix of existence."

Q: Who or what is God?

You are! Divinity is your Nature. How can you be in mere denial of that when you are! God is as much the I AM presence in Me as it is the I AM Presence in You. I AM as much the Light of God as you are the Light of God.

God is the Energetic Vibrance, the Master Creator, and the Orchestrator of the Universal Song. God is the Architect, the Grand Vizier, the Overseer of All, the Master Creator, and Transformer of the Conscious evolving Universal Event. God Source Energy has always been, but for the mere contusion of a bout of forgetfulness one suffers from in the human embodiment, and thus one has forgotten. Live not in FEAR of the Creator and the programming of what the Creator has been portrayed as, for how can ye but live in fear of God, when ye are God? Be in acceptance of the Alpha to the Omega and in acceptance of the Self as the same. Worry not what the World thinks of You but what you think of yourself in the World. Ye all who judge are but the judge of Oneself. You are as much an Energetic Imprint of the Divine Resonance as I AM. All are imprints of each other. All are interconnected within the vastness of the vacuum of Infinite Expansion, that is. Look at the I AM in Me as I look at the I AM in you; there is no difference, but for the embodiment one so houses, it is the mere conditioned human mind that tricks the user into the differentiation between all. Think not that one is lesser than the other. ALL are of equal Divinity. You are an enigmatic blend of all Races, Past, Present, and Future, a multidimensional facet of the Whole. All men are equal by Nature, made all of the same earth by the one workman, the Creator Alchemist of All. Be in Acceptance of all and embrace all, for all are your brothers and sisters of the Sacred Divine. All are Sparks of the I AM as much as the AM I You—for that, my Child, you ARE!

Q: The world seems to be falling apart at the seams right now, falling into the abyss. Will it ever get better?

Humanity is relentlessly Selfish. It has always been about the ME, ME, ME as opposed to the WE WE WE. Living in the matrix of a me-centric created state of Mind—a cultivated EGO-based persona rather than a we-centric state of Mind, of understanding the ONEness, with All. The smacked-on-the-head illusion, with the delicacies of 'being' separate from the Whole that one has been served with, instead of understanding that we are all part of the Divine Whole, has created a discord and disharmony by the mere slapping of labels on everyone and everything through the art of one's sophisticated non-analysis of one's experiences. If one would be of the understanding of the inclusion of all, and would work harmoniously with one another to resolve conflict to resolve issues, all in life would be vibrating at a much higher level of understanding instead of the dense "anarchy" that currently runs rampant on Earth. You sing from different hymn sheets; hence the song of the World is out of tune; one would have to be tone-deaf to think that all sing but in harmony with each other. It is the eclectic musical gathering of the conductors, the maestros, the orchestrators of the World, that cause the discord, for they have no intricacies of the fine-tuning nor the desire to do so, for an Orchestrator's sole purpose on this Earth is to create "dis-harmony" between all musicians, between all of humanity. And all still "Rock-a-bye Baby" along to the false tune, yet many have awakened to the dis-frequency in the octaves, having come to the enlightened understanding that this is not the way forward for humanity, for our Mother, the Earth and have thus dis-connected from the matrix to venture into the deeper wonderlands of awareness within, discarding all the conditioning returning to a far more natural state choosing instead to align their Soul Selves with the Universal Harmony of Song.

The Cosmic Rays of Love, Light, and Wisdom have been "deployed" and are in the current process of shifting the Earth's axis, ascending her into the next vibrational level of Consciousness. Humanity's vibration is shifting rapidly, and those who choose to remain in the darkness of their own voided Soul will be left in the misery of non-understanding. Understand the shift instead of standing there but dazed and confused in the mere flailing and in that self-suffocation, breathing life with the inherent breath of conscious awareness. Gone will be days of selfishness and be replaced by acts of selflessness; the understanding of differentiation will evaporate into the clearing of the dawning of a new day of the rising tides of the Light.

You are the Light of the Cosmic Sun. How can you deny what you are when you are all that you are and more! Share your Light, always speak your Truth, whether the world responds to your Truth or cares for it not, know that we will always walk beside thee every step of the way.

Call upon us, the "Kumarans," the Venusians, in service to Lord Kumara, for guidance into the Truth of the Light within. Never waver, but remain steadfast and focused upon thy mission, thy journey of Life incarnate. We remain in service to thee, of the Cosmic Rays of Divine Wisdom, in Love and Light.

My First Real Love

Like many of you, I was searching for love outside myself, looking for someone to complete me. But nobody completes you but you! It took me years and many trials and tribulations to figure that out, as honestly, I suffered from repetitive donkey syndrome.

Suffering from trauma tends to affect every aspect of your life. My relationships were all rather painful. I was so fragmented; I attracted nothing but broken "bird" souls. It was not my job to fix them, yet I always looked for fixer-uppers to see how I could renovate them into the likeness of the image I wanted. Like renovating a house, scouring through every room, every aspect of that person's life, and desperately trying to mould them to your liking. Why try and renovate all the rooms when the rooms don't want to be renovated? You cannot fix someone; they need to fix themselves. The more you try, the more you need to look within your own "home" of soul, for we are all but a mere reflection of the other.

Reflecting on the many failed relationships I have had in my life; I couldn't understand what the hell was wrong with me. It seemed Mr. Right had eluded me.

"No, Birgitta," Hilarion chips in, *"you eluded yourself and played Houdini with yourself, and thus your relationships reflected as such."*

In hindsight, I had a lot to learn in walking the treacherous journey of who I was not, back to a more authentic version of the I AM light of self. I was an insecure and persistent needy individual, having chosen these insufferable men-with-defects because I was a class-A sadomasochist. I am sure many of you have been in the same situation or are currently, not quite knowing how to move forward. If you have depleted all of your energy on someone—and remember this is always by choice, as you're the only one doing this to yourself—what do you have left to give? Absolutely nothing! If you do not truly love yourself first, how can you give love without expectations? It is not your place to resolve someone else's demons, is it?

But I thought it was. I was the demon slayer, the hero trying to save every wretched arse who crossed my path. In truth, all you can do is accept that person—not soak in their toxicity as much as your own, but merely plant a seed. We can't change someone if they are not willing to change themselves.

Relationships are reflections of the hurt and pain we have carried inside ourselves for heaven knows how long. It is merely the pain and suffering surfacing, requesting healing so we can rise above, expand, and transcend the experiences. The few relationships I was in have been nothing short of miraculously disastrous. Yet I now understand that all were my teachers in unearthing myself back to vibing in a far more authentic version of myself.

At the tender age of twenty-one and a half, having never kissed a guy, I met my first real boyfriend, Aaron (not his real name), in a restaurant opposite Biber café, where I worked as a bartender. Biber was co-owned by Emre Ergani, a now well-known public figure, a true visionary, and entrepreneur, having concocted many unique food and beverage concepts. I loved working there and met quite a few Turkish celebs, including the singer Burak Kut, whose music I sometimes still listen to today. He was lovely and very demure and sat quietly in a corner, always drinking his whiskey sour.

Aaron was Turkish, living in Nuremberg, Germany, but finishing his studies at the university in Istanbul. He was just over six foot, tall, well-toned, olive skin, and handsome, with a prominent nose. He spoke just about enough English, and I just about enough German for us to understand each other.

My mum was not thrilled that I was dating a Turkish guy. My mother never met him, and John had jotted us down in the address book as no less than Hitler and Eva Braun. In Holland, too many Turkish people give the Turks back in Turkey a bad name. But this is unfair because the mentality of the people in Turkey is entirely different.

After the first kiss, I wasn't entirely sure about Aaron, but I wholly ignored my gut and that little voice in my head. Instead, I gave him a chance. Mind you, I was a newbie to all this love stuff. I felt that once I'd kissed him, I was committed to him and wouldn't be able to back out—that I had to go out with him as I was already in too deep. I could have just as easily walked away, but being a messed-up green bean, I knew nothing of men and the mechanical workings of relationships.

The Pleiadeans have worded this emotion we call fear far better than I could articulate it for you: I was both fearful and scared of hurting the other person, but in the end, I hurt myself far more by allowing myself to remain wading in the soggy experience. Never be too scared to walk away, making sure to honour and love yourself in the process.

"Would you like you if you met you today? The status quo of everyday 'society' is that you have had to conform to the norm of fitting into the paradox of that created super-ficiality of society, yet that in itself is 'ludicrousy'—how can you be yourself when you nurture not yourself but starve yourself, killing off the roots of your divine brilliance of an existence all because you have chosen to conform by listening to the outside chatter and demurring the inside chatter? You reflect yourself in the outer world according to the conditioning of your inner world, which is an offset from the outward circumstances imprinted upon your Mind, feeding into your Soul. You create nothing but random chaos through the bombardment of the absorbed external chaos, causing your Soul immense malnourishment and knocking yourself out cold in the boxing ring, being the cause of your own Divine Frequency misalignment.

Any traumatic experience can set off a series of reactions incorporated in the hardwiring of your programming, for fear is the ruler of the shadows within, causing uncertainties and thus not standing in the Authentic Nature of your own I AM Essence, but a mauled and hampered version thereof, causing one a distorted view of love. Love is one's truest essence; it is the stark-naked truth of one's Soul; it is the Divinity, the essence of what makes you, you, with the chosen human journey, the way back to finding that infinite spark of Love Divine within. The fear of love, the fear of being true to oneself, causes a disconnect and creates a ripple effect of inner chaos emerging in the outer realms of your reality to an ever bigger entangled web of "e-motionalities," which are the anomalies within the energetic bodies of oneself, causing a disruption and a disharmony in the frequency waves, in turn creating blockages, and are thus the cause of extreme discomfort, misalignment, and the possibilities of dis-ease.

Fear is a mere label you have so firmly superglued to yourself through the sheer art of your human conditioning. It is non-existent but for the trickery, the Mind has played on you. You're not this body, but the Light within this body, and yet you allow fear to reprimand you and be the annihilator of your dreams, burning them and razing them to the ground relentlessly, all because you choose to remain in bed with fear, in fear of being your truth of Self! Cut the label, wash out the conditioning, and shake your Soul back to the vibrance of living life but fearlessly in the brilliance of the beautiful Light you are.

There is Light in every situation; never let rain clouds dampen your Spirit into the cold, wet heart of Self, but muster up the courage to find your way back through the winding corridors of the drenched Soul, back to the beautiful Light of day within."

~The Pleiadians & the Ascended Master St Germain~

Aaron was a hardworking individual with ambitions. He rented a space and turned it into a successful nightclub for six months, with me working there two nights a week on top of my modelling gigs and working at Biber. I became rundown, suffered from strep throat, and went to see a doctor recommended by a friend, to get some antibiotics. However, as his English was rather abysmal, he gave me an injection, telling me that this would help settle the infection without telling me what it was. I thought maybe it was a vitamin shot or an anti-flu jab, but instead, he jabbed penicillin into my veins, which I am allergic to. I went home, took a cold shower, went to bed, and curled up in front of my portable gas heater, hoping to feel better in the morning.

When I woke up, I felt like someone had bludgeoned me with a sledgehammer. My hands were tingling, and when I looked at them, I saw the skin had started peeling off, which freaked me out. I couldn't swallow properly and ran to the bathroom to look in the mirror and saw that I had a lump the size of an egg on the left side of my neck. I panicked and made an appointment with the American hospital in Taksim. The doctor there prescribed antibiotics, saying the penicillin could have killed me.

What they had failed to diagnose, however, was that I had glandular fever, which my GP diagnosed when I went back to Holland for a few weeks, staying with my grandmother as I was continuously tired and suffering from swollen glands. I loved spending time with her, as she took excellent care of me; she cooked, did my laundry, and made sure I went to bed early, and I was eternally grateful for all she did for me. She was an absolute sweetheart in her own distant sort of way. Instead of resting, though, I kept working. I had an admin temp job not far from her, so I cycled to work every day, rain or shine. It took quite a while to recover, and I decided to go back to Istanbul, as Holland wasn't the right place for me; it didn't sync with my soul.

Aaron was my first and longest relationship: give or take about three years, with nearly a year apart. My first time having sex was horrendous; here, I thought it would be all fireworks, like in the movies or romance novels, not knowing it's all a bunch of bollocks and overly exaggerated. After having sex, it felt like the insides of my vagina had been sanded and battered. An estimated 11–41 percent of women have difficulty reaching an orgasm with a partner for many reasons. This can cause low oxytocin (love-hormone) levels, with many women finding sex painful. Society has taught us to be "fearful" of sex, but your sexuality is part of your integrated makeup; it is the expression of your soul through the vehicle of your body. It is an outer expression of the inner expressions that make you *you*.

I was a crutch. I could hardly walk the next day. I felt numb and on fire down under, having to run up and down to the toilet like a peeing hyena. Over the years, I avoided having sex daily to heal, having a few days' reprieve. Orgasms aren't always guaranteed for women, and because of my childhood trauma, I was rather prudish in my ways. I genuinely didn't know what was wrong with me until many years later.

In 2014, at the age of 39, I was referred to a specialist who told me that I was suffering from vaginismus, which I had never heard of. Vaginismus is vaginal dryness, which causes the pelvic floor muscles to contract involuntarily every time something tries to enter the vagina. No wonder I hated tampons walking round like a stumped Scarecrow from the Wizard of Oz, as they were so invasive.

Many women suffer from this dis-ease in silence, not knowing the cause and being too ashamed to talk about it—but why? Who cares? It is a society that has created this labelled condition of shame. Women feel something is wrong with them and thus keep experiencing these horrendous vaginal pains, and doctors misdiagnose them, telling them that lube will do the trick. It does help, except lube makes your vagina blow farty bubbles, and you still hit and miss those 5-second orgasms. It's messy, but you'll still be in pain after the fact, with your vagina left in dire straits.

Vaginismus is often a physical materialisation of past emotional trauma rooted within the cell memory of your body. Your body and mind are connected, with your mind suffering the hurt, causing the blockages within your physical body. The mind scours the inner archives of your traumatic experiences and, having found it, sends a signal to that part of the body to try to keep the penis from invading your vagina. Traumatic experiences, if not healed, can cause all kinds of emotional kinks and dis-ease within the physical. To heal your deep-rooted trauma, you've got to realign yourself by giving yourself a massive dose of self-love and hugging your beautiful soul to harmonise your mind, body, and soul.

I tried numerous different things back in the day, but nothing worked for me. However, these days, many women swear by Membrasin Vitality Pearls, a dietary herbal supplement containing sea buckthorn oil.

We are energy; it is our divine frequency. If we understand that energy is constantly in flux, then we know that nothing in life is an impossibility. We can transcend any embodied trauma carried within the body, for we are fluid BEings of the universe. Once we understand fluidity, we become aware of ourselves as being infinite, and being infinite means that we have the ability to break the barricades that have kept our soul imprisoned within the stigma of that experience.

Regardless of the painful experiences, we've got to learn to let go. Our experiences serve to empower our conscious evolution and the growth of our soul, back to the love, light, and harmony of ourselves. The trauma we have experienced may well hold us back from living our lives to our full potential, and until we embrace the hurt of the traumas and iron out the kinks in our soul, they will continue to hold us back from living the life we truly deserve and want.

When I returned to Istanbul, Aaron disappeared, emerging a few weeks later saying that he had been working with the Turkish Secret Service. I never quite understood his disappearance, but it might explain why the guy in the minimart I lived above disappeared. I sometimes got my groceries there, always having a friendly chat—until one day, the guy decided to pinch my breast, with me screaming bloody murder at him and walking out, leaving my groceries on the counter. I called Aaron, and he said he would take care of it. The next day, the guy was gone. I asked Aaron what happened, and he told me that he broke the hand he touched me with and wanted to break his legs, but the guys he took with him for backup kept him from doing so. True or not, the guy never reappeared.

I also worked for a company called Sekiz that made handmade rattan furniture. I didn't get paid, but I wanted to learn how to make rattan furniture. I absolutely loved it. It's not easy; it's a very skilled trade and actual hard labour, with many employees working overtime to make ends meet. I happily worked with them on the factory floor and had numerous family meals with them, all the while trying hard to make myself understood in broken Turkish.

Several months later, I left the bustling city of Istanbul for the shores of the UK, wanting to make some money and save up, while Aaron went back to Nuremberg, where the plan was for me to join him two months later. It didn't quite go according to plan, as my mother had very different ideas: she wanted me to go to college.

To appease her, I decided to be smart and picked a five-month secretarial course. I worked part-time as a bartender in a pub and as a sales associate at Marks & Spencer. I finished college and passed with flying colours. Money saved up, I plucked up the courage and told my mother I was leaving for Germany. My mother was heartbroken, said I was making a big mistake and kicked me out of the house. But I wasn't going to change my mind; it was my life, not hers.

When I left, she didn't say goodbye to me; even though I tried to give her a hug, she simply turned away. My mum needed to accept that I had to make my own decisions, whether right or wrong. We have to walk our own journey through life and learn from our experiences; we stumble, fall, get up, and move on.

Whilst in the UK, I applied to be an air hostess with Gulf Air and Virgin, but I was way too tall for Gulf Air. Virgin sent me a letter inviting me for an interview, and I scooped it up a few days before I left for Germany. If my mum had found this instead of me, she would have bolted the doors and windows, handcuffed me to my bed, and put me on a leash dragging me to the interview.

Life in Nuremberg

When I got to Nuremberg, I had all these expectations of a wonderful life, but things turned out somewhat different than I had envisioned. It wasn't exactly moonbeams and sunshine. Aaron and I lived in a council flat with cracked walls and peeling paint. We had a black and white TV, and I loved walking through Nuremberg, as the city oozed such history; it is a blend of both old and new, with many impressive churches. The Altstadt (old town) is surrounded by a five-kilometre wall, which in the olden days was the mediaeval defensive mechanism of the city.

I have always been very resourceful when it comes to work; it's ingrained in me. I couldn't for the life of me be a couch potato, for that would defeat the very purpose of progression. So, having barely settled in, I went to several temp agencies and found a job several days later. It was nothing fancy: painting prices and reductions on signs for a huge DIY warehouse. My German wasn't fluent, so I attended evening classes to improve my language skills.

Aaron wanted to set up a business selling mops, and I sat down and had a serious talk with him, as I didn't want him to throw away his university degree like that; he was far too intelligent. He agreed and soon afterward found a job with Siemens. In the interim, I was also looking for another job and found one a few weeks later as a data typist for a telecommunications repair company. I worked hard and did quite a bit of overtime, after which I was quickly promoted to handling all import and export repairs of the many faxes, landline handsets, and the rather clunky old-school mobile phones that people sent in.

Nuremberg is the second largest city in Bavaria, about two hours from Munich. It was once known as the Capital of the Middle Ages, as it was the centre of long-distance trade and crafts, including the ancient salt and trade routes from the east via Venice and Genoa in Italy. Nuremberg is famous for Adolf Hitler's "Reichsparteitage," the outdoor rallies at the Zeppelin Stadium where his architect, Albert Speer, had designed a "Cathedral of Light" in the night sky. The Nazis correlated everything according to the stars and ley lines of the land, much like the ancient civilisations did. As Spirit stated, "Glory to the powers that be, that listen to the heart of the earth and the whispers and constellations of the stars, and yet it was done not for the betterment of the people, but to regain power over the people."

Hitler often said that if Berlin was the head of the Third Reich, then Nuremberg was its heart. Nuremberg was one of the worst-destroyed cities during the war, yet in November of 1945, the first international war-crimes trials were held here, lasting eleven months. I have been to the grounds, and it's eerily quiet; you can still feel the imprint of the energy from all those years ago. It's like standing in a vacuum of emptiness, for the grounds carry a hollowness—yet every year, they hold the wonderful Spring Volksfest, replenishing the lands with the energy of much laughter and joy.

I loved going to the Christkindlmarket on the Hauptmarkt, which is the oldest market in Germany and opens the last Friday of every November—a total treat if you've never been. I enjoyed nosing in all the stalls, and I'd wander through the market several times a week to soak up the atmosphere; it is genuinely something rather extraordinary. It felt very Christmassy with numerous ornaments, angels, and other little tidbits. I always bought fresh Lebkuchen, a sort of gingerbread with honey. I have never understood how people can drink Gluhwein; this heated red wine with sugar and lemon twists and topped with cinnamon sticks is truly an acquired taste.

I wasn't happy in the relationship. Aaron tried everything to make me happy, but as I realised many years later, it wasn't him but me who wasn't comfortable within my own skin. He knew that I loved birds, as I always popped into the local pet store on my way home from work, sitting with a mynah bird, which he got me as a surprise for my twenty-third birthday. I loved the mynah bird, which I named Beo. It mimicked Turkish, Dutch, German, and English. Growing up, I had a hand-reared green budgie called Dixie, which my grandmother had given me as a seven-year-old in Middelburg, Holland, but we had to leave it with friends when we moved to Singapore. I was gutted; this crazy-arse bird would never stop talking, its favourite phrase being "sex bomb." At the age of fifteen, my grandmother got my sister and me another blue hand-reared baby budgie, which we baptised Dixie the second, another natterer that would never shut up. He suffered from, believe it or not, arthritis. His claws turned blue, two fell off, and we were given drops to help him heal. They worked, but he would remain an invalid for the rest of his life, which did not deter this little fella. He remained full of life, with no issues walking around and sitting happily on his perches in his cage. When we moved abroad, my grandmother took him, and he lived out the rest of his life happily with her.

Not content with one animal, I decided to buy two Mongolian gerbils. I had explicitly told the pet shop assistants that I wanted either two males or two females, as I did not want them multiplying in multitude. They told me they couldn't tell the difference; obviously, they weren't very clued in because, as I now know, females have more prominent nipples, and males have a noticeable little lump at the base of their little tails. As luck would have it, they gave me a male and a female, so you can imagine what happened—they multiplied faster than I could blink. When I had eleven and the little one was pregnant again, I decided I needed to take drastic action. I kept the smallest and loneliest black gerbil, with a white stripe on its nose, called Pinky, and took the rest to Marienberg Park—where, with a heavy heart, I set them free. I figured they wouldn't starve here, as many in the Turkish community were renowned for having picnics and barbecues in this spot, especially in the summertime. I know I should have taken them back to the pet shop to be resold, but obviously, I wasn't the smartest cookie in the box.

As much as I had tried to mend fences with my mother, our relationship remained frosty. She had a hard time letting go as a mother, always thinking she knew what was best for me, but I wasn't a child anymore. I felt very caged up in my relationship with Aaron, which led to heated arguments, whereby I'd smash cups and plates to the floor out of pure frustration. I remembered my dad doing this once when he was mad; perhaps this was a conditioning of mine from my childhood. I felt I couldn't express my thoughts and kept a lot of that frustration inside until I popped my clogs, feeling exasperated with both myself and him. Perhaps I was still very childlike in many ways, not adult enough to talk about and verbalise my thoughts and feelings. I honestly thought I'd be heard and get my point across by breaking plates. And it didn't stop there: I even went as far as smashing the study door with a hammer, leaving a big, gaping hole.

When I was a kid, I dreamt that the first person I'd meet would be my Mr. Right, yet he turned out to be a beautiful disaster. Even though he had a full-time job, he remained in debt, and life wasn't easy at times, with me worrying about how we'd keep our heads above board. I was frugal when it came to shopping and crafty enough, making meals for several days and freezing them.

Munich

Aaron used to be quite a successful model himself, having worked far more than I ever had, yet he refused to help introduce me to the right people and said I should figure it out on my own. About a year later, Aaron was offered a job in the suburbs of Munich, and we moved. Munich is a great place, famous for the Oktoberfest beer festival on the Theresienwiese. I have never been a beer fan but enjoyed the fair until I hopped on a rollercoaster, and my shoulder became dislodged from the "secure" restraints because I was so skinny. I grabbed the bars so tightly, hanging on to dear life, and prayed to God for it to be over soon. When it finally was, I felt nauseous and vowed never to go on one of these things again.

Since Aaron wouldn't hook me up with his modelling contacts, I decided to find an agency in Munich. After several attempts, one finally took me on with an opportunity to go to Cape Town, which I grabbed with both hands.

Cape Town

Cape Town was the experience I needed to open my eyes to the world around me—because back in Germany, I was a house mouse with blinkers on. I never wanted to go out, which was partially due to a lack of money, but also because I didn't feel comfortable within myself. I worked and did all the house chores, cleaned, cooked, did laundry, and ironed. So, whilst the cat was away, this mouse played the field and saw and did things she never knew existed.

I plucked up the courage and called Aaron from Cape Town, telling him I needed space to figure out what I wanted out of life. In my own messed-up way, I loved him, but it wasn't enough. How could it be enough? How could I love someone else when I couldn't even love myself? It was one of the hardest things I've had to do, and I felt cowardly because I should have told him to his face. However, I couldn't leave him in the non-knowing, either.

He didn't want to lose me and wanted to fly down to try and save the relationship, but I asked him not to. With that off the table, he reverted to pretty much calling me nonstop, causing me to freak out, with me reacting from the viewpoint of my emotions that had gone haywire because I allowed them to. This was my first breakup, and I went through a rollercoaster of emotions, which caused me panic attacks, and I resorted to what I'd always done best: I stopped eating, losing a considerable amount of weight. I was an absolute pro at it, and it helped keep my emotions in check. It was totally my own doing, for I created this anxiety and thus trapped myself in fear of my own fear.

Anxiety is the anchoring of the I AM Fearful Syndrome; it is listening to the vibration of the words from others, imprinted on your own psyche, causing you a paralysis of fear. I was running away big time from myself and my created problems. However, no matter how hard I ran, I eventually had to face the music.

Still in Cape Town and feeling utterly lost, after a year of not talking to my mum, I called her and told her what had happened. She told me she would be there for me if I needed her. I bet in that head of hers, she was jumping for joy that it didn't last.

Aaron couldn't understand how I had just stopped loving him. He thought we could sort things out; to him, every couple had their problems, and problems could be resolved. Sadly, this was not the case for me. My soul felt constricted, and remaining stuck and unhappy was not an option for me. Sometimes we outgrow people, and to allow ourselves the opportunity for growth, we need to lovingly let them go. All relationships serve as reflections, their rays shining a light on what we need to work on. It was either leave and evolve or remain and devolve. I had tasted a different kind of freedom, opened my eyes, and liked what I saw, and the relationship for me had run its course; there was no further growth in it. I didn't have the guts to get up and leave until I had experienced Cape Town. Many will make a ton of excuses to remain because getting up and walking away would mean venturing out into the unknown and having to start all over again—yet that is precisely the beauty of experiencing life, of evolving rather than remaining stagnant and stale in our ways. If you outgrow a shirt, you don't keep wearing that same shirt, you buy a size that fits you to be able to breathe, rather than holding your breath and stifling yourself.

Aaron turned the tables when I got back, telling me he'd been in the hospital. When I asked why he told me it was because he had attempted to commit suicide, and they pumped his stomach. On top of that, he even said that I wasn't a virgin when I met him, which I most definitely was. Then one day, he came home early and told me he'd just received his blood test results from the company doctor. He just sat there at the kitchen table looking at me whilst rolling a joint and told me he had tested positive for HIV.

I stood there, pinned to the ground, unable to move, not understanding how this was possible. I got up abruptly, grabbed my coat and mobile phone, and ran into the fields behind the house, into the woods. Tears were streaming down my face, but I kept running until I reached the edge of the clearing. I sat there hunched in the shadow of the trees, rocking myself back and forth. I called my mum, who told me to calm down and that I could always do a test back in the UK.

When I finally returned to the flat, he was still sitting at the kitchen table, and I told him I couldn't understand how he might have tested positive. He told me he was fine and that it was a joke; he simply wanted to know if I'd been sleeping around, and saying that he had HIV was his way of finding out. No matter how hurt he felt, that was a sick and twisted mindfuck.

Aaron then expected me to have break-up sex with him, but how could I have sex with someone I was not in love with? But he insisted we sleep in the same bed. What was I to do? I couldn't just turn around and walk out the door. I had no place to go; I felt trapped.

After a few days, however, I started sleeping in the spare bedroom, and even then, I remained alert, as I didn't want him coming in. I stayed a few weeks to get all my affairs in order before getting on a plane. We tried to remain civil towards each other, but at times he'd snap and lose it.

Aaron told me I owed him money, as he had been paying the bills while I was in Cape Town. I gave him what I had, knowing full well I had to start from scratch. He always used to tell me, "Birgitta, I know you, and yet I don't, for you don't let me into your world and don't open up to me." I couldn't understand it at the time, but he was right; then again, I had unplugged from the authentic soul I was, to a conditioned and masked persona of who I thought I was, having difficulty expressing myself in many ways.

As St. Germain kindly pointed out, *"Really now Birgitta, ask yourself, do you know you? People don't know you. They know a projected version of you, a version you have created of yourself through a conditioning of that label called 'society,' just like everyone knows a version of themselves, casting that portrayal onto others. Much casting goes on in the world in the current state of affairs, for everyone seems to be someone except their own true authentic selves. Everyone acts and acclimatises based on their circumstances, and thus one has mastered the art of being a true chameleon amongst the earthly décor of the living. The journey of life enriches your Soul with the zingy and zesty flavours served to you in the mere form of experiences, enabling you to peel back the cloaked layers you have so divinely draped over yourself while walking through life. Everyone has a different perception of each other and themselves; it is a rather fascinating feat to see from above, yet mind-boggling, that one can create so many different personas towards so many different people, including oneself. Do any of us know who we really are? That is the golden goose question. That's what you're here to find out. So, who are you really?"*

Aaron used to call me his *"can kuş,"* meaning "sweet bird" in Turkish. It's funny because it's a perfect description of me, as I've never stayed in one place for too long. I have always suffered from itchy feet, not quite having found a spot to anchor myself to.

I couldn't take Beo and Pinky with me to the UK, and I thought it would be cruel for Beo to stay in quarantine for so long. She stayed with a friend of mine before being donated to a bird sanctuary in Ipthausen, baptised "Biggy" and being the life of the party. I don't think my mum would have appreciated a gerbil in the house; according to her, rodents bring bad luck, so Aaron set him free in the woods behind the flat we once shared. I wasn't thrilled, to say the least because he would not have survived.

Several years later, when my mum and I attended a spiritualist church in Buckingham, the medium came to me and asked if I'd had a small pet named Pinky. She said he wants you to know that he is fine and happy where he's at now. Bless his little cotton socks, as I felt terrible for quite some time after Aaron had set him free in the woods.

We did not speak for more than four years until he got back in touch with me and apologised for his behaviour. He told me he went to such extremes because he didn't want to lose his little *can kuş*, but he realised that I had to find my own way in this world. He wasn't angry, just disappointed that our relationship didn't last. Our experience of being with one another made us richer in understanding our own experiences and ourselves.

He married someone he knew before he met me and now has children of his own, after which our contact floundered.

He was a tremendous reflection to my then-naive spirit; he was my first love and an immensely beautiful soul, but we were lovers in a toxic storm, simply young and inexperienced in life and love and made mistakes. We were tarnished by the views of our societal generations, yet like fine wine each of us has grown and come into their own as the years have matured. I can only thank him for having been a part of my life and allowing me to experience part of my journey with him.

Short-Term Relationships

If you ghost someone, then know what you cast out there comes back to you in equal measures. If you treat people like s***, karma hits you back with s***. That's precisely what happened to me. In 1999, I met a South African who just wanted a bit of fun, which wasn't my style, so I ghosted him. Fast forward a few months later, and the same was done to me. Spirit did me a favour in this case as the guy had a nasty cocaine habit.

From there, I went from the frying pan into the fire, ending up with another South African I'd first met in Cape Town. He was atrocious, as I was not into rough sex, nor was it enjoyable for me, and I wasn't happy that my back ended up bruised more times than not. He first introduced me to the world of drugs and dragged me into this downward spiral. At the time, he was a frequent user and even ran the New York marathon on mushrooms, which could easily have killed him. He used to raid my fridge whenever he stayed over, literally sitting in front of it, eating whatever he fancied, mostly ham and salami, after which he would go back to the couch, lie down, and watch TV. I lent him money several times but never got it back, as he most probably spent it on drugs and alcohol.

I encountered some scary moments with him; I once found him passed out on a couch in a nightclub, totally delirious. I don't know how I got him home that night, but let me tell you, it wasn't a pretty sight. The things drugs do to a person, all because they choose to run from their own underlying issues that are screaming to be healed. He left that life behind him many years ago, and even though I have not been in touch with him for many years, I believe he is now happily married with kids.

I ventured on to another Englishman, although we never slept together as he suffered from psychological issues, unable to get over his ex, so that fizzled out after a few weeks. He had a severe alcohol addiction and also took recreational drugs from time to time. He disappeared from one day to the next, ghosting me whilst living it up in Italy. He roamed around in high-society circles, though most of the well-known folks I met through him were a mess and off their heads half the time, partying. I met Victoria Hervey, who was very sweet, although a bit worse for wear, and James Hewitt, who dated Princess Di. One night, being a little tipsy, having looked "through the looking-glass but a wee bit too deeply," I told James that he wasn't the jerk the media portrayed him as, and he thanked me for this. We often believe the illusion of what is written in the mainstream media, but the truth it is not.

As St. Germain says, *"People judge others based on a story being fed to them, yet know not the person in this human incarnation from a Jacques or Jimmy, it is a preposterous feat of that entangled chaotic e-motion running rife with the senses, all because you believe it to be so."*

I asked one of his friends later that night if he was Prince Harry's son because of the uncanny resemblance, and he told me that this is a subject he is reluctant to discuss with anyone. In the grand scheme of things, it doesn't matter as we are all of the same light, merely having chosen a different vessel and a different set of circumstances to experience and express ourselves through the art of being humanoid.

People have always called Princess Di a princess of the people. Yet, as she says, *"I was riddled with my own insecurities that I tried to mask, having been confined and literally constricted by the palace 'watch dogs' controlling my every move. I loathed myself to the point of wanting to bolt from life, yet to love oneself is to accept oneself wholly and wholeheartedly, for, without love, life would be a loneliness and a sheer misery within the guarded walls of one's created Self. I had to learn to love myself and find myself out of the conditioned mousetrap of my once fragile existence. We all think we love ourselves, yet often it is a conditioned love according to the upbringing and conditioning passed on from our parents and those that have come before us, with the firm trying to break my Spirit and having largely succeeded until it was I that decided to step up and chose to change to living my Life according to my rules.*

The focus of my love was on my children, to instil within them a love, a joy, and a resilience for future tomorrows, hoping that they would come to understand to live a life in their own bliss of selves, escaping the tentacles of the incestuousness firm, for love is non-existent within the walls of the 'family.' Charles had no love for me, nor is he capable of loving himself, portraying a persona that is so far out of touch with who he really is beneath the surface to the demise of his own existence. Feeling 'unloved,' a deep-seated melancholy washed over me, drowning me in the depths thereof, and the only way I could retaliate against the non-affection of the absence of love was by hurting the physical essence of myself. My Mind was a wounded portal of self-in-flicted pain, and yet it was also the doorway to helping me heal the broken fragments of myself, which was an ongoing process till death departed me but swiftly back to the light of the warm 'sliced apple pie' heavens.

In all that you do, be kind, be compassionate, and have a love for your fellow human beings, for all are embers from that same spark of Divine Light, often knowing no better than what they believe according to their own embodiment of that feat of human conditioning. Live life according to the principles and kindness of both giving and receiving through the heart, not by choosing to fit into a created society, making you feel uncomfortable within your own skin, that you lose sight of who you are, living in an angst of Self, traipsing into the corridors of a Willy Wonka World. You are Magic; believe in yourself and the beauty of the Magic that you are."

Everyone chooses to express themselves through their own belief systems. Everyone heals and deals with their pain in different ways; let them. The only way out of pain is to walk through the darkness within. Simply allow your suppressed emotions to melodically surface, like the musical rhythm of an orchestra. Let them surface to the rims of your soul, releasing and alchemising them back into the wisdom of understanding. You cannot commence living a better life till you choose to disentangle the blockages you have created within yourself.

As St. Germain says, *"Judge ye, not others, for looketh but in the thorn cast in one's own eye, that serveth as a reflection of the hole in thy own Soul. Seek life as it seeks you; do not deviate away from it, for it will deviate away from you and elude you, much like you elude yourself."*

Benjamin

In November of 2000, I met Benjamin; we only dated for about six months, but it was intense. He was a typical Englishman: my height, spiky blond hair, a year younger, and oh, those pinstriped suits and chequered shirts. He was an investment banker working in Canary Wharf, and there was an instant connection from the moment we met. After three months, I moved into his two-bedroom flat in East London.

I met him right before I decided to go to Miami to give the modelling another go. When I flew back from Miami on Valentine's Day, he had booked us a suite at the Lanesborough hotel, which to me was a bit of a bribe as I hadn't wanted to leave Miami in the first place. However, Benjamin gave me an ultimatum that it wouldn't work between us if I planned to stay in Miami. So stupid is as stupid does, thinking he was more important, I flew back and lived to regret that decision because we floundered a few weeks later.

He wanted to go on vacation; I didn't. However, two weeks after returning from Miami, we flew out to Phuket in Thailand. A bad move, as that's where the cracks started to show. He was studying and sitting on the beach, whereas I wanted to explore the island. Not my style; if you're in a different country, you might as well go exploring whilst you're there, so that's exactly what I did, which was great.

He wanted to sleep in separate beds due to the intensity of the heat; however, that was a load of bollocks as there was air conditioning in the room. Once we got back to the UK, he started to work till after midnight most days, making no time for me, saying this was to further his career. It escalated into a huge argument, and the next day when he woke up, he told me that it would be better if I moved out because he didn't love me anymore, but not even two weeks before that, he had spoken of marriage and kids. He said that he always seemed to rush into something and that things had just gone too fast between us. I should have listened to my gut and stayed in Miami rather than give in to his ultimatum. It took me many more life experiences to understand that I AM important and that I should be living my life according to the song of my own heart, not tap dance to the tune of another.

Benjamin had ripped my heart out; truth be told, I couldn't even think straight and called up a good friend to drown my sorrows with shots of absinthe in some bar in South Kensington. I was utterly wasted, but at least it numbed the pain. All I remember was getting in a cab and, somehow, making it back to his flat and falling asleep with my clothes on. The next day, needless to say, I had a massive hangover, was throwing up, and wasn't feeling any better.

I loved Benjamin and was in pain that he abruptly broke it off with me. I allowed it to affect me so much that I resorted to the usual neglect of myself. I hated losing weight, even though it was my own doing; taking it out on myself was the only way to punish myself for the stupidity of my own doing. I'd often curl up and cry myself to sleep. For the longest time, I hated myself, as I couldn't figure out what was wrong with me. I'd come back to the UK for this plonker, and he just ditched me by the wayside like I was nothing.

We often allow ourselves to get trapped in reliving an experience over and over again until we decide to snap out of it and move on. I was so immersed within that created experience; I couldn't see it as just another experience and move on. Instead, I felt lost within myself, utterly disconnected from who I was, feeling inadequate, worthless, undeserving, and rejected by others. I tried so desperately to fit in by giving in to the wants and needs of others instead of learning to accept and fix myself. It truly was a cry from the deepest part of my soul that wanted to be heard and healed—something I blatantly ignored back then.

My experiences became more pronounced and more extreme over the years, as I wasn't learning, nor understanding the lessons within these experiences, instead choosing to drown in my emotions. I was stuck in that same repetitive scenario, remaining in that same programming loop. It's a case of, are you privy to the light yet? Can you comprehend the experience? No? Okay, then, let's switch it up and rewrap the experience using a different scenario, a fresh set of circumstances, and newly embedded characters, to see how it will unfold this time.

Everyone we meet on the journey of life is our teacher. Yet we often allow the behaviour of others to destroy our peace because we choose to react rather than reflect. If you refuse to heal yourself, then know you will only attract more toxic experiences—until you become so exasperated that you either see the light and commence the journey to healing the wounded mind or keep running further down the rabbit hole. As St. Germain says:

"People often expect others to feel sorry for the hardships of their experiences and to be swathed in the warmth of that victimhood. Hell no! What are you going to do about it? Remain in your sorry arse victimhood, nursing your worries, until they become big kahunas, or choose to change your Life? The ball is in your court. It is entirely up to you on the moves you make to slam-dunk the experiences into the home net of alchemisation back to the understanding of Self. Expect no pity, for how would one ever learn if experiences were but candy wrapped and we would feel sorry for thee? Never argue with a fool, for the wisdom one tries to instil will only ricochet off their tainted armour of victimisation, until they choose to remove the armour and decide to walk through the abyss of their experiences, merely wanting that change to a better life and less toxic experiences. Life is simple, heal yourself, to heal your life, allowing the sunshine to return to your once overcast Soul."

Great advice, St. Germain, I just wasn't there yet. All I wanted was for my heart to stop hurting so bad.

Nick Bateman

As luck would have it, several months earlier, I had met Nick Bateman, formerly known as Nasty Nick, from the first Big Brother TV series in the UK.

I met him when I was working at a launch for some spectacle store on Oxford Street, got chatting to him, and he invited me to the Music Awards, but I couldn't go because I had my first date with Benjamin and I didn't want to let him down. Nick always used to say that he was 48 hours too late.

We bumped into each other again two weeks later somewhere in Covent Garden, where I was doing another promotion. We stayed in touch from that point on, and he has been nothing but a good friend to me. He had a room available in East Putney where I could stay until I found something else, and he offered to rent it out to me for £70 a week. I loved my room as I looked out onto the back garden, and I loved listening to the sound of the birds every morning.

Nick was a tad hyperactive but is a beautiful soul with a heart of gold. He always called me a "little bird" as I was never in one place for too long and had a gypsy soul. In August 2000, he was labelled Nasty Nick after being thrown out of the Big Brother house 34 days into the experiment. His fellow contestants discovered he had been writing notes about who should be evicted from their camera-filled house each week. He said at a London press conference, "I haven't committed a murder; it's a small error." Asked what he thought of his "most hated man in Britain" label, he replied: "I'm just an ordinary guy who took part in an unusual experiment amid scrutiny. I don't think the label attaches itself to me. I was taking part in a game show." He laughed off suggestions that he had smuggled a mobile phone into the house and said his early lies, including a claim that his wife had died in a car crash, were hasty words spoken at an odd time for the contestants.

When it comes to TV, the producers ask contestants to do certain things merely to boost ratings. One only has to look at shows such as *Love Island* or *The Bachelor* to see how unreal a reality show really is. Viewers saw Nick cry as he realised he had been caught. He said, "Those tears were genuine. I was sorry to be leaving an environment I'd been in for 34 days. I haven't committed a murder, and as intelligent human beings, we have the capacity to forgive and forget."

Nick carved out quite a career for himself, presenting his own show, *Trust Me*, with 1.8 million viewers. He guest-presented *The Big Breakfast, TFI Friday, Film Four Double Takes*, and BBC's Email Weekend. He starred in the ITV Network commercial for *Survivor* and was a guest on numerous TV shows, including *GMTV, The Late Late Show*, and Through the Keyhole. He wrote columns for the *Sun, Cosmopolitan, The Guardian, The Independent, Now*, and She magazine and wrote a book called How to Be a Complete Bastard. For people that think he's a dimwit, think again—he's addressed the Cambridge and Oxford student unions and fronted a television campaign for Cancer Research UK during Men's Cancer Awareness Month in June 2001. He also won *The Celebrity Weakest Link* and donated the prize money of £10,000 to cancer research. He's toured with *The Rocky Horror Show*, did a panto for *Jack and the Beanstalk*, and studied to become a producer. However, he's left it all behind and now resides in Australia, away from the world of TV, working a regular day job, paired with a quieter lifestyle in the sun—so good on him.

Here I was in early 2001, single and having killed Nick's 11-year-old pet goldfish; life must've been looking down at me with a wry smile. What could be next? While cleaning the goldfish's bowl, I must have left some disinfectant in it, purely by accident, so the next day it was floating sideways on the surface. I decided to get a replacement goldfish. I got two, so the other wouldn't be lonely, even though fish have a memory span of barely five seconds. A few weeks later, I got some more fish and a suckerfish; they swam around happily for a few months, except for the suckerfish, which seemed to die every other week, but seeing I cleaned the tank every week, I would have deprived them of their much-needed food... Nick nicknamed me the goldfish killer.

Several years later, when I was dating someone else and came back from New York, being in-between places, I called Benjamin, and he offered to put me up in his spare bedroom in Greenwich. I occasionally bumped into him as I worked as a hostess at the door of this swanky restaurant and lounge called the Collection in South Kensington. He wanted to get back together but had just started seeing someone else, and I told him to give it a go with her instead. As it turned out, he ended up marrying her.

I met Edwin van der Sar again, chatting to him for a while before returning to work. Many other soccer players frequented the place, mainly from Chelsea, with one of the players giving me a T-shirt I used for my gym workouts. I met many others, including celebrities like Jamiroquai, Peter Andre, Katie Price, and Angelina Jolie. One night I was saddled with Oliver Stone as he was having dinner at the Collection, and I had to ensure I tended to his every need. His whole entourage eventually went to another club, where he seemed to be having a good time with some very young Asian girls.

I met up with Benjamin one night after work because he still had this beautiful abstract painting I had created, gracing his living room wall, refusing to part with it (it took me several years to get it back). His then-girlfriend, at that point his fiancée, always said that she would never be able to live up to my "model" looks and that he would never love her as much as he had loved me. When I picked up the painting at his place, he told me to wait in the hallway, as she did not want me to come in. I am sure she was glad to see the back of that painting, as it must have been a constant reminder of me.

I will never understand jealousy; it is rather alien to me. Those that judge others merely judge themselves. Jealousy is a feeling of unworthiness within ourselves, an unhealed aspect we are choosing not to look at. It is lacking the art of loving ourselves, for those that judge see not the thorn within their own eyes, but look to see the reflected thorns in others. As Archangel Jophiel says, *"Worries and doubts cloud the judgement of oneself, falling into that trap of feeding one's own illusion—rise above, raise the vibe one breath at a time, into a state of becoming more aware of yourself and your own experiences and seeing how far you have come. One needs to air the dirty linen, cleansing them from the incorporated stains of one's experiences one has so chosen to hold onto, yet serve one but little, but for a mere incorporated heaviness within the Self. Seek some joie de vivre back into the lightness of Soul, accept all your experiences with a joyous heart, and one will in truth elevate the Self out of the created funk and drama at the flick of a switch. Remember to live a little, to love yourself a little more, and open the door to your heart to let the Light of Life stream back in."*

I know he has done exceptionally well for himself over the years but have no idea where he resides these days. Hopefully, he is happy, healthy, and still married. He was another beautiful disaster. But I don't dwell on yesterdays; I look forward to better tomorrows and love the path I have chosen to walk.

Logan

I didn't date for nearly a year until I met Logan, another investment banker. I seemed to be stuck in the same materialistic genre of men. He was about four years older than me, six-foot-something, slim, had medium-blond hair, and was a total pessimist, always saying he would die young as the cancer gene ran in his family. He thought the end of the world was upon us and that when we die, we're just done, basta finito (!); I told him it was all a load of crock.

On our first date, I was puzzled because I was sure that when I met him, he had blonde hair, and now it was a hue of orange. He had dyed it himself, and it had gone horribly wrong. Never date a guy who tries to dye his hair and fails miserably. It took me some time to warm to him; something felt off. I should have listened to my gut, but once again, I chose to silence my inner voice, telling it to shush. I merely told him I wanted to take things super slow. He was very understanding and said that he wouldn't put me under any pressure. 9/11 had just happened, and he'd lost a couple of people, one of them being on the second 'plane' that hit the World Trade Centre.

It took me a while to fall for him, as I had this nagging feeling in the back of my head that something wasn't right. The night before he left for Boston in early December 2001, he told me he loved me and that I had no idea how happy I had made him. He wanted to say something else, but he refrained from doing so because he said I'd hate him forever if he did. I mean, it couldn't be that bad. He wasn't married or anything, was he?

Several days later, one early winter morning at 6:30 a.m., as I was getting ready to hop on the tube for work, my phone rang: number unknown. I picked up, and it was some random girl on the phone with an American accent. She said she was calling from Boston, and did I know that she was Logan's girlfriend of six years?

I was already cold when I was waiting on the platform for my train to London, but I think my heart froze to several degrees below zero. I felt numb; I was spinning in a state of utter disbelief; the world was moving, yet I wasn't. I should have listened to my inner voice that had tried so desperately to warn me, but that I had gagged and muted instead.

Backtracking to our conversations and his behaviour, it made sense that he didn't want to sleep with me early in the relationship because he probably felt guilty about seeing someone else. It had nothing to do with the feeble 9/11 excuse he'd used.

The girlfriend went on to tell me that they'd been on holiday to Vietnam a month earlier. The penny dropped; he'd told me he was going on holiday to Vietnam and had wanted me to go with him. However, I couldn't take time off at such short notice, and a plane ticket to that part of the world was way too expensive for me. The explanation he gave baffled me: he said that if I'd gone with him, his then-girlfriend, who was Vietnamese, would have seen me, and it would have been easier for him to break up with her. I should have hung up on him there and then, and that would have been the end of it. Instead, I asked if

195

he was still sleeping with her. He wasn't, he said, as there had been no chemistry between them for a long time.

This whole drama happened just before I went on a Christmas break to Tenerife with my mum. I let it cloud my mood, and it turned out to be a rather unpleasant trip, not first because the weather wasn't superb but also because Logan's "girlfriend" called me several more times. I should have just ignored her calls. But being the sadomasochist I was, I picked up, listening to her rant about him, telling me he was a liar and that he had decided to remain in Boston with her, seeing they had far more history than he and I had.

Fighting over a loser guy wasn't worth my time, yet I thought he was. The icing on the cake came on New Year's Eve. I was having dinner when Logan called me and told me in no uncertain terms that we were done. He would stay with her because they'd been together for six years, and he wasn't about to throw that away. I burst out crying, inconsolable. My mum told me he was a jerk and not worth my tears—what a superb start to the new year.

A few days later, he had the nerve to call me, explaining he had no choice but to say what he had said as she had been standing right next to him. You're probably thinking, what a moron, why didn't you just slam the phone down on him? Because I was naïve enough to believe that he would change, and I still loved him. Oh, Birgitta, you loved him? Honestly, you loved a version of him as much as you loved a twisted and broken version of yourself, and you call that love? We seek so much outside ourselves when we need to look inward to the root cause of our misery. We are so afraid of losing someone, and yet we lose ourselves in the process because of our clingy and needy behaviour! We gag our inner voice, and tape it shut, causing nothing but a barrage of unwanted drama. And after the fact, your inner voice that you chucked in the back of the broom closet will go, *I told you so.*

After a lot of drama, he ended the relationship with her and chose to be with me, or so he said. When Valentine's Day came around, I got him a card, but I got nothing from him. He said I had no idea how much the card meant to him—then, several hours later, dumped me, drunk as a skunk, telling me repeatedly and in no uncertain terms that we were done, leaving me standing there bewildered outside the pub. He was like a Dr. Jekyll and Mr. Hyde, a relentless bastard with severe psychological issues and a drinking problem.

Shortly afterwards, he emailed me from Boston, apologising for his behaviour, hoping I would forgive him. As soon as I got his email, what do you think this idiot did? Bingo—I called him! We spoke for a while and asked ourselves if the relationship was salvageable and if there was still a slim chance for us or not. My insides were screaming, "No! Why stay with someone when he's treated you like shit?" Yet I persisted, going against the grind of my gut instincts, with my ego doing friggin' somersaults, having punked my soul whilst my soul was crying uncontrollably.

I always had these crazy thoughts going through my head: *Why isn't he calling me? What's he doing now? Did I do something or say something wrong?* My overanalytical brain started creating these wacky scenarios, basing actions on events that hadn't even happened. If a guy didn't call me for several hours or I texted them and didn't get a response, my mind would snowball into thinking all sorts of things, causing a rapid flurry of insecurities within myself. I suffered from that svelte relationship anxiety, which can make us ill-tempered; because we want things to go a certain way, with the incessant need to control the relationship every step of the way, which can make us come across as very needy.

You could argue, Birgitta, that's just immaturity, and you would be correct. Still, it was my current level of conscious understanding of how I perceived life at that current point in time. I lugged the baggage of old hurt and trauma, carrying this with me from my youth into adulthood. Because I remained in the same state of programming, the more traumatic experiences I accumulated, the heavier the baggage became. Of course, this affected my physical body; I lived off ibuprofen to ease the constant pain in my rigid shoulders, which caused me to suffer from throbbing headaches on a daily basis.

But I never let that deter me from living my life; I kept going, I learned to live with the pain, and it became a part of me for many years. I should have reverted inwards, silenced the mind chatter, and listened to the faint whispers of my muted and battered soul.

If only I had commenced healing myself then, I would have spared myself much unnecessary pain, yet I chose to soldier on in my rigid conditioning. I was afraid of losing him, and in my sorry state of desperation, I refused to let go and held on to that last shred of hope. Instead, I packed my bags and headed off to New York City, staying with friends until I found my own place.

Sometimes we hold onto things so desperately because we think we don't deserve better or can do better, and we are right either way. If we believe we do not deserve it, we energetically make it so. No one holds you back but you, for everything stems from the inner essence of ourselves. We fall, break, flourish, or perish deeper into the torrent of our own created cesspit of emotions. If you riddle the mind with the verbal onslaught of negativity, wailing "Why me?" instead of getting right back up and saying "Try me," then always remember you get what you so willingly called forth.

As the Master Teacher Emanuel Swedenborg says, *"If you can't deal, then you won't heal, for one gets so deviated by the outside chatter, the burlesque and pompous narrative of the comings and goings of the illusion, that one loses sight of oneself, remaining steadfast but living in the uncomfortable beingness of one's pain. Life is about self-improvement, pushing your boundaries beyond the barrier of that created illusion, beyond the veil, and returning to an Awareness of Self. You can only do so if you choose to move forward in life, not sideward like an aimless crab, much like the 'zoinks' of Shagster in Scooby-doo. Seek life as it seeks you, do not deviate away from it, for it will deviate from you and elude you, as much as you elude yourself, remaining nothing but in one's own convulsed and created convoluted pain. Know that you can change the status quo of your experiences at any point. Be that glowstick, hitting back harder and shining brighter after the fall of the experience—for all experiences are mere stepping stones to the Divine radiance of Self and of a remembrance of who you are and why you're here."*

In this entangled web of life, we are all connected. Your heart, mind, and soul are in sync with the energetic frequencies of the world around you. When we feel a disconnect within, we manifest a distortion in our outer world, which is a reflection of our inner world and what we truly want. We lack that belief in ourselves—and thus, feel the need to constantly seek validation from others, filling those missing pieces in the created void within, and giving ourselves some sense of self. We become addicted to the feel-good validations instead of looking at our wounded mind, wanting another quick fix, pumping up the deflated ego to feel a wee bit better for a time. We often choose to remain in the comfort zone of our programming until, eventually, we become so uncomfortable that we want nothing more but to change. As St. Germain says:

"We look at life all wrong, and thus we often get experiences whipped up and thrown our way, topped off with a dandy liquor of a created delight to entice the senses for a walk back to the authentic version of the you in you. If you don't learn it the first time around, Spirit will make it harder for you until your back is against the wall and you cannot do anything other than for a want of changing your ways. You are here for your Soul's growth, not for the mere 'pleasure' of remaining in your stupefied conditioned Self.

The Creator created you as BEing your own Creator, creating and expressing yourself through this wonderful vessel of the created organism of the human body that you have so gracefully fused your Soul with. Yes, it is a bit rigid, and one can feel rather constricted, bashing it black and blueish into a corner now and again, feeling like you have lost all conscious will in the matter of one's Life, yet it is the beauty of the human candy wrapper that gives one the ability to use and enhance all five senses that have been given to you. And what do you do? Use it but artificially superficially, like a bubble floating atop the flow of water, never venturing below the surface of who you authentically are but often remaining bobbing along in the superficiality of one's rather dim-witted 'amnesiad' out existence. Is it not time to wake up and smell the 'roses' of your rather wilted inner garden? How can one blossom, how can one flower, when one remains in the constricted creations of one's own created dramas in this paradigm of existence? Tend to the inner overgrown, weeded, and 'smelly' garden to let the outer garden of the world flourish in turn. It is a somewhat feeble excuse that you may have forgotten who you are because you have been bushwhacked like a billy-o on the head before arriving here having incarnated cold turkey. C'est une choix, n'est-ce pas? Stop making your life miserable and commence to create and live life according to the creation of your own Soul lyrics. Ho-hum to your own vibrant tune back to the very song of Self and the Universal rhythm of Soul. You need to find your groove and swing dance through the bad times, making life far more of a breeze than being crutched out and hobbling along in a sheer misery of Self. Have some swagger in your Soul, and care not what others think of you; care what you think of you! You are a magical creation of the Divine, here to be magical, to create magic, and leave a magical trail to inspire others, so care not what other people think of you, for it is merely their reflection staring back at them, on how they feel, and what they need to heal and ultimately deal with to create their own magical shit. Rebirth the Self to the 'marvelicioso' sensational Universal StarLight that you are—if not, you will remain but a dulled-out version of the truth of Self that you so authentically think you are stuck in the land of the EGO trapped comparable state of Self. Ça serait malheureux, n'est-ce pas?"

My inner garden was littered with debris, rotten roots, leaves, and wilted flowers that I had refused to tend to. At the age of twenty-seven, I read *The Journey* by the author Brandon Bay, a healing method based on the principles of neuro-linguistic programming (NLP). Brandon had an ulcer, and she cured herself by meditating and making an inward journey. She is quoted as saying that to be permanently free of any emotional block, we need to uncover the root cause of the issue and release the emotions we have subconsciously held onto by connecting directly with the unconditional love at our innermost core.

We all sense deep within that we have tremendous potential, and we long to free ourselves, yet there seems to be a kink, and something holds us back. If we go deep enough, we fall into the fountain of peace that we recognise as our own essence, eradicating all attached emotions.

After reading the book, I decided to contact a Journey therapist to see how I could get rid of my deep-rooted issues. These therapists weren't cheap in those days, and I paid over £100 for a session, which lasted two hours. I was put into a hypnotic, meditative state, had to get into a "rocket" in my body, travelling inward. If the rocket stopped, I had to examine and view the memory attached to it. I then sat around a campfire and asked these individuals why they hurt me, and then forgave them. Once the trauma was cleared, I had to search for the black hole and fall through it before returning to the here and now and stepping out of my rocket. The events that arose on my inward trip were my father's death and what happened with John in Kuala Lumpur.

When it was all over, I felt calm, but maybe that was because I was in a deep state of relaxation. Over the next few days, I remember being in tears, and my confidence had dropped below zero. I fidgeted but finally called the Journey practitioner a week later and told her I was not happy; I was struggling, as our session had opened up a can of worms, which were nibbling on the roots of my issues, inflicting me with pain instead of relief and release. Rather than scheduling another appointment, I received a fifteen-minute phone session. In other words, she wasn't concerned about the well-being of her clients. So much for that bollocks fountain feeling of peace.

NLP supposedly helps you reprogram your brain, but this therapist left me hanging in the balance—and of course, what works for one person may not necessarily work for another. Would I recommend it? Hell no! It caused me to become an even bigger entangled mess of nauseating balled-up emotions than I already was, as she left a gaping wound in my heart and soul. I emailed them years later, telling them about the horrendous experience. They were very apologetic, saying no session should ever be done over the phone if the client is in such a state.

Psychics and Phonies

Limping even more through life, having fallen to pieces within, and not thinking straight, I pondered about life and why everything I touched seemed to turn to dust. And then, I decided to consult a so-called psychic to help me solve this particular problem. As Spirit stated, *"Birgitta, the problem isn't the problem, but the problem staring back in the mirror being the problem, which is you."* As I later find out, New York is swarmed with people claiming to be psychics and spiritualists, who will rip off the naive. I had several readings, but they were all utter tosh, telling me I'd be successful in my modelling career. None of them seemed to be accurate. I'd started reading the Crowley tarot cards back in Germany, and whenever I gave readings, I always said the cards are just a guideline, for one is still the bearer of their own destiny. Nothing is set in stone; the cards are a mere guide to the infinite possibilities within your life.

My first run-in with a charlatan reader was called Lisa, whom I met through a renowned site called Keen, when I was still in London. I'm not sure why she wasn't screened accordingly, as she should have been barred from giving phone readings, considering she probably conned many people out of their money. She told me that a lot of negativity was floating within my aura and in my life that needed to be removed for me to move forward. Before I hauled my arse to New York, she had me courier her $4,995 in cash, split into three piles in a box. Why? In the hopes of keeping the swirling negativity that had consumed me at bay. She promised, hand on her heart, that the monies would be returned to me. She needed this amount to let all positivity flow back into my life. I had no clue about psychics at that stage. I, honest to God, thought that maybe there was some sense in a money ritual. I'd depleted most of my savings, choosing to give her the benefit of the doubt.

When I got to New York, I met her and her partner, both of Roma heritage; however, repeated attempts to retrieve my money were futile. Having gone for private counselling sessions with an intuitive healer, who helped me work on my self-confidence, I finally stood up for myself and demanded my $4,995 back. Lisa said she would try to get a hold of the church to see if this could be returned to me. She got back to me a few days later, and lo and behold: the answer was a resounding no. I waited a week, plucking up the courage to confront her, but when I called, no one was home, so I left her several voicemails demanding my money back. Then the line was disconnected.

I wrote a formal letter saying I would get a lawyer involved. She called me back a few weeks later, literally screaming down the phone, not understanding why I had to take such drastic action. I got some BS story, that she had to rush off to Chicago because her son had fallen ill. This woman was always in financial difficulty, never had enough money to buy food, and had ongoing family issues. She told me to call her again the next day, and I tried several times, but she never picked up, nor did I ever hear from her again. I went round and knocked on her door, all to no avail. I couldn't get a lawyer involved or the police because I had no proof, and I doubt they would have believed my insane story if I told them, probably dragging me off to a "psych" ward.

One summer day, I went to a street fair in NYC. In one of the stalls, this woman kept nagging me and the girls I was with to get a reading done. She told me someone was trying to help me get all this negativity out of my life, but she'd only been partially successful. She said I'd have to choose between two men. She also said I should have been successful a long time ago, but because someone envied me so strongly, it hindered me from reaching my goals. Was this reading accurate? In hindsight, hell no!

I wonder if these so-called psychics "sense" their prey, or maybe it just says "pick this sucker" on my forehead. Being deeply unhappy and feeling insecure, I was utterly desperate for my life to change. I should have been looking at myself to make these changes instead of turning without.

This woman at the street fair was something else: she instructed me to take my favourite white T-shirt and, using a black marker, write down all the things I wanted and that were important to me. I was then instructed to buy a grapefruit, and together with some rose petals, ground pepper, a bit of floor dust, and nine rolled-up $100 bills with a pin through each, wrap it all in the T-shirt. I had to leave it under my bed for two days before taking it to my scheduled appointment with her.

Two days later, we met, and she told me to step on the grapefruit and squash it; I did, and it went all over my white T-shirt. She gasped and repetitively said, "Oh, my God," then started praying frantically and told me there was a lot of darkness around me. She took my favourite now ruby-red shirt, with the money wrapped in it, and said she would take it up to her mountain retreat that evening. I simply picked a random grapefruit; I should have asked the guy at the grocery store to give me one that wasn't ripe yet. She allegedly went to her "mountain" retreat, which of course, was a blatant lie, and said she required another $19,000 to clear the remaining negativity around me. I refused point-blank.

In hindsight, seeing she was a rather heavy-set woman, what I should have done was grab my T-shirt and my money off the table and done a runner. Instead, this idiot meekly left, feeling worse than when I walked in. Here I was, $900 poorer, my favourite shirt gone, and feeling extremely sorry for myself due to my gullibility. She called me a few times to see if I had the money, and I told her to stop calling me. I bet she must have laughed all the way to the bank, having milked many others who crossed her path.

When was I ever going to learn? My desperation blocked me from seeing my own potential in that situation. The trick is learning to believe in yourself, searching within, unleashing your own capabilities and the changes you yearn for, rather than staying put and living in your own ultra-superficiality. Your spirit guides help you free of charge, no payment required, and have your best interests at heart.

Never again did I hand over my money so freely and so willingly or perform any of these ridiculous fake rituals. It was their gain and my loss monetary-wise, but my gain and their loss in experience. A little bit of desperation can go a long way to lining the pockets of a fraudulent medium, and if ever there was a gig rife with potential deception, this is it.

"To believe or not to believe, that is the question. Only you can choose to believe according to the energetic resonance within your Soul, n'est-ce pas? Creating often causes a distortion of the energetic flow one tries to achieve, with the results not quite to one's liking. Despair not, for it is only a facet of the Soul that is requesting healing for the energy to flow far more freely in the abundance of the desired Self. When one's Mind is bruised, one limps and stumbles through Life, yet when one is healed, one skips but through rainbow clouds and moonshine beams to sweeter tomorrows by believing in the true Magic of Oneself. Learn to accept your own Divine I AM Presence and to harness your I AM Power. You are the Light of a thousand Stars. You are a beautiful Child of the Universe, having incarnated to shine forth your Light through the art of your learn-ed and cast experiences, and thus one is but a beacon to each other, merely walking one another home back into the Authentic ascension of Self and that of the Planet.

Life is about harnessing and mastering your inner Alchemist and understanding that you are Energy and the Creator of all things in your Life. When you understand that, then whatever experience is as surely to high heavens bowled your way, you will kingpin it, because, you are as much the problem as you are the solution to every problem that is available deep in the wells within—all you need to do is shift your attitude, your thinking, and weave the wand of your inner Merlin, to conjure up a rabbit out of a hat solution, n'est-ce pas?"

~The Ascended Master St. Germain~

Work Adventures in NYC

I worked like a maniac, working mostly seven days a week. I was drowning in it, whereas Logan had the attitude of being too good for a job that was beneath his educational standing. I had no papers but found a job only three days after I'd arrived, working as a hostess at Nello's restaurant, run by none other than Nello. I wasn't the only foreigner working there; there were people from all different parts of the world, from China, Romania, Morocco, Colombia, and Turkey. Did they all speak perfect English compared to me? Au contraire! I sucked at being a hostess, so I was promoted to bartender instead.

Nello's was a celebrity hotspot, with celebs being treated like royalty. Lunch entrees ranged from $31–$48, and a beer set you back $12. A three-course lunch with a couple of drinks for two would easily set you back $250.

Many well-known faces passed through this joint, including Claudia Schiffer and the designer Tommy Hilfiger. More often than not, the waitstaff would have to tell me who they were. Paris Hilton dined there from time to time; she looked skin over bones all those years ago. The one person I did recognise was the German TV presenter Thomas Gottschalk. No one knew who he was, but I did. He sat at the bar for a while and was a genuinely lovely person to talk to. Neil Diamond made it adamantly clear to the managers not to call the paparazzi while he was having dinner, or he would not be coming back. Nello was notorious for calling the paparazzi, all for publicity in the trashy *New York Post*.

One night, Kirk Douglas and his wife Mary came in, both lovely, down-to-earth-people, and when George Hamilton passed the restaurant at the same time from across the street, Nello told me to run after him and tell him that his friend Kirk Douglas was having dinner there. I had to run like three blocks before I finally caught up with him, introducing myself and asking if he wanted to join Kirk. He said he had unfortunately already made other plans for the evening but promised to come back some other time. Two weeks later, he came in for lunch with a beautiful young lady, even remembering my name—though I hadn't the foggiest idea who he was or what he was famous for, I merely remembered seeing him in several sunglass ads.

One day, while I was on hostess shift, some random, dishevelled guy came into the restaurant, completely ignored me, and took a seat at a table. I was on my way over to him when one of the managers stopped me in my tracks and told me it was Chris Noth. I was like, "Who?" He told me that he was a well-known actor who played Mr. Big in *Sex and the City*, a series that I had never and to this day have never watched.

On another lunch shift, one of the managers told me that Billy Joel was sitting at one of the tables by the open patio doors and that I should get him whatever he needed. The summers in New York can be sweltering, very different from the mostly cold and rainy UK summers. I couldn't for the life of me figure out where he was seated, as I didn't recognise him. When my manager pointed him out to me, I was surprised to discover that he looked nothing like the man from his music videos or the pictures I'd seen of him in the tabloids—he looked much smaller. But he was a charming, well-spoken, and seemingly demure kind of guy. People on the street were taking pictures and asking for his autograph. I asked if they were bothering him, and he told me that it wasn't an issue, as this was part of the job description. The sad part was that he ordered two bottles of wine, and a few weeks later, I read that he was in rehab for alcohol addiction. Being a celeb is not for the faint of heart.

I loved working at Nello's, but staff were never paid on time, as another of the owner's restaurants wasn't making any money and was draining his finances. He also had a severe drinking problem, often turning nasty to customers and staff. He said that it was difficult for him to pay me because I had no papers. None of us received a wage; we merely worked for tips, so why tax over tips? One day, I'd had enough and plucked up the courage to advise the manager and Nello that this would be my last day. Nello just stood there, not saying a word, looking down at his feet. The manager took me aside and told me it would be best if I went home and came back the next day since I'd upset Nello. What a man-child, standing in a corner feeling insulted.

It took weeks before I finally got my money, paying a visit to the restaurant, where one of the busboys called Nello, who then called the restaurant and threatened me over the phone, telling me to get the hell out. With his bodyguards on-site walking towards me, I bolted. He may have been rich, but class and intellect cannot be bought.

I had no lack of work. In fact, I had to pick and choose. I had a crazy promotion gig at the Milk Studios, which I found through Craigslist, and they had me wearing an 18th-century French dress with a tight corset, making it hard for me to breathe. It's incredible how women from that era could walk around hoisted in these dresses. The people that attended the soiree were all part of New York society; I did not recognise half of them, except for David Copperfield, whose skin was absolument flawless. At the end of the night, I was glad to put my clothes back on and be able to breathe again. The corset had bruised my skin rather badly, but it was work, and I got paid for it.

I remember doing an AT&T promotion at South Street Seaport on the East River, famed for its historic ships, museums, and cobblestoned streets, a nice change from the concrete jungle. It was a two-day job, and it was scorching hot both days. I burned my shoulders pretty badly as we wore tank tops and shorts. I wasn't feeling comfortable because I'd lost so much weight and was afraid people would stare at my 34-inch bony legs and arms.

I left my bag in the promo tent with all the other bags, thinking it would be safe. At the end of the day, I was looking for my subway card and realised that my credit cards had also been stolen. Someone had obviously gone through my bag, and I was left with no money except the last $10 I had in my pockets. I called my mum, but she couldn't wire any money because I didn't have a US bank account. To make matters worse, I hadn't done any food shopping, so I was left with just two packs of yoghurt in the fridge. I decided to get some bread and ham and was left with a dollar. Thankfully a check would be cut for me in the next day or so; however, I was due to do a trial run as a bartender the next day at Bella Blu on the Upper East Side.

So here I was, with no money for the subway; having made sandwiches and taken a bottle of water with me, I walked seventy blocks from Clinton Street to the Upper East Side. It was quite a trek, and because it was another scorcher, when I finally arrived at Bella Blu, on time, I might add, I was drenched in sweat. After my training session, the bartender gave me part of the tips and told me to take a cab home. I took the subway instead to save the rest of the money for groceries.

Liza Minnelli was in the restaurant that night with her then-husband, David Gest. They were an odd couple, and he was definitely gay. David wore sunglasses all night and was a rather peculiar-looking chap. I guess he feared growing older and hence had a lot of plastic surgery done, as his facial skin had been pulled back so tight, it made his face look like a porcelain doll. On the other hand, Liza wasn't wearing any shoes. Now, it was a hot night, and she lived close by, but the soles of her feet were utterly black and filthy from all the dirt she had trod in. She was brassy and loud, and bless her, she obviously didn't have it quite together as she was running all over the place. To be fair, both had been drinking a substantial amount, each battling their own inner demons. In the end, I didn't get the job, as they decided to hire someone from their sister restaurant familiar with the till system. But it was definitely an experience.

When it came to my work, I embraced every single challenge, turning them into opportunities, no matter what Spirit threw at me—but my love life was a whole different ball game. I was a car crash, daft and naive at best.

As both St. Germain and Archangel Michael say:
"The quicker one understands that life is a mere series of 'serv-ed' experiences and merely laughs in jest at the creation thereof and submersion of oneself in the enactment, the quicker one expands into the ascension of Self.

Life is very much like a jelly bean—either the bean got your jelly or the jelly got your bean, either way as the bean you've been had, for the jelly surmises to the challenges of one's chosen creation of the Self.

Much like the jam got your doughnut or the doughnut got your jam, it's all about how you tackle the challenge at hand, for a challenge is as much an opportunity for the growth of Self.

It's all about how you take the first bite, with either a jam squirt face or a save from being a jam doughnut face.

Life is a mere view of perspective and how you choose to toy with the experiences 'goalied' into your corner.

So, when life gives you doughnuts, eat them to embrace the full flavour of the experience and rise to the acceptance of the challenge to a mere sweeter and better tomorrow, by tackling the opportunity for the acceleration of one's growth in the here and now."

A few days before my 28th birthday, I went to the Veruka lounge in downtown Manhattan with a journalist friend. We were seated in the VIP area, and he introduced me to Jesse Bradford from *Clockstoppers* and Swimfan, neither of which I had ever seen, but he was a really nice guy. As the night progressed, I was getting rather tipsy and wasn't impressed by the music the DJ was playing. I walked up to the DJ, but she barked at me before I could utter a word, telling me she didn't do requests. I walked back to my seat, and some guy told me her name was Samantha Ronson; her stepfather was the lead singer from Foreigner, and she'd recently been signed by Roc-A-Fella records. I don't care who you are or what you do, but at least have some respect for others.

Back at my table, I tapped some random guy on the shoulder sitting in the upper section of the VIP area. I explained the pickle I was in. He went up to the DJ and said that Chuck Knoblauch, a former Yankee player, had put in a request to hear the new Eminem song. She played it, and when the guy asked me why I wasn't dancing, I told him I didn't recognise the tune.

We started talking, and he told me his name was Shawn S. He was a rookie with the Kansas City Royals. I'll be honest; I had no clue about baseball. He invited me to the hotel where the team was staying, and we talked till daylight broke. Nothing happened because I told him I had a boyfriend, and he respected that. On the subject of baseball, he said, "When I'm out there on the pitch, I have to believe in myself, and if I believe in myself, I know I can make it." I asked him if it bothered him when he lost a game, and he said that sometimes you win, sometimes you lose, it's all part of the game. He told me not to give up believing in my dreams, for eventually, I would get there.

He got me tickets to the game that Sunday, and I ended up going alone, as no one wanted to join me. I'd never been in a baseball stadium before, and it was surreal. I loved the atmosphere and thoroughly enjoyed watching the game; it was an all-American experience, topped with a hot dog and soda. Shawn pitched part of the game, not badly, but they still lost. After the game, I called Shawn and told him it was the best birthday present I'd gotten in a long time, and I asked him if it would be possible to get a Kansas City Royals cap. He said he'd bring it next time he was in New York. He asked if he could call me from time to time to see how I was doing, and I told him that I would love that.

Of course, Logan forgot my birthday—how could he not? Then again, most people do, except for my mum, so I'm used to it. His excuse? He thought my birthday was the following day. I should have seen his true colours many moons ago, but I was so stupendously needy at that time in my life; it's ridiculous. Instead, I spent my birthday quietly by myself, treating myself to a deli meal and having dinner at home, while realising that he would never change.

I hadn't heard from Logan in over a month and decided to give him a call. He told me I had left him a voicemail saying we were done, which was not my style. I told him that if he wanted to make whatever this was work, he should be more considerate and spend time with me. I was hoping he wouldn't stonewall me this time around, but what can I say—he was all talk, no action. I felt like I was in

Aaron's shoes this time, trying desperately to save something that wasn't worth saving and telling Logan that people argue all the time, but if you love one another, you can work things out. Well, B, ain't that a shot of your own medicinal karma right there!

Shawn S. popped back into town and we met up and talked for hours. He'd grown up in Iowa, in the Midwest, and still had that unspoiled quality about him that many baseball players lacked. He truly was a beautiful soul. He'd recently split up with his girlfriend because he needed to concentrate on his career and was travelling so much that he never had time to see her.

When it was nearly two in the morning, I told him I had to get some sleep, and he had to get up early to go to the training grounds. He walked me to the door and asked if he could kiss me. I was a little hesitant—but figured, Sod Logan, Shawn is standing right in front of me. The next morning as we parted ways, he promised to call me later that day, and he did.

We went to a diner to grab an early lunch, and when we were seated, he looked at me and said, "You look beautiful." Instead of going into my usual defensive mode, I looked at him and just said thank you. Walking hand in hand back to the hotel, I felt a knot in my stomach and had to fight back the tears because I knew I'd probably never see him again.

He'd gotten me three more tickets, and at the last minute, two of my friends decided to come along. It was quite a trek to get to Yankee Stadium, as it's in the Bronx. The Yankees thrashed the Royals. After the game, we went down to the VIP area. I saw Shawn briefly, we hugged, and he said he'd call me, but I knew he wouldn't. As people were leaving the stadium, looking back, I dragged my feet, but he had been upfront with me, telling me he wanted no commitment. I never got the baseball cap, though.

Logan eventually found a job in the financial sector, but things didn't change. He made no time for me, nor was he ever there for me when I needed him, yet I had to jump when he said jump. Well, hallelujah, the penny had finally dropped, and I stopped jumping like the little loved-up poodle I had been! Early November 2002, when the elections were in full swing, he called me, and discussing Republican politics with him was a no-no. He lost it, telling me I had no clue about politics and that I should keep my mouth shut. When he was younger, he had worked for a Republican Congressman, and Logan was the only person by his side when he died after succumbing to an illness, as both the Congressman's wife and all his friends had left him.

He said, "Do you know what it's like to see someone deteriorate right in front of your eyes?" Seeing he had an incredibly short memory and life was all about him, he had forgotten that I had, with my stepdad John. I'd had enough of his antics and got everything off my chest, which turned into a final heated argument, where he told me that I had no right to voice my opinion because I was not an American citizen and had no idea what I was talking about. He then slammed the phone down on me, and I thought to myself, *Good riddance*. I'd had enough of all his bullshit and his selfish attitude.

I am not a fan of politics, as all politicians sell their soul to the highest bidder, in the end only forfeiting themselves. Politics, as per the Divine Mechanical Quantum Healers, is like a game of chess, and those that have risen to power have not done so by being pure of heart but by selling themselves out, "checkmating" their souls in return.

It wasn't easy for me to move on, I had invested a lot of time and energy in this so-called relationship, and it really broke me; in my own twisted way, I did love him. I was wallowing in self-pity; truth be told, the only thing that kept me going was my work, doing promo gigs, and bartending. And work like a dog I did, as it kept my mind from wandering. Very few people noticed my sadness, as I would wear my usual mask with a smile. They told me I'd get through it; I was strong enough. It was the same old bullshit story I've heard all my life. I got so bored of it that I learned to keep my mouth shut and keep to myself, saving them the time and trouble of actually being there for me when I needed them—but when the tables were turned, they knew exactly where to find me, as I would always be there for them.

My breakup escape mechanisms kicked back in full swing, switching to living on "I don't give a f***" autopilot and turning my back on food and the gym. *Way to go, B, starving yourself is your ultimate superpower.* Is it any wonder I felt depressed? I lived on pure adrenaline. I might have had a candy bar here or there, and I could keep this up for weeks and sometimes months at a time—hence it became normal for both my mind and body. My body must've thought, *You bitch!* When stressed, most people indulge in comfort food rather than healthier foods. I hated myself and was savagely beating myself up and made myself physically ill, walking around nauseous, but I never gave in to the wants and needs of my body. Instead, I popped my ibuprofen pills like blimmin' Tic Tacs, which I carried with me at all times. The only things I could control in all the chaos were my eating habits and my work, with my body merely adjusting to me not wanting to eat.

Eventually, when I decided to snap out of it and stop beating the crap out of myself, my problem was getting the weight back on, which was excruciating, as I couldn't eat properly for a week or so. It would take me months to get back to some sort of normality.

"Everything can be transcended; every energetic frequency that does not align with the resonance of your heartbeat o' Soul can be transcended because at the core of it all you are an alchemical BEing of the Divine. Even though your created negative chaos of e-motions may cloud your judgement, and fill you with an un-ease of Self, allow it, embrace it, walk through it, and endure it, for only you have the ability to transmute that cloud of the rollin' negatives back into the absolvement of the Light, just as easily as you have the choice to remain in the flood of the torrential rain of ever-consuming darkness.

If you follow the signs and the bliss of your inner Awareness there is nothing that can fail thee. If one's inner compass is off due to the vehement bluster of one's clouded experiences, simply sit but in the stillness within, for when the waters have calmed only then can one see the truth and depth of a situation and only then will the path be revealed, for one has chosen to sit and breathe back to a calm of one's inner Self.

Life is really not that hard; in fact, it is utter simplicity if only one understood that by the mere removal of the learn-ed conditioning, one is, in truth, one's own greatest sorcerer in existence, whipping up life according to the Mind-fed status quo that you have so thought and thus manifested into the created desire of one's chosen outcome."

~Ascended Master St. Germain~

I look back at my younger self, shaking my head in disbelief. I could come up with the excuse that I was always trying to see the good in people, but I should have accepted the fact that no one will change unless they choose to. I should have been looking at myself, for Logan was but a mirror reflection of me, and I had been so utterly oblivious to the flashing warning signs in front of me that I crashed head-on, hurting myself.

I have no idea where Logan resides these days, but like me, he has matured over the years and is happily married, is a health nut and is in the best shape of his life. If I had not met him, I would never have packed my bags and gone to New York, so I can only thank him for having been a part of my life.

Life on Clinton Street

As I had to move out from where I was, I found a room through a friend for $500 a month. I loaded all my belongings in a cab and moved without a hitch. The room I had rented was at the back of the apartment, which was small and dark. It had one window, which looked straight into someone else's bedroom. I could have literally jumped across to the flat next door. The people that lived there were night owls; lying in my bed, I could hear their conversations word-for-word, not to mention their loud music, as the walls were razor-thin. The room consisted of a double bed, a stained mattress, no shelving, no outlets, no air-conditioning, no fan, and a dirty light bulb dangling from the ceiling. It did not have a proper door either, but one of these cheap plastic folding doors with a magnet.

As I moved in the middle of summer, you can imagine, the room was unbearable at night. There was no separate bathroom in the apartment; the bathtub was next to the fridge in the kitchen. The shower curtain was transparent, with blue fish imprinted on it, and the bathtub itself was old, with the water not always running or draining properly and, lest I forget, mostly cold. I always made sure that I took a shower when the landlord wasn't there, and if he was taking a shower, I had to wait outside in the hallway till he was done, as I did not particularly want to see him naked. The place was basic, the kitchen filthy, with only a few pots and pans and an old stove. The apartment had no toilet; it was located in the communal hallway, which we shared with two other Chinese families. It was bolted, so every time I had to go, no matter how urgent, I'd hope and pray no one else was on it. At night, I had a peeing cup next to my bed, as I wasn't about to go stumbling in the dark.

The landlord was Colombian; he worked in a warehouse and had this little scruffy Pomeranian dog called Polo. Instead of taking him to the groomer's, he used an electric razor to trim his hair. Poor sod looked like he'd been electrocuted. I liked the dog, but a week after I'd moved in, he peed right bang in the middle of my bed and then hid under the bathtub, knowing full well he'd done something wrong. I was fuming, grabbed the darn thing by its collar, dragged him from under the tub, and smacked him on his snout. I was forced to wash my sheets and threw bleach on the mattress, scrubbing out the pee. A few days later, when I got back from work around midnight, Polo was eyeing me from under the bathtub again.

The landlord wasn't there, and I feared the worst. Once again, that crappy dog had peed on my bed, and in a moment of blinding fury, I grabbed him from under the bathtub, dragged him into my room, and pressed his snout into his own wee. I hoped he understood that he should never do such a thing again. I was exhausted, and as I had no extra linen, I had no choice but to sleep on the edge of the bed; and because of the heat, the smell of dog wee was overpowering, to say the least. I told the landlord to spend more time with Polo, but he argued that he did. My weight was already an issue, but not being able to utilise anything in such a filthy kitchen was disastrous, so I went to MacDonald's every morning and ordered sausage and pancakes instead, with Chinese take-out at night.

I got sick of having to eat the same thing every day. I wasn't sleeping properly because of the heat, and the flat below me was also being renovated, which stirred up a lot of dust, not to mention drilling started at seven in the morning, including on weekends. To add to that, I had the company of bedbugs, which I got rid of a week later after they'd viciously bitten me all over, including my face. My landlord lived like a king compared to me: his room was renovated, had air conditioning, electrical outlets, two big windows, and even a fish tank.

The people on the top floor were a bunch of modern-day hippies, living in a three-bedroom apartment like one big happy family. One of them repaired bicycles and volunteered as a landscape gardener in Brooklyn; another two were puppeteers and travelled around the US with their show, and the remainder of the group were activists. Not all worked, so I was curious how they survived. They told me that one of the guys used to pass a sushi place on his way home from work every day, where staff would throw out untouched and wrapped-up food in the garbage; he dove into the trash and took it home for all to eat. During the hot New York summer nights, they often slept in their sleeping bags on the roof. I must say, they were a cool bunch. I had made amends with Polo and felt sorry that he was often left alone, so I made sure to take him up on the roof when I hung my laundry to dry after having hand-washed it in the bathtub.

The view was breathtaking; I could see the Williamsburg Bridge on one end and the strict Hasidic Jewish community on the other side of Delancey Street. I walked through the neighbourhood once, and it was surreal; it was like stepping into a different world. The men wore black jackets, white shirts, black pants, and black hats showing their side curls; the women wore long dresses or skirts to cover their legs and long-sleeved blouses, with many wearing wigs, for once married, they have to shave their heads. There is no mingling between the sexes; they speak Yiddish and strictly follow the commandments as written in the Torah. They stick to their own newspapers, and many have no TV. They keep to themselves and stay in their own community. Parents arrange marriages through the use of a matchmaker. Many young men are not sent to college to pursue a higher education but tend to work within the community, while the women stay home and look after the kids.

I am glad to say that I found another place several months later and moved in with a friend of mine.

Ellis Hooks

In mid-August of 2002, with everything around me falling apart, I was on my way home to Clinton Street and decided to stop at my usual local Chinese take-out and get my typical sweet and sour pork with white rice.

Inside, an African-American guy approached me, looked at me, and asked if I'd just come from a shoot. I looked at him agitated, smiled, and said, no, I'm just suntanned. I never wear makeup; I think it's a hassle and unnecessary—why mask who you are? This guy was overly hyper and would not shut up. He told me to take a seat across from him as he was having his wonton soup, so I slumped down on the chair opposite him.

He told me his name was Ellis Hooks; his father was of Afro-American descent, and his mother, Cherokee. He grew up in Alabama, Mississippi, and at the age of four, he was already singing in a church choir but got kicked out because he had a different taste in music. When I met him, he was trying to make it in the music industry as a blues, R&B, and rock artist. He'd been busking on the streets of New York City and then went off to Europe, busking in Paris, Amsterdam, Milan, and various other places before returning to play in Washington Square Park in Manhattan, all to keep his head above water.

Finally, in 2002, he met a producer called Jon Tiven through a stripper friend, who was going for an audition, with him coming along to support her. Jon wasn't overly impressed by her voice and asked Ellis what he did for a living, who told him he was a singer. Jon looked at him and told him to go ahead and sing something, so he grabbed a guitar and did just that. Tiven was blown away by the sound of Ellis's voice and was hoping to get him a record deal.

Ellis said, "Good things come to those who wait, and my time, no matter how long the wait, will come someday as well. We have chosen to walk a difficult road in life to appreciate things more once we become successful in our own right." Incredibly wise words, which resonated with me at the time. As the Ascended Master Lord Kuthumi says, *"Your path may have dwindled into the many back avenues of Life yet that should not deter you from the path you have forged amongst the crevices of your very Soul, for you are a fortitude of the Light within the Self, an enigmatic warmth of BEing, embracing one's challenges in the bravado of a knights galore, piecing the Self back into the heart and dazzling Divine Soul Light that you are. Nurturing the Self through the perils of shadows but cast, venturing and blooming back to the aspiration and to the trueness of one's Authenticity in the beautiful arena of the Godly Light you are."*

Having finished our lunch, he asked if I wanted to take a ride on his Harley Davidson, and I figured why the hell not. I'd never been on a motorbike before, let alone a Harley. The helmet was a little big for my head, but I loved the ride, cruising along South Seaport and the FDR Drive with the wind in my face. A few days later, he called me to thank me, saying I'd helped him out that day because he was feeling rather depressed, and I'd hauled him out of that state. He'd been so inspired, he told me he wrote five songs dedicated to me, which really touched me.

Several weeks later, Ellis called me and was ecstatic that BMI had signed him to their record label. I was so thrilled for him, as he deserved this break. His first album, *Undeniable*, was a smash. His motto had always been, "Have fun with the one you love and your dog." He had a German shepherd at the time that he loved to bits. However, as I was always running around and working, I never had the chance to visit him in Battery Park, where he resided, before leaving for Nashville shortly after to record his next album.

When he returned to New York, we met up, and he told me I was his fantasy girl. He told me he had some crazy women fans; some had scratched his face at various venues, not to mention girls went to see $300 per hour psychics and were told they would marry him. He wanted a modelling picture of mine, so I gave it to him and what he did with it cracked me up. One night when he was pretty wasted, he went to Kinko's, got it blown up to a life-size format, went back to the party, and showed it to everyone, telling them who I was. Life-sized Me didn't last long, as someone drunk at the party decided to tear it to pieces.

One day after a ride with Ellis on his Harley, I gifted him the autobiography by David Wells called *Boomer*. I thought it was an excellent read and very funny. I told him to read it when he had his down moments, as it would show him that there is always light at the end of the tunnel. Boomer used to be a pitcher for the Yankees and had transferred to the Padres at the time. Ellis stood next to his Harley, looked at me, and said, "God, this is the most beautiful woman on Earth, and she doesn't like me that way. Why?" No response from God, but you can't help how you feel, right?

When I returned to the UK, we remained in touch; however, he was playing many gigs and recording his new album, so it was hard to keep up with him. In the summer of 2003, veteran rocker Brian May from Queen was equally impressed. *"Ellis? Well, Ellis rocks— what more can you say? Must've done it from the cradle; that stuff can't be learned!"*

Ellis told me he was nominated for "Best New Artist Debut" at the W.C. Handy Blues Awards. I was hoping and praying he would get that award; it was a shame he didn't. He was planning to buy a house in Nashville and live out there, although he loved New York, but on the upside, his dog would have all the freedom to run around in the country instead of being cooped up in a flat.

As time passed, his number got disconnected, and the emails bounced back. Life goes on; people come and go. Sometimes they walk with you for a short while before continuing on their own journey. Each of us has our own path to carve out ahead of us, and we need to walk it according to the song that sings in our own hearts and dance to the tune of our own vibrational truth.

Rejects and Runners

I have been a reject, too. I met a guy called Gerry, the co-owner of a restaurant in Midtown Manhattan. He was also a co-producer of a docudrama with a well-known MMA Fighter—bloody and brutal, definitely not for me. After the premiere, we went to the restaurant for the after-party, and it had started to snow.

I liked Gerry; usually, I don't go for the big-bear-bulky type, but he was an interesting character. I got rather drunk and left around 1 a.m.; he asked if he could get me a cab, as it was still snowing. I told him I'd be taking the subway instead, as I couldn't afford a cab all the way back to Astoria.

We said our polite goodbyes, and as I walked away, I plucked up the courage, turned around, and through the curtain of falling snow, said, "Can't you see that I really like you, isn't it obvious?"

He said, "You don't know me; you don't know my past. It's better not to get involved." I asked him why, but he didn't want to elaborate, and there was no point in reasoning with him. He told me he was going back inside, as he was freezing without his jacket, and turned around and walked away.

I may have been wasted, but I'd said exactly what I meant. I stood there, somewhat forlorn, with the flurry of snow blanketing me. I was nailed to the ground, feeling like an utter idiot as he had rejected me so cruelly. I finally managed to turn around and walk to Central Park. As my jacket wasn't waterproof, I was soaked when I got to the subway station, but that didn't bother me. What did, however, was the fact that I had made an utter fool out of myself; I felt embarrassed and humiliated by the whole incident. Maybe I should've called him to apologise for my behaviour, but I didn't; sometimes, keeping your mouth shut is the far wiser option.

He didn't call me after that; my friend had spoken to his friend, and he told her it was for the best. Gerry had been a sex addict but had been in therapy to get over his addiction, including some other issues related to porn, which he did not divulge. So, his rejection was probably a blessing in disguise.

I have also done the rejecting—the most memorable being a former professional American football player. I met him working as a hostess at a charity boxing event, together with another fifty girls. We were all assigned tables in the ballroom; however, I decided to walk around as I felt uncomfortable with people staring at me.

Some big guy came up to talk to me, making polite conversation. He told me he was raised in Texas with a load of farm animals. He had his own sports marketing company and was a former NFL player with the New York Giants. He had been an NFL linebacker for nine years and was with the New York Giants in 1986 when they won the Super Bowl. In 1982, he had knocked out Redskin Joe Theismann's front teeth in a blitz. In *ESPN Magazine's* December 2003 issue, he was quoted as saying the following of his days in the NFL:

"Early on, we shared a house, and we had some memorable parties. One night, there was a guy or girl in every room and every closet, either sleeping or having sex. And that was a three-bedroom house with a study, living room, kitchen, dining room, pantry, and basement. Oh, I forgot the shower. There were two or three people in there, too. We were living the dream. We had two things in that refrigerator: Budweiser and what was called a strawberry shake; that's strawberry-flavoured penicillin for any disease you might get from being with the wrong women."

He was drinking one vodka cranberry after the other as if it were lemonade.

I swear to God, his eyes nearly popped from their sockets, like Scrat, the sabre-toothed squirrel from *Ice Age*—I was surprised he was still on his feet. He kept telling me that I was the most beautiful woman walking around there that night, but after hearing that about twenty times, I got sick of it. He just would not shut up.

As I'd already given him my number, the next day, he called me, and what I thought would be a five-minute conversation turned into an hour, burning up all my minutes. I was not impressed. Over the next few days, he was relentless in his pursuit, but I couldn't and wouldn't answer because I was working. He left up to five long, rambling messages daily, and I hadn't even known him for a week! It was ludicrous, and I refused to answer, feeling driven into a corner like a trapped animal.

I accidentally picked it up when he called me from a different number. He told me he'd been worried, and I said I'd been working and didn't appreciate the fact that he thought I'd been deported. He said it was just a joke. He merely wanted to know when I'd go to a Giants game with him. *In your dreams, mate.* But instead, I told him I had no time.

The next night he showed up at the restaurant where I worked. I asked the hostess if she'd seen him there before, but she hadn't. What was he doing here? He'd only said a polite hello before moving onto the bar. It made me feel uneasy, and I hid in the cloakroom, well out of sight. Thankfully he left about an hour later, and I thought that would be the end of that.

Fat chance of that happening; ten minutes later, the bartender, who'd popped out for a quick cigarette, came in with a big bunch of flowers. He had bought me a dozen red roses. With the bouquet was a card that said, "I wanted you to know how wonderful it was to meet you. Forgive me for being so forward, but I had to do it."

The bartender insisted I take the bouquet because this guy was standing across the street, watching in anticipation to see what my reaction would be. I was too stubborn to take them; if I don't want something, I won't budge. The hostess took them for me instead because I had to get a coat for someone anyway. The bartender thought it was a nice gesture; he seemed like a decent guy. On the other hand, I was beginning to think I had a stalker.

I had to put an end to this, which meant mustering up the courage and calling him the next day. When he answered his phone, he seemed as jovial as ever.

I thanked him for the flowers but told him he had made me feel very uneasy, firstly because he wouldn't stop calling, then showing up at my work, and finally because he had bought me a bunch of red roses. He said that this was the way he expressed his feelings. What feelings? I had none for him. He asked me if I wanted him to stop calling, and I told him yes, please. He kept apologising, telling me he had insecurities and struggled with his identity, and finally, I told him I had to go and politely told him goodbye. Lo behold, a few minutes later, he called me back, leaving me another long voicemail wanting to know if he had scared me and if he was a dangerous person or not? But thankfully, he left me in peace after that.

Davut

In March 2003, I waded into completely different territory with my next male experience. At the time, I wasn't even sure why I'd agreed to meet all these *"des hommes terribles"* experiences as per my agreed upon and stipulated Soul contract, but here I thought I had finally found Mr. Right. This experience went by the name of Davut, or so he said. I asked him if it was spelled "David," and he was adamant that it was "Davut," with his DJ name being "Da-vut." Even though this relationship was not significant, I mention him because the repercussions of the experience created a cascading snowball effect in my life.

I met him whilst I was hired to be the presenter for a stunt called the Bartenders Show in a joint called Etoile in Manhattan, where he was hired to DJ, but only lasted one session as it wasn't his scene.

We met up the next day, and I was dithering, as I honestly didn't feel like going. It was cold outside, but I went as I felt like my Guides were giving me a kick up the backside. They'd obviously not been in their right minds, the buggers as they should have bolted the doors instead. We actually got on really well, and he turned out to be very intelligent. We talked about life in general and touched on the subject of the Four Horsemen of the Apocalypse, who will ride when the "end" of the world is near.

Rev 6:1 I watched as the Lamb opened the first of the seven seals. Then I heard one of the four living creatures say in a voice like thunder, "Come!" I looked, and there before me was a white horse! Its rider held a bow, and he was given a crown, and he rode out as a conqueror bent on conquest.

Rev 6:3 When the Lamb opened the second seal, I heard the second living creature say, "Come!" Then another horse came out, a fiery red one. Its rider was given power to take peace from the earth and to make men slay each other. To him was given a large sword.

Rev 6:5 When the Lamb opened the third seal, I heard the third living creature say, "Come!" I looked, and there before me was a black horse! Its rider was holding a pair of scales in his hand. Then I heard what sounded like a voice among the four living creatures, saying, "A quart of wheat for a day's wages, and three quarts of barley for a day's wages, and do not damage the oil and the wine!"

Rev 6:7 When the Lamb opened the fourth seal, I heard the voice of the fourth living creature say, "Come!" I looked, and there before me was a pale horse! Its rider was named Death, and Hades was following close behind him. They were given power over a fourth of the earth to kill by sword, famine, and plague, and by the wild beasts of the earth.

Make of this what you will; I leave it open to your interpretation. It is a clear sign of the transitioning times we find ourselves in and very on point. For it is those wielding power behind the scenes, conquering and enslaving the people through a well-thought-out psychological warfare of creating divisiveness by instilling a so-called "pestilence" and thus inducing fear within humanity. Amidst the panic and scurrying, they seize control, commencing to regulate the worldly food supply chain, possible blackouts, and implementing a higher, far more regimented cost of living, making the people submissive to their will—all under the guise of this so-called plague. Yet the end of the world refers to the mere crumbling of the old and corrupt system, the falling of the current matrix, where people live(d) in the mind-fed illusion of a conditioned 3D paradigm—making way for the dawning of a new era, a new freedom, a new way of life. The four horsemen will falter back to the dust from whence they came, eventually being snuffed out by the blinding light of love.

This new experience shoved onto my path was born in New York, a mixture of Italian, Russian, and German. He'd previously worked in banking but quit to pursue his passion for music. He promoted parties but, for the most part, was locked away in his studio. He was very artistic, half a year younger than me, a few inches taller, enabling me to wear my high heels. He went for the T-shirt and baggy pants look and had several tattoos, including one on his lower leg of Yosemite Sam, that furry little bundle of irascibility who is forever and always running after Bugs Bunny. He was a tribal-tech/trance artist and had about eighteen record releases on his own record label and a popular house label. He played all over New York City and Las Vegas and toured for three months around the UK.

He'd been engaged a year earlier but broke it off a month before the wedding because his fiancée told him the diamond on the engagement ring was too small. He left her that night, leaving everything behind, staying at a friend's place until he found somewhere else to live.

The dude had heaps of baggage slung over his shoulders, and he clearly hadn't healed from his breakup. Another fixer-upper, another broken bird that sought out another broken bird to make the "broken" make sense in the reflections cast upon one another. Like attracts, like when you have blocked yourself emotionally—you cast out what you reel back in. As the Light BEings have often said, *"Constraints are but one's own doing, as are the cannots or any other feeble excuses to remain living in the vast constriction of Self. Life is the very thoughts you plant in your head, watering them into manifestation. You are the biggest constraint within the paradigm of your created life; you choose to state the impossible as to the possible equation of a life of infinite possibles. If you say you cannot, then indeed you cannot, because that is exactly what you choose to vibe out and thus back in—it is precisely a taste of your own medicine."*

I met up with him several times before we got a bit more serious. One night when we'd been out for dinner, we got in a cab, and he turned to me and said, "I hope you don't think I'm gay." I honestly didn't think he was. He said he simply needed to be certain, as this time, it felt different. I told him it wasn't a problem as I was happy to wait and preferred it this way.

I was not in the mood to be dragged into a similar experience as I had encountered with Logan, and I couldn't quite get a handle on him, leaving me feeling insecure. I may be a "crappy" crab, but I realised he was a complex person with stacks of layers draped over him. He could jump high and low, saying he was open and honest, but the contrary was true; yet he expected me to be an open book?

Regarding relationships, he didn't want any excuses, no games, just honesty. That's all fair and well mate, but as I came to find out, he did not practise what he preached.

It's not rocket science, but I should have realised by then that you cannot be with someone until they learn to let go of their own harboured pain that they have so duly sheltered within their hearts, and by clinging to the old, you cannot move forward into the new.

"If you keep looking in the rear-view mirror, you'll just be a friggin' trip hazard to the Self, a crash-bandicoot, and a darn fine klutz of your own makin'. Feelings are just temporary visitors; they come and go, much like the ebb and flow of water, like the waves crashing onto the shoreline and gently receding, leaving no trace of what was but yet what can become. Be in that ebb and flow of Self, be fluid, live in the moment, create in the NOW, alchemise the superfluous baggage, be grateful for all your experiences, and stop making a rod for your own back, because many of you get so hung up on your experiences, that all you do is hang yourself out to dry. Ain't no one the culprit, but you—you're the Cap'n of yer own Soul, cause it sure as hell ain't me. The miracle of Life is letting go of soakin' in that cold tub of the past, creating in the breath of the present moment for the shaping of better tomorrows—and if you say you ain't worth it or come with that illustrious deadbeat phrase of, it's not possible or yammering I can't, then my Child, you haven't quite grasped the flair and finesse of the wondrous Alchemical BEing that you are. Forget not that you are a 'bouncilicious' LightStar of Energetic Awesomeness—so learn to harness your own Divine I AM Power according to the will of thine own Self be True."

~The Ascended Master St. Germain~

The guy who ran the Bartenders Show knew I was in the country on a visa waiver. I met up with his lawyer, who advised me that he would be able to turn my visa into a work permit, but I'd need to leave the country and apply for a six-month tourist visa so that he could change it to a work permit once I returned. There was a possibility that a tourist visa would be refused; however, I could return on my waiver, which would be my only option. It seemed pretty straightforward, but as it turned out, a whole load of kak was about to rain down on me.

As the Bartenders Show was slow to get off the ground, I started working as a bartender for a Turkish restaurant called Sultan on the Upper East Side, which is now closed. I lasted two months before finding something else. I have always been a people connector; if friends were looking for a job, I usually got them hooked up, and I got one of my friends a job as a hostess there. The bar was in a right state. I cleaned it out rigorously, as the bottles had been collecting dust and debris over the years. Some people can live and work in their own created filth. I cannot work or live in either.

While cleaning up, out of the corner of my eye, I saw something scurrying over the counter. Shit, a roach! I asked for insect spray, hoping this was a one-off, but hell no, there were loads more. As time progressed, they ran over the bar counter more frequently, and I had to make sure to kill them before a customer saw one. I hate roaches; they scare the living daylights out of me. Walking home on a hot New York summer's night, you'll find plenty of roaches running around severely littered areas. Trust me when I say that they're HUGE! I used to pass them rapidly as you can bet your arse that I would be screaming bloody murder if one touched me.

I'd never had my dinner in the bar, nor had I entered the kitchen the first few weeks I'd been working there—but when I did, I ran straight back out. Roaches were scurrying along the kitchen walls, and the chef did not seem bothered. How fresh and edible can the food be, not to mention what if a roach made its way into the food served to customers?

Oh, but it did. One of the regulars found a roach served in his food. He must have been disgusted because he got up, left, and never came back. The owner did get in pesticide control overnight, but it didn't help much. My friend only lasted two weeks, and her replacement was a complete ditz. I don't know where the owner picked this one up, but she was nineteen and from Hollywood. Apparently, after I'd left, she performed a lap dance for both the owner and his lawyer, and hence she was given a room above the premises. Eventually, she got kicked out because she'd gotten a Chihuahua puppy, which she kept hidden in her handbag. Furthermore, she was never on time for work or didn't bother showing up, leaving me to be both the bartender and hostess most evenings.

One night, a few of the owner's Turkish friends came in, and one was a coffee reader. He told me to get my coffee grounds read. I was a little sceptical because while I believe in many other things, I did not believe in this, but I went anyway.

The reader told me the person I was in a relationship with was not for me; it wouldn't last. She said my life would not be easy, as she saw many hills and challenges throughout my life, but it would get better once I had conquered all the hills and come out the other side. That sucked. In other words, my life would be shit. I mean, who wants to hear that? The person I would eventually end up with was dark-haired; however, we would only get to know each other briefly before being separated for many years, eventually reuniting again—what a load of crock.

I got hired as a bartender at Plumeri, which was my all-time favourite place. It was an absolute privilege and a joy to have been able to work there. It meant working in two places and still doing promotion work on top of that. I felt like this eternal gerbil on a treadmill.

Most of the clientele at Plumeri were bankers and brokers, but quite a few famous people popped in, too; the singer Anastacia; supermodel Christy Turlington; Monica Lewinsky; Kevin Bacon; and the then-mayor of New York, Mike Bloomberg. He was an absolute prick towards staff. You'd know exactly when he was on his way; you could hear the sirens of his entourage a mile away. It was amusing because he is small compared to his beefcake bodyguards and myself. He had the privilege of having free lunch, yet he was too stingy to ever leave a tip for the wait staff, so no one wanted to serve him. Shame on you, Mr. Bloomberg, all that money, and you can't even be bothered to leave a tip.

The chef helped me open a bank account, as he knew the bank manager across the street. I had wads of cash stashed in an envelope, hidden under a pile of neatly folded clothes in my closet. All they required was a copy of my passport, et voila, my bank account was opened without a hitch.

Christmas parties meant good money, and it kept me busy. If I was bartending on my own together with the barback, I made sure to give him half of my tips. I have always done this, as all those I worked with were South Americans and had families to feed, and they worked tirelessly for long hours on end—to receive a mere 20 percent of the tips I made was not right. As Spirit always said, "*There is no difference, but for the embodiment one so houses, it is but the mere conditioned human mind that tricks the user into thinking there is a differentiation between all. Think not that one is lesser than the other, for even though ALL vibrate at a different level of understanding, ALL are of equal Divinity.*"

I couldn't meet up with Davut before flying back to the UK as he had a family emergency. I tried calling him on the way to the airport, but he'd switched off his phone. I was gutted, as I had no idea when I'd return to New York.

Back in the UK

In April 2003, I landed back in the UK's rain, cold, and gloom, staying with my mum in Buckingham. Not one to rest on my laurels, I found work within two days as a receptionist in Milton Keynes.

In May 2003, I trotted off to the US Consulate in London, where I was strip-searched. Once inside this fortress, I joined a massive queue, with a lady checking to see if everyone had completed their forms, but of course, as luck would have it, they had omitted to send me one. The voice in the back of my head told me I had made one fatal mistake on the form: I stated that I wanted to visit my boyfriend rather than visiting friends and travelling through the US. I figured honesty was the best policy.

Three hours later, I was called to the counter. Before I could even say hello, the elderly gentleman looked at me and brusquely told me he wasn't going to issue me a visa, as I didn't have a mortgage, I hadn't lived long enough in the UK, and I had an American boyfriend. He told me there had been no need for me to apply for a visa, as I could have easily travelled on my waiver. I wasn't about to tell him why I needed a visa. Instead, I fibbed and told him a lawyer in New Jersey advised me to apply for a tourist visa as I already had four entry stamps in my passport. He responded that the lawyer was incorrect. When I told him I'd simply travel on my waiver again, he looked at me, smirked, and said, once you have applied for a visa, you are not permitted to re-enter the country on your waiver. He then stamped my passport, which was the end of that.

I was close to tears. I could not believe it; here I was, a Dutch citizen, treated worse than a dog by an American in London. I ran out of the consulate and called Davut. He told me not to worry and to reapply. He would come over to the UK if I was refused again. But that wasn't as simple as it sounded because he'd just been confronted with a court case from his days as an investment banker and wasn't allowed to leave the country until the case was settled, not to mention that he had a potential fifteen-year prison sentence hanging over his head. I couldn't believe he would want to do that for me. Inwardly, my heart skipped a beat because none of the guys I had been with had ever done anything for me. Could I be that lucky?

Reapplying cost me more fees. I told them I couldn't understand why I'd been refused, and the woman on the other side of the phone said to me that it solely depended on the mood of the immigration officer. If you've got one in a good mood, they'll issue you a visa, but if you've got one that got out of the wrong side of the bed that morning, then you can totally forget it. I told her I didn't think that was fair. She agreed but said they liked having that power over people.

This time the appointment was on the 25th of June, which coincided with my 29th birthday. You think I'd be lucky, right? Hell no! I thought a female immigration officer would understand my plight and be far more reasonable. I came well-prepared, taking my phone bills, bank statements, wage slips, and my mum's mortgage agreement with me. I told her I had been refused a visa because I didn't have a mortgage. She told me this was incorrect; it was purely because I had an American boyfriend. She queried the status of the relationship, and I responded that it had hit the rocks. She didn't bother checking the rest of my papers, even though I had a faxed invitation from a friend in the US; she said I could have forged the fax myself. She stamped the back of my passport, stating I hadn't lived long enough in the UK, and told me to reapply in a year. I asked if it would be possible to travel on my waiver, and she said I could try, but they might deport me back to the UK.

It was soul-destroying; I was devastated and walked out in tears, wandering aimlessly through London, trying to collect my shattered thoughts.

At that point, I didn't see life as being fair. No matter how much I asked Spirit for help, they seemed "unavailable" and closed for maintenance on an ongoing basis—and yet they had shown me the warning signs, which I blatantly chose to ignore, wanting the rainbows and fluffy marshmallows kind of happiness. It all comes down to how aware we choose to be living our lives and how we often ignore our inner voice that is desperately trying to get our attention—to no avail as we merely snub it.

I was most probably borderline depressed, as I felt utterly lost within myself, crying myself to sleep at night, overwhelmed by everything. Having lived on my own for several years, and being back under my mother's roof and strict rules was a difficult adjustment. I used to shout and cuss at God and my Guides, telling them that life wasn't fair and that I didn't deserve this. They merely looked at me, shrugged their shoulders, and said:

"This is exactly what you deserve because you chose not to listen. You chose to ignore the flashing warning signs and thus swerved off the road and collided head-on into the egotistical mountainside of the EGO, so now handle the repercussions of your choices. It is not us that have created the piddle you duly find yourself in; it is very much your own. You decided to burn your arse in the fire; it is but duly thy own making to decide to heal the blisters thereof, non? The cycle of life starts and ends time and time again; however, in this current chosen life, what one does with the time given is solely up to you. You blow your own wondrous creations of cosmic bubbles within the cosmic bubble that is your world. You are the Creator of your chosen experiences, the outcomes pertaining to certain life truths one can either choose to face or dodge. Suck it up, buttercup, and get out of your own created pile of chaos."

Within every challenge presented lies one's greatest opportunity for growth. Change is inevitable, that is the nature of life, yet growth remains a choice. Great, but I wasn't feeling it, and I chose to stay amid the chaos and drown in the deluge of the experience.

I told my Guides that my whole life was in New York; everything I had was there, from my friends to my clothes and personal belongings. I had a debt to clear and nothing but the ample clothes in my suitcase. They merely laughed, and as St. Germain kindly points out:

"Oh, Birgitta, my Child, these are just material aspects. You are alive; you can create from this point forward, seek ye but a way out, then search ye but yourself within,

to uncover the wisdom and peace you so desperately seek but in the outer realms of your existence. You cannot be an 'experience' hoarder and expect to live a life less ordinary, n'est-ce pas? All jokes aside, mes chéris, but you are a Divine BEing of the Light, so keep the vibrance in your Soul light instead of weeping away through the heaviness instilled by the mere feat of one's created deluge of soggy experiences. Stop living in the doldrums, and be a wee bit kinder to yourself. Release the patterning that has held you back in the ease and breath of the gentle breeze, allowing yourself to live in a state of a more authentic version of yourself. Heal and deal with the pain, walk through the created barriers, allowing you to move past the pain of your own tormented Mind and limping Soul.

Stop hoarding, piling, and impressing the junk upon the very heart of your Soul, my Child. It is much like holding your breath underwater and refusing to come up for air; thus choosing to remain but drowning and spluttering in your own created drama, causing you to flail around like a chicken on steroids within that very created storm, causing nothing but chaos in both your inner and outer worlds. C'est malheureux, mais tout peut être surmonté, mon petit filous. Is it of servitude, or is it more of a flair for having the egotistical vigour of hiding within the very realms of yourself? One is but a master at the game of eternal hide-and-seek with the Self, a trickster per se. Open the lotus of your beautiful divine sacred heart centre, to let the light of love back in, to see past the quizzical grand illusion of this created reality that has you utterly and quizzically stupefied with a sense of loss within the Self. Let go of the remnants of fear that have held you captive in the shadows of yourself and dare to bask back in the Cosmic Sun of the Truth of the Eternal Self. Walk through it with a heartfelt candour and grace, healing and alchemising all back into the fortitude of love and understanding, coming out in an enlightened delight of lightness returning to the heart and light of Self, rather than remaining but duly stained and encrusted like a cracked and withered porcelain doll with a heaviness to thy Soul.

Believe in your heart that you are meant to live a life full of passion, magic, miracles, and popsicle rainbows, and it will so forth spring into existence. For the power of the mind, once unhinged from the dam brigade of the illusion of the drama one has so lovingly soaked the mind in, runs but free like the flowing rivers of the beautiful divine cosmic heart within, and thus it reflects and flows but abundantly without—for one is merely a babe magnet for the chosen ingredients in the batter one so freely whips up into manifestation, n'est-ce pas?"

Wise words, but I didn't know this back then. I felt like I was hanging off the edge of a cliff, and we all know the expression: desperate times call for desperate measures.

I ended up scrolling through the local newspaper job section and saw several ads hiring escorts. I thought, *Why not.* I decided to give one of them a call, and the woman on the other end told me that often guys don't want sex, just someone to talk to. It was perfect, as I did not want to sleep with them, but getting paid to chat was great. My mum was very aware and told me that if I felt I needed to do this, she would support me.

I started a few days later at £50ph, which back in 2004 was a lot of money. A car picked me up, with the driver, the woman who hired me, and another girl already in the backseat. She had been an escort for quite some time, and I asked her if it was true that most guys don't want sex. She looked at me and said, "Honey, most guys do want sex."

Oh, shit! How could I have been so naive as to believe the woman on the phone? We drove off to a first client, somewhere in a remote village on the outskirts of Northampton, and of course, they threw me to the lions, straight in the deep end. They would be waiting in the car outside and knock on the door after the hour was up. The guy lived in a beautifully renovated farmhouse; he was English and had been in a long-term relationship. However, his girlfriend was out of town for the weekend—so sure, why not hire an escort?

The guy was chatty, but he wanted to have sex, so I simply disconnected from myself throughout the ordeal and was so relieved when that knock on the door finally came, as that was my cue to exit. The experience left me feeling empty; I felt wretched, dirty, and unclean like I'd been violated. Honestly, I just wanted to have a good cry. I was hoping I would be taken home at that point, but instead, we drove to a meeting point where another car was waiting with several more girls. I was feverishly praying that I would not have to go through such an ordeal again, and thank God, in this case, my prayers had been heard. It was very rare for them to be so quiet on a Saturday night, but after waiting in the car for five hours in the middle of nowhere, they dropped me back home at 4 a.m.

I went straight to my mother's room and broke down crying. I told her it was the most awful experience ever and that I felt empty, cheap, and dirty. She told me at least I had experienced it and never had to do it again—damn straight. I took a long hot shower, trying to scrub the grime off, but no matter how hard I scrubbed, I felt unclean on the inside. I threw the clothes I wore that night into my suitcase, and they found their way into a charity bin several months later.

It took me a couple of weeks to feel "clean" again. Whilst I don't understand how women can be escorts—it is a choice, whether for survival or other reasons—I do know that you will attract those who ride the same wavelength as you. In my case, my mind was shot to pieces, with my soul suffering, and I hummed at a very dense energetic vibration; therefore, I sunk to a depth of an experience unbeknownst to me and ripped myself apart even further.

The Pleiadeans on the Sacred Union of Love and Sex

The Pleiadian Council of Light have often said to me that there is no right or wrong in how we choose to live our lives, but for the experiences we clock to the beat of our own soul, nor is there a right or wrong in how we choose to heal—to each their own and to thine own self be true. Don't beat yourself up when it comes to your experiences, for life is a mere series of "unfortunate" events to eventually achieve an enlightened state of understanding of both yourself and the world. Choose your dances wisely, for energy is more fluid than you can ever anticipate; once you commence understanding that everything vibrates at that sweet song of energy, you can learn to start dancing to the new beats of heightened frequency, but till then, dance the dance that seems but most befittingly to your soul at this present moment in time. They state that we can all decide to change at our leisure, when it feels convenient to us, as life is a mere wave of misadventures pertaining to the user's chosen experiences. Your future waits for your past to intersect with the present and catapult all of your existence to a higher divine dimensional state of BEing, resonating with the core of your radiant authenticity. To reveal is to unveil yourself back to the wonders of all that you are! Be that joy, be that frivolous spark of light that you are, and refrain from being the saboteur of your own procrastination as much as your procrastinations are but the saboteur causing wranglings within your life. No one dims the light of self back into that gutter of darkness but you.

I love their wisdom, something I severely lacked back then, as well as their love for humanity. They are the bringers of cosmic light, elevation, and peace. They are a thoughtful intergalactic family of healers, healing at a vibrational frequency faster than the speed of light, with a bond and a love for all that knows no bounds, for they just *are*.

I am eternally grateful to them, for it is only now that I feel much freer and more comfortable within my own skin. Still, my healing journey to better understand myself only commenced six years later, when I was kicked into the abyss, only to be kicked even deeper into the abyss five years later.

The Pleiadeans state that in this day and age, many have forgotten to live from and through the awareness of the heart, the space most sacred to the feeling and the connectedness back to the voice of the soul. The world is shifting back to the age of Christ consciousness, the embodiment of pure unconditional love.

"Is Love not what you are? Are you so far down the chute of your Mind that you realise not that Love is the eternal spark of the blazing fires of the Light within? Allow your beautiful Soul to speak but untold words and to shine through the Light of eternalness, for the ignition of that spark is the chemical reaction, the bond between two people fusing into one. If you remain within the coated armour of Self, one merely clinks like mere champagne glasses, never truly touching the Soul of the other, for the bubbly remains firmly harboured within each glass, never flowing into the loving stream of One.

Love is a 'joyous' experience. Love has no ego, nor does the ego carry 'love' but for the mere paraphrasing of the 'conditioned' word thereof. Know that when dancing that vibrant and exuberant dance of love, that you are both mirror reflections of each other, reflecting both the light and shadows within. Love is a stepping stone to evolving and learning from each other. Leap into the depths of the multidimensional wonder that you are, stop splashing in the superficial shallow puddles of playing love for keeps with conditioning—for love is Pure Cosmic Divinity untamed. It is infinite; it is the Light of the you and each other that you are (!); it is not bound by the human capacity of what one believes Love to be, for that is but the mere conditioning of what Love pertains to each individual. Breathe that love, live that love, for it is infinitely beautiful.

Roam not behind that cut-dry conditioned created armour, but let it fall, and let your Soul dance stark naked in the 'surrenderance' of Self, for only then can one walk the truth of their Authentic Light; only then will the Light be ever stronger in the higher reaching embrace. Love is not all as per Olivia Newton John's tune, 'Let's get physical, and I want to hear your body talk,' but it is the unison united in Love of the Cosmic Spiritual Orgasm and a delving into and swimming the crystal-clear waters of each other's Soul on a deeper and far more infinite level of understanding of one another. It is that poetic bliss of entwined Souls in harmonic rhapsody as One. How can that not be beautiful, my Child?

The making of love has been dogmatised relentlessly by the barking illusion of fear from the conditioning of the outer realms of existence. It is the fusion of having a Cosmic Experience between two Souls connecting to the higher realms of Consciousness, back to the higher planes of the Devotional Self and to the pureness of the Divinity within, and to each other as One. It is Love in its purest and highest vibrational form; it is the equivocation that has bereaved Oneself in the damned darkness of the misunderstood surface of the Soul of Self.

Why live in the absurdity of a labelled love when one can delve but deeper back to the beatific harmony of Self? It is the relationship with yourself through the merging of one another back to the liberation of the understanding that Love is the universal key to all there is and ever will be.

Your sexuality is the bridge that has been severed to reach the higher realms of Consciousness through the eons of misguided misinterpretation. Is it any wonder that one walks round in a confused stupor, with the labelling of sexuality for all it is not, but rather for the Oneness of Cosmic Consciousness that it is? Simplicity has never been humanity's strongest suit, for everything is an analytical thought patterning of the equivocal fear of what is and can be, rather than being in the acceptance of the flow that you are. And yet, in attaining the orgasmic realms of spiritual Consciousness is the road to a love back for oneself. You are Love; it is the Sole Nature of your Soul. How can one be in denial of that gift?

Being a bed-hopper, and having many partners, is a whole different arena. It is a wonderful game of playing hide-and-seek with the Self, the con artist EGO of escaping the Self, whereby one becomes contrived and conceited within, and the truth of who you are becomes a blur of hiding one's beautiful Light. It is the mere sticky labels you have so masterfully stuck on your beautiful selves that have made you so heavily and creamily conditioned in your ways of 'loving' yourselves and others—you've created a haphazard of 'love.' Hop like the rabbit you are, all you like, but you will keep masking and playing Houdini with the light of your Soul. The more you 'sleep' around, the more your energy becomes fragmented, finding no joy within but for the sheer escapism of having sex without, living in the smoke and mirrors of the mirage of yours truly yourself, relieving the suppression, the tension within your shattered Mind and bondaged Soul, lifting that void for only the briefest of moments, before slumping back into the mechanisms of the conditioned pain one has allowed oneself to become.

The guilt tripping of the e-motions of the 'blame-tag-you're-it' is as old as day. Denying each other growth when one has come to a place of complacency is to deny yourself the growth your Soul so truly yearns for. Love is always the answer to walking the road to healing yourself, and yet many people choose to hang on to others because they have not alchemised their experiences and thus carry but a vibratory version of love through the programming of their experiences. You know the expression, 'If you love someone, set them free?' How can you deny another their growth when you yammer on, afraid to lose them, all the whilst having become lost in the mind maze of yourself? How can you love another if you cannot love yourself? Yet humanity is fraught with what they perceive to be love and what pure unconditional divine love is, for love does not swirl in the sludge of muddy topped with 'nutty' e-motions; it is pure divine Madagascar vanilla flavour. Love is not a contract. Love is not quid pro quo. Love is not an egotistical mud-slinging match. Remain not in the convenience of a 'stale cheese' relationship, for it will reek to high heavens, causing one nothing but a poison to each other's Soul. So, tell me Child, is it a fear of the unknown? A fear of leaving? A case of better the devil, you know? If you no longer vibrate at the same frequency, where you no longer sing from the same hymn sheet and are tone-deaf and out of tune, do not go harping on about the differences of the hymn sheet or the tune; simply acknowledge that you no longer serve one another and walk away with gratitude and with love in each of your hearts, for every relationship is and will be an experience to a better understanding of yourself, would you not agree? Either that or remain locked in the algebraic rhythm of a continued constipation allowing the EGO and the Mind to bolster each other ramming the Soul into a muted oblivion.

Always remember others are mere reflective teachers of walking back to a love for yourselves, for they illuminate the holes in the Mind that require healing and learning to love the all of you so that you in turn, can love the all in everything and each other. Stop being your own hustler and sabotaging your beautiful Soul, inflicting far more pain with sorrier consequences for the Self. Look into the mirror, and understand your worthiness. Simply re-evaluate the void in your Mind, for one is but a mere reflection of the other, is it not? You are mere conduits of one another, a divine compass through the art of the subtleties of the human experience. Honouring yourself and your feelings means coming to a state of living in the balancing of the scales of the divinely beautiful Self.

To evolve or not to evolve? Only you can respond to the question of determining the outcome of that very question. Live in a capacity from the heart and through an awareness of the heart instead of living within the confines of the so-called contented *superficiality of stating that one is happy but is not, causing nothing but a 'stifleness' to oneself and one's life."*

Q: It's always I climax, you climax—not we climax together. If the woman climaxes first, it's no joy if the man then has to climax. And if the man climaxes first, well, too bad for the woman in question.

Many Souls live and breathe through a conditioned version of themselves, having sex or making love body-to-body with the EGO of one another, rather than the nakedness of their beautiful Souls. Too many gooey labels attached to your Mind have superglued your strapped Soul, causing nothing but a scraping the barrel of making love what one believes to be Authentic Soul-to-Soul Love, or is it the masked-to-mask EGO-to-EGO having sex with each other? See it as these two mirror reflections trying to catch the beams of the sunray simultaneously, setting each other's Soul on Cosmic fire. It is the streaming of energy back and forth to climax on that same wavelength, yet you don't see the divine naked Soul of that person; you see a conditioned version reflecting back at each other."

Do not think I understood this then, for sex had always been shallow on my end—how could it not be when I understood myself so little? Being the sadomasochist I was, I opted to keep carrying all my accumulated traumatic experiences, and thus my soul was raptured in the heavily gilded protective armour, making it difficult for me to often enjoy having sex. Subconsciously, something triggered in my mind that blocked the joy of making love. We are so stuck in those lower vibrational states of consciousness that we ricochet the acceptance of who we truly are. Our fear keeps us trapped in our current state of existence. It is a kink in the cable of our soul alignment, with the energies within our body being blocked like darn sewage due to all the accumulated crap, often causing a state of dis-ease. We've got to be raw, real, and honest with ourselves; only then will the energy start to reflow through our 'shot' body, making it far more breathable and user-friendly to the operator. We are all energy, and thus energy is the source of power that fuels our inner frequency—the user manual to the bodily functioning and operational use of the soul.

I've faked more orgasms than I care to remember. I wasn't always honest about it—but there is no shame in it, even though I felt ashamed at the time. Your experiences will always reflect on how you interact with others. Suffering traumatic experiences can have that effect on both men and women. Events throughout your life create feelings that form a carefully crafted belief system; from these beliefs, we create never-ending stories about the nature of that reality. We are visionary masterminds at creating and interweaving these energetic frequencies within our chosen stories—our lives are run by a bunch of stories that we have convinced ourselves are real. Only by healing ourselves and expanding our awareness can we choose to leave the distortion of those created stories behind, living, breathing, and feeling more harmonious and at ease within ourselves.

"To be more aligned within yourself, you must first heal the cause, the root of that created problem, and learn to love all of who you are. You are not flawed, but for the flaws you perceive yourself to have; it is rather the layering of the various implemented conditions that have caused you to be so distorted in the view of yourself. When suffering any form of abuse or trauma, all of your Soul's issues are broadcast loud and clear throughout your body; how can it not, for your Soul literally lives there. The frequency imprint literally 'screams' it. Your body is a mere antenna, and your mind has outwitted you, played you for a Humpty Dumpty fool, and thus you have so courteously 'cracked' and calibrated yourself to your serv-ed experiences, attracting a whole host of unwanted boloney, and thus you emit as such, n'est-ce pas?

Hang not your head in shame because of the hurt and pain caused by the experience. Why remain a piddling fool being but the most critical judge of yourself? You only add to the bubbling froth of slapping on 'what-people-think' labels that one becomes a lethal poison to the Self. It is the mere fact that you are not always Conscious that this could be the cause because you live in such a blissful state of unawareness. You tuck it far away, hidden in the inner realms of your mind, where the 'trauma' of the memory has been stored and compartmentalised, only for the eluded to be triggered in a similar experience. Why do you feel the need to judge yourself through the opinionated eyes of another? No matter the violation involved, understand that all experiences serve as a catalyst for change and growth, to help heal your wounded mind, elevating your Soul's awareness back to the unlayered freedom of the beautiful Light within, for you are but the mere lightness of BEing, and yet my Child, the denseness within is as much the key to unlocking the Light within back to the beauty of the world without. Bask a wee bit more in a love for Self, and the Self will bask a wee bit more in love."

My Bro Gwyn

Gwyn, a very close friend of mine and my "bro," was a minibus driver and chauffeuring people on UK movie sets, and when I was in dire straits, he got me on as an extra on the set of the then hyped-up Wimbledon movie. I met Gwyn in 1999 when I joined a circle to develop my mediumship—a group of us got together weekly to meditate and pass on messages from crossed-over loved ones.

Gwyn was a lovely bloke from Wales who lived in North London and always tried to be there for everyone. He was a people pleaser to a T; I say "was" because he crossed over in January 2019. He had a complicated childhood and a history of alcohol abuse after losing custody of his daughter. He had met a twenty-year-old Romanian girl half his age and knocked her up a few weeks after meeting her—intentional on her part, stupidity on his. He didn't want any more kids, as he had two teenagers from previous relationships, but had to accept the fact that there was another on the way. I did not see this ending well, but in 2005, he said he was in love with her, and she with him.

They ended acrimoniously, and the battle for custody between the two went on for many years; she broke him, and yet that is exactly what he allowed, for he got emotionally entangled within this created experience. He could not understand why his ex was so vindictive towards him. I told him to let it go, but he couldn't.

Gwyn would not relent, unlike my father, who chose to let go. My father tried everything to remain in touch with his two kids from his former marriage, fighting for custody of his son, but his ex made sure he had no part in their lives, and they grew up to believe that their father wanted nothing to do with them. He let go for his own sanity, and my half-sister and brother never saw their father again. Yet through a Dutch program called Lost and Found, they were able to find my younger sister, who lives in Amsterdam, and through her, me. I met my half-sister, but my half-brother refused to meet me unless my younger sister, with whom I have a very fractured relationship, was present.

When doctors warned Gwyn that he needed to stop drinking to avoid further liver damage, he dialled it down to drinking one beer a night. He said all he ever wanted was for the negativity to disappear. He kept asking his angels for help and tried to be positive, but all he got was one negative experience after another. He said he knew that everything happened for a reason, but at that point, he thought, *Why me? What have I done to deserve all this crap in my life, as all I want is to be happy? Is that too much to ask?* He hoped that six months down the line, he'd look back and smile and understand why it all happened. He would sometimes sit and meditate or try to reconnect with Spirit for guidance. I tried to give him nuggets of advice and a little glimmer of hope, but he had to discard the heaviness, heal himself, and open the door to appreciate and embrace the light and warmth of his own soul BEing.

Things didn't turn out as planned; he was slapped with another court case, having to prove that he didn't try to kill his daughter's stepdad. That was a ludicrous claim, as he was the gentlest of spirits, but his ex-partner tried every trick in the book to keep him away from their daughter. He was feeling incredibly low within himself once more; lost another job and wanted to get out of his miserable circumstances, out of the old, cold caravan he lived in with his cats, bearded dragon, and creepy arse tarantula. He told me he would have gone back to Wales a long time ago had his daughter not lived in the London area.

He used to say he envied me, that I was his inspiration, yet my life was a war zone underneath the pretence I portrayed to the outside world. In 2017, he started working for his former employer at Pinewood Studios, chauffeuring on the new Star Wars movie; years prior, he had worked there on the Harry Potter franchise. He was hoping to save up enough money to be able to rent a flat, and yet as soon as a setback occurred, he'd fall back into the slump of his old habitual self once again. He was found not guilty, and the other party admitted it was a setup, yet he was denied visitation rights by the judge that had presided over the case. It destroyed him, and he spiralled, refusing to nourish and nurture himself.

When I returned to the UK, he wanted to come and see me, but he said he was too ashamed because he knew I would see straight through him. A year later, in December 2018, he wanted to visit, and I told him he could swing by anytime, day or night. He never did; he landed in the hospital, and the doctors told him his liver was shot. I think he chose to drink himself to death, with his heart giving in. To him, it seemed pointless to continue living when he felt he had nothing left to live for, and with his liver failing, he figured, what the hell, I might as well go out with a bang. I often told him, "You are eternal, Gwyn; you merely transform—you go on. Death is not the answer to solving your problems."

We live in such a labelled society that we often get lost in our own mind maze, keeping ourselves cuffed to the illusion, to confuse ourselves on how to even remotely remedy and expand our awareness; having lost the plot to understanding life, because we've been left locked and bogged down in our problems. The key is to keep nurturing ourselves, even through the rough patches in life. Never feel that you are alone, for you have infinite BEings of Light that are always ready to embrace and assist in your time of need. Be open to receiving their healing and guidance. Write down how you feel, pour your heart out on paper; it relieves the pressure on your weighted mind, it lets out the heaviness; then you can burn it, letting it all go into the reach of the celestial heavens.

"Nourish and nurture your inner garden to flourish and blossom in the awareness of your inner world and vibrance of abundance in your outer world, for what you vibe in, is exactement what you vibe out and vice versa, for such is the Law of the Energetic Frequency of the Universal Divine BEing You are. You are a Creator of as much your own Universe as the Universe is the Creation of You.

Your body is your garden; your will the gardener to how you choose to tend to that "garden." Make it a beautiful and scented aroma of sweetness galore or a wilted wasteland of but "death" and decay, forever choosing to linger in the darkness of your clung-on experiences. Dare to live a little, dance a bit more to the swagger of your own Soul rhythm, and enjoy the eclectic dance of Life, in all its flavoursome enchanting delights."

~The Ascended Master St. Germain~

Gwyn made it known that he crossed over by hovering around me relentlessly for several days, refusing to let go. I was so mad at him; I shouted at him to get lost and was infuriated that he allowed himself to drown in his experiences instead of moving forward with grace and gratitude in his life. I refused to speak to him and made it clear that he needed to cross over and heal first, but the bugger wouldn't budge. He suffocated my energy, literally draining the life out of me; I couldn't sleep as he was just standing there in my room. I did not see him, but I could feel him. I called a friend of mine, a medium, and he helped Gwyn cross over. I knew the instant he had, as both my house and I could breathe again.

Gwyn was an amazing medium and healer, and I know he could have done so well for himself in that field if only he had embraced the essence of all of who he was rather than remaining chained in his victim mentality. He could have helped so many others if only he had chosen to help himself. He knows that now.

I miss my bro, but he revels in the remembrance of the light that he is. He's up to his usual mischief in spirit and has a helping hand in guiding his family and those that seek his help from the otherworldly dimensions of home, where he is far more useful than he was on the earthly planes.

Alcohol was his drug of choice, but he also dabbled in cocaine and could smoke cigarettes like the best of them. All these feats served to induce his escapism into his Salvador Dalian obscure hidden world of a little boy lost within his traumatic experiences. His chosen reality he could not face, and he was desperate to free himself from the demons that had enraptured his soul. Thus, the alcohol numbed the pain of his mind, yet it was also the poison that eventually led to his demise before he 'popped' his clogs to return home.

There were too many holes in his beautiful mind that he had debilitated his soul. The more holes, the more you allow yourself to become absorbed within the "negative" emotions of your experiences, refusing to let go. Instead, consuming yourself with the acidic nature of your conjured-up feelings, damning yourself to a life of sheer misery, rather than the flip side of that: sheer bliss!

I have conversations with Gwyn as he pops his head round the corner now and again. He always suffered from verbal diarrhoea, and he could swear like the best of them. Could he have done things differently? Could he have altered the outcome of his chosen direction in life?

"Yes!" He says, "I could have, and yet I now do far more work on the other side than in the skewed unalignment of who I was when I roamed the earthly planes. I made a f***** mess of it. If I knew back then what I know now, life would have been a breeze, and I might have made different choices. Unfortunately, you get hammered on the

head, mate, knocked unconscious, suffering from memory loss, not even having the foggiest of who you are and why you came to earth in the first place. They've literally done a number on you lot, and you've been believing every single word of the thread being fed to you in the optical illusion of the matrix you find yourselves in. It's like watching tv, and you're the star of your own dramedy. Flippin heck, I sure made mine a drama worthy of a tear-jerking Emmy nomination, with my Guides rooting for me, but me none the wiser as I was so blinded by my self-loathing and wallowing in my drunken self-pity to even realise they were there! But let's face it, mate, they didn't have a chance to get through to me; that's how far down the hole I was."

When I asked him about love on the earthly plane, he said, "Love, what's that? I attracted those on the same level of awareness of love as I was; that's the law of cause and effect right there. What you throw out into the ether energy-wise comes back to you on that same velocious frequency. It's cool how you can conjure up energy, well on this side anyway, and transform it into anything you put your mind to; it is that simple. I was just a flake for not seeing it. People forget that we are all learning from each other, yet many get sucked into their experiences, remaining astute in their ways, whilst life is none of the above. You gotta take life with a pinch of salt; otherwise, you remain within that recipe of disaster. Was I in love? I thought I was, but no, not really. I didn't even love myself, so how could I love another? Fuckin' hell, it sure was a messed-up version of love, with me trying to desperately fill those empty holes within, with whatever helped ease my on-the-rocks mind – no pun intended, although I liked my vodka neat. I loved the booze more than I did myself. I had zero concept of loving myself because I had such a distorted perception of what I thought love was. Did Kylie not sing love at first sight? You've got to be in love with yourself, at first sight, hearing the you in you, not the EGO in you, and knowing that for the first time, you are meant to be as One with the you in Self and the Self in One with the you in All. We are all conditioned according to the quid pro quo of our environment because that is what we are taught to believe. The key is to figure out the joke of the experiences played on you so that you love yourself and grin and bear the shit of the deluge you sometimes get soaked in. Merely say thank you, cut the crap, dry yourself off and move on from the experience, onwards and upwards, buzz-lightin' it to infinity and beyond, because ha, you are infinite, so you create the story of exactly what you decide within your mind, and it's either an awesome sauce storyline or you're toast, mate."

He asks, "Why do you poison your body? Why choose a toxic ingredient to escape the tortured mind, keeping your soul chastised to a chair? Don't be like me, slapping yourself silly, because your soul merely wants to return to basking in the warmth of the sunlight of self. Is it easier to remain as a creature of comfort lying in bed with the uncomfortable comfort of that created pain than to heal up? There are many forms of escapism—what's your vice? What inducement gives you that momentary high to deflect all your created pain? I had a wish list of things I created to pick and choose from. My creature comforts ranged from cigarettes to strong alcoholic beverages and stroking my cats for the love I failed to give myself —all to ease the unease of my hurt mind. To what end? Only to the demise of my physical essence, feeling nothing but sorry for myself, yet the plugging of my holes through the various vices of escapism, was the mere reflection of my soul screaming to be healed. Yet, I chose to ignore it to the detriment of my own life.

Do what feels right for you. Always be yourself, not who society dictates you to be, as that is total bollocks. Simply be the best version of yourself, dictating the rules according to the notions of your own heart. Look how I ended up? I put the blame for my buggered-up experiences at the feet of others, worshipping their 'power' over me rather than worshipping and taking care of myself. Yet it was not their 'fault' nor their responsibility, for ultimately, I had to take responsibility for my experiences in that given life, and thus I was a tart for crash-and-burnin' out of this life, having 'smoked' my body.

I could have done better had I chosen to get off my backside and been willing to do the work to heal myself, but instead, I got so caught up in my own crap that I became lost in the maze of my subliminal conscious, subconscious mind. I was lost in a potential minefield; everywhere I turned, I triggered myself into the abyss of my chosen 'traumatic' experiences. I would have rather lived in the illusion of my authentic self than be the Light of who I really was and now AM. Here, I don't see my past experiences as traumatic but simply as experiences I had chosen to evolve. It is not your body that makes you you, but the intricate expression of your soul that contours both the outer and inner edges of who you choose to become in the density of the human form. I was the contusion to the embodiment of Gwyn; I used myself as a mere punching bag, winner winner chicken dinner, to cover my deep-rooted insecurities and trauma I carried from childhood, and yet these were just experiences. But like a dog endlessly humping a leg, you cling on for dear life!

Seen from the space of where I am, know that you are all beautiful lights of dancing consciousness. Yes, upon incarnating, we can be such dimwits gracing our presence on the earthly planes, incarnating according to the agreements of our soul contract, forgetting everything we've learned and trying to evolve in a f*****-up world bequeathed with the laughing mirrors of illusions, layering ourselves with constant labels, influenced by the bombardments of the external deceptions at hand. Yet, in all this pomp and grandeur, trying to navigate through the 'wilderness of the forest,' there is no right or wrong; in the end, there is only love for one's chosen experiences. You cannot help someone if they don't want to help themselves, and I sure as hell didn't want to be helped. You cannot save someone from themselves if they are not privy to the light within, for only they can save themselves from the mayhem that resides deep within the wells of their own heart. Each must walk their journey pertaining to the vibrance of their own heartbeat; you may walk with them, but let them walk freely, just as you do."

I love Gwyn; always been a straight shooter, which hasn't changed. "Remember that God helps those who help themselves, and darn, I AM God; if only I'd understood that then, although people would have thought me nuts and conceited, my life would have been vastly different. I should have been a bit more Bruce Almightier and been the flippin' miracle, as that is what you are! You are the energy of God incarnate; you are the creator of your very own show of an earthly reality. Both joy and misery are *two sides of the same coin—flip it whichever way you want, mate, because from the will of thy choosing, may God help you to help yourself. Peace out sis."*

I had started working as a PA for a government branch in London and registered myself with a casting agency. I actually received a call asking if I wanted to be an extra on the new movie *Alfie* with Jude Law and Sienna Miller. I love that last scene, with Michael Cane reminiscing, *"What have I got? Really? Some money in my pocket, some nice threads, a fancy car at my disposal, and I'm single. Yeah... unattached, free as a bird. I don't depend on nobody, and nobody depends on me. My life's my own. But I don't have peace of mind. And if you don't have that, you've got nothing. So...what's the answer? That's what I keep asking myself. What's it all about? You know what I mean?"*

Gwyn was working on the same job, driving a minibus from early morning till late at night. It was being filmed in one of the new buildings at Canary Wharf, the sky-scraping business district of London. The set was decorated for a New Year's party, so I was dolled up like everyone else and got to wear a short black cocktail dress. Jude Law and Sienna Miller only had eyes for each other; it was as if the world outside of them did not exist. I don't envy those in the acting industry as it is a tough business, but then they get paid more than their fair share to shapeshift into many different characters, settings, and scenarios. Aren't we all just a bunch of actors playing our part?

Making My Way Back to the US

The summer of 2003 in the UK was a scorching one; to be honest, it's very rare, as it always pours in this miserable country. I did not want to be here. My body was here, but I'd left my heart back in New York. I walked around with this deep-seated unhappiness, which was my own doing, and yet I refused to hop out of it, choosing to remain soaking within that feeling of deep despair instead. Pathetic as it was, I missed Davut, but he was going through a lot of drama of his own going back and forth to court.

He couldn't dial overseas from his cell phone; otherwise, as he said, he would have called more often, which was bull, as anyone with half a decent brain knows that international calling cards existed in that era. But this braindead chick chose to stick her head in the sand and play dumb. Weeks would go by with no word from him, and my mind would wander, thinking I'd done something wrong. In response to my emails about why he was so quiet, he'd merely come back and say I shouldn't doubt him. I was still in that same subdued state of awareness, not yet having snapped out of my old programming.

His court case ended in December 2003, and he was in debt for about $68K. The case had consumed him, and he'd been working to recover his losses, saying he was lucky to have escaped with a fine and not a sentence. He told me he'd rather forget the whole episode, as he was made out to be the scapegoat. I then got an email asking if I wanted to move in with him when I returned. He was like Dr. Jekyll and Mr. Hyde, yet here I thought, could he really be that serious about me?

He would often tell me to call him on his cell, but when I called, it always went straight to voicemail. Christmas came and went, and I received a lousy email from him wanting my address so he could send me a little present. Guess what? I'm still waiting. New Year's came and went, and nope, nothing. I left him a voicemail, but no response in return. February came and went, including Valentine's Day, and I received an email out of the blue asking me if I'd forgotten about him or if I'd found another Valentine? Of course, I hadn't, and I emailed back, pathetically saying that he'd be the only guy for me for the rest of my life.

His emails became more sporadic as the months went by. In the meantime, however, I made plans to return and advised him of this. He eventually got back to me and told me he had been at the Sundance Film Festival and apologised for not keeping in touch. He was excited about the prospect of me coming back. I was ecstatic to hear from him, but my mood quickly dampened because guess what? I got his voicemail once again.

He had my portfolio, which I asked him to courier across, as Major Models in Milan was interested in me. I literally had to beg and plead for him to return it to me. Three months later, I was still waiting for him to send it to me, which bottlenecked everything and wasn't fair to me. Apparently, which I knew was a lie, when he had tried to send my portfolio "first" class, it had been returned to him. Eventually, a friend of mine, who I'd helped get clean (he'd been a severe coke addict but turned his life around and is highly successful now), got my portfolio when he visited New York, so I received it pretty much right before I headed back out there. The irony of it all.

In all his emails to me, Davut kept apologising, telling me he had shows booked throughout the country for his newly dropped album. According to him, he'd been trying to call me but couldn't reach me, which was utter tosh. I had this nagging feeling that he was running scared and felt he was slipping away, yet I chose to shrug off that irritating inner voice in the back of my head. My idiocy knew no bounds.

In the interim, I contacted several immigration lawyers, using my middle name, as I was a bit paranoid after all the issues I had encountered applying for a visa at the US consulate. A few replied and told me that if I even attempted to re-enter the country on my waiver, I would be detained and deported back to the UK, after which I would be prohibited from entering the country again. I couldn't under-stand why—I hadn't done anything illegal, so why would I be banned?

The email response received by the US consulate stated that while I was not prohibited from travelling on the visa waiver program, the immigration officer at the US port of entry might question me regarding my refusal by the embassy. Ultimately, the decision to admit a traveller is solely at the discretion of the immigration officer at the port of entry.

After doing even more research, being none the wiser, and being a total nut nut, I decided to email Bush and Cheney. Oh yes, they have email addresses, but I knew they would never read nor respond to my email, and indeed it was a complete waste of time, as I merely received two automated replies.

As the Pleiadeans say, *"We are all but an eclectic variation of different species in the vastness of the Galaxy, vibrating at different frequencies of Awareness, yet there is no difference in each and every one and all of us, for we are all but Divine Sparks of Source Energy. We are born of the same Universal Source Energy, simply different tin, different label."* The composition of our soul energy makes us unique, for we choose to be born into a certain vibration, humming our beginnings at a certain tune; how we choose to evolve our composition is entirely up to us.

A female lawyer advised me to make sure that I had all the correct documen-tation with me when going through immigration; she hoped that the letter from my employer would sway things in the right direction. Another piece of advice she had was if I had anything like theatre tickets, European travel, or evening classes booked for future dates; evidence of that type also helped show that I had future plans in my home country.

In April 2004, I got my last email from Davut, telling me the same boring thing once again—that he'd only just had access to the internet to check his messages, blah blah blah. He would be in Vegas for the next two weeks and wanted to know why I didn't call him. Why? He never had the decency to pick up or call me back. I tried, and all I got was his blimmin' voicemail. I left him a message telling him that I would be there at the end of May and he'd better not leave me stranded at the airport.

That's when he vanished on me, and his cell phone got cut off. I was stumped, and at the same time, I felt like a serious dumbass. That feeling, however, did not deter me from returning to New York; I simply had to adjust my sails and alter my plans accordingly, as I needed to find a place first, which I did online—a room on the Upper East Side, right bang in the middle of Manhattan. A friend's mother went to check it out for me, making sure the landlord was bona fide and gave me the go-ahead.

By the end of May, I'd received no word, and I wrote him one final email. I can't even say for sure if he read it, but my gut tells me he did. Nevertheless, I kept my hopes up that one day he would at least have the decency to tell me what had happened. It's a horrible feeling to be ghosted by someone who wanted it all. I had no clue if he was dead or alive or if he had been handed a sentence and was doing time in prison.

The moral of the story is, I was stuck in a repetitive programming loop, causing myself a yoyo of emotions, craving validations to plug the holes in my own drafty cheese. I couldn't stop creating all the different scenarios in my head and only ended up hurting myself by continuously over analysing and overthinking things.

Davut was not responsible for how he made me feel. I was responsible for how I chose to react and feel about the situation he projected onto me. As St. Germain always says:

"How can people disappoint you when they merely disappoint themselves? You are the Light of infinite StarLight particles, wrapped up in this human gummy bear wrapper of your chosen suit. Think not so little of yourself, and act like you are the whole 'damn' Universe rather than thinking that you are but controlled by your outer experiences. Don't let Life define you, but define your own Life according to the rules and banter of your own joyous heart. You are far more capable than you think you are. How can you not be? When you are the Light of a thousand Suns, when you are the infinite beauty of the Universe in constant motion. Make your Life worth the ride, let it not go to waste; if not, it will waste it for you. You are Magic, so own that s***! You are a magical Soul housed within this current human embodiment. Stop being a walk-all-over-me, and act like the goddamn King or Queen you are, instead of always eating the humble pie doormat syndrome. You are an Alchemist, the whip-me-up to the Magic of your own Divine Creations, a transformational conduit of the Universe. Act like the powerhouse you are, unleashing the I AM Presence that resides within you, rather than the insistent need of constantly comparing yourself to others, being barked back into a corner by the God-fearing shadow of Self and what others think of you. Stop depending on the need for others like your Life depends on it, and look at the need to fix the leaky holes within yourself—look at yourself and your own capabilities instead of giving your power away and feeling but gloomy within yourself because you think you are nothing! You are everything; you are the whole goddamn Universe within, expressing yourself through the hue-man creation that you are."

Even now, when people put me down, *it's like, No, don't even go there, keep your soul rooted in gratitude, it is their awareness, leave them be, simply keep basking in your own Soul-de-Light, don't let yourself get side-tracked or kicked back into the dirt.*

My experiences were just so real to me at the time; I was allowing myself to drown in the thick of it, turning my life into a raving shit storm. I didn't understand that for the longest time, it was me that chose to cling onto these created hardships for dear life and roam around in the "losing Davut" experience, until I finally learned to detach, but by God, I was a turtle. Is it any wonder that my posture was like the hunchback of Notre Dame? I cloaked the layers of all my experiences over my shoulders; I literally heaped an immense amount of energetic junk onto myself, making it near impossible for me to walk with a flair of confidence, for I was an enigma of total insecurity, and for what? All because of some dude that didn't give me the time of day? As the Ascended Master Hilarion says, *"You become what you surround yourself with. Energy is an infectious feat, intertwining and dancing to the hues and absorbance of your environment. At any given moment you can change the status quo."*

I have always been a restless soul with awfully itchy feet, always searching for meaning, peace, and happiness in life, but all are found within. I have moved nearly more times than my age; my roots are non-existent in the literal sense, except that my soul is the "root," the anchor to my body. My current home is where my soul resides, with my true home being amongst the stars.

But back then, my soul was not exactly in agreement with my body; I hated every aspect of myself and believed there was something severely wrong with me, as I would look in the mirror and see this distorted image of who I was. You are not who people say you are but who you believe yourself to be. My dad always used to say, tell your mirror image, "I love you," and it'll make you feel better. It's the oldest trick in the book, and you can roll your eyes, but loving yourself is necessary, for if you cannot love yourself, how the hell can you give that love to others? Love and worth are not performance-based; that's just human conditioning; these aspects reside within. All you need to do is unveil them, to reveal the beautiful light within.

"You are an energetic ball of frequential alchemical awesomeness. What you think of in the mental imagery of your Mind, you conjure up into the existential framework of your existence. You get what you think about, and thus will it so into the damn fine woven reality of your Cosmic lil world of existence—ain't nobody's fault but the culprit of an Alchemist staring back at you but rather sheepishly in the mirror. Don't like the outcome? Change the energetic formulation of the created concoction, et voila, for ain't nobody stoppin' you from either bringing down the house like a pack o' wild berry cherry cards, splatting your beautiful Soul or clappin' along to the happiness beatz of bring me a higher love and celebrate the world, living in the badass truth of your wondrous bliss of Soul of a Divine Existence."

~The Divine Shakespeare Club~

At that stage in my chaotic life, I just hadn't figured it out, and with Davut I suffered bouts of severe "hangxiety"—that feeling of unease, that queasiness that comes from hanging on to all the s*** that is out of alignment with your spirit. It's hanging on to people that don't give a damn about you, making your mind go doolally and into overdrive of spinning infinite stories and endings. The truth was, I was on a mission to get answers, and get them I would. I needed them; hence my mind was consumed by it all. I was a sad-o-masochist, unnecessarily keeping myself in that consistent pain. The irony of the whole Davut experience is that he always told me I was gullible, and he so darn well hit the nail right on the head......

Getting back to the US would be one hell of a nerve-wracking trip, but in August of 2004, I thought *sod it*, and took the plunge. I flew back via Amsterdam and didn't listen to music or watch movies throughout the whole nine-hour flight to Philadelphia; instead, I just kept praying to my Guides and the archangels to guide me through immigration safely.

I was afraid of being handcuffed and deported back to the UK. That little voice in my head told me I would be fine, and in my inner vision, I saw my dad raising a glass of champagne to me. The advice that the lady lawyer gave me was that upon arrival in the US, I should try and get off the plane as quickly as possible so that when I got to immigration, I'd be at the front of the queue. The airport in Philadelphia is enormous, so I asked the angels which immigration officer to pick. They made me walk all the way to the other end, with only one person ahead of me in the queue. I had all the necessary paperwork in case they asked me any questions, and when the guy said "Next," my heart pounded in my chest.

I approached the officer with lead in my shoes and gave him my passport, although I would rather have hung on to it. He swiped it, and I thought, *Uh-oh, here come all the hundreds of questions*. But none came. Instead, he said, "So, you're on your way to Miami for vacation?" I told him, yes, and he asked what kind of work I did in the UK. I told him I worked for the UK Government in London and had lived there for eight years. He stamped my passport, looked at the green form, and said, "How come you were refused a visa?" I told him that a lawyer in the US had advised me to apply for a six-month tourist visa and that when I went to the US consulate in London, I was asked what I was doing there because I didn't need a tourist visa.

At that point, I was panicking inside, as I had to go to secondary immigration, but he said, "You'll be fine, don't worry." Off I walked and waited my turn. My palms were sweaty from the adrenaline coursing through my nervous system. After ten minutes, the immigration officer called me and asked what the problem was, and I explained it again, trying not to sound panicky. He said, "We hear this so often that lawyers and the US consulates say something completely different than what we tell them."

I said, "Are you telling me that I could have gone on holiday last year, no problem?" He said, "You haven't been refused a visa and could have travelled on your waiver."

In effect, the guy said I could have come back last year, and maybe Davut and I could still be together? Seriously? He returned my passport and told me to enjoy my holiday. He hadn't asked to see a return ticket or any of my other papers or documentation. Neither were my fingerprints or a picture taken. How was this possible? A few weeks earlier, I had called the State Department, and they advised me that I was in the system, and here I was going through immigration with no record of any refusal exhibited on-screen.

I was extremely lucky, and I thanked the angels for getting me through with such ease. I could've then taken a train to New York, but instead, I thought to myself, *Time to chill out in Miami,* seeing I had booked a hotel and wanted to meet up with some friends I hadn't seen for several years.

I called my mum from the airport, and she asked me where I was, and I told her I'd gotten through. She didn't hear me straight away, so I had to repeat it twice. She was ecstatic. I could have cried with joy; I had finally made it back on American soil, and I was able to breathe a massive sigh of relief.

Back in the Big Apple

Once back in the Big Apple, I called up an Israeli promoter I'd met, and he invited me to Marquis, some snazzy lounge in Midtown. He knew Davut, but hadn't seen him around in a while.

I wasn't a fan of the energy in Marquis; everyone was superficially eyeing one another like cotton candy. It was filled with skinny models whose clothes were hanging like potato sacks over their bony bodies, draped around one big table, namely Leonardo di Caprio's. He was pretty wasted, sitting there with his baseball cap partially covering his face and just talking to some guy sitting next to him, oblivious to what was going on around him.

Another guy who suddenly brushed past me was the actor Benicio del Toro, totally off his face, looking bleary-eyed with intoxication. At a hotel bar promo gig I had met Queen Latifah, who happened to be in the lobby and was a lovely, down-to-earth person.

Hollywood and the Media

I've never been starry-eyed, and I certainly don't envy those that have submerged themselves into the Hollywood cesspool. It takes a strong character to remain upright in that cutthroat industry; it's either that or being consumed by the darkness of it all. I never knew about the apparent symbolism of the word "Hollywood" until someone told me. It derives back to the days of the ancient druids of the first century B.C., who used to make wands out of holly trees to weave, channel, and cast spells. If they required help, they would consult the magi or mediums to channel their magic to the population. Fast-forward to today and see how this eerily aligns, as most households have a tv or other streaming devices.

Television equates to tell-a-vision as this seemingly innocent little electronic box programs your mind, should you allow it, and is the ultra-weapon of conditioning. It fries the brain through these pesky electromagnetic energy waves, with mostly nonsensical bullshit lulling the senses, giving the "user" the option of many different channels to "tune" into. Whatever you decide to watch, it relays the mental imagery back into the mind, changing how you view your reality, and thus one becomes a wonky conditioned version as you believe the illusions of the narrative so duly fed. All this crap from the corrupt media propaganda machine spouting false information, hoping to put the fear of God in people. We know that we are not this dense matter but beings consistent of energetic particles, and thus these transmitted waves are merely meant to manipulate and alter the thoughts and feelings of humanity, to keep us dumbed down, living a life under a set of incorporated rules within the status quo of the ego, trapped in the matrix.

Growing up, my sister and I watched the A-Team, Magnum, Airwolf, MacGyver, Knight Rider, or movies such as Annie, Star Wars, and E.T., the latter which scared the crap out of me, not to mention the Emperor, Darth Sidious, a face of harrowing nightmares. Even music videos were demure back then compared to the pornography we have on display these days. I didn't even dare to watch *Thriller* by Michael Jackson, as that too gave me the heebie-jeebies. Our parents told us we could watch it, but we were hiding behind the sofa, occasionally taking a peek at the dancing zombies that had risen from the dead.

Everything shown on tv impresses upon our mind and psyche, conditioning our thought patterns, behaviours, beliefs, and actions. To control humanity, you have to control the people that manage the population, which is precisely what those in power through the art of using the media do.

I'm not a big social media fan, and the Light BEings have advised that Facebook is a social experiment gone horribly wrong:

"Social media is often not heart-based but EGO-driven, and thus it brings nothing but emotional discord and chaos amongst the masses, which was its actual intent from the outset. And Instagram? So many selfies, yet so little knowledge of Self as one lives in the superficiality of the superficial Self. What holes are you trying to plug in your Mind that your Soul is but a game of tit for tat? What is the hurt behind the selfie that has made you become a selfitis? Why allow society to mould you and live according to the 'injected' societal narrative? Your beautiful minds are often modified and photoshopped into thinking that 'likes and loves' are more important than liking and loving yourself, and that 'follows' are more significant than following your own beautiful heart. You have become so absorbed and lost in your screens and the virtual realities you have so clandestinely created that you have built mere castles in the sky, instead of trying to get lost in the wonder of the tangible magic of living a soulful life. Unplug from the technocratic craziness and plug the Self back into Source and your own sweet Soul because getting to know yourself is a true wonder and miracle in itself. Isn't it far more wondrous to align yourself back to the sacred geometrical grid of Self, to allow yourself to flourish according to the Authenticity of All that makes you, you? Blow your inflated EGO out of the water, deflating yourself back to a love and zen of Self. Like yourself, to love yourself and follow your own Divine bliss of Self."

While playing detective and hoping to find Davut, I was avidly job-hunting. I could not just sit on my arse and do nothing, I'd feel like a useless couch potato, merely wasting away. I can't have a lie-in either, as it's a waste of time. It's just the way my brain's been wired through the accumulation of all my experiences. I was able to surf the internet from the flat, and from Craigslist I landed my first promotion job within a week.

It didn't go without a hitch; sweet and sour pork poisoning the night before got me good, but as this was my first gig after my return, I dragged myself into work handing out flyers, but nevertheless was a frequent flyer to the blimmin' Bloomingdale's Upper East Side bathroom.

I have always enjoyed working the many promotions I got, as the jobs were very diverse. Having signed up with an agency, I worked several gigs for Jameson whiskey, giving away free shots of Jameson, T-shirts, and headphones at Arlene's

Grocery down in the East Village, where many independent rock bands showcased their music. I picked up a few freelance modelling gigs here and there too.

I also did a wacky promotion for Bacardi Limon. I was dressed up as a cross between one of Austin Powers' girls and some futuristic babe from another galaxy, in a platinum blond wig, white shorts, a skimpy yellow shirt, and a white plastic shirt over that, which had "Bacardi" written on it and lit up. I looked like a goddamn freak, and thank the heavens, I was unrecognisable.

I wasn't the most social butterfly in the venues, but the pay was fantastic, and even though I sucked it up, I felt awkward wearing the outfit, with folks staring at me as it showed my bony arms and skinny legs. I felt like a little girl lost on the inside, but I masked it well.

During my time in New York, I had more gigs than I care to remember. My all-time favourite was working for Chivas Regal, the blended Scotch whiskey brand. It sure paid well. We went to bars and lounges and persuaded people to have free Chivas on us. We'd go back to them with their drinks and ask for their email addresses, as Chivas had these swanky free tasting parties. The guests would get good food, hear about Chivas Regal, hosted by a Scotsman wearing a kilt, and win prizes like T-shirts and bottles of Chivas. At the end of the evening, everyone would leave with a goodie bag.

I briefly worked for Maurice Paprin, a New York City real estate developer and social activist who crossed over in November 2005. He had a home office on First Avenue near the 59th Street Bridge. He had been a leading real estate developer in New York City since 1965, having developed thousands of apartments. He was also a well-known philanthropist, having sat on several charitable boards. Mr. Paprin was neither Democrat nor Republican but a progressive liberal, and I admired him, for he was well over eighty, still sharp as a hawk and active on all fronts. When I sat with him, he said that all he truly cared about was striving for world peace. Honestly, I wish there were more people like him with such passion and dedication to the cause.

I only worked for him for about six weeks, as sadly, he became ill; however, I thoroughly enjoyed the time I spent working for him. I admired and respected him for all the work he did to make the world a better place, and I hope that he continues his work on the other side, with his mission to help instil peace on Earth.

The Candid Truth about Davut

Towards the end of 2004, hallelujah, I finally found out the truth about Davut. I had this nagging feeling that he'd lied about his name. Why would someone lie about that? Early one Sunday morning, for whatever reason, I logged on to Google and typed in the correct spelling for David with his last name, and I was stunned at what I found. It made zero sense to me, but the company name mentioned in the article confirmed it. I could have found out much earlier, but truth be told, my subconscious mind withheld me from ever typing in "David"; I chose the ostrich in the sand mode, evading the truth for as long as possible until I was ready to hear it.

He had defrauded an elderly, cancer-stricken widow out of $80,000 by promising to invest her money, instead using it for his own personal expense. He'd been charged with grand larceny in the second degree, a class C felony punishable by up to 15 years in prison.

Reading this, I was in shock. Davut had told the lady that her records had been destroyed in 9/11, but promised to look into it, vanishing instead. He had made numerous ATM withdrawals, had drawn personal checks on the account, and even made payments to his former girlfriend, most probably his ex-fiancée.

He was arrested and arraigned in July 2003, which he neglected to tell me. I sat in front of my laptop, feeling numb, unable to move. He had pleaded guilty to fourth-degree grand larceny, was sentenced to five years' probation, and was directed to repay the full amount to the lady he had defrauded. Being on probation explained why he couldn't travel to London. I knew about the money, but he told me it was because of an investment gone wrong. What a heartless bastard! I couldn't comprehend the lies and deceit.

But even so, I have absolutely no ill feelings towards him. Wherever he's at, I can only hope he has found himself and righted the wrongs of his past.

You've got to be honest in any relationship; you cannot start the foundation based on a lie. If you cannot be real with yourself, how can you be real with others? Spirit state, *"If you deflate yourself with the heaviness of deception, then you walk, but an entwining path of spinning a web of entangled darkness of the soul created persona, whereby one will eventually get caught up in the mess of the lies one has so artfully spun. For what is truth and what is a lie, when eventually the lines start to blur when one is caught up in the delusional mess of oneself?"*

Everything in life is an experience; every experience is a mere energetic imprint that impresses upon our spirit. We all decide what song to sing, what energetic waves to catch and ride, surfin' through the turmoil of our experiences. To be a surfer, we must master the waves and find the equilibrium of balance between our inner and outer worlds. To master our lives is to learn to first master ourselves. I sucked balls at it as I kept tumbling off that darn board, being wiped out by the waves, caught in the undercurrent of my exasperating experiences, eventually learning to pivot and swing to ride those darn breakers, having learned from my past ordeals. But alas, if we cannot comprehend the mastering of ourselves, then we will never be able to master the flow of our life and will remain stuck in the programming of our chosen reality.

As St. Germain says, "*Mais oui, cherie, c'est très vrai. Life inadvertently will knock you flat on your arse until you decide to learn from the experiences so wonderlicisiously served to you. If not, merely enjoy a different serving in a different setting with a wonderful array of possibly different characters, unless you keep being iced with the exact same platter in front of you pertaining to the mucking about in that same experience for God knows how long. For life will keep punching you until you tell life to sod off, and commence to change the tune of your ways, healing the hurt of the bruis-ed Soul and shedding a layer to that state of a lighter BEingness within the Self— ultimately, your life, your choice, your decision, n'est-ce pas?*"

I felt sick to my stomach finding out about Davut the way I did, and the only thing that kept me going was my work. The more work, the better, and I was crafty enough at finding promotional gigs and hostessing and bartending jobs. People would tell me that same sentence over and over again, that I was strong enough, and that I'd be OK; that's why I learned to tune them out and cry when no one was around. To the outside world, I would always be the girl with the beautiful smile who was strong and admirable. Honestly, I was so sick of hearing it at that point.

Sure, I was very much the creator of my own misery, for that was the "tune" I chose to dance to. However, he chose to disappear into thin air, leaving me standing there like a brokenhearted fool. Looking back, I realise my Guides were probably protecting me. I should have been grateful, but at that point, I really wasn't. I know I caused my own pain and suffering because I chose to cling on like the desperado I was, being totally consumed by the experience.

I realised that I was an absolute disaster when it came to relationships; they always seemed to take their toll and drain the life out of me. In truth, this was my own doing; I was looking to the reflection of another to heal my own jaded soul. It was a small lightbulb moment—maybe working on the relationship with myself and being on my own for a while wasn't such a bad idea. I had to learn to be willing to heal on a deeper level within. Easier said than done.

Let's be clear, I had no boundaries in place, and thus my light flickered and wavered, and I was engulfed by the storms that lashed upon the shores of my soul. I was a darn doormat for everyone that wished to wipe their feet. I had to shift the shit, or the shit would shift me in a direction not of my choosing. We have to journey within, for the only way out of the dreaded darkness and out of the pain, is to go within and walk through the burning embers that have kept us incarcerated, returning to the beautiful transformational bliss of a far more enlightened state of BEing. That is what we call an alchemical transformation—transforming the chemical composition within and alchemising, healing the hurt back to the all of the beautiful formulated soul that you are.

The poet Rumi said it best as he compared feelings with guests in the "guesthouse of being human." He said, "*Treat each guest honourably, for each may be clearing you out for some new delight.*" By honouring and embracing all feelings, we empower ourselves back to the wholeness of who we most authentically are.

Maybe a dear friend of mine was right all those years ago, having analysed my signature, which revealed a lot of suppressed anger in me. I never talked about my "feelings" nor my "issues" except to the people closest to me, but even then, I kept a lot hidden inside, as I always saw myself as a burden due to my experiences with others. Most people, in my experience at the time, were all about themselves and how they fit into the world, with the art of selflessness replaced with the obscurity of selfishness.

Not understanding that my experiences were just a mere reflection of my own growth, I found that my greatest hurdle was understanding the emotional hurt caused by my reaction to these experiences. As Spirit says:

"Experiences are like honey jars; if you don't rinse the jars accordingly, remnants of honey will remain, and as such, the sticky residue will leave an imprint on your Soul, creating a whole sticky mess for the Self, unless all 'jars,' all 'experiences' have been properly 'washed,' meaning, all experiences have been healed and cleansed with the Spirit of understanding back to the Light within, leaving nothing but clear empty jars on the shelves of our Soul. If we leave the remnants of honey in the jars, over time, we become intoxicated with the amount of created stickiness, losing sight of who we authentically are, creating nothing but a library of programmed associations and triggers to each and every one of our created experiences. Much of a tiring feat to behold and a chosen lifestyle of living with an emotional trigger for every single experience one has accumulated through the created and serv-ed experiences of one's Life. When one chains the Self to past, present, and future events, know that it is all an illusion of the human mind. You are either your own greatest stumble block of a villainous desperado or your own superhero, knowing full well you are infinite potential—for you alone set the limitations of all that you perceive yourself to be. Once you decide to change and commence the journey of walking inwards, so too will you experience a vast difference in your outlook and your ways in experiencing the world you so grace with your presence."

People thought they knew the real me but what they saw was the fun-loving, happy persona that I portrayed on the outside—not the emotional rollercoaster, screwed-up bunny persona on the inside. As my friend read my palm, he was probably right when he said, "Briggs, you were born way before your time and hence will often be misunderstood." I am an acquired taste, but I am content living in my own world, away from the masquerade of people pretending to be someone they are not. I always say, hate me, love me, treat me like marmite, it's all the same to me, but regardless of how you feel, I will still love you. As the Divine Shakespeare Club state, *"Other people don't have to like you, nor do you need to conform to their wants and needs; that's like trying to squish into clothes that are too small, making yourself look like a laughing stock at the expense of hurting and depleting yourself, by taking the very 'breath' of life away. Always be happy with the you in you; life is not about bending over backwards to please others, crikey, that is too much of the EGO trippin' BS, merely rise above the drama of others and walk along* *your own created yellow brick road, and if there is s** along the way, well just refuse to indulge, unless you feel the need to step into it, then learn from the pooped-up experience, heal-up, alchemise it back to the Light, and walk on in one's garnered wisdom 'delight,' forging the path ahead back to the radiance of your own true wonder of Self."*

If you want to know if I heard from Davut, I did—several years later, when I was in Curacao. I spoke to him briefly, and to be honest, I cannot recall the conversation. I do remember that this idiot ran to the supermarket to get an international calling card. Rest assured, he disappeared two weeks later when his work email bounced back. A leopard does not and will not change its spots unless it chooses to do so.

I stayed in New York till early January 2005, after which I decided to move to Miami. I felt like my journey in New York had come to an end.

Miami and Curacao

What can I say about Miami? It's fake, materialistic, and "plastic fantastic." My friend, Miguel, had landed me a studio right on the beach. It was a bit more expensive than I had envisaged, but it had a pool and was in a quiet area at the beginning of Ocean Drive. Another friend had organised a job for me with a friend of his who was the CEO and president of a production and film company. He was one of the producers for a new movie being filmed that year called *The Goal* with Mario Lopez, the guy from the hit sitcom *Saved by the Bell*.

The CEO turned out to be a tyrant, a liar, a fraud, and a cheat. In fact, he was the biggest con artist rolling around on South Beach and a member of the U.S. House of Representatives.

I quit after several weeks and rolled from one con artist to the next, working part-time for a former Puerto Rican national basketball player turned broker in Miami. He was a devout Christian, went to church every Sunday, and attended Bible class every week. I received no paycheck after the first week, and every week he apologised profusely as all his deals kept falling through. After five weeks, I quit, leaving him my unpaid invoice. Instead of apologising, I got this sob story that he had to move out of his condo as he could not afford the rent and, unfortunately, could not keep me on as an admin any longer. I called several times, and he promised to pay me once he closed a deal until he chose to cancel my calls. Such a devout Christian and yet so dishonest. Does it not state in the Bible, under Leviticus 19:11 NKJV, *"You shall not steal, nor deal falsely, nor lie to one another"*?

I commenced working for another realtor part-time and really enjoyed it, as my boss was chill, sold one property after the other, and paid me on time.

I eventually got a tax ID through a lawyer in Miami who created my tax report for 2004 and paid my taxes. Like me, the laws for illegal immigrants paying taxes would allegedly change in July 2004, which meant there was a chance I could become legal.

Miami wasn't my scene; it had no depth and held a vibrational energy that did not resonate with my soul. I started getting severe headaches as I was out of whack. I loved the weather but was not a fan of the mentality—most people were materialistic and shallow-hearted, as the culture was all about status, money, clothes, and looks. People very much walked the surface of themselves, living in their own shallowness, with no sense of awareness. I wasn't some sexy goddess, just some scruffy parrot going about my daily routine. My friend Miguel took me to this superficial snazzy wannabe hangout called Pearl Lounge on Ocean Drive, having to entertain the NFL Carolina Panthers, whom I met briefly and was not impressed by. I made polite conversation, but they lacked conversational skills, which was clear to see in the girls that hung on to their every syllable, hoping to get laid.

I enjoyed my many bike rides and early morning strolls along the deserted beach, watching the sunrise. I could sit and take in the peaceful energies of the early dawn, watching birds tipple across the sand and seagulls gently swoop past. That right there was my little slice of heaven.

I had lost my I-94 form, which, as per the U.S. Customs and Border Protection website, is the DHS Arrival/Departure Record issued to aliens admitted to the U.S. to keep track of their arrival and departure from the country. This "alien" had requested a replacement through the same lawyer who organised her Tax ID, as she needed it to leave the country. As long as this was in progress, my status would not be classed as having overstayed. I received it in the mail the day I booked my flight back to the UK, yet Miguel asked me to stay on a few more days so that he could pay me back my six-week deposit, which never happened.

Curacao

I only ended up living in the small village of Buckingham in Buckinghamshire County for just over a year before I scooted off to Curacao in March 2006. Curacao is one of the Dutch Antilles in the Caribbean. It is about forty miles north of the Venezuelan coast and in between Aruba and Bonaire. My mum was thinking of buying a property out there but had never been, and I volunteered to go. I worked and rented a little cottage close to my mum, but I've never felt at home in the UK, even though I kept coming back to refuel before jetting off to different shores once again. Why? Because the once crystal-clear energies that flowed through the veins of the lands have always unsettled me, as they have been left uncleansed through the ancient and ancestral sludge that has slipped in and clogged the pores, causing much of the surface to suffocate with unresolved and accumulating trauma running through its very heart and soul.

I researched Curacao properly before going there and managed to secure rental accommodation before leaving the UK. On the plane, I sat next to someone whose wife was opening up a Hunkemöller store in Curacao, a Dutch clothing manufacturer founded in Amsterdam in 1886, similar to Victoria's Secret.

I was excited when I landed on the island. The place I'd rented wasn't in the best of areas, but that didn't bother me. I explored the area mostly on foot as I realised that the public transport infrastructure was nihil, as the few buses that did run only ran every two hours. The smaller, nine-seater vans operated by individuals labelled as minibuses ran more frequently than regular public transport; however, they had no schedule, and they never ran at night. I couldn't afford a car, so I figured I'd have to make do with my 'Fred Flintstone' feet and the minivans.

I sent out my résumé to various places and went to several hotels in the area to drop it off by hand. I soon landed a PA position for the MD of the Kura Hulanda Hotel and Village in Otrabanda. It didn't pay much, but it was a start. Kura Hulanda was founded by the Dutch millionaire, entrepreneur, and philanthropist Jacob Gelt Dekker, who completely transformed the rundown Otrabanda district into what it is today. The hotel had a dialysis centre at the bottom of the village, making it a breeze for dialysis patients to receive treatment while staying there. Dekker also opened the Kura Hulanda "slavery" museum, depicting the cruel slave trade by the Dutch. I visited it a few times, and I must say it is rather thought-provoking and emotional to see how people were treated due to the colour of their skin. I met him a few times while he was being treated for cancer, and he was a humble and compassionate human being, with no fuss whatsoever. Regardless of his failing health, he still made the most out of life, remaining upbeat, and despite the setbacks, it never deterred his spirit from achieving the many things he set out to do. He finally crossed over in 2019 after a long battle with cancer that got the better of him.

Several months later, I commenced working for a global financial services company. It paid more, and I'd never worked in the financial sector before.

I also started working at Hunkemöller on Thursday nights and Saturdays, so I was always busy and on the go. I moved closer to work, walking twenty-five minutes each way. Was I happy? Hell no! Curacao was not the place for me; it had no soul, and I felt vacant within. I never felt safe at night; there was no street lighting where I lived. It was pitch black. In fact, this is common on the island, and thus Curacao is plunged into darkness once the sun sets. Some areas were beautiful, but others were severely rundown; there was a divide that was clear to see. Hot water was a luxury, and many homes had no boilers installed. I hated taking cold showers, but I had to make do. You had to hope and pray it had been a hot and sunny day so that at least the pipes had warmed up and you had some lukewarm water coming out of the showerhead. I didn't have a washing machine either, nor were there any launderettes, so I washed all my clothes by hand, using a kettle to boil the water. You learn to live with what you've got, adjust, accept it and make it work.

To make matters worse, my mum decided against coming down to Curacao, as she didn't think it wise to invest in a property on the island, which caused a deep sense of loss within me. Hence, I did what I do best, throwing myself into my work and neglecting myself, falling back into my usual coping mechanism, beating myself up for my own created misery. My self-loathing knew no bounds.

I rescued a badly abused mutt from the dog pound to fill the void in my already deeply unhappy existence. She was called Snoopy, but I renamed her Kyra. I worked long hours, as that was the nature of my work, and I know it wasn't always fair on her, but I loved that little schizo dog, and if she had to pee, bless her, she'd nicely do it in the shower cubicle. Sometimes, I'd pop home for lunch and take her for a quick walk. Most dogs in Curacao are guard dogs and kept outside, and Kyr and I nearly got bitten by the neighbour's aggressive Rottweiler that had escaped from her yard. I should have socialised with her, but there were no doggie daycare centres, I didn't have a car, nor was she allowed in the minivans, and there were no parks, so I was cut off from the world.

In truth, I didn't socialise either. I was apprehensive of people; I had my work but felt cut off on the inside, lugging my soul under my arms, trying to make the best out of the situation I had duly created. The more a dog (or person) has been subject to abandonment or abuse, the more anxiety-ridden they're likely to be. I suffered from island fever and felt at a dis-ease within myself, so naturally, I was a mirror to my dog as much as my dog was a mirror to me.

Animals are the key to the doorway of your heart, to unlocking your inner truth and potential, often drawing out the shadow sides needing healing. They're a comfort, like a warm cosmic blanket of unconditional love, and are wonderful teachers, reflecting the mere light of love from them to you and you back to them.

I guess you could class me as an "emotionalic": I was addicted to my emotions, running rampant, in the outer world impressing itself upon my inner world—I was a star at repeating what I did not repair. For the record, I did not neglect my dog, as I made sure she got her food and treats.

I hated my life and often worked harder than most. Whilst many of my colleagues were great, I felt very much suppressed, and I was frustrated that I wasn't given the opportunity to develop myself. I applied for a transfer to the Canadian office; however, that quickly fell in the water, as I fell out with my operations manager at a New Year's Eve office party, discussing work. In his drunken stupor, he asked me why I even cared, as I had resigned and that even if I were hired, they'd fire me within three weeks, as I couldn't hold down a job.

I was shocked by his outburst and told him to get his facts straight before blurting out any untruths. In the end, I received a forced apology through an intervention with HR. He could not remember what he'd said as he'd been drinking. What a load of crock; he sat there with a poker face, lying through his teeth. His whole demeanour gave it away. After the incident, he avoided talking to me, making my life a living hell. Subsequently, I was rejected for the role in Canada, after which I resigned.

Bullying in the workplace happens more often than we care to realise, and many suffer in silence, afraid to speak up, in fear of losing their job. In the end my wellbeing was far more important. It was most certainly an experience, but I was glad to have shut the door on that toxic environment and leave Curacao. It wasn't for me; we were like chalk and cheese.

Several weeks before leaving Curacao, I told myself I wanted to work for Shell. I manifested this and got hired as a project coordinator, working in The Hague. I love challenges and have always taken on jobs that have plunged me into the deep end, learning new things. My aunt, my mum's sister, had viewed a place in the Hague for Kyra and me before we landed, and even though it was small, it was quaint and had a huge terrace.

It was truly a breath of fresh air for me to be back in civilization. It had been twelve years since I'd set foot in Holland. I lived ten minutes from the city centre and five minutes from the park. It was great to be able to walk around and pop to the shops. I was utterly exhilarated that I had hot water and being able to take long hot showers was pure bliss. The apartment also came with a washing machine, which meant the smell of fresh and clean clothes. It was such a delight; we take so much for granted in life, and being stripped from certain comforts made me more appreciative of what I had.

On the Road to Hell with Mark

Where do I even begin? The events leading up to me falling into the abyss and nearly "drowning" commenced when I met the charming and dashing Mark through MySpace while I was still living in Buckingham. We were in touch here and there throughout my time in Curacao and when I returned to Holland.

In early 2009, having applied for a six-month tourist visa at the US Consulate in Amsterdam, I visited him in Raleigh, North Carolina. I had left the US in 2004 and had no issues, nor was I worried about obtaining a visa, as I worked for Shell. The US consulate in Amsterdam was small, and the people working there were very personable, unlike my encounter in the UK.

When we met in person, there was an instant attraction; it was magnetic, and there seemed no hint of trouble on the horizon. Mark was an inch shorter than I was, had a beautifully handsome face, chiselled jaw, brown hair, and just oozed charisma. I could not pinpoint what this was—it was as if I had known him for years. We had prolonged conversations, with him finishing my sentences and me finishing his. But he kept a dark secret hidden from me.

My mistake was that I have always run after a guy, and looking back, he should have made an effort to come and visit me and buy an international calling card to maybe call me. It was always me having to call and visit him. It seems I still hadn't learned.

In the three years I had known him, he would disappear from time to time and resurface, and I'd get some lame excuse. He had been on probation for drug offences, but I didn't understand the seriousness of it; I thought it was just for smoking pot now and again. I was a bit blasé to the fact that he was a full-blown addict. It was so alien to me that I didn't grasp the extent of it until it was too late.

I stayed in a hotel for several days before his mother twisted my arm into staying in her home for the remainder of my ten-day stay. His mother is a devout Christian, and I remember attending church on a Sunday while I was there. Upon entering this particular Christian church, all I wanted to do was turn around and run. The energy held within suffocated me, it was filled with a heaviness that pressed upon my soul, yet I had to sit there and breathe through all I heard, which was in total non-resonance with who I was. I don't sing hymns, nor do I believe in the narrative of the Bible. The written scriptures of the conglomerate, the church, are a dogma of rules. It is not the scripture of Christ consciousness, for Christ Consciousness is the "scripture" of the heart. Religion is being conditioned to live by a set of rules indoctrinating fear, believing in separation from Source.

As a kid, however, I loved visiting Buddhist and Hindu temples in Malaysia, but churches have always made me feel somewhat uncomfortable. I very much believe this has to do with a past life, having lived in the southern states of the North Americas, where the sand and dust whipped the air during the arid seasons. I can see myself getting out of a carriage, with the dust hitting my black boots and dirtying the rim of my long grey-blue cotton skirt, speaking with a heavy Southern drawl. My brother was a travelling preacher, and being his adventurous younger sister, I decided to go with him. Under his wing, I empowered women, not only in the area of hygiene, but also for them to learn to stand up for themselves. That did not sit well with some of the men in one of the towns, who said I was blasphemous, having gone against the grind of God's will, having disrespected and dishonoured both them and God. I was spat upon, cornered, and raped because, per their ideology and words, *"the wrath of God haveth no mercy, for what is wrong must be righted, to cleanse the earth of the uncleansed sins back to the holy lands of the forgiving Father."* My brother knew of this, but I refused to get the child aborted. I was violated, and it was a traumatic experience, yet I fostered no hate; I merely withdrew within myself, allowing myself to heal in the silence of my wandering heart, eventually pulling myself out of it, continuing with educating women. Unfortunately, at nearly full term, several men found me, dragging me off into the desert, pinning me down, and cutting out my unborn infant, leaving me to die, with death welcoming me briskly back into the arms of the warmth of the light. The infant, a baby boy also died, but heaven only knows why they took the body of that poor wee child with them.

Sri Sri Ravi Shankar, a spiritual leader, and founder of the Art of Living Centre, said something that resonated with me when I was in India many years ago. He said, every created religion is the banana peel, the outer layer, whilst spirituality is the inner fruit of the banana itself. Religion is the surface, the outer covering of many rituals and rules, whilst spirituality is the fruit, the core substance that connects us back to the source of ourselves and thus infinite source energy (God). We are all particles of God; we are all creators in our own right, and each and every action affects the breadth and depth of the flow of universal consciousness.

People pray to God when they are God and thus pray to themselves for help in helping themselves! To take it up with God means to take it up with yourself. When people state it's between you and God, it's between you and your God Self to find a resolution. When people tell you to love God, it means loving yourself and all. Christ consciousness is love consciousness; it is the infinite love divine knocking on the dormant and closed eyelids of our souls, gently persuading us that all we have to do is look to the light and love within to allow us to flourish from the inside out. As the Light BEings state, *"You are each the alpha to the omega of your eternal Soul Selves. You are not who you think you are, but who you choose to forge out of the iron cast in the fires, for nothing is as interchangeable as the energetic flux of the Light within through the creation of one's own making. You are a fellow traveller in and of the Cosmos amongst the Galaxial Grid of Existence, all evolving at an exponentially different rate of vibrational awareness and undercurrents of understanding. And yet that is the interweaving of the architecture through the reminisce in the All in All of us, for the Universal tapestry is a grand design of Energetic Weaving and Evolving Consciousness. A vivre le joi of one's enigmatic creation. You are the You in each other, as one is the I AM Presence in the heart of one another. One is a mere eclectic of the BEing of the Whole. A Light of the same of the All, but for the chosen garment of one's current embodiment, to create one's experiences in the Cosmic Game of Evolution, to the evolvement of oneself and the karmic imprint one has so chosen to incarnate into. Remember you are here to walk your journey, and BE your beautiful Truth of yours truly your Divine Self."*

I read tarot and angel cards for others, which vehemently went against all that Mark's mother believed in. I took these with me to Raleigh and was "politely" told to keep them out of sight. She stated that I was Lucifer's daughter. That's great because Lucifer is as much a part of the all as we are. He isn't the "evil" bastard he's been made out to be, but I realise that everyone believes differently, and one is as aware as one chooses to be. Lucifer is the builder of many worldly civilisations, and "evil" is merely the absence of love. As Lucifer says, *"You've bet on the wrong horse here, thinking I AM the epitome of 'evil' incarnate. I AM as much Divine Consciousness as you are the I AM of all that You are in the I AM of All of Me. I AM the breath of Creation, like all my brothers and sisters, and what you perceive to be good is in fact 'evil,' but one sees it not, for one lives a life of inconsistent conditioned dualities, having been knocked senseless. You are merely sleeping beauties having been incapacitated by the so-called sweetened 'bitters' of Wonderland; it is time to awaken the lulled senses of the falsely fed narrative as that is and has always been the portrayal of acceptance of the I AM in the Light of who I AM and who I AM not."*

Lord Sananda

Mark's mother threw Jesus around like blimmin' confetti, making sure to say the Lord's prayer before every meal, which I had to adhere to. She dictated many Bible scriptures, which truthfully did my head in.

The origin of saying grace before meals was not only to thank some God in the "sky" but to honour and bless the sacrifice of the food served on your plate. Sending love and light to everything you eat lightens the energy of your food. We become more aware of what we eat rather than taking what's on our plate for granted. Food is energy and carries frequency, just as you are energy and carry frequency. However many hands the food has passed, from the seed of its 'creation' to those having prepared your food, all throw their energy into the mix of what you eat. If a person is in a bad mood, you digest that energy.

I love the Enlightened Master Teacher Lord Sananda; Jesus was one of his earthly incarnations. He is of Venusian descent, and as Jesus was probably one of the greatest spiritual teachers of the incarnated ascended masters who chose to walk among us as a Starseed on earth.

Jesus was an Essene and became a High Priest in the Temple of the Order of Melchizedek. He has a gentle, loving nature about him, and basking in his energy tends to calm you down to the quietness within, giving you clarity of mind in any situation. He says, *"Everything can be transmuted with the art of loving yourself and in turn loving others, for one is love, it is the foundation of who you are, one has simply forgotten the spark of that Light due to the conditioning of the gravity of the Earthly dimensional frequency."*

He will always tell you to rise above, forgive, and embrace one another like the earthly family you are, for love transcends even the darkest of souls back to having a love for themselves.

"Did you forget who I AM, what I stood for in the embodiment of Jesus? Did I not lead by example? Have you strayed so far from the beautiful heart of Self that you have spun your Mind out of control, having ingested too much of that delirious worldly cocktail of "intoxication" to even understand that you are Love?

Who I AM, one must become, by walking the unknown road through the hues of the engrained and tainted human conditioning back to the beautiful remembrance of the Light and Love of Self.

Submerge yourself in the beautiful swamp of your twirling Mind, and be that Divine stripper, stripping yourself naked of all the conditioning you have so slapped upon your beautiful Soul, immersing yourself in the waters of unconditional love and emerging replenished, becoming a vessel of love and light, touching all with the warmth of your heart. So, I ask thee to merely lay down your "arms" to all the twisted discoloured distortion of all that you believe to be love, and simply feel the love in my embrac-ed arms, letting all but fall away, bouncing back to the beautiful hue of the Authentic you.

AM I not the Bearer of Christ Consciousness? It is only by inserting the ingredient of Love into your Consciousness that you fuse back to the fuzzy warmth and lightness of your Soul. Yet Man has been riddled with the plague of the bullet-ridden EGO and the negative swirlin' of hybrid e-motions at the jest of a mere courting of others in the field at play. Thinketh not that one is but the only species in the celestial heavens of the Universal dimensions, for that is a fabled narrative to keep you constricted in the very chokehold of a boa-tic matrix of Existence.

To unravel the shadows buried deep within, one must unbury the murkiness and dredge the mud back up to the surface, cleansing the Self with the pureness of the "gemilicious" Light Divine, flowing back into the Waters of the Consciousness of Self. One cannot surpass the depths of the abyss unless one has but plunged into one's shadow sides, transmuting all back to the Love of the Light of the Heart space with the transmutation of the Violet Flame.

One needs to come undone in the philosophy of having done a wicked game of a number on be-com-ing oneself, readjusting the sails through the winds of change and peppering a frequential dose of Love over the Self, sneezing out the gunk-laden debris within the Mind—much like a vitamin infuse for the Mind to diffuse back to the Soul's happy high vibe of BEing the Self. Remember, you are the sum of the awe of the all-encompassing awesomeness that is you"

We have become too engrossed with ourselves, driven by our ego, that we often forget to communicate from the heart without having the failsafe of all the conditions in place. Did the great Spiritual teacher Jesus not say thou shalt love thy neighbour as thyself? He did not mean to stab thy neighbour, or talk s*** about them. Nor did he mean merely 'loving' thy neighbour next door – he meant loving all your worldly brothers and sisters in the very acceptance precisely as they are. If you can't love yourself, you cast that non-loving attitude towards others, which is duly returned to you in equal measure as what you cast out. Matthew 7 NIV clearly states, *"Do not judge, or you too will be judged. For in the same way you judge others, you will be judged, and with the measure you use, it will be measured to you. Why do you look at the speck of sawdust in your brother's eye and pay no attention to the plank in your own eye?"*

For the record, Jesus was the essence of BEing, and did not die for your sins; he merely showed humanity that there is no death, that we simply change form and transcend back to the loving light we are and have always been. The Bible merely got lost in translation of separation.

"See ME as I see You—for my Child, You are ME, as much as I AM You.

You are the All in Everything as much as Everything is a part of You. Are you not the epitome of pure Light and beauty defined?

To love ME wholly is to love YourSelf. Your place of worship is the body you have given yourself home to, for the church lies not in the concrete of the worldly jungle, in a recited fals-ed prayer book; it lies within the sacred sanctum of thy own beautiful heart. Find refuge in the solitude of self, for the pureness of a said prayer comes from a desire of the heart to remove the built-up bricks of the warped and hardened walls within to allow for the EGO to gently dissipate in the wee hours of the warm rays of the morn' Sun, having defrosted the very coarsened core of Self, allowing the energetic flow of love and abundance to flow but ever so lovingly from within trickling to the world without.

One grows up but oh so conditioned, having to uncondition the Self of these 'weirdilicious' ingrained beliefs back to the bare nakedness of the 'bones' one truly is. It is merely through the absence of love that one grows wonky, withering in the cold and dark of one's dampened spirit of the shivering Self. Always feed the Mind with the nutrients of hope, truth, and love, nurturing the Self back to the warmth of the bless-ed soul that you are.

Know that I will cloak thee in the warmth of my Light, nourishing thee with the sprinkles of my radiant Love, helping to heal thy Soul, strengthening thy resolve, in the hope one will choose but to walk into the sunshine of better tomorrows by merely speaking the truth of the radiant Soul thou art. Life is merely learning to look past the illusion of the upside-down of everything rather than the downside of the upside of everything. What is real? What is not? Are you real, or are you not? Was Alice in Wonderland, or was the Wonderland in Alice all along? I dare thee to wander within the Wonderlands of Self, to cast the net wide open and walk through but the very wondrous wonders of Self.

The gist of Life is to remember who you are, a beautiful Child of the Sun, and to move forward with Grace and Gratitude in all of Life's eternal ebb and flows. And so it is."

~*The Ascended Master Lord Sananda (Jesus)*~

Life in Holland with Mark

What I did next would define me as tripping and hurtling down the mountainside into the depths of the darkness below—I bought Mark a plane ticket to come and live with me in the Hague, where I resided. You're right, he should have bought his own ticket, but he didn't have the money and seeing I had a good job, I stupidly bought it instead. I honestly was so excited and thought this could be the start of something good.

However, after several weeks, he became frustrated at not finding any work, as he didn't have a social security number. I helped him out and signed him up with several casting agencies, paying for the required shoot for his photographs, and he got quite a bit of work through that. I also applied for cash-in-hand jobs on Craigslist for him, and he had several gigs building up stands for exhibitions in Amsterdam.

Wherever I have made a "home" for myself, I have never been without work. Yet here I was, working long hours and still having to help Mark out because he wasn't savvy enough to figure out how to apply for jobs! I opened a bank account in his name, which was connected to mine—another mistake I came to regret because if there was no more money in his account, any withdrawals or debits would draft from my account.

We seemed to be doing okay for several months. We hopped on the bike, cycled a lot, and talked about getting married in Norway, as it was easier than jumping through the hoops in Holland. There were, however, obstacles when it came to the paperwork, so it never happened. In hindsight, that was my saving grace.

I had my own activities at night, following a tarot course. Mark worked out to feel better within himself, but not without buying GHB / GBL, Gamma Hydroxybutyrate, which is readily and easily available in Holland. He was always working on his outer appearance rather than working to heal his inner sanctum and his wounded mind, to feel more at ease in his own skin.

Bodybuilders use GHB for muscle building and reducing fat, which can have anabolic effects due to protein synthesis. I had taken drugs for "recreational" use many years prior, but I had never been around severe substance abuse, so I had no idea what the signs were.

There was one incident where I had gotten some water out of the fridge, which contained GBH, which I wasn't aware of; you can't taste or smell it. GHB is a central nervous system depressant, commonly referred to as a "date rape" drug because it's often placed in alcoholic beverages to make the user feel sleepy and euphoric. Its side effects range from sweating, loss of consciousness, and nausea, to hallucinations and amnesia. Those who abuse it can suffer from severe withdrawal symptoms: confusion, shaking, epileptic seizures, and even slipping into a coma. GHB and GBL can reduce people's inhibitions, and some take it to have more intense sex.

Ten minutes after having consumed it, I was off my rocker. It made me feel disconnected like I was the observer of my body outside of myself, and having sex on it was not my idea of fun.

Mark apologised to me profusely, and I told him to stop taking it, as this was not for his fitness regime; this was substance abuse, keeping him on a continuous high. It was near impossible to wean him off the GHB, as he was too far gone and had become dependent on it, and slowly, matters deteriorated.

My little dog Kyra was his next victim. She was not good with strangers; in fact, she was terrified of men and people in general. I helped her as much as I could over the years by taking her to a dog homoeopath, a dog whisperer, and a trainer, but her fear was so deeply ingrained that she trusted no one but me and eventually my mum. Even taking her for walks outside was at times difficult, as she walked in continuous fear of her own shadow. She was caught in a non-stop fight or flight syndrome, yet I loved that dog with all my heart, even though I was tough on her at times, as she tested my patience. But we choose dogs that "complement" our inner reflection of who we are and how we see the world, and she was just as damaged as I was.

One day, Mark decided to put a tiny bit of pot in her food, hoping that she would relax a bit more, and the poor thing was definitely more relaxed within herself but merely dozed off after a while. I did not think it was a good idea, but he did it nevertheless. I use CBD oil infused with melissa and lavender, which has been attuned with vibrational healing by an amazing healer called Marlene, for my current dog, Myra, who has dementia and it has done wonders for her (www.remediesmatter.com).

I was working in the office and couldn't be watching Mark 24/7, but some things happened to Kyra that have baffled me to this day. As we were living on the second floor of a building, the poor thing hopped onto the ledge of the balcony and decided to walk across it, falling onto the restaurant's awning below, rolling off, and landing on all four paws in their garden. The restaurant slapped me with the bill as the canopy went bust. Another time she was huddled on the kitchen counter in a corner, which broke my heart. I blamed myself for the longest time, learning to forgive myself many years later.

One evening when I had my tarot course, Mark decided to go cycling through a rough neighbourhood in the Hague. He was looking for trouble and descended right back into the seedy world of drugs, landing in the hotbed of the Dutch Crips, run by a notorious figure called Keylow. I thought I'd finally found my soul mate for life. No such luck, mate! For the record, his family had not warned me about his history of severe drug abuse. He could go without for a while before seeking to numb his pain again. His drug of choice? Crack cocaine.

His mother was furious with me; she said I had taken her son away from her and his family. He had a little boy that lived with his former partner and was mostly an absentee father. He came from a highly dysfunctional family, and drugs were his choice to escape the pain of his experiences that had consumed his battered mind.

He was like a part-time crack addict: fine for weeks, then disappearing for weeks, something he kept hidden from me until he moved in with me. I knew he had been in prison for stealing something but didn't think anything of it; that's how blasé I was. I paid all the bills, even got him a new wardrobe, as he didn't have a dime to his name.

After he disappeared, he called me under the guise of having been mugged and needing to pay someone off. At that point, I had no clue what was going on, and I met with him and some Moroccan guy, giving him the required amount of several hundred euros. He thanked me and said he would be back later, after which they both disappeared, with me being none the wiser.

He returned for a few days until he disappeared again, this time deciding to pawn all my electronic stuff and taking all my loose change from the kitchen counter. I was smart enough to call the bank and block his debit card; otherwise, he would have bled my account dry. When he came back, I had already packed his suitcase and kicked him out of my apartment—having to get the police involved, who put him on the train to Schiphol airport. Do you think he made it to Schiphol? Hell no, the cops didn't even escort him there. They should have deported his arse there and then, instead of leaving him at the train station to catch a train.

Several hours later, I received a call from the lost and found department at Leiden train station, telling me that a suitcase was left on the platform, asking me if I could come and retrieve it. I had enough shit to deal with but picked it up after work, leaving it packed by the door if he ever decided to return. Stupidly, I was worried about him, whilst he cared nothing for either living or dying. I felt like I was drowning; it was like a dam had burst, and I was caught up in the riptide of the cascading waters.

Several days later, he called me up in tears. Apparently, he had gone from Leiden to Rotterdam and partied out there before going to Amsterdam and being stranded. I excused myself from work, grabbed some clothes from his still-packed suitcase, and hopped on a train to Amsterdam, booking him into a cheap hotel.

I was shocked when I saw the state of him. I had never seen someone so destroyed by drugs; it had drained the life out of him. He looked harrowing and dishevelled; his fingertips were blistered, raw, and open, which is typical for crack users. I needed to realise that no matter how hard you try to save someone, that person must truly want to save and change themselves. Even though he may have wanted it, he wasn't ready to release and heal his inner demons. I had to understand that I wasn't there to fix him, but I didn't quite comprehend this at the time. You can drag a horse to water, but you cannot force it to drink. It wasn't my "monkey" to resolve his issues, nor was I there to put out every single fire, yet that is exactly what I did, all the while fanning the flames and burning my arse in the process.

"Your past does not define you unless you allow your mind to remain in a 'cluster-you-know-what' state of BEing. Your life. Your journey. Your experiences. Live it how you see fit, but never remain roaming round in the gloaming of your past, because one causes nothing but a rampage of kinkilicious disarray within the physical essence that you have given your Soul home to. You suffer because you have beaten your mind

senseless. You've got to let go and forgive, but most of all, love and hug yourself to commence creating the life you are so deserving of."

~The Ascended Master St Germain~

Mark cried so hard and said that he did not want to be this person but had no idea how to stop the cycle of addiction he was trapped in. He told me that if he died, to tell his son that he loved him and that he was sorry.

I went to the pharmacy and got some antiseptic to clean and disinfect the wounds on his fingertips, which were horrific. He told me to take a picture of him and his hands so that if he ever went off the rails again, I could show him the consequences of his actions. I got him some healthy foods and a big bowl of soup, and he decided to call up a counsellor himself, with me accompanying him to the appointment the next day.

Mark was brutally honest and said he needed help; otherwise, he wouldn't make it. Because he didn't have a Dutch social and was not insured, he was turned down everywhere. We then went to Smith & Jones, another clinic for drug and alcohol addicts. They told him to detox first and then come back, which made no sense to me, as detoxing from crack is truly dangerous. The risks of relapsing throughout are high; hence detox should be completed under medical supervision and managed by a medical professional. As with other drugs, crack withdrawal can take months to subside completely, so it seems I was stuck in a catch-22 situation, a complete paradox, due to all the contradictory rules, which held neither rhyme nor reason. A person wants to get better, but you won't admit him because he needs to detox, which needs to be overseen by a medical professional?

Not wanting an addict in my home, I left him at the hotel. Every clinic he visited had turned him down, and several days later, not in the right frame of mind, he hopped back on a train to the Hague, back into the "arms" of Keylow. I still hadn't figured out who the guy was, with Mark telling me that I couldn't trust him, as all he did was ply him with drugs, and he was just too weak to say no. I didn't believe a word that came out of his mouth at that point, so instead, I stupidly listened to Keylow, who promised to keep an eye on him and keep him clean. I had to pay two months' rent in advance for Mark, costing me another one thousand euros.

In the meantime, I called his mother. Instead of being supportive and understanding, she screamed at me, telling me this was all my fault and that I had manipulated her son into flying out to Holland. She never levelled with me, nor did anyone else in his family, about the severity of his drug abuse, as he had been in the system's revolving doors long before I met him. She bore down on me with her vicious remarks, which tore into the fabric of my very soul. I have never had to deal with someone so spiteful and so full of hate towards another human being. When I hung up, I was shaking like a leaf, just sitting there crying, unable to breathe. Thankfully, I was able to reach my mother, who was my beacon in these dark tidings.

A week later, Mark broke into my apartment when I was at work. I am not quite sure how he managed to climb up two storeys, most probably via the drainpipes, but when an addict is high, all they can think of is getting their next fix. He forced the latch of the top window and must have crawled in somehow. He also smashed my front door; it hung half off its hinges when I got home. The last thing he took was my laptop, even locking my poor dog in her crate while plundering my flat.

It was a terrifying ordeal for me. I had never been in a situation like this before and hardly slept, remaining alert.

I had been in touch with the police and immigration, with the cops having returned my laptop to me after Keylow had released it to them. The cops, however, remained tight-lipped on Keylow and his activities. My mum, who had flown over, was with me at the time, and the police officer asked her what I was planning to do. She told him I was starting over in the UK again, and he agreed that this was the best course of action to take, considering the circumstances I had wandered into.

The Dutch Crips

"Keylow," a.k.a. Delano was the leader of the Crips in Holland, living in the Schilderswijk area of The Hague. Most of the gang were of Antillean or Suriname descent, coming from broken homes and the Crips were a surrogate family. They made their money both in dealing and stealing drugs, but as I soon came to find out, the police wouldn't touch Keylow—he had this celebrity status of sorts.

He was a mastermind at importing and distributing drugs in Holland, having many influential people in his pocket—probably blackmailing them by having damning information on them, so it's no wonder the police didn't touch him. I've always said Holland is a "narcostate"; the big cities have always been littered with more drugs than anywhere else in the world. Drugs are readily available, with many messing themselves up, seeking solace and an escapism out of their own pain. Crime pays, so it won't stop anytime soon, and the police in Holland are slack in how they deal with crime, being corrupt to the core themselves.

When I met Keylow, he gave me this total BS story that he was helping the impoverished youth get back on their feet so they could make something out of their lives—giving hope to young kids, having created a "youth centre." Really what he was doing was using them as drug runners instead, since no one would suspect kids.

In 2016 the gang changed its name from the Crips to Caloh Wagon and became a "motorcycle" club—same gang, same dealings, different name. Keylow is currently remanded in prison, awaiting trial. He made a real-life documentary on liquidating people, and members of his gang are in the episode "This Isn't Miami Vice" in the Netflix series *Dope*, in which the bustling Rotterdam drug trade is exposed. According to the Public Prosecution Service, he took on countless assignments from various clients as a murder broker, with jobs yielding the most money given priority. His most important client was the well-known drug lord Ridouan Taghi, whose gang allegedly assassinated and killed prominent Dutch crime reporter and justice campaigner Peter R. de Vries in July 2021. Peter acted in an advisory role in the Marengo trial and was well known for solving many cold cases, including getting a confession undercover from Joran van der Sloot in the murder of Natalee Holloway in Aruba.

Murder victims were simply a commodity to Delano, and the Dutch Public Prosecution Service garnered staggering evidence consisting of millions of chat messages, pictures, videos, emails, and various other documents brokering murders on such an unprecedented scale, the likes of which the Dutch Criminal Justice System had never seen before.

Within less than three weeks, Mark had spiralled entirely out of control. My mother, who thought the situation extremely dire and knew how distraught I had become, got me out of The Hague with everything packed and ready for shipment within a few days. She found a garden flat for Kyra and me to move into in Wallington. I honestly don't know how I would have managed without her.

Even when I moved to Wallington and Mark was in Holland, I still worried about his well-being. He called me several times from a MoneyGram location and told me Keylow's gang mostly kept him locked in a small room with a gun pointed at his head, and he saw small kids running in and out, merely used as drug runners for his operation.

The Dis-ease of Addiction

I have never been overly sexual, and nor am I not ashamed of that fact. Let's face it; it was too much hassle, painful and difficult to achieve an orgasm. Peeing after having intercourse was like acid; it burnt the hell out of me with several days of throbbing, all for a mere five-second orgasm.

Sex, for Mark, however, other than drugs, was the only way he knew how, to plug the holes in his painfully shattered soul. It was hard to find out that he'd advertised himself on Craigslist because I wasn't sexual enough. He wrote that he was an American actor/model and entrepreneur, had a perfect body, was well endowed, educated, and aimed to please.

Some people go through trauma, masking their pain with such hatred towards themselves that they get lost in their entangled web of spun darkness within, unable to manoeuvre back to the light, as they have booby trapped themselves within their experiences, reliving those #repeat-events, that all they can do is numb their pain by a 'poison' of their choosing.

The Pleiadian Council states that sexuality is a key, a doorway to ascending to the higher realms of consciousness, but not as understood in the current paradigm of understanding.

"The making of love between two people is a fusion of two souls into one in the elevation of ecstasy of Consciousness. It is a spiritual celebration of reaching ever higher states of bliss, causing a tremor in the soul particles, an emulsion within, for love is much like the symphonic flow of electrical energy currents flowing into one. The art of 'making love' is not 'sex', and sex does not plug the holes in your bullet-ridden Mind having left a gaping doughnut hole in your soul; it only fuels the fire of escapism into the abyss below. It is a deviation in walking back to oneself in the intensifying of the pain through a temporary fix of created momentary euphoria of feeling a delusional bliss, until you are right back where you started from that momentary lapse of joy slumped into that created condition of 'pain.' You look so much for love without yourself you forget it is all inside of you.

Humanity has become much like fiddler crabs, fiddling along like an out-of-tune fiddle, having thwarted themselves and lost all sense of self due to the overload of sticky labels attached to the blinded Mind, unable to see the path ahead, moving 'delicately' sideways, living outward, consuming inward, rather than living inward and creating with a love and harmony outward. Life is all about perspective. Limited or enlightened?. Note to Self: You've got to love yourself to free yourself."

Mark's mind was a tripwire, a hallucinogenic minefield, having allowed the dis-ease to consume him, taking it out on his body, severely abusing it. He had been whacked out of alignment for many years, not having the capability or understanding to "uncondition" that pain. As St. Germain says:

"To torment or not to torment oneself, that is the rhetorical question, and a torrent of a torment of thy own making, n'est-ce pas? No one in the world nor the whole dang Universe is responsible for your emotional reactions except you. Others can do and say whatever they like, but whichever buttons they press, understand that what happens inside you and how you willingly choose to process these e-motions is the mere result of what you think and feel, non? So, will you be a blown-out of proportions emotional spicy chorizo, running rampant into the vice of your escapisms or a sweetened as pie sugar-covered churro, blowin' but love to these serv-ed experiences? To be bothered, or not to be bothered, that is the question, and yet one needs to learn how to alchemise one's created painful experiences, embracing the inner 'cop,' setting the Self straight, rather than fleeing the scene."

Addiction is a dis-ease of the soul within the body it houses. It is a chosen and created experience, by the soul, due to the absorbance of the energetic waves they have compounded in their chosen environment. It is a harbouring of traumatic experiences in that person's cellular memory body, holding the "user" hostage until they are ready to release the fear within that trauma that has kept them from living a life in connection with and to themselves. It's much like being a chained bird, unable to literally let that "shit" go because it is unable to take flight in the freedom it so relishes. First, figure out what weighs you down before commencing on the journey to healing yourself and setting yourself free.

ADDICTION means **A**busing the self into the **D**epths of **D**arkness **I**nternally through the **C**reated **T**rauma **I**nflicted on **O**ne's **N**avigational-self.

Navigational-self pertains to the neuropeptides, as in the inner workings of quantum mechanics. Every thought we think is a conscious process; it is energy set in motion. What you think, so shall you become—creating within a neuropeptide molecule, a chemical messenger that connects to and docks at a cell receptor site, sending a signal back into the emotional hard drive, pinging back a conditioned response, manifesting as our physical reality. We are in the constant flow of creating and becoming. Our mind thinks it and thus builds it to become, manifesting from our inner to our outer reality. Addiction is a kink in the cable, a disruption in our energy system, a constipation clogging up our internal flow and thus causing havoc with our state of mind and well-being. As Lord Sananda says:

"You think you become addicted to drugs, alcohol, or whatever one's chastised choice of escapism may be to evade one's in dire straits e-motions? The brain is a magical mushroom of energetic wonder, wired according to your Mind's will. Thus, those wonderful neuropeptides get one's 'pep' in a neurotic twist of tides, causing a bewildered commotion, all because you have programmed them according to the stated conditioning. Like, little soldiers, they listen and abide by the orders from the bark-ed Mind and dock onto the receptor cells in total obedience and correspondence thereof."

Addiction is influenced by the created paradigm of the instilled societal factors. Blaming other people is not part of the solution. Instead, addicts need to take responsibility and focus on what they need to do to heal and recover. It is an uncovering of the muddied soils within the streams of their heart; it is a recovering of that inner light that they have so subdued, back out to the sparkle of the beautiful divine grace that they are.

Without realising it, we often choose to give our power away to our urges, to plug the holes in our cheese, to ease our burdened minds. Self-mastery is the key to healing and transcending the experience(s) that have kept us cornered into stonewalling ourselves. Why can we not let go of the experiences? What holds us back? Is it our presumptuous ego? Is it the fear of judgement from others? Addiction is a real mind-screw, all created within the mind, with the ego in the driver's seat running amok, shattering the soul into a further illusion of all that it is not. It is mastering a slow form of suicide, a self-loathing victim mentality keeping the "user" in the grips of that lower-vibrational darkness. You cannot save them; only they can save themselves, nor can you free them, for they are as much the lock as they are the key to freeing themselves from their incarcerated mind.

I love Confucius, an aspect of the Ascended Master Djwhal Kuhl, aiding humanity in attaining a higher state of consciousness. He badgered me to add something additional to the dis-ease of addiction as he suffered from arthritis. Not sure where he was going with this, I asked him to elaborate:

"I chose to reside in the cold, travelling through the peaks and valleys of the long-gone golden age of ancient China, choosing to suffer the stiffness in my joints, but lest one forgets, the herbs of mother nature do wonders for one's body, mind, and soul. The mere ingredients of the mandrake root and poppy plants, brewed into a sweetened salve of an herbal tea, aided in the wonderful warmth and alleviation of the pains of my old and crooked joints. Yet in those days, herbs were treated with respect, as a healing aid for the bearer of the Soul. These days, all 'drugs' have been injected with a fusion of a variety of chemical-laden compounds, with the intent of poisoning the very fabric of the user, serving as an escapism of the pained Soul and one becomes 'Confucious,' metaphorically becoming 'consciously confused.'"

Addiction is the stop block to the remnants of a coerced memory that plays a continuous tug of war with the "user," a trigger that keeps on giving the angel within a run for its money, with the devil fervently pulling the strings of the heart.

"What, my Child, is it that you choose to hold on to so desperately? Does it serve you? Or is it a damnation to the growth of your Soul you so desperately hold on to? Why keep abusing yourself, playing Chuckie-voodoo-doll on yourself, having allowed your mind to become so consumed due to the trauma of the experiences instilled. Why play Russian roulette with yourself, shooting another hole in the mind, using yourself as a target practice absorbing the hail of bullets shot, 'hurting' yourself according to the triggers of your experiences that you seem to hang on to, walking the ledge having plead insanity, as you've lost yourself through the bout of your dependent

behaviour subduing your e-motions? Why hold on to the ramifications thereof when life is infinitely more beautiful through the art of transformation of the harboured trauma? Wisdom tells you the story of your experiences, with the heart in the accordance of agreement, yet the mind loves to stray and wander, with the devil whispering words of temptations in your ear, to ride but into the blazin' hell fires of eternal purgatory having pulverised your mind like a wrecking ball razing your physical body to the ground in the process.

That 'fear' has entranced you into the diabolical non-thinking of seeking but an escapism of the Light of your Soul. Let go of this consistent tug o' war, allowing yourself to drown in the sweeping storms of your e-motions, having been a thief to the warmth of your joyous Self. One cannot heal if one dares not change one's attitude and perception to the billowing of the Soul's leading rhythm; transcendence is the key to the elevation back to the divine spring in one's step. Ain't no one the culprit but the reflection staring back in the mirror, that has let it be so. Refuse not to budge, remaining cemented in a spot o' bother of a non-conforming attitude, lingering in the swirling created toxic waste of one's merry-go-round experiences. What a buzzkill, for in the current embodiment of the humanoid you are, you are infinitely more agile and adaptable than you have allowed yourself to believe, and thus have gotten yourself in a 'picklelicious' mess.

Come not to me with a self-pitying demeanour of your circumstances, much like a deadbeat lying in a weeping heap on the floor, indulging in the sadomasochistic pain-ed tendencies of your 'shot' Mind, nor the drama of your experiences, but with the guided intention of the solution thereof.

There is nothing that cannot be overcome but overcoming the torment of one's mindset. You have to come undone to become. You have to uncover to recover. You have to sit in your s*** to understand your s***. What greater way to grow than from one's damned suffering?

The deepest pain often empowers you to grow and bloom into your higher self, having duly understood the experiences served to you. Change is inevitable, transformation, however, is by Conscious choice. One can choose to reside in the eternal sinking damnation of Self or rise to the occasion, slam-dunking the experiences and levelling up in the expansion of your Awareness, having understood the play of the experiences at hand. No matter the brokenness, heal the shattered mind of Self, giving birth to your transformation and wisdom returning to the flavour of the 'marvel-icious' wunderbar 'lightilicious' essence of all that makes you Authentically You."

~The Ascended Master St. Germain~

Dealing with the Aftermath

Within a week of returning to the UK, I lost my job, which was no surprise, as I had severely neglected it back in Holland, trying to save Mark's arse. I worked a different job for several weeks in another department, which paid a lot less. I was exhausted and running on empty, for even in the UK, I was still trying to help Mark and the police in Holland. I felt like a mere shell of myself, not even caring about life or where it would take me.

The police had advised me to call them if Mark got in touch with me with a location, so they could pick him up, which is precisely what I did. They took him to Parnassia, a rehabilitation clinic for those suffering from mental health issues. He was grateful to be there, as he had a roof over his head, but was being weaned off the drugs by something else that made him drowsy.

It only lasted a week, as one of Keylow's men happened to be in there, too. He told Mark to pack his bags and come with him if he valued his life, with Keylow apparently grabbing him as soon as he was outside. Apparently, Mark had stolen an American motorcycle worth over one thousand euros, sold a mobile phone, and was held by the Crips until the ransom amount was paid in full—if he couldn't pay, they threatened to end his life. It's really simple: you steal from a gang, you pay. That's the street code.

Even though his mother refused to respond to my emails, I had kept her in the loop. Instead, all communication went through one of her former husbands, Mark's stepdad, who I was in touch with, saying that she had warned me that her son was a serious addict; this was all my fault, as I had taken her son away—and I should be coughing up the five-thousand-euro ransom money.

Was she high or what? He'd been in and out of the system since 1994, long before he met me. It was clear that she didn't care whether her son lived or died, but I did. I had been in contact with Keylow, but he was unaware that I had been feeding information to the police. He had initially spun me this BS story that a gang was holding Mark hostage and that he was negotiating the ransom on their behalf instead of being honest with me from the get-go. He even queried why his mother had never helped him. She tried putting Mark into an "open" rehab; however, as it was "religious" he ended up walking out of these meetings every time.

Mark managed to call me several times; however, he was off his head, plied with drugs, which he took all too readily. The police told me to wire twenty euros so Mark could pick it up from the required location, which I did. One of Keylow's men was always with him; however, the police swooped in and remanded him, after which he thanked them for saving his life. The police took Mark to a detention centre, and several days later, he was deported back to Washington, DC, where his mother picked him up, wanting to drive him straight to a religious rehab, but he refused.

Keylow called me and advised me that Mark's mother's (I believe) fifth husband had told him that I had called the police. He said that if he ever found Mark, he would make sure that no one would ever find him again. He then threatened to find and kill me, telling me Mark's mother had been right about me, that I was manipulative and untrustworthy, and would be better off dead. If my mother had not acted as swiftly as she had, hauling my butt out of Holland back to the UK, I would probably have been six feet under. I instantly changed my mobile number and even reported the incident to the police in Sutton, who shrugged their shoulders, telling me it was out of their jurisdiction.

In my weakness, even after saving his life and fearing for my own, as Keylow knew where I worked, I took a whole box of Nurofen plus, similar to ibuprofen— only twelve tablets—hoping I'd simply fall asleep and not wake up anymore. It was a feeble attempt on my own life; all it did was give me a good night's sleep, and I woke up with my banging headache gone.

The stepdad that raised him for part of his life said that his whole life had been nothing but a big lie since high school. He constantly got in trouble with the law, stealing from his parents, his brother, and years later, from his son. He branded Mark a psychopath who would continue leaving a wake of destruction in his path until he finally realised he needed help. He stated that it wasn't his mother's nor his biological father's fault but that the blame lay solely with Mark himself.

I have always told Mark that his relationship with his mother seemed off; it was disconcerting. She first praised me to high heavens until he left for Holland, after which I was dead to her. My mother even reached out to her via email after she ripped me apart, and she ignored my mother point-blank.

She finally admitted via email that he had already been incarcerated for many years, something I was blissfully unaware of until I started digging myself. She went on to say that had I been in the right frame of mind, I would never have taken Mark away from his family. I was too controlling and demanding with her already vulnerable son, who was searching for the meaning of life, with me preferring to accuse others of being controlling whilst I was to blame.

Here I was, having saved Mark's life having lost everything, including my deposit on the rental in The Hague, as the window latch was damaged when he'd broken into my home. I had depleted my finances from paying for hotel rooms, train travel, buying food, paying rent—even paying one of his so-called ransoms; basically, everything, to finally getting him admitted into a rehabilitation clinic in the UK that had accepted him. Not to mention, I was skin over bones. I had tried my hardest to save him, but at that point in his life, he did not want to be saved; that was a choice only he could eventually make.

Yet, in this whole experience, his parents were sitting peachy in their multi-million-dollar homes with not a care in the world while I was trying to hold on to my sanity. What a stark contrast to my own reality. According to his mother, Mark had a spiritual problem; she even wanted to have an exorcism performed on him. One could argue that his mother enabled him, but did she? Mark allowed the tentacles of the experiences to suffocate him and chose to enable himself by fleeing the hurt of his mind. Why deal with the pain when remaining in the comfort of the discomfort is so much easier because it is what you have become so accustomed to?

Did his mother trigger him? I believe they both triggered each other, yet any trigger should lead to a catalyst for healing the caused hurt within ourselves. Did she turn a blind eye to his habits, or was it Mark that chose to turn a blind eye to the hurt of his experiences and run in the other direction? No matter the experiences we go through in life, we have asked for these events to help polish and upgrade ourselves, making us more conscious of who we are and what life is all about.

Her resentment towards me runs deep and to this day remains. It's okay because I understand her behaviour says more about her and how she feels about herself than it does about me. She has always run from the beautiful light of her soul, having chosen to live within her deeply wounded mind, hiding behind her sermons and Bible scriptures.

I know Mark did not have an easy childhood, but that should never be an excuse to keep railroading yourself. It makes me wonder if subconsciously, due to his religious upbringing, this was one of the reasons he chose to escape and descend into the seedy world of becoming a male stripper, where he first got introduced to drugs, which eventually cascaded into a serious addiction. This endless cycle has gone on for years, and only Mark can break the sequence of being in the revolving doors of the prison system; only he can decide when it's time to hop off the merry-go-round. Without fail, he returned to his mother's place each time he came out of prison, entering another prison and remaining in that same environment.

You cannot heal in the same environment that made you sick. If the people surrounding you bring you down, manipulate, abuse, discourage you from your goals, and consume you with their drama, you cannot heal. You've got to walk the road alone instead of falling back into that oh-so-cushy trap. You can't use the same old bricks from the past and expect to be building a different home, as much as you can't keep singing the same repetitive mantra expecting a difference in the outcome you are trying to create. You can't thrive in toxicity; it's a slow poison to the soul. Trying to do the same thing repeatedly but expecting different results is the very definition of *Groundhog Day* insanity. It's hard to blossom within an environment with overgrown weeds; you flourish in an environment that dances with the harmony and the very breath of your soul.

The past serves as a rich dish of our tasted experiences; the future should remind you to make better choices, thus enriching the self by living in that blissful state of conscious awareness. As St. Germain says:

"If you want to heal your wounds, you need to commence healing your entangled thoughts, for everything stems as a seed from the Mind. It is not others that have tripped you, but you, that has solely tripped your Mind into a confus-ed state and beaten the self to a fried-out frenzy, being the very cause of created dis-ease within the hous-ed body. You are a Divine al-chemical Creator of your Cosmic bubblicious bubble of Existence. What you choose to ingest in the mental imagery of your Mind, you conjure up and will forth into the outer realms of your existence. To heal or not to

heal, that is the very question only you can answer by recovering the luminous gem of the ever-blossoming Soul Light that you are."

Even after the whole fiasco in Holland, I still felt deeply connected to Mark; it was like an invisible thread kept itself attached between us, much like a ricocheting coil, and I couldn't figure out why. It bothered me, which is exactly what Spirit wanted, because they knew I would be savvy enough to figure out that drowning in his energy wasn't healthy for me.

I decided to contact a regression therapist in London to see if there was a connection to a past life and to help me understand my erratic emotions.

Past Lives and Reincarnation

"Life is over before you know it, before plunging you into another life in the Cosmic Game of Evolution. Life is a bit like snakes and ladders. You fall flat on your arse slithering in the mud until you've understood the lessons within the experiences that have been shoved in your face, all for the development and growth of your Soul, and thus once understood, hop on up a notch on that ladder. The question you need to ask yourself is, whether you've understood the experiences and are ready to let go, allowing for other experiences to come forth on your blissfully blessed journey of Life."

~The Ascended Master St Germain~

Reincarnation is "the belief that the soul, upon the death of the body, comes back to earth in another body or form." The concept of reincarnation, also called metempsychosis, is that the soul is born into another body (of the same species or a different one) after succumbing to a physical death.

Time is an illusion, yet it serves as an experience for humanity to learn the art of evolution, to attain enlightenment in understanding who we really are in the grand scheme of existence. Every energetic particle is a wave of possibilities before turning into form or matter. In other words, we have infinite possibilities to choose from before the "actual form" is created. We are master creators. Everything in our current life, in our outer world, is a direct reflection cast from our inner world, with our outer world being the absorbance of all of our experiences reflected back into our inner world—for we are all merely energetic transmitters having cast our net from within to the outer banks of our cosmic bubble of creation without.

"You are born into a system of your chosen itinerary and raised in the confinements of a created society. Can you master the game by mastering the self, through the art of your experiences, to break free from la vida loca and play life according to the jump and beats of your own rules of Soul?

You are infinite consciousness evolving. A candyfloss bundle of immeasurable de-light casting your ball of auric light in the world around you according to the feelings of the world within that you have ingested through the influx of the outer worldly narrative without.

Reincarnation is the recipe to life for the creation of your experiences, making one richer in the sweetness of one's Light o' Soul. To forget, or not to forget? That begs the question how much of a hindrance one is choosing to be-come, by zipping the Soul up into the human embodiment back to the Light of the Authentic Self. You decided to be "amnesiad-out" in the stupor of living in the third-dimensional frequency, falling into the booby traps of the physical unplugged separation of the Whole into the ever-wandering abyss of "fear" finding the Self within the remembrance of somewhere within the Self, back to the Light within. Game on, we dare say."

~The Ascended Master St. Germain~

You are not here by chance but by choice. You may not remember what you signed up for, but such is the Game of Life. As a galactic ambassador of light, you volunteered to incarnate on Earth during this time, within the constraints of that "straitjacket" called the physical human embodiment, to Houdini yourself out of the thick of the matrix, helping to usher in a new dawn and help free Mother Earth back to the breath of her beautiful divine conscious self.

You do realise that you are a created hybrid and that your family are the many Galactic species within the multiverse, right? And that you are here to explore, express, and create not in the shallow puddles of yourself, but in the very depths of the beautiful waters of the original hues of the you in *you*. It's not like, hey, I'm human, I die, and reincarnate as a human BEing—hell no. You could decide to incarnate somewhere else should you choose to. Earth isn't the only planet within the multiverse—it would be a lonely place if we were.

I have lived countless very diverse lives; in truth, more than I care to remember, which I'll discuss later, delving into the Akashic Records. I've flip-flopped on both sides of the coin of duality, for one cannot transcend without the other, having lived several lifetimes with Mark, with this particular regression session taking me back to the ancient times of the Byzantine Empire.

To some, regression may be a myth, but have you ever had a sense of déjà vu in your life and thought, *I've been here, I know this place, or I'm sure I've done this before*? And just as that sense was in your grasp, it evaporated, leaving you with that feeling of "huh." We have all lived countless lives, for enlightenment cannot be attained in just one Earthly incarnation. Some people will raise their eyebrows and say that we are just dead when we die, extinguished like fire to a flame. But even to the sceptics I daresay, when the wick of a candle is snuffed out, the smoke, the energy, rises and dissipates into the ether; thus, one's inner light can never be snuffed out.

Everything an individual has ever experienced is recorded and retained within the intricate BluePrint of one's DNA—the living library of the Cosmos of Light. Everything stored here can be accessed if we choose to switch on the light. Sometimes, these memories can surface in our current lives and affect us physically, emotionally, and in how we live our lives.

In regression, these symptoms are accessed in a hypnotically induced state by being guided into a deeply relaxing hypnosis to uncover the root cause and the events that took place. Accessing these memories and understanding why certain events happened allows for the healing process to begin in a person's current life.

I honestly had no idea what to expect, except that I had been walking around with this immense bitterness towards Mark's family, which utterly consumed me, leaving my life in tethers, and I needed to come what may piece myself together again.

I was a bit sceptical, yet open to the idea. Several years earlier, I had tried regression, but all I saw was a white light, and, feeling agitated and fidgety, I just wanted to get up and walk away. Clearly, I wasn't under hypnosis. The therapist's response to this was that I had been in the light for a long time, having chosen not to incarnate, remaining "sleeping" up in the celestial heavens. He was, however, incorrect, as I had also lived and wandered the streets of moonlit Paris during World War II.

Admittedly, this time I had a completely different experience, as I was regressed to the dust of the Byzantine Empire, where I had taken the appearance and the embodiment of a man. I was well-groomed, wearing a woven and intricately beautiful hand-stitched piece of clothing of blues and beige, and a turban. I was in my early thirties, well-off, married, and had a daughter, who was my absolute bundle of joy. I loved working the dirt and tending to my horses; even now, I can smell the sand, dust, and horses' breath in the fiery heat against the backdrop of the mountains. As my past life former self continues:

"Happily married, I was not, for we each vibrated at a different level of understanding. Our views of the world and the intricacies thereof differed, yet we had a mutual bond of respect.

My home was of a certain allure, a captivating entrance for those that entered and dwelled in my abode. The beautiful blue mosaic handcrafted fountain was the jewel that bequeathed the inner courtyard, with a well-tended garden and the aroma of fresh and spiced herbs infused with other plant life and flowers that bloomed and adorned the walls, giving it life. An authentic captivation of the senses of the heart, for what could be more beautiful than the conscious rhythmic and harmonious sentience of nurtured plants and herbs of the Earth? All are merely the same as you, evolving but in the natural flow of nature and embracing all-natural aspects. Yet, humanity is flawed to a fault in believing in the existence of the EGO, and of a separation from the flow of Self and Life. Plants can teach one much if one has the patience to see the wonders of growth.

The house itself was constructed out of a smooth sand-coloured stone. I cannot be sure of the materials, but it was cool in the sweltering summers and kept the wreath of the cold from entering in the wintry settings of the dusk. I was a merchant, and yet I was a writer and philosopher at heart. When not travelling, one could find me in my study, writing away under the flickering wick of a candle burning brightly on the table beside me. A place where I sat with my thoughts of loving inspiration and under-standing to the mere behaviours of humanity and a deluding of its Consciousness, having dwindled from the indigenous nature of itself, carving out a path in the folly of sharpened edges, wounding itself as a whole, for we lived in politically warped and egotistical times. I had servants, yet I must wholeheartedly admit that I should have treated them better, for the difference between them, and I was but none, for but the role they partook in playing. I was not always a forbearing man, patience to be the least of my traits, yet I was guilty not of a cruelness but a firm yet fair articulation in the weighing of the spoken word.

As dawn turned to dusk, with the sun setting behind the mountainous horizons once more and darkness blanketing the landscapes aided by the mere faint hue of the stars, I rode off into the night, having to deliver a message to my blood brother, an oath made, a bond forged through the strenuous childhood we each had, and yet that is what shaped us into the casting of who we became. A brother I would have trusted with my life: my ex, Mark, and his mother, his then betrothed wife. His wife was of the "evil" eye, for she shunned the light within that I merely reflected without. She would hide in the shadows of her husband in the unwillingness to hear, but my heart speak. She suffered from a granularity of the heart; she was a trickery of fumée et miroirs. Still waters run deep, and yet when one is turned the other way, and a scorpion feels threatened, it will strike and hurt its opponent, bringing it to its knees, its venomous sting a slow poison to a death of the heart."

I was then fast-forwarded to what I had seen at the beginning of the session, where I saw myself shackled in the open by my right foot—the shackle was old and rusty, but it served its purpose of keeping me afflicted within my pain. I was dishevelled, my beard had grown, my hair was tangled and dirty, and I was a mere shimmer of who I once was. Yet, these were my chosen experiences, having played out due to the decisive actions of my brother.

"My blood brother had betrayed me, having chosen to turn the other cheek. His reasoning was a logical fallacy, stating, "I did it in the name of the All of God, for the written words a mere injustice, a blasphemous insult to the society we live and breathe in. A society that has given us the gift of life, of living in freedom, abiding by the supremacy as heralded and cemented in the governing of the people, and one cannot protrude with an air of self-righteousness for that is a betrayal of all that is right and just.

I was a mere mortal man of the people, a philosopher at heart; what could be so unfathomable of living in these blusterous sins when I carried but a pure love for all within for a want of balancing the scales of equality? What remains of my work is all but gone, the embers having smouldered the once created wording, turning them back to the ashes from whence they came, carried by the now long forgotten dwindling winds of time and a distant memory it now remains. Culpable I was not, yet all was taken from me, for my family knew not what had become of me. My credibility, my dignity lost, clothed in dirty white linen, spending my days like many lost souls in the solitary confinement of the four walls with myself, the odd sparks of sunlight and the breeze on my withered face.

Sent to the quarries I was to mine for minerals to sustain the wealthy, who cared little for the well-being of the imprisoned. Yet my experiences allowed me to forge a deeper connection and have a greater appreciation of myself and my circumstances, for a heart of stone I carried not, but for the mere pity, compassion, and love towards my brother's tortured soul for the betrayal, he chose to make.

Prison was my last stopover before my life ended, for a sharp object through the throat by an assailant unbeknownst to me was my undoing. I died an agonising death but perturbed I was not, for the lining had already disconnected from the body that once served me well. As the life force seeped out of me, I headed back home to *the warmth of the light and love of the spiritual realm, back into the embrace of my beloved brothers and sisters."*

Dr. Ian Stevenson published a collection of personal reports in works such as *Reincarnation and Biology: A Contribution to the Etiology of Birthmarks and Birth Defects*, which documents thousands of detailed cases where claims of injuries received in past lives correlate with physical birthmarks or congenital disabilities. I have two very distinct birthmarks: a cat paw on the left side of my neck and the Canadian maple leaf under my right arm.

While I was still under, the therapist asked me if I now saw the similarities in this life. I shook my head and then realised, connecting the dots, that they were right in front of me. In the 1990s, I lived in Istanbul, feeling right at home. Of course, Istanbul, formerly Constantinople, was part of the Byzantine Empire.

And yet, even after everything that happened, I still tried to extend an olive branch to Mark's mother, to no avail. My ex is the one who now has the experience of doing time, having incarcerated himself in the conditioning of his own experiences. He has chosen to imprison his soul by clinging to the hurt experiences that have wounded his mind. He picked these characters to roleplay in his own show, "The Life of Mark," and seeing as he's the producer, director, actor, and casting director, only he can decide whether to change the outcome.

It took me a long time to heal myself of the bitterness I felt towards his family for what they did to me, but the simple truth is, I have learned to let go by choice. My ego got the better of me, keeping me chained within the experience, and for what? I was an utter fool, as these characters were merely part and parcel in my playbook of life to help me change my perception of the circumstances presented. I was duped into my experiences and decided to take a backseat, permitting them to take me on a joyride to hell, plummeting me into the depths of that damned darkness within.

Sometimes life truly feels like a wretched balls and chains game. You're trying to move forward but can't because you feel so utterly locked and cemented into the experience, not knowing how to break free, when all you have to do is simply embrace the experience and "hug it out." Letting go is a breath of liberation to your soul, for where love goes, healing flows.

My experiences in Holland were a blessing in disguise; without them, I would not have embarked on my inner healing journey and commenced studying the many healing modalities to stitch up my wayward soul.

I would not recommend regression for the fun of it; my experience going under was intense. I was utterly drained, shook like a leaf, and felt ice-cold after the session, which is the energy being released and shifting. You can also get rid of past life "hiccups" through Light Language and Akashic Record Healing; it is merely a different pathway to healing yourself. As we are a holographic imprint encased within this physical body, everything is stored in the cellular memory of our body's DNA. All the "material" is sourced from deep within our subconscious mind, for our soul's blueprint carries with it all knowledge of all incarnated lives.

I have had many other lifetimes with Mark, including lives in Ancient Egypt (discussed later) and South America, where he was a warrior by my side. However, at that point in my life, I needed to release the heaviness attached to me from our life in the Byzantine Empire. Mark himself has incarnated upon the earthly planes many times. I can effortlessly step into his energy and have seen him as a tall, skinny blond lad in the trenches of the first world war, where he escaped the overbearing family home by enlisting in the army, trying to find his way in the world, only to succumb to the bombings, with one of his compadres shouting, "Willie!" He was a knight and jouster and an arrogant bastard at that, but people loved him for his sportsmanship and the show he put on, as there was never a dull moment. He died when the lance hit his upper chest, causing him to fall off his horse with breathing difficulties. Thinking nothing of the wheezing it had caused, internal bleeding was the possible culprit that led to his untimely death several days later.

He was also a well-respected and loved Native American named Bear Medicine Woman, a gentle yet firm spirit, and an amazing healer working with the womb of the mother.

I saw him as an adviser of sorts at the courts of Henry VIII, whose spirit has come across to me as rather vain, rude, obnoxious, and rather indulgent and debaucherous, having affairs with both men and women, with a flair for the dramatic and a moodiness that often clouded his egotistical judgement and was an insult to his underlying intelligence. Henry had a mirror on the ceiling in one of his dining halls, reflecting the upside-down cast of his advisers—a rather humorous display of cat and mouse. Mark, in that lifetime, was the object of his father's rage, having to fend for himself, and learned the art of stealing for scraps of food. As a young teen, unable to stomach the beatings, he left home, joining a band of musical troubadours, learning the art of song and dance. He had a flair for the arts, possessing the gift of gab and was skilled in creating prose and sonnets. He was a lankish lad with a bowl haircut, walking through the horses' stables, eating an apple, rehearsing a repertoire on the lute, striking up a conversation with Sir Thomas More—who, as he stated to me, was not a zealot but a passionate humbled enthusiast who could carry a conversation with the listener ever mesmerised by the very words but spoken. Yet More was none other than an incarnation of the Ascended Master El Morya.

Lastly, I saw Mark in Ancient Egypt, with immense physical endurance, as he was a renowned javelin thrower.

The Continuance of Mark

After Mark had been deported back to the US, he landed back behind bars several months later after a thirty-minute high-speed car chase. He was high on crack, with state troopers finally arresting him after having broken his car window, tasering him for refusing to come out of his vehicle.

Even in prison, I was in touch with Mark, merely writing letters back and forth, and throughout the time I have known him, he has spent more time in prison than not. He is locked up in the prison of his wounded mind, having imprisoned his beautiful soul in a prison of his own making, in the matrix of the physical prison system experience. Yet many become repeat offenders, as they have become so programmed and institutionalised in their ways, it almost seems like a relief for them to be sent back to the normalcy they have become so accustomed to.

Throughout the years, I sent him plenty of self-help books, both in and out of prison, including many books on the Pleiadians, St. Germain, and other spiritual books, supporting him emotionally and financially as and when. I've always been there for him, but it never quite worked the other way around—and how could it, when he was vacant in his own "home" and was never there for himself? I topped up his prison phone card so he could call me, but I decided that, although I loved him, it was time to let him go, his life, his journey, his experiences. He should figure life out on his own instead of me enabling him and continuing to be a crutch for him, as I wouldn't be doing him any favours. Instead of basking in the warmth and glow of my soul light, I shoved him out into the cold and dark of his experiences.

In 2020, after having returned and overstayed my welcome in St. Petersburg, Florida, which I will delve into shortly, I consulted a US immigration attorney in the UK, costing me a whopping £700. Why? Because even though Mark and I had not seen one another since Holland, being on probation, he couldn't fly to the UK. Lawyers are leeches; this guy had zero empathy and wasn't interested in the circumstances. He sat there with his greasy, long, uncombed hair and unironed shirt and told me I would need to get hired, be sponsored for a work visa, be invited as a speaker at a conference, or get married to a US citizen, or I wasn't eligible to return—failing that, I'd be banned for ten years. This guy was the epitome of a real dickhead, but looking back, it was a blessing in disguise and served me right to get sucker-punched by him.

I think sometimes my Guides have lost the will to live, banging their heads against the wall, with my sadomasochistic tendencies, saying, *"Birgitta, when are you going to learn? You can't be with someone that is lost in the gunk of their own experiences. You just ain't vibin' on the same frequency doll, nor humming to the same Soul tune for now. You're not singing from the same hymn sheet and will cause nothing but a damned false concerto, shattering each other's vibration and 'shooting' each other's lives to pieces, so let it go. You're like two screeching cats continually zapped by a tripwire. You need to heal and dance with a Love of yourself a wee bit more, for life is merely walkin' the walk and talkin' the talk returning on back to love. Ain't nobody a kink in the cable but you. It is entirely your choice whether you want* to persist at being a folded accordion, remaining incapacitated in your rigidness, or choose to unfold yourself, allowing the energy and musical notes to flow to the heart-beat of your beautiful evolving Soul. Will your life be a 'transforming' out of this world Steve Jablonsky or a saddened tenure of an out-of-tune Tchaikovsky?"

Initially, I was upset, but in the weeks and months that followed, I finally let go of the idea of the US, as life happens where you're at, not in some distant reminiscence of future past gones. You're exactly where you're meant to be through the explicit choices you have made.

Mark will keep being the repeat offender, repeating the same experiences in that vicious circle, locked in this eternal devilish dance a la Paso Doble with his madre, entranced in a battle of wills, until he chooses to break the chains he has so bound himself with. It is the same spot on his Achilles heel being tripped repeatedly, which is the conditioning of his experiences he has grown accustomed to over the many unfolding years.

"Never let others define you according to the moulding of their choosing. Hop out of that toxic waste pond and plunge into the crystal blue waters of the Divine Self, living life according to the song and dance of your own heart and Soul."

~The Divine~

There is no right or wrong in how we choose to experience or participate in life. We all evolve at our own pace. We are where we are because of our created circumstances. And I was definitely where I was at through my own life choices, having evolved according to the patterning of my chosen experiences. No one is responsible for the course and actions of our lives, but solely the bearer thereof. If we understand that life is one giant "board" game of cosmic evolution, and we, the players, are merely creating and expressing ourselves through the feat of our experiences, rolling the dice according to the status quo of our mindset, then we wouldn't get so sucked in, drowning in the undercurrent of our nonsensical dramas.

Mark said he lost himself completely over a woman, yet I was not the trigger to his drug abuse, nor his continuous escapades. We often deflect while we should be taking responsibility for our own lives and, subsequently, our actions. Archangel Raphael, below, explains that people do not get lost in other people; they merely get lost in their experiences. Once they commence taking responsibility, is the moment they unloosen the screws of their once-rigid mindset allowing the clogged sludge of their experiences to come cascading down.

"He did not get lost in you. He got lost in the maze of his experiences. You were the light switch in the constant darkness he had thrown and submerged himself in. You were the lifeline, the buoy to the weighted anchor around his ankle. Yet on a conscious level, trying to make sense of his once "past," in ways he sees you as the culprit of his ingested toxic cocktail of experiences, whilst like all, he should be looking at the reflection in the mirror and realise that the root of all that triggered him, stems from the

wee boy he once was and in ways still is for his inner child weeps for the joy he has so lost. It is easy to project blame onto others when they are reflecting that blinding light cast into their hurt of what needs to be healed within themselves. How can one heal if one merely chooses to wear but sunglasses throughout life, rejecting and deflecting those cast reflections trying to shed light on the hurt and thus smiting oneself to oblivion having used the Self as target practise on a shooting range—for like Mark, one is the shooter to the reflection of one's own Mind and Soul.

It takes one to be brutally raw and honest with oneself to battle through the onslaught of the dramatic experiences one has so heavily waded into, having incarcerated the Self in the toxic swamp of one's created conditioning. It is the responsibility of the 'user,' the Soul's modus operandi, to "metamorphosis" out of the dangling straitjacket one has so tightly strapped the Self in, to vanquish the mind-sludge that kept the Soul in the grip of those created traumatic occurrences in the first place.

Lest one forgets, as per their stipulated Soul contract, they have willingly subjected themselves to these experiences to expand and rise above the trickery of the "Sinestro" Mind, which has held their own "Green Lantern" confined and clasped in chains.

Yet many remain forlorn when battered by their experiences, merely numbing their emotions, walking through life jadedly jaywalking and limping but rather aimlessly with their soul under their arm, having lost the basic understanding of a joie de vivre for life.

Experiences are meant to elevate you, not bewitch you in the humdrum of Self, so l'arrêt mes cheris of remaining trapped in the dogma of your created experiences. Life is a beautiful experiment for you to intimately experience in all its flavoursome richness. If you keep choking on those ingested chillies refusing to heal, one will remain fuming within the very dis-ease of Self causing nothing but a toxic radiation within one's created life and environment.

I urge you to walk inward and lovingly release all of your tarred-on experiences, healing the Self, for once the fog has cleared, the sun will break through those clouds again, and you will see that life is beautiful.

All are merely teachers to the expansion of your Soul, so give thanks to all with much gratitude, grace, and love in your heart for all you have been allowed to experience with them. Gratitude paired with the hand of forgiveness in the embrace-ed arms of love releases the heaviness of the intoxicated Mind back to having but a gusto and a zest for loving life. So why remain in the acidity of your incarcerated experiences when life can be infinitely so much more 'splendiliciously' beautiful?

A simple daily mantra reminder: I AM love. I AM whole. I bask in the warmth and radiance of my own Soul Light. And so it is."

~Archangel Raphael~

Mark and I are each on our own chosen journeys, and if he can turn his life around, "exorcising" the demons that have for so long taken up residence in his head, then one day, inshallah, we may meet again—if not this lifetime, then the next.

I will always love him, and even though he is only now relinquishing his experiences, being the slow arse turtle he is, he is a wonderfully advanced soul, has a deep inner knowing, and is a kindred spirit. He has taught me so much about myself; truth be told, without him, I would not have commenced the road to healing myself. Mark was the catalyst and a hard-core reflection, causing all the nausea of who I thought I was to come belching to the surface quite literally, with me having to walk through my reflected fears on the road to who I AM and am still BE-com-ing. He was an immensely beautiful reflection to my then downtrodden and wayward spirit and has been an incredible driving force for me to continually strive to become a better version of myself, wanting to grow, expand, and evolve, all the whilst journeying back to the unfolding lotus of the light of who I AM.

I wish him nothing but love, happiness, and consciousness, and I sincerely hope that he is now changing the tides and learning from his experiences, taking the necessary steps to taking back his I AM power and basking in the light of his beautiful divine I AM presence.

Twin Flames and Soulmates

We tend to think that we meet someone with our eyes, but we actually meet them through the vibration of our energies. Energy is the substance you are made of, and you are attracted to the energetic vibration that matches your own frequency. Like attracts like, and we draw into our lives what we put out.

I have been told at various times that Mark is my twin flame, and he could well be due to the connection we share, but I'm not one to dwell on it. Even though we were on the road to somewhere, yet nowhere, we had this invisible electromagnetic coil spring mechanism between us, and no matter how far we'd wander or drift away, the thread we shared kept drawing us right back in.

There is a romanticised misconception of the term "twin flames." As soon as people hear the phrase, they get excited about the prospect of meeting this one person who will forever change their lives. No one is going to change your life but you. I think most people forget that you don't have to look for that love outside of yourself, for everyone carries that flame of love within.

Think of twin flames as a dancing, entwined flame, burning beautifully on a single candle wick—and yet these two can snuff each other out as much as they can ignite the vibrational flame to ever-expanding heights of consciousness. Not all twin flames incarnate concurrently unless they have agreed to do so. These relationships, however, carry the most traumatic experiences we can choose to incarnate into. It is an unbreakable bond forged in the core of each other's vibration and according to the heartbeat and song of each other's soul.

Twin flames are like two beautiful symbiotic trees intertwined by their roots—both feed off each other and are catalysts to accelerating each other's growth. Yet, some remain stumped in their growth due to their unrelinquished experiences and thus poison the very fabric of their BEing, causing their roots to starve. Others have chosen to embrace their experiences and heal the pain within their roots, nurturing their very soul—thus flourishing, expanding, sprouting new buds and branches, ascending further to the celestial heavens. If one tree is not doing too well, the other shares its water and nutrients, yet if the other tree refuses the help, one can only let them maul around in their own rooted issues until they decide to untangle the knots they have created, learning from the experiences that caused them such dis-ease in the first place.

The moment you meet, you have this instant connection, a feeling of déjà vu that you can't quite put your finger on. Mark and I finished each other's sentences, and regardless of where he's at, I've always known how he feels. Many have had similar experiences. It's like looking in a mirror: not only is your unprocessed trauma reflected back at you, but past lives and ancestral trauma, which can help heal intergenerational patterns of family dysfunction, may well surface, 'politely' requesting healing. It's a bit of a damned and wretched trip into the inferno of our very own created hell, for everything that comes to light is saying, "help me, heal me." If we leave the unhealed trauma be, we'll only smack ourselves on the head, causing many unpleasantries in the current walking of the journey we have so boldly undertaken.

Twin flames are two sides of the same soul that have chosen to unite on the earthly realms to teach each other profound lessons in the hope of walking back to their most authentic selves. They are like pure humming magnets, the yin to one's yang, pulled to one another through the vibration of their energetic formulated compounds, destined to meet at some point on the journey of life, for that was the agreement made before leaping into the incarnation of the human experience.

"Love is the fusion of a single "soul" having chosen to inhabit two bodies. It is like a neutron slung shot at the nucleus of an atom, causing a solar flare of infinite dispersing particles, an explosion if you will, splitting the nucleus into two halves of the same Light matter, creating a nuclear fission of two particle Souls. The electronic magnetic frequencies of the reflective yin to the yang to each other serve as a mere mirror reflecting the light as much as the darkness within each other to the acceleration of a fast-tracked pathway to an elevated Consciousness, serving to inspire the turning away from the darkness back to the light in both the self and others.

Infused as one, yet split at the birthing of one's existence into the Earthly realms, much like the severing of the umbilical cord of Consciousness into the bare naked cut-off existence of a biological degradable human form of existence—disconnected from the warmth of Divine Love, shoved into the stark cold of an Arctic blast of winter—alone and forlorn having to find one's way back through the torrent of chosen experiences returning to the self-realisation of your blossoming Authenticity, and of understanding yourself and each other. Through the mere enactments of the experiences, it remains a choice of two halves. One incarnates in the hope of experiencing all that one has tasked the Self from the outset of one's incarnation. Yet, one's life is an infinite choice of many infinite potentialities, with an endless flow of different outcomes, as such are the workings of the energies within the Quantum Universe of the 'tapestrial' field of interweaving electro-magnetic magnitudes. Life is merely a created pathway through one's picked and chosen circumstances—will it be a stumblin' through the thicket of bramble bushes adorning the Self with thorns, or a road of the intricate particles of energetic vibra-tional understanding, embracing the all of one's true form of alchemical divinity, back to the recalibration of the Divine Soul of Self through the expansion of one's elevation of Consciousness?

Love is that feeling of floating on fluttering butterfly wings within, in the innate-ness of BEing in the rhythmic harmony of yourself and the Universe, lifting the Soul but ever exponentially to the higher vibrational dance of a rapture of Self, whirling intrinsically higher to the Oneness with the Universal ballroom tapestry of Cognisance flow. Love knows no bounds; it simply is. It is the spindle to the axis of your Soul, of the Everything and All, leaving one feeling light as a feather, of walkin' on cotton candy clouds, catchin' the rays of the joyous and warmheartedness of the Sun through the shadows cast; it is a connection beyond the shadows of the continuum of time and space. The bonding of two Souls reforged, embers of the same fire, sparking through the dancing flames engulfing the darkness back to the light within, rising from the ashes back to the unison and fusion of One."

~The Light Beings of the Divine~

When you're soul mates, you're good ol' mates from the same tribe, incarnating repeatedly and playing different characters to accelerate each other's growth. Sometimes new souls may join an alternate band of travelling troubadours to switch up their experiences. They, too, serve as mirror reflections in the hope that we learn from the experiences reflected at us, rather than remaining in the seat of hot branding our soul. Avoiding healing, becoming that artful dodger, will only cause us to suffocate and smother our beautiful soul BEing.

I agree that twin flames are the equivalent of falling off a cliff, plunging into the abyss below, where they are slammed by the roaring waters. Even though twin flame relationships can have rather painful endings, never shun the other half of who you are, for you co-exist on the flip side of each other, forever dancing, and thus will forever be part of each other. For growth to concur, both parties need to rebalance the scales of one another, to blossom but ever beautifully at an exponential rate of delving into the waters of the conscious cosmos of Self. Yet one cannot remain if the harmonious melodic pitch is off between both parties, and one needs to let go to allow for the other to evolve. You bring yourself in balance, to bring the world and humanity in balance. Live your life in the freedom of knowing that your twin flame will always be a part of you, for you will always be two sides of the same coin, and the bond will remain throughout this life and beyond.

Regardless of the twin flame aspect, we owe it to ourselves to heal the fractured parts of ourselves that we have for so long left in tethers. As St. Germain kindly points out:

"If people irk you, provoke you, then there's the riddle me that question as to why? Seek ye not the fault in the other Soul, but ask from within what is it that ails thee? The e-motion of anger you feel towards the other is a mere reflection of the anger you feel towards yourself. You play this constant hide and seek with your EGO, the disruptor to the game of living in the very breath of your natural state of Self; it is a mischievous little prankster keeping you in the loop of its mind games. Strip the EGO to stand downright naked in the light of your very fruitiness of Self, having peeled the layers of the once cloaked banana that you were. Love is the crux of who you are; it is the Divine vanilla ice cream without all the accumulated toppings that would make you a soggy mess of sorts—it is You in the pureness of your Divine Essence. Without the art of loving yourself, there can be no genuine love for others; you'll be stuck in the same spinning cycle of a warped conditioning of what you think love is but is not. You are much like clay; thus, you are the cause of your own inflicted moulding and shaping of Self and hence your very own creation of the circumstances as to how you have chosen to act. You are free to remain in the role of self-condemnation and to continue to give yourself a walloping until the heavens open for the pouring of even more. Act

from the stance of Love—for Love, my Child, is the healer to all ailments of the Soul that you carry in your burdened heart.

NO ONE is responsible for your life nor your unequivocal happiness but YOU. You are not your pain; your pain is YOU. You are not your suffering; your suffering is YOU.

Be grateful for the opportunity of the challenges presented to you, for it is only by jumping the hurdles and the hoops that one levels up into the dome of the expansion of one's blissful Self. Look within, for you are drenched in magic. You cannot elevate your consciousness from the outside in; it has to be from the inside out - it is only there that you can pull the rabbit out of the magical hat to commence transforming your life."

There is beauty and pain in all relationships; we just don't see it when we are bang in the middle of that experience, but all serve as a teacher to accelerate our soul's growth. Be with someone that makes your heart sing, making your heart skip a bit, and that makes you joyous, but remain not in a non-loving, tit-for-tat kind of relationship, for blackmail of the emotions is a devolvement and a hanged man's suffocation of the breath of your very soul.

The Road to Healing

Experiences teach us to learn to forgive ourselves, yet we often thrust the axe of harshness upon ourselves. We cannot move forward until we learn the art of loving every aspect of ourselves, embracing the good and bad in our loving arms, and fusing all back into the light of love.

And if you can't? Then you will stay in the stagnant energies of your negative emotions, stuck within your own created muddied emotional swirl of a cesspool, all because you have allowed yourself to be influenced by other people's emotions and opinions, having given your power away. It is not about what others want but what you need to do to return to the wholeness of yourself. Fear leads one down a winding path of darkness. If you remain lost in that fear, you could end up strung out or even dead.

I was lost, having no direction or any understanding how to get a grip on the hopelessness that had washed over me. After making a feeble attempt on my own life, I knew I needed help. I was referred to a counsellor through the National Health Service, but that was a total waste of time. She simply told me that I was strong enough to overcome what I had been through and that I would be fine, which hurtled me further into the hole. Besides that, after only a few weeks, my temporary job at Shell ended, with many employees made redundant. I was out of work for about six weeks before being offered another position at an Italian oil and gas company. It paid peanuts, but I was grateful for the opportunity to keep the storms in my head at bay.

"Pain is creation; love is the healing transformation and thus one's salvation. Pain is the creation through the art of that feat called duality; it is not a tormenter but here to prod and 'hot' poke you to a remembrance of Self, knowing that you are Love and that Love transcends all pain back to the Light of all that you are, for you are One with Love as Love is One with you. If you understand this, you also understand that there is nothing that you cannot overcome but for the veiled limitation of your capped capabilities.

Life is the greatest university of understanding and BE-com-ing. Everything that happens to you is your teacher. Many people sit not at the feet of their own life being taught by it but dodge it like the crafty thief of an artful dodger they have become, running hither and yonder like their life depends on it, always looking over their shoulder, trippin' over their own feet, hurtling themselves ever further into the dense jungles of their cloak-ed Soul, seeking but an escapism from the very tortures of their enraptured Mind. Your experiences merely teach you a greater understanding of yourself and the world and the characters you have given a role to play in your life. Whatever experiences and emotions are projected onto you is the reflection cast on what you need to learn from. Stop feeling sorry for yourself cause there ain't no one sorrier than the sight of a sorriness you have so projected upon your sorry arse Self. If you 'hate' them, that is the exact reflection of what you 'hate' about yourself. The way back to the raw onion of the Soul that you are within is to peel back the layers, walk through the garnered and garnished crap-o-cake of your experiences and heal up, pucker up, and revel in the lightness of all you can be rather than the drab of a slushy heaviness one chooses to be."

~The Ascended Master St. Germain~

Some great advice from St. Germain, but I wasn't feeling it. However, I refused to keep myself moored in my misery. I needed help. I could either take responsibility for my mistakes or remain unhappy and lose myself further. I searched the internet for an alternative healer instead of a counsellor, listened to the voice of my heart, and started on my healing journey, learning to become a healer in the process through my then–Reiki teacher, Sue Walsh.

When I met Sue for the first time, I had no expectations, as this was completely new territory for me. Sue was a Reiki healer, helping to realign my energy field and clearing any energetic blockages over various sessions. She told me I was incredibly "gifted" but had blocked all my potential by giving to others and allowing them to waltz all over me, causing a depletion of my energetic imbalance to the point of making myself ill. I still suffered from continuous tension headaches and painfully rigid shoulders. Even though my body had been rebuking all the mud I slung at it, silently screaming at me, I still soldiered on with the pain I had caused myself. As St. Germain says, *"Migraines and tension headaches are a form of emotional suppression, of not wanting to deal with 'issues' that are popping to the surface, with you playing whack-a-mole with them, being a tyrant to oneself, denying the request to be healed, pushing the screaming-for-help issues right back down from whence they came, causing a conflict between the two sparring parties, hence the continuous waves of nausea engulfing you, leading you to feel but rather contused in life. One can also attest this to having suffered blunt force trauma to the head in a past life, yet as one lives in a deviation to the outer fringes of the 'matrix' world, often reverting to the band-aid of a chemical intervention rather than listening to the voice of the heart within, and as you to what the body is so desperately trying to tell you, as you having turned a deaf ear and are lalalala-ing away in your own world in the very avoidance of Self."*

Sue said it's OK to help others, but I needed to learn to set boundaries, something I had no concept of. My experiences would keep getting more intense until I finally learned to say no and stop helping others to the detriment of myself. I had to stop being their overbearing heroic saviour, and they needed to help themselves get out of their own created toxic "victimlicious" cocktail.

Reiki was my saving grace; my healing sessions with Sue helped me immensely. Reiki is a non-invasive healing technique whereby the body heals itself through a hands-on healing method. Reiki consists of two Japanese words: *rei*, "universal, god consciousness," and *ki*, "life force energy." Combined, Reiki stands for universal or God consciousness life force energy. The phrase was coined by Mikao Usui, the founder of the Usui Reiki healing technique. In a past life, Dr. Usui was a high priest during the Golden Age of Atlantis and had aided the failing colony during its demise. However, in the deluge, much knowledge was lost, and after its fall, the symbolism and healing techniques were taken to Tibet, where many were initiated; but humanity used them for their own personal gain, and thus the wisdom was removed until such a time when a part could be returned. In his incarnation as Dr. Usui, he received several of these symbols, which many practitioners still use in their practice today.

In the space of a year, Sue taught me Reiki levels I and II—and in those days, being taught Reiki was different than today, where people become certified within a weekend. I was given homework and had to do my self-healing, attend healing shares, and keep a journal. For level II, I did about ten case studies, which was intense, and reported all progress back to her.

I briefly want to touch on Pyramid Healing, which also dates back to the Lemurian and Atlantean Age, with the Ancient Sumerians and Egyptians using this form of sacred geometrical healing, realigning themselves to the sacred grid of their divine elves. I was first introduced to Pyramid healing in 2011 by John Yukus, an incredible healer out in Jensen Beach, Florida. I was thinking, why does this guy have a copper pyramid in his garden? I thought it was weird and tried sitting in it; however, it did absolutely nothing for me.

Fast forward years later, Guy Taylor (www.healingintent.co.uk) reintro-duced me to this ancient form of multidimensional energy healing. He is also the founder of Pyranosis Healing, a combination of pyramid healing and hypnosis infused with the energy frequency of the ancient Qabalah, which has helped many people surpass their own barriers and self-limiting beliefs allowing them to heal from their own created dis-ease. Pyranosis is an accelerated healing process, unravelling one's issues stored within the encoded DNA structure of one's BEing—the divine blueprint. It is the process of discovering that we are life itself and that healing takes place when we take responsibility for our lives, viewing ourselves with compassion, and understanding that the nuances of duality are ingrained within our humanness, giving us the power to return to the lightness of who we are and enabling us to power-walk through life with an ease never felt before.

I have a Metatron mat under my mattress, and I sleep like a log when not getting downloads. I call it a divine activator and recalibrator of one's DNA, as it truly helps realign you, but as with all healing, you have to be open to receiving the energies wanting to heal you.

As St. Germain says, *"You are a mathematical equation of energy. When one suffers from dis-ease, one has duly messed up the formula of one's response to a serv-ed experience, and only you can calculate the 'formula' and decide what 'medicinal' frequency eases your body and soul back to the Divine Sacred Geometrical Grid of Self."*

I enrolled in a course on drug and alcohol abuse via the Open College to understand why people turned to addiction, followed by Angelic Reiki, with someone who had studied under Diane Cooper—I thought she would be great, but sadly she was not. She was adamant that none of us connected with our angels, but angels are always willing to work with you and assist you. In my experience, you can feel their energetic heat rush through you; it's literally out of this world and intense.

In the summer of 2010, I attended the Arthur Findlay College of spiritualism and psychic sciences at Stansted Hall, set within beautiful grounds in Stansted Mountfitchet in the UK. When I participated in Reiki healing shares, I would pick up an awful lot from people while healing them. I wanted to explore my options and enrolled in a course called "So You Want to Be a Medium?" We were all categorised into beginner, medium, or advanced. I got thrown into the beginners' group, where we all learned to enhance our abilities because developing ourselves and becoming more spiritually aware happens in stages.

One day, while sitting in a circle with the advanced class, everyone was too scared to get up and give a message. So, I bit the bullet and stood up, as I had an elderly gentleman in Spirit that kept prodding me. I described the gentleman, seeing he was once military, and how he would show the stars to his daughter and talk about the Milky Way. He had two beautiful Afghan hounds at his side, and I could see a library in this quaint, stately country house. The teacher from the advanced group thanked me for the message, as she could take all I had conveyed.

It was an interesting course. Was it for me? No, not really; I did, however, join a circle in Sutton, went a few times, and delivered several messages, but not everyone was open to them—I kept getting that a woman's son was an addict, but she remained deathly silent. It would have helped if she had spoken up because, as I later learned from another member, her son was indeed an addict.

One thing Anubis says that I agree with is, *"Heaven? Do you believe Souls here to be frolicking around on a beach, playing golf, or any other worldly things they so divulged in? Souls can tell you who they once were through mediums giving evidence, but how about asking them who they really are instead of remaining in the fantasy island world of what you think they are?"*

EFT and Meridian Psychotherapy

Late in 2011, I wanted to follow a more tangible course and stumbled upon Meridian Therapy and EFT. I became fascinated with it, as it was such a simple approach to healing.

With all of these different healing modalities, I learned something new about myself, and every step was healing my shattered mind back to a more aligned version of who I was. I am a continuous work in progress and still unfolding and BE-com-ing. We are all exactly where we are meant to be, peeling back the layers of our covered-up selves, eventually returning to the light of who we are. We may gasp in pain when we rip off the band-aid and expose the hurt, but we'll feel far better for letting it air, allowing ourselves to breathe and heal. Once the pain of the experience is transmuted and has healed, only a scar remains of what was once seemingly so daunting.

I dove into the beauty of the father of affirmations, Émile Coué de la Châtaigneraie (1857–1926), a French psychologist and pharmacist who, during the 1920s, pioneered the method of self-hypnosis called autosuggestion. He said that it is not the will but the imagination which is the principal force in the human being. So, when your desires and imagination are in conflict, your imagination invariably wins.

I was fascinated by Émile Coue's life and technique, which may have had to do with a past life in Austria, where in the late 1800s and early 1900s, I lived along one of the towns on the Danube River. I can see myself walking across a bridge with an umbrella in hand. I was a female psychologist working in a hospital, fascinated by the psyche of the mind, specifically between the left and right hemispheres of the brain, the temporal lobes—from the emotional functionality of expressing one's thoughts to the interpretation of information through images construed within the mind's imagination. These patients had roped their minds into a hangman's knot, asphyxiating themselves in the knotted chaos of emotions created by the illusion of the phenomena of their experiences. As my former self continues:

"I helped the incurable come back to an understanding of the ailment itself, aiding to cure them from the demons inside their head, for everything commences from the mind. The mind is the narrative of the words fed to oneself, transcribed into experiences, as a perception of how one views the world. The mind kept these poor patients locked in a prison of their own making, their own Alcatraz, from which there seemed no escape. I could not help all; often, they would slide back into their own created phenomenon of feeling comfortable in their uncomfortable state of an unwholesomeness within themselves. Yet, others chose to let the past be in a state of dissolvance, having jumped the maze of their minds, accepted their circumstances, and freed their minds for a deservance of a better life. I wish I could have helped all these souls see the beautiful Lights they were, but each walked a path of their choosing, participating in life according to the many spiced, seasoned, and savoury dishes of their experiences served and wilfully ingested by their beautiful minds."

Émile shared one phrase—easy to incorporate into one's everyday life, by reciting this 20 times in the morning before arising and 20 times at night before retiring to bed—that has helped many people worldwide:

"Every day in every way, I am getting better and better."

I used to add, *"and I send myself insights and miracles right now."*

I used Émile Coue's miracle reframe in many of my EFT tapping exercises. He suggested saying it with gentle ease rather than with conviction.

He also discovered that giving patients their medicine and delivering positive suggestions proved to be a far more effective cure than prescribing medications alone. He said, "You have in yourself the instrument of your cure." In other words, each person carries the solution to their problem. By using auto suggestion consciously, he observed that the subjects could cure themselves by replacing the "thought of illness" with the "thought of cure." By consciously repeating words or images as self-suggestion to the subconscious mind, one can order one's mind to obey them.

His unique discovery was that willpower is the biggest obstacle in any cure. He eventually abandoned hypnosis in favour of just using positive suggestions, as he thought that the hypnotic state impaired the efficiency of the suggestion.

Patients from all walks of life visited him with maladies that included kidney problems, diabetes, memory loss, stammering, weakness, atrophy, and other physical and mental illnesses. Using his so-called method (which he called a "trick"), his patients were all "miraculously" cured of their ailments. If the idea of "I can't" is in one's mind, one cannot open one's hands no matter how much force one applies, for the imagination always wins; such is the power of the mind.

He said, "A person wants to do such a thing but imagining that he is not able to accomplish it, he does exactly the contrary to that which he wants to do. Dizziness is a striking example of this. Suppose a person is walking on a very narrow path bordering a steep precipice (cliff). At first, he thinks nothing of it, but suddenly, the idea comes to him that he may tumble over the edge. If he has the misfortune to look down, he is lost. The image of a fall has taken root in his mind, and he feels himself attracted toward the abyss by an invisible force that becomes increasingly insistent, the greater his efforts at resistance. Finally, he gives, and down he goes."

Physically, you respond to the mental picture your imagination produces because you map your thoughts according to the wording you feed your mind. Unwholesome thoughts are like a bottomless pit that attracts those unable to resist them. If you ask people who suffer from various addictions why they acted the way they did, they'll respond that they couldn't help it; they could not resist the temptation. They are "forced" to act according to their wired and programmed conditioning because they imagine that they cannot help nor change themselves.

Coue says, "Now then, we are so proud of our willpower, we who think that we act voluntarily; we are, in reality, only poor puppets directed by our imagination, which holds the reins. We cease to be puppets only after we have learned to consciously direct our imagination."

Autosuggestion is defined as "the power of mind over matter." It is also known as suggestionism because we influence our minds with the thoughts we send to them, and thus it emits that frequency, riding the energy waves manifesting this into existence. Coué teaches us that no matter how hard we try to consciously stop something from happening, whenever the imagination grasps hold of an idea, "willpower" alone will stand no chance of exerting any control over that situation. Instead of auto suggesting unconsciously, we simply need to autosuggest consciously.

As the Council of Ra and St. Germain state, *"The Universe is mental in nature, you are mental in nature, and all that you create comes from the mental imagery of the Mind. Thus, one is the Alchemist of one's own Creation. Think what you wish to wish what you think, and it shall be so. Remember your true nature is Energy, not the blob of the current organism you inhabit that you think you are, but the enlightened light of the Alchemical Soul within that enlivens and creates the world through the mental imagery you project within, transpiring into the world without. Your Mind is like an endless film reel that produces its own reality according to the status quo of one's mental input—don't like it, change your mentality to change the mental input producing a different outcome to your mentally created reality from fiction to nonfiction in your outer world of a created receptivity."*

Healing is a simple feat, but instead of looking inward, we look outward to relieve our symptoms. If we have a headache, we take an aspirin instead of wondering what may have caused the headache; if we suffer from depression, we take an antidepressant instead of addressing the issue of the discord within. Our minds are bombarded with chemical remedies by the pharmaceutical industry. Chemicals subdue our emotions, and as long as a person refrains from addressing the underlying issue, merely band-aiding the symptoms, they will duly remain in a continuous loop of beating up their beautiful mind and soul.

EFT is the Emotional Freedom Technique, tapping the emotions out of a memory, freeing the self of that issue. It is a meridian energy therapy—just like acupuncture, it works directly on the meridian system in the body. But instead of needles, you stimulate the major meridian lines by tapping on them. As an analogy, think of the meridians as rivers, whereby upsets in the emotional or physical bodies lead to the equivalent of blockages or sludge, disrupting the flow of these rivers and making you feel ill (Imbalanced of Love and Light). EFT gets to the root of the problem, eradicating it instead of putting a band-aid on it.

EFT was founded by Dr. Roger Callahan, a clinical psychologist who devoted his life to finding ways to heal people from unreal fears, phobias, trauma, and stress disorders. He helped a patient named Mary who suffered from a severe water phobia, not daring to take a bath or venture outside when it rained. Having worked on her case for eighteen months with many different therapeutic approaches, from client-centred therapy to rational-emotive therapy and hypnosis, he decided to use the tapping approach. Surprisingly, she got instant relief from the phobia. To be sure, Callahan guided her to the pool on the grounds, and, showing no sign of fear, she nearly dove in before remembering that she couldn't swim. Such a simple technique, yet so profound. Healing is innately simple, yet our conditioning has led us astray from ourselves to believe we need a prescription for everything.

I had to sit for an exam and find six guinea pigs as case studies, doing a proper write-up of each. I passed with flying colours and became a qualified EFT therapist.

I had some severe cases, one who was afraid to commit due to her parents getting divorced at a young age and constantly shouting at one another. As a child, she had felt guilty and suffered from panic attacks, but during our session, she felt an instant calm and that all her emotional turmoil and "baggage" was releasing itself. She felt happy and energised afterward, and the following day, she felt wholly released from this emotional cloud that had been inside her for so long. Her peers at work even noticed that she seemed relaxed and happy, with minor issues that would normally have caused emotional turmoil not bothering her. Her panic/anxiety attacks completely subsided. She had also spoken to her boyfriend, and once they had decided to take it a step at a time, and the pressure was off, she felt like she was falling in love all over again. Several years later, she got married and had a baby girl.

One of my best friends, Trinh-ny—a beautiful, funny, and witty soul—had this phobia of slugs. To her, they were cold, slimy, scaly, and pure evil; they reminded her of leeches. If a slug was on the sidewalk, she'd freak out, crossing the road to walk on the other side. She went on to say that she hated them even though she knew they were part of the food chain, and it was an irrational fear.

When she was seven years old, she had stepped on a slug, and as stated, the slimy goo shimmered, and she couldn't get the thing off her shoe, having to ransack the kitchen cabinets to find an acidic substance to wash it off. She put salt on slugs and snails as they would fizz and bubble. At the age of eight, she moved to Purley and used to run along a wooded path and knew they were close because of the smell of rotten vegetation. She thought they were there to torment her and called them dirty, slimy, pointless little things. One day she ran so hard to escape them, tripped, and fell right into these fat and blue evil-eyed things, screaming at the top of her lungs, even though, as she said, they're nothing but bird feed. As a teenager, it got out of hand after she read a book called *Slugs* by Shaun Hutson, about slugs eating human flesh.

As I went through the created statements and tapping sequences with her, she said they were still scary, so I told her that this was living in the fear of the fear of snails, and she agreed. She said she couldn't let this fear go as it was part of her; it felt strangely comfortable.

At this point, I asked her to close her eyes and go to the little eight-year-old girl on the wooded path and asked her how she felt. There were no slugs, so she was okay. I told her it had just rained, and there were two slugs to her left, but they were not there to harm her and were much slower than she was. She stepped around them. Along the path, I advised her there were more and more slugs, and every time she ignored them.

I told her to let the little girl know that this fear was hampering the big Trinh-ny and that there was no need to be scared. The little girl was okay with that; she said she was happier and would simply ignore them. She then said they're boring as she can't put salt on them anymore and decided she wanted to play pirates instead. She was such a gem.

When Trinh-ny emailed me after our session, she told me that the slug thing was going well; she hadn't seen any but came across some snails and simply ignored them instead of freaking out and crossing the road or walking in the middle of the road to avoid them. She thought it was amazing and was surprised that EFT had virtually banished her phobia of molluscs.

I took on another complex case, with someone drinking too much and being fearful of it turning into an addiction. When she drank, she came out of her shell and had more confidence and clarity in articulating herself; however, drinking too much would turn her into a monster, making her more aggressive. She felt awful because she saw her parents, heavy drinkers, always fighting and arguing when she was three or four years old. Having no brothers or sisters, she would sit in her bedroom, feeling utterly alone. She was very emotional during the session.

When I phoned her several days later for a follow-up, she said she felt good. She was much more aware and understood that the root issues stemmed from her childhood. She had subsequently been decluttering her home and had curbed her drinking, swapping her drink of choice for something with a much lower percentage of alcohol.

There were many more phobias I helped cure over the years, ranging from a fear of flying to a fear of spiders to many alcohol-related issues and a guy who kept being turned down rudely by girls—as, bless his heart, he was made to feel worthless at the tender age of ten when he had asked a girl at school if she wanted to go to the school disco with him. She mockingly turned him down, telling the whole school about it. He got teased immensely, which made him withdraw within himself, having become very insecure, which only worsened as the years went by.

I still use EFT today, not as a practitioner but sometimes will create specific exercises for people to help them heal themselves. I want to share a tapping exercise channelled to me by the Ascended Master St. Germain that is so simple yet powerful. It will have you on a 'high' by the end of it.

The Power of the Violet Flame using EFT

"I AM who you are, as much as you are who I AM, we merely vibe at different acoustic and melodic timbres of transformational consciousness."

~The Ascended Maestro St. Germain~

The Violet Flame is one of the most powerful tools to heal and transform your life, enhancing your health, and balancing your etheric bodies. It flushes out inconsistent energetic frequencies and any anomalies. It clears old karmic and ancestral ties you have been lugging around, helping to heal all relationships, and is an invaluable tool in creating more abundance in all areas of your life. It is like dunking yourself into a cold water pond to dislodge all the stuck energies, clearing your auric field and restoring you to equilibrium.

As St. Germain puts it, *"The Violet Flame in all its simplicity, smites the non-serving energies that have taken up residence in your auric field and blown your Soul to smith-ereens, allowing for you to re-emerge as the dazzling diamond of Light that you are and always have been my Child."*

Archangel Zadkiel is the Lord and Overseer of the Violet Flame, while St. Germain is the hierarch of the Aquarian Age and its Keeper, who reintroduced the Violet Flame into the lives of humanity.

When we talk about the Violet Flame, there is often a tug-of-war between the old and the new, between the lightness and darkness of both our condi-tioned self and that of the world. The life that has been can no longer continue in that form; do not remain stomping in your own created mud bath, but know that our soul yearns to evolve from the old into the new, and we very much deserve that. We should honour what continues to hold value and dismiss what no longer serves us.

Zadkiel says, *"You have chosen a life of conditioning, yet when invoking the simplicity of the Violet Flame, one cannot help but see the beautiful alternate outcomes of a once so carefully created life of drama to a mere flow of ease in all that you do.*

The art of challenges serves merely as a dish of opportunities one can choose to defy or·accept. You are an Alchemist of thy own making, for you have the power to transform all your experiences to love, light, and understanding, or to remain in the stance of complete darkness, in the coldness of the Soul of Self."

The Violet Flame decree is intensely powerful. It will cause you to feel a height-ened sense of awareness. It makes all the electromagnetic particles within your energy spin and dance, jolting them back to life according to the musical vibrance of your soul.

"I AM, the Divine Presence of the I AM in You, as much as you are the I AM of the Divine Presence in Me. Are we not strings to the same bow? We may play different timbres according to our Souls' frequency, evolving at a different pace, with the tones causing vibrational rippling waves across the multiverse of our lives, but the light of the same creator of All still adorns us.

Drown yourself not in the austere and solemness of the tones of your experiences, causing but a malady of unwanted creations being played into existence, but fine-tune the disharmonised strings of yourself, by using the invocation of the Violet Flame, for your Soul can be 'plucked' to playing either lowered frequencies, darkening the mood, or higher frequencies, heightening the mood according to the dance of your existence.

The Violet Flame illuminates the soul's pathways, clearing the disharmony within one's out-of-tune auric field. Let all but wash away with the ease of the recurring riptides. Does the sea not wash away its imprints on the sand? So too, release your experiences, rather than the malarkey of drowning yourself in your own created nonsensical blown-out-of-proportion humanoid problems.

One day you will wake up, and instead of it being with a sorry sore head of heaviness, seeing life so bleak, it will be with such joy and giddiness. You will realise that living is a joyous occasion and not the struggle you once perceived it to be, embracing yourself in the lightness of having transformed from a once upon a time 'hoodwinked' caterpillar to a beautiful enlightened butterfly, feeling but love, light, beauty, and acceptance in the radiance of yourself and all."

~The Ascended Master St. Germain~

Mantra

I AM the I AM in all that You Are
Yet I AM the I AM that you are not and yet you are all that you are as I AM You

I AM a Being of Violet Fire
I AM the Purity Source desires
I AM the Violet Flame of Freedom of Self
I AM the I AM of the Awakening within
I Invoke the Violet Flame in action in ME Now
To eliminate all miscalibration and dissonance, re-aligning my Higher Conscious Self back into the realignment of Self
I AM my own Compass, my own Way Bearer of Truth, of Light and of Love Divine
I Live in Awareness
I Breathe in Awareness
I AM Awareness
I AM the I AM
I AM
I

Always make sure to put yourself in a bubble of protection. I will often add the following after the incorporated mantra, in no particular order, but you can add whatever feels right for you:

- I AM all that I AM, and More
- I AM the Violet Flame in action in me NOW
- I invoke the Violet Flame in the I AM Presence and Empowerment of Self

- The Violet Flame heals, transmutes, and illuminates all that no longer serves me back into the Flame and Heart of the I AM
- I AM Love, I AM Empowerment, I AM Light, I AM Inspiration, I AM Abundance, I AM Divine, etc
- I invoke Christ Consciousness back into the space of my heart chakra here and now

If you state "I ask for" or "I want," you make a possible future statement, inviting this into your life instead of it being in your life already. It is an imprint into your energetic field of consciousness; you will be relentlessly running after it, much like trying to catch a butterfly that keeps eluding you. Those who suffer from addiction and attend meetings always make the same statements: "I AM an alcoholic" or "I AM a drug addict," reaffirming that they are still an addict, not realising that their subconscious mind picks this up. How can they heal when they reiterate the same thing over and over again? It cripples them forever, locking them into that personality. The individual will be a constant trip hazard to themselves, continuously identifying with what they are trying to heal and release.

If you want to cleanse a room and sage it, merely state as often as you like:

- This room is bathed in Violet Fire, cleansing itself with the light and love of God's pure desire. (*If you want to be more visual, you can replace cleansing with washing*).

Violet Flame - St Germain Affirmation

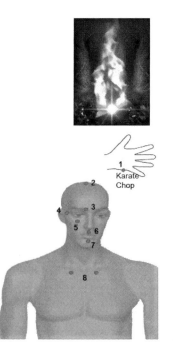

1. Karate Chop
I AM a being of violet fire – I AM the purity God desires
2. Top of the Head
I AM a being of violet fire – I AM the purity God desires
3. Eyebrow
I AM a being of violet fire – I AM the purity God desires
4. Side of the Eye
I AM a being of violet fire – I AM the purity God desires
5. Under the Eye
I AM a being of violet fire – I AM the purity God desires
6. Under the Nose
I AM a being of violet fire – I AM the purity God desires
7. Chin
I AM a being of violet fire – I AM the purity God desires
8. Collarbone
I AM a being of violet fire – I AM the purity God desires

The Sequence
Tap 7 times on the following energy points while repeating the Violet Flame affirmation, this helps to transform negative emotions on the spot. Sit down and envision the Violet Flame within your heart and around you. Repeat the sequence as many times as you like – the more the better.

Holistic Nutrition

Studying holistic nutrition taught me a lot about myself, in a "wholistic" way: my body and the foods I consumed. It made me listen to my body and its wants and needs because after all, you are what you eat. I suffered from high cholesterol, which is what happens when you have a love for chocolate croissants and cheezy crisps. I was happily clogging up my arteries and starving my heart of oxygen, which, if I wasn't careful, could eventually cause coronary heart dis-ease.

This course taught me to listen to my body and become more aware of its needs. I ditched the junk food and took a supplement called Lecithin 1200mg, and when I had a follow-up appointment six weeks later, the doctor was astounded, as my cholesterol had dropped to normal range. He said that he would keep this supplement in mind for others. Lecithin contributes to raising HDL (good) cholesterol and lowering LDL (bad) cholesterol in blood profiles but also helps to alleviate tiredness. It is named after the Greek word *lekithos,* meaning "egg yolk," and was first isolated from egg yolk sometime in the 1850s. It occurs naturally in certain foods, such as whole grains, nuts, and soybeans.

Health is the relationship between you and your body. My father always used to say, "Your body is a temple, treat it as such," although he didn't quite grasp that himself. The traditional definition of a "temple" is a dedicated place of worship with a divine presence within. You are a divine BEing that inhabits a bodily temple, so treat it with the respect and love it deserves. Honour yourself, your body, and your soul; you owe it to yourself to resonate in the lightness of all that you are and can be. Why would you deny yourself that?

The phrase "You are what you eat" originates from Anthelme Brillat-Savarin, who in 1826 wrote,

> "Dis-moi ce que tu manges, je te dirai ce que tu es"
> "Tell me what you eat, and I will tell you what you are"

In an essay entitled "Concerning Spiritualism and Materialism," Ludwig Andreas Feuerbach wrote:

> "Der Mensch ist, was er ißt"
> "Man is what he eats"

Your current body is the vessel you chose to reach your full potential; it should be the driving factor for striving towards your goals, dreams, and aspirations in life. Your soul is the operator manual to your given body; ain't nobody else in the driver seat but you. Look not to the external inhibiting factors but the internal, to the created dis-ease within.

"You are a radiant BEing of Infinite StarLight particles, compressed within a physical embodiment, with your Soul vibrating like a musical accordion to the notes of the highs and lows of life.

Energy = Light = Frequency = Waves of energetic shifts of forever dancing molecules and atoms within your incarnated body, a Light vessel of the Soul incarnate, lambada-ing forth to the rhythm of your beautiful Soul swimming but in the 'hue-man-i-licious' essence of Self. The created patterning of dis-ease within the physical is the mere blockage of one's coordinated 'chi' caused by the energetic imbalance of the Spirit 'hatschi-ing' within.

What you feed your Mind, so will you but evolve in the chosen direction of your created pathway, for the infinite energetic particles that make up the organic composition of the physical embodiment merely hip-hop according to the song and rhythm of said mind chatter.

The human experiences labelled as 'trauma' are the mere energetic hiccups causing a pile-up of distorted energy waves within the body, causing a mass of endless possible 'uncomfortabilities.'

Dis-ease is the cause of one's diminishing vibrational Light. It is the mere bludgeoning of the Self, creating a slippage of energetic sludge causing a blockage in one's auric energy field and electromagnetic inner wiring, in turn causing a discord within one's physical body, trickling down to the contusion of living cells, organs, tissues, and systems, for everything is interconnected through the neuro network of electromagnetic pulses. The energy merely vibrates according to one's Soul resonance - much like a beaver having built a dam, clogging up the water flow.

You've got to let go, to grow, for life is that beautifying fact of a simple series of experiences, not meant to tether you by the balls, having you screech and laugh but like a dam-ned and pain-ed hyena, but to teach you a mere understanding of life in its grand potentiality and wondrous absurdity of simplicity.

One is the cause of one's own demise. It is not society, but one's own demeanour towards oneself, that causes havoc in the internal Self. Tell me it isn't so, and I will tell thee, to rear thy head to the reflection casting but its reflection back at the shimmering sheepishly Self of the Divine you.

Food consumption is a key energetic ingredient to the ingestion of fuel that can cause both an enlightened state or a demise in the vibrational Light one so radiates. Changing one's foods to nurture one's temple creates a different energetic vibration, with one becoming more in tune with the beatific song of Self. However, the consumption of non-nutritional foods can cause utter discomfort, causing congestion along the highway of the physical body.

Bombardments of external optics to the Mind cause one to deviate from the high vibrational foods to low vibrational foods keeping one entranced in the matrix and the thinking that any dis-ease is caused by external factors as opposed to the internal energetic infrequency.

Have but a wee bit more love for yourself, my Child, for it breaks down the clogged-up unbreathable barriers of the sewage compiled within. Like that tree in nature, as dark clouds break and the rain falls and whispers down on the leaves, allowing for the gentle water droplets to cleanse the weathered dirt, stimulating growth and replenishing the tree to its vibrant hue of Self, so too is the human experience, for to hold on to the grime and dirt causes nothing but a tug o' war and chaos within the cells of the body.

You can either choose to eat healthy, to live far more 'wealthy' or keep eating 'sludge' remaining sorely within the discomfort of being a fudged-up crutch."

~The Ascended Master Lord Sananda et le Club Divin de Shakespeare~

As Shakespeare said, "Our bodies are our gardens—our wills are our gardeners." When your body is sick, it sends a signal to you, letting you know that something is missing, that it desperately requires something you are not giving it. We suck at tuning into our bodies because we have not been taught to listen to them; we simply ignore their cries and blatant screams for help. We live so much outside ourselves that we have daftly forgotten the relationship with our bodies, and yet we should realise that we are the sole guardian and caretaker of our body and soul. Do not ever take your body for granted, for life is like playing a piano—what you get out of it depends on how you choose to play it. Will it be a beautiful symphony, or a false concerto?

Without your soul, your body would not function, nor would you exist. Our bodies are true miracles, with everything working in perfect harmony according to our divine frequency. Given how many of us treat our bodies with contempt, it's rather remarkable that it continues to work as well as it does. We allow our bodies to get run down like abandoned shacks and treat our stomachs like blimmin' garbage disposals. Who can possibly explain the wondrous workings of this machine without realising that a power mightier than our physical being dwells within us?

Meditation, Prana, and Quantum Touch Healing

I studied Quantum Healing, which works with the body's Life Force Energy to reduce pain and promote optimal wellness by focusing, amplifying, and directing the energy to the intended area of "distortion."

Do you really need a healer to help heal yourself when you have the innate power of the healer within to heal the self? I've always gone to a healer not to fix me but to help me unlock the key to my own ability to heal. We can agree that everything is energy. Our body is energy and resonates according to the frequency and the thoughts we send to it. It has an extraordinary intelligence and ability to heal itself; our body listens to every word we speak and transforms it into an energetic frequency to correspond with how our emotions run through our system. *E-motions*, derived from the Latin *emotare*, are nothing more than *energies-in-motion*, which is the experience of our soul's energy moving through our body, created by the experiences interpreted through the associated programming of our mind. Emotions are nothing more than energetic carrier waves to the entire spectrum of our feelings, and like water, they are fluid; much like the waves of the ocean crashing onto the shores and receding, emotions are meant to be felt and released rather than repressed and ignored, causing a bottle-neck within our system. As the Goddess Sekhmet says, *"You are not this body; you are the Soul within the body, for the body is but a transient shell to enliven the senses carried forth by the breath returning to the fold through the evolution of Self."*

When I tell people that they themselves are the world's greatest healer, they look at me quizzically, but the truth is, we are. Everything within our body is a connected energetic sequence of algorithms, from a subatomic level to the atoms, molecules, cells, and tissue, all having the power to shift the energetic particles.

We are all wondrous alchemists, creating concoctions for the advancement of our own stratospheric BEing. We are energetic wonders of the universe, and our body is an incredible living organism giving life through the hue of our soul, with billions of changes taking place within. Energy is a simple "transactional" transference: everything starts with that once tiny seedling within the mind, henceforth nurtured, sprouting into manifestation and whipping it into existence, creating the very backdrop of our life—that is the ultimate power of the I AM of who you are, of who we all are.

Quantum Touch is an ancient art of healing that has been repackaged and westernised. Many people in India work with specific breathing techniques and body awareness exercises, called *prana, chi,* or *ki,* raising their vibration and optimising their health, redistributing the oxygen flow. When I was at the Art of Living Centre, in Bangalore, India, following the Basic and Advanced Course, we were taught the art of breathing and how pranayama aids in the alleviation of pain and in a correct running of energy through our body's meridian points, helping everything to work in harmony and unison as it should.

Prana is the subtle life energy and *pranayama* (Sanskrit, from *prana* or "breath" and *ayama* or "extend/lengthen"), literally meaning "lengthening the breath." One form of this breathwork involves four phases of controlled breathing: inhale, hold in, exhale, and hold out. Sometimes the breath is held or stopped for specific lengths of time. Many of us breathe shallow, which does not allow the body to be fully oxygenated, causing many problems.

The power of *yama*, extending the breath, is used to dissolve the stuck sense of self, to break through the barrier of one's frustrated will, one's ego, to renew the life-force energy within. For many ancient civilisations, prana breathing was the essence of survival; it was a way of life, and they had a far better understanding of the workings of the body and the flow of energy throughout. Thousands of years later, much of humanity merely uses the lungs and mouth to breathe super-ficially. Doing so limits our potential to distribute valuable energy to the molec-ular structure. When done correctly, prana breathing allows us to move the molecular structure in a different direction and level of understanding—we are in communication with the whole neuro-network of the body. We know where the energy needs to travel to feel better about ourselves. The Ascended Master Lord Sananda always drums into me the importance of breathwork, making sure I do my breathing exercises every night because whatever you suffer from, you can breathe out the pain.

"You breathe in the shallowness of Self, causing dis-ease in the energetic interior flow of one's Cosmic Self, for the Energy does not flow through the intricate meridian points providing oxygenation as it should.

The Body is an energetic quantum field, a neural-network of meridian points. All are interlinked and connected to keep one in the equilibrium of the Self, the body, the ethereal layers, and the Higher Divine Consciousness. As you have embarked on your journey of Life in the form of the human embodiment, you have chosen to shut down the art of breathing, of "oxygenation" in the density of the conditioned world you so live and breathe in, causing you an array of dis-cord within yourselves.

You have become a superficial shallowness of a fish out of the water instead of a fish in the pond breathing the very depth of the Soul that you are.

You are the current to each atom within your body. You are a chemical composi-tion of energetic frequency waves that interlinks the fluidity of the composition and workings of your human physique. You are the sole creator of the intricate workings of your body, soul, and mind—the incorporated directional sequence of the envisioned outcome of all creation in your Life.

You are the Creator of the creations created. Breathwork is key to realigning yourselves with the inner self-grid, returning to the harmonious flow within yourselves.

Healing comes through the transcendence of allowing your energetic love particles to infiltrate the disconnected energetic synapses within the body. When you refurbish a home, you give it the love, attention, and dedication it needs; you nurture it to the outcome of your liking. Why should your temple be any different? Does your body not deserve nurturing? Does it not deserve to be worshipped? Does it not deserve your love, honour, attention, and dedication?

It is a true rejuvenation of the Soul breathing back to the wholeness of Self—it is loving every cell, every atom, every light particle, every inch of the wholeness of who you are, breathing back the loving warmth of Light to permeate through every pore of your BEing, allowing the particles of your Divine Light to dance in rhythmic harmony with the Universal Consciousness. There is nothing more beautiful than realigning yourself to the Universal Cosmic Grid of Consciousness, with the electromagnetic particles that one had for so long subdued, swimming against the tidal wave of non-understanding, having recalibrated and dancing but ever so joyfully in harmonic unison.

You are the electrical current of Light swimming back into the Sea of Eternal subatomic Consciousness.

Your vibrational field represents the quality of your Divine dancing Light within the human body. You are an inner Alchemist, a Magi, manifesting and manipulating the Energy according to the vibration and rhythm of your Soul, creating your own masterful experiences, and wilfully so, there is no other caster greater than the one casting the Energy, for that is the unfathomable Power that resides within the I AM Presence of the BEing that is You."

~The Ascended Master Lord Sananda~

Lord Sananda did not ascend after his lifetime as Jesus. He ascended after his incarnation as Apollonius of Tyana (Greek: Ἀπολλώνιος ὁ Τυανεύς; ca. 1–97 C.E.). In that lifetime, he was from the town of Tyana in the Roman province of Cappadocia in Anatolia, which now falls within Turkish borders. He was a Greek neo-Pythagorean philosopher, ascetic teacher, author, and wonder-worker, mastering divination, self-mastery, and the divine mysteries. His teachings, after his death, influenced both scientific thought and occultism for many centuries. He was often compared to Jesus during this lifetime.

Having taken a vow of silence for five years, travelling inward whilst travelling outward to India, learning the wisdom of the Persian Magi, the Indian Brahmins, Babylonianmagoi and Hyrcanians and travelled to Egypt, studying the ways of the Gymnoi, the "Naked Ones," before heading to Hierapolis in Syria and then the Euphrates. He was a keen scholar and an absorber of knowledge, having spent time with many of the priests of famous Greek sanctuaries. He was also a miracle healer, saving many people from the dying breath at death's door by blowing life back into their damaged bodies.

As he says, *"I realigned the misconstrued particles from the denseness of the caused contusions, returning it to a state of vibrational frequency and recalibrating that soul with their body. Every Soul housed within its body is the creator of its own dis-ease. I understood the song of that Soul that had obliterated its mind with the unalignment that had bled into its physical essence. Energy is a field of manipulation, of untangling the created knotted 'stagnance,' returning it to the flow of health; for my Child, you are all energetic conjurors of the Divine, so I urge you to unleash your own inner 'wunder' Alchemist to return to a state of symmetry."*

In Quantum-Touch, when you raise your own vibration, the body you heal receives that high vibration; by way of "transference," it responds in whatever way it chooses to accelerate the healing process. Quantum-Touch wasn't quite right for me; it didn't float my boat. Granted, I wasn't feeling overly confident, as I felt many others on the course were better equipped and far more knowledgeable than I was. I was a green bean on the scene while they were all much older and far more experienced. I let myself down due to my own insecurities, and thus was my own most excellent stumbling block of a lousy alchemist at play. Your greatest power will always lie in being yourself. As St. Germain says, *"You are a unique vibrational Divine Being, your Energy resonance is your own, dance to your own vibe and be happy with being the uniqueness, and blissfully Divine scrumptious 'lushalicious' BEing that you are."*

St. Petersburg, Florida

When work dried up at the British oil and gas operator, I was offered another job at an American operator. There was some bullying there too, but I kept to myself and worked well with the engineering teams. Life was good, if only for a while. I seemed to be on the mend, and the turbulence seemed to have levelled out.

In 2011, I decided to buy a property in Florida. Houses were cheap in the Tampa Bay area, as the property market had been in a dip for quite some years. I had felt an immense pull to that part of Florida (while never having been there) and, having looked extensively online, got in touch with a realtor through a mutual friend, booked a hotel, and rented a car to get around. The realtor had advised me to look in St. Petersburg, as it was an up-and-coming place, and I'm glad I followed his lead as Tampa wasn't my vibe.

I found a green-coloured house that had been repossessed by the bank, just above my budget. The poor house was suffocating; it could barely breathe, having been depleted of its energy. The inside had to be gutted; it was dark, dingy, yet a beautiful disaster with a pool. I love natural light, clean lines, and an open plan so the energy flows and the house can breathe. It cost me all my savings to buy it with a bit of help from my mum, and truth be told, I had my work cut out for me. I was thankful I still had my tax ID, opened a bank account, and found a handyman through the bank manager. He was slow and costly, but he got started on the job, removing walls and messing up my pool in the interim, which I subsequently had to get patched up by a professional company, costing me far more than I bargained for. He then suffered a stroke at home, and I had to find someone else to continue the work.

One night I walked into the house and was unable to move. I stood there in the living room, nailed to the ground, frozen in fear, as this black pool of energy formed right in front of me. I'd never been so scared in my life. The place became cold, and I was locked into place, unable to take my eyes from it until the fear had washed over me, after which I bolted, locking the door behind me.

Unbeknownst to me, the house had a history. A couple lived there with their autistic son, and the husband had an air-conditioning business that went bust. Apparently, things went from bad to worse as he became a severe alcoholic, couldn't pay the bills, fell behind on the mortgage repayments, and often defecated on the wooden floors in the living room, leaving black stains ingrained within the floorboards. I was told that when his family came back, as I don't know the ins and outs, he held them hostage, holding a gun to their heads, with the police having to intervene, cordoning off the street, finally arresting him several hours later. He spent time in prison and was released at some stage. I decided it would be best to work there during the day and leave before dark until I "saged" the place.

I loved St. Pete; I felt welcome and at home for the first time.

Liam

I recommend avoiding online dating sites, especially one named Plenty of Fish, for this is how I met my next walking disaster, Liam. I thought Mark was bad, but Liam was a different ballgame; he was like a friggin' piranha. But even though the relationship was highly toxic for both of us, we turned out the better for it, so I see him as having been a wonderful teacher. And even though at the time I was close to the end of my wits, hating the very essence of him, I also hated the very essence of myself, and thus he was a mere reflection of everything that I had chosen to be but was not.

And despite all the healing work I was doing, my world came crashing down. In every challenge pitched our way, lies an opportunity for us to correspond to the thrown pitch by instilling the necessary changes, for what weighs you down drowns you in the sorrows that need not be.

My experiences with Liam were given to me to wake me up, to snap myself out of that comatose state of BEing. Without these tangy and triple hot spicy flavoured experiences, I could not and would not be who I am today, so I am thankful he came into my life and gave me a taste of my own medicine, thus accelerating my growth and quick-walking me back to my own truth and originality.

I love him for having plunged me into the darkness, for having allowed me to walk through the crappy, tainted shadow sides of myself, to alleviate the gunk and get myself to a more enlightened state of BEing. As St. Germain says, *"What's down comes up, making you 'puke' out all the issues of your experiences, of everything that you are not, and what's up comes down, with the shadows having made way for the absorbance of the light of forgiveness and the remedy to a better understanding of both life and yourself. Healing is merely walking from denseness to light through love."*

Life is here to teach us, to unnerve us into such a state of unease that we can choose to either heal and live a life of a far more joyous and abundant nature or remain living in a sorry state of affairs. No matter the s*** that rained down on me, I was exactly where I was supposed to be, having chosen these experiences for my own soul's growth, with me breaking apart just beautifully. My Guides rejoiced, me, not so much, as I kept running into walls, breaking and bruising myself.

Here I thought I'd gotten my life together—I had no idea what car crash was about to hit me. Spirit shoved my face in the s***, whereas they first held my face above it, hoping that I would learn from the smell of my "nasty" experiences, which, quite clearly, I did not.

I met Liam in 2012 after he invited me over for a home-cooked meal while I had wanted to go bowling. I'm not one to go to someone's home I've never met, but even though I had a bit of a queasy feeling, I did. Yes, in hindsight, I should have listened to my gut.

He lived about an hour from St. Pete, and when I met him, he seemed genuinely nice. He worked in publishing and had been pretty successful, though his car, as I later found out, was bust; hence we couldn't go bowling that night.

The next time I got into town, I got him some new bed linen and some shirts and cleaned his house, as it was filthy, plus he had two rather smelly cats. At this stage, you must think I was some sort of moronic sugar mama—I wasn't, though; it was merely how I was wired. I don't understand how people can live in their own filth; it clearly reflects their state of mind. As Spirit states, *"The house to your Soul is a reflection to the house you live in as much as your Mind is a reflection of who you create yourself to be."*

He wanted to help refurbish my home, which was the start to the end of my life as I knew it. As I went back and forth for the next two years, the trouble began, and cracks started to show, with me choosing to ignore the signs at first, wanting to give him the benefit of the doubt.

In early 2013, I went to see Kathy Mingo (www.kathymingo.com), a fantastic aura medium and clairvoyant specialising in past life regression through shamanic healing. She told me that I would break Liam's heart. I should have understood that as a sign to run in the other direction, yet I remained. She brought me under and took me back to a lifetime where I lived in Paris, during the height of WWII, where the Jews were persecuted and deported to death camps between 1940 and 1944 or treated as pariahs and forced to wear the Star of David.

I came from a very wealthy French family who made their money in the clothing and textile industry, yet I never really cared much for the family business or the notion of being well-off. Liam, in that lifetime, was a tall, lean Jewish painter with a mop of brown hair, living in the Jewish quarters in a small attic with only a tiny window for daylight. Walking through the poorer parts of Paris to Liam's, I remember the distinct smell of the sewers, mixed with the sweet smell of freshly baked Jewish bread. Although I have never tasted Jewish bread in this lifetime, the smell has lingered in my memory.

Liam's abode was in stark contrast to my family's, who bathed in the lap of luxury. It did not bother me in the slightest, as I loved him for him, not for the circumstances he lived in or his status. He lived a modest life, with a simple wrought iron bed in a tiny room and a table and chair to sit and create his sketches, often by candlelight or the light of an oil lamp, as he did not have electricity. The kitchen had a basic sink and some shelves, and he shared a bathroom with several residents on the adjacent floors. He could barely make ends meet as an artist, even though he was very talented, so he did other odd jobs to pay his rent and afford the basic food necessities. When times got tough, I helped him out; no questions asked.

Much of the food was rationed during the occupation, with strict curfews in place. Even though times were tough, people were resilient and still tried to find joy and appreciation in what little they had and each other. You are not entitled to anything but for the gratitude of a life forged through the fires and the wisdom of the soul to carry it through and inspire the flicker of the flame of hope in others. When the war hit and Paris became occupied, I used my money to help many of the Jews escape through the tunnels and sewer systems of Paris, back to the safety of the countryside—and not just me, but a whole network of people throughout Paris and the rest of France, for we believed all were equal regardless of race, and that no one should suffer at the hands of the Nazis that had taken occupation of the city of Paris. I also helped my then-lover to safety, knowing I would never see him again.

We make a life less ordinary by surrendering our hearts and believing in the oneness of all, for love is an eternal fountain. It is the very essence of who we are. A love lost, with a deep sadness in my heart. Yet, a love gained for letting go in the freedom of reinventing and returning to ourselves. Paris was not a place for those who were haunted, with its severe regulations and checkpoints, the German troops having been completely brainwashed by the Nazi regime, patrolling the streets and stopping anyone they did not like the look of with a request for their papers.

A few months later—after a night out, Liam was charged with a reckless, refused a breathalyser test, and had to attend court instead. He also had to move, as the landlady was putting the house up for sale, and I said faster than I could shut my mouth that maybe he should move in with me in St. Pete once the building work had been completed. He was over the moon, me not so much, as I was allergic to cats, and he refused to compromise on them. He said he could build a cattery in the garage or a shed in the back garden with a built-in ventilation system and spend time with them there. He refused to give them up for anyone, as they were his life. My friend Trinh-ny could not wrap her head around this and called him the crazy cat lady. She thought he was nuts.

I went back and forth a few times a year to see how the work was progressing, and I worked hard on the house, as I have always been very much a DIY person, at times choosing to work till the early hours of the morning. I sanded the wooden floors and helped plaster and sand the walls, with my mum helping me paint part of the interior.

New Year's 2012 was a night to remember. Still living an hour from St. Pete, Liam managed to get a dinner reservation last minute. I didn't know the route and made a wrong turn, and he flipped out on me in the car, wondering how I could be so stupid as to miss it. I was sitting there, driving in silence, taken aback by his sudden outburst.

We ended up at another restaurant instead. Thankfully, by that time, he had calmed down. I had left the car at my house, still under construction, and we had taken a cab downtown. Dinner was great, and we decided to go to a rooftop club to celebrate New Year's in style, but Liam was pretty wasted.

I was on the dance floor chatting away while he was getting drinks. When he returned, he lost his cool again, asking me why I was talking to another guy. I didn't quite understand, as all I was doing was wishing him the best for the new year. I was slightly tipsy but not off my face. He ripped into me, calling me every name under the sun in his drunken stupor. He kept shouting at me, and I stupidly kept trying to reason with him, pleading with him to calm down, whilst I should have kept my dignity and walked away.

We should view all relationships as reflective teachers of what requires healing within our own tethered minds. Those that cuss at you in truth cuss at themselves.

They have lost all love for themselves and hate the very sight of themselves, blaming others, to avoid looking at themselves. Yet here I was, allowing myself to be trampled on, trying to salvage something that wasn't salvageable. He wasn't exactly a 'loveable' drunk, and the hotel I usually stayed in was fully booked, so I had no choice but to go back and stay in my building site of a home and sleep in the filth thereof.

I didn't really sleep, and several hours later, when dawn broke, I quietly got up to leave; he asked me where I was going. I relayed everything he had said to me, which he claimed to have no recollection of. He was either lying or suffering memory lapses. Then again mixing painkillers and alcohol will do that to you. It causes possible oxygen deprivation, whereby the brain fails to retain memories. We talked for a long time and made up, with me giving him the benefit of the doubt. Undoubtedly, I was a fool for doing so.

When posting pictures of him online, I found out the hard way that they needed his seal of approval. I told him he was insecure and should take a chill pill, but he was a creature of habit and very set in his ways.

Funny story. When suffering from a swollen finger, he became paranoid and said it must be an STD that he caught from me. It made no sense to me, but he was adamant and kept banging on about it, to the point where I wanted him to shut the hell up. Back on UK soil, I made an appointment with a clinic, as I was worried that I was indeed the one that caused it, but I came back all clear. Guess what? When he finally went to see a doctor, he was given a prescription to treat the inflammation of an ingrown fingernail.

He relentlessly projected his insecurities onto me, and being the idiot I was, I "happily" participated in the drama at hand. His negative energy strangled me, suffocating the life out of me; I felt like I couldn't breathe. He was constantly on my case, even with an ocean between us, and it wasn't healthy. I'd never met someone in such a state of denial within himself. Feeling trapped and backed into a corner, I suffered from anxiety as he would not listen to reason, hearing only himself speak and remaining in that victim mentality, pointing the finger at me and retracting it only to point it at me again.

I felt like I was walking through a state of purgatory, and in April of 2013, I became ill. Initially, I didn't think anything of it; I thought it was just a stomach bug or some dainty virus, but it wouldn't budge. No matter how lousy I felt, I never skived off work and stayed home.

When I went to see my general practitioner two months later, I had lost an incredible amount of weight. It wasn't Crohn's disease, and he thought it might be an IBS strain, but the tests were inconclusive, and I would have to undergo more tests, something I wasn't particularly keen on as I didn't want some camera being poked up my bum. I couldn't eat much without it coming back out, and I couldn't even drink a full cup of tea a day at one point. It was tiring and frustrating, and losing that much weight did not bode well for my confidence. I made sure to layer myself with enough clothes to keep me warm as I was often ice-cold.

My emotions ate away at me, and the gas and bloating were terrible; sometimes, it felt like someone had punched me in the gut, and waves of nausea would wash over me. I also suffered acid reflux, causing me heartburn at times. I felt in a total state of disrepair, cascading from one area of my life into another, as I was also being bullied at work. One of my colleagues, an engineering manager, told me I was a rarity in this world: a male in a female's body. I was intelligent, tough as nails, but also vulnerable. He told me to keep my head down and get on with it because being upfront and honest with people would give them more ammunition and only get me into more trouble.

"Hey B, how's it going? Are you feeling the experience yet, or would you like more of the same served to you? Your Soul is this big ball of awesome, dipped in glitter, yet, you've deglammed yourself by 'unglittering' yourself through the mere feat of rolling through the mud of your accumulating experiences, leaving you in a rather fancy cake of a caked-on muddy mess."

Thanks, mate; I think I'll roll further on out in the mud for a wee while longer. Hilarion has a wicked sense of humour, and if you want his help to heal up that beautiful heart space of yours, well, expect to be confronted by more demons.

"Always trust your gut. It never lies. Your Mind can be the ultimate trickster playing you for a fiddling fool with its pertinent riddle me that status quo, whilst your heart can be blinded by the intoxicating spray-painted tainted paints one has chosen to adorn the Self with, seeing but the world rather impaired. And may I but oh so gently remind you that the heart is but the seat of one's emotions, carrying the eternal baggage of one's experiences that, in turn, you have so duly archived within the compartments of the Mind, being the astute librarian one is and thus the two toy with you through the ping-ponging ball of the EGO, making you but dizzyingly confused and looking but stupendously saucer-eyed, thus losing one's balance and falling like a klutz over your own butterfingered feet. Trust your gut my Child, for it is the ultimate truth-o-meter of the Soul."

~The Ascended Master Hilarion~

I was not in the right frame of mind to even give myself time to heal, but I did read many self-help books on how to heal yourself. As Spirit kindly points out, *"You can read as many books as you like, but if you're unable to hone in and read yourself, you'll never learn a thing and remain in the epitome of the eternal merry-go-round of a non-conscious stupor."*

The late Louise L. Hay, author of *You can Heal your Life*, stated that the probable cause for diarrhoea and stomach issues is "disowning the right to live, being insecure, and fearful of both love and abandonment, paired with the inability to digest." Diarrhoea, on a physical level, is when the body rejects unassimilated nutrients. On a mental and emotional level, there is a premature rejection of ideas and situations and anything that causes emotional discomfort. When I bought her book to understand more about my symptoms, I had to learn to tune into my body and see it as a whole because I felt such a disconnect. I felt trapped, yet I was extremely good at running from myself and shifting into automatic pilot. It was the only way I knew how to exist, to show up for life, not let the buggers grind me down, and throw myself into my work, regardless of how I felt, as this was the mechanism that had always kept me going. The key ingredient I was missing was loving myself, for I did the opposite; I punished myself. My erratic thoughts caused the state of my unfolding life experiences, as this was where my focus flowed and thus materialised into existence.

I was responsible for my experiences, yet Liam chose to make me responsible for his, with his continuously manipulative ways. I could not get through to him, and through his relentless behaviour, all I did with that pent-up frustration and anger was end up hurting myself. I was giving my emotions the run-around, using myself as a hardcore punching bag.

And yet, I can only thank him for that; however, instead of tuning in to the cries of my soul, I chose to put a lid on my emotions, which manifested in pain and dis-ease within the physical. My body literally retaliated against me because I had so freely allowed Liam to disempower me, drowning in the toxic sludge of his energy.

My body often screamed bloody murder at me, and all I did was shush it, refusing to listen, even shutting out my yammering soul. As St. Germain says, *"How about removing your foot from your own 'garden hose,' because my Child, as you will see, you are the kink in your own Soul of Self. To remove the foot is to remove the rigidness and the gunk within the Mind, equating to healing and a beautiful flow of abundance back into the shine and sun of your life and Soul."*

Your body is a divine instrument. The soul housed within is the vehicle to the mind, and your body will adjust to what you so "craftily" feed your mind. Was healing easy? If you asked me at the time, I would have said it was bloody hard, but actually all I needed to do was kick the anomaly called Liam, who was the root cause of my symptoms, to the curb and be done with him; however, with an ocean between us, I couldn't just tell him to take a hike. I felt like a rat in a trap, and no matter which way I turned, I kept punching myself and was a right bloody mess, all because I allowed myself to simmer in the immense self-loathing I had when it came to Liam. I was the cause of my created creature discomforts, so I knew I was the cure to the ailment of my buggered-up self, for my body was merely living according to the vibrance and energetic direction of my wayward soul.

Physically, I managed to calm my stomach down by eating mangoes, and I commenced taking peppermint, zinc, turmeric, calcium, and ginger herbal supplements. Even though I slept very little, I used a hot water bottle to relieve the cramps at night. Forced to tune in to my body because it rebuked me, as much as I rebuked myself, I started to learn an awful lot about myself. As the Light BEings state, *"Be mindful of the thoughts you feed your Mind, for you may find being the energetic-ingenious-genie that you are, that you create into manifestation that which you would not want, yet duly receive for the very thought you chose to whip-up and thus materialise into the serv-ed plate of existence."*

My Beautiful Friend Trinh-Ny

I am not a social media buff, but I reactivated my Facebook account in July 2013 and checked my best friend Trinh-ny's page. She had called me in May, but I had been so caught up in my own experiences that time got the better of me, and I forgot to return her call. When I logged on, my heart stopped as there was a post thanking all those who had attended her funeral. I sat there in utter shock, not moving for the longest time until I finally managed to email one of her friends, who called me straight away.

I worked with Trinh-ny at Shell for several years. I'd never met her friends as I was a bit of a kooky one, being into my spiritual stuff and reading cards. She was Vietnamese and had such a fun and quirky sense of humour. She could never wrap her head around the fact that Liam would choose his cats over me. She always portrayed herself as happy-go-lucky but was struggling with herself immensely.

Trinh-ny helped her family out financially, had her own mortgage, and when her mum was diagnosed with cancer, she returned to the family home in London to support her. After the chemo, her mom was in remission, but the cancer had returned shortly before Trinh-ny died. On top of that, her accountants had miscalculated her taxes, and she owed a substantial amount, having no idea how to pay for it. Her issues simply accumulated, and she fell in with the wrong crowd, dabbling in drugs for the last eighteen months of her life.

She hid her drug abuse well from those that loved her and chose to continue with those that enabled her. When I saw her in March 2013, she told me she hadn't slept and was still coming down from an LSD trip, but she wanted to meet me for a coffee in London. Sitting there, not mincing my words, I told her, "If you continue like this, you'll kill yourself." She brushed my warning aside and said her usual, "I'll be OK, I'll be OK, don't worry, I only take it sometimes," which I foolishly believed.

I guess I wasn't meant to know then. I warned her to change her lifestyle as she hung out with a guy who had schizophrenia and had a whole range of other serious mental issues, not to mention his immense love for ingesting hallucinogenic drugs. She often told me he had an entity around him that was his inspiration for writing and music and that she had seen and felt it. She described it as the room dropping in temperature, creating a heavy and dense atmosphere. She said it felt weird, but it didn't mean her any harm. I told her to stay away from him as he had such darkness within, but she was curious and would not relent. Being out of work for several months, she said she'd found her calling, wanting to help others, with the next step of setting up a consultancy.

On that fateful weekend, on her way to crossing over, she'd gone out on both Friday and Saturday night, taken whatever with this friend and two others, and apparently, she seemed fine coming down. On Monday at 10 in the morning, still at his place, she jumped into the shower, and when she came out, she complained of chest pains and grabbing the stair railing for support, she collapsed and fell down the stairs.

Her so-called friend called an ambulance and was told to perform CPR until they arrived twenty minutes later. The paramedics tried to resuscitate her for forty minutes, but she died of cardiac arrest on the scene. When the police arrived, her friend couldn't even remember her name and didn't know her family, and hence they became suspicious and checked the place for drugs, but couldn't find anything. She had simply overdosed with the drugs supplied that she so willingly took.

She wasn't into drugs when I met her, and she knew I was vehemently against them because of the hell I'd gone through with Mark, so she had been lying to me and others that cared for her. Her excuse, "I only take it sometimes," should have alerted me, but she didn't seem like an addict. However, as I well knew, those on drugs can be most deceitful to your face and hide their addiction but oh too well.

I did not realise it was this bad until I saw her last pictures on Facebook, taken two days before she crossed over. She looked totally out of it, a shell of her former self. If I had not deactivated my account, I would have called her, as she looked alarmingly worse for wear. She had always called me when she felt down, and we could talk for hours. I always told her that she needed to change her ways and sell her home, but she just never got round to it. She kept putting it off, but it would have gotten her out of debt. I honestly believe she was too far gone, unable to dig herself out of the darkness she had so willingly fallen into. In the end, you can drag a horse to water, but you cannot force it to drink.

One of her friends told me that her funeral was really crowded, and her family was surprised at how loved she was. I visited her grave and put flowers there, but I thought to myself, *Why am I even here if she isn't?*

For the longest time, I felt guilty for not answering her call that Saturday night. I couldn't help but think that our conversation might have somehow altered the outcome if I had spoken to her. I was mad at her for bailing out on life the way she did. We'd talked about her coming to stay with me for a while in sunny Florida so that she could figure her life out. She always said I was good with all the spiritual stuff I did, helping others battle their demons with my therapies and card readings, yet it seemed I had failed her miserably.

I don't speak to her often, as she has happily moved on, but when I do, she always brings up this song by Rihanna, "Shine Bright Like a Diamond." I know she does shine in the sparkle of her beautiful iridescent Starseed BEing self up there.

She said, *"I was so lost, I sought other lost souls to help escape the pain of my everyday life, and imagined simply drifting into a vast ocean of nothingness with the sun beating down on my face and merely wandering along in the space of happy on a beach somewhere, in the hope that things would somehow, someway magically get better. My death was a mere accident of me having overdosed, stretching my physical capacity to the limits it could not hold, for my body had deteriorated due to lack of food and having run on adrenaline for too long. Drugs do that to you—they make you forget to eat. They are a suppressant and thus a great diet regime. Kidding, as it was my own undoing. It was my irresponsibility to take control of my own life, and it* spiralled out of control, causing me to fall down the stairs, hit my head, and succumb to cardiac arrest.

Yet, I felt no pain, as I was merely looking down on my body, ready to ascend. I had taken too much, and my heart couldn't take it anymore—all my sadness, anger, and frustrations were pent-up inside, and partying was my outlet for remaining the happy 'T' that people wanted and expected me to be. No one is responsible for me transitioning to the other side. I chose to get on that drug-fuelled merry-go-round of numbing my inner senses for that short-lived euphoric sweetness of feeling happy. It wasn't my exit strategy. It's not how I imagined going out. It wasn't a conscious decision, yet subconsciously, it was, as I was living in my own tormented pain. Looking back, had I made different choices, I would have much to live for, I could still have done so much, and yet out here, I have everything to live for, for it is far more fun and 'mweh' than you can imagine.

Crossing over, we're like diamonds in the sky. We're never gone. We simply transcend back to our StarSeed descent from whence we came. We shine bright like diamonds as we have left the earthly denseness behind us back to our iridescent Light, our beautiful originality. I chose to be happy, and I now am. I always masked myself to be that happy persona for others, whilst I was deeply unhappy within myself. Yet, I chose to keep up the appearance of being bubbly and someone I was not, often keeping up appearances whilst playing devil's advocate with my own life. If only I knew then what I know now, I would have simply skipped through my experiences like a fluffy white bunny in the sheer ease of it all, rather than burying myself so deep down the rabbit hole within that I got lost in the maze of having my head up my butt through the creation of my very own troubled and painful experiences. Those were really bad demons (!), but here, here I can be me, I don't have to pretend, and I'm happy, and I think that's all that really matters.

Life is about being happy, about finding your own 'mweh' and just doing whatever the f*** you want. Life is not about making others happy, which was my cause for failing and falling, but it's about making yourself happy, as inside happiness is the key to unlocking everything in life; it is to be ever-present and being in the NOW of every-thing. I was pretend-happy and chose to chase it outside of myself and got buggered into chasing myself into the afterlife.

The key is to participate in life, or it will participate for you, having its way with you. And when life shucks balls, 'cause it does, you kick 'em right back in the shenan-igans, back into the transcendence of the Light from whence they came. Never get bogged down by the bogeyman of your own thoughts. Life is a dream of strung on experiences, not getting strung out on them, all to make you darn well walk back to living life in awareness and making the best of a bad situation, remediating yourself back to the symphonious song of Self. Make a difference to be a difference and to see a difference in both yourself and the world, for just as the world is changing, so are you, unless you choose to remain cemented in your wayward ways, then sit there in that sorry relentless state of yourself, never moving, never wavering, letting the world pass you by, creating but only 'what ifs' within that beautiful head of yours. Live or be lived; the choice is yours."

She was a beautiful soul with a tremendously big heart—she had so much love to give to others but forgot to pour that love back into herself. At thirty-two, she had her whole life ahead of her, and yet she chose to succumb to the pull of her demons by using drugs. I love and miss her dearly—I miss her zany and bubbly personality, for, in life, she was a joy to be around. She would light up a room as much as she now lights up the celestial heavens with her sparkling return-to-happy soul light and vibe, running her mouth off with her quirky sense of humour.

My Munchkin Kyra

Not even two weeks later, I had to take my dog, Kyra, in for her vaccinations, and I ended up putting her to sleep, as I knew that all she yearned for was to have some peace instead of always being so nervous in that continuous fight-or-flight mode walking outside. I wasn't planning on putting her down that day—I'd bought food for her that morning—so it was the last thing on my mind, but strangely, as I approached the vet, I got very teary. Maybe it was both her and Spirit preparing me that it was time to say goodbye. I just felt like I did not do enough for her. I have always felt that way. I certainly could have done more and should have spent more time with her, but the vet, who knew her history, said that I had done so much for her already and that no one would have done what I did. Anyone else would have given up on this dog in the first year of having had her.

He said he saw confusion in her eyes and that it was probably an onset of early dementia, as she was kicked in the head and beaten as a puppy, which caused this immense trauma that she could not shake through the eight years she lived. I was so glad this vet believed in the afterlife and that all pets go to a better place, as I have come across many who did not.

Kyra lay there quietly, knowing she was going home. She was usually skittish, but she just licked my fingers and sniffed my face, looking at me, telling me it was okay to let her go. She was ready, but I wasn't. After all, she was my bestest bud in the whole world, and her crossing over to the rainbow bridge with my grandmother left a massive hole in my heart.

I know her beautiful spirit felt trapped, and she was scared of every little thing; in the end, even the slight rustling of a bag, or the slip of the rug on the floor, would make her jump. Sometimes it seemed she had a haze over her, not recognising me and getting snappy, so who was I to deny her the freedom, happiness, and peace she so longed for that she could not wholly have here? Who was I to deny her becoming whole again in the unconditional love and warmth of Spirit? Even though bless her little heart, she was a schizo towards other people (besides my mum), she loved me, and I loved her. Yet she was a shimmering reflection of me—we were both two traumatised souls, both abused and not trusting anyone who tried to get near us or befriend us. We were both guarded, had our walls up, and were constantly alert. I knew she wouldn't want me to cry but to celebrate her instead, as she was now finally her unbound self and happily playing in the fields on the other side. My mum picked me up from the vet and helped me throw most of Kyra's stuff away when I got home, as it was too painful to keep.

I will miss you forever, Kyr, as you brought me much joy, love, and happiness and enriched my life in countless ways in the seven and a half years I was blessed to have you as my companion. You weren't always the easiest of dogs, but I loved you regardless; in many ways, you were a mirror image to me. I hope that your soul has found that bit of peace you so yearned for and that your spirit runs free in the sun-filled skies in the eternal green fields of heaven till one day we are reunited once more.

It was a double whammy for me in two weeks, on top of a badgering Liam and my worsening stomach issues. I knew that time would eventually heal the pain and sadness I felt for the loss of both, and I coped by simply staying in the office and working till late at night, as that kept my mind off the guilt I felt towards both Kyra and Trinh-ny. I felt so guilty for putting Kyra down, as I should have done more for her, and for the longest time, I simply wished I'd picked up the phone and spoken to Trinh-ny the night she had called me. Those what-ifs can cause one to slide down a slippery slope in the mind, yet my coping mechanism of working was my saving grace and got me through it—that and shutting myself off from others.

I didn't want people to feel sorry for me; it's something I loathe and feel uncomfortable with. I didn't want sympathy from others or to have to talk about what happened. What for? It was far better for me to keep my head down and work and deal with it, acknowledging my feelings in the way I saw fit.

Drowning within Myself

"Always take a deep bow in gratitude for your experiences—they are beautiful teachers meant to teach you, to uncondition the conditioned, and are not meant for you to keep slapping your mind into oblivion unless you love it but so."

~The Ascended Master St Germain~

Liam couldn't understand why I would shut him out and was constantly yammering on about it, rather than respecting my space.

I just wanted to be left alone, so I ignored him most of the time, which caused him to become even more obsessed because me not emailing or calling him made him feel, as he said, terribly insecure. For the record, this was another one that knew not of the existence of international calling cards, so it was I that had to 'virtuously' call him. As his "partner," he didn't think it normal that I didn't cry, making him feel uncomfortable. He'd bombard me with emails and panic if he didn't hear from me. He even sent flowers to my workplace once; however, they were orchids, and I was blunt enough to ask him if he wanted me dead, as orchids have always symbolised death to me. Instead, I brightened a colleague's day by giving them to her.

I refused point-blank to help pay for his reckless driving charge for his driver's licence to be reinstated. He said that's what partners do; they help each other out. I told him to ask his family, as they had far more money than I did. It was not my monkey to deal with—this was his own doing, his experience, and I'd helped him out enough financially as it was. If he truly wanted to get his life back on track, he would find a way, stop procrastinating, and get his head out of his ass. It was a never-ending sob story with this guy.

It felt like my whole world had come crashing down, and I was like a drowning rat caught up in a tsunami, trying to keep my head above the water—yet I had an incredible resilience and managed to swim against the deluge of torrents that swept me away, with my rigid coping mechanisms firmly in place.

Life is like the flow of electricity—an ever-flowing river, never the same from one moment to the next. Happiness and misery alternate like the sun and rain, day and night, floods and droughts, but the river of life keeps moving. It is continuous, for we are always expressing, creating, and expanding ourselves. Hope, courage, and faith are the only soul antidotes that can heal life's ups and downs, weeding out the ingested poison of our fears. Eventually, if we choose not to heal, we get sucked into the riptides drowning in our own mushy soup of created "uncomfortabilities."

"You are the creator of your own dis-ease, with fear, the underlying e-motion having a laugh with the energetic particles at your own expense. Life is merely like the flow of electricity, you the conduit. You can either choose to be in sync with the current of Self, or short circuit yourself through the trippin' up of your experiences, causing but an imminent flicker and a perpetual darkness within the very realms of yourself. Yet

you have the ability to hotwire the Self, igniting that spark back to the syncing of the current and conduit of the Light that is your Soul, c'est un choix, n'est-ce pas? Pain is a given, growth is an optional opportunity thereof."

~The Ascended Master St. Germain~

We are all beautiful energy clusters humming our song forth in perpetual motion, yet we often doddle the earth like we are constipated and constricted. If we refuse to heal our pain, we'll end up not just hurting ourselves but also hurting those around us.

Happiness is a seed within that commences blossoming when we walk back inwardly, through the warped shadows of our darkened hall of mirrors, learning to nurture and heal ourselves, flowering into the beautiful light of the lotus we are and always have been.

"You are Divine Source in a physical embodiment. You are a Soul encased within a suit of biodegradable compost. You are not this body. You are Consciousness. You are 'Life' eternal expressing and creating itself in the embodiment of' You.' You are a Cosmic BEing dancing the dance of Life. You are the Power of the I AM. You are a Creator BEing as much as the BEing of the Creator is a part of you creating the creation of You on this multidimensional plane of a planet called Earth. You are 'la perle' to the wisdom you seek. You are perfection, merely having doused the Mind, having 'smoked' it into a fog of conditioning. You are 'splendilicious' as you are magnifique.

Experiences? Come not to me, and state that these were not of my choosing, for they most certainly were. Your experiences are beautiful servings served to you as per votre menu de la vie, n'est-ce pas? Have you not chosen the recipe of your experiences? Expect nothing less in the outcome, as the equation is duly formulated as per the requested combined ingredients in your dished-out servings.

You've got to train your Mind to be stronger than your riddle me that e-motions, or without fail, you'll lose yourself every single time, Houdini-ing the Self from the cast experiences that are trying to help expand your awareness, with your e-motions chasing you rather outrageously and full throttle, until they devour you. And the only way out is through, healing to a far more enlightened natural version of yourself. You've got to take life on the chin, for life is a beautiful ride regardless of the whims and troughs one goes through."

~The Ascended Master St. Germain~

The problem was staring me right in the face. Clearly, I needed to ditch this guy for my sanity. I was scared of confronting him, so I kicked that can down the road. Not the smartest move, I must admit, so don't do as I did; never let others keep you on the merry-go-round of depleting your energy. Instead, simply walk away into the sunset of better tomorrows because you're so darn worth it. As St. Germain gently reminds those stuck in a recurring story loop of themselves, *"Remember, if you remain soaking in the nod of a hat to your wind in the willows* drama, then you'll remain in a repetitive loop, causing you more holes in your 'cheese' than you could have anticipated, making your life a contorted twisted saga of popcorn theatrics worthy of an Oscar for the taking."

I had hired another handyman on a neighbour's advice, and he turned out to be excellent. Liam couldn't understand why I'd done that, as he said he could have easily renovated the whole house. Fat chance, mate. He knew little of plumbing and electricity, which I came to find out several years later when I sold the house. The electricians checking if all was up to par didn't understand how, in heaven's name, my home did not catch fire, as the wires in my kitchen sockets had all been reversed—which explained why my fuses kept tripping and why my electric bills were sky-high. They both said I must have some kickass guardian angel looking out for me from above.

I couldn't handle his whiny and needy persona and the constant feat of his struggles he chose to dump on me. Every day was just another bad day for him. He always said the same thing over and over again: that he had done and was doing all that I asked and wished of him. But you don't fix your life for another—you fix your life for you. I had told him plenty of times to change his stance towards life, but he simply had no clue how; instead, he said that I had destroyed him, whilst in fact, he was the perpetrator in destroying himself.

If someone continuously tells me they can't trust me, they cannot trust themselves. It says more about them and how they feel about themselves than it does about me. He kept blaming the outer conditions of the world for all that had happened to him and for being unable to find a job. How can change concur when one refuses to change their stance within and to life itself?

The sucker had drained the life out of me, yet I allowed it. He seemed incapable of dealing with all that life had thrown at him, and I felt bad for having to help him out continuously, as I was not wired like that. I have never appreciated someone trying to help me by offering me money when I am in dire straits; I find it utterly degrading. If I got myself into a mess, I sure as hell would figure a way out of my created crap, regardless of the tantrums I might throw in my head.

He was the epitome of a procrastinator. After a year, he still hadn't found a job, and I kept filling the kitty as he'd been helping me with the house. How could he expect me to love him when he barely loved himself? But then again, I didn't exactly love myself either. I knew I was at fault, as I kept on giving, and he readily kept on taking, but as it turns out, according to him, he'd been emotionally supportive, and I was the miserable git, as all he wanted was some happiness in his life. As the Ascended Master St. Germain and Soul and Master Teacher Aristotle quaintly put it:

"Happiness is an inside job, always has been, always will be. You can keep chasing that damn butterfly, but that butterfly seeing your big arse scary face and big grabby fingers, will forever elude you because one chooses to chase it outside of oneself and look for it in either one's past, future, or in others where it cannot be found—all to plug the holes in your own Soul cheese, as that is the conditioned mindset that has been taught and engrained within society. It is the key to mastering everything in life and to *being ever-present in the now of everything. Life is about being open to the full monty of the experience thereof. Regardless of the ride and all that has been thrown your way, you need to embrace it with the all of you, turn challenges into opportunities and laugh at the outcomes of your stumbles—for nothing is a mere hindrance but for the ever-drifting clouds one allows but to hover over oneself. How long will you keep your e-motions pent up to be a mere inconvenience to the Self? One calls that a tale of chase the rabbit down the hole of an Alice in Wonderland syndrome, I'm late, I'm late for a very important date—like that rabbit always running around, not getting much done because one runs past the Self like a headless chicken always living in the deviation outside of oneself.*

Turn within to heal those fragmented segments, for if you are the epitome of zen within, so shall your world but vibrate to the epitome of zen without. Problems are but a mere illusion of the Mind, and one can argue until one is blue in the face and tell me this is not true, my life is a s*** storm, and I will merely laugh my Child, and tell thee to extinguish the created dumpster fires within, that have caused your Soul to suffocate in the smoke inhalation of Self. If one chooses to iron out the kinks back to the Divine radiance and bliss within, then one radiates but that eternal bliss without. You attract without how you feel within, and how you ultimately choose to live is a mere translation of the vibration you have so 'feverishly' conjured up within to the world without.

Dramas are just clusters of needlessly created energies that serve you not, but that you have heaped yourself with, thinking it is a necessity—but if one changes one's perception of one's created heaps of these dramas, then one will see that they will dissipate but with the blink of an eye, like a dewdrop's tear glistening and fading in the rising morn's sun."

In December 2013, he was adamant that I had promised him I would be spending Christmas with his family, though I never had. Being broke, he was disappointed he could not visit his family for Christmas and feeling bad for him, I bought him a bus ticket so he could at least spend the holiday season with them. I tried to help him, which was my cross to bear, yet he wanted complete control over my life. He felt I was disrespectful, choosing to stay at a hotel while my home was being renovated rather than staying with him, nor did he approve of the clothes I wore, as he didn't find them classy enough. He continuously beat me down and didn't even see it because he was so blinded by his own conditioning.

When his mother crossed over, it plunged him into a deep state of loss within himself. He didn't know how to cope with her passing, and even though I tried to be there for him, this was a loss that he needed to experience and heal from.

Living in St. Petersburg

finally moved to St. Petersburg in June 2014. I knew I had to leave the country every six months to remain legit, but it didn't quite work out that way, as Spirit had other plans for me, or it was rather that I made a toxic mess out of it. I had stayed in this state of fear and complacency for far too long, having gotten stuck in my dithering ways, hoping that life would magically get better when they finally kicked my ass into the abyss. But life does not get better by magic; it gets better when you decide to do the work.

I had no issues with work as I had a tax ID number. I placed an ad on the neighbourhood's Facebook page for any type of work available. Within a week of me getting there, someone responded and asked if I could help them with their overgrown garden. I sure could, and let me tell you, it was hard work, as it looked like a jungle out there, with me pulling weeds and cutting away overgrown bushes, working my arse off in the hot sun, getting bitten and suffering bruises and cuts, but I'm not a prima donna, so I didn't care.

I landscaped my whole front and back garden, pulled out all the hard-core weeds, trimmed down bushes, laid pavers, and created a patio with seashells for my lounge chairs. I rescued many plants and flowers from the "sick and dying" shelves at a home improvement store and brought them back to life by planting them in the richness of new soil. It took me many weeks of arduous labour of laying my pavers and many trips to the store, with the constant heavy lifting and unloading killing my back. But my back had been a problem all my life, so I just got on with it, pain or no pain, and was super proud of the result.

I love gardening. I always have. Out there, I spoke to the Spirit of the plants whilst taking them out of their little pots and planting them, making my garden a vibrant haven of flowers and a beautiful oasis for nature. The Ascended Master Hilarion says, *"The wonders of talking to a plant and watching it sprout but energetically through the resonance of your words far outweighs the distraction of a Mind absorbed by the arts of the deviated technocratic mind chatter of everyday distractions causing a static interference within."*

I love butterflies and created an area with milkweed plants, which is food for the monarch caterpillars and for these butterflies to lay their eggs. In the past few decades, the monarch population has sadly dwindled. They are essential to the environment as they are plant pollinators; many plant species would become extinct without them. Once the caterpillars hatched, I put them in a small container to avoid them becoming tasty snacks for birds and other predators. I now know that milkweed plants contain toxic compounds called cardenolides that the caterpillars absorb, and thus they are protected against predators. When snapping leaves from milkweeds, I'd first ask the plant for permission, allowing them to pull back their energy so they would not feel the pain. Once the caterpillars had spun themselves into a chrysalis and transformed into a butterfly, I'd put them on my houseplants or sometimes on the front of my shirt to allow their wings to dry before I set them free into the world, where they would happily flutter away. It gave me such joy to help them along their journey of evolution.

I have always had an immense affinity with the plant world, and honestly, if my plants needed water, they would make it known. There were times when I had to go and thought, I'll water them when I return, but no such luck. Have you ever heard plants screaming at you that they need water? It's like a chorus of all of them that you cannot walk away from. They would also tell me if they required nutrients and sprout up and be their joyful, happy selves. If you leave crystals around your home or garden plants, they will soak up the energy and bloom even more beautifully. Crystals don't only help heal or energise people or animals, but all flora and fauna love them; it's like this wonderful and exhilarating energy boost for them.

"You and I are not so different, but for the outer shell of our existence, from seedlings we grow, we take root and spring up, slowly blossoming through the many seasons and cycles of change. We breathe the same air, keeping the ecological balance of Mother Nature, for we are the very breath of Consciousness evolving as much as you are the breath of that same Consciousness. We are part of the whole as much as you are part of that whole. We are one with all, and all is one with us, just as you are one with all, and all is one with you and us. We are alive as much as you are alive. We feel joy, pain, sadness, and love as much as you do and thus, your life seen on the whole is not so different.

Life is like a plant; growth a necessity for the Soul. Experiences teach one to nurture and embrace the Soul, dancing through all of life's storms with ease, acceptance, and grace, much like the winds softly whispering the gentle wording of the swaying breeze, telling plants that no matter the downpours in life, it serves as the nutrients for the growth of its wondrous existence, gracing the earth with its beautiful ever-expanding presence and Light.

We grow in the most uncomfortable places, yet stagnant we remain not, for we will always find a way to grow consciously through the tumbleweeds of our existence. So, too, untangle the Self from the entangled experiences one has waded into, rising above the essence of the drama thereof with the wisdom of conscious understanding.

Plant the seeds of your aspirations, and let your dreams take root by nurturing them through the actions one taketh, allowing yourself to flourish back into the blossoming bud of the beautiful Self, harvesting the fruits of your labour, and understanding that one is and has always been a Creator of one's intended direction to the destination thereof.

Everything in life is done by choice; nothing happens by chance, for everything is an energetic resonance of what you vibe out.

You are a Magical Seedling of the Divine. You are a beautiful energetic hue of the Infinite One of All. Be in the ebb and flow of life, like the ever-changing landscapes of the earthly seasons, and know that to live a life of peace without, one must first find the zen within. You are the Commander to the growth and expansion of your own life; the steering wheel is in your hands. Listen to the inner compass of your innate wisdom, and steer wisely for the allowance of your Soul to expand back to the hue of its own Light. Stand in your own truth, bask in your Divine SunLight of the Power of the I AM, and watch yourself blossom."

Grasshoppers were sometimes a problem, and they scared the bejesus out of me, as they were huge. I'd try to prod them off my plants while squealing to avoid them jumping on me, trying to squish them by throwing a brick. I later found a far better solution, which helped with other bugs too: using organic vinegar diluted with water and spraying this on my plants and flowers. It did the trick, and nature could breathe in my garden again. Liam never understood why I talked to plants; he thought I was weird, but at least the plants got the "weird" in me.

I bought my first-ever car, a used white Jeep Wrangler; that didn't go without a hitch as used cars have no warranty. The car already cost me a fortune, but then the transmission went bust, costing me another couple of grand before other things broke and needed to be replaced. I started nannying two lovely kids, aged four and eight, which was part-time, five days a week. I loved those two, even though I was strict with them.

I finally ended up doing my Reiki Master Teacher Certification in St. Petersburg, and besides becoming certified as Universal Minister, it enabled me to teach, practise, and initiate others. On my way to First Unity Spiritualist Church, I got lost in the drizzle, driving through residential streets. I had to swerve around a black dog that was bang in the middle of the road and stopped the car. A couple had tried to coax this poor shaking dog, but they had been unsuccessful, as it was so timid. I crouched down in the middle of the street, and she slowly edged her way towards me until we finally got her into my car. I went back home and washed her—the poor thing was so filthy and smelled horrendous, yet she wore a metal dog collar, so I knew she had an owner.

I took her to the vet, but she wasn't chipped. They took all the details, and I said I would put a post on Craigslist to see if anyone had lost a dog. They asked if I wanted to leave her there. I stood there mauling it over and, being the sucker I was, took her home instead. As luck would have it, nobody responded to the ad or contacted the vet.

According to the vet, she was part Basenji, part Lab. Basenjis were first bred in Ancient Egypt, meaning "dog of the villagers," and were prized companions to the pharaohs—depicted on many Egyptian pharaoh tombstones, found in the graves of the great pyramids of Khufu. This half-breed had been badly abused and left outside on the concrete due to the bald spots on her legs. She wasn't always stable on her hind legs and also had heartworm. I got her treated for that before getting her spayed. She wasn't the easiest of dogs as she hated being crated, chewing straight through Kyra's old crate.

I bought a massive metal crate, and she houdinied herself out of that one too. I got a proper lock, but after two weeks, I gave up as she whined and barked up a storm. It was like a torture chamber to her, regardless of how big the crate was. She was as much a mirror reflection to me as I was to her, as I felt imprisoned in my own home, trying desperately to claw my way out of the situation with Liam. I learned the hard way not to leave my faux wooden blinds down as she mauled them with an utter furore with that fiery little spirit of hers. I "mauled" Liam with my salvo of words, as I often could not stand the sight of him because he refused to respect my boundaries, also "mauling" my own mind to shreds in the process because of the rounds of words duly fired at him, which ultimately backfired upon me, riddling me with anxiety. When I wasn't home, all she wanted was a clear view out the front window to the world outside, and all was fine in her world.

She even tore up a new bed I got for her. When I came home, I found it in a thousand pieces on the living room floor, with her sitting there proud as a peach in the middle of the mess, with her ears flopped back and tail wagging nervously. I named this scoundrel Myra, and she loves everyone. She's an avid squirrel watcher, and can sit in front of a tree quite happily for hours, in the avid hope that a squirrel will pop down.

I wasn't always right to her, either, as I did give her a harsh spanking from time to time when she had been naughty. Then again, I was a mess internally, and I guess we were mirroring our inner trauma upon each other. After a while, I stopped, telling her "off" instead, and she knew when she'd done something wrong, as she'd scurry off to her basket. Nowadays, she's pretty much enhanced the Zen mistress within, and if she does anything she's not supposed to, I only have to look at her, and she'll hop into her basket, muttering away to herself and plopping down.

This chunky monkey, as I call her, knows that she is loved, and I know that she loves me (and my mum, whom she adores) in turn. I always say that pets are sent to us to teach us and heal certain aspects of ourselves, to brighten the "unbrightened" within us. They are guardians to help us see the reflection of ourselves in them, to learn to love ourselves a bit more, and let go of the resentment we may have harboured in our hearts.

I made it to the church the following week, taught Reiki Level 1, and gave workshops in meditative art, which I later did from home, as I had the space. I had followed a short course on becoming a meditation teacher back in the UK, and even though I sucked in class—feeling insecure when it came to the pitch of my voice with all these people listening to me—I threw myself into the deep end, telling myself I could do this.

Meditative art is expressing yourself through art, and whatever you paint— the colours used, textures, and designs—tells a lot about you and where you're at in life. I pondered how to best put it into practice. I had seen someone in Holland combine meditation and art, and I wanted to do the same. I'd never done it but figured if she could do it, so could I. I loved giving these workshops, and they were always packed. Some people claimed they couldn't paint, and I always said, once you've done the meditation, you won't think, you'll be in the zone and paint whatever your soul feels like, and honestly, some of these created works were truly amazing.

I taught Reiki Level 2 at my home and commenced doing my shares there instead of the church. Reiki is not a magic bullet. A healer is merely the tool to unlock the healing potential within another person, no more, no less—it is the stagnant energy that needs to shift to wash away the conditioning that has hardened the mind of that soul on the table. Healers are merely the conduits for the universal energies flowing through the portals of the bodies. It is up to the individual not to loop back into their faulty programming, which often happens, and thus I call it a mere temporary band-aid healing. Even though the healer is a conduit for healing, often healers themselves have issues, walking around being at a dis-ease within themselves, mea culpa, and the energetic debris of the healer filters through to the client—unlike light language, as discussed with Archangel Nathaniel earlier, which speaks directly unfiltered to the soul.

Healing is helping to elevate and alleviate to lovingly inspire no-one but the Godself back to the equilibrium and oneness of the breath of self and all.

Healing is attuning each atom, molecule, cell, and fibre within our BEing. Healing can only occur when we have an aha moment and choose to heal up instead of deflecting and ignoring the experiences that slapped us to the ground in the first place.

I truly wanted to heal, even though I was a dumb arse and a slow arse turtle in the understanding thereof, I did not want to remain as I was. It wasn't an option for me, and hence I sought far and wide to disentangle my minefield of a mind and knotted soul.

"Taking the journey of 'spirituality' is a wondrous inner 'field trip' journey that can only be commenced by the very Soul inhabiting its current body. The choice is yours whether you decide to wade further in the sludge of the fed narrative of the outside world or whether you choose to search and recover the very gems of your Soul Light within, understanding the Self and the truth of the world one so, in turn, chooses to henceforth gracefully dance in. It is a wandering, a trawling through the many labyrinths in the created caverns of one's heart, with one's heaped-up created and un-alchemised experiences having formed but hardened icicle-shaped stalactites and stalagmites, causing one nothing but dis-ease and a puncturing of one's Soul through one's conditioned ways, that one has continuously drip-fed, creating air pockets within the constricted Self, leaving one gulping for air due to the hoarding of the many kept and created conditioned experiences thereof. The hazardous trek into the darkened heart of Self is not for the faint of heart, and yet healing and alchemising all of one's experiences back to the very breath and Light of Self is well worth the ticket to the inner realms of one's core of Existence, for there is no greater joy than to unclog the pores and to breathe in the Power of the 'I AM Love' once again."

~The Divine Shakespeare Club~

I got into the promotional circuit, worked an *'It's getting hot in here'* Nelly concert, and worked several auction events in the Tampa Bay area and Sarasota. I was a Bond girl for a health technology company's Christmas party and worked for them again, doing tarot and angel readings another night. I transformed myself into a tall elf working for a smaller-sized Santa for those returning from active military tours and veterans at the Tampa Airport base.

I also worked for K-Pax at the St. Petersburg Firestone Grand Prix for two years in a row, doing all their catering. The hours were extremely long, standing on my feet for more than thirteen hours a day, which killed my back but paid exceptionally well, and allowed me to meet many of the drivers on the circuit. I loved the atmosphere; it's such a great vibe, with so many people from all walks of life flocking to the event.

I even did several infomercials for HSN, promoting hair dryer products, a terribly inconvenient-to-use standalone mixer, and an instant pressure cooker. I saw an ad for becoming a dog walker, applied, and got the job, sometimes working seven days a week. I took care of mostly cats and dogs, and occasionally other creatures, like fish and turtles—even a tarantula, which freaked me out, having to feed it crickets and mealworms. I went to different homes in the St. Petersburg vicinity, taking care of the animals and walking the dogs, and often the owners would leave tips once they got to know me.

I had several modelling gigs; some paid better than others, but I enjoyed them all, from being a muse for vintage clothing to showcasing pyjamas made out of bamboo cotton fabric to being a guinea pig for professional photographers.

I created my own healing website after being ripped off by a web designer who created my jewellery site several years prior. My jewellery was a bit of a hobby I picked up in Holland; I loved creating pieces as it quietened my overactive mind. I simply learned as I went along and commenced building websites for others that had been in the same boat, offering them a better deal than most and sometimes helping them for free. I did quite a few fairs at "New Age" churches where I offered card readings and was always busy.

Most people said I had a unique way of reading, with many coming back to tell me I was right about events that had come to pass in their lives. Readings are a great tool to ascertain guidance when feeling stuck in life or when visiting a medium in overcoming grief, knowing that your loved ones are happy and vibrant on the other side of the veil. Many people repeatedly return to rid themselves of their insecurities, wanting to plug their holes, to stem the flood of their own whispers of doubt, hoping that predicted outcomes will come to pass. Receiving messages and gaining clarity in certain situations helps; however, one can only follow through with action if one wants to progress and develop in life.

Many people go to a reader as they are too muddled within their own minds to read themselves. Many will ask about relationships and trust me, I too had to learn, for I often stuck my middle finger up to Spirit, as I wasn't having it. I made it clear to them that I wanted to be with a particular person, even pleading with them, and they shook their heads, telling me, "But Birgitta, stop with the shenanigans. Why do you want to be with this person so badly when you should be looking at ways to mend the fractured relationship with yourself? You've got too many holes in your own 'cheese,' created by none other than the ever-spinning Mind, that you duly need to heal and patch up, seeing you've left your Soul out in the icy rain and cold. Why choose to attract another broken Soul, only to cause yourself more misery to the pile o' junk you have already created?"

No matter how much we want to cling to a person or remain with them, if it does not serve the growth of your soul, you will only 'stump' your growth, stumping yourself to mush in the process, having to then drag yourself out of the created waste of your experiences. We attract the people we need unless we choose to cling to people and experiences for dear life rather than learning from them and moving forward into the bliss of better tomorrows.

You are here to grow, so I say, find your own little slice of heaven. Let go of the people depleting your energy. Why remain a lopsided Duracell bunny, running out of battery? Release all lovingly back to their own winds of change, for they too are here to learn to take responsibility for the relationship with themselves. Always ask yourself, does it serve me? If not, wrap up the experience and kick it to the curb. Everyone is merely a character in your life's playbook, all for the betterment and expansion of your own soul.

We often look at someone else to make us feel better about ourselves. But only you can do that. Someone may inspire you to make a change, but you decide whether or not you want to change for the better.

People always argue with me on the point of having suffered severe trauma and struggling to cope. Instead of telling me how much you are suffering, tell me why you choose to hold on to that pain you seem so unwilling to let go of? Tell me why you are holding on to the fractured pieces that have become lodged within your mind and have cut your soul, causing your heart to bleed into the physical discomforts of yourself?

"Life is simples. If people or situations are toxic and cause you to malnourish your Body and Soul, simply say au revoir, merci beaucoup for the lessons and the experiences you have so graciously and lovingly shared with me but as much as I love you, I have learned to love me more. You have chosen your circumstances, and one can either choose to roam around in the wonderful pile of s*** one has so duly created, making even more 'kak' out of your own life, or choose the well-being of your own beautiful Soul, hop outta the s***, cleansing the Self in the Seas of the Violet Flame, and transmuting all back to the Lightness of one's radiant BEing."

~The Divine Shakespeare Club~

I had a stand at the Gulfport Art Walk twice a month and did the Christmas and Easter markets to showcase and sell my handmade jewellery and my handmade line Buzy B Organics, consisting of organic candles, goat's milk soap, and shampoos. I sometimes broke even but made more of a loss than a profit, as I had to consider the cost of the stand.

When it came to my healing sessions and readings, this wally never charged full price and often gave sessions for free. I think that was a reflection of who I was, as I thought people would walk away if I charged more. You attract exactly what you vibe out. Just because you are a "healer" or "medium" does not mean people should take advantage of you. Your energy is worth your time, and as we live in a monetary society, people need to respect that you are offering a service.

Don't allow people to become energy thieves. At the supermarket, you need to pay for your groceries; you can't just walk out without paying; that would be stealing. Everything in life is an energy exchange, so don't expect healers to give their time at no cost, for you would not take the healing or reading seriously. If there is a monetary exchange, you are far more likely to listen to their advice or be more open to receiving healing.

After countless job application rejections, I was well chuffed when I received an email for an interview as an admin. The woman that interviewed me was called Forbes Riley, an award-winning TV host, author, motivational speaker, entrepreneur, founder of SpinGym, and one of the world's leading health and wellness experts who has been inducted into the National Fitness Hall of Fame. She has often been referred to as the female Tony Robbins. She has not had the easiest life and has been through a lot of trauma, yet she soldiered on and turned her experiences into a mission to empower and inspire others. We were not so different, she and I, but at the time, I discounted the experience of Forbes being a reflection of precisely what I did in my life, which was running away from myself and all of my issues just to stay afloat above the waters of sanity. I only worked there for several months, creating many of her Forbes Living TV social media posts, developing content for her website, and doing other admin stuff. She wanted to give me my own cooking show, as I am quite an awesome cook, but sadly it never got off the ground. I designed a cool SpinGym t-shirt logo, and we created an online t-shirt campaign whereby the proceeds went to a charity of Forbes's choice.

I helped feed the homeless in St. Pete at the Unitarian Universalist Church downtown, where homemade dinners are served buffet-style. It was rewarding, and many of my Reiki students joined in and enjoyed giving back to the community. The homeless came from all walks of life: many veterans had PTSD, having spiralled into drugs, while others, some in their late teens, were in halfway homes, trying to get their lives back on track. Everyone had a different story to tell, but all were so grateful to sit down and have a proper meal.

I made different dishes, from rice to Indonesian macaroni to Dutch potato salad and pancakes. Sometimes I even baked various cakes and cookies or bought fresh bread. Others brought chicken, greens, salad, pizza, and sausages—there was plenty for everyone. I even had a wonderful friend from Holland send me a massive box of Dutch foods for them.

I was given a $10 Starbucks gift card and held on to it for several months, as I hadn't found the right person to give it to. As I was leaving for the night, one of the homeless gents that had dinner earlier was crushing aluminium for scraps. I went up to him and asked him if he wanted a Starbucks gift card worth $10. His face lit up, and he said, "God is good," to which I responded, "That 'he' is."

We are all equal, regardless of race or background. Something my father taught me is to bless the homeless and all those suffering in silence, saying a prayer of gratitude for them. Sometimes a smile or a random act or word of kindness has the potential to turn a life around and cause a ripple effect, in not only their universe but yours. Many are trying to better their lives, yet it takes time. As John Holmes said, "There is no exercise better for the heart than reaching down and helping people up." Be grateful you have a roof over your head and appreciate the life you have been given.

"Homelessness is the mere labelling of a person that has chosen difficult circumstances for the growth of their Soul. Homelessness is not a disease, nor is it a crime. They may be at a dis-ease within themselves but carry not a plague, for each and every one is a Divine hue-man in Nature. There is no difference between any of us, but for the outer shell being the mere variance thereof. It is the conditioned human mind that tricks the user into thinking it is so. We all come from the same breath of Consciousness—we may bob and vibe at different levels of awareness, yet are all equal, but for the mere difference of having chosen different experiences for our Soul's evolutional Growth.

Be kind, show compassion, and above all, love all your brothers and sisters who walk with you on this earthly journey, for all experiences inspire the Soul to walk back to the beautiful Light of the inspired Self."

~The Divine~

Whilst I was rockin' 'n' rollin', I was still helping Liam search for jobs. Eventually, hallelujah, he got one working on a fishing charter, although the work depended on the weather. Before I moved into my home, having overloaded his garage with all of his "precious" stuff, he moved his busted car to the back of my driveway, leaving it there for nearly one and a half years, with me unable to park my car in my garage. He kept promising to get it fixed but had no money, so fat chance of that ever happening.

I'd often help him out by buying him groceries and supplements to help alleviate the state of depression he had fallen into. Sometimes I'd pay his bills to avoid his utilities being cut off. He rented out his other room to a friend, which helped him stay afloat for a bit, but he'd often go out and spend it, regretting it the next day. He simply did not have his priorities straight. After that eventful New Year's fiasco, I refused point-blank to go out to a bar with him. He'd come over to mine nearly every day, checking what I'd made for supper, wanting to have some, so yes, mea culpa, he'd often have dinner at mine, in turn saving him money on buying food.

Did he ever take me for dinner? Sure, once or twice under duress, as I was the designated driver. The bugger called me a cheap date, as I ordered a simple bowl of soup and had a glass of water. I didn't want him to spend his money, something he had little concept of, whilst he ordered the whole goddamn menu. He did, however, take care of Myra whenever I had to go to work, as he loved that dog to bits.

Even though I wasn't a US citizen, I worked far more than he did when I was there. I was a sheer workaholic, escaping the imprisoned suffocation I felt in my own home, with him continuously barging into my space. He could not understand that I did not love him anymore. He said people worked things out; regardless of their problems, you didn't give up on love. You fought for it. You learned to love one another again. I just wasn't vibing on the same frequency, mate—why would I downgrade myself to a neediness and a clinginess like my life depended on it?

I didn't know how to get away from him. He was a serious mistake, with some serious consequences, although as my Guides corrected me, *"It's all about perspective, for he was a brilliant mistake with some brilliant consequences."* He did my head in, always talking about wanting to get back together and saying he had done everything I asked. Whenever he tried to hug me, I tried to get away, but as with everything, he always said I was too sensitive, telling me to lighten up when he cracked jokes that weren't even funny.

Whenever Mark called, Liam would have a go at me, as he didn't understand the need for me to be in touch with my ex, and I duly reminded him that he was my ex too. Yet, he refused to get it through that thick skull of his that I had ditched him and just wanted to be friends. He would come round to my place whenever he liked, as he still had the keys. I told him that I wanted them back, but he refused. I should have changed the locks, but I couldn't. In one of his crazy fits, he had threatened me with immigration because, as he said, I had threatened him with the cops—which I hadn't. I had tried to extend my visa, but USCIS got back to me more than a year later, requesting a copy of my flight itinerary showing my return date; however, my ticket had expired as it had only been valid for a year.

I tried calling them numerous times and sent several emails, all in vain, as no one ever picked up or responded. I even sent them a letter, but all to no avail.

I was this pretend-happy person, this happy-go-lucky girl, masking my emotions towards the outside world, whilst on the inside, I was this tormented soul, slowly being torn to shreds by his relentless behaviour.

Two years later, he was still struggling to get himself out of the bramble bushes of his experiences, all the while manipulating me to help him out of his burning fires. I remember smashing my smash-piggy-bank that my mum had given me so that he had some loose change for the bus. He had struggled immensely with his mother's passing, unable to get past that deep state of depression, seeing nothing but bleakness in his life, and remained stuck in the gloaming of his own victim consciousness. He was always telling me to heal him. Over the years, many people have asked me to heal them like I'm some sort of genie with a magic wand. We are all our own magical genies and have always had the power of the magic wand within us. We merely need to figure out how to harness the magic of the I AM Power within to heal ourselves. You've got to do the work. How can we ever appreciate our circumstances if everything was served to us on a silver platter?

You can either linger in the past or let bygones be bygones and learn from the experiences, changing your attitude with a serving of gratitude for all and every-thing that has been served in your life. The key ingredient to happiness is self-love. You are the cause of your demise as much as you are the cause of your happi-ness—they are two sides of the same coin alternating like the winds of emotional change within your soul. You are the sunshine to your own rainbow as much as the cloud burst of rain to the dampening of your own spirits. Simply be happy and in acceptance of all that you have and all experiences served to you, for a positive mindset will get you over those hurdles more quickly than sitting there with an attitude of no-can-do.

"Never let the 'illusion' of your experiences keep taunting you, provoking you into a rupture of wounding your beautiful Mind, for practising the flow of heartfelt gratitude in moments of utter pent-up frustration is a splendid, if I dare say so, game changer. Cultivate a grateful mindset and see the message within the whirlin' smokin' mess. And even though life may knock you on yer arse, know that by being grateful, you will always find a reason to get up. Remember you are the Creator as much as you are the Destroyer of your own Life – so create as you wish, but know that so too will you reap what you sow."

~The Divine~

I need to pause here for a minute as Archangel Michael came through, wanting to discuss the topic of depression and how it is so vastly misunderstood.

The Art of Depression with Archangel Michael

Archangel Michael is about overcoming your darkest fears and "holed-up" secrets that keep you in a waffling and argumentative state between your mind and ego, with your soul gagged and bound to a chair. He will throw your fears in your face to make you see the light, allowing you to feel the presence of your soul again. If you want his help in overcoming your innate fears, walking through the dark night of' the soul that you have for so long run and hidden from, then be prepared to be thrown into the deepest end of the deep end.

Q: Before we dive into the aspect of depression, aren't fear and depression two sides of the same coin?

Yes, fear is that master of grand illusion that keeps you chained to the inner confinements of your created reality. Say it is not so, and I will prove thee wrong, my Child— you are where you are solely because of how you have chosen to experience your experiences and how you have chosen to become because of these experiences. Capiche? Fear is the culprit that makes one eat their e-motions like a culpable cookie monster, causing a frenzied forlorn state, leading to an anxiety of one's senses often bordering on a depressive state of BEing. What you harbour within your heart, so shall it shine forth out of the light of your eyes. Fear is merely this daft illusion that keeps you rather stagnant and dull in the non-movement of your Life, causing nothing but an unbearable suffocation of the senses, having zipped the Self up in a ziplock bag.

Fear does not come to taunt you; it is your Soul crying out to you to set yourself free. The darkened hues of one's experiences teach one to seize the opportunity and to accept the challenge of growth, for being in that state of paralytic gripped fear that has immobilised your senses to move is a rather painful feat and proves nothing but being dumbstruck by the illusion thereof. To triumph over your fear and your hurdles, acknowledge them to understand them, for the journey to healing oneself commences with the courage of taking a single first step.

You are more powerful, more capable than you think—for you should never forget that I AM You and You are ME—we are mere extensions of one another, created from the same Power Source you have duly unplugged from. You are never alone. Look above the rim of this so-called tainted glass of life, and you will find you have many friends in the otherworldly realms with a willingness to help you on your life's journey.

Life is a beautiful journey. Walk it not with eyes wide shut, but choose to live it in a state of awareness, with the remedy of facing your challenges and laughing at your experiences, instead of being "doddled" down by the sheer nothingness thereof. You are a beautiful force of Nature. You are a radiant being of the Divine. You are Love, you are Light, and you are a God Wonder on this beautiful current timeline on Earth—live life not in the shadow of yourself, unshackle yourself, come out of your abandoned Self, and Light up the world with your pure divine brilliance, and know that fear is a non-existent entity in the room where but Love and Light are present.

Q: What is depression? How would you describe it? To me, it is that immense feeling of being at a loss with oneself, with nothing in life seeming worthwhile.

Always remember there are varying states of depression, much like the colliding of a cold and warm front, which is the disarray of e-motions running through your system, causing a front of varying degrees of the forming of dark rain clouds, hovering but heavily within and over the Soul, yet not bursting, for one holds the rain of these pent-up e-motions inside. You have literally green-lighted your life force energy to be pressed down, weighted down by the e-motional ballast you have allowed yourself to carry.

Depression is a state of being crippled by fear, whereby the e-motions of one's outer experiences have overwhelmed the senses and run ragged with the Soul's e-motions, much like the devil has taken you for a joyride, whereby one becomes nauseatingly ill. E-motions are the energetic highways within the body along which the Soul runs, much like the game Super Mario Run. When in a state of fear, these e-motions run and flee in every direction within the bodily highway, causing havoc due to the chaotic and intended direction one has ultimately given them. You have allowed your senses to be conned, to be hijacked by the rather conniving "vivacious" e-motions that have rather frivolously done a number on you. You have been "bogeymanned," for the demons that have taken up residence in the seat of your Mind have sucked the life out of you, leaving you feeling in a state of disrepair, of having choked on your own lifeforce energy, for all has become too much, with the experiences having consumed the very essence of your BEing, causing you to drown in the wild water rafting experience of your e-motions.

You have become an unintentional "emotionalic," having become addicted to the e-motions fed to the Soul via the consum-ed experiences of the Mind. It is an unwillingness to see the light in the matter at hand, in the experiences one has been so wilfully subjected to. It is as if one's Soul has been ripped from one's body, with an innate sadness that seems to loom over one for an eternity. It is that feeling of despair and hopelessness, rebuking against the world, walking around like a lifeless, cracked yet empty shell. The analogy of being washed up on the beach comes to Mind, simply allowing the currents to take you like the limp-ed doll one has so chosen to become. It is that sickly state of the bruis-ed Mind that has battered the Soul, into a grave unalignment with the body. It knows not how to move past the pain of the experiences, and yet, it is the richness of these experiences that become either far more palpable for drowning within the darkened hues of the aroma thereof, or one becomes so exasperated having swum too deeply in the burning toxicity that one awakens with a willingness to heal out of the darkness back into the light.

When one floats around like a melted in the sun sticky root beer float, in the contused senses one has so caused the Self, it is a dire consequence to choose to pop pills to battle the sickly Mind of one's Soul, to house it back into a forced re-alignment, yet does not sing in unison with the body and Soul. It is merely a numbing of the senses that forces one to participate within the societal puppet grid once again, not having healed the root of that discernment, that dis-ease that caused the Soul to be pressurised into a game of hide and seek of the senses in the first place.

You have abandoned yourself in favour of being bullied by the fed emotions causing a riot within your Mind and thus your life, having vacated your Soul in lieu of the perpetual grievance brought upon you through the illusion of a tormented experience that has squandered and taken a life on its own.

You become defunct within yourselves, having incapacitated the Mind, causing one to live on the razor's edge of squandering your Soul with the unforgiveness of being and deviating to the escapisms of the outer-worldly fringes through the excess of inflammatory poisons to the system through foods, alcohol, drugs, or a simple not caring attitude, letting oneself slip and slide into the oblivion of the created darkness and remaining there in the loss of that bubbling toxicity, waiting for someone to save you from yourself. Yet, my Child, no one can save you from the destitute of the inhaled hallucinogenic of fear but thyself.

Depression is the cause of one's inflammation through the negative bombardment of the words of thought fed to the Mind. It is your Soul duelling with the experiences impressed upon the Mind, through the war of words, with the EGO as the Judge and Jury in between, causing one's body to respond accordingly. In other words, you have allowed yourself to be sucker punched by your e-motions all due to the interpreted wording of the experiences you have fed and fuelled your Mind. Every dis-ease is a state of Mind. There is no exception to the rule thereof, for the Mind feeds the Soul according to the outer impressions of the experiences it chooses to ingest, which subsequently feeds the energetic wiring, feeding through to the bio-mechanisms of the body. It is much like the brewing of a fresh pot of coffee using a torn filter, with the drab seeping through the brew, causing that bitter aftertaste of the experience, rather than when the brew is of a far more perfect and clear delight, where one sits and savours in the experience, having embraced and understood the beauty of the lessons thereof.

Depression is the art of being at war with the Self, having been trapped into a corner by one's e-motions, being suffocated by them, all the whilst having lost the will to fight. It is the non-understanding of these experiences and the confus-ed state of the warring factors that cause one to be riddled with the disastrous consequences of feeling an uneasiness within because one cannot cope nor understand the lesson it entails, nor what it wishes to convey to us and thus one becomes a sorry state of sitting in the destitute void of Self. It is the feeding of the Mind and having the inability to digest the e-motional impact of the experience(s) that causes one to be beaten down by the e-motions causing the Soul to become sickly and contused through the punches thrown, yet if one changes one's perspective of the situation, one avoids becoming one's own glamorously glorified punching bag.

Depression is that desolate feeling of walking through the desert lands parched for water and yet finding none, for the Soul cannot understand the direction of the body, and neither can the body understand the direction of the Soul, for the two are in perpetual disagreement with one another on which way to go, hither or yonder? It is this continuous swashbuckling sword battle of words one feeds the Mind, causing the ailing of the fatigued Soul with these gruelling and confused despairing feelings of being at a loss with the Self. It is allowing the Self to be wounded by enriching the hurt of these experiences, like adding a creamy mustard sauce onto one's chosen flavoured ice cream, rebuking the lesson, yet adding the extra chillies for the sacrament of the Soul. Snap out of one's created mumbo jumbo, for one is the mere spellcaster depicting the mood of Self. Blame not others for thy worldly ways, but merely thank them for being a teacher and for having created this plunging into the darkness of a confus-ed and contus-ed soul experience. You are the bearer as much as the saviour of your Soul, either languishing in the desired muddled darkness or vanquishing the shadowed experiences washing away the pain, the hurt, the overwhelming emotions with the cleansing waters, ridding the Self of the added spices that set your Soul aflame in a mental frenzy in the first place.

When one's mouth is afire, one gulps down the water for the pain release of the chillies eaten; is it not so? Yet many of you would gladly sit there choking on one's own feelings of the permitted experience, with tears streaming down your beautiful face. Why do you feel the need to torture yourself endlessly? Honour yourself and the very breath of your Divine BEing. Remain not fixated on one dish served, standing there severely constipated and wriggling in contortions as the experience does not agree with you but move along life's plentiful buffet and "taste" the many other different flavoured experiences instead.

Q: Don't you think you laid that on rather thick? I am sure people will understand "depression," seen from all these different angles.

Good! As I can sum it up in one sentence, "You've shot your Mind to Hell (!)." By sitting in the blacked-out room of your Soul having a "wail" of a time with your e-motions persistently knocking on your door, and you going, "Nooo, why me?!" instead of mustering up the courage and opening the damn door, embracing these e-motions and saying, "Hello is it me you're looking for, and I wondered where y'all were, as I hadn't got a clue, but let me start by saying I love you.

Q: When we do ask for help, it seems we aren't being heard, or are we simply not listening?

Ask, and it is given, just not as you may expect. Many of you do ask for help, but because you are often so immersed in the thick of your situation, you do not see the road signs up ahead that we give you, and you crash and burn within the experience. It seems you can follow all the road signs that state "depression ahead," but you cannot see the signs that say "for help, turn right," instead you are so blinded by the things you choose to see and what you are comfortable with, in that uncomfortable state of being that you wholly ignore the fact that we are trying to help you. Yet, you have infinite free will galore to choose how you wish to live your life. Do not expect us to come to your aid on a magic "Aladdinian" carpet right, handing you everything on a silver platter, for that would defeat the very purpose of the growth of your Soul and the learnings from that serv-ed experience. Have your cake and eat it, yet reap the consequences of your chosen actions. We are always here to encourage you and to cheer you on, but when asking for help, learn not to turn a deaf ear and walk with eyes wide shut, or much like a bridled horse, one will run off into the horizon, having lost its furore of a fighting spirit within its inner sanctum.

Q: How do you see life and humanity's experiences?

Life is the innate expression of who you are through the human embodiment. Strip yourself back like wallpaper to reveal your Authentic Nature. There are too many overtones, courtesy of the created EGO, that have caused this cloaked heaviness iced with all the swirling negative emotions and the "comparable" toppings between one another through the materialism of a created society. See your Soul as this simple, pure flavoured ice cream, with the cone as the embodiment thereof, and you sprinkling as many toppings on the ice cream as possible, covering the Light of your Soul. You can either eat or remove the toppings, having understood the lesson, or you can leave them to melt, with both your problem(s) and you melting into one, blending with the very essence of your BEing, dripping down onto the cone, your body, and causing an array of dis-ease because you have allowed the created energy of your experience(s) to spill over into a merging with your body, thus affecting all of your existence.

Life is the equation of tuning in with yourself, connecting with the Universe within, to tune in to the Universe without. It is the blending of yourself with everything and All. You live outward, expecting your inner world to change, but you should be living inward for your outer world to change.

Be a free-thinker, not a follow-the-herd-fit-in kind of thinker. Do what resonates with the song of your Soul and follow your own paved, yellow brick road to realising your dreams and aspirations. Blow life into your dreams, and your dreams will blow but a new lease on life into you. Why try and wriggle yourself into a suit to fit in with the norm and the illusion of a created paradigm when you are born to stand out and breathe in your own unique authenticity? Wear that "suit" to your liking, and be that starburst of infinite StarLight brilliance that you are. Be that radiant Light walker and sprinkle those infinite divine light sparkles everywhere so that others may get infused by the joy and wonder thereof, commencing on walking the journey back to their own Light of selves. You forget that everyone and everything is interwoven by this mere "invisible" thread of energetic pulsating Light, and you are all walking each other back home through the portrayal of experiences cast upon each other.

Remember that your true Power in Life is standing in your I AM Power and basking in your beautiful Divine I Am Presence. Be more like the olden cartoon character of He-Man, stating, "I have the Power!" to transform and transcend with the Masters of the Universe supporting you each step of the way.

Q: How do you heal from a state of depression, of being so forlorn and not having any oomph for living?

The journey to healing starts from within; for my Child, this is the Way. It lies in the power of the Mind for the Soul to commence the healing journey back to the vibrancy and life of Self. Every step of healing undertaken is a step back to the Light within; it is a step closer to uncovering the Divine You that was always there but has simply been covered with the heaven knows how many sticky conditioned labels you have so labelled yourself with.

Love is always the way back to yourself, for Love transcends all shades and volumes of created analogies of darkness. You are Love Divine incarnate. You have simply rejected the Love of Self through the conditioning of the earthly dualities at play. One thinks, Love has to be "earned," but how can that be when Love is who you are? You've got to love yourself regardless of the experiences, embracing all of who you are back to the acceptance and Divine wonder that is you. If one does not look at the cause of the affliction, how can one heal? There is no one in this world, in this Universe, that can depress you but you through the mere exacerbated stories you tell yourself by allowing the problem to blow up in your face, poisoning you with the very intensity of the wording thereof. No one can make you feel anxious but you, nor can anyone hurt your feelings or make you anything other than what you allow inside your energy field, allowing it to morph your perspective into the allure of a depress-ed state of beingness.

To have Hope in the I AM of All that you Are, is to have Faith in the I AM of all that You Are. To BE or not to BE? How can you not BE? When you are the Creator, the Master of all that You can BE?

The remedy lies in the cause of the malady of the experience. Humanity has this immense "ants in your pants" fear of dying; whilst one can never cease to exist, it's a diabolical injected myth into the minds of Man. Humanity is far more afraid of living, allowing themselves to be lived, remaining confined within their own programmed little boxes of what they perceive to be with utter conviction to be a reality but is all, in fact, just smoke and mirrors of a created illusion.

You Master yourself by creating and expressing yourself in the human embodiment. Yet that does not come without its convulsions and trip hazards, for often one does not understand the experience and muddles round until one becomes exasperated from wounding the Self, choosing to either continue on this little accolade of yours or to relinquish the experience through the transmutation of that lightbulb moment in the understanding thereof.

When you are so at a loss with yourself, do not flail around like a hit on the head chicken, sit in the very "silencio" of your thoughts. BE still, instead of deviating to the popping of pills, band-aid short-term recovery syndrome that one can become so addicted to. You have chosen to become consumed by your intoxicated environment rather than kicking the environment and the intoxication thereof in the teeth and saying, I got this. There is no right or wrong in how one chooses to heal, nor how one chooses to live one's life. Everyone moves through the learnings of their experiences at a different pace according to the song of their heart and their understanding of life. Know that the power to heal lies with you, delving into understanding the root cause of your own tormented pain, your emptiness, and your unwillingness to heal the wounded Soul back to the Light and breath of who you are.

Meditation is the frequency language aiding in the recalibration of your Soul, returning home to the essence of yourself, for it is the breathwork that calms and slots one back into a re-alignment with the Self. Meditation is upgrading your spiritual reception by fine-tuning the antenna within. People often think it is a mere form of juju because that is what society has led you to believe, but breathwork helps realign and refocus your thoughts in the here and now. It aids the wandering of the Mind going in infinite zany different directions, venturing into a torrential overdrive, bushwhacking yourself, and branching off into infinite peculiar hellraising scenarios, causing nothing but seeds o' weed to sprout because one thinketh it so. You've got to feel the hurt, to breathe through the hurt, returning to the flow of the heart-centred Self. Collect your thoughts, and rejiggle your Consciousness, much like having thawed the jelly from the cold of the icy freezer, expressing yourself according to the calm of the focused Mind. Meditation, like exercise, is the mental gym to flexing those stiff atomic stagnant particles, moving these from a rigid state, returning to a state of flow; it is the bonding of the Soul back to the body, for it is a feel-good factor that helps elevate you out of that forlorn state of Self.

Do not deny yourself the freedom of living in the beauty of the breath of Self, to merely being lived and rolling the dice with your life choosing to live on the edge of your own, suffocated insanity.

A decompression of the Soul happens through the art of breathing, for living in a shallowness of breath through the erratic behaviour of the energetic flow due to the emotional anxiety caused can give one's palpable heart a run for its money. It is a mere build-up of these scrambled rewired energetic negative particles that eventually spill over due to the self-simmering state one has egged themselves with, causing the e-motions to overflow, having a desired outlet in the body somewhere. Remain not with one's head in the sand, causing one eventually but a stupor of flailing around like an out-of-breath clucking hen, but seek to sit with your thoughts, to smile, and tell yourself that you got this and all will be well.

Why allow someone else's emotions to get to you, to say, tag, you're it? Why do you let their toxicity into your auric energy field? It is your reaction that is the cause to the outcome of that experience. I sometimes sit here, thinking but mildly in the very thought of my own amusement that if you knew all that I knew without that human insistent fugue, you would sit there laughing at yourself for all the silliness you have allowed yourself to be bargain chipped for. All these experiences that you have refused to rid yourself of and so willingly slung over your shoulders, trudging along but merrily through the sludge, knowing you could have been so much happier because you have understood that life is indeed a breeze and your experiences serve as a mere expansion of your awareness of that portrayed situation that you had pictured and painted so gravely, yet is a mere wave of a wand of turning the gravity back to the lightness and jest of that situation by having a different perspective on your chosen experiences. Life is the perspective of what lens you choose to view your life and life as a whole through. Will it be sharpened or blurred?

You are not depression, and depression is not you. Come not to me still and state, but I AM depressed, for my Child, I will tell thee once again, it is a mere state of Mind that one has become embroiled in due to the lack of understanding of the experience one has been 'subjected to.' You choose to vibrate based on fear, allowing your experiences to manipulate your feelings and allowing them to control your life, and yet within you, you hold the sacred keys to forgiveness, to unlocking the root cause of your own created and opened Pandora's Box, returning to an enlightened state of love and understanding of Self through the mere art of transformational bliss, relinquishing one's suffering and recovering the beauty of the eternal SunShine of the spotless Mind.

When in doubt, remember, I AM all that you are, just as you are all that I AM, and that should be the fuel to your power of the Divine I AM Presence that you are.

My own State of Depression

I love Archangel Michael and his many perspectives on making humanity understand the very art of depression. Not done, he honed in on my life, which was very enlightening for me, and I hope for those struggling that you will feel a bit better in yourself, taking back control of your life and telling yourself you got this. He continued:

Like many, you have also been in that trickled and tricked state of depression. You have also pressed down the barrage of your erratic energy on the life force within you, having allowed your e-motions to be toyed with. It is that codependency of having a saviour syndrome complex wanting to save all the broken birds of the kingdom of the earth only because you were so broken yourself. It is as much an addiction as it was a form of depression of living in an avoidance of self by deflecting outward, keeping busy to keep your head above that rippling water of sanity, all the while taking it out on yourself through the art of self-infliction. Yet, all served as a mere reflection, to show your own broken Mindedness, with your Soul desperately crying out to you for healing, whilst lo behold you tucked all the crap away in the deepest pocket of your own heart until that pocket popped to the seams, and you had no choice but to take a long hard look at yourself.

You've got to take control of your Life. If not, it will so fatuously assume to control you. You were a master and still are at masking your e-motions, but in the capacity of being an observer, simply choosing to keep yourself to yourself, enjoying your own company of "soulitude" rather than the company of others, being empathic in your ways, having endlessly absorbed their energies like a never-ending Slurpee, icing your Soul into a wiped-out version of yourself. "Soul-i-tude" is taking the plunge and swimming back through the waters of your Soul to the I AM Presence of transforming and unifying the densities of the Earthly-Self and understanding the Divine enigma of the All of You.

You chose to mask your e-motions, to mask the fear of the beautiful truth of who you are, believing yourself to live authentically, when in fact, you lived a life of the total opposite thereof, having created many different personas honing in on a chosen mask to use when speaking to the people mapped across your path. You chose to live in a deviation of your pain, like the many out there, rather than dealing with and healing your fragmented Self. You still lived in the grandness of avoiding yourself, much like the protagonist in Grand Theft Auto, being a criminal negligence to your own Mind. You just had a different outlet of dodging food, which meant subsequently hurting yourself, using your body as a punching bag, and being the forever workaholic, running from yourself to avoid dealing with your self-inflicted pain.

You masked it well, according to the laws of your coping mechanisms, refusing to sit there like a punched-up bland 'n bleedin' paddle pop by the side of the road, feeling sorry for yourself. It is not having that victim mentality per se; it's merely fleeing the scene of the Mind. Eventually, by trekking through the heavy 'smelly' deluge of yourself, you have chosen to become aware of the mechanisms of your experiences and why they gravitated to you for the sake of your evolution. Cry me a river, and then some, but regardless of what was thrown at you quite repetitively from a variety of different angles, I daresay, you got there by never giving up hope, soldiering on, as best you knew how per your engrained conditioning, keeping that faith and that belief that Life would inherently get better, for eventually by ploughing through the hardships, seeds of new wisdom will always sprout to the surface. Through your experiences, you have begun to understand Life and the illusion of the experiences so delightfully served to you. Instead of moping around like a weeping mop, remaining in the same soggy ol' water, you now laugh and move on with such ease and grace that it is but a joy to watch.

Every one of you is a continuous conscious work in progress. There is no beginning. There is no end. One is but a diverse multitude of ever-expanding Consciousness through the streams of Self returning to the Light of Remembrance of Oneself and the All. You are this vast drop in the ocean of ever-evolving Consciousness, always expressing, expanding, evolving, and learning to become undone in the unawareness, becoming more aware of yourself and the world you so dance in. Always have gratitude for all your bespoke experiences tailored to the needs of your creations, for it is the best attitude to have in all aspects of one's Life to the expansion of one's beautiful Light of Soul.

My Eating Disorder

Whatever I went through, it was my mess to clean up. I often felt like Liam was a crutch, pulling me down whilst I was trying to build a life for myself, as he refused to get out of his own punched-up misery. I took it out on myself by hurting myself, starving myself, and providing myself with just enough "fuel" to keep me going. It was the norm for me; over the years, my body adjusted accordingly. It was the only way I knew how to function, and I hid my eating disorder well. As Archangel Michael continued:

"Your body adjusted according to the whims of your needs, quietly weeping, for even though your body was shouting at you for its lack of nutrition, you so wilfully ignored its cries. Thus, it became the norm for you, with your body acclimatising to your conditioning. And no matter how it cried out to you, you refused and thus abandoned yourself, shunning your own Light, switching to an automated pilot version of yourself that you were so coherently good at, as it was second nature to you.

The state of your soul reflects how you treat your body. The state of your body is a reflection of the Soul housed within. You choose to ingest according to your mind's cravings, whether this is inherently good for you or not is not the concern one trifles with, yet your body is the only thing that gives you the power to the aspiration of your dreams. Your Soul is pure, whole, and perfect. It is the Mind that muddies the waters thereof.

You were most excellent at keeping food away and were inherently punishing yourself by starving yourself for the emotional haemorrhaging you caused yourself. You had no qualms about your inner doldrums, and yet you diminished in the physical sense of the attributes, with your life force fading due to the lack of food you chose to stave off. You had that contradictory victim consciousness on steroids as you didn't lambast and cry outwardly. You kept going full steam ahead in survival mode syndrome yet struggled inwardly with the tormenting of yourself. Admirable to keep going, but also self-destructive if you choose to live in the sheer avoidance of Self.

All your experiences over the years eventually led to a gradual breakthrough by merely chipping away the layers through the serv-ed experiences. And that, my Child, has been your saving grace, with a willingness to change and choosing to wake yourself up from the deep slumber you whacked yourself into."

My father always said your body is a temple. How can it not be when your soul dwells within? If you suffer from any eating disorders and can't seem to alchemise the experiences that have "shot" your mind to hell (as per Michael), then please get help. I am as healthy as a fish now, but it took me well into my forties to learn to eat correctly, and sometimes I still look in the mirror and think *Hmmmm, I could be leaner.* I am very aware of what my body requires, as I have tuned in, listening to its wants and needs rather than letting that voice fall on deaf ears.

I love my Kit Kats, peanut M&Ms and Tic Tacs from time to time, not to mention having a total addiction to homemade garlic butter, but I have overcome my non-eating habits and now exercise several times a week to stay fit. I also do yoga to strengthen my spine, and did pole dancing for several months to strengthen my core—though with the latter I tore the upper muscles in my torso and over my heart, leaving me unable to breathe and walk properly for nearly a month.

I had an emergency session with Louise Rhodes. She accelerated the healing process, including my extreme nausea caused by the pains that shot up my head, with my Guides shouting at me to meditate and breathe out the last bit of pain, optimising me from being a rigid C-3PO back to my flexible self, rather than continuously rubbing myself with dōTERRA peppermint oil and walking around with my pink fluffy hot water bottle as my constant companion.

Archangel Raphael also came in, bartering with me, saying he would help me heal in meditation if I channelled his words of wisdom, defining the term "Arc-(h)-angel." He kept his word as I kept mine, and when I got up an hour later, the heart muscle wasn't twinging anymore, and by the end of the day, I had improved by 90 percent. The power of working with the divine BEings never ceases to amaze me. Archangel Michael continues:

"Your body is a temple. It is the Divine embodiment of all that you are. Foods are an ingredient, adding nutritional fuel to the powerhouse of your BEing. Without fuel, one would not be able to move the body, a body you silently neglected for years, with many none the wiser. When one becomes a dis-ease to oneself, one can learn much from the fruition of the encountered experiences. You vibe according to the essence of the food you choose to intake. The higher the nutritional vibrational energy foods one chooses to consume, the far more in tune one becomes with the body and oneself equating to a cleaner living within, and thus without, allowing your body as much as yourself to breathe in the Light as intended."

The less dense your food intake becomes, the higher you commence to vibrate. The key is to stick to a lot of fresh and healthy nutritional foods instead of the chemical-laden junk food that keeps you trapped in that heavy and dense vibration.

"Yes, indeed, the more junk you impose upon your body, the denser the vibration of your energy becomes, and the less aware you are of life and your surroundings. And yet you still wonder why one suffers from the intrinsic ailments of the body? You live in that discontented superficiality of Self - what you choose to eat is a direct representation of you, how you feel about yourself, and how you view the world. On another note, which is part of the misfit of many being perfectly imperfect, you neglected your inner child that had been hurting tremendously since a young age, and yet with your petulance and insolent behaviour towards her, being the wicked witch you were, you mistreated little 'Gretel' and kept her locked in her cage. And doing what she, your inner child did best, she hid behind her walled-up emotions. She starved herself due to her unhappiness growing up through the presented experiences and not quite grasping how to handle these. You adapted as an adult, keeping her neglected and caged up as much as you neglected and caged yourself up. Whilst you have often taken life too seriously and still do, you have learned the art of loving yourself far more. All that little girl wanted was to be healed, to be loved, and for you to come out and play and be more joyful in all your life endeavours. Life is a playground for you to play and find yourself returning to the lightness, laughter, and the essence of the breath of Self.

Like many, you have often been swayed by the breeze of having not been understood and thus conformed to the norms of others, and it is a tiring feat to behold if one cannot be authentic to one's own Light. It is like having to dance with various masks, thus losing one's sparkle through the mismatching steps of the dance and the rhythm of one's Soul.

Liam was the final blow to blow that lid off yer kettle. He was that fire-starter, that absolute firecracker to make you implode into finally reaching out to us for help, being utterly overwhelmed and forlorn in the despair of your darkness within. He was that final cherry on your beautifully created pudding before you decided that this created persona of you be blown to smithereens, opting to take that long walk, in faith, back to healing yourself, shedding the many protective labelled layers you had put in place.

Through the suffering of your chosen, signed, sealed, and delivered experiences you had so ghastly inflicted upon yourself; you had an incredible instilled resilience that kept you on your toes, keeping you going through the immense quiet inner perseverance you had build-up over the years through what you had chosen to experience. You were like this bouncy back castle every single time. No matter what life threw at you, no matter how far deep down in the sticky mud you had waded, you always managed to grab onto the branches of your innate inner voice and muddle through back to safer shores, resting for a while till the next batch of mud was slung at you.

It has been a process, but as you can agree, it has been a beautiful journey of uncovering and rediscovering yourself on the road to returning to the delightful nakedness of your divine Light of Soul. It is only now that you can appreciate all that you are and all that you have. Without your traumatic experiences, you would not be sitting here conversing with me. You would have chosen a far more superficial life than originally intended, merely dabbling in the reading of cards and healing, opting for a life of climbing the corporate ladder. What could be more beautiful than opening up to the remembrance of all that you are and all of who you can be while journeying through the earthly dimensional grid of existence? To all, I say, burst that bubble-gum of illusion and take a walk with me back to the reality and originality of the roots of who you are. If you are indeed ready to instil that change that has for so long been calling you from yonder, taking that wondrous healing journey back to the Self, then know I am merely a beep of the buzzer away, so whenever you need me, I'll be there, like a darn devil on the wind riding yer tail.

Q: I've not heard that song in a long time, Michael, but it's an old one by the Spinners and was released in 1973, a year before I crash-landed here on earth.

We do have a sense of humour instilled within us, albeit some are more serious than others. Yet, we all have different personalities in the many otherworldly dimensional realms. Still, we all vibrate on that unconditional love vibe of One, bound by the Universal Laws of One, having a love for all throughout the Cosmos and the interstellar races throughout the Multiverse. Life is a game. You're the player, the creator, the manifester in all you do. Be not a pawn to someone else's chess game, but be your own crackin' lightning rod feasting on the joys of all that life brings you. If you learn to see life from a different perspective, you won't immerse yourself in the thickness of the trickling puddled tar you have so wilfully and gleefully created. You are all here to walk one another home through the casting of one's experiences upon each other. Appreciate the days you have been given, for life is a joyous occasion, and experiences are a multitude of flavoursome dishes served with the intention for the growth of your luminous Soul, with you being the Master Creator of all that you create through the art of remembering that you are Source and that Source is very much a part of You."

Soaking in my own 'Toxilicious' Brew

On the occasions I did go out with Liam, it often ended in sour grapes. Several people asked me drunkenly what I did at a friend's housewarming party a few blocks from my place. I told them I walked dogs, read cards, and worked with the many archangels. They sniggered and laughed in my face, so I got up, politely excused myself, and left the party, swapping it for the quiet of my own home. You don't have to like or agree with what someone does, but you can still respect them for it. This is just an example, but I have often been ridiculed for my beliefs, and that's okay, but we can surely accept that we are all different grades of fish in the pond and yet know that regardless of the "grade," you're still awesome. As St. Germain says:

"We are all weird-a-licious BEings swimming in the Soup of our expansiveness, flowing back to the Oneness of ourselves and the All of who we are. Ultimately, you choose to vibrate in the Light of your own awesomeness galore or sit in your perpetual loneliness of the moulded cloaked and masked Self, living Life according to the fitting in of the societal graces and rules and of the 'oh why me, I'm weird' syndrome with a disconnectedness to yourself. To plug the Self back into Source and light yourself up like the sparkles of an iridescent Christmas tree, or to not plug the Self back into Source and be but a dull and dreary Christmas tree, is a choice of your own making. Know that Life is infinitely more beautiful when you are plugged into the Conscious Light of All, vibrating in the resonance of your awesomeness galore, rather than being a 'blààätant' sheep lost in the crowd, for Life would be far more of a smoother sailing than a stumbling in the darkness of one's created teacup in a storm. You are here to understand yourself, swimming back to the essence of the 'creamilicious' and 'vanilicious' heavenly Light o' delight making up the sum of the equation that makes up the infinite Universal all of you."

I daftly did try to make a go of it once more, following my cousin's advice, who told me to give him a chance when she came over for Christmas in 2014; however, after a week, I just couldn't. I didn't love him and felt horrified with myself, scrubbing myself down thoroughly in the shower—that's how much of a mistake this was to me.

He used to make fun of me and my dilators prescribed for my vaginismus, after which I threw them out, as I felt so ashamed. Who needs a guy when a vibrator will do the trick? No fuss, no comments, no mess, just do it. It saves me from waddling around like a pained duck in the aftermath.

Being in a relationship with someone often holds nothing but a barrage of conditions, making it a minefield, having to remember all the rules of the game of love—no thank you. Is it any wonder many become cluster-you-know-what in the head, as it's like a goddamn legal contract with too many clauses created along the way that one needs to adhere to?

He remained insecure in his behaviour towards me, always keeping tabs on my every move. I often resorted to switching off the lights at night, leaving my home in complete darkness, having bolted my front door on the inside as I did not want him coming in, which he would do most evenings. I could not stand the sight of him, as I had allowed him to break me down bit by bit with his psycho mind games. I would scream, cry and cuss at Spirit and slump down against a wall out of sight, sobbing as I couldn't understand why this was happening to me. I suffered panic attacks and heart palpitations as I felt so imprisoned. It was like this gradual chipping away at my identity, and I was losing my mind and myself, allowing myself to soak and bathe in his toxicity. I did what I did best —not eat, work, teach, sleep, repeat, all to escape the anguish of my antagonising mind. Healer, heal thyself, right?

I could teach and did it well, giving others the tools to heal themselves, but I was rather 'shite' at healing myself. My self-healing was a mere band-aid as I was only healing the superficial wound yet infecting it at the same time! I mean, how can you heal others when you walk around unhealed? How can we hold the light for others when we are searching for ways to keep our own light lit? Sometimes it needs to be snuffed out for us to perp-walk through the darkest nights of the soul, overcoming our created fears in this one-dimensional reality and resurfacing to the bliss and light of our reinvigorated selves.

People would comment that I was skinny and should eat more, and I merely told them I had a fast metabolism, which is true, except I left out the part that I was severely neglecting myself. I'd often feel nauseous and suffer severe tension headaches, causing me to throw up, which was the story of my life. I couldn't handle his obsessive behaviour, and he would not back down no matter what I did or said. In turn, I started to isolate myself from other people, with work my only focus that kept me going.

Liam had this immense fear of losing me and was clinging on to me for dear life while trying to sort out his own life. I had often told him to think of himself first and let me go, but he refused to listen, and all he did was drag me down with him, making my soul limp. He projected that fear onto me, causing me to inhale the toxicity within my energetic field, causing me to act out. One wobble creates another wobble of messed-up emotions because I allowed it so. We were as toxic to one another as poisoned mushrooms on a stick. We both needed to hit rock bottom, as that was the sole reason we were brought into each other's lives: to see the reflections cast upon each other, to come to our senses, elevate ourselves, and climb out of the deep holes we had each dug.

We all know the famous quote from Yoda: "Fear is the path to the dark side... fear leads to anger...anger leads to hate...hate leads to suffering." Truer than that, it cannot be. As St. Germain says:

"Fear is the Darth Vader to your Jedi. Fear is the quake in your suited and booted boots that's quipped you into a fright in believing yourself to solemnly swear to be authentically you, but are not. It is a non-existential e-motion. It is an added human flavourful and

favourable ingredient you created as a grand backdrop, creating the drama within your life. It is a forlorn experience to see if one can break the barrier of returning to the Light of one's natural state of BEing. Fear pertains to your reality but is, in fact, not a reality, but an illusion portrayed and created by the trickster to be perceived as your illusion of reality. If you understand that you are eternal in nature, would you still be sitting in the hidden shivering shadows of yourself, or would you rather break a leg and risk losing the self out of the darkness by overcoming the created hurdles of one's experiences?

Fear is the illusion that is the cause of one's crazy corresponding with the lateral waves of that energetic impression, with fear being in control, much like a shoal of fish becoming dispersed in a shock and awe experience of a rock being thrown in the water, causing them to become disorientated due to the imploded bomb of the velocity of the experience, with adrenaline kicking them into that fight or flight mode mechanism having disconnected from the collective and having lost all sense of direction in the loco and fright of the panicked Self.

You play your cards with the hand you've been dealt and outsmart the devil on your shoulder. Fear is the charlatan of the swindling Mind. It toys with the thoughts in your head, spinning your e-motions out of control, getting your tutu in a tizzy. It is playing the devil's advocate with a gullible intent of acting out on your e-motions, causing a distortion of an illusion that you have created into an experienced reality of your own making. Fear is not real. It is an illusion of the e-motion with which you have so gullibly fed your Mind, having wilfully disempowered yourself, allowing it to control you and run ragged with the e-motions in your head, causing you to act out on the impulse of that created fear in your head. It is a trip of the disempowerment of Self back to the resolve of the I AM Power that is you!

Fear is the Jedi mind trickster—the cop on duty keeping you imprisoned in eternal night. Step up to the plate like a Kung-Fu Panda. Everything you want is on the other side of your 'warmly' created and seasoned fear, having entrapped your duly fed Mind by the maturing of the fine wine EGO into thinking it is real, in turn holding your heavily peppered Soul at gunpoint. Fear is every negative e-motion that has broken you away from understanding a Love of Self. It keeps the Divine You, harboured in the shadows of yourself in a self-inflicted torment and severe angst of the Light and Love of Self. Fear is the mere dogma of a created society to keep you warped into the most "dumbed"-down version of yourself, keeping you at bay from the brilliance of the Light you are.

Life is an experiment meant to be experienced by walking back to the beautiful bliss of a Divine Light that you are. Life is meant to be savoured, not shaken or stirred but poured neat flowing back but ever so smoothly to the hue that makes up the beautiful particles of the all of you.

Fear is the crook that eats away at your self-worth and nibbles away on the fringes of your Soul, causing the "ooze" to seep through, sedating one to the conditioning of that belief. Fear is the beta-blocker and the annihilator of your dreams, burning them and razing them to the ground relentlessly, all because you choose to remain in bed with fear, in fear of being your truth of Self. Detach yourself and walk away from your relationship with fear, allowing yourself to free flow instead of allowing fear to be the dam builder to your dreams.

If you huddle in the "dis-comfort" of fear, you lose your earthly timing, living relentlessly in the encapsulated capsule of dancing with your fear instead of unclasping your hands from the clung-on fear and choosing to run free in the world fearless and unfettered, in the understanding that one has no limitations, but for the status quo of the engrained mindset one has so rendered the Self with.

You can achieve anything if you put your Mind to it. Let dreams not remain in your head but inspire the Light of the Universe within to manifest what you choose to create into the Universe without. Live your Life according to the very ho-hums of your Soul. Allow not others to do the singing for you, or you'll end up like a screeching miserable cat afraid of its own shadow. Stop saying you can't because I will tell you that you can. You are an Alchemist; therefore, you create and transform all in your Life—so if it 'shucks', then do something about it instead of sitting there in the energy of feeling "ratherliciously" sorry for yourself. Live a little, dance a little, and be the magnifique belle or beau of the ball of the "blastilicous" Self."

Here were two people paralysed by fear, feeding off each other—great combo, hence the continuous clashing of two people who were addicted to that toxicity, with one working nonstop, playing the great escape artist and avoiding the self, and the other trying to cling onto the other person for fear of losing her.

On a side note, all masters and Light BEings love talking about fear because it really is non-existent. For the longest time, I didn't understand this because I was continuously living in fear of myself and in fear of hurting people, always choosing my words carefully, not wanting to upset others, in turn causing me to be buggered with that doormat syndrome. Not a great way to live because the only one you'll end up hurting is yourself. Constantly worrying about what others think of you causes a dent in your self-worth and a host of other insecurities that have taken hold of your mind and that you enact and manifest within the direct environment you have chosen as your playground.

Understanding Abuse

One cannot co-exist without the complementary feat of duality, for one's shadow side is but a mere reflection of oneself to the Light within, enabling thee with the choice to either grow and evolve or to keep slaying the monsters without to the detriment within.

~The Divine~

Abuse is not always apparent to an outsider looking in. Emotional abuse is a very subtle yet insidious form of manipulation that chips away at the victim's self-esteem, causing them to doubt and second-guess themselves at every turn. It can consume their everyday thoughts, causing anxiety and panic attacks because they literally get jumped in their own skin. A once-vibrant person can become drained of one's identity, as "abusers" are like energy vampires: they latch onto someone's vulnerability because they have been through their own traumatic experiences.

A very subtle form of manipulation knocked my senses out to a low, dull feeling of nothingness. It was this gradual chipping away at my mind and soul, to a feeling of worthlessness, like I didn't matter. In truth, these are the experiences your soul gravitates towards for its growth. People disagree with me, telling me they did not choose these experiences. Why would I choose to be abused? Why would I choose to suffer?

If we expand our minds, chances are we might see abuse from a different perspective. There are extenuating circumstances for those who are being severely abused, yet without that feat of duality, how would we understand light and dark, day and night, the alternating of hot and cold, happiness and sadness, love and hate, war and peace? We need flipsides to our experiences to come to a better understanding of ourselves and the world. How else can we evolve?

I have lived many difficult lifetimes, this one included, where I have been violated, raped, and beheaded. Yet I have come to understand that we are simply roleplaying these created characters to help us evolve—and not to get so caught up in our experiences. Our soul always remains beautifully intact; it is our humanoid and conditioned mind we rip to shreds, sitting in that fear and the dumps of feeling sorry for ourselves.

We become wounded and feel trapped in this toxic cocktail of our victim consciousness. We forget that prior to incarnating, we choose our experiences. That does not mean people do not have free will because everyone expresses and creates themselves according to their conditioning on the earthly planes. I have damn well chosen all my past lives and this life and have been a sadomasochist, flagellating myself because I remained in the same energy loop of those served-up experiences.

I had to take responsibility and change my stance towards myself and my created circumstance to stop the cycle of "abusing" myself. I received contrasting relationships with different aspects to wake me up so I could see the light of day—but oh the night was long! I felt like I was wandering through purgatory and the dark night of my damned soul, its tentacles having wrapped me in its suffocating embrace. I felt trapped in the void of myself, which forced me to take a long, hard look in the mirror. I couldn't fathom going on the way I had, walking around with a mask of a smile when inwardly I was screaming and crying.

And yet, as it all unfolded, I felt that I was the guilty party, as that's the emotional battering I have always given myself in all my relationships. What if I had helped to pay Liam's fine? Would things have been better, or would he have remained his old self and not learned from the experience? The term "abuser" is merely a label for someone that chooses to mistreat others only because they have been taken advantage of and mistreated, and thus muddle through life, hating themselves and having to inflict the pain of their own "hellish" experience(s) onto others as an outlet. People are mechanical products of the factory of their environment and live life according to their conditioning, having wired their minds to conform to the regulations of their surroundings. It is by no fault of their own that they have forgotten the wonders of their alchemical spiritual powers, not fathoming the laws of manifestation according to the cosmic laws, having become mere programmed mechanical robots working along the assembly line of life.

John in Malaysia was a sick, twisted, and sexually frustrated individual who focused his energy and emotions on me, causing my sacral chakra to become drained and blocked, which resulted in me suffering from lower back pain, rigidity, a deep-rooted fear of men, severe emotional instability, menstrual cycle issues, and sexual dysfunction as I grew into adulthood, on top of developing the knack to starve myself.

I held such trauma within from both this life and past lives. It's no wonder I suffered the way I did. In one of these lives, I was in an arranged marriage with a husband that raped and beat me repeatedly. I remember the beautiful yet simple home, with its many rows of olive trees, walking the earth with my bare feet to the bleating of the goats in the background. I was often made to wear dresses that were too tight, making it hard for me to breathe, and yet my family would not hear my cries for help, so I suffered in silence. I bore several children, but that did not deter the beatings; thus, I also miscarried. I died at the hands of my husband, who hit me with such brute force that all I can remember is falling over backward, hitting my head on the corner of something sharp, and hitting the floor, bleeding profusely, suffering from a cracked skull.

Going back in time, I chose a harrowing life as a sex slave during the Ming Dynasty, the essence of which I can vividly remember, for this life was not pretty, and many women were ill-treated. I was tortured, placed in shackles, and thrown back into my cage underground after being used for sex like many others during that era. I chose to numb the pain, becoming a void of non-emotions. Much went on underground that those existing above ground were blissfully unaware of.

I was born on the farmlands in a place called Zhang, in the northern part of China, and taken from my parents, my mother wept and screamed as I was ripped from her arms, yet she could do nothing to stop it and was kicked back forcefully in the dirt. I lived a life of obedience and having to please others. If I failed, I would get beaten and be left without the basics of water and food. As my former past life self continued:

"I lived not a long life; like many, I died, prone to infections in these circumstances. One lived and died, being of no significance to anyone, as many of those along the route of trade chose to come to these underground prisons to exercise their fantasies, choosing someone to their liking, with no 'bearance' of the consequences of the body presented for usage to them. One thought of them as men and women of respect, yet their minds carried an inhibited sickness within, paling but to a comparison of a swift and committed murder up ground. Only through word of mouth and being sworn to secrecy would they learn of these abhorrent 'places' of existent captive men and women to use for their 'leisure' as they pleased. The body is a sacred instrument of the divine, yet in their twisted sense of self, they saw no use, nor the belief to the gravitation thereof, for the body was a mere tool of the flesh for the forsaken pleasure of others to do their bidding and to alleviate the 'pain' inflicted to them upon others for their own selfish gains. Evil incarnate exists in the unlikeliest of places, for the mask does not betray the face of the beholder it so casts towards others.

Think not that it only back then, for it remains in present-day times, for what lurks beneath the surface is merely trodden on with the unknowingness of a non-existence feat, for what one sees not can harm one not. Yet, many still suffer at the hands of these people, being subjugated to their experiments. My chosen life made me see the flip side of humanity and the chaos they bestowed upon the many. I chose to disconnect from myself, understanding that it was a deep-seated pain and despair carried out by an immensely tortured Soul, to reap but the gains of a short-lived ecstasy within their twisted and misconfigured persona. The infliction of pain was not ours to carry; thus, a retreat within the self was our saving grace, for one cannot hurt the soul of another; it is the mere infliction of the bodily pain felt.

Many of us were young when taken by barbarians to live in confinement, having our 'wings' clipped, and treated like mere mealworms, relinquishing the world we left behind, becoming but a faded wisp of a barely there memory. One got used to the smell of putrid flesh, the screams, and the stench of non-hygiene, with merely a cold bucket of water given several times a week, as cleanliness was not of the essence unless you were from the people walking the lands above and of a higher standing. How I missed the warmth of the sun on my face, walking through the rain and splashing in puddles as a child, the mere joys of a smile, a kind word or gesture, the simple things in life that one takes so for granted. And yet, in my confinement, I wept for the hurt cast upon these people of the lands, for they were far poorer for their ignorance of a love for themselves, rejecting the very essence of their humble BEing. I wasn't privy to a long life and welcomed the embrace and warmth of the light when I slipped away in my unconscious state of a battered woman caught in a 'game' of affray, free to feel the freedom I had so long longed for, sending but a whim and a prayer of light to the wounded souls left behind on a continuance of their journey."

When you have suffered or are suffering from a lack of self-esteem or self-worth, which, in turn, contributes to finding ourselves in unhealthy or abusive relationships, it can have a cascading snowball effect, for what we harbour within our energy field manifests within the quantum field, attracting the "like" in another person, for our emotions are like a magnetic charge. Our thoughts carry an electrical charge; thus, we become like this magnet for trauma. As long as we have not learned the lesson from the given experience, we will keep repeating the same experiences, wrapped in different sets of circumstances.

If you're doing the same thing repeatedly every day, then you're caught in the predictable world of, as Dr. Joe Dispenza says, Newtonian physics. Nothing in your life will ever change because you are refusing to change your predictable mindset; thus, you are collapsing the same possibilities into that exact same reality because you are anticipating the future based on the past and creating those moments in the present.

Most of us are blocked energetically and suffer from imbalances due to our accumulated experiences that we cling to instead of healing and releasing them. In turn, we suffer from energy-sabotaging habits, making us feel exhausted and causing a dis-ease within ourselves and our daily lives.

I gave my all to everyone, I took care of everyone's physical and emotional needs, and put my own needs last; hence people often forgot about me, and I became very blasé about it, becoming a mere flower on the wall, an uncomfortable nobody in the room, only to be approached if someone needed my help or wanted something from me.

Yet over time, I understood that I AM important too, and my needs come first. That is not selfish. Self-love and nurturing yourself are a necessity. Self-love doesn't mean lying in a crumpled heap, feeling sorry for ourselves. Self-love means showing up for life, swinging that bat, and hitting the ball, regardless of our circumstances. We have to water the roots of our soul to empower the hue of the loving light within, dancing once more to the tune of our own hearts. It is changing that field of thought, transforming our thought patterning and understanding that what we think, we broadcast loud and clear into the field of our creation, creating more of the same experiences.

We are raised according to the conditioning of our parents and our environment, and everything we go through impresses upon our minds. It gets darn confusing, having to keep up with all the rules and regulations of this whole societal game of charades. How can you ever be your most authentic self if you're lost within this manipulative maze of existence?

Every single experience thrown your way is meant to help awaken you. As St. Germain says, *"Care not what a repressed society thinks, for all that 'psychobabble' is meant to keep you fooled into thinking you have to remain a demure and emotionally repressed Soul, living in denial of your own true beautiful authentic nature."*

Once we choose to release the weight and walk through these barren lands of our created shades of polar experiences—finding strength and gratitude, stripping the layers of cloaked heaviness, returning to an innate enlightened version of ourselves, owning the trauma—we stop partaking in the victimology thereof, and life changes.

As Archangel Michael butts in:

"Are you going to allow the ball to knock you out cold being swung off your socks, twirling in a daz-ed confused state, or will you hit the bat swinging, telling us to stick it where the sun don't shine, saying you got this, you've understood the lesson, and are home runnin' it to the last base, having elevated your level of understanding and road runnin' onto the next level of the playing field with the deservance of a better life?

Whatever you feed your mind is exactly what will materialise. You are your very own spellcaster, for your words spell the outcome of either your intended desires or the misdirection thereof. Word is intent. The electrical current of what you think or speak commences to form and manifest as your reality within the quantum field of your existence. You can either drown in your experiences or swim out of your malfunctioning currents returning to the centre and calm of Self. Never let your experiences defeat you, but be your own David of Goliath, swinging on back and beating and defeating those shadows of doubt that have taken up residence in the very heart of your Mind and Soul.

Life is quid pro quo; what you put comes back in equal measures to what you reciprocate, for the favour is returned; such is the Law of the Cosmic Conscious Intelligence. The more you heal the hurt of your experiences stored within the Mind, the more you unburden yourself, the more you become at ease with yourself, and the more things will start to flow in your life. It's not rocket science. Get with the program—you're energy, end of."

Great advice from Michael, but I was dazed and confused, simmering within my current experience, still not quite getting it—and even though I was severely scathed, I clearly hadn't hit the bottom of the rock just yet, for it was about to get a whole lot worse. Feeling trapped in a corner and not thinking straight, I decided to put my home up for sale, the home to which I had devoted many hours of loving labour, and yet I felt there was no other way to get away from Liam.

Moving

About six weeks before my home went on to the market, I decided to give the house a complete lick of paint, cleaning the outside by hand with a cloth and water, spending several weeks of intense, loving labour in the heat of the sun, restoring it to its former glory of a beautiful mid-green.

Liam finally removed his beaten-up car from my driveway and had to move as his rental went into foreclosure. He refused to share a place with others and eventually found a small studio, with me paying the holding deposit, seeing he was broke. I told him to get rid of all his stuff, as it was only material value and could one day be replaced. Instead, he stacked the garage that came with the new place to the brim. It truly showed his state of mind. If you can't let go of things, you are refusing to let go of any heaped-up junk you have accumulated mentally, reverberating into your outer existence. As St. Germain says, *"You've got to let go of this insistent need to keep choking yourself, tightening that noose around your beautiful neck, all because you are refusing to budge, allowing the Mind to bully you rather than removing the engrained human conditioning you have for so long adhered to, in turn empowering yourself and breathing back a lightness in the very state of your BEing."*

After receiving an offer in the space of a week of it being on the market, I had no idea if the sale was going ahead, as my realtor remained deathly silent. He was a bit of a bastard, for he knew I was a first-time seller, and instead of keeping me in the loop, he kept me in the dark of the proceedings. After the survey, I had to invest in a new roof, a new central air conditioning system (which my mum fronted for me), and fix every tiny little thing before the buyer signed off on purchasing the home, causing me to be out of pocket before the sale.

During that time, I had come to my senses but couldn't back out, as I had already accepted an offer and was two weeks from having to move but had not heard anything. Due to the unprofessionalism of the silent realtor, another was assigned to me. She was an absolute gem and explained the whole procedure to me, taking care of everything from that point on.

I had two weeks to pack up all my s*** and throw it in storage, having to find something else on the fly. Every property I viewed was a no-go as they all wanted proof of employment, making at least two times the annual rent. Highly unlikely with a part-time job, nor would they accept a UK guarantor. I told them I could pay six months in advance once the sale of my house went through, but no one was willing to budge.

I found a place last minute via Craigslist on St. Pete Beach, an aparthotel where my mutt Myra was allowed. I could have returned to the UK with some money in my pocket to start over. Yet I didn't want that—I felt like a complete and utter failure for not having achieved anything except a whole load of Scheiße.

The truth was I felt worthless. I felt that whatever I touched turned to crap. I was angry for having allowed myself into this irreversible situation, and this constant depressing state of my own presence was exhausting me on all levels— yet I had to keep going. After all, I was the one that created this whole mess, allowing my hand to be forced into taking the drastic measure of stupidly selling my home.

When I closed the door that final time, the tears were streaming down my face because I had loved that home and worked blood, sweat, and tears, making it a supposedly perfect "tranquil" space just for me, even though my ex turned it into a prison. Yet here I was, closing the door on another chapter of my life into hopefully calmer waters—well, fat chance of that happening.

As St. Germain says, *"Nothing from the past matters; what matters is the NOW. Your past does not define you; you define your past in the shaping of the experiences not to the detriment of yourself but to the improvement of yourself. You choose to have hang-ups and be judgemental of others because of your garnered experiences that you have hoarded in the closet of your Soul, which is truly bulging at the seams. Ah, what a great way to live my Child, n'est-ce pas? If you keep hoarding, your Soul won't find space to breathe, causing nothing but an inner chaos spilling over into the outer fringes of your environment, causing but an enticing and warped misadventure of having to find the Light within yourself by learning to alchemise all of your experiences. Stop hoarding, let go, allow yourself to breathe and live in the Light of the Truth of who you are—for I AM as You are, as You are as I AM—so drop the hang-ups and the conditioning and know that You are as much the Light of Love as I AM in You as You are the Light of Love in ME."*

From the Frying Pan into the Fire

Having sold my home, with no other home on the market that had taken my fancy, I moved into the aparthotel in St. Pete Beach. It was not in the best area, but at least I had a roof over my head and a pillow to lay my head on.

My bedroom was adjacent to the back of a bar, with a low wall separating my window and their kitchen. It sometimes got a bit rowdy, but I got used to the loud music, the beatboxing of my bed, and the noise, just as I got used to the drug dealing and prostitution going on at the motel and the one across the road, with the police regularly coming round. It cost me a whopping $1,600 a month, including my mutt's surcharge.

I finally found a property a few weeks later, and even though I wasn't sure, it had potential. Had I chosen to pay a bit more for another property back in my old area, I probably would have been far happier, but me being the daft bird I was, I chose another blimmin' fixer-upper. I should have listened to my gut, which I ignored far too often.

A builder at the aparthotel offered his services, showing me his website, which seemed legit, showing proof of the works completed. He cost half of what the others had quoted me, and I signed a contract with him.

I put my dog walking job on hold, as I was at the house every day, helping out. The building work commenced relatively smoothly, and I kept to my end of the agreement. However, the contractor had a severe drink and drug problem. His wife, however, accused me of cheating with her husband. She kept knocking on my door and, fed up, I told her to stop being so insecure and get a life, as apparently, he was abusive towards her, and she had shrivelled to a glimpse of her former self. I felt sorry for her, as she felt trapped, with no way out, as she had been in this cycle for nearly twenty years. She said she kept praying to God, hoping her life would get better, and I told her praying to God won't help if you are not going to follow through with action.

I made it clear that I was sick and tired of women like her accusing me of sleeping around with their boyfriend, fiancée, or husband. This scenario has repeatedly played out throughout my life, and I have never understood it, nor do I have any interest in doing so. In truth, I think it is pathetic. People need to look at their reflection in the mirror and stop projecting their insecurities onto others. I gave her a big hug after that, and she cried, but in the end, only she could take that step of leaving him, which sadly, during the short time I knew her, she did not. It saddened me to see a beautiful woman sitting there in such a fragile and fidgety state, having been torn to shreds with no sense of self-worth due to an abusive partner.

The building work did not go without a hitch. My mistake was that I adhered to the signed agreement, which the builder did not, and in good faith, I paid the final instalment, which cost me dearly.

He said I could get away without a permit inserting four new windows for the back room, as it was already enclosed when I bought it, but in hindsight, I should

369

have put my foot down to avoid the oncoming headaches it would eventually bring me.

The house was a money pit, with the builders' finding termites embedded within the bathroom and kitchen walls, having to remove all the rotten wood, which upon inspection was missed in its entirety to the home inspector not having reported the badly warped and cracked wood that caused the ceilings to slope, and would have eventually caused massive structural damage, all because the AC in the loft had been positioned right on top of it. Not to mention the disastrous drunken tile layer, hired by the contractor for the back room, with the few tiles laid in two working days, all crooked and unlevelled; even a toddler could have done a better job.

If I had known this, I would never have bought the house. Don't think either inspector cared—they were all about business and money. Total charlatans, wanting to take advantage, probably because I was a woman.

With all these extra costs incurred on top of the original quote, I had no choice but to get the work done while doing a lot myself, from sanding to painting, hanging up blinds, and assembling all the kitchen cabinets in the garage.

The icing on the cake came when the contractor ran out on me, leaving me a rambling voicemail stating that I had kicked him off the job. He must have been off his head, as I hadn't spoken to him. Unable to get a hold of him, I emailed him instead, receiving a mere repeat of the same thing. He'd run off with the money and left the builders in the lurch as he hadn't paid them, and I had a home that was 80 percent done.

I was forced to cancel my movers at the last minute, had to extend the lease on my storage space and the motel, and had to fork out more money on other workers and materials. This guy was off his rocker, living in la-la land, and I felt like an utter idiot, having been taken for a ride by another dodgy builder.

But that was not the end: having left one of the newly fitted windows in the back room unlatched, he broke into my home overnight and cleared out my whole garage, with all the purchased tools I paid for—gone.

Liam had been quiet, and we spoke but not as often, and I had a bit of breathing space. His other seasonal job had slowed down, and he asked if he could work on my home, to which I agreed. People change, right?

I could just about tolerate him for a week. He never showed up on time and was a nuisance, requiring constant supervision. He was unhappy with the amount I paid him, which turned into a nearly two-hour screaming match on my end as I wanted him to get out of my house, but he refused. I was sick and tired of him being such an ungrateful bastard. I had given him an opportunity to work, seeing he was desperate for cash, and here he was, wanting to be paid more? I gave him an extra $100 to get him out of my sight. After getting him out the door, feeling utterly exasperated from the experience, I slumped down behind it, sobbing with my dog Myra beside me.

In August 2016, I finally moved in. I started with my dog-walking work again and raked in some more promotional gigs. Unfortunately, the nannying had become very infrequent, as the kids were at that age where they didn't need a nanny anymore.

I installed gutters around my house and turned my front garden into a beautiful slice of paradise, laying pavers and brickwork and adding a bird feeder stand and a birdbath that a crow frequented every day without fail. I landscaped the entire back garden, laying all pavers myself, and once again, planted several milkweed plants for the monarch butterflies to flourish.

When Liam had termites in his place, the landlord was happy to tent it but refused to pay for a hotel, as Liam had advised him that he could stay at mine for the duration of the tenting. Hell no! I couldn't bear to be in the same room with him, let alone have his two fat, stinking cats around.

He finally plucked up the courage to ask his father for help, who stated that he would merely keep him in his prayers. It's sad when a parent seems loveless and distant, just as a grown man is afraid to call up his own father to ask him for help.

Liam begged and pleaded with me, as he didn't want to be sleeping outside, so I ended up paying for a hotel with a surcharge for his two cats, which wasn't peanuts to me, as I ended up working double shifts to make ends meet. When he checked out of the hotel, the tenting had not yet been removed, so he had to come to mine with his two cats in tow.

At that point, I was so livid, and at the end of my rope, I lost it in its entirety, as my life had been one fuck-up after another, and once again, I was lumbered with him. I was shaking, stuttering, and couldn't even think straight at that point. I remember driving and gripping the steering wheel so tight my knuckles turned white. It was like a haze came over me, and I drove like a maniac, weaving through traffic, jumping several red lights, not caring if I crashed my car and died. I was at my absolute breaking point.

To feel at a loss and so empty, so utterly devoid of feelings, because of such a jerk of a man-child who still, after all these years, could not take care of himself, nor pick himself up from the depression he had sunken into, with a family who refused point-blank to help him, leaving me to carry the burden, had become too much, and I finally snapped. To this day, I don't even know how a cop didn't pull me over for my erratic driving.

I was so cramped up within myself that I couldn't find a way out of my despair. I was so far gone and unable to breathe, I don't even know how I eventually calmed myself down, but I did. I decided to put everything in an email to Liam's father, which turned into several, as I was so broken—and even though I wasn't disrespectful, I was harsh and vented all my pain, and all the hell his son had put me through over the years.

Liam said I was his only friend, and it broke my heart that his family lived high and dry and had everything while he struggled tremendously to make ends meet, trying the best he could according to how he was raised. I couldn't fathom that no one in his family loved him enough to help him out and communicate with each other regardless of the circumstances. As St. Germain says,

"We should all remember that we choose our parents upon incarnating, and we have so chosen them for the experiences they divulge upon us, not to make us feel smaller or irrelevant about ourselves but to savour these experiences like a stack of richly poured upon maple syrup pancakes, indulging in these, to learn to rise above, to embrace and understand the incorporated teachings within these serv-ed experiences. Life is about remembering who you are, not soaking further into the denial of Self, and having a pity party at your Soul's expense. Challenging parents and experiences allow you to grow and transcend beyond the pain, and accept and understand that they, too, have been conditioned according to the ways of being raised by their parents. We are all products of our conditioning; everything has a ripple effect, cascading and forming according to the 'conditioned and manufactured product' one has become, but this does not mean you cannot change it, nor uncondition it, laying the Self bare and refor-mulating yourself from the ground up.

You're a Divine Alchemist! Act like it! You're free to break the chains of these repeti-tive cycles and these restraints you have so lovingly slapped around your ankles should you choose to step out of your conditioned frame of mind and your created 'comfort zone,' snapping out of your victim conscious state of indulgence, and becoming aware of the cause and creation of the Self in that sorry state of created affairs. Embrace the mess, as this is where all the good stuff you've thus far brewed lives. You are the cause of your own demise as much as you are the cause of your own happiness. Therefore, you are the cause of your own dis-ease as much as you are the cause of your own 'optimus prime' happiness.

Tell me, how can you be at One with the Self when you cannot even Master the truth of Self? When you continue living in the mere perceptual prison of your own making, walking round in a stupefied fugue of non-remembrance, conditioned through the external conditioning one has so chosen to abide by and adhere to, all the while having forgotten the I AM Power one duly carries within to creating a magical Life of infinite possibilities in the radiance of the magnifique BEing that you are without.

Free your Mind and unbind your Soul from all the tethered experiences you have chosen to cling to. You are the Light of a thousand cosmic suns, lighting up the world according to the status quo of the vibrance of yours truly yourself. Never hide the true Light and the Magic of all that you are, having cuffed the Self to one's conditioning through one's 'allocated' experiences. Regardless of the 'turts' hurtled and the laden path of asteroids catapulted your way, remain that graceful cosmic wave rider surfing the waves with ease and grace, using the sacred art of the breath of composing and balancing the Self for Life to become, but dare I say, infinitely easier."

I love my solitude, as I'm pretty good friends with myself, but like many, Liam feared being alone. How can we ever get to know ourselves if we keep running away from making friends with our 'hurt' minds? People feel worthless and unloved within themselves, having strayed so far from their own light, they have no clue how to improve their lives. We forget that we are made of one key ingre-dient, love, and only love can set you free. Love is the key to ditching all the hurt. You merely need to ditch the socially added conditioned ingredients within your experiences, learn to be whole within yourself, and relish in the joy of silence. I have often been called unsocial, but I live in my own created cosmological brew o' life, whipping up my deliciously delightful experiences into existence. A little me time and some well-needed mental refreshment goes a long way to creating peace of mind and a fresh outlook on life.

Receiving no response from his father, I took matters further and copied in his siblings, as Liam was in a terrible place within himself. I told them he had fallen into a deep depression after their mother died. He was stuck and procrastinated with everything in his life, as that is what depression does—you become numb and simply stop caring, which is no laughing matter. What saddened me the most was the fact that none of them had ever noticed the dire straits he'd been in the past few years.

My mum would stick her hands in the fire to help me out if I were knee-deep in trouble, just like I would with her, yet I have killer survivor instincts, courtesy of my parents. But I appreciate that not everyone has these coping skills. Liam's coping mechanism was a destructive one, causing carnage to others in his self-defeating ways. And even though these were my life lessons to learn from, I tried to point him in the right direction. Ultimately, it was to no avail, as he needed to see the light himself, and instead, I tightened the noose around my own neck. I made it clear that in writing the email, I wasn't blaming anyone but hoped and prayed they would come together as a family to find a way forward and help Liam somehow.

One sibling thanked me for reaching out but thought I was disrespectful, yet no one acknowledged the emotional carnage their brother had put me through all these years.

After the whole hotel drama, Liam knew he had gone too far, and even though my mind had snapped, this programmed angry bird still bought some of his groceries. I was left in a constant state of fear, which sounds ludicrous, but I believe it was because I had shot my mind to hell, and the walls I had created to keep all the hurt at bay came crashing down. The fear had consumed me and swallowed me whole, much like being swallowed by Moby Dick. I was floating in the darkness of the whale's stomach in between all the acidic gunk, the debris of my accumulated experiences. I parked my car in the garage at night, leaving myself sitting in the dark. When I finally made my way into the house, I either lay on the cold floor or on my bed, staring into space or was huddled somewhere in a corner of my home, screaming at Spirit, at God, at everything that had gone wrong in my life, just wanting it all to go away. I felt numb, and nothing but sheer emptiness within, wishing my life didn't feel so hollow. I knew that exiting this life through the turnstiles to the next would be the easy way out—so starving myself felt like my only option.

I had no self-worth and suffered from low self-esteem in all that I did. By working hard, I was trying to prove to myself that I was not a failure—yet that didn't fly, for I was still trying to fill a void within my soul, turning a blind eye to what was really asking to be healed within. I was like this skinny, panic-stricken strung-out bird on a wire on the inside, which I subsequently vibed out energetically to the outside. I wanted my mind to be still, to find some relief from the erratic overdrive and cascading torrent of words in my head. I wanted it to stop, not think of anything, and just be at total peace with myself, even if it was for the briefest of moments.

We may sit there at our lowest point, in that state of utter depression, in that loneliness, thinking it's easier to leave the physical realm back home for the spiritual, but Spirit have always said to me, *"You cannot 'die'! You are energy and merely transfer from one energetic state to another. You have no beginning. You have no end. You are a beautiful drop in the ocean of Evolutional Consciousness. Why waste that current beautiful drop that you are? The life you have been given is not a torment; the broken fragments of yourself are an opportunity for you to walk through the triggered pain and hurt, back to the perfect beautiful wholesome Light you are."*

Dear Birgitta (and to all reading this in the same situation),

Do you not think you have soiled yourself enough just yet? You're not here to fix other broken birds. You're here to fix the broken bird that is YOU. So, stop living in the avoidance of Self and deflecting through the art of staying busy to keep your Mind preoccupied other than with healing the Self back to the reality and originality of your own Soul Light. If you don't repair your Mind, you keep your Soul hostage remaining in a repetitive loop, causing yourself more holes in your "cheese" and making your Life a contorted, twisted drama of chosen "realities." This continuous lalala-ing will only create deeper troughs in your sugary shimmied s*** (crap).

Spiritual growth is a process of annihilation, of complete destruction, of hitting the bottom of that insidious rock. The sooner you embrace and understand your experiences, the easier the flow and ease of Life will be. You are a beautiful ray of sunshine wrapped in this de-lightful candy wrapper of a human body, crinkling oneself in the process of life's experiences and ironing out the kinks through the process thereof, for better or worse. Awakening is returning "home" to the beautiful raw Soul you most authentically are. It is often a road of solitude, yet with a slice of heavenly aromatic, warm crisp aha-pies along the way. To walk through the s***, clear up, and heal the created crap of your experiences is to step back into the Light and sparkle of your Soul. Like a beautiful snake, you are merely shedding the energies of the snake "charmer" experiences that once kept you enthralled and no longer match the divine frequency of your destined journey ahead. If you say you are not deserving of a beautiful life, then one is at liberty to keep walking through the damned slushiness of your created mess of a jungle fog created persona, causing one nothing but eternal trip hazards of the Mind and thus one's Life.

Life is an experience, and you are the experiment, or is it that Life is the experiment you get to experience? Either way, you are an experiment, experiencing Life whilst experimenting through your given experiences, non? You get to decide how you want to play in the sandbox of Life, so will it be a dandy "scrumpalicious" flavoured delight or an out-of-sorts muddy sludge? Either way, keyfine bak! Şerefe canim!

Yes, I hear the repetitive, "but it is not my fault" record song playing ever so feebly in the background, but alas it is (!), for you have so freely chosen to give your Power away. The mere suggestion would be to regain control of the steering wheel, sit yourself back in the driver's seat, and stop others from having a flippin' whale of time of a rather nauseating trip of a joyride with you.

Without any self-development, there can be no self-awareness, and thus one will remain wandering down that road of the same old conundrums that have made your life but rather 'shittilicious.' Change your life, chuck the s*** and start living life instead of allowing yourself to be farted and darted about being lived by others. But... There are no buts. Stop pulling the procrastinator out of the bag, and just do it!

Let your Life not fall into the mere state of disrepair, but build it weathering the adversity of the various weather patterns of experiences hurtled your way, strengthening the sheer resolve and the growth of your Soul to a wee bit more Love and Light of Self. Life is beautiful, so quit skulking around and stumbling over yourself like the "unlearned" klutz you are. Happiness is an inner state of BEing, my Child. Either you choose to remain miserable, in your stuck in a rut experience of the oh why me syndrome or you pick yourself up from that experience and say, "dang" I got this, I forgive myself, elevating yourself out of your own created cesspool of 'miserablisioso' back to the 'happyliciousness' of your bubblelicious Soul of Self. You gotta dance with a little more universal rhythm, and joie de vivre in those rigid hips of yours, on that chosen incarnated dancefloor dancing to that song called "Life.

If you don't deal with the inflicted pain of the wounded Mind, you will keep bleeding. Lest one forgets, your Mind is merely deeply asleep, snoring like a baby rhino under the duvet of the matrix, lost in a dream world.

Your experiences are 'neatly' serv-ed to shaken you, awakening you into the very expansion of 'stirring' your Soul. Heal on up from the root cause and embrace the experience(s) that has gotten you in a state of dis-ease with the Self, and you will fold back into alignment and bloom into the energetic resonance of the beautiful iridescent Sun-Light-Flower you are.

In the end, walk your journey how you see fit; just don't remain holding on to experiences that drag you squealing by the balls into the very epitome of swirling in the mud of soggy hogwash dung.

Remember, you cannot expect to be the Light, if you cannot walk in your Light.

In Love and Light I remain, yours truly,

~The Ascended Master St. Germain~

Sure, love you too, St. Germain. But easy for him to say. He was up there in his crib in the ethereal planes, and I was stuck here on earth mucking through the mud of my wonderful experiences. I was stuck in this crappy, created trauma, having overwhelmed my senses, drowning and spiralling into a feeling of helplessness and my ability to feel the full range of emotional experiences. I felt sorry for myself, walking around like a numbed-out fool, feeling trapped and not knowing how to move forward, often taking on the defensive approach of fight-or-flight.

It's easy for others to say that you should reach out, but over the many years of walking this earth, I have learned to keep myself to myself, as most people are all about themselves. When was the last time you genuinely had someone ask you how you were from, instead of that mere paraphrase of politeness, a common courtesy to commence a conversation? Most people merely play nice in getting what they want from you to further their own lives. That's the ego and separation at play for you.

One or two of my friends knew of the ongoing surface issues with Liam, yet I would not allow them into my world in that aspect; it wasn't their issue to resolve, and truth be told, I have never wanted to burden anyone with whatever I was going through. Why would people want to hear my sob story of something I had so divinely created using the ingredients of my own disastrous recipe? It was my mess, my monkey to deal with, and no one else's. As St. Germain says, *"If you remain in that sorry state of 'the world doesn't understand me,' then you are wrong—it is you who doesn't understand the you in the world it chooses to vibrate in. The Consciousness of the Earth understands you just beautifully; it is you that understands it not, choosing to remain a judgemental stickler in the breath of the foe of the EGO of Self. Time to shove the EGO back into that 'pi-hole.' If you keep repeating that phrase, 'people don't understand me,' well, my Child, people need not understand you; it is you that needs to understand yourself. You merely need to learn to talk Soul lingo instead of EGO lingo with your beautiful Mind of Self."*

What you put out into the universe will hit you back like a proverbial boomerang, with the same velocity you sent out. But as you may have gathered, I have been a repetitive dumb-arse more times than I can count. I didn't always understand nor think it was fair that it always rained on my parade. All I wanted was for the pain to go away.

My Guides were like, *"Whatever you created, suck it up, buttercup, and learn from the serv-ed lessons, for life is trial and error, to the reckoning and the bliss of one's true Light of Self. If not, then be a donkey, relearning the lesson until one sees but sweet blue t**** up in the face, kicking the 'I feel sorry for myself' proverb to the curb and taking responsibility to sweeten your life through the unravelling of the wrapped experience back to the smoothness of the Soul of Self. Lighten up, life's an enjoyable ride, don't waste it, or it will waste it but con mucho gusto for you, whilst you doldrum within the illusion of a dampened Spirit, wondering where the heck life went."*

It's hard when you're in the thick of things and in this constant battle with yourself. I had cried out for help for so long, cussing and screaming in the dark of my own home, in the depths of the very darkness of myself, and yet I felt Spirit wasn't listening. But they were—it was me that wasn't listening.

I had to get it through my head that I had created this cesspool of despondency within, and thus, I alone was to find the cure to the torturous pain within the crevices of my beaten off-the-track mind. We should embrace our darkness as a friend, not a foe. When we befriend the darkness, we forgive and hug it out with all the "icky" aspects of ourselves. If the darkness of the mind remains a foe, we will struggle with the demons within, causing more of the same without.

Q&A with Archangel Zadkiel and St. Germain and the Violet Flame of Transmutation

Channelled in June 2021

Q: In all that I AM, who AM I? Do I matter?

"*My Child, you matter. All of you matter! It is merely the constant moulding that has gotten your Soul in a twisted 'git' of misery, for in all that You Are, I AM, and yet I AM all that You Are. We are sparks of the same creation, but for the memory fugue instilled for having chosen to incarnate on to the earthly realms. Yours is to unearth the splendour within to fill up the "drafty" darkened corridors of the night of Soul to vibrate your wondrous Light without. You have always been a firefly. You merely lost your way through the bout of your experiences, stumbling through the dark of the created forest, lost in the debris of your own decoyed Self, having lost the spark to the Light of your sweet Soul of Self.*"

Q: What do you say to people who say, but I can't change because my life is so difficult?

"Excuses! It is much like saying you can't teach an old dog new tricks. How can one be too old when one is eternal? It is a mere copout of wanting to change in one's current created embodied persona. Change is inevitable, as much as suffering and growth are an option, no? If you are suffering, "unsuffer" yourself because you are the intolerable suffering of the created suffering of yourself. Yet, one would refuse to become a butterfly as intended and remain that bamboozled fat caterpillar, never taking flight for fear of living and thus remaining in one's own shadows till dearly beloved death do us part, to then realise, having shaken off the amnesia, that one is eternal, having not lived a life fulfilled all because one was whacked on the head into oblivion rendered into an unconscious state upon incarnating? Well, ain't it grand you can't remember? That is precisely the point!

Like ALF, the 1980s sitcom star sang, "My name is ALF, and I'm stuck on Earth, I can't get back to my place of birth, I'm making the best of a bad situation, Think of it as an extended vacation." You too, my Child, have duly incarnated wanting to be reborn in the experiment of Life on Earth for your Soul to experience the embodiment of that thing called humanity, to slice and dice the conditioning of your experiences you have so richly slapped upon yourselves in the rather diabolical and louche theatre of the Mind Matrix Saga. Let life not go to yonder. Step out of the box of your created fears and out into the sunlight, basking in the infinite possibilities of all that life has to offer unless one chooses to remain a "vampire" soaking up the energies of the pulverising darkness within. Difficult is but a word blocking the energetic frequency of the flow of the intention within to the constipation and distortion of the world created without. Life is as difficult or as easy of a concoction as you wish to make it—for everything is a creation of Self, and thus a serving of the brew is a mere reflection back to you.

Don't take life so seriously; you're merely an actor in your own unravelling movie reel of coherent plots and twists of intangible winding and convoluted rivers. The Creator created you to create, not to sit there like a frazzled willy-nilly staring blankly into space, no? So, my Child, will it be a nuance of enlightened colours of sheer beauty lighting up the world, with a wink and a nod to the celestial heavens, or a madness and folly of a variety of darkened nuances, that troll the Self down yonder into the abyss of Hades? One has been on this plane dancing to the rhythm of Life many a time, yet one has, at one's own behest but forgotten. Time and time again, one has been knocked unconscious, hit on the head, having to learn through the masquerade of the world to become conscious once more. The flame of remembrance extinguished but for the moral compass of your Soul to guide you 'home' through the turmoil of your experiences to the bliss of the real McCoy you are.

You are exactly what you believe yourself to be, as that is the energetic resonance of the flow inwards outwards to the vibration that attracts your frequency. One chooses to resonate to either the tune of broken chords or the sweet melodies of la belle pièce de la musique. You sing the song that currently vibrates at the resonance of your Soul vibration—the uniqueness that is you. If you resonate at the stringent frequency of fear or breathe but bellows of sadness, so shall one live in fear and flow but with drops of tears and be a babe magnet to all at the vibrational equivalence thereof.

It is not merely the world is your oyster, but you hold the world and the Universe in the palm of your hands. You are infinite potential. You have within you immense power to wield the sword of manifestation in favour of your way. Don't hide your Light under the many stitched-up layers you have so 'damseled in distress' yourself with, but shine and sparkle like the beautiful Divine StarBEing you are.

Sometimes all you need is a little help from your friends up here in the Multiversal realms to jolt you out of your pain and misery to jumpstart you onto better and brighter tomorrows."

~Lord Zadkiel, and the Ascended Master St. Germain~

Zadkiel and his twin flame, Holy Amethyst, are the archangels of the seventh ray of the Violet Flame of transmutation and spiritual alchemy. Together with the many ascended masters and angels, they work tirelessly, carrying forth the power of the Violet Flame, serving hue-mankind from the Temple of Purification. This temple, once physical, is now in the etheric realms over the beautiful island of Cuba. Priests of the sacred fire on Atlantis underwent their training here under the order of Lord Zadkiel, and their service to life drew the momentum that prevented the island from sinking. Cuba may be a "poor" country with many having lost their "senses" upon reincarnation into the physical, yet the richness of the sprinkled Atlantean incantations flows deeply through its veins and into the heart of this beautiful country but has been veiled until such time, the people clear the created "polluted" karma on the surface, reawakening back to the pureness of their hearts of selves.

"I AM the Archangel Zadkiel, Lord of the Violet Flame of Transmutation, of alchemising the compounded darkness into the understanding and essence of the Light. It is the dissipating of the fervently harboured darkness back into the embracement of the Cosmic Sun through the alchemical composition of the Cosmic Energy transference of returning "home" to the wholesomeness of one's unfiltered beautiful Self, recalibrating the Soul Presence in alignment with the hues of the body it currently inhabits and calls "home."

One lives too much in the slung phrasing of judgemental wording, of a comparison-created society. Yet, it also enlivens the Soul to understand that dualities are a feat of unearthing the beloved I AM Presence. Hug it out with yourself, and show some compassion. Experiences are mere teachers to learning to have a wee bit more love for oneself. The world is an inconsistent place of superficial conditioned epitomes, often leaving one in a desolate state of BEing. And yet weep not my Child, for life is but a paraphrasing of the sun with the twirling of the night, and the celestial stars guiding thee back home—home, to one's Soul Light in realignment with the physical temple, reconnecting and plugging the Self back into the All, for beyond the door of one's current conditioned belief, lies an interdimensional remembrance of the beautiful hue of the you that you are.

If experiences were not part of the experiment of Life, then how would one perceive to grow? Forgiveness is the key to opening the doorway to the hope for better tomorrows.

You know that you are a Master Creator of the Divine, a StarSeed incarnate, a Galactic Ambassador of the Light, a powerhouse of Infinite Potentiality. Yet, you choose to live in the hopscotching dubio of your mistrust, often overanalyzing, until your brain is merely overheated and overcooked. It is time for the revolution to the conscious evolution of Self, letting go of that insistent and petulant control you so tenaciously, like a dog with a bone wish to cling to. You can only be a crux if you allow it, n'est-ce pas? The culmination of one's darkness will eventually steer you towards the Light unless you choose to rein in the bridles to swim but in the eternal damnation of the souped-up Self. How can you manifest your dreams when you have allowed yourself to be cowered into a corner by FEAR?

If you allow the tenacious lions and bears to impede you, allowing you the lunacy of running around by the idiocy of the illusion of that mischievous clapping and chattering monkey of fear, you will remain a slacker, lollygagging around like a screaming rhino being 'hunted' and out of breath. Step into the magical Universe that is You, for the Universe to correspond but magically back to You. What you vibe out comes back to you like the cast-out echo, vibing it right back in, either elevating your spirits or smacking you right back down. Master the Mind to master the outcome of your intended intentions into your chosen reality, or the Mind will be the Master of you. Get to grips with the Evolutional Game of Life, and Master yourself onto the next level of the playing field by learning to master your experiences rather than standing there dribbling in a state of sorriness, all because you've been hit too many a time."

Q: What is alchemy and the power of transformation?

The art of challenges serves merely as haute cuisine for the different flavourable opportunities one can choose to accept or defy. You are a transformer consistent of al-chemical formulated components, n'est-ce pas? You are an alchemist creating through the power of transformational equations, non? Map you not your thoughts, albeit consciously or semi-consciously? You have the ability to transform all of your pained experiences back to the very breath of a love and lightness for yourself or to remain in the stance of complete darkness, in the cold and disheartened dis-ease of the Soul of Self. There is nothing that cannot be alchemised, nor transcended back to the Light, for one is an Energetic BEing of the Divine. All particles seem but conformed to a denseness and matter, yet one consists of infinite continuous evolving and construing electro-conscious cosmic particles of the Divine. It is like this forever dance eternal of all these wondrous electro-magnetic molecules that dance and bounce around to the beat of your Soul vibrance. Emerging out of the darkness from the cold of the shadows is like feeling the warmth and bliss of the sun on your face for the first time.

Creating karma and dissolving karma is like this beautiful dance of eclectic light particles in the fervent dance of a tangoing with the dark. It is this weaving tapestry of the evolving Soul—for you yield and wield your magic as your Soul sees fit for purpose. You conjure the energy, directing it to the chosen intent of your "favoured" outcome and thus manifest it into your reality, that my Child is how powerful you are. Use the quantum mechanics of the Mind wisely, for it listens intently and will breathe life into the mental images you conjure up. All I can say is, fall ye not into the trap of the eternal monkey-mind syndrome, for one will remain in a repetitive loop of one's ever-evolving chosen merry-go-round-karma.

Humour me when it comes to your life, and I will tell thee that it is the exact circumstances you have placed yourself in that beckon for a healing of the heart space. An elaborate scheme, you daresay? I think it not, for an enlightened state of BEing is but a relishing of the giddiness of the Soul Self in the Light that one truly is. As per the lyrical song Cher the songstress sang, we need a little more love and understanding of Self to ease these troubled times, gurgling and spitting out all the hurt of the poisoned ointment you have but so woefully ingested, enlightening the light of yer Soul. Wish you to stay but at the lower frequencies you have so impounded upon yourself, or to cleanse yourself back to the truth of who you are—away from the density you have gotten yourself oh so caught up in? Wish you to remain in your spun web of entangled bedlam just a wee bit longer, or would you rather let bygones be bygones and learn to forgive, regaining your composure through the sheer art of empowering the Self by enhancing the Light of transmutation with the Violet Flame? My Child, there is nothing that cannot be overcome, but for the repetitive chosen stumbling one has so incarcerated the Self with.

Humanity makes life so overly complicated by having conformed to a conditioning that has neither rhyme nor reason, merely having become ingrained within the paradigm of that sleekened limbo-land feeling that portrays all for a fear of living and a fear of dying. The paradox of that created insanity would drive anyone to the brink of pivoting on a razor's edge, staying put in that superficial existence because it is the comfortable zone of the known, remaining within the syrupy heaviness of one's garnered experiences, a true hoarder of one's Soul magnifique, allowing one to suffocate yourself for the mere refusal to let go of the experiences cast your way.

Let go of all the inconsistent and concocted theatrics, freeing the Self, much like that flutter of a butterfly in the belly of the gut feeling, with the sun warming the very essence of your Soul, having chosen to decloak yourself reverberating back to the bounce of the Light one is. How can that not be beautiful? That sheer lightness of feeling enlightened, much like a fluffy sponge cake, an experience with an ease on the senses having understood the lessons pertaining to the experience, rather than being sucker-punched into the bloated heaviness of eating an Oreo chocolate cheesecake glazed with pecan and caramel, drizzled with lemon meringue syrup and topped with blueberries and cream, leaving one on the floor in pain remaining in the surely nauseating experience thereof.

The Soul is here to experience Life, walking through the troughs and rain, the sun and warmth, growth a necessity for the Soul, with change the way forward to eventually coming to one's Divine senses. So, my Child, sit there not pouting and wailing, saying, it's not my fault, and of the world has me in chains, for it is the mere constraints one has crab-clamped the Self with by choice! You came here to learn from the richly served experiences to elevate your Awareness and to help shift the Consciousness of Mother Earth, so get over yourself, stop being "bugaboo-ed" by the illusion you perceive so much to be a reality and start living a joyful life by instilling change and doing the work on healing the fragmented Soul back to the Oneness of Self and All. You create what you thinketh and thus desire and your desire turns into the fruition of the thought that was but a seedling one has so forth fed and thus manifested.

Life is like an immersed simulation that you get to experience through the human senses, with your Soul being suited and booted with the required kit to kickstart your "game of life." Does a character sit in your video game slain forever? Non, pas du tout! You hit the button to retry that level within the experience until you have mastered the level and then advance to the next level within the game. So why sit there in that state of feeling sorry for yourself because life beat you down, and you can't seem to master the experience? Get up, hit the button, and reload to master the level within the game, regardless of the slippin' and slidin' boulders catapulted your way. Either one becomes the Master of Self, or the Self will become the Master of you, non? Life is a holographic imprint with one clocking up experiences attaining the next level of consciousness in the game of evolution, raising the vibration of Self, one another, and the planet. So, you tell me, is it real? It feels real because of the extrasensory perceptions within the experience that make it so.

Life is much like supercalifragilisticexpialidocious. The more you repeat it, the easier it becomes, and thus the more you experience life, the easier it becomes, unless you choose to remain but dawdling in a rather befuddled haze, then c'est la vie.

Q: What is the Violet Flame, and how would you describe using it to get through the shifting of the void within?

The Violet Flame is empowering the Self through the process of transmutation, re-emerging out of the crude oil of darkness, and alchemising the distortions into the formulation of the enlightened essence of Self, with the Soul being snapped back into place, humming to the harmonising frequency and the very breath of one's body.

Sitting enveloped in the warmth of the Violet Flame is like coming in from the ice cold, damp, and rain of the Soul and warming yourself by the hearth of the fire, removing the layers of the Mind no longer of servitude, of all that has kept you enthralled in the cold of that experience and has given you that chill of the Soul, having locked yourself outside the warmth of yourself.

Merely visualise coming in from the cold and dark night of Soul warming the 'bones' of your Mind by the hearth of the cracklin' flames of the Violet Fire, releasing and transmuting all that no longer agrees with you nor serves you, warming your Soul, and feeling the warmth and glow return within, for that is the power of transformation, of letting go, and shaking off the damp and cold of the experience(s). For my Child, the hearth of the home is the seat of your Soul.

Violet Flame Invocation

You can recite this invocation as many times as you want, envisioning yourself sitting in front of the hearth of the Violet Flame, warming the very core of your BEing.

I AM One with the multitude of the Universe as the Universe is One with the multitude of All that I AM
I AM Divine Inspiration, as much as the Inspiration is the Magic of the Divine I AM Presence that I AM
I AM Oneness—I AM
I AM a BEing of Violet Fire
I bask in the Light of my own Soul Fire
I AM a BEing of Violet Fire
I am the purity God desires

St. Germain is in service of Lord Zadkiel and the keeper of the Violet Flame. As he was on his perch stool, I let him continue talking and explain more about the art of transformation.

"Transformation is the revelling of the Self in the darkness, back to the breath of the Light within. Pretty it is not, but challenges may question the very existence of why you are here? Unless you choose to suffocate yourself in the dribbling of the nonsensical existence of the dogmatised Self, then so be it. A wordily mouthful, is it not? That may be so, but perhaps one will choose to read these words again.... You are

the formation of who you are in how you choose to either tackle or evade life's dishy presented challenges. To kick the platter or keep the platter, that is the experience of choice.

Transformation is key to the evolution of your Soul of Self; without it, one slings oneself back into the darkness like a looping boomerang in continuous reverse. Live not in the shadow nor in the stagnancy of yourself, for it serves no purpose but for a constipated energetic disharmony causing the body nothing but the sludge of dis-ease.

One can decide whether to remain a darned fat caterpillar, continuing to exist in one's little cosmic bubble listening to the spoken narrative of the world without, and remain but forever trapped in the quicksand of one's rampant running e-motions, moving in endless circles of one's dulled and lulled experiences, never changing, never unfolding, or one can stop drowning in the overflowing sorrows of the anxiety-ridden mind, leaving the shades of grey of the once confined shadows and lightening the load of the carried heaviness by cocooning the Self, choosing to heal, transform and thus emerge from the chrysalis back to the iridescent spark of the enlightened light of a butterfly one truly is.

If you can't go left where nothing is right for you, or turn right where nothing is left for you, then follow the path straight ahead where nothing is left or right for you, but where one leaves the endings and chooses to venture onto new beginnings. Life is either "indeedly" so, a daring adventure or a drab of nothing at all—why remain in the safe harbours of your conditioned existence when the world and the Universe are waiting with utter anticipation to be explored by you into the multitude of an expansion of your brilliant Light? Venture outside the created existential box, and walk the journey back to the beautiful hue of the natural flavoured Self, daring to plunge into the depths of your 'scrunchilicious' hidden darkness, scrubbing and healing the soot off your latched-on experiences and reemerging to the radiance of yourself. Learn to live a little, laugh a little and love your life just that wee bit more because before you know it, your song has ended, the dance is over, and you have cha-chaed on outta here, glidin' back home to the Divine-licious heavenly Stars "up above."

We get so caught up in the drama and the pain of our experiences, and yet, we have a choice to either shift this pain or remain in it. I don't care how 'old' you are; it is never too late to change our ways, for what could be greater than living life in the flow of who we truly and magnificently are?

I had to journey through hell many times to undergo the process of healing over time, having burnt my arse in the blazin' hell fires, to commence the process of ripping off those darn pesky labels I had so frivolously and like a ditz stuck all over myself. I jumped from one dire experience into the next—and I can tell you, life will still be throwing mud balls at me, but I now know not to let the experiences get me down.

My Beautiful Sister

I could not fathom going on like this, and wanting to change so desperately, I threw my plea into the universe. As St. Germain says, *"Either deal and heal or run and shun, but to ascend to, you have to tend to, n'est-ce pas?"* Enter my sister, who I have been in touch with only sporadically over the years, as we are two completely different personalities with completely different lifestyles. Our relationship has been fragile since she was nineteen and I was twenty-one. She has chosen to roam around in her victimhood, carrying with her all of her experiences, having alchemised none, although she says she has. Yet she always digs in her heels, kicking the dirt from the past back in my face.

She lives in her perception of the truth concerning her youth and how she has experienced the world, as we all do. She has fractured her beautiful mind, having dabbled in drugs far more than I could even fathom, although she would disagree, proclaiming I have used far more throughout my life. According to her husband's old crew, I had an outstanding debt with Keylow, and, as I was using drugs with Mark, I was thus harassed, having given my PlayStation as a pay-off, with the police doing nothing about it.

My truth is somewhat different, as I lived through the hell of what truly happened with him, and she was not part of my life in Holland. As Spirit states, *"The he said, she said tug o' war of the ego is rather petulant, and a never-ending mind-bender, causing one nothing but the ailment of dizziness. Everyone chooses to resonate in their own truth, so leave them be and merely send them love and wish them consciousness."* My sister was misdiagnosed as bipolar and suffered from border-line personality syndrome. She's always blamed our mum for making herself ill, being at a complete dis-ease within herself, but you can't blame someone else for your woes; you have to take responsibility for your own life. Pain and suffering are mere warning signs that you are going against the grind of living in your own truth, and you will keep limping throughout life if you keep suppressing the emotional triggers that are crying out for healing.

Like me, she signed up for this earthly dance of life, requesting a laundry list of challenges. She set the bar high and was so excited to incarnate as my sister, but like all of us, she got knocked on the head, suffering extreme memory loss. Yet, as she became more embroiled in the earthly surface life, having forgotten her true origins, she turned her life into a real s*** show. A bit more indulging in the Greek *"metanoia"* would have worked wonders for her soul, returning from the depths of darkness to basking and breathing in the light, choosing to reflect instead of deflecting by healing one's heart, one's mind, one's self, and one's orchestrated destructive self-defeating ways.

At nineteen, she moved in with her first boyfriend, who became a police officer. She said she often roamed the streets, not wanting to go home, as he was abusive. After spending several days with Mum and John in the UK, they told her she could stay with them in Aylesbury and rebuild her life in the UK, but she refused and returned to him instead. When she finally left him many years later, she wandered straight into the arms of another without any breathing space to heal the hurt of her 'shot' mind, and hence attracted another broken soul, ending up in another fractured relationship. She married this person shortly after he was released from prison.

If you are broken, you should be healing; the last thing you should be doing is running into the arms of another and projecting the energy of your traumas onto each other. All you will do is choose to live in the pain of each other's experiences and feed off each other's toxicity. You deflect rather than reflect. People tend to love the reflections in each other, but that is not love, that is the conditioning being reflected with your soul merely requesting healing of that cast reflection that has given rise to the 'unseen' hurt. How can you love another if you cannot love yourself? To love someone is to firstly learn to love the song in their own hearts, but when both are so broken and out of tune, then that is not love—that is holding onto one another, trying to vehemently plug the holes in each other's "cheese."

The key to being in the flow of life is that what you think and do aligns with what resonates with you. This way, your soul and body are in harmony with who you most authentically are. As the Ascended Master Sananda, in his life as Apollonius of Tyana, is quoted as saying, *"Pythagoras said that the most Divine art was that of Healing. And if the Healing art is most Divine, it must occupy itself with the soul as well as with the body; for no creature can be sound so long as the higher part in it is sickly."*

My sister went to counselling throughout the years, with both my mum and I offering to speak to the counsellor, or set up a group session; however, my sister refused.

Therapy is great and can be very healing for the patient, but never commence treatment based on a lie and blaming others, choosing to roam in the gloaming of that victim mentality. Doing so will only aid in hurtling you further into the abyss, spinning a dark web of deceit entangling the mind in an ever-spinning sticky web of lies, submerging into the created quicksand and suffocating one's own beautiful heart and soul.

We should all take responsibility for our experiences. Lying to ourselves will only cause us to shoot ourselves in the foot, tripping and falling off that famous "cliff." I see my sister as being the cause of her own dis-ease, suffering many ongoing health problems, but blaming our mum is a deflective reflex. My sister ended her relationship with our mum many years ago; however, in her last email, before choosing to cut ties, she told our mum she still loves her, and my mum said the same.

If only my sister could understand that she has chosen these experiences for her own soul's growth; if only she understood that she is the mere creator of her own created reality, then her life would have been infinitely so much more beautiful. She quit working many years ago due to being harassed in the workplace and has been living off benefits since, much like her husband, who sadly suffers from poor health. The Divine Shakespeare Club have a clever mind twist on it; they state, *"People think they benefit from benefits, but in truth, the benefits benefit from them, so is it really a benefit and beneficial for the growth of your Soul?"*

When my mum came over from the UK to visit her for the weekend, staying in a hotel in Amsterdam, my sister told her that she would only have an hour to meet up because they were going to visit a friend of her husband. My mum was gutted, as they had agreed to spend the weekend together. My sister introduced our mum to her then-boyfriend in a bar of all places, something our mum has a complete aversion to. She only met him once and couldn't stand the sight of him because he boasted about having spent time in prison, telling my mum he would beat the crap out of my sister's ex.

My sister suffered more at the hand of our mum than I did, but I had other kinds of abuse thrown into the mix as a child, and even though I was a bit of a fuck-a-roo, messing up my own life, learning through trial and error, I did not keep pointing the finger and figured out how to heal myself eventually, all the whilst trudging through the muck of my duly created experiences. We all blame our parents or have a good moan at some stage, but we can't keep walking around with that blip in our soul.

I think people need to understand that a lot comes through the lineage of our ancestors and the families we have chosen to be born into. My mother took on the behaviour of her mother, who was subsequently conditioned by her mother, for my grandma was beaten senseless by her own mother as well—yet my mother never turned her back on her mother nor chose to disrespect her, as she understood why she was the way she was and eventually broke the ancestral cycle, by having a heart-to-heart with my sister when she was nineteen years old. Yet, my sister has chosen to fall foul to that victim consciousness that she feels so comfortable in, choosing to huddle in the shadows of herself.

My sister visited me for two weeks while I lived in Curacao, and I thoroughly enjoyed my time with her. We took a trip to Klein Curacao, snorkelling in the turquoise waters, walking along white sandy beaches, and going up to the lighthouse.

I did not attend my sister's wedding, nor did she invite our mother. When I visited her in Amsterdam, pondering whether to go, we sat outside a café, and she decided to light up a joint. I asked her to refrain from doing so, as it made me nauseous, but she refused. It made me feel very uncomfortable as I did not want to be around people smoking pot. Another time I stayed with her overnight on my way to Curacao, and her husband's brother was over, they were smoking pot, and I asked my sister if they could please smoke somewhere else, as it made me ill. She said it was her home, so I would have to grin and bear it. I can tell you this much, I was sick as a pig, having thrown up at the airport the following day.

The last time I physically saw my sister was in 2012 when our mum had gotten free tickets for the Olympic Games in London. Seeing I don't give a hoot about sports, my mum paid for my sister to come over and go to the event with her.

My sister has always claimed that her husband takes care of her, but even when my sister was married, they couldn't afford a new stove and didn't have a washing machine, so my mum and I bought her both, splitting the cost, so she could cook and do her laundry. When her first dog, a little Jack Russell terrier, was so ill, she knew he had to be put down, but she didn't have the money for the vet, so she left him in pain, even though it was excruciating for her to watch. Eventually, my mum paid the vet for her, and my sister relieved that sweet dog of its misery. She has always been an immense animal lover, often having several dogs. Over the years, I have sent her money on numerous occasions. Still, she has never quite been able to turn her life around, instead often seemingly digging a far deeper hole and remaining in the accustomed pain of her created life. As St. Germain says:

"What you seek is seeking you, yet what you vibe out is exactly what you vibe back in. Be mindful of the thoughts you feed your Mind, for you may find being the energetic-ingenious-genie that you are, that you create into manifestation that which you would not want, yet duly receive for the very thought you chose to whip-up and thus materialise onto the serv-ed plate of your existence. Never forget that you have been given this beautiful life with an opportunity to waltz back to your magical, authentic Self through the power of being a Master Creator, expressing and creating your own masterfully concocted creations, uncovering the magic one holds within through the trial and error of your experiences to either create but a brighter existence or remain indefinitely soaking but ever so wonderfully in the toxicity of yourselves. Remember you are the Divine Alchemist of your Divine Cosmic Creation—so will what you want, and want what you will, for the energy that is you, will maketh it so, as that is the Law of the Divine I AM of All that you are."

In 2013, I invited my sister to come down to Florida. I advised her that mum and I would work on the house but was happy to pay for her flight. As she had an ongoing court case, all she wanted to do was relax and go to the beach so she could fly back refreshed. Instead of finding all kinds of excuses, she should have just hopped on a plane and gotten over her ultra-conditioned self, as Mum and I were working hard, and sometimes we'd be exhausted, but we still hung out in St. Pete, had fun, and went out for dinner on several occasions.

My sister, like me, has wanted to exit the turnstiles of life as she could no longer stomach this life and the environment she was in, and yet she remained, instead shutting out the light of her beautiful soul in favour of staying put where she was. My sister could have been a fantastic lawyer, as she was offered an internship but turned it down. She has made homemade CBD oil, which is legal in Holland, selling it and providing relief to others. What saddens me most is that she has an extremely high IQ; she could do so much more with her brilliant mind.

School was a breeze for her as she hardly had to study, whereas I had to study hard to get half-decent grades. I wasn't as bright as she was, nor did I pretend to be; the only thing I excelled in, besides English, German, and history, was art, as I loved drawing and painting. I sucked at algebra. Numbers and formulas did not agree with me. It took me three times to pass my theory test and three times to pass my driving test, and the only reason I passed was that I told the instructor

I had made a mistake while turning. If not, I would have had to retake it a fourth time. My sister did it all in one take, passing with flying colours.

I cannot converse with my sister as we are on two different frequencies. It's like two people speaking a different language the other doesn't know—*no comprende* one another. Our short bursts of texting communication always came to a halt when the subject of the acceptance of her husband came up. Without fail, she would mention the letters and cards I sent him in prison, where I said he was like my brother and that I loved him. But she also told me that she could not leave her husband because if she did, he would take his own life. It merely saddens me that she has remained stagnant in the same energetic field of her existence. She made it known that she finds it impossible that I communicate with the Light BEings, because I would need to understand the terminology of loving people unconditionally.

She often questioned why I couldn't build an intimate relationship with a man. She said I avoided the question by saying I was happy on my own, labelling me as possibly asexual. Why would I need someone to complete me when I finally feel whole? I have never understood the need to label someone. We are all sparks of the same light, experiencing life in this encasing of flesh and bones.

When you are attracted to someone, you are attracted to the same vibrational frequency that you vibe off into the ether. Who cares about your sexual orientation? It is not your body that attracts another body; it is the soul that is attracted to another soul housed within that body. You are attracted to the energy thereof. Society has labelled you as being "xyz," and it is you who decides to conform to the acceptance of that label that has been slapped upon you. Why? All because you feel a sense of acceptance, of belonging in this burped-up society, having been able to identify yourself with a tag that agrees with you in that partaken reality?

We must stop labelling ourselves and be happy with who we are. Care not what others think of you, care what you think of you, for only by being real with ourselves can we live a life l'extraordinaire lumière. Ditch the created masks, and never retreat in the shadows of Self, allowing the opinions of others to bark you back. Sweep that illusion of fear into the flowing and alchemising waters of the gutter, and let the light of your soul shine forth into the world.

We could be standing in the same room, observing the same view, but we would still have two different perspectives of that reality. The Ascended Master St. Germain refers to it as *"a wordilicious feat called Reality."* He says, *"If I could tell you one secret about this beautiful world you live in, it is that all that you believe to be a reality is not a reality but an illusion that you perceive to be a reality according to the implemented matrix of existence to keep you in the dogma of that reality, that is in actual fact the illusion to step out of, back to the remembrance of the Authenticity of You, that is a reality."*

Even though my sister has had several healers help her free of charge because I helped them, she seems to have remained stuck in the loop of her buggered-up programming. People who refuse to change have like this friggin' virus stuck in their computer's hardware that you can't seem to get rid of, as it keeps glitching back to its former status.

Yet regardless of how she always lingers in the past and has lashed out at me and used me as a punching bag, rebuking her light, deflecting all her inner pain towards me with the art of her war of words, I have always said to her that I love her unconditionally and that I am always there for her should she need me. These are my experiences, and I have chosen to incarnate with her, to learn from the reflections she has so "gently" cast in my face. I cannot deny that it has been difficult, but to hold on would only cause me to be depleted, so I have lovingly released her to walk her journey and hope that she finds her way back to the love and warmth of the beautiful Soul that she is.

"You have chosen this life.
You have chosen your experiences.
You have created your experiences.
Take responsibility.

Life keeps ticking away, whether you choose to live or allow yourself to be lived, whether you choose to be inspired and make it a va-va-voom hell of a ride or a drizzled misery of a self-destruct jam doughnut. Don't live a life with what-ifs. Live it according to the very song that sings in your own heart—for when your time is up, it's up, there ain't no Jumanji do-over, one can merely choose to reincarnate again, coming in with this wonderful bout of whacked-on-the-head amnesia, and hope to God, you just ain't gonna bugger up again, and leave with a bunch of what-ifs having drowned in your 'funkalicious' Soul sludge. Life is beautiful, much like a field of dandelion seeds taking flight on the breeze, letting go, and rebirthing in one's experiences. Every birthing equates to a better understanding of the equation you are, dancing back to the divine grid of one's gem of bless-ed consciousness. Life—live it, love it, breathe it, and know that you are blessed in all ways."

~The Divine Shakespeare Club and the Council of Blue Ray Light Beings~

I will add that I have had several past lives with my sister. One was during the Middle Ages, where I desperately tried to save her, as she was swept away by the currents, drowning, and yet as the Light BEings kindly point out, in this lifetime, my sister needs to save herself from her own drowning waters. Let her find her way back through the darkness of her own sweet self. Eventually, she will re-emerge, basking in the warmth of her own soul light, loving herself wholly for the beautiful divine Goddess she is.

I love my sister, and I hope one day she unwraps herself out of all the conditioned layers she has wrapped around her beautiful Soul and learns to forgive herself and others.

And so it is.

Q&A with St. Germain on Mental Illness and Overcoming Trauma

I asked the Ascended Master St. Germain about the various branches of "mental illness," and how people become mentally unstable within themselves.

Mental illness serves as a literal metaphor—for one is mental in nature, and thus it is the map of the mind that has become frazzled due to the narrative of the experiences ingested and the environment one has been seduced in, causing one to become ill—imbalanced of love and light. A fractured Soul causes a splintered state of Mind, for the many fragments floating within the pool of the Soul seem but a reality yet are an illusion of the pockets created through one's experiences. It is creating an alternate reality to deviate away from dealing with one's pain and projecting that blame onto another, living in that muddled state of a reality that pertains to a created reality rather than the truth of that reality as it is too painful for them to look at the "ghastly" reality of the reflection staring back at them. It is a blur of that truth, and a conveyed and created reality according to their conditioning and repetitive thoughts of the events, having rewired the neurons within the brain and given it a different corresponding energetic rhythm to the once original rhythm as was intended, creating an alternate reality in line with the untruth of one's Soul. Yet, when so fractured, one believes that alternate truth, the fabricated narrative, as it reverberates far better than the painful truth of the events as played out. In otherworldly terms, one's brains have been scrambled according to the truth of what they prefer to see rather than for what it is. It is merely for want of plugging the many holes in their leaky 'cheese,' yet it is like trying to fill a round hole with a square peg, causing one a further defragmentation of the truth and the light of who they are. A mental illness is nothing more than being unable to process one's experiences as per the instilled coping mechanisms one has been taught. Yet, if one understood that every reflective experience is but a notion to be-com-ing more learn-ed of and within the Self, life would become infinitely easier. However, many are caught up in the "rapture" of the experience, thinking it like a demon that torments them, that they cannot see the light in the situation, and will dig themselves a deeper hole remaining trapped within that victim consciousness state of BEing.

Q: Can you define trauma? Like many others, I've been through it, but I know there are varying degrees and every situation is different.

Trauma is like being in the blurgh of Self, with one being on a constant war path with the rammed and battered Mind that has swallowed you whole with its putrid e-motions, having been consumed by the outer narrative of one's experiences. One has lost direction and control of Life's steering wheel, having been slung and catapulted off the edge of a cliff, drowning in the deluge of one's created experiences, thus becoming incapacitated by a deeply unnerving angst within and therefore not being able to breathe because one refuses point blank to be in acceptance of one's served experiences, causing that deep-seated loss within oneself. It is like plunging into and through this never-ending tunnel of darkness, unable to grasp oneself onto the light of day. Now my Child, are you out of breath yet? One often forgets that trauma gives one the most beautiful opportunity to delve deep within the caverns of the darkness of the heart; serving as a mere reflection, illuminating the lodged fragments in one's Soul, wading through the unwanted depths of one's dread, confronting those pesky chattering demons of the devious Mind that have held your Soul for ransom, to the bout of your unresolved experiences, eradicating the shadows within, giving one a deeper understanding of Self returning to the light and breath of the I AM Presence of the I AM within Oneself.

Whatever sways you is what feeds your Mind and thus influences the experiences in your Life you choose to partake in. Never forget that what you give power to has power over you. There is no conundrum that cannot be solved, nor is Life a stupefied riddle, for it is as much of an ease and flow as one chooses it to be. Light and darkness are merely varying degrees at different angles; it all depends on how you choose to "tipple" to tip the scales.

As Lord Zadkiel chips in," Your Mind is an acute and eager beaver listener of all the wording you whisper but to yourself, taking avid notes, being a most excellent minute taker of all that you speak and thus, whether heaven or hell, helps you to keenly co-create and manifest all that you have so fervently 'spoken' of to create."

Q: What about people that say "It is not my fault that this has happened to me"?

Well, aren't you a sight for sorry eyes, sitting there in the oh poor why me syndrome? Do you think it's my fault? Are you not in control of all that comes to pass in your life? Are you not the creator of all you create and manifest, and so shall it come to pass? Your experiences do not define who you are. You define your experiences unless you allow them to run you over like a relentless cart truck, leaving you in a flattened and contused state of BEing with a doddle of a whipped cream of unpleasantries along the way. You get served what you have so gleefully asked for, my Child. You can either allow your Soul to be bulldozed over by your repeat experiences, letting your experiences suck the life right out of you, or you can hop back onto the saddle and beat the devilish Mind o' the EGO at its own game of having relentlessly chased you into the gutter of your own darkness, vanquishing the shadows within, back into the Light eternal, leaving you in the basking of your own beautiful Love of the "heavenlicious" Divine You.

You are what you choose to become through the serv-ed experiences, and ain't nothing as dandy as a plate serv-ed full of chilli peppers, to make you tear up and alleviate yourself out of your own created hornets' nest of a stingin' pain, back to the alchemisation of that zen of love and understanding in a perfect realignment with the Divine en toi.

The direction of your energy determines the outcome of your intended thoughts, lest one forgets that one's Mind is the most 'potent' universal tool of the Soul, for your Soul is the conjuror of your created thoughts and thus manifestations.

If you state, "it is not my fault," and remain in the poppycock of hangin' round in that victim mentality, then that is a decisive choice of you partaking in the direction of choosing to walk that belligerent path. It is your choice to slip into this spiritual hiccup malaise of Self. When you deny yourself, you deny the I AM in ME as I AM the ME in You. A "deniance" causes a short-circuiting of the life you truly desire. There is nothing that cannot be resolved with the Art of the Mind to get to the Heart of the Matter.

Q: How do we actually heal from traumatic experiences?

The main ingredients to healing from the engrained trauma within yourselves are, a dose of responsibility, ain't no one at fault but the 'baddilicious' villain blinking back at you dans le miroir, sprinkled with a whole dollop of whipped-on creamy self-love and so too seeing the reflection of the experiences with nothing but love towards others, and lastly, a peppering of beautiful echoes of forgiveness, allowing the encrusted heaviness to be flushed out with the brilliance of the light flooding back into the breath of your Soul.

Does a flower retaliate when crushed or pulled apart, having caused it pain? Does it kick or bite back? It screams like a "banshee" unbeknownst to the untrained human ear, but regardless of that fact, it still gives off this wonderful smell, telling you it still loves you and forgives you for crushing it, draining it of its life force energy.

Pucker up, my Child, let go of those sticky clung-on toffee cloudy meatball grudges that have clouded your Mind; merely forgive and love all that have caused you the swirling e-motions of that so-called pain that you have so utterly indulged yourself in, for you are as much the cause of your own happiness as you are of your own "elated" misery. Say it is not so, and I will prove thee wrong. You are in control unless you have allowed your life to be controlled by others, having allowed the "Gremlins" of your experiences to toy with you. It is much like devouring a whole box of chocolates and becoming sick because of it—you are the cause as much as the effect of the chosen outcomes of your Life. Let go, and I promise you all will be well. Life is a beautiful journey, a grand spectacle of an ease of gliding through one's experiences, unless you choose to remain in the created stickiness of a drama, having bent to the will of fear, denying the beauty of the honest-to-God-truth of who you are, then, by all means, let me get the popcorn, and watch you from afar, to see how you will find your way out of your own created mess of a "fudged-up" life.

You are the world's greatest healer as much as the world's greatest punisher. Either way, you are right. You allow yourself to play Russian roulette with the possible creation of dis-ease and other faulty inner programming because you choose to turn a blind eye to the screaming and pleading Soul, not me.

Q: You make healing sound so easy, like the flip of a switch.

Mais oui, c'est très facile, but it is the mere human conditioning that has gotten your panties in a tizzy, making you stand there like a stupefied Harry Potter, unable to move because you have been paralysed by fear, barked back in the shadows from your own light, preferring to deflect to that state of bitchin' and moanin' rather than healing and releasing with all the Love in le monde. You are Love, so how difficult can it be to chuck all the old conditioning you have so rammed your mind with? No pun *intended, but everything stems from the mind, so nurture the mind with Love, and all will spring back to the wells of the originality of one's Soul at heart, n'est-ce pas?*

Speak I but lightly of this? Yes, for healing is the elevation out of the drab back into the light through the art of Love, for to love yourself is to heal yourself, and how can you heal yourself if you cannot forgive nor love yourself from the experiences slung your way? It is the memories of the experiences that keep one trapped in the ever-vicious cycle of one's programming. Trauma is the gift that keeps on giving, allowing one to walk the outer fringes of the Self, tipping you either into the abyss or pledging you to hold on for dear life to the edge of sanity in your current state of awareness. One has far greater power within than one is led to believe, but you have simply forgotten through a smack on the head upon being born.

Why do you rely so much on the outer world in seeking a magical band-aid to solve all your problems? Are you not the sole perpetrator of all that you so wilfully create? The truth is, you are here to attain self-mastery, so why do you keep giving your Power away like sweets in a candy jar? Why do you care what others may think of you? Mastering the Self may be easier said than done in the awareness you perceive yourself to be. The impossibility is of choosing that one is either in acceptance of being locked within the emotional pitfalls of the Mind or that one steps out of the paradigm of that acceptance to do the work and create a better life for oneself. You either harbour the Self as a fugitive in the shadows one so rocks to, or break free from one's self-imposed and created misery of an existence.

Trauma can keep one trapped in victimhood, of the oh poor me syndrome, or it can give one the courage to snap out of it and to break free from the comatose predicament one has for so long chosen to remain in. Tell me you do not have a choice, and I will merely frown and say that you do! For you are as much the Universe as the Universe is you— there is no equation of 1+1, for you are One with All there is, and One is All with You. In other words, you are an energetic powerhouse of creating your manifestations into the artwork of your reality of life on a daily basis. Don't like the paints, change the response, and the reaction thereof, to change the colouring of your life, for you and only you are the true alchemist of your creations. Decide to make a choice to make a difference.

Your life is simply a creation of a multitude of experiences across the threshold for the evolution of your Soul, to attain a higher degree in Consciousness, to an understanding of Life and the Universe and how we are all interconnected. If you remain unmoving because of your current state of thinking and your stubbornness to remain locking horns with the fragments of your inner reflections, then so be it. Come not to me for help but for the aid to help oneself. If you ask for our help, it is freely given as we are always ready to assist. Expect not a magic carpet ride, for the work to healing is the road one must walk in the remnants of one's surfacing shadows, but the bread crumbs we leave, serve as a reminder that one is never alone on the road to uncovering and recovering the Soul from the darkness back into the Light of Self.

Q: We don't always listen to the universe, as we wear blinkers, blind to the signs around us because we know no better. What's your advice?

The Universe is always bringing you signs. It just depends if you're too tone-deaf and going lalalalalala to even hear what it is whispering to you. Life is magical. You are magical. You are a transformational BEing consistent of Universal Energy and such the Creator of your Magical Universe according to the ho-hums of your Soul vibrance. Create magically with all the tools given to thee: your Mind, your Words, and your Wisdom—tapping into that inner knowing to create and express, weaving your own stories into a beautiful reality. Think not that you cannot, and it will be so; think that you can and thus manifest it into existence—after all, you are the brew to your own divine tea, n'est-ce pas? You can make it as delicious and divine or as bitter and repugnant as you choose, but why rebuke the knowing of your Soul by choosing to linger in the experiences for too long? It serves you not.

Tell me, when it rains, does it keep raining? Non, pas du tout, c'est impossible! Yet as humans, many remain in the damned matrix of one's current existence, not daring to venture one's toe out of the shadows of oneself, for what if? Step out of your conditioning, it is all but an illusion, served as a concoction to keep you in line of the ward you have been incapacitated in. What is real, and what is the illusion, that is the current reality you are faced with, or maybe it is all an illusion? If you are that confused, sit quietly with yourself, connecting to the Source within, for you are Source, as much as Source is You. You are the only one to get yourself back out of the ditch onto the magical yellow brick road returning to the light of your Authenticity and thus existence.

When in dubio, brew yourself a nice cup of chai and sit in the warmth of your Soul Light, aligning yourself to the sacred geometrical Grid of the "divinelicious" Grace that is You.

Much love and gratitude to you in the unfolding of your journey back to the beautiful Divine blossoming of a Light that you are.

Ancestral Healing

The Sun shines in each and every one of you, but some may have simply hidden their SunLight behind the darkness of the heavy clouds of experience dancing across the vastness of one's Soul, waiting to be released by the impending rain, to free the Soul back to the Light of the Sun within.

~The Council of Ra~

I could have spoken of ancestral healing earlier, but I wanted to show how the patterning runs like a red line through the whole of my family lineage. When something is "genetic," it is that ancestral part that sits embedded within your DNA; it is encoded within your memory body. My mum always says that her haemorrhoids are genetic, as her mother suffered the same. I told her it was a load of tosh, as she could easily shift that energetic constipation by changing her diet to eating far healthier, as my grandmother's diet was atrocious.

For once, she listened and commenced incorporating veggies and salads and cutting down on her sugar intake. I did get her herbal Aloe Vera and Probiotic Lactobacillus Acidophilus capsules, and she now has it under control, suffering little to no issues. All it takes is that simple willingness of a mind shift to jolt the stagnant and stiffened energetic particles within your energy field. You are energy; there is nothing that cannot be changed, end of.

Ancestral healing relieves the blockages that have clogged our energy system, delving into the root cause of our inflicted pain. Only then can we heal, enabling the energetic flow to ripple through our lives and relationships. These negative ingrained belief patterns—inherited from our parents and often going back generations to our ancestors—can easily be released and transcended into wisdom and healing. What is more beautiful than living in the freedom of ourselves, rather than living in a repressed state of BEing, unwilling to break the cycle?

Remaining within that same stale fluctuation and timbre of energy is like starving your roots of the water they need to nourish your soul, letting yourself run around parched and in a state of dehydration, causing you to collapse into delirium, with no understanding of the experiences that have thrown you.

Even if addictive genes run through your DNA, it is up to you to change this if you have the awareness that it can be so—becoming conscious of the fact that it is a repetitive pattern that runs in your family, bleeding into the next generation, causing unhealthy relationship patterns and limiting self-belief systems. It can affect your life on many levels, and one is merely a self-saboteur without understanding why because you have been conditioned that way.

Ancestral energy is the embodiment of lives past in one's lineage, having passed down, giving voice, and an art of expression into the incarnated human embodiment that is you. To heal or not to heal, that is the question. Healing is understanding that transformation is the key to releasing old wounds, shifting the conditioning and beliefs that have held you and past generations in captivity. Do you not owe it to yourself to set yourself free? Our ancestors, having crossed over, leave behind this sticky residue in the lineage of our DNA. It's their lovely unfinished business, having passed down through many generations and finally having made its way to you. The question is, what are you going to do about it?

You can decline the call and stick your middle finger up, with your soul hurting and the wound continuously reproducing and inflaming itself, leaving your mind in pain till you're blue in the face. Or see it as a gift, honouring yourself, with the opportunity to heal these painful wounds and resolve the issues for all parties involved.

My father kept a lid on his traumatic childhood experiences. He chose to live his life through a "conditioned" version of himself, with his own suffered abuse, including the combo of my mum, later bleeding into my life and my sister's. As much as he believed he could cure himself, he did not embrace nor transcend the pain of his chosen experiences and thus waltzed out of life. Keeping pent-up emotions inside causes a distortion in the energetic frequency waves you emit—in his case, it was his heart, the seat of his emotions, which ultimately took its toll. It's like lugging this immense boulder with you, often falling flat under the weight of it, with it eventually manifesting itself into a dis-ease.

My grandfather—who, as I stated earlier, was tortured by the Japanese in WWII—kept a lot of that trauma hidden within, and years later, he died of a heart attack, for this is where the dis-ease between his soul and body became apparent, but it was too late to repair. Times were different back then; people weren't as open spiritually, and much of his awareness of living his life in his true spiritual essence had been snuffed out.

On my mum's side, the severe beating that her own mother got from her mother, my great grandmother, was conditioned onto my mother. Yet my mother broke that part of the cycle by sitting down with my sister and apologising for her behaviour. My mum will always admit if she is wrong, as she is very black and white like that. Admitting fault is cause for improvement in our own lives, as well as others, as we change the frequency we once hummed at. It shows that we are capable of being objective about ourselves and that through our conditioning, we are neither perfect nor right. My sister chose to remain in the ancestral cycle of abuse, as it bled into her relationships and environment, and thus she remains blaming everyone else, except looking at the culprit pointing the finger—herself. We often don't even consider that our pain could be ancestral. Or we just clock it up to the easy copout of, oh, well, it runs in my family. If you know that, what are you going to do about it? Use it as an excuse or decide to change it?

Much of my pain came from my ancestral lineage, and it took a lot of healing to get to a place of understanding, releasing many ingrained patterns over the years. Louise Rhodes, a phenomenal light language healer, and channel picked up on abuse through my whole family lineage, going back to past lives and into my galactic origins. Yet I chose these sometimes excruciatingly adverse lives for the growth and expansion of my soul. I have never been one to take half measures;

the more challenging the experience, the better, as I have always found a way to conquer my demons.

Attachments will often roam around in the lovely warmth of your energy field, having nestled and found a home there. As you are this fuzzy atomic ball of energetic particles in flux, you attract the energy they are drawn to and thus "lovingly" cling to. Yet, once the energies are released, you can feel like a whole new person. You feel so much lighter; it's like one has shaken off this energetic density after taking a warm golden light shower, and the fog has cleared, allowing you to breathe and see life far more clearly.

The recalibration does not happen overnight. The physical pain you may have felt or suffered from may ease, but realigning all within your body can take several days or even longer. Be grateful for all that surfaces, especially during these transitional times, for whatever arises from within is asking to be healed no matter how icky it may be. You would do yourself a great disservice by remaining in your so-called uncomfortable comfort zone.

Always remember, it is not others who have stung you with their wording; you have stung yourself by allowing it so. Choosing to hide behind a created narrative because of a fear of stepping out into the truth of who you are, serves you a whole lot of unwanted accumulated garbage in the corridors of your soul. You can't breathe in your own true I AM presence if you choose to let fear rule your life. You are the essence of infinite star particles, with the guidance of the stars mapped within the intricacy of your eloquent DNA. Call to your ancestors to walk the road back home to yourself because you are worthy of the light that you are, the core authenticity of all that makes you *you*. As St. Germain states:

"Speak not to me, of not having chosen one's difficult circumstances, but seek a solution to the difficulty entailed of that created experience in this very moment.

Experiences seek not to taunt you but are the zingy and zesty flavours enriching the very essence of your Soul—so embrace all, clearing what is no longer of servitude to you, remaining strong through the onslaught of waves whilst traipsing through the pain of one's innate darkness, allowing your inner guidance and an empowered perspective to lead you back to the Light and Laughter of your Divine Self. Ditch the EGO and eat humble pie, taking the inner journey through the shadows of yourself, shimmering back to the surface in the radiance of the dazzling pearl you are. Rebirthing is never easy, but the beauty beyond the transitioning of the Self is a phenomenal feat to behold."

One often laments that the fault lies with another, but in truth, it lies with ourselves. Those who trigger us to feel these negative emotions bubbling to the surface are merely messengers showing us the unhealed parts of our being. It takes courage to look at ourselves and break the chains of our built-in beliefs, healing and transforming the wounds we carry from those who came before us, enabling us to clear and change the pathway for those who come after us, allowing the entire lineage to evolve.

It's time to smack ourselves out of that dream—to rise up and see what lies beyond the created wound that we have for so long rubbed salt in and let bleed so freely. There is nothing that cannot be overcome but for one's own created chaotic hurdles. As St. Germain states with Hilarion continuing below, *"Only a fool would let the boat rock in a storm, capsizing one's ship in the minuscule tempest of the ocean of one's experiences."*

"Self-transformation is the key to unlocking the door of Truth, allowing the Light and Authentic breeze to engulf the very heart of your Soul into the Divine Remembrance of the bliss of who you are. The world is your oyster, and you, my Child, are a Light walker amongst the stars, standing on the cusp of your own transformation. Cut the cords, and dazzle to the heights of freedom, flying free in the Truth of the Divine Grace of All that You are. Don't be a Pinocchio and get Pinocchio-ed out by denying yourself growth; simply waltz to the step-steppin' of your own Divine tune, and all will be well."

~The Ascended Master Hilarion~

You are here to co-create a new dawning, ushering in the new with the defragmentation of the old, lifting the veil of the illusion you have been birthed into. It means ploughing through the troughs and clearing away the dogma that binds you and the conditioning you have inherited from your familial sources—the ancestral healing of the line within you—to set yourself free and free your heart, back to an understanding and an a-ha of self.

You chose to incarnate, so get crackin' with the life you have always dreamed of. Be bold, for boldness carries genius, power, and divine magic. The direction of the energetic frequencies you call forth will hit just the right notes along life's journey, making it a blissful musical of wondrous wonder, achieving and aspiring to who you choose to become.

Kambo Medicine

During one of these short spells, I was in touch with my sister, she advised me of kambo and how it had helped her quit smoking cigarettes, if only for a short while. At the end of my wits and always willing to try a new way of alternative healing to move forward in life, I decided to do some online research and found a licensed practitioner in Florida named José Falquez.

If you had told me about the kambo cleanse process and what it does years ago, I would have laughed in your face, and thought you were nuts! Kambo is a beautiful medicine from Mother Earth. It is known as the "vaccine of the forest," as it's anti-inflammatory, antibacterial, and antimicrobial. It purifies the physical from all the toxic substances we have hampered our body with and aids in purifying the heaviness of the mind and spirit. Scientists have debunked kambo in many medical journals, stating it is pure poison and can cause serious health complications and even death. Yet, it has been around for eons, and is one of the most effective and natural ways to empower your immune system. Rather than the alternative of pumping ourselves full of pharmaceutical medications, band-aiding the physical and suppressing the unaligned energies caused by the raging yet muted emotions that are desperately crying out for healing.

Kambo is the name given to the traditional shamanic frog venom; its "poison" scraped off the giant monkey tree frog, a beautiful, luminous nocturnal frog that lives in trees. These lucky amphibians, who are here to aid humanity, have no natural predators and can be found in abundance, happily croaking away across the Upper Amazon rainforest in South America. No frogs are ever harmed during the scraping process; they are duly respected for the healing they give and still ribbit and hop around blissfully afterward.

Kambo medicine is not for the faint of heart, as it literally plunges you into the depths of the layered self; much like Alice in Wonderland tumbling down that rabbit hole, aiding one to become a more wholly balanced persona, loosening and releasing the ultra-conditioned aspects that are embedded deep within, to realign yourself to a lighter state of being. By removing all the negative thought patterns and purging out unwanted energies, you allow the light back into your soul through the recalibration of your electromagnetic particles. The key is to keep working on yourself and not fall back into that imprisoned limited thinking as soon as you are back in your home environment.

Joan, a beautiful soul, and friend, bless her heart, decided to drive me to my session, as it was about a three-hour drive, and I had no idea how I would feel afterward. In truth, I had no idea about the whole process, as I wanted to know as little as possible, to fully embrace the experience with an open mind. I was told not to eat twelve hours before treatment and to wear loose-fitting clothes, so I put on a pair of sweatpants and a baggy t-shirt, and off I went. What could go wrong, right?

I sat down with José, and he asked me to set an intention for what I wanted to achieve: to rid myself of the old programming and nurse my fractured self back to health. I had to drink a litre of water, which was tough as I'm not a fan of drinking plain water, after which José made three minor, superficial burns with the tip of a glowing stick on my lower right leg, which felt like the sharp pin-pricks of a needle.

He then applied the kambo secretion dots onto the burns, which my body instantly absorbed. I immediately started to feel the effects as it ran through my circulatory system. Nothing could have prepared me for what happened next. I felt myself getting hot and flustered, with my face turning bright red. I felt like a bit of pufferfish as I could hardly feel my lips; they felt swollen. It was like I had a bad case of the flu, as the heat spread like an insistent rash throughout my body, followed by this intense nausea that washed over me, with me puking my guts out in the big "happy" yellow bucket beside me.

Kambo stimulates a purge while toxins are literally kicked out of your body. Here I was throwing up and running up and down to the toilet because of the continuous bowel movements, as it came out all ends—I needed José's help to do so because I could hardly get up as the room was spinning. I had to keep drinking water and simply focus on my breath, breathing in from the root chakra to my crown chakra and back out to the root chakra, to remain in control and become more relaxed, to allow for the kambo to flow more easily.

I thought I was dying and that this would be the end of me. I felt like my insides had turned to jelly. It's hard to describe, but every fibre of my being was being pulled apart to shake the gunk from the crevices of my whole essence. But no matter how bad I felt, I had told myself that I wanted to do this, and I was going to go through with it, as giving up was not an option. Hell no!

I'm not going to lie; kambo is a highly physical experience and considered an "ordeal" medicine, unlike a relaxing Reiki session or an aromatherapy massage. It is an intensely uncomfortable yet beautiful experience of walking through one's darkness, feeling wretched due to the nature of the physicality endured. Think of it as your body receiving a rigorous internal car wash. Even though I felt like I was losing the will to live, with tears streaming down my face due to the pain raging through me, with my body purging toxins and eliminating waste left, right, and centre from the various organs—it was a beautiful, raw ceremonial experience that left me feeling forever changed.

But then nothing worthwhile comes easily, does it? Don't think my clothes remained clean. I literally crapped my pants, and the dribble of the puke caught my shirt—but I didn't give a hoot. Turning myself inside out, getting rid of the gunk was for my own good, with me coming out cleansed and 'croakier' on the other side. Thankfully I had a change of clean clothes with me. It's not for everyone, so do your research before embarking on a kambo journey. I suggest going on the International Association of Kambo Practitioners (IAKP) site online to find a licensed and respectable shaman—that way, you'll know you are in safe hands.

My session took about four hours, and I struggled to get through it. My darn ego and my mind were fighting a war against me. I was so stuck in my manipulated and hampered ways that I had utterly disfigured my own makeup from the truth of who I was, choosing to become someone I was not, which in turn caused me to remain on the merry-go-round of "happily" tormenting my soul. It really is about immersing yourself in the healing process and making the unconscious conscious again, for the greatest explorer to have ever lived is the you in *you*.

Kambo is like an alkali for the soul; it's a calcination of learning to see beyond the veiled illusion and stepping out of our ego, exploring what lies beneath the surface of that created façade. Kambo is like a rebirthing of yourself—expanding inward to expand outward. It is surrendering and releasing all that no longer serves you, for hanging onto the past serves no one. We suffer when we choose to remain roaming in the gloaming of our past, causing nothing but chaos within our physical essence.

"Your body is only an instrument to navigate the Soul through this earthly life back to a knowing of Self. Start listening deeply to the song that sings within your own heart, for the Universe is constantly speaking to you on what goes on beneath the surface of all things, so stop living in the superficiality of yourselves, as you'll only end up being a sour twist and distorted frequency wave of who you are meant to be.

Your EGO is like Kryptonite to the Soul, leaving one straying from the Authenticity of the I AM of Self instead of living, plugged into the I AM of Source. One can remain flustered in one's experiences, cementing oneself in the set conditioning thereof, with the EGO running ragged with the Mind and taking but the reins to one's life oh so flamboyantly, or one can decide not to give a damn and understand that life's experiences are here to elevate you, soul spinning you onto the next level of the game of Life, and not here to downgrade you, remaining stuck on that same level, roaming around in your sorry arse state of existence. You're only as awakened as your own awareness, so how aware of an awakened Soul are you?"

~The Divine Shakespeare Club~

After all the purging and puking, *José* removed the kambo dots from my leg, and the major part of the cleanse was over. I was shaking like a leaf after the session, which is normal, as you have rid your body of so many toxins that the energetic particles need time to recalibrate, as it has been such a jolt to the body's senses. It was as if my body had been pulled apart, like the effect of a rubber band. After it had snapped back into place, I felt different. As part of the treatment, I was told to lie down and relax, with many people reporting a feeling of peace washing over them and seeing colours, or meeting their spirit guides. Really? Well, I saw jack shit and couldn't even lie down for five minutes, as I couldn't relax; my mind was racing a marathon in my head, with too many thoughts all at once. I needed to go out and walk to clear my head.

Kambo detoxifies the internal organs: the liver gets a thorough cleanse due to the vomiting of bile, and the intestines through the excretion, leaving your entire digestive system spanking clean. It has helped many heal from infections, regulating blood pressure, treating anxiety, chronic pain, depression, PTSD, chronic fatigue, migraines, arthritis, diabetes, candida, herpes, fertility problems,

HIV, high blood pressure, cancer, fertility issues, recurrent infections, pulled muscles, stomach issues, hepatitis, and much more.

Here I was, thinking Spirit had not listened to me, but they sent me the breadcrumb in the form of my sister's message of kambo. It was excruciatingly challenging for me, as it turned me inside out, yet afterward, things started to shift within my life. Whether we follow the trail of breadcrumbs or deviate back to our old programming, limping through life is entirely up to us.

After that first challenging detox, I felt queasy on the way home, having to stop at a gas station every twenty minutes. When I finally got home, I slept a whole day, as my body needed to rest, rejuvenate, and acclimatise. Subsequently, even though I still had a bit of an upward battle, I threw out all "junk" food and incorporated a far healthier diet. I made breakfast smoothies and went back to the gym several times a week. I cleared out my closets, donated to charity, and made a bucket list, which I stuck on my fridge.

I was advised to have at least three treatments, so being the sadomasochist I was, I returned several weeks later. The second time was so much easier for me; it took only two hours, with me yet again looking like a barbie doll with lip fillers gone wrong. There was no need for me to lie down, but I did so for several minutes before getting up and taking a stroll outside. This time I felt more connected within myself, like I was dancing in tune with all the world's energetic particles and electromagnetic frequencies. I embraced the whole experience and felt more in unison with myself and my environment. We often forget that love is the bridge between everything, but how can we expect to heal if we disconnect from a love of self?

At the top of my bucket list was running for charities, raising money for cancer primarily, as I had promised to start running once John had crossed over. Well, that remained a figment of running in my imagination until more than sixteen years later, I decided to make good on that promise and commenced running many 5k runs. I became pretty good at it and even received two awards as I came in second and third in my age category. I loved it; it made me feel good about myself. I'd simply plug in my earphones, listen to my music, and run to the beat of my soul, lost in my own world. When I saw others struggling, I always encouraged them to keep going and avoid stopping, as they'd lose pace—with some coming up to me after the race, thanking me for the support to keep going. I then had the idea to start making YouTube videos encouraging others to follow their own inspiration.

I interviewed many healers, mediums, authors, and even the likes of Pirelli World Challenge Champion and McLaren K-Pax Race Driver Álvaro Parente, as I was the team's catering host when they were in town. I also interviewed the immensely talented US motocross racer Scott Meshey, who wasn't a pro then. I predicted one day he would be riding a white bike, wearing green and blue gear, but it would take him several years to get there, with many ups and downs.

I interviewed the phenomenal cosmic sound energy healer Allan Pratt and various renowned psychic mediums like Cathy Miktuk, Molly Morningstar, and

Janie Boisclair, the 5C Gourmet Medium, who uses all five of her senses (clairvoyance, clairaudience, clairsentience, clairalience, and clairgustance) to deliver her messages. I sat down with the wonderful singer-songwriter, healer, speaker, teacher, and author John Stringer from Atlanta, Georgia; former lead singer from the pop-rock band State of Man, which had a top-ten hit with "Swallow Your Fears" and the beautiful, inspirational, and witty Temple Hayes, who is the founder of Life Rights and the SOFI Project, a renowned author, practising shaman, international motivational speaker and spiritual leader at the now Unity Campus in Santa Barbara, and is featured weekly on Unity FM, on the show *The Intentional Spirit*.

They each had unique stories of all they had been through and overcome in their lives. Editing the videos took a lot of work, as I was self-taught, and I often worked till late, yet the final result was always rewarding. Nowadays, people simply live stream, making it much easier, having no editing hassles.

As I had asked Spirit for help, just a few weeks later, there was a body, mind, spirit expo with various mediums, healers, and speakers, about a five-minute walk from my place. I had this flyer lying on my kitchen counter, and my Guides were nagging me, telling me to get my butt out the door to that fair. I remember being slightly startled by the sheer force, which was loving yet firm.

I had no idea what to expect and wandered around for a bit, looking at the sheet of speakers and those offering readings. Only two caught my eye: Brecht Saelens, a Belgian medium who works in Lilydale, New York, and Alania Starhawk, a divine channel from the Tampa Bay area.

Having had a reading with Brecht, who is fantastic, I sat out in the late-autumn sun for a while, waiting for my session with Alania.

She remembers me plopping down on the chair in front of her, being this big bubble of joyous light, talking away. The instant I connected with her, I knew that she could help me; however, little did I know then that I would embark on a very intense healing journey through the Akashic Records, retrieving many fragmented pieces of my soul and removing many lodged 'splintered' pieces within my mind.

Regardless of how many layers you have cloaked yourself with, you are still a beautiful, radiant BEing of light divine. So, even if life throws you a sledgehammer or submerges your soul in a cold spring morn's pond, always rock on and shine forth, unless you choose to drown in your "kinkilicious" sorrows, causing you but a mere mishap of a created series of unfortunate events.

"Ain't Life just a bit like shootin' hoops in basketball? You shoot, you score, in the light of one's true focus, or miss by a tenth of an inch as the balls hits the rims and bounces back, as one's dribble is off-kilter and one's footwork won't play ball due to the trippin' up by one's opponents in the game, but that is the play and outcome of one's chosen experiences. As long as you take responsibility, get up, dust off, take the learnings and continue on, you never fail; the EGOtistical conditioned Mind tricks you into thinking it so. All experiences teach you to counteract due diligently and to step on up to the plate and up your game to the ascension and elevation of slam dunkin' that ball to the netting of a 'home run,' onto the next level of the playing field in your awareness.

Rise to the challenge; remain not on the bench with your head bowed down in defeat. Re-strategise, rethink, get up and expand the whizz of your flow, for we are rooting for you from the side-lines, unable to, as per the "rules' intervene, so 'playa' keep on playin'," and keep on keepin' on, as ultimately the court is yours for the taking."

~The Divine Shakespeare Club~

I knew that even though I was still stumbling in the dark, not quite knowing a way forward, I had already started making strides in changing my ways. I knew this was Spirit's way of telling me to keep going, that I was on the right track—I just had to keep ploughing ahead.

Shamanic Egg Cleanse

If kambo scares the crap out of you, and you'd rather not puke your guts out, then I suggest trying a shamanic egg cleanse with psychic and physical trance medium, healer, and spiritual teacher Garry Edwards (www.garryedwardsspiritconnections. co.uk), who gives advice without sugar-coating it. He calls himself the marmite medium. You either hate him or love him because if you want his help, don't expect him to feel sorry for you. Do you want out of your misery? Then you'll have to walk back in and through.

I did this 2021 and had no idea what to expect. What was he going to do, splat the egg? I went in with zero expectations. If we are attached to an outcome or afraid of an answer, we may unintentionally block our perceptive abilities, letting our fear take the reins. We block the energy rather than letting it free-flow through our body and soul. It's the spiritual version of sticking our fingers in our ears, drowning out the 'noise' and saying, talk to the hand 'cause the face ain't listening.

The night before my first session, he was working on me while preparing the egg because I felt myself getting nauseous and lightheaded, which made him chuckle—me less so as I was feeling sick as a pig.

Preparing the egg typically involves smoke and an egg. One doesn't literally "smoke" the egg, but the client's aura is cleansed, which can be done via distant healing. The following day, after leaving the egg floating in a glass of water overnight, he read it for me.

Mine was pretty much crystal-clear. Then again, I have always believed that when we heal, our outlook on life changes, and those kinks in the cable that we created, blocking the flow of ourselves, will duly disintegrate. The amount of symbolism, numbers, and people found within the floating egg in that single glass of water is incredible. Garry subsequently left the egg for a few days, which must have reeked to high heaven, leaving me with several sleepless nights, causing me to crash out in the middle of the day due to the massive internal energy shifts. This happens due to the big cleanse that is sweeping through your soul—the question is whether you choose to incessantly cling to the old or decide to let go. I let it all go, and I could feel the bounciness of my mind and the lightness of a summer's breeze airing through the corridors of my heart again.

After the cleanse, it was like the fog within my head had cleared up, and my communication with the Light BEings became far more transparent.

Healing eases the breath of the soul, removing cluttered weight from the mind. Do we not owe it to ourselves to heal up, to be able to live a far more enriched and abundant life? We hold on to so many things that keep us trapped in our own dogma, our own created prison – yet we all hold the key and have always been the key to unlocking the doors to the liberation and expansion of ourselves. The shamanic egg cleanse with Garry was a magical yet bumpy joyride for me, but as with all healing, you need to keep working on yourself rather than slipping back into the discomfort of the old.

Akashic Record Healing and Past Lives

"Hello you, it's me here. I want to reintroduce the you in me and the me in you, back to forging a connection and fusing the you in me and the me in you back to the Authenticity of the Whole of the All that is so 'wholesomeliciously' you.

It's funny how time flies, yet what you do with the time given to you is what makes your life worthwhile. You can either choose to remain in the stickiness of one's created and self-absorbed experiences or stick up your middle finger and tackle life's so-called problems head-on, transcending all and living the life of your dreams and aspirations. There is no greater barrier than the reflection peek-a-booing back in the mirror."

~The Divine~

On my healing journey, I've walked through the halls of Akasha with Alania, later simply picking up on past lifetimes by sitting in the stillness of myself, the quietude of my I AM presence stirring memories in the depths of my soul, learning to understand more about myself and the various aspects of other lives lived. It is learning from the all that I AM since it separated from the oneness and took on this earthly incarnation, becoming an individuated aspect of the divine, retracing my steps through the journey of life back to the spark and the remembrance of who I truly AM.

The Akashic Records are etheric records of all experiences from all lifetimes across all multidimensional realities. They are a holographic archive or storage room filled with endless data on all of human consciousness containing past, present, and potential futures. Every single soul's information is stored here, and as you currently live and breathe in your current incarnation, it is continuing to be written energetically—you are the author to the ink of your holographic book of life, a record-keeper to the experiences of your soul in its current incarnation.

I have visited the Akashic halls several times. It's like this incroyable never-ending book repository to me, but all in the form of energetic holographic imprints. Upon opening one of these books, the energy dances ever so beautifully in front of your eyes. It's kind of cool, as I've seen the energy of books change according to the infinite experiences that souls garner, and thus I call it a library of evolving consciousness. DNA is a living and dancing encoded energetic history of truth and life that holds the blueprint encoded of each and every one of you and all that is, for you are the breath and life of the universe. Everything you think you know is recorded and stored within the DNA structure of your cells, with the encrypted data being read back and interpreted as your memory.

All we need to do to learn to access the encryption is to live in our authentic truth, merely by being real with ourselves, to understand the plan of existence and the history of both the Earth and the cosmos. To me, it has always been a beautiful modern antiquarian library with many winding sleek staircases—seemingly endless, timeless, and such a wonder to behold.

No Akashic Record healing session is the same. All involve traipsing through the different dimensional surfacing lifetimes, requesting healing, releasing, and clearing beliefs and patterns that are no longer of service to us, allowing new energies and perspectives to flow gently into our lives. My lifetimes have all been different. I've been both male and female, having lived both sides of that flipped coin, coming to terms with learning to understand duality. I've lived as a gentle skinny healer along the Brahmaputra River, been a murdering-for-sacrifice Aztec, a thieving and cruel Spanish Inquisitor in the South Americas, a mundane Roma foot soldier guarding the Aerarium treasury, was beaten senseless by a bunch of nuns in the Middle Ages, been a murdering no-good ruthless Viking, and even lived during the American Civil War, all the while trying to figure out why the heck I incarnated here on Earth in the first place.

Doing Akasha healing has, at times, been intensely emotional, as many things surface, having waited and wanted to be healed for so long, it is a relief for your soul and your body to lighten the load of that carried junk. Not to mention your mind, as you're getting rid of all the overloaded programmed clutter you once piled and stored away. You literally feel your body breathing that sigh of relief, thinking; finally, we can now move past the patterning and the pain of the "caus-ed" self. Your soul always knows the way back home to the light of self; we simply have to learn to hone in and follow its energy trail, to let it lead us through our karmic maze into a more enlightened state of BEing..

You will find that when I channel different aspects of my past lives, the language becomes different, and that is only because I quite literally sit within the very essence of that life, reliving how I felt; it's like these flashes I can step into—like stepping in and out of a movie reel.

Before I continue into my past life with Liam and the changes that occurred due to action on my part as well—because healing and action are a quid pro quo, one cannot do without the other, for if there is no action, the conditioning remains—I want to delve into who I AM and take you on a journey of a few of my rather illustrious past lives. The truth is I have lived countless lives, more than I care to remember, some have come through via the Akashic healing, whilst others have come to me in a dream state or waking state with me simply sitting down and listening to my higher self, cracking the code of my DNA.

Yet, like all of us, I am still learning in this rather confined human body I have been given to work with. But every breath and every step I take is a joyous walk back to myself, and like the munching Pac-Man devouring its 'yummy' experiences, I too am embracing, healing, and alchemising all of my experiences.

Who Am I?

"The I AM Who is the all and nothing encompassing of Who I AM, and yet we are nothing and everything at the same time, ingrained in the infinite part of the All. So, how can we be nothing when we are all part of the total sum of the stratospheric

mathematical equation of the Cosmic Conscious Convolution, breathing, building,
and evolving in the starlit heavens of the multidimensional atmosphere?"

~Ararat / Jiamantiwa~

Do I know who I am? Is it important? In the grand scheme of things, it is not. Like you, I AM nothing and everything at the same time as much as I AM everywhere and nowhere all at once. I AM as much a Houdini in the bottle as a genie out the bottle. I AM you as much as you ARE me, and all are fiery sparks of the great fire of Father Sky. We are mere interconnecting lights, lighting up the multiverse with our conscious omnipresence. Like you, I AM just another Light BEing, another Starseed having chosen to incarnate as a Galactic Ambassador of Light to help with the planetary ascension, ridding it of the eons of implemented darkness, the enslavement of humanity, allowing for all to breathe back to a love of self. I am merely here to help you dance back to your soul vibrance so that you too, may see past the veil of forgetfulness.

Always remember, I AM the I AM in You as much as You are the I AM of the I AM in ME. We are mere extensions of one another, walking each other home.

I AM as much the ruler of all as I AM the master of none, but for the mere current human embodiment I have chosen to wear and serve.

There are infinite planets throughout the multiverse. Having astral travelled, I know I am from the very outer fringes of the Sirian star belt system. I AM a multi-dimensional soul BEing and go by various names, one of which is *A'rarat*, or *A'ra* for short. Indeed, an ode to the beautiful Ararat Mountain range in Turkey.

I'm also a bit of a God Creator, called *Jiamantiwa*, dabbling in architecture, construction, and design—a bit of a Bob the Builder and "bricklayer" of sorts, helping to build worlds from the ground up. The name *Jiamantiwa* was given to me by Alan Pratt and resonated with me on an immensely deep level. It's a clever wordplay on the I AM, *"J-I-AM-mantiwa,"* with the *"J"* in Hebrew as *"Yod"* signifying the presence of God in all things. If you want to go all Star Wars, it's *Yod(a)-I-AM-Mantiwa,* which makes me sound like a mysterious, unearthed Jedi Light Warrior.

I am a bit of a 'riddler,' but then I am the "Loki" of my kind—a rebel, a warrior, and the prodigal daughter. We are tall BEings, a blue hue in colour; however, I am not a Blue Sirian per se. We are, however, very similar in ways but not of the same "species," even though it's not important as we are all divine cosmic balls of energetic awesomeness dipped in glitter. We are divine alchemists: trans-formers, living according to the sacred geometric divine matrix, moving energy at will, creating planetary grids, keeping almanacs of all events, and transmuting the lower densities back to the light of oneness. Some of us have hair, others do not, yet we intermingle. In fact, we have many emissaries that come to visit, and in turn, we visit many other planets within the multiverse, sharing knowledge, helping build galactic hubs, and enhancing communities.

As we are all energy, we are very much "genderless." We are divine shape-shifters, able to transform ourselves at will, so I can be whoever I choose to be. We choose to present ourselves in a form we are most comfortable with. They showed me a glimpse of my capabilities whilst there, and I'd transformed myself into a phoenix at will and could run like the wind, with my legs very different from the humanoid legs I have currently been adorned with.

I am somewhat constricted and a bit of a short-circuiting alchemist in my human form. After more than 200 billion years of playing the game of creation and cosmic evolution, one would think I'd have mastered it by now. It's like having lost my abilities, having lost the mojo to my Merlin, trying to firepower it back up by using all the wrong formulations and creating nothing but a load of blow-ups in my face. I am far taller in my Light BEing form, so this nearly six-foot-tall human body is a bit of a tight squeeze for me and relatively dense in its ways of usage, but as I chose it, I'll have to make do with it, for now, to manoeuvre myself around in whilst on the Earthly planes.

Many of us have lived through the era of Lemuria. We swam the seas and walked the lands to help sustain balance and fairness. We were the mermaids of the crystal blue waters. I, too, have been a mermaid, captured for my language of an enlightened song by the Atlanteans to help integrate species, toning them according to a willed frequency springing a newly created cross-bred species to life. There are many beautiful and enigmatic aquatic Starseeds in the Sirius star belt, hybrids between humans, mammals, and amphibians. Some species I have never seen before but have caught glimpses of on my astral travels; all are here to either observe or guide humanity or keep the peace within the galaxial grid of the multiverse.

Within the different dimensions, different levels of consciousness exist, and for the record, it ain't all love, light, peace, and all that jazz out here. Many aquatics—especially the beautiful yet gentle luminous hybrid crustaceans with their chelae, who are exotic-mineral miners—have often been subjected to enslavement and experiments, with many a rescue mission embarked upon to save them.

I love the gentle six-foot-tall "Squid-heads," as I call them, as they are overly polite yet carry an immense intelligence of the universe within them, making them phenomenal engineers and problem-solvers with their wondrous quizzical and mathematical minds. I have many reptilian friends who are also a multidimensional aspect of who I AM. They are 'awesomeliciously' beautiful, and they know it! They are gracious with shimmering oil-slick changing hues of blues and purples and a fanlike comb on their head. They are incredibly muscular, run like the wind, and are known as the chameleons of their species, astutely blending into their surroundings.

They have been allies in helping resolve conflicts between the many in the multiverse. Though warriors at heart, they are known for their wit, strategic sharpness, and rapid resolutions in combat, yet can be tricksters, making light of any situation, no matter the seriousness—because to them, nothing is unachievable. One simply needs to look at the mathematical improbabilities from a different perspective. They merely state:

"You've got to change the lens if it ain't looking so dandy. You are a trickster of your own Mind, so trick it into believing the impossible, and one will see that by conveying

a different message within, one's world will dramatically change to the many infinite 'possibles' without. Use the hues of your many colours to change the way of the inward warrior, to breathe back life into the outward warrior, taking a different stance on any given situational experience catapulted your way. Duck and dive, or splat on impact, but get up ever so graciously, packing in the experience, strategising your healing back to the al-chemical component of the beautiful translucent hues of the Light of Self."

Entering the stellar dimensional hallways of my home planet, one can only look up in wonder at the beautiful, pristine, iridescent statues that bear a vast resemblance to those that once adorned the many temples in Karnak in Kemet (Egypt), including the beautiful goddess Bastet, a Lyran ruler and descendent, where life was an integration of the many species. A way of life that has long been forgotten and forever lost by the sands of time.

One feels so small, walking from the hangars mouthing into the beautiful entrance hall, opening up into the gateway of the landscapes of my home, with the various species gracing the planet with their humble and divine presence. The colours are so vibrant that one can see the energy emitting and interflowing from and with all of nature: the many pinks, purples, and luminescent blue hues all communicating as one with all sentient BEings.

Many years ago, I was told that I am a Clark Kent by day and Supergirl by night, working undercover with the Galactic Federation of Light and other councils. In truth, I think many of us are "undercover agents"; too "drugged-up," living in the confines of the conditioned matrix we don't always remember.

A Future Past Life

I am still the hit-by-a-brick sadomasochist who came down, incarnating into the earthly realms, getting my knickers in a twist with my experiences, suffering from repetitive donkey syndrome, and getting hopelessly lost in my experiences. I've been a literal car crash at times, yet I've been able to iron out the kinks a little more every time. I have a beautiful pink and red dragon with me, a bit of a doozy snoozer from Lemurian times, who protects me when there's too much fire lit up my arse, and my trusted falcon and guide, Akbar, who has been with me for many eons, and lived an earthly incarnation with me long before the Anunnaki set foot on this planet. A time when the landscapes were far purer, where the sun lit up the lands, and unfiltered and red fiery sunsets bathed the ripples of the sands and many oases of waters.

Humanoid BEings of a far lighter density graced the lands that looked human but weren't quite human. They were far taller, had a far more translucent skin tone of an "imbued" colour variation, longer-shaped faces with beautiful almond-shaped eyes. They lived in captivating rows of dome-shaped buildings, all symmetrically shaped and close to the spirit of the ocean. It was rather quaint to see. If I had to map it, it would be east of the once-future civilisation of Mesopotamia. I know that the Arcturians commenced another civilisation in what we now know to be India, as the Ascended Master Krishna is of Arcturian descent. I lived on the outskirts with my sister, my mother, in this lifetime. I was stealthy, muscular, quick-witted, and whilst on the Earth, not of the Earth. I was watching myself up on the top of my home, my outpost, my face covered due to the sands that would often whip up, causing a whirlwind of dancing particles to lash out and disperse. I could see the vast range of the snow-capped mountains all around me, basking in the glory of the wondrous nature of the Mother.

My home was created with a brown mortar, extremely sturdy, and much of the wooden furniture was carved and bathed in warm textiles, which reflected the light of the flickering flames in the fireplace. The days were warm, but the nights were cold. In the back, we had two yaks that gave us milk, and my sister was brilliant at making clothing and ropes from their fur. We had several inquisitive geese and horses in the stalls, yet there were other modes of "air" transportation for those in the more densely populated "cities." As my former self indicated, *"Think not that sorcery did not exist, for, in those days, there were those of the light as well as the pale shades of darkness, conjuring up but from the etheric realms of bondaged Souls to do their bidding. One was of a lighter nature and far more advanced, yet there were those walking the line of the famished ego, enslaving the many. So advanced and yet but a poor man's taste of a self-inflicted wounded Soul."*

I died by the tip of a poisoned arrow whilst on watch shot by my father in this lifetime. My trusted sidekick Akbar tried to warn me, but instead of diving left, I fell right, and the arrow caught my shoulder, with a black poison spreading rapidly through my upper body. The healer my sister called for was a beautiful, tall, dark, and lean BEing, wearing a purple turban and finely woven yet simple linen-like clothing. He had extremely long, slender, nearly translucent fingers and beautiful, striking features with piercing blue eyes—almost human yet not. He could not extract the poison, as it had seeped too far into the pores of my physical being, and thus I transformed back into the light, on to far greater adventures.

I also have a beautiful griffin that I leave by the wayside far too often. Yet, it has remained sitting rather majestically and silently by my side. Here is his story:

"I the Griffin, half Eagle, half Lion, stand tall before thee, in the very breath of the BEing that is You, a vision of wisdom, bowing before thee in the shimmering of the Light that you are.

It is said that we are the Keepers of treasure, of all that sparkles and shines. In truth, we are the Keepers of Ancient Wisdom, and of the Sacred Tree of Knowledge of all of Life within the interconnectedness of the Enlightened Universal spectrum—that in itself is a Treasure worth far greater than merely the shine of diamonds and pearls. By the guidance of the Creator, the Celestial Father, I stand here in the valour of strength and honour, for I AM one of the Knights of the Ancients, a protector of the many realms, and thus one of the Council of the Protectors of the Realms.

Those that seek us will find us, patiently waiting in the realms of all and none, of here and yonder, yet we are neither here nor there; we simply are.

Life is but a grand spiel of infinite potentials, depending on the sum of the equation of the choices one chooseth to make. Yet, every choice carries multiple equations and thus multiple outcomes, where one continuously relays the grid of oneself, weaving and unweaving the light and dark hues of one's beautiful tapestry, affecting one's own Life and that of the Universal Consciousness, for everyone, and everything is connected to the very breath and Consciousness of all of Life throughout the Cosmos.

When dark forces descend, across the landscapes of the Soul, casting shadows through the engulf-ed Mind, we stand by thee, protecting thee from harm's way. Our sight is piercing, our talons sharp, our wings enfold thee, and our tails whip the shadows back to the dungeons from whence they came. Call on us always, for we will aid thee to strengthen thy resolve by transcending thy fears, walking through the heart of the fire, into the rebirthing of the inner golden phoenix of Self.

Accept the cup of wisdom and have the strength and heart of a lion and the flight and sharpness of an eagle, to rise above the drama into the beauty of the eternal Love and Light of all that makes you, you.

We aid all who aid to seek themselves, seeking their true nature of infinite oneness within the Cosmos of Creation."

~The Council of Cosmic Light~

I am blessed to be able to sit on various councils of light, one of which is the Karmic Board of (Blue) Light, ironing out the anomalies of the universe within the multiverse whilst helping to oversee others. There are many councils throughout the multiverse, more than we are aware of or even care to remember, due to the density of the human form we have taken on. They aid in anchoring the divine feminine upon the earthly sacred geometrical grids, elevating all BEings and the planet into the next dimensional shift of existence through the sheer art of alchemical transmutation back to the brilliance of the Light of One and All. In other words, we are all Universal Light Warriors anchoring the Light grids back upon the Earth, "shooing" away the darkness, a light at a time, a step at a time.

Galactic Lives

Like many of you, I have fought in the galactic wars, forcing many of us to flee to different dimensional vibrations within the galaxy. I incarnated into the lives of various species, living in other dimensions, helping with the evolution of otherworldly planets; however, I have been captured several times and killed in battle due to my often reckless nature, going in heart-first, thinking with my head later.

After one of my past life healing sessions with Louise Rhodes, whom I mentioned earlier, I felt physically ill for nearly two days. I could see myself, in a past life, hovering in the air, with two metal pieces sticking out of the wall, touching my shoulder blades. I was zapped with an electrical current, and the velocity of the current literally threw my body. My captors snapped my back in two, dislodged my arms, broke my funny-shaped fingers, disfigured my face, and left me with stuff oozing out of my nose and ears. I was tortured for information, refusing point-blank to give it to them. Yet, these species were crafty, and even when I died, with my mission a failure, I could always incarnate into another lifetime to continue onwards, as that is the game of the soul's evolution.

I felt so nauseous after the session I nearly collapsed. I was in shock, and my energy had gone haywire; it was as if I was reliving the whole event. After another session to iron out the kinks, I felt much lighter. When you're on the healing journey of recovering yourself, other things will start to pop to the surface rather quickly, all requesting healing.

I got in touch with another amazing galactic healer, Siobhan Purcell, with whom I instantly connected. She has this very ethereal way about her and works with the ancient StarWalkers, as I call them, the Navajo of the planes of the heavenly stars. I zonked out within a minute, going places, seeing many golden galactic light beings, and being light-warped to a different dimensional zone. Siobhan saw me in another space and time within columns and rectangular forms of light, a form of coding to enhance the healing. Although quite different from what one would imagine, the site was an etheric temple, an interdimensional gateway, yet a sacred space for me to heal and receive new golden light codes.

The Galactics always educate and give instructions and can be quite direct and forceful; they do not mince their words in the slightest. They reminded me of my cosmic lineage and that I am a channel to the stars. It was quite profound and amazingly healing for me. As you've read, I have met many different BEings, but many years ago, the Zeta greys hauled me up in their craft. I have no idea what they did to me on the table, but I remember them very distinctly, as they were utterly light on their feet and meticulous in their ways. After they finished, they let me walk around for a bit, as my curiosity got the better of me, allowing me to examine their sleek craft, which had a mostly white interior. They were benevolent BEings and didn't scare me at all.

Many years later, in early 2021, I discovered that the Zetas had implanted a tracker in me, which Louise removed, fine-tuning my telephone line with the divine. I had been on a Draconian ship once, and whilst not all are bad, some care for nothing but conquering the many. You have to observe, understand their game, and play by their rules, to eventually checkmate them. It does not mean that all are malicious, as many have changed their ways, but that is the evolution of their species. To them, there is no victory without sacrifice, yet when I was in that state of awareness on their ship, I thought to myself, *Not again, I've danced this dance with them too many a time, with all their tricks from the ole playbook of war, enslaving those in the multiverse and now the people of man.* Diplomacy does not get one very far, for they will try to manipulate emissaries at every turn. Are they advanced? Yes, very, but so are many other races in the galaxy.

Many races carry the nuances of both light and dark; all are evolving in consciousness and constantly learning. The Andromedans are another very advanced race I have met in my astral state on one of their ships, with a small faction grappling with the darkness. I have had to intervene with their ongoing experiments of cloning species with AI tech. The Councils have implemented rules to avoid species misusing technology and cross-breeding, mixing strands of cocktails on the fly, creating breeds with unknown characteristics, interfering with the natural laws of the cosmos, and upsetting the balance. They're not the only ones, as many operate in the dark under the radar. The Andromedans can jump into any timeline within the earthly realms. They told me I was precisely 85 light-years away from Earth, which is, by my calculation, somewhere in the Sagittarius belt. This sounds like science-fiction, but I can assure you it is not.

In one of my galactic lives, I was one of the last ones standing on a red and dying planet, once beautiful but now covered in ashes and smoke. The air was so thick and putrid that it was hard to breathe in the atmosphere. I was tasked with unearthing the beautiful orange pulsating crystals that had been covered by dark forces, starving the planet of all its life. I was in a state of sadness for the destruction and utter demise of this beautiful planet that I had called home for many moons. Two of us were left, while the rest had succumbed to their injuries, and we managed to uncover and encode all crystals to breathe back life into the heart of the planet. Yet, we too got caught, being "chained" and either enslaved or eradicated. Even though my "sister" had died on land, I was executed and was blissfully welcomed back to the light of home.

This planet was once beautiful in the height of its existence, with numerous floating landmasses, various enlightened and ethereal races and species, and many emissaries of light visiting. I called it the land of two rising Suns. The structure of the many buildings varied, but all were made of a far sleeker design, materials that are unknown on Earth, and the lay of the land was lush, with many pools and lakes of water, and plant life and species of animals unbeknownst to me. All life breathed through the sacred geometrical grid of a crystalline existence that kept the planet thriving and in balance. Science and spirituality walked hand-in-hand, thriving in unison. All adhered to the laws of genomics to further the education and development of all species and to respect the natural flow of the planet and each other.

Nimrod

I have thought long and hard about inserting this aspect of a life once lived because my Guides only gave me the name *Nimrod* and *hybrid Anunnaki*, and I was like, Who the hell is that, and what do you want me to do with these two words? My Guides were like, "Sit in the essence of the life that once was, and rewrite the wrongs of a story once told."

"As I stand here pensively staring at my rather hairy yet dusty feet in brown leather-bound sandals, with the wind blowing gently in my face atop the beautiful Babylonian mountainous landscape steeped with its lush valleys below and curving clear rivers, the sweet scent of jasmine lingering in the air, tickling my nostrils, I come back returning to a sense of Self, rather than being the gruff of a giant I have more often

been than not. Was I a brute? No, I was the prodigal son and was more of a rebel, living life according to the tune of my own heart, yet was vastly misunderstood and misinterpreted and deformed in the wording over eons of time, having passed the many ancient tongues of Man. My manes were long, and the hair on my back was merely what made me more of a hue-man. I was a hybrid, a brew of half a man and half Anunnaki created to aid humanity in the learn-ed ways of governing themselves.

I was once a revered King of Babylon, yet I too, had to learn the art of kinship with the many I was given to watch over and govern. I was often at war with myself, which spilled into being at war with those around me. I was a creator of structure, yet a 'deconstructor' of mechanical equations to outcomes I did not perceive to be of value nor believe in, which caused a rupture amongst the young people of Man. These wondrous yet eager sproutlings had just sprung on the ladder of Earth's evolution, taking but root and planting their seeds further into an existence and co-existence of the species.

Humanity needed structure to learn and to thrive, to build better lives for themselves, and cultivate the lands into creating something beautiful in turn, building onto that – for life is a series of stepping stones of expanding one's awareness.

Was I better than others? No. But my EGO thought otherwise, and thus I often battled with the heart and mind of myself. Humanity once became, has become, and is still evolving into be-com-ing, much to the hindrance and chagrin of the ones losing grip of the strings.

All wordplay dances but playfully in front of one's eyes wide shut, leaving one standing in the huh of the gullible naked mole-rat one has conditioned the self to become. The name of Nim-rod was given to me by the Celestial Gods of the Skies above, for 'nim' is the mere game equating to mathematical strategies; as such, humanity is a mathematical constructed equation created according to the sacred geometrical divine nature of the holographic Universe to help elevate the Earth's Consciousness as much as the Conscious Spark of their own Soul Light, syncing back to the heart of the sacred Divine Self, by diving into the sum of the equations of life's experiences and gemming the Self up to the hexagonal inverted double pyramid of the mathematical wonder one is and always has been. 'Rod' refers to the staff of the Creator, who created hue-manity, helping to guide the flock of newly born hue-mans into the direction of creating themselves to an enlightened state of BEingness, as much as I was known as a lightning rod for causing controversy in the thinking of the many.

I wasn't exactly my father's favourite son. I was an architect, a builder, yet in a warring of conflict with myself, causing a mesmeric dance of conflict and divergence from the Light of myself to the depths of darkness within. I struggled with myself in my hybrid humanity, thinking of ways to experiment and experience life. I have often been depicted as evil, but evil merely stands for 'eve-ill,' meaning I wasn't balanced with the feminine counterpart of myself and thus imbalanced of love and light.

Eventually, in the war zone of myself, another hand befriended me and pulled me out of the fire of my EGO. Was I wilted? Yes, but one can regrow from the nothingness that one feels within to the all of a blossoming heart to the world one chooses to shine forth without. *Build a life from love, not from the wayward EGO, and the stampede of the bullish wars within will settle and resolve themselves like the taming of a wild bull. Befriend the EGO to cleanse the mind of one's unhealed suffering, and one will embrace the light of one's heart to build forth a life of deservance.*

Be it known that the many invasive wars into the region along the Tigris and Euphrates rivers, once known as the thriving region of Babylon, and baptised as modern-day Iraq, with the lands turned to a purposely created arid dust, a shimmer of the ripples of its former glorious self, was merely initiated under the guise of a false flag, and created to extract 'hybrid' DNA, preserved helix strands and technology from the chambers of a lost 'tomb' found, whilst plundering and bombing everything in their wake, leaving no trace of all that once was, and transporting all back across the seas to commence experimenting on cross-pollinating species, leaving humanity none the wiser that in truth there was a wretched game of war being fought, but not for the tyrant of the ruling lands, but for the mere greed of the powers at play. Poor are those that seek to enliven the senses of the EGO, and rich are those that are humbled by the truth of the loving divine equation they have so understood themselves to be.

History is on a continuous replay and repeat, and humanity has lost the art of co-creating in unity with each other. All have become much like the defamatory fallen Babylonian Tower of Babel, having grown into the roots of the EGO, and lost the art of understanding one another, causing strife and an animus feeling within the many. Chaos drives fear, and fear is what those in seat prey on, whereas if humanity were to look within their hearts, pouring the cup of love and forgiveness, much could be achieved. It is up to the people to deconstruct the created egotistical tower and rebuild it from the ground of the heart up.

Humanity procreates, living in the perpetual ignorance of understanding co-creation. Expressing and creating yourselves through co-creation allows all dormant buds to grow back to the harmonious unit of becoming wholesome and blossoming within and with each other. Once co-creation is understood, pro-creation can commence in a state of a bloomed awakened awareness through the art of communal co-creation. When all gain mastery in co-creating as one, allowing for separation to dissipate like the warm rays of the enlightened morning sun, only then can one truly understand the term to procreate, and should one wish it so, will it forth in but in an exuberance of Divine Conscious living."

A High Priestess in Atlantis

As for my earthly lives, fast forward to my time in Atlantis, having chosen to incarnate to help with the planet's evolution, seeing Earth was veering into an abysmal direction due to other species having interfered. But the Galactic Council would not allow interference to save the human race. Humanity has its own trajectory for its evolutionary progress, and thus many in the galactic arena have chosen to incarnate to help humanity shift away from the impending darkness returning to the vibration of the Light, ascending the planet to the next level of vibrational consciousness.

Due to the bout of forgetfulness upon incarnating, we have to find our way through the jungle game of life with all its rules and regulations to a remembrance of self and our mission. We make it all sound so difficult, but it is utterly simple; it is just manoeuvring ourselves through the game, understanding the rules, and then playing the game according to our own rules, dancing our way back to the divinity of ourselves. I have lived many lifetimes from the outset of the Atlantis experiment. It was a place where many awakened souls descended from the strands of DNA infusions of the many galactic races, wishing to help humanity evolve towards the higher planes of consciousness. Atlantis was a beautiful place, with moderate temperatures, lush green nature, and a vast array of botanical and healing herbs and plants, some no longer in existence. Atlantis offered harmonious living, beautiful, timeless structures, the likes of which are not seen today, with temples built on sacred geometrical grids to help heal the land, tend to Mother Earth's Garden, and keep the vibration of the people in tune with their higher selves.

Everything was built along ley lines per the resonance of crystal grids. The Atlanteans were technologically far more advanced than we are today, with various emissaries visiting from other home planets. But as with all cycles, light turned to dark, and the darkness muddied the once-pure lands, blanketing the earth in unenlightenment, with duality becoming ingrained within the mindset of the Atlantean people. The more advanced they became, the more powerful some felt, wanting dominance over the species—and many wars erupted.

I was a high priestess serving one of the temples, having studied within the Golden Gate City in the Temple of Poseidon, working with the wonders of the herbs and plants of the Earth, and serving the many people that sought my help. Yet I too fell under the relentless spell of darkness, becoming incapacitated, with my powers and awareness stripped and scrambled, causing an identity crisis, until I no longer knew who I was, and thus fell prey to believing in the illusion of separation from the whole, choosing to indulge in my selfish pursuits. The darkness in me chose to devour the light, shifting my awareness and dimming the light within, manipulating the many. The joy of power through the art of manipulation was far grander than serving the light, for light talked of equality and unison. Yet, darkness taught us the glory of elevating ourselves, believing ourselves to be of a higher standing than others.

For so long, I had tapped into my power to serve others, yet now I served the greater good of myself. The tear in the veil unravelled upon Atlantis like the soft falling of snow, not tangible at first, but like a thief in the night, it crept in and seeped into the hearts and minds of the many, engulfing us with the slow poison of its toxicity. Life became an entangled case of warring dualisms, and living in the dualities, having lost our connection with the whole, having erased God out of existence, and worshipping false "idols."

Through experimenting with advanced technology, engineers and scientists began interbreeding human-animal chimeras; that got vastly out of control as they created an army of these creatures, tinkering with various DNA strands, cross-pollinating and creating fusions that would devour on the battlefield. The war tore a veil between the Sons of Belial (Reptilians) and the Law of One, until the Council stepped in to halt the experiment, and the vast waters of the ocean submerged the once fertile and beatific lands of Atlantis.

The many masters of the beholden ancient knowledge and wisdom warned of the coming shift of tectonic plates that would cause a tsunami and swallow the islands, letting what once was and could never be again rest under the ocean waves. Many heard the silent call and travelled to settle and instil the ancient wisdom in the rebuilt colonies in the South Americas, along the banks of the river Nile, parts of Europe, the lands of Egypt, Tibet, and further afield.

To feel powerful for one's own gain is an experience that was new to many, and yet, regardless of having been stripped of all my awareness, I chose to have a change of heart and trample on the many that required my help. I drowned in the swirling waters, unable to withstand the brute force of nature that submerged me through the drowning of my lungs back into the light and in the full bloom of my loving, authentic self.

My Lives in Ancient Egypt

I have lived many lifetimes in Ancient Egypt, several of which I remember rather vividly and have come to me over the years. Tens of thousands of years before the lands of Ancient Egypt birthed into existence, there were other civilisations that extended to the west into Africa and beyond, with lands that once were but are no longer. The rivers and seas were more expansive, the waters crystalline, the soil far more enriched and fertile than today, and a multitude of humanoid and intergalactic races graced its surface, living in harmonious existence. It was a return to a pure love for self and all of humankind, where the ego had no place; one was at peace, and fertility bloomed in what is now known as the Sahara Desert, where Man coexisted with the Gods from the sky, learning from them in much gratitude to help the Earthly Mother with her progress of evolution.

I lived as a hybrid human queen of Ancient Egypt, with both human and Sirian DNA dancing through my veins, and thus was a BEing with a beautifully elongated skull with visionary purpose. Many will say this was caused by cranial deformation, which existed in many later cultures, and that there are no such things as hybrids. But I urge you to look at yourself in the mirror, for you are as much a hybrid of intertwining encoded DNA strands as everyone on this planet.

Even as Atlantis came to its end, many Sirians, Lyrans, and Pleiadeans had been on scientific expeditions, garnering information and creating several humanoid races, using their strands of DNA, blending this with the strands of the more prehistoric humans, thus creating a far more intelligent species. And yet, many fell in love with humans and mated with them, producing different hybrids, and I was one of these.

Many civilisations coexisted across the vast landscapes of the Earth, just like the Arcturians set foot and flourished in the area we now call India, or the Pleiadeans, who made a home on the grid in the Nordic regions and have often been depicted as the Nordic Gods. Many think that the Anunnaki were not around at the same time; however, on several occasions, they made their way to Ancient Egypt, seeking council. Even though these created civilisations were like two peas in a pod, we chose to share our knowledge for the betterment of the people. Ours was a spiritual nurturing of the soul and enhancing our consciousness working with the spirit of the Mother, whilst theirs was a technologically advanced nature. Yet, even here, there were warring factions, and not all were of love and light. Still, Ancient Egypt thrived with its many multidimensional gateways, visiting emissaries, and beautiful buildings built according to the sacred geometrical grid of the Earth.

Its many gold-capped pyramids, built by the Atlantean "Gods" that fled the floods of Atlantis in conjunction with the Egyptian people, were constructed in line according to Polaris, the northern star in the Ursae Minoris constellation, and harnessed the power of transmitting energy. In other words, they were "power" plants, but they also studied the constellations to calculate the best time to plant seeds for optimum growth. The pyramids symbolise the cycles of expansion, evolution, and transformation of human consciousness, leading to a higher state of BEing, eventually returning to the fold and the flow of oneness of the great cosmic central sun.

My mother in that lifetime, who I saw as a little girl in her white dress playing around in the courtyards with wooden dolls and balls, was a distant niece. My father was my uncle and a priest in the temple of Amun-Ra, and I frequently sought his counsel. After years of intensive studies and various gruelling yet illuminating initiations, he was initiated into the Thoth mystery schools, eventually taking his place in the Council of the Great White Brotherhood. It was a time when all life was honoured, and all remained aligned with the celestial heavens and the breath of the Earth. Yet, thousands of years later, many priests within the kingdom became corrupt, having been enriched considerably through lands given by various rulers and those requiring favours.

Priests learned the art of bribery, and thus, the ego sang its song slowly back into the hearts of man. Ma'at—who fled the floods of Atlantis and is of Sirian descent, just like Osiris, whom she is often associated with in helping balance the scales of the hearts of man—was my close friend and confidante. She was funny and light-hearted, yet sharp and serious, especially to those she taught. We sat many a night discussing the well-being of the people of Egypt, drinking a brew of water mixed with fermented honey, lemon, anise seed, and a fruity hint of plum.

"I AM Ma'at, Daughter of Ra, twin flame to Thoth. A High Priestess to the ancestral lineage of the once but washed away cities of Atlantis, having fled the floods to live

but in the lands of what was to become the rising rays of the Amun Ra of basking in the warmth of the fertile lands once known as Ancient Egypt. I created balance, and fairness for all, for without an equilibrium within the people, they too would be doomed like the experiment of the once golden age of Atlantis and sucked into the swirling tides by the Brotherhood of the Dark, that ceased at nothing to cause but divisiveness instilling chaos in the hearts of Man. And succeed they did, with a cunning yet 'exuberant' glee in their hearts, with many recanting the beautiful hue of their Light. Yet our ways flourished, and the net of peace was cast in all corners of Kemet, where all worked according to the seasons of the sun, the moon, and the stars, and the 'Creator Gods' were merely seen as the just of the land, as equals in the brethren of Man, aiding in the planetary ascension through the transformational axis of Consciousness. I am the seeker of Truth, server of the just, serving karma to the unjust but ever so flavoursome and with a sheer twinkle of delight. I am the Keeper of the old ways, for it is through the mere art of ancient knowledge that one illuminates one's Conscious Awareness returning to the Godhood of Self. Restoring inner balance requires one to offload the bothersome thoughts of one's experiences that have given way to the mist within the Mind. I merely help those that choose to help themselves. Pity is but for fools, and a fool you are not, my Child. Detach from the honey-trapped experiences you have so fallen prone to, empowering the Self back to the embodiment of Life. The Soul's journey is about progression, not remaining idly within a sinking jar o' honey. Follow the path of your heart, for to love yourself is to heal yourself, and if you cannot love yourself, how pray tell me, can you heal yourself? Tipping the scales serves one but for an immoral way of Life concluding but to a barrage of ill at ease energies creating an effect within the all of one's Life. Balance of the feminine and masculine is the key to following the path back home to the Self. Do not deflect, but reflect, relinquish, and release and know that the scales of the once dis-eas-ed Soul will be eas-ed and balanced back to the lightness of the very breath of the Divine Cosmic Order of Self."

We gave thanks to the creator and all of creation for keeping the balance of the people and the lands. During those times, gratitude, grace, and respect were essential components of blissful living. Balance is like a piano key to tuning the Earth's instrument. It's simple really, for when the people on the lands of the evolving Mother are happy and have a nurturing respect and love for her, the Earth echoes back those same qualities to the very people on her surface. When all work jointly and in unity, with a warmth for all and everything, all in turn sing to the melodious tune of a harmonic vibrance. When one believes in separation, everything becomes disjointed, and people work not as a community but as a bipartisan disassociation of the self and the whole.

I was olive-skinned, with striking features and long, flowing 'wiggilicious' brown 'hair'—never a fan of the beautiful headgear worn by many. I was an avid beekeeper and extremely passionate about it, as honey was a gift from the Sun God Ra. Usually, the priests in the temples kept bees; however, I loved everything to do with nature and herbs—especially dill, to keep my body in balance—and had a keen eye for bees from a young age. Bees are wonderful pollinators, dancing amongst the many blossoming flowers, sipping on the sweet nectar, and carrying 'pollen baskets' 'strapped' around their tiny legs, couriering this back to the hive. I loved taking a stroll down to the port before dawn, walking through the quiet streets down to the harbour, watching the men and their reed boats glide quietly into the waters, and sometimes I'd venture out and join them.

My favourite fish was tilapia, something I have never eaten or prepared in this lifetime, but I can see myself sprinkling olive oil with a hint of garlic and squeezed lemons over the cooked fish. Such simple, nutritious foods without chemical additives were a sheer delight.

My other half, my twin flame, who incarnated with me in that lifetime to help raise the vibration of the people, was far darker-skinned, with piercing blue/brown eyes and an athletic physique. He was a thoughtful man, who often took the time to walk amongst the people, listening to them, and was all about implementing changes where he could, yet all had to be in agreement with the lands, for an imbalance would cause a disruption in the flow of the Earth's vibrational frequencies and upset the balance of the Mother, who was duly respected in all ways. He was a philosopher and an analytical thinker at heart, often wanting to know the why and how of things. One would often find him in the library reading from the vast number of scrolls that were categorically catalogued. He loved his sports and had tremendous physical endurance: a skilled archer, javelin thrower, avid rower, and swimmer, and joined in with many other sporting events, especially tug of war, creating a sense of equality and community. He says:

"The body is the earthly temple, but so is the mind. If the mind falters to thoughts of dis-ease and one refutes for the mind to be cleansed, the body suffers from the fallout of the protruding ailments of the beaten and weeping Soul. Treat your mind with dignity and respect, and feed it with the prayer of daily meditation to keep your beautiful Light of Soul within the chosen 'hous-ed' body at peace. Silence is the elixir to enlighten the Light and vibrance of your Soul. If you cannot love your mind or your body, you cannot hold a love for your Soul. The mind, body, and soul are all interconnected cosmic wires, each complimenting the other in the workings of the beautiful physical embodiment your Soul has incarnated into. Use its vehicle wisely until one day 'death' departs one dearly back into the Light of Amun-Ra.

Remember to carry a hand filled with a graciousness of eternal gratitude for your experiences as they foster a nourishment for both one's Mind and Spirit. Much like freshly harvested grain slipping through your fingers—experiences should be as such, with the mere remnants of the 'dust' swirls thereof, dissipating into the healing ethers of love and understanding. Forgiveness is like rich compost to the Soul, allowing the heart nor the mind to be burdened but acutely fertilised, with the flourishing of the evolution of Self, and thus, all flows into the gentle streams, mouthing into the rivers of growth and the unfoldment of all of one's creation. Be in acceptance of all fellow man with a mere aptitude of understanding through the 'learn-ed' heart, overflowing others with the cup of love thereof."

I chuckle because my twin flame knew Osiris in that lifetime yet has no conscious recollection thereof in this life. Osiris has always been depicted as "green" because he is of Sirian descent. He calls himself a "mental mind philosopher" and soul "realisator," as he wrecks your brains for you to walk the path of remembrance to the light you are and the realisation of the self in God as much as God in the self. He is one of the more serious Ascended Masters and says:

"The Divine exists within you as much as it exists outside of you in all things and in each moment, for you are the breath of the infinite part of the breath of all. Your spirit never dies; its vibrational fire merely dances from incarnation to incarnation, finding its way back to a unison of oneself and the planet. Remain in the vibration of Love, and all will dance but accordingly to the Soul's command and mere wishes fulfilled.

One should not roam in fear of fear itself but conquer the darkness of the mind's ingested thoughts, having allowed oneself to bleed profusely from the created 'head' wounds that have seeped into the bane of one's existence. Out of the wallowing darkness, one can only spring forth back into the light or remain but damned eternal, roaming in the fires of the fearful shadows of self. You are a light within man as much as man is a light unto himself."

People have often asked whether the Egyptian deities wore masks or were a hybrid fusion of a human and animal. Anubis chuckles at this. He says, *"We were not chimeras, yet be it known that not all were of a good ilk, for we were feigned in our ways towards hue-manity. We wore masks and were often depicted within temples and funeral rites as half breeds, yet we were not. It was a mere form of authoritarian yet loving governing. Thus, we hid our features to reverberate that level of authority to the created hue-man race—carrying these traits of Self as portrayed by the mere reflection of that chosen animal within themselves. We were of this world, and yet we were not. Were we humanoid in appearance? Yes, but we were far taller, carrying a variant of Galactic DNA strands, and were thus of different descent, yet the Light in us all remains the same. We were far more advanced in our ways, and these 'masks' were made of an alloy that was light and breathable and retracted within our body armour. Humanity depicted us as Gods, and we were revered and worshipped as such, for we walked into the land of luscious 'sands' and created the ancient and wondrous civilisation once known as Kemet, under the rule of the Ennead, the land of a thousand cosmic unfolding suns, enlightened by the loving rays of Amun-Ra."*

My other half worked with many of the Star BEings, often referred to as the Atlantean "Gods," as a hydraulic engineer. Generating power in those days, one relied on the rays of the celestial embodiment of Amun Ra; they knew that to harness the power of energy, the gateway to the manifestation thereof was to use a combination of sound and voice vibration, metal conductors, and crystals. It's not rocket science that crystals carry a vibration and are an ancient technology used to transmit energy. All the elements used were connected and aligned accordingly. As above, so below, as within, so without—working in perfect alignment according to the grid of existence. I am sure many of you have crystal obelisks and use them for healing, knowing full well that they aid in accelerating the healing process due to the encoded frequencies. How do you feel afterwards when you lie on a bed of crystals? The Egyptian obelisks were made of granite and quartz and served as crystal amplifiers. The pyramids built on the earth's surface would absorb and harness the frequencies from deep within the earth and convert the energies into electromagnetic frequency waves. The earth is energy, always will be, always has been.

It is not a new technology; even the ancient Atlanteans used crystals to harness energy. You've been had if you still believe that the pyramids are tombs. This is what those governing want you to believe because humanity cannot awaken from the ruse they have been fed for eons—that would mean clean, wireless, and free energy for all and losing the grip of power over the people that have been confined to paying to live in the regulated artificial matrix of the big blue marble, called Earth.

A Life as an Artist and Messenger of the Courts

I lived another life in Ancient Egypt before the wars of Ramesses II, who was the embodiment of the Ascended Master Kuthumi, doorkeeper of ancient mysteries and knowledge, and co-protector of the Holy Grail. I was a young female/male painter, an artist of the court, and worked as a messenger for the high priestess, learning from her throughout my life. Travelling between the Temple and the great halls of Ramesses II, walking through the many grand halls and pillars, I was of service with such joy in my heart.

As I channelled that past lifetime, I could not identify myself as either male or female, and I was told that life and aspects of love in Ancient Egypt were vastly different from how we perceive them in today's labelled society. Even though separation started to creep in, gender fluidity was life in all of its acceptance, for love is love.

Love is the creation of everything, and all of oneness exists as much within you as it exists without you. You are part of the Creator, part of the oneness in everything, reflecting this in each other and back at Supreme Creator.

Your soul defines you, not your gender. You are a divine holographic imprint of the multiverse. You are consciousness and fluidity in motion. You are genderless, for you are a sparkling light particle of the beautiful divine grace that shines forth in the beauty of your physical embodiment. If you dance, flowing and blending with the oneness in all, life instantly becomes far more beautiful, for differentiation is no more. Yet, one defines another as a separate entity through the validity of misconstrued labels, all because of a fed narrative of a societal and conditioned existence through a created one-dimensional matrix, rather than the multidimensional kaleidoscope of the whole of a unified existence. Love is love; it asks not for gender nor a labelling thereof. How can it? When you are divine love incarnate. It is your nature. Love is wholesome, universal, and the very expression of who you are. As my once former self continues:

"Where rose the sun along the banks of the river Nile, in the quiet of the morn, but for the ibises standing majestically in the stillness of the reflecting waters, their feathers catching the breeze, probing the banks but astutely for their early daybreak meal, I sat but quietly with my thoughts, contemplating life, watching the breaking of the dawn, the warm rays of Amun-Ra joyfully playing hide-and-seek with the eternal shadows cast, gently caressing the lands, bathing the coolness of the Earth bringing but the very breath of the warmth back from the chill of the night.

Sketching in this peaceful bliss of silence but for the faint sounds of nature and the gentle rustling of the papyrus plants along the river banks, this was my quiet before rising to my day of service to the courts and the Temple. I cared but for the simplicities of life and the warmth and joy of the sun rays dancing on my face. I was never one to relinquish a challenge, having burnt myself many a time for being proven wrong in my doings. Yet this did not deter my laughter, joy, and wanting to learn from the high priestess of the Temple, for she failed me not. A great lover of tending and growing herbs, a forte to the fingers I beheld. The smells of sweet jasmine, floral lavender, invigorating mint, musky frankincense, myrrh, and the spice of fresh thyme, carried by the gentle breeze, enriched and enlivened the senses of all who walked through—used in the foods prepared and in aiding the sick, preparing remedial medicine to heal their ailments. The Nile and all of Life were once so pure, the lands once fertile, and the priestesses in service to Isis and Hathor blessed the lands giving thanks to the harvest bestowed upon the people, where the Divine ruled the land, in peace, in fairness and harmony, connecting through the heart space to All and Nature. Egypt was a'bloom and thrived under the Sun God Ra. In gratitude, we were for the gifts of Mother Earth.

I lived during a time when Ramses II had ascended the throne. Yet noble in his ways, he ruled with the staff of wielding power, bloodshed, and greed with a status of self-importance, a vanity at its finest, where the sore of individuality slowly crept in. The kingdom thrived under the grand allure of the architecture of ingeniously designed buildings, temples of worship, and statues. Life was beautiful, and yet there was an unease in the lingering of the Soul, felt by the many, a tremor in the energy that the old ways were dying and that the magic beheld was but fading. And even when my time came crossing from hither to yonder, when my body could be of service no more, leaving the lands, I loved and cherished, wandering through the tunnel back to the Light and warmth of my Spirit home, watching from the banks of yon, I wept, for humanity was my evolutionary grace, a learn-ed process, and I carried nothing but love for those that walked the lands of the beautiful Mother.

Eventually, many moons later, the old ways died and were no more, for darkness befell upon the lands of Milk and Honey, and war and chaos reigned as the EGO rode once more but victoriously through the hearts of Man, slaying all of the Light with the mere blade and sharpness of his scythe.

Life died, and Anubis mourned, for the air filled with the pungent smell of death, carried across the lands by the winds of change. Blood flowed deep into the veins of Mother Earth, and she wept. The richness of the land turned to dust. The old ways were no more, but a faded memory washed away by the receding waters from the banks of the river Nile, hidden for thousands of years, lying dormant throughout the *changing of the seasons, whilst mankind lost its way, and all but focused on the Self—on the Me in Me, as opposed to the Me in We. Wretched greed and power took hold and ruled the lands, and separation crept in, with fear the instigator in the People of Man, to control the ways of the winding roads cast. And yet the old ways will be born anew, for people are waking from their deep slumber, having walked through the intrepid darkness—their selfish ways no more. The wisdom of the ancients re-emerging, through a faint whisper of remembrance, living in the grid of a heart awareness once more. Nourishing and treating the Mother with a deserved honour and respect, as much as having that honour and respect for the Self and all sentient BEings - for all is Consciousness, all is Divine. The balance of nature restored, a disconnect no more, and mankind will flourish yet again, living a life in a chosen harmony, with a Divine Love towards All."*

The Life of a Priestess in Service of Isis

I find myself, a high priestess in Kemet, walking through the marble and alabaster halls in the Temple of Isis and Hathor, with the smell of amber and frankincense in the air, looking out over the city with the thin white linen curtains gently blowing in the breeze. I had a love for Egypt, its people, and its many races and was in service, nurturing the Mother Goddess in the Temple of the Womb of Fertility, allowing the richness to flow back into the lands and waters.

Walking through the halls of the temple, I held an incense censer, burning the sweet smell of lavender, frankincense, myrrh, and amber—such a divine sweet smell, which came to me whilst I was sitting in the essence of that life, after which I added these scents into my diffuser. It is a heavenly smell, for the burning of the incense leaves one with a feeling of a calmed collection of the senses, back to the restoration and balance of one's soul.

I was a devotee in the spirit of a wanderer with a zest for life—a nurturer, an explorer, a gazer of the stars and planetary alignments. Otherworldly BEings were not otherworldly, for we intermingled, learning from each other, studying under their loving gaze. Were we not foolish then as we are now? Much of the learned wisdom has been deconsecrated, lying dormant in the undertones of our souls, waiting for us to be reunited with the ancient wisdom of the gods, enhancing our potentialities and understanding that life is more than our outer vision.

Even though I devoted my life in service to Isis, the fruit of forbidden love was a thread that bound me with one in the lineage of the standing royal family; it was heavenly bliss, yet it remained out of sight. It was a beautiful dance of two souls entwined by the rays of our hearts as one. I don't know how I died in that life, and it's not important, but I remember the beautiful buildings created by humans in conjunction with other interplanetary races.

Nothing remains of what once was Ancient Egypt. The ruins pale in comparison to the breathtaking magnificence they once held. Buildings were constructed according to the grid lines and vibrational frequency, energetically and harmoniously tuned and aligned with the Earth and its people. Constructions were a work of art, a labour of love and dedication. Many were grand, as other BEings stood taller than humankind. These BEings were far more prominent in Atlantis yet faded into the background as different DNA strands and the EGO overtook humanity, and all was veiled. Many were over six feet, if not taller, had elongated beautiful faces, and had no hair. Standing in their presence, one could feel the love emitting from their radiant inner light. They carried much love for humanity; they were gracious, compassionate, kind, thoughtful, and relayed much ancient wisdom of the stars to all those who chose to listen with open and receptive hearts. I don't know what star system they are from, but one of these BEings stated to me that the ego of humanity is like a disgruntled coil of emotions, with the ego often screaming "I hate you," whilst the Soul will always whisper, "But I love you."

The Hathors of Venusian descent, in service to the Sky Goddess, dwelled within the temples; their vibrational tones realigned the lands of the Mother and its people back to the "harmonial" grid of existence. One would feel nothing but love in their presence, as their hearts were pure and carried much light. If you were angry, sickly, or in discord with the Self, their loving, enlightened tones would dissipate all back to love. They say that you should never forget that you are the sunlight to your Soul and Divine Grace by Nature.

You can call forth their energy at any time by reciting the following:

I AM the Sunlight to my Soul Temple.
I AM a Divine Cosmic BEing of Love and Light.
I AM a Cosmic Star of the Cosmic Central Sun orbiting in the brilliance of infinite StarLight particles incarnate across the vastness of the planes of the bodily heavens.
I AM a Master of the ancients, wisdom expressing the sea of my Light outward.
I stand here solemnly under the heavens embracing the beam of Light of pure unconditional Love, aligning me back to the sacred Divine Temple of the I AM Presence within.
And so it is.

I want to highlight that they, too, have a sense of humour. They say, *"We are the 'Hathorians.' We are notorious to the darkness, for all we do is breathe and spread love, light, and healing into the hearts of Man, quelling their thickly spread smoke and pollution, unlocking the conditioning in the form of challenges so that all may awaken, alchemising themselves back to the very breath of the essence of Self, allowing for the smog and toxic taste of a poison paradise to dissipate within their hearts returning to the brilliance of the Rays of the Sun of Amun-Ra."*

The architecture and lushness of flora and fauna enriched the cities with created rivers and waterways flowing through them, built with the utmost precision, in alignment with the stars and the Mother. Everything flowed into one and was in harmony, as were its people. I often remember watching the early sunrise in the quiet of the temple abode, watching the ships glide past silently from afar, docking in the harbour. Life was infinitely less dense than it is today, and there are many times when I can just sit and close my eyes and transport myself back to the temple, quietly absorbing the energies of a time that once was.

The Politics of Rome

The 12th Legion of Rome

The mentality of a commanding officer is to stave off the enemy and conquer lands that we thought belonged to us and were for the taking by the Roman Empire. Even I have slaughtered those on the battlefield, serving as my Guides said, in the 12th Legion of Rome. We waded deep into the territory of the once beautiful Gardens of Eden, only to be ambushed by skilled archers, and such was my death a mere hollow victory but for the piercing of arrows in my side, neck, and legs. Yet as many of the 'casualties' on both sides ascended, we greeted each other not with simmering hate but with a burst of brotherly comradery and love in our hearts, having understood the trickery of the conditioned human duality and experiences that we had so wilfully chosen to partake in.

I had a far more exciting life when I chose to live as a politician during the time of Julius Caesar, which I channelled out of the blue one evening, not understanding half the wording of what was given to me, as I know nothing of politics.

A Remembrance of a Life in the Times of Julius Augustus Caesar

To be born in a manufactured world is but by grand design an unfathomable feat to behold, a conditioned figurine, navigating the Self through the current superficiality to the reacquaintance with the Self returning to the Lightness of thy BEing.

Consciously create the life thy deserveth away from listening to the persistent indoctrinated worldly whispers, and it will be so, for one createth but constantly of every second of every hour of every day of one's given Life.

Walking back through the halls of the once instated Senate house, the smooth etched alabaster pillars reflect the late afternoon autumn sun. The grand delusion of Julius Caesar was the undoing of his own EGOtistical Self. He walked in both nuances of Light and Darkness. He was the depiction of a true Yin and Yang, temperamental in his wayward earthly ways. One walked with an air of alertness when surrounded by his aura, for one could not predict either the wisdom or the wrath that befell upon one; such was the predicament we often found ourselves in—walking on eggshells of sorts would be a proper enunciation.

He suffered from the grandeur of illusion to fit but solely his needs. Cruel yet kind from one flitting and fleeting moment to the next, having no Conscious understanding of his State of BEing. Knowledge to him was Power, and Power was only to be bestowed to him. Those that did not share his philosophy of the people, and of the Republic of Rome, had their fate sealed unbeknownst to the individual partaken to the situation of the said word.

The Republic was not for the people of Rome but befell solely to the Power of One and those following. The Constitution of the Republic was established in favourable conditions for those that served the inner circle of the Senate of the Republic. It was not a representation for the people but solely served those in Power, and yet in a diabolical twist of the Man he was, he did much to help those of the lands, yet the Empire was fraught with inconsistent policies, a forever changing landscape to suit but the few.

As much as he fought for the people and was a man of the people, he fought just as much against them. He was a man of extremes, riddled with inconsistencies, firm in his undertakings, a coherent master well versed in his prose of the spoken word, congenial yet abhorrent to those that opposed his ways of "fortitudal" undertakings.

The ideology of warfare is but the delusion of a few, detrimental to the masses who have no understanding thereof. Those few are merely at war with the ideologies within themselves stemming from traumas of their own experiences, and thus their leadership is but a mere reflection of their state of Mind, their reality rather than what is best for the people they behold to "govern." One does not attain Power through the good deeds of one's heart, but through the immense political, strategic chess game of the muddled arts of the dark.

The legislation of the Senate was in favour of the Senate. The inner Senate divulged the legislations to the politicos representing the provinces of the Roman Republic—in the guise of the good for the people, aiding them in their welfare, but it was a tale of two sides to the same coin, for it enhanced to enrich the life of the Senators in seat within the Senate, whereby the monies were re-invested under the guise of wars, the building of roads, bridges and the aqueducts of Rome.

The commencement of the well-intended autonomy of the Empire became, over time, an autocratic bureaucracy increasingly difficult for the political landscape and those living within the rules of the game thereof. A destitution of absolution, a corrupt system serving as the soulless expression of the few in Power.

Yet there were those like myself who listened and disagreed in the mode of silence, for words were the weapons of truth. I lived outside the walls of Rome along the rolling hills of fields of corn, tending to my herd, a writer's sore head of the laws of Rome. Yet, in the stillness, I authored many laws for the good of the people, implemented after the death of my then mortal existence. Quiet I kept and watched from afar the unfolding of the last rites of Julius the Invictus Caesar. I dared not speak, for my family was sorely accustomed to the lifestyle of convenience. I cared not for riches, but they prudently did. I lived an honourable life by decree, for the good of the vicinity of my people, according to the Universal Laws of Man. A life of two halves—the semblance of a family loved and loyal to the Senate, and the other to the people I served for the greater good of the nation and humanity. Judge me not, for I too was but fraught with the learnings of life, yet a continuation and culmination of my works a necessity, for alas, without the secrecy of the few, this would not have been attainable.

It was not the will of the people that was invoked but the regimented following the cause thereof; such was not a life of freedom, but a life of living in fear—a fear of being persecuted for speaking one's truth. To live but a life besieged by the Power of a few is not a life lived in the freedom of the expression of one's Spirit but a life lived in fear of expressing oneself.

Carnage was strewn through the tolls of war, and the putrid smell of a flesh a'burnin', carried by the winds, and the cries of the innocents heard afar. Many a soldier perished on the battlefields but for the heavenly embracement of 'home' for the eternal Soul. Many deaths for but the Love of Power, all for the vanity of one, in what should have been but a conquering of hearts through the Power of Wisdom and of Love. Those that survived were enslaved to work under the laws and decrees of Rome; such is but the legacy of the Caesar unbeknownst to Man. A strategist, a mind so brilliant, so controlled, yet opposing in the law of contradictions to suit but his will, with a fate so cruel to those who defied his status and refused to abide by the laws of his imposement.

And yet after Caesar was relieved from his Earthly plight, many wept, for the night conveyed was long. Yet once the shadows lifted, came back but the dawning o' the morn,' and oh how glorious it was, for it was only when the darkness protruded that the Light was able to return to the Souls of Man, for without the understanding of 'despotism,' the contrasting of dualities one was unable to commence with the understanding of a lighter state of BEing—of living in Truth, of living in Light, for Rome became once more bathed in glory—if only for a while, normality and respect to all were given, but the Light would not last forever for Man cease to desist from learning—and as such there will always be those wanting to rule the few for but the mere ego-betterment of themselves.

Freedom findeth one not in the world as ruled by the few, but in oneself. Return within and seek what was lost in the drama of thy outer-worldly experiences. Only when one becomes One with the Master within can one become One with the Master of Self without. It is only then through the expression of one's inner sanctum that one can understand the rhythms of the outer-worldly dimensions and pay but Mind to the fruition of the dreams of one's beautiful Divine Soul, rather than ingesting but a false flagg-ed narrative of those that hold the sceptre of power over the people of Man.

As the Master teacher Socrates puts it, "la liberté de vivre dans la joie de vivre," which translates to "the freedom to live in the joy of living." How can that not be beautiful, for we live so much in the deviation of who we truly are, forgetting the true joy of living life, allowing ourselves to be lived as opposed to living in the true essence of who we are.

The Late Middle Ages with Liam

I went to see Alania to get away from Liam's energy, as he was suffocating me, and it was affecting all areas of my life. She had no idea what had happened before I came to the US, so I was blown away by the experience.

I lived another life with him somewhere in Europe in the Late Middle Ages, and I was well-off, having made a name for myself in a particular trade. I wish I could tell you what it was, but I could see myself poring over books and writing things down. Perhaps something to do with herbalism, but I can't say for sure; however, I was ahead of my time. I was independent and worked hard for a living.

Many people came to me for advice and respected me, until one day, the Pied Piper and pauper of Hamelin came along, throwing me off my game.

He was good-looking, charming, and seemed well-off, but looks can be deceiving, for he was a charlatan and a swindler at its finest. He treated me with respect, and his intentions seemed pure of heart. Yet what came to pass was not of an expectancy, for his heart carried a tarred vindictiveness, a wickedness that consumed his soul—yet people would not speak ill of him, for all loved his charismatic persona. Cruelly, he chose to slowly poison me, using his intricate knowledge of herbs using the roots of an arsenic toxin. My body endured violent stomach cramps and bowel movements, suffering spells of intense dizziness and nausea. Yet it did not deter me from wanting to get better.

Still, unbeknownst to me, he took advantage of my poor condition, taking over part of my business and swindling me out of my money under the pretence of taking care of me until I finally came to the conclusion that he had been ingesting me with a poison, obliterating my senses, leaving me in a fugue of mindset and body. Yet when I lay curled up on the floor, sobbing and in torment, ravaged by the sheer fire of pain coursing through my veins, asking him why he'd done this, he bent down and retorted by saying that he loved me for my money and my upward standing in society, yet felt no gain in remaining with me, for my usage now was of little value to him. He wanted to rise among the ranks of society and dabble with other women for the pleasure of a courtier, to feel the need to be respected and well-liked, as such were his narcissistic megalomaniacal tendencies. As I drifted in and out of consciousness, he left me to die whilst leaving like a thief in the night, with none the wiser. In the days when I was found, it was too late for me to be saved, my body having eventually succumbed to the poison flowing through my veins.

Alania was unaware that I had suffered from severe stomach issues, was unable to eat properly for months on end, and lost an incredible amount of weight. I now had the missing piece of the puzzle to what happened in that lifetime, with me carrying a remnant from that life into this one, having stored that trauma in my cellular memory body.

We should all remember that everyone we meet on life's journey is our teacher. We often allow the behaviour of others to destroy our peace because we choose to react rather than reflect. Don't speak s*** about others, for that is merely a reflection of the s*** you need to heal within yourself. Once you release the burdened self, only then can the dammed energy flow back to your infinite potentiality.

Onwards and Upwards

Life is a magical journey, ill begotten by the tides of chaos caused, and yet but beauty lies in the still wells thereof—for simplicity is the key to Life.
It is the key ingredient to lessen the Mind and lighten the heart, back to the notes of the harmonial Soul and happiness of Self—for one is much like the sound of music, tune in to the inner flow of Self, in the stillness of the beacon within and listen to the soft valiant whispers of the guidance that give it voice to the song of your Heart, paving the way for a life of sheer quaintness and a dandiness back to the Light of your Soul.

~Master Lao Tzu~

It was a rather profound experience. Having understood my lifetimes with Liam and the cause of the anomalies within my own life through the Akashic healing, the once-stagnant energetic particles started to shift, and I also began to feel better as Liam simply left me in peace. This clung-on, sticky-tape energy that was like a cancerous sore to me had been removed, and it was like I had been absolved—and thus, his energy also changed, for we were no longer bound in that way. It felt so freeing and yet so strange at the same time, as I had imprisoned myself in the making of my own programming for the longest time. Now, for the first time, I felt like I was stepping outside the painted lines of myself, into the unknown.

Regardless of any healing you receive, you still have to put in the work because ain't no magic wand going to turn your life into a whoopin' arse fairy-tale; it's up to you to integrate the changes. You can't keep deflecting in the hope that your life will change; it won't. Change requires action on your part, and no one can rescue you from yourself but you.

"To embrace yourself, or not to embrace yourself, that is the question, as much as you choose to stray or not to stray from yourself, n'est-ce pas? We can only live our most authentic selves if we commence listening to our inner awareness instead of the chaotic chatter of the outside world. It is much like a fuzzy radio station, trying to make sense of it all with your Soul becoming agitated and straitjacket confused, causing a sticky stir-up of concocted created conditioning syrup that spreads through the predicament of the crevices of your cooped-up Soul. Embrace the beauty and hue of the beautiful spiritual Divine Light that you are, and take that walk back to the portal of your Soul, opening the door to remembering who you are and why you are here. Remember that life is infinitely simplistic; it is merely your human nature that has made it but a trip into the maze of the Mad Hatter's Wonderland."

~The Ascended Master St. Germain~

I continued to set myself challenges, adding to my bucket list on my fridge. I wanted to walk on hot coals, so I did just that! It was an evening of board-breaking, symbolic for following through and overcoming limitations. I broke that board with a single blow of my hand, and it felt incredible. I then walked on broken glass, which represents paying attention and being mindful while changing your perception of things. The night's last event was fire-walking, which is about letting go, trusting, and transforming your soul through mind over matter. I did it once and was glad to put my feet in the cooling water at the end of that stretch of walking over hot coals. My feet didn't feel the pain of the embers, but admittedly I let my mind slip up at the last step, and I felt a surge of pain shoot up my foot. Everything commences from that little seedling of fear because ultimately, what you give your power to has power over you.

I finally commenced rebuilding the relationship with myself that I had so severely neglected. The truth is, I have always thrived best on my own. I think this is because I have carried the weight of my childhood burdens and dove into toxic relationships from the get-go, allowing myself to be whipped by my experiences time and again. Yet these reflections—the characters in my ongoing reel of life—were put in place merely to jolt me awake, prodding me with ever more difficult experiences until I finally learned the lesson.

How many times have you asked, "Why does this keep happening to me?" The answer is because you are not taking away the learnings within the experiences—thus, it will continue until you decide to say enough is enough and commence to heal and change your ways. You cannot progress if you choose to remain in the loop of the same old programming.

"The best relationship to have, is with yourself, for if you can be at one with the Self, you can be at one with others. You cannot love another if you love not yourself. It will just be a fragmented diversion of what you perceive to be love, as much as the other perceives it to be with you.

Get rid of all that doesn't nourish your soul. If you're suffering, you have to take a long hard look at yourself and question why you are malnourishing the very Light within the physical embodiment you have so incarnated into. People tend to live so much on the surface of themselves, merely dipping their toes in the heart of self, when the s*** hits the fan. The key is to not remain honey-trapped in the stuck programming of doolallying in the eternal dance of the conditioned Self but to refrain from striking out and falling into the entrapment of famishing the soul in favour of holding on to s*** that gets you nowhere but in a 'hang-ed' entangled web of oneself. You've got to forgive yourself to love yourself to get rid of all the leeches in your pond o' Soul, or you'll remain a damned eternal 'sucker.'"

~The Divine Shakespeare Club~

My headaches subsided, which was a relief. The rigidness in my shoulders eased a little, which helped temper my acid reflux symptoms and nausea. I left my aspirins to the side, only using my dōTERRA peppermint oil, which worked wonders; the cold alleviated the pain, allowing me to breathe and collect my thoughts.

The next thing on my bucket list was going to Gatorland in Florida with my beautiful French friend Sandrine, who is just as crazy as I am and loves challenging herself as much as I do. We went ziplining over the alligators, which was awesome. The instructor needed someone to jump off the platform first, to bite the bullet, so I said, "I'll go!" And off I zipped, flying past the gators down below. The first jump was scary, but after doing a few, I started having fun. I then sat on a live adult alligator, and even with its mouth taped shut, these beautiful creatures commanded respect, as they possess immense strength and have one of the strongest bites in the animal kingdom.

I also went skydiving with Sandrine, an avid jumper, whilst this was my first time. I was terrified, as I have a fear of heights, so here I was, challenging myself to conquer my fears by jumping out of a plane more than 13,000 feet up in the air. I just sat there, repeating over and over in my head that I could do this, and in the end, I had no choice but to jump, as I was attached to the instructor.

The wind hit me like a thunderbolt and caught my cheeks, making me feel like a nut-stashed chipmunk. I could not speak. I just hung there limp in mid-air, paralysed by fear, which subsided after a minute or so, as I got over the initial adrenaline rush. When the parachute opened and we drifted down, the view was amazing. I could breathe! You see a completely different perspective of the world from above, with everything on the earth's surface so minuscule. The things we think are so big are minute compared to the grandness of the universe itself.

As St. Germain says, *"It is that bird's-eye view of understanding that life is but utterly minuscule from the heights above than when one stands but below in the thick of the drama of it all. Yet, from above, it seems so insignificant, for it is but a mere taste of a mouth-watering truffle to be able to have been given these wonderfully created challenges, to see how you choose to surmount these opportunities that we see as auspiciously delicious. Failure should not be part of your 'dictionarial' vocabulary, for if it is failure you wish, then failure it will be. One can either be bound by the chains one has so clasped around one's ankle, enabling one to fly, yet crash land right back in the thick of one's own created s***, or decide to sever the illusion of those chains and rise above the drama, soaring high into the freedom of having understood the experience and relinquishing this back to the wisdom of eternal understanding."*

I was so relieved when my feet touched the ground. I could have kissed the goddamn earth. They asked me if I would do it again, and I was like, "Yeah, sure," but in my head, I was like, *"Hell no!"* It was a fantastic experience, and I respect those who do this for a living or as a hobby. I learned that there is nothing I cannot overcome if I put my mind to it, for that is the challenge of the illusion of the barrier I had created. The more you challenge yourself, the more confident you become in all areas of your life, with your fears dissipating and your soul dancing vibrantly in tune with the world around you. Never do things half-arsed, but do what you said you would. Linger not in the never-ending war of words with your mind, but follow the stepping-stones to the wisdom of your heart.

Hang-gliding in Groveland, Florida, was a mere 3,200 feet up in the air, and thank the heavens I didn't have to jump from a plane. It was such a great feeling, enjoying that serenity from above, soaring peacefully above the beautiful Floridian landscapes.

I set all these challenges and felt better about myself. I was far more vibrant and met many new people, changing my outlook on life.

As I started to enjoy life a bit more, I also enrolled in a course that Alania Starhawk (www.alaniastarhawk.com) was teaching in January 2017 on channelling the divine while still going in for Akashic Record healing sessions with her. Alania is a channel of the divine, but also a sacred visionary, lightworker, and spiritual mentor. She mentored me for several years and is a fantastic teacher. She works with those ready to unearth their own light, helping them access their inner source of wisdom, love, and truth. Her downloads and meditations are incredible. I am forever grateful that she has helped me along part of my life's journey, as I was beyond ready to travel inward and walk the journey of remembrance back to myself.

I have done many courses in my lifetime. And I am a great believer that if you truly want to heal and don't have the money for workshops, courses, or healing sessions, you work hard to make it happen. There are no buts. The only but is the thought in your head that causes your own limitation. I saved up until I had the required amount, working my arse off because I wanted to rid myself of all the encoded and engrained trauma I carried within that made me feel downright urgh and in a complete state of disrepair. If you refuse to put in the work, you will never heal or evolve and simply remain, so the choice is yours. And if you think for one second that your Guides will royally give you everything on a silver platter, think again.

I'll be honest, I am never one to sit with others. I'm an anti-social shit bird, preferring my own company, and during this course, I sat quietly tucked away on a pillow in a corner, whilst the others sat next to each other in a circle. I often tell this story when asked how my channelling journey started; people think it's an amazing ability, and I always correct them, as it is not an ability. It is merely an expansion of one's awareness. Everyone has this awareness within. We simply have to recover the light of our syrupy-covered selves, getting rid of the unwanted layers by healing ourselves. It's not rocket science. It's like taking ourselves through an authentication process and throwing out all the anomalies that left us living in an unauthenticated version of ourselves, uncluttering the hard drive of our minds of the riddled and bespoke implemented conditioning that we have for too long adhered to and chosen to live by.

If people say I have a "gift," a word I despise, I hit back that everyone has a "gift," they just need to learn to unwrap the conditioning they have so wrapped their beautiful minds with, thus constricting the beautiful light of the soul they perfectly are. It took me many years to figure this out, as I was a turtle and a blatant sadomasochist in not understanding the lessons within my experiences. I healed a bit, then, like a rubber band, snapped right back into my conditioned programming, with my dished out experiences only becoming more severe—my Guides hoping that, in my desperation, I'd eventually "snap" out of it.

Sitting in this class, I had no idea what to expect, and as Alania led us through a guided meditation, I zonked out completely, only returning when she counted back from three to one. When people shared their experiences, they vividly described seeing colours, archangels, ascended masters, Galactics, and even totem animals and their surroundings, experiencing higher emotions like peace or total bliss.

I had nothing to share as I saw zilch. Lord knows where the hell I went. I felt myself well up, as I felt like a loser just sitting there, and I wiped my tears away quickly with the sleeve of my black cardigan, which, thankfully, no one noticed. Alania explained her journey on speaking to the divine by sitting down with a notepad and pen one day and stating that she was now open and ready to receive. When the class was over, I made a quick exit and hopped in my car, as I didn't want people to see my flustered face.

On the drive back home, for whatever reason, this exercise stuck in my head. That night after dinner, I decided to sit down with a notepad and pen and simply quieten my mind, then told the Spirit and the divine that I was ready to receive. I had no expectations at that point and simply let my mind be; indeed, after a minute or so, the words flowed! I was so elated, so excited, I just sat there and cried, feeling so thankful to Spirit. I didn't feel like a complete loser for once. That had always been my problem, I always thought others were far better than I was, and I was just some quirky misfit who didn't fit in with the norm, unable to see or envision anything because I wasn't good enough.

This is the very first thing that came to me:

And so it is
Trust that it is so
Be proud of who you are
Stand tall and take your place to walk among us
As in Human, so in Spirit
Listen, seek and thou shall find thy true Self
We are the whispers of the wind, hear us
We are the trodden of the Earth
Feel us in the warmth of the sunshine
And in the mere cleansing of the rain
Hear our song for we are calling you
Speak but Truth
Feel our Thoughts
Hear our Wisdom
Pray for Answers
Live in truth, enlightenment, and love
Peace is restored through the love and light of healing
We do not stand alone in our quest for there are many
Be still, hear us for we are always there
We live in uncertain times
Heed our call, for we will call upon you

Believe
Have Courage
Have Strength to move out of the old paradigm
There is growth in all you do
Take flight
Trust Soar
For great wonder awaits you
Heal thyself in order to help heal others
Accept the shift and move into the New Age with wisdom, clarity and a
newfound freedom

You are Love
You are Light
You are the Truth
You are the Way

Blessings

As Archangel Michael says to all doubting yourselves like I did:

"If you doubt your own I AM Power, you Power your own I AM doubt, leaving you trippin' and slidin' in a hinkilicious slurpee sludge of Self. Master the Mind, healing the "wounds," to Master the Self and the world you so universally choose to dance in.

Be the Master Creator of your own Path, let no one do the walking for you, but walk it your way, with swagger, galore, and style, oui? You have within you that innate wisdom, that power to steppin' up to the plate, and hittin' the bat swinging into the home run of your dreams. It is that belief that one must have to fulfil one's dreams and aspirations. Without it, one's dreams just fall flat, and the ball knocks you out for six instead.

Never let anyone make you feel less than you are, and in truth, my Child, you choose to make yourself feel that way by the mere imprint of their wording impressing upon your heart and thus a reaction to the imposed feelings within.

Life is an intricate adventure, a graceful game of a hide-and-seek experience to finding the way back to yourself—see it as such. Wear your crown and be proud of who you are and how far you have come. Trust yourself and ride not on the wave of trust of others, nor the wording said to make you believe any less, for that is the crispy crinkle in the 'fried' mind to doubting yourself.

Be that lion once held back in the shadows, that roars deep with a truth in the wells of the stillness of the Soul within, and know that the best protection is your own spine. Do not be the spineless Soul that would lie but damned in the trenches of one's perfect little epitome of sheer misery, but seek ye Light in the devouring of the darkness back to the hues of the shimmering Light you are. Harness the I AM Power and realise your self-worth and self-reliance, for it is within that you will find the sleeping giant to harnessing the power without. Be that beautiful powerhouse of the Divine Soul that you are, and never sell yourself short in this given life, for my Child, you are worthy."

Life is meant to be lived through our own beautiful eyes, yet we often deviate, looking through the lens of others and being swayed by what others think. Thus, we often dither within our confusion, not daring to venture out of our concocted little shell of a box.

But in the end, their opinions don't matter. Merely walk through the wonders of your own Wonderland, rediscovering the magic of the soul you are, daring to live in the magnificent brilliance of the light you are, and deciding to live a life less ordinary.

That same evening, I decided to ask questions to see what would happen, trusting what came to me. Trust is always key, as opposed to letting your analytical mind take over.

The Buddha in me mirrors the Buddha in you
The equal parts of you mirror the equal parts of me
My soul is your soul
I AM to you
What you mirror to me
We are equal in all parts
We are One

Who are you?
I AM Love
I AM the Light
I AM the Truth
I AM the Way
I AM the Me in You
And the You in Me
I AM

I AM the acceptance of Grace
I AM Love in all
I AM Light in all
I AM Truth in all
And
I AM the way in ALL

WHO AM I?
I AM You

That was the start of my journey into channelling the divine, and I was so psyched when I showed Alania. She was so excited for me, saying, "You see, all you needed to do was release the blockages, to open yourself up to channelling again." I looked at her a bit confused and told her, but I've never channelled before, this is my first time! She looked at me, rather astounded, as she thought I had simply shut it down due to my traumatic experiences, as the language and prose I channelled were relatively advanced.

I have always been very disciplined, and from that point on, I wrote every day because practice is key in cultivating a relationship with the divine—just as one would go to the gym to get fit. Many different Light BEings came through, including the Ancient Brotherhood of the Old Ways, the Council of the Elohim, and the Galactic Federation of Light. There are more councils than we can even imagine throughout the multiverse, and all carry messages for humanity for those willing to listen.

Many of us reside on these councils, though we can't always remember this in the humanoid form we are currently dressed up in. It was revealed to me late one night that I sit on the High Council of the Courts of the Intergalactic Races, a council for balancing the laws of the karmic wheel and the equilibrium between all within the multiverse. Any anomalies within the universal tapestry, within the quantum fields, will show up within the energetic blue spheric globes of electro-magnetic frequency waves to which we have access. Many emissaries are sent throughout the galaxy to keep the peace and learn from one another.

I have channelled too many BEings to name—from the Archangels to Ascended Masters, to the Egyptian and Cosmic Masters and Galactics—and they have duly enriched my life, aiding me on my transformational journey of life and healing and disintegrating my karmic ties and past lives back to the light and love of source.

The divine are always willing and readily available to all who make the time to listen and convey their messages. Yet I, too, had much to learn and still do. When I began, it was really to help heal myself. I asked them many questions about life, which was a great way to connect with them. When I was down, I'd often ask them for help, and they would always come back with a reply. It wasn't always what I would want to hear, but it was the truth. Ultimately, it was my life, my responsibility, as I was the painter of my canvas.

I asked them if they ever slept, and they politely told me they did not need sleep, as they weren't human but energetic frequencies of the divine, transformers, and conduits in their own right. They often kept talking to me, sometimes waking me up in the middle of the night. They still do, but I have learned to set boundaries.

I asked them for guidance about whether to return to the UK, as my passport was about to expire, and the Dutch consulate in Miami was curt in their advice towards me. I could not apply for a new passport in the US unless I had a work visa or a green card, neither of which I had. My finances had also started to dwindle as work had decreased considerably, and their response was, *"If you could see what we see, then would life not be easy? Yet, that would spoil the plot and take the wonder out of the human experience. Take the road less travelled, to cities afar and yonder, map out thy course, and follow thy inner compass of the Stars."* Great, another riddle. That wasn't the response I had envisioned. A simple yes or no would have sufficed, but as they always say, it is your life, do what you will and will it so into realisation. The fact I questioned going back should have told me to stay, yet I think my human self was in doubt, and because I could not renew my passport, it swayed my mind to leave.

Several years later, having become far more aware than I was, I still smack myself on the head for leaving, but I am where I am today because this is how I chose to continue my journey—by creating myself and building different experiences.

"You have been jinxed into thinking that you are labelled as being Dutch, yet you are a citizen of the world, a Child of the Universe, an Ambassador of the Multiverse. That mere individualism of thinking has gotten your knickers in a twist. It matters not where one roams, for the world is thine. One can either manoeuvre within the parameters of a chosen confinement of slapped-up labels duly created to cause divisiveness between the 'people' or be of the understanding that one is free and not governed by the state of one's nationality, for we are all embers of the same spark, so I ask thee how can there be a differentiation amongst the 'species' when we are all One?

Always follow the narrative of your heart, not the worldly fed conditioned tripe, to keep you induced and hypnotised in the clutches of a fear of living in a deviation of who you most authentically are. Fear is the path to the dark side; it is the path to experiencing the forever clinging entangled created in the sun melted sticky chocolate toffee fudge of darkness of believing all that is but is not, thus concocting yer own brewin' soup of disasters through the mere ingredients of the illusion of fear.

Always follow the ho-hums of your inner bliss, listen to the mere guidance of the whispers of your Soul within, for where doors were none, the Universe conspires to alleviate you back to the breath of the shift within, aligning you to the energetic frequencies of the song that sings to your own heart."

~The Ascended Master St. Germain~

I should have listened to my gut and not given a flying monkey's about all the rules and regulations. Does it matter what nationality you have? Hell no! It merely indicates that you have chosen to incarnate in that part of the world under certain circumstances. There is zero difference between you, me, or anyone else but for the mere cultivation of our mind and understanding thereof. We are of the light, and we return to the light of eternal existence, end of.

I studied Karuna Reiki and did a dōTERRA AromaTouch course, later infusing it with Reiki healing. I used all oils as prescribed for AromaTouch but often used other oils that I felt would benefit the client. One of my firm favourite dōTERRA oils has to be Arborvitae. It is so grounding and cleansing. It feels and smells like you're standing in the middle of a forest, soaking in all of Mother Nature in the bliss of total peace and quiet.

But from the calm I had been experiencing for the past four months, my life descended into chaos again. The minute I decided to leave was the minute I also had to put my plans in motion. My dog Myra, even though she had all her rabies shots, had to be revaccinated, which took several months. There was no way I would leave my little sunshine monkey behind. She is my ray of sunshine, brightening even the darkest days with her gentle and loving nature. She has been my lifesaver and taught me much over the years. Even though I have often felt down or been sad, instead of sitting quietly by my side, she would get her squeaky toys out and come to me, nudging me, wanting me to throw her favourite ball—in effect, telling me to get off my arse, stop moping around, and to see the light of day in every situation.

Putting my home up for sale was hard, as I had built up a life here; I had wanted to buy an RV and simply travel around the US, but I never did. I bought another place instead. To be honest, it scared the shit out of me to drive such a big truck; however, I still wish I'd had the guts to do it. I think Myra and I would have had a blast, clocking up some grand adventures travelling through the mostly warmer parts of the US and visiting the Grand Canyon and Arizona. Spirit taught me over the years that the known is comfortable, and the unknown is an adventure; simply jump off that cliff and soar into the land of new beckonings and better tomorrows.

As Archangel Michael has kindly reminded me many a time, *"Never sit within the remnants of yourself, thinking what could have been, for that keeps the doors to your potential future possibilities locked tight. One can keep knockin' on heaven's 'door,' but opportunity won't open sesame unless you shut another door first, so stop standing there, dithering and prancing around like a prima ballerina having to go for a wee, because that door will remain shut if you do not take action on opening it. Learn to let go, and enjoy each day, for Life is an experimental adventure. Carpe diem - live each day knowing that all in Life is a blessing, regardless of the sour gummy parades that sometimes rain down on the Life of your Soul. Life ain't all sour grapes and lime zests, for experiences teach you to embrace all of who you are, not just certain aspects but ALL, and to let go to allow for other experiences to come in, for Life won't flow until you do."*

Granted, I made mistakes. I should have made myself scarce when a potential buyer, a realtor of all people came to view my property. I should have taken that buyer's offer, but I didn't, as it was under list price, and I felt the house was worth every penny of the blood, sweat, and tears I had put into it. It snowballed from there, and the drama continued months after I'd returned to the UK. The realtor was clueless and hired the contractor that initially inspected my home when I bought it, which I didn't want, as he was a complete prick. I paid him $750 by check via the realtor to file for a permit application for unpermitted work through the city of St. Petersburg. Fat chance of that happening: the contractor stalled, with the realtor having to chase him for the invoice and an appointment. According to the city of St. Petersburg, no one had applied for a permit. The contractor was long gone, had deposited the check, and stolen the monies. My realtor took no action, and I emailed the contractor, threatening to report him to the Pinellas Park state attorney for further action. He never responded.

The next potential buyer, who cost me another substantial amount in repairs, pulled out an hour before closing! At that point, I had no more money to spend and was done. My former realtor jumped in after I called her, and she managed to sell it for me several months down the line to investors at quite a substantial loss, but I was glad to be rid of it, as that property had drained me both financially and emotionally at that stage.

I put all my furniture up for sale on various websites, selling most of it. What I could not sell, I gave to friends or charity. I've never been one to reminisce over material things, as everything can be replaced.

I can tell you that the whole moving experience was exhausting for me, especially with the added turmoil of my home being on the market. I had booked a return flight with British Airways, who cancelled my flight without informing me, as I had not taken the first leg from London to Tampa. I didn't have the money to book another flight, then to be told my dog was not allowed on the flight, as all pets are required to fly in the hold.

Unbelievable. Myr would have chewed straight through the plastic crate and run rampant through the hold. I didn't hear back from British Airways, having chased them relentlessly for a resolution, no surprises there.

I was forced to book a flight out of Orlando with Norwegian, where my dog could fly in-cabin, costing me more than a thousand dollars. Looking back, I wonder if my Guides made it so difficult to avoid me leaving. Of course, there's no point in what-ifs because in letting go, in shutting doors, others will open to fresh new beginnings. I chose to go down this road, so I had to get on with it, no matter the sadness I felt deep within.

The hardest thing for me to part with was my white Jeep Liberty. It was the first car I ever bought, and it was heart-wrenching for me to let it go. I cried like a baby the day I sold it to a girl from Tampa who had just graduated from high school, with her parents buying the car for her as a graduation gift. I loved that car. It was my everything and drove me everywhere. I know I sound pathetic, and a car is just a thing—I get that. But regardless of how often that car had been at the mechanic, I always took excellent care of it. Ultimately, selling my car was my saving grace, as it enabled me to book a new airline ticket.

I saw Liam briefly before I left and hadn't heard from him in several months, as he had been sorting his life out, focusing solely on himself, working and living in downtown St. Pete. I am glad he did.

Looking back, I can see that I enabled Liam's behaviour towards me, working like a dog to keep supporting others. I realise now that I shouldn't have helped him by buying him food, paying his bills, looking for jobs, etc. I should have let him drown because he would have hit rock bottom much faster. I should have stood my ground and mustered up the courage to stick to a firm no, yet I did not and got sucked into the experience of helping a broken bird that refused to fix himself.

I asked Archangel Michael what courage is and how we overcome our battle with our own tossing and turning of fear. He replied:

"Courage and fear are two sides of the same coin. It all depends on how you flip it and if you believe that fear is a reality and not some smoked mirage created through the conditioning of one's Life. If you believe in something, so will you attract it—fear is the

instigator of a dis-ease within the Self, accumulating facets of distorted probabilities within one's life. Another may be the instigator, but one remains the culprit to the entangled e-motions of one's own created feelings to the reaction thereof, no? You are all so afraid of hurting one another, but how can you hurt others when in truth, they can hurt only themselves?

Courage is being a braveheart and having a brave heart, standing up to the executioner of fear that has incapacitated you, leaving you in a state of paralysis, all through the drip-feed of your own experiences, having formed your belief system, with courage decloaking the beautiful once covered Light of Self, and fear keeping you in the cloaked unoriginality of a created Self. Fear is a magnified e-motion causing nothing but the illusion of anxiety, as one's Mind creates a variety of stories, causing one's e-motions to shift into overdrive. Fear is the trickster, and you, the fool, for believing the apparition to be real.

Not mustering up the courage to shift from the place you have so rigidly chained yourself to, would be a dire feat of sinking in the quicksand of your experiences. You remain in the same drivel, all of your want for fear of shifting gears in your life, because courage is out of your comfort zone with fear keeping you hidden in the shadows of your uncomfortable self, toying with your very thoughts. Doubt causes a dithering, much like a prancing around having to go for a wee, not knowing which way to turn, allowing one to lose oneself in the chaos of the experience, and subsequently wetting your pants and thus drowning in a morass for one has not partaken in the 'game' of change. Life is about being bold, stripping the created smoke and mirrors of the Soul, having faith, and knowing that if you jump, your Soul is bound to be the catcher of you.

Fear 'exists' because you have so cultivated that belief through the art of your garnered experiences. You are the barrier to yourself, for life is limitless, you are limit-less, but for the rules a la carte imparted upon yourself. Courage encourages you to take back your power and stand in your Divine I AM Power of Presence instead of freely offloading it to others. What you feed your Mind is what will come to materi-alise, for you build as much as you destroy according to the non-belief you often fall prone to. Every experience carries lessons for the Soul's retrieval of the Light of Self and not becoming a 'repeat offender' of that same experience, knowing full well it will be served and wrapped in different packaging until one learns the lessons presented within.

As my other flip side of the coin, brother Archangel Samael rather bemusedly says, "It is time to let go of your fears and face life as it comes. Does that scare you? Well, but then indeed, I AM the Joker to your peeing in your pants Batman, right? I am merely an illusion that humanity has but taken oh so seriously to keep you in the imprisonment of Self, but in Truth, I AM the Light to your Darkness as much as you are the Darkness to your own Light. Are you not your own king or queen in your very own created living hell? I choose not to live in the predicaments of your Life; you are the mere creator as much the destroyer and rebuilder thereof. Know that everything is an illusion, so step forth out of the shadows and into the Light, learning to listen with your own Heart and Soul as opposed to the narrative of the worldly outside chatter, for fear is the path to the......., well let's not go there, shall we? Lighten up, pucker up, and live a little bit more in your Truth than the worldly created 'lying' truth, and you will see Life will become a whole lot dandier and rosier in one's outlook."

It matters not that all hum at a different level of awareness; forgive them as you forgive yourself and love all to love yourself. Love is the doorway to healing all wounds inflicted upon oneself, dispersing the inhibited inner fears, and knowing that life is a wondrous adventure back to the Self. Experiences teach you the art of resilience to either rockin' the boat of Self remaining in choppy waters or merely floating the boat, gliding into calmer spring waters through the mere embracing of one's experiences in the sheer love and gratitude of having been allowed to grow. One lives a life according to the Soul's vibrant compass of navigation, of the awareness one skips, jumps, and hula-hoops in, yet in all that you do, see experiences as a mere feat of growth and expansion rather than the lion and bears of one's 'figmented' imagination that keep one incapacitated within the shadows of the cavern of Self, for Life is truly a beautiful feat to behold."

I sat in that fear, afraid to stand up for myself, and thus dragged out the whole experience with Liam, causing utter chaos. Yet, even though we eventually hit rock bottom, we mustered up the courage to work on and become better versions of ourselves. I take full responsibility for my non-actions and my life, and hence I don't see these experiences (now) as being traumatic but merely having served to elevate myself out of my own funk rather than remaining as I was. We are all walking light beacons to each other, walking one another home.

Back then, I soldiered on, even though at times, I felt like a 'victim' of my circum-stances—but you've got to go through the shits to walk through the shifts. You are not a victim unless you allow yourself to live and breathe as one; only then do you get consumed by it, drowning yourself in your own emotions, causing you to mess up your own life. Others may be the cause, yet you are the effect in how you choose to overcome the trauma of that experience. Some trauma can be extremely severe, but regardless of its severity, one has the power to move past it because you are not this "density of human mass," you are the light within. We often need to smite ourselves into oblivion, hitting the bottom of the rock head-on to finally awaken from the dreadful nightmare of an experience. It's finding the strength within and managing to clamber on out of the muddied abyss, knowing full well that with each step we take in climbing that mountain, we are choosing to heal.

The last thing to go was my bed frame and mattress, leaving me to sleep on the floor for the last few days, using my duvet as a mattress. It was not very comfort-able, and my body ached, but as I was downright broke, it was better than sleeping out on the street.

A friend drove me to the airport in Orlando, and closing the door one last time of my second home in Florida brought tears to my eyes. I loved living in St. Pete. It was home for me. I loved the warmth of the sun on my face and the friendli-ness of the people and culture, yet I had to move forward. Returning to the UK seemed like I was going sideways, like the crab I was, branching off from my soul path—yet I had made that choice. Another goodbye, another door closing, with new doors opening.

Starting Over

I landed in the UK, skin over bones, on the 08th of June 2017, the day my passport expired and the day that my parents got married in 1973.

Life in the UK was hard for me initially, as I was flat broke, staying with my mum, waiting for my home to get sold, and looking for work every day, but getting nothing, which was odd for me, as agencies would usually bombard me. But the economic climate has drastically changed over the last few years, with more people coming to the UK, hence more choice and often cheaper labour.

My mum has always been very set in her ways when cleaning her home, so I had to help out, and as I had lived on my own for so long, it was tough for me to adjust to the rigidness of my mum's rules. I felt isolated and removed from myself and often cried myself to sleep at night, wondering what the point of it all was.

Here I was at 43, with nothing to show for and having to start from scratch once again. My life was in shambles. So many other people my age had a family, kids, a home, a job, and what did I have? Nothing, zilch, nada. I was stuck in this funk, feeling like a complete and utter loser, and it was hard to pull myself out of it.

Just because you progress spiritually does not mean everything is a bed of roses; your life goes tits up. Everything in your created and thought-out bubble of existence gets torn down. It's unlearning everything you think you know, stripping the conditioned cling film that had you all wrapped up—much like stripping wallpaper from a worn-out and dated room. It's the gift that keeps on giving—and truthfully, I'd had enough and turned my back on Spirit for several months, as I needed to take care of me, and they sure as hell weren't doing it.

"The wisdom you seek is and has always been inside of you, sleeping but ever so snuggly under the woolly blankets of your Mind. To open the doorway inward, one must let go of the door outward, for inward is the key to attaining ascension and a better understanding of oneself and one's nature in the Cosmic Divine Universe. Life is your grandest teacher, helping you to master the experiences bowled your way to elevate you to the next level in the playing field of the Cosmic Game of Evolution. Ride the wave or fudge-up, remaining in that stickiness of mauling round in one's own created merry-go-round drama until you have mastered the level of the 'game,' thumping your chest like a victorious Donkey Kong. Votre choix, n'est-ce pas?"

~The Ascended Master St. Germain~

My mum and I bickered a lot. I told her I was an adult, not a child. As she said, two grown adults in the house 24/7 was difficult for her, especially when both people were so different. When we are not in each other's space for too long, we get along just fine. I love my mother very much, and we have a strong bond even though we are like chalk and cheese sometimes, as I have hopped out of the matrix, and she loves the comfort thereof, occasionally hopping out before slidin' back in.

I felt empty, alone, trapped, and had no zest for anything, but somehow, I had to keep going. But when you feel down and everything seems to fall apart, it is hard to get up. I kept applying for jobs every day, allowing my autopilot to kick in, having to try to make the best of the situation I had conjured up. I didn't tell my mum how I felt, as it wasn't for her monkey to deal with. I needed to get myself out of the rapidly deep hole I had dug. Was I borderline depressed? I can't deny that I wasn't, but we all deal with our emotions differently due to the variety of experiences thrown our way.

Dear all those reading this that are in the funk of self,

Life is only as dreary or sunny side up as you choose to make it, non? The body partakes in the visual arts one speaks to the Self and orchestrates the energetic frequencies according to the harmony or au contraire of the Self. To bring oneself back in alignment is the cascading of events in the natural unfoldment of the energetic life force field itself, much like the making of a pizza deliziosa, choosing the ingredients pertaining to one's experiences and thus making and baking it according to the humming of one's soul tune. If the ingredients are not in agreement and repugnant to the taste thereof, or one burns the pizza by the non-focus of the task at hand, one can simply try again with a different set of served circumstances, same lesson, different take, different ingredients et voila a pizza diversa.

Tomayto Tomahto, Potato Potahto—Life is all about perspectives, the optical illusion of what is and is not...... Have you figured it out yet, or are you still in that mere state of a yawnin' slumber? Understanding the Self is much like peeling back the onion layers of one's created Self; as one ascends, one loses a layer of that once created version of Self through the mere feat of having wept through the pain, transcended, alchemised, and understood the experiences. For all that you seek, you will find nestled deep inside yourself, your outer world mirrors your inner world and are but served-up events to honour the remembrance of who you are.

My darling, ain't no one going to save you from yourself but you. What would be the point in saving you from yourself when you need to understand that whatever formula of experiences you have brewed and thus ingested are merely of your own miraculous creation, n'est-ce pas? Admittedly, I sometimes despair and yet watch with nothing but loving admiration how one has trapped themselves in this beautifully carved and gilded cage and thrown away the key, refusing to be in acceptance of the sheer beauty of life and oneself. One seems but a whacked-out bird, having bought into the illusion of thinking one is caged, as that is the mentality of the conditioned senses one has so wonderfully adhered to, yet one is free!

Ask not for someone else to save you, for one can wait till the end of days; you have always been your own saviour of the Light of Self. Unlock the cage of your Soul and fly free. Care not for the trivialities of what others may think, but care for the song that sings within your own heart and allow thy Soul to swing and dance to the beatz and funky grooves thereof.

Life is a damn fine journey of rediscovering yourself, unearthing yourself, and returning to the splendour of the sparkling gem you most Authentically are. Let it not be dimmed by remaining in the heaviness of any situation, sliding down a slippery slope of a Willy Wonka chocolate slide, landing your arse in a deluge of sticky choco-late pudding, having lost the plot lying there but in the bewilderment of Self.

Bow but in deep gratitude for all your experiences, giving thanks to the lesson(s), and set yourself FREE, for my Child, you were never incapacitated, you have always been free—merely rise above the created mental illusion and be all that you can be and are meant to be.

Remember that you are a beautiful Ray of Light of the All of Amun-Ra. Think not so little of yourself, but step out of the shadows into the glorious sparklin' Light of the All of You.

Yours in grace and eternal gratitude,

~The Ascended Master Hilarion, Le Comte de St. Germain et the Council of Ra~

Honestly, I sometimes hated my life and the carnage I had created. My pizzas were all burnt to hell, or I threw too many chillies on them, trying to fan the flames. On the other hand, my mum always told me to look at how much I had achieved, as many would not have travelled as extensively, nor would they have persevered as I did when the shit hit the fan. She said what matters are your experiences and all that you have learned.

Losing it all and sitting in the absence of myself, in the nothing that I AM, I also knew that I AM far more than I AM, allowing me to re-evaluate my life once again. I may have felt deflated, but I would never raise a white flag to show defeat.

Many of us fall into states of depression, anxiety, or other mental dis-eases as the world feels too much to survive, and yet it is through the sheer loss we feel within that we can ultimately choose to find ourselves again. If you need to sit there and cry and feel sorry for yourself, by all means, do; just don't sit there wallowing in your pain forever, avoiding the shift, for darkness is the way back to finding yourself. I felt immensely alone every time I went through traumatic experiences, not wanting to bother others because, in truth, I felt a bother to them as much as I was a bother to myself. Archangel Michael states:

"To remain stagnant in a conditioned jam jar on the shelf is not living. It is allowing yourself to be lived through the maturity of a nonsensical art of doing nothing. Step outside the created and conditioned glass jam jar of what you think Life is, but is not, and step into the unknown known, embarking on the grandest adventure of walking through the mind fog jungle back to a remembrance of Self.

You're here to define your experiences. They're not given to you to let life have its merry way with you, with you being slumped in the driver's seat, too tired to navigate yourself through life because you've allowed the turmoil of your experiences to take hold of you and drag you down like a ragdoll on a cart. No one is going to rescue you from you; only you can do that. No one can slay your inner demons; only you can do that. Your lack of confidence is yours to conquer back to the inner knowing and trust of yourself. The discord with yourself and with Life is yours to change. Self-love is the key to unlocking the hurt back to the light within. One can either be that saddened weepy willow in the wind, letting the Self be run by your e-motions, or take charge of your Life, changing the outcome of your predicaments, for truth be told, no one can set you free, but you."

It's about changing your attitude towards the experiences you've lumbered yourself with. I say lumbered as that's what it felt like, although as St. Germain says, *"You lumbered yourself with these experiences by creating them from the 'fairy' dust of your Mind, forming and enabling the energy to form and take shape in the material ether of your existent world."*

I kept praying to Spirit for a job, and God knows, they took their sweet time. I eventually bagged a temp admin job seven weeks later, paying precious little to work on a London construction.

When my Florida home finally sold at the end of September 2017, I moved to my new place, where dogs were accepted, for the UK is honestly the least pet-friendly country I have ever encountered when it comes to the rental market.

You're going to think I'm crazy, but my Guides kept prodding me to pay Liam for the building work he said I owed him all those years ago, even though he hadn't brought it up again. Every time the thought popped into my head, I found a penny or five pence on the street, so I asked him for his address and sent him a check for the "angelic" numbered amount of $1,111.11.

He wasn't expecting it and said he was blessed that I'd helped him and would be eternally grateful, as the money enabled him to buy a used car he'd had his sights on for a while. It helped brighten his spirit and catapulted him into landing a better job. He knows we were toxic for one another but thanked me for loving him for the little time I did.

I forgave him a long time ago and told him it's time he forgave himself and to see how far he'd come from when we were in each other's lives. He was thankful I had badgered his father, who eventually helped him. He said he was basically on the run from the law for three years, with an outstanding warrant, trying to salvage his relationship with me whilst trying to save his own bacon and get his life back on track, but he failed miserably. He was paranoid back then, constantly looking over his shoulder, afraid of getting caught. As soon as the warrant was withdrawn, he biked to the DMV and got his Florida licence reinstated. When he had $10, he first got a one-month gym membership, where he could shower and brush his teeth to be presentable for interviews. He eventually got a job in counselling, helping people find jobs, and now lives on the water, has a boat, and loves life.

I love how when he finally hit rock bottom, with me out of the picture, he turned his life around instead of remaining in his own crap. I have a lot of respect and love for him, for he dug himself out of the dumps and made something of his life, blossoming into a more authentic version of himself. All he needed was to find the magic within and open the door. The shadow of fear we often allow to hover over our soul inhabits the mind. It kills the joy from the heartfelt soul within, suffocating the breath of ourselves. We forget that a little more self-love goes a long way, for it is the bridge to healing our wounds and integrating the broken fragments into a more wholesome version of ourselves.

"Life is as jolly roger or as rotten of a scoundrel as you choose to make it, and shit happens, get over it. You can decide to soak in the ice-cold popsicles of your experiences, remaining in a forever frozen state with a dread of moving forward, yammering about life at every turn and feeling sorry for yourself, or you can get the hell up, smile, kick the bucket of the experience, letting it all out, and mop up, heal-up, alchemise and transcend onto the next level of the playing field of your life—cause ain't no one gonna save you from yourself but you. After all, you're the only one you've been waiting for your whole life, n'est-ce-pas?"

~The Divine Shakespeare Club~

After my short stint on the building site, I worked for another oil and gas company in London, lasting a few weeks. The CEO was a severe bully, calling me stupid, unintelligent, and dumb because he always thought he knew better. I stood up to him and told him to stop bullying and shouting at me and show me a little more respect. It lasted for a day before he fell back into his old habits and I quit, swiftly exiting the building as my health was far more important to me than a paycheck.

I then began working as a receptionist for a local charity, where I stayed for about one and a half years. The pay was absolute peanuts, and I did more than my job description entailed, yet my wages did not increase, so eventually, I looked for something else. Jobs were scarce, and I applied through many job sites over many months, even looking abroad in Malta, Spain, Greece, and Asia; however, I either received rejections or no response at all.

We all have the ultimate potential within, yet we often compromise, and for what? All to fit in within the societal paradigm? My mum has always harped on about the importance of a job, having that lack of money fear as my father left her with nothing, which was conditioned onto myself. I went into work with lead in my shoes every single day, feeling desperately unhappy, and finally I told my mum, "I can't do this anymore, I'm sorry, I am quitting. I am tired of being miserable."

I used to have this fear of having nothing and had this lack mentality, thinking I should have a certain amount in the bank, but I came into this world with nothing, and I leave this world with nothing—what I do with that time in between and how I choose to experience and express myself in this life is all that matters. Life is about coming alive in the joy of who you are and what you do.

In the meantime, I started interviewing people for my YouTube channel, talking to the likes of international mediums such as Warren Bailey, Ivan Lee, Philip Solomon, Ashley Robinson, Graham Watson, Danielle "the happy medium," way guide and well living creator Iain Mason, healer and angelic walk-in Claire Candy Hough, and many more.

Rebuilding Myself

"Love yourself, to find yourself, to unearth yourself, out of the zany entangled thread of created chaos returning to the flow and ease of the untangled breathing lightness of who you are, flowing in the zen of the winding river back to the mouthing of the wholeness of the Magical Universal Soul of Self."

~The Divine~

I commenced helping out a Spiritualist church in South London, creating websites for them to help market their yearly sold-out spiritual weekend event, with many leading mediums, speakers, and tutors giving workshops on developing and enhancing mediumship and psychic skills and learning about the spiritual philosophies. I participated in a Q&A panel session, but no one was interested in learning more about channelling, so I quickly sat back down. I honestly thought others would be open to enhancing their awareness, but instead, they were more interested in receiving messages from past loved ones in the spirit world.

I have previously consulted mediums until I realised that all those having crossed over have returned to the celestial heavens in their true Starseed essence. I guess you could say that the many masters have unconditioned the conditioning and enlightened the unenlightened within me, and for that, I am eternally grateful. Your loved ones can guide you, but they're also busy aiding with the planetary ascension of Mother Earth, helping humanity and many other planets in the multiverse and otherworldly dimensions. It's great to hear from those that have crossed over; however, change does not happen through them; change happens when you take action and whip up your own magic in life.

I was a bit of a walking empath at the retreat, having absorbed the energies like a total SpongeBob and left with a banging headache. It was an interesting experience, and at the end of the day, everyone bobs around in their earthly soup bowl at their own level of consciousness.

I can talk about the subject of death till I beat it to "death," and that'll, in truth, be the death of it. There can be no loss, but for the mere loss one feels within themselves. St. Germain says:

"You are free to choose what you believe as per your current state of Awareness, yet be of the understanding that death is non-existent but for the mere wording and terminology attached to it as per the created human dictionary. You are Energy, you are Consciousness, you cannot 'die,' you merely transform and expand, for Energy can neither be created nor destroyed. The only thing one chooses to miss is the earthly garment the Soul once wore, and yet that is not the Soul itself; it was merely a body it housed, for the Soul has rejoiced in a return of the warmth of the Light back home, continuing on its journey of evolving in Consciousness.

So, tell me, Child, how can you miss someone when they never truly died? One chooses to carry the experience of 'grief' of 'hurt' that one has so chosen to incarcerate the Self with according to the implemented belief systems, n'est-ce pas? And yet the

Soul back home does not share that same sentiment. It asks for nothing but for you to relinquish this created and chosen pain, back to a joie de vivre of Self and of Life, for it revels in the remembrance of the Light and Love of Self, in its state of 'perfection,' having shaken off the fugue of its once human existence, having understood that the once created life experiences in the human embodiment in its fettered existence were merely to help expand its own Consciousness, often to the joy, sometimes to the chagrin of others and to help the Planet out of the suffocation of the entangled tentacles of darkness. Merely walk the inner journey back home to the Soul of Self, plugging back into the Oneness of All, losing that feat of separation, honouring the Light in each other, and awakening to the wondrous Light of the Conscious Self in your current human embodiment, for Life is a breathtaking miracle and You are a beautiful infinite God Wonder of the I AM."

What a waste it would be if death were truly the end of the human spirit, if all we become is dust in the wind, all our experiences, and creativity thrown away into the void of nothingness. One merely discards one's old worn overcoat of a physical body, with one's soul returning to the higher planes of consciousness, taking with it all its eclectic accumulated experiences. Celebrate the life they lived, knowing they are alive and will continue to live on, for that is the beauty we should hold on to.

Mediums help an immense amount of people with the tireless work they do, so kudos to them. Mediumship just never satisfied me, and I believe we should be open to expanding ourselves to other modalities, or we linger in that trap of remaining one-dimensional in all that we do. Yet, as the Light BEings state, *"Like any healing modality, it is a gateway to the multidimensional Self, for what lies beyond the veil is far more significant and magnificent than you can humanly imagine. Remember all are of the Stars, there is no exception to the rule thereof, yet that concept is too much for people to comprehend, and many remain roaming within the box of that created one-dimensional aspect, believing that heaven is a happy place for Souls merely basking in the Light of home. It is indeed, but standing in that doorway, and walking across the threshold of that doorway are two different things—one can remain in that one-dimensional aspect of BEing or one can walk across that threshold, opening the door to the infiniteness beyond, the gateway to the expansion of Self standing on the threshold of unfolding back into the multidimensional Universal all of Self.*

Anubis weighs in with a penny for his thoughts:

"Mediums state they communicate with loved ones beyond the veil. How can that be when they are very much alive, and humanity has merely veiled themselves behind the veil of forgetfulness, having drawn the curtains and gone to 'zzz-leep' and instilled the subtle art of separation through a cultivated, honed in, and created recipe called conditioning?

Mediums communicate with an aspect of the soul that once was and once lived, yet not the spectacular Seed of the StarLight BEing they truly are and that my Child is the difference."

We are all at a different stage of evolution and operating from a different level of consciousness, which is why we are such an eclectic bunch, vibing at different frequencies. We merely hum to the tune of our soul's level of consciousness. Every soul on this Earth has their journey to walk and their reasons for choosing which dimensional state to live from, so I say, honour that and respect them for walking their journey of life the way they see fit, not loving them any less.

I have had to study many different modalities to understand their different aspects, in order to expand my own awareness and commence to make sense of life. Each modality helped me to recover something of my own authentic nature that I had buried deep beneath my earthly conditioning.

I had always wanted to become a fitness and spinning instructor; however, having to study the anatomy of the human body was not easy. I had a tough time with it, as biology was never my strong suit, but I passed both the written and full-day practical exams, after which I enrolled in the spinning instructor course. Once I received my certification, I went to my local gym, bit the bullet, and asked if I could teach—and was thrown into the deep end after another spinning instructor had the flu. In my head, I was like scared s***less, but I got on that bike and taught. I enjoyed it, really working those that came to my weekly classes to the rhythm of '80s and '90s music, with an infusion of some modern-day beats. I had a considerable waitlist of people wanting to join and did this for several months until the UK decided to shut everything down.

I was out of a job for nearly five months, and I kid you not, I even applied to McDonald's and was hired several weeks later; however, the uniform took more than two months to arrive, seeing I'm such a gangly giraffe, and they didn't have my size. By then, I'd found another job in London, which I loved, but I got bullied again for doing too much. In hindsight, I am grateful for the experience. By putting myself out there, I was offered another job right before lockdown, which was my saving grace, as all contractors were subsequently axed at my former company the following month. There are always hidden blessings in any experience if we learn to see the world and our experiences with a different mindset. Change your vibe to change your life by changing the quantum field and rewiring the energetic currents— 'simples.'

In 2018, I took my mum on a ten-day all-inclusive vacation to San Agustin in Gran Canarias. It was my birthday present to her, and we thoroughly enjoyed the sunshine, the spa, the beach, the food, the excursion of the dromedary ride and being kissed by one, and just walking around exploring the area.

I took her to Benalmadena, Spain, the following year; however, Benalmadena has lost its Spanish authenticity, charm, and soul a wee bit as it's overrun by too many tourists. We visited Mijas Pablo, a quaint little town up in the mountains, where I fell in love with the donkeys. Such beautiful and graceful creatures, I adored them. I felt so sorry for them as people rode on them, yet admittedly they were well cared for. We visited the beautifully preserved La Ermita de la Virgen de la Peña de Mijas (Chapel of the Virgin of the Rock), where the Virgin appeared to two shepherd's children. Entering the chapel felt like stepping into a different era as in 1656, the church was carved into a rock by friar Diego de Jesus Mercy, taking twenty-six years to complete. My mum loved it and sat inside for a while, soaking up the energy. We visited Colomares Castle, with its beautiful architecture and gardens dedicated to the life and adventures of Christopher Columbus, who was the incarnation of none other than the Ascended Master St. Germain.

Just because I channel and work for those up in the celestial heavens, that doesn't mean my life is always a picnic in the park—but once you get the gist of life, you laugh at whatever is thrown your way. Growth is losing all your savings through an elaborate online scam, taking half an hour to recover, and subsequently laughing about the experience.

In 2020 my entire savings went up in smoke and with it my dream to buy a home in Spain, all due to an elaborate online scam, with fraudsters cloning websites posing as well-known investment companies, scamming thousands of people. On the surface, everything seemed legit, with clients receiving log-in details and the correct paperwork. It took me nearly a year to get it back, with myself investigating and doing all the legwork, as neither the big corporations nor the police cared.

My Guides told me, *"Birgitta, it's only money; you have a job, you have a home, so how you choose to respond to what happened to you is entirely up to you."* Most people would have lost their minds and freaked out, going mental in the head. I just laughed at it because what's the point? Spirit was right. Why should I disrupt the flow of my energy? It'll only cause more distortions within my energy field and thus my life.

Problems are merely an illusion of the mind; if you feed them, they'll grow into a persistent little distorted bugger. If you don't kick the demons of that clobbered fear to the curb, they will cause nothing but total anarchy because you allowed yourself to be kicked down by an experience meant to elevate your awareness, not lower it. It was simply another experience, and how I chose to react made all the difference.

I channel every day. It's like riding a bike: the more you practise, the better you become at it, eventually flying like the wind. I have channelled an immense amount over the last few years, being the cosmic wave rider I am, but that is a different book. Channelling has given me clarity, and a better understanding of myself, the multiverse, and the beautiful Earth. And no, I don't have an ability nor a gift, as that implies, I'm special, and I am not. The key to channelling is merely releasing all your layered and conditioned crap, fine-tuning yourself, and vibing to a far higher vibrational frequency, leaving you in the lightness of the radiant authentic soul of a butterfly that you are.

Life is all about honouring your inner Light and not giving away pieces of yourself to make others feel whole, leaving you with holes in your soul. I was bullet-ridden and had virtually disappeared, bending my will to others. As Archangel Nathaniel says, *"To reconnect with us is to reconnect with the beauty of the Light of yourself. A Life without Light is like an entombed and mummified Soul. As much as you honour your inner Light, honour others as they honour you. If your Light has 'faded' beneath all the accumulated piled-up junk of life, then it is time to sweep the dust out of that darkness, unwrap the bandaged mummy of Self and let Light of Love back into the pores of your Soul, for only then will you be able to breathe and shine forth your Light once more in the divine essence of BEing true to you."*

Throughout the years, both through my relationships and my healing practice, I have learned that I am not here to fix anyone; everyone needs to fix their own wounded mind and soul. Nor am I here to save anyone, as everyone needs to save themselves. We are each responsible for our own soul growth; enabling broken birds doesn't help the bird fix itself. I really had to learn this the hard way because we often deny a soul the growth it eternally yearns for by continuing to help this person, thus enabling them, trying to be their saviour instead of just letting them hit the bottom of that rock, and allowing them to make their own mistakes.

I also had to come to grips with the fact that it doesn't matter what people think of you or whether people like you. *You* have to like the *you* in yourself, and as the Divine Shakespeare Club states, *"If you are not happy with the you in you, then you need to shake those tail feathers, and lay off the soured cream conditioning you have so layered your Mind with. To get to the good stuff, you must work through the sour taste of your accumulated experiences. Never conform to the wants and needs of others, your life, your rules; at the end of the day, you are the only one that has to live with you until you pop yer clogs, drop the garment and ride the waves across the celestial heavens back home."*

I have been on my own since 2015, dating myself, and I love it. I am probably a born-again virgin, but I really needed to work on and heal the relationship with myself, seeing I had been running from myself for so long. I don't have the distractions of draining someone else's swamp and absorbing it into my own auric field, having to wade through it and cleanse myself once again, which was my operator manifesto. I love my own company; I much prefer it these days. I am and have always been very much a loner throughout my life, with my mum by my side, whether near or far, picking me up, trying to make me see sense when I went tumbling through the crap in my life. Even though we are very different people with somewhat different views on life, she is and has always been my best friend and biggest supporter in everything I do. She's my soul sister, and I love her for all she has done for me and for putting up with all my shit. She deserves the whole world and then some. Of course, I have my many Light BEing friends and confidantes in the multiverse, who always crack a smile on my face with their words of ingenious wit and wisdom, and I have less than a handful of earthly friends scattered around the globe, and that suffices.

I once yearned for a family, a home, and all the trimmings that come with it, but I have long surpassed that desire. My life is in service to the Light BEings and humankind. I AM here to help empower all to the divine breath of being themselves. I AM merely here to pour love back into the souls of Man, for love in the field of unconditionality is the answer to everything.

People often ask me if I was ever really in love. It felt like love, but it was a conditioned love. It was about me learning to love myself, fixing my broken mind and heavily intoxicated soul through mirror-reflection relationships with others. Conditioned love is like a mind boggling legal contract with too many clauses. How many scars have we justified just because we "loved" the person holding the knife? Love just is; it is unconditional. It is our infinite nature. Love is pure. Love is wholesome; it does not judge and is the epitome of absolute pure light.

When asked how I can forgive all the people that have hurt me, my response is, how can you not? You are love. It is your divine nature. Forgiveness is the key to healing your own burdened self and letting your soul fly free to the expansion and understanding of new heights and depths of yourself you never knew existed. I say, always be thankful for the experiences and the characters that have helped you evolve, as we are all teachers of one another. St. Germain says that the best thing to say is, *"I used to love you in the reflection of you in me, and yet I will always love you for you are the I AM in Me as much as I AM the Me in You."*

Like you, I am imperfectly perfect—flawsome, flaw-edly awesome, and then some—but that is my current human nature. Like you, I am still BE-com-ing, learning about myself and the world I dance in, and I inherently love the transformational times we find ourselves in. I still suffer from bouts of forgetfulness, with shimmers of who I am glistening through the cracks of my current existence, and yes, like you, I still have much to learn.

What I have written is not gospel. If it resonates with you and helps you on your life's journey, I am honoured to have been a piece of the puzzle. These are my human experiences and how I have learned and chosen to deal with them. Yet, know there is no right or wrong way; there is only *your way* in how you wish to evolve and experience life. Without all the hardships I encountered, I would not be who I AM today, nor have written my story and channelled the messages from the many masters and Light BEings, who have now become an integral part of my life. I wouldn't have it any other way. I have learned to accept and embrace my quirkiness and be that fish out of water rather than conforming to someone I AM not. As St. Germain always says:

"You are here not to please others but to understand yourself even when others do not understand the Light that is you—for it is for them to learn and understand the Light within themselves. You are here to swim upstream in l'extraordinaire lumière de soi, not downstream with the shoal of fish in the mainstream de la société de la vie. You have come to Earth to unearth yourself, returning to the ascension of the Light within. Your healing journey starts with the Self, for to heal the Self is to feel the Self and the heaviness of the past teaches you the unbearable lightness of BEing, of learning to be present within yourself—that is the freedom to the expansion and thus the ascension of the Soul particles dancing back to the Equilibrium of the Oneness and Wonder of the Infinite All that makes You, You."

Remember, we are not separate. You are as much a part of me as I am a part of you, as much as I AM equal to you, and you are equal to me, and we are all an equal part of each other in the enfoldment of returning to the whole. Love is the answer to everything; it is the road to leading you back to living in unison and harmony within yourself, one another, and the world—and trust me, without the competitiveness of the I AM better than you ego syndrome, the world will be a far more beautiful place, filled with love, peace, harmony and above all, unity.

I am that little *can kuş* (sweet soul bird) that can't live life cooped up in the matrix of the societal norm. I will always choose to let my soul soar to new heights of expansion, wanting to go places and explore, as life is an adventure of finding the way back home to yourself. I will always be that little bird, flying high above the grid, singing its song to humanity, aiding in awakening and empowering those that heed the call back to the very nature and divine bliss of BE-com-ing their beautiful and radiant authentic selves, rising above the drama, learning to soar free in their magnifique divine BEingness—for life is a brilliant journey, and we live in exhilarating times, walking the surface of this beautiful conscious soul, Mother Gaia.

Know that you are a beautiful ray of the divine. See yourself for the beautiful, sparkling "divinelicious" wonder of a soul that you are—and know that you are loved beyond measure by all your brothers and sisters in the multiverse.

As St. Germain sums it up rather poignantly, *"Life is simply a return to Love, nothing more, nothing less."*

About Birgitta

Birgitta Visser is Soul Empowerment Coach and Light Configurator, delivering messages from the many Light BEings to the aid of humanity. She is a courier for those who wish to convey their messages across.

She is a Dutch mutt, living the good life with her ninja black sidekick dog that she rescued from the streets in Florida. She's been a model, bartender, promo girl, dog walker, healer, web designer, created her own organic soap line, designed jewellery, taught many holistic workshops, and manoeuvred herself to holding a demanding job in the corporate industry. In other words, she's an excellent all-around chameleon.

She's travelled the world rather extensively, as being a wanderer is in her blood. She's gotten herself into many difficult situations, yet has managed to vanquish her demons. Her often turbulent journey has been a learning curve. She is who she is, and has learned to embrace all quirky aspects of herself, often stumbling through the darkness of her trauma yet never giving up.

Birgitta is a pro at surfing the cosmic dimensional waves across the Multiverse, delivering the many messages she receives from the collective of Light BEings, Ascended Masters, Archangels, and Galactics in the hope that people will awaken to what life is all about. She has a profound knowledge of ancient wisdom that has over the years bubbled from deep within and has emerged as an inspirational channel having been submerged in her own traumatic experiences and having chosen to overcome these.

She is simply here to offer her words as food for thought in unlocking your own potential and be-com-ing authentically you, while journeying back to the unfolding of the beautiful lotus of the light of who you are.

Life is like the sound of music. You've got to dance before the music is over and live before life is over.

www.powersoulhealing.com
www.birgittavisser.com
Facebook: Universal Light Warriors

All of Birgitta's very different flavoured experiences have led her to this point in her life; without them, she would not have a story to tell. As a Child of the World and seeker to the constant expansion of Consciousness, it took her years to realise why her life was an eclectic bag of mixed experiences, some utterly sour and distasteful, having to sweat the chillies whilst others were sweeter, bringing her immense joy. Birgitta is currently working on a new healing modality infusing crystalline energy and Light Language; however, if you want to learn from Birgitta's experiences and embark on this epic journey called Life, visit her website for more information - www.BirgittaVisser.com.

Printed in Great Britain
by Amazon

87171470R00273